BILL BREWSTER & FRANK BROUGHTON

THE RECORD PLAYERS

THE STORY OF DANCE MUSIC TOLD BY HISTORY'S GREATEST DJS

Virgin BOOKS

10 9 8 7 6 5 4 3 2 1

First published in the United Kingdom in 2010 by DJhistory.com

This edition published in the UK in 2012 by Virgin Books,
an imprint of Ebury Publishing

A Random House Group Company

www.randomhouse.co.uk

Addresses for companies within The Random House Group Limited
can be found at www.randomhouse.co.uk/offices.htm

The Random House Group Limited Reg. No. 954009

A CIP catalogue record for this book is available from the British Library

The Random House Group Limited supports The Forest Stewardship
Council (FSC®), the leading international forest certification organisation.
Our books carrying the FSC label are printed on FSC® certified paper.
FSC is the only forest certification scheme endorsed by the leading
environmental organisations, including Greenpeace.
Our paper procurement policy can be found at:
www.randomhouse.co.uk/environment

Printed and bound in India by Replika Press Pvt. Ltd

ISBN: 9780753540688

To buy books by your favourite authors and register for offers, visit:
www.randomhouse.co.uk

For the dancers of Low Life and
the curmudgeons of the forum.

Contents

Introduction
Listen to this!

It's *your* record. You discovered it. You didn't make it, but you found it and brought it back from the dead. No-one else knows about it – it's yours. You love it for the feelings it conjures. You just know what it'll do to them.

You saved it for tonight. This is the perfect crowd to play it to. It'll have them in bits. The atmosphere in here is starting to crackle. You've brought them up slowly over the last hour, now you're finally mixing it in. It's 30 years old but for everyone in this room it's a brand new tune. As it starts you notice a few people look up, they can tell it's something special. And it sounds so great on this system. The percussion kicks off, that brilliant *chakk-chakk* noise. It's like an invitation. That little lick of guitar and horns. And then the bassline. Devastating! *THuuuuNNNNGling!* – into your chest. And the melody. It's started. It's here. People going *crazy* now – jumping, whistling. You look around. Everyone's smiling at their friends, smiling at you.

It's so great seeing them get it the same way you got it. As exciting as hearing it for the first time. It's that same thrill bounced round the room and back at you times 300. Sharing a song, there's nothing like it. *Listen to this!*

The rhythm steps up a gear. The guitar pushes its way to the front. The room gets crazier. The strings make a couple of people close their eyes. It couldn't be better: everyone's loving it, everyone's right here. The whole dancefloor is wrapped up together, lost and found in your beautiful song.

And then, just when it couldn't be any more perfect, those wild stinging vocals scream in. And you know it's coming, so you're watching for their reaction – here it comes... NOW! And the piano, too. Everyone loses it. The whole room takes a breath... and *roars*. You knew that would be the moment. You're grinning so much you're almost crying.

A couple of lads ask you what it is; you show them the sleeve – and you're all smiling that mind-blown 'Ouch!?' expression, because they think it's unbelievable too. 'It's not hard to find,' you say, happy that they asked, sharing that great tribal feeling with them. Now, what are you going to play next?

Thirty years ago some now-forgotten musicians cut that record. Without them this brilliant song wouldn't exist. But without you – a DJ – that record would still be in a bent cardboard box in a basement, and tonight's incredible musical moment would never have happened. This is the thrill, and the compulsion, of DJing. This need to share music, and to constantly find *new* music to excite people with, this is the primal force of DJing.

It's not just DJs who have this urge. Music exists to be shared, nature invented it to bring us together, at least that's what the evolutionary psychologists think. They see music as glue for humanity. The neurologists too, they've found bits of our brains which only exist to interact with music. We're *designed* to love music and to want to hear it with others. This explains the skirmishes over the stereo at house parties, and why the kids on the bus prefer tinny mobiles to headphones. It feels great to spread your music just like it feels great to spread your genes. You have a music urge just like you have a sex drive.

The DJs whose lives we've collected in this book were all chasing this feeling. They made finding and spreading music the centre of their lives. And in their quest to share great records with their dancers and listeners they changed the course of popular music. Disco, hip hop and reggae, house, techno and drum and bass, were all created by DJs, by the ones who were brave enough to try something weird and extreme and different.

Some DJs championed a silly amount of amazing new songs. For others it's been about digging for forgotten treasure, rediscovering the thousands of terrific records eclipsed in their time by the few hits everyone knows. Some DJs devised wild new playing techniques to make the party more exciting. Or perverted technology to make a devastating new noise. Some collided styles on their turntables that previously had no business together, like crashing jump jive from the city into down-home hillbilly to give us rock'n'roll. Others waded into the vast gene pool of music and homed in on a particular sound so precisely that pretty soon they'd selectively bred an entirely new species. Ever since music could be recorded, it's travelled way faster than the musicians who make it. That makes the DJ central to music's evolution.

And once technology caught up with his aspirations, the DJ was a musician as well, sampling and sequencing, programming and thieving, chopping, mixing, even occasionally learning an instrument. Who knows better what makes people dance than someone who's spent a lifetime staring at a dancefloor?

If you're a DJ yourself (or have tendencies), this book should inspire you. Here are DJs who've risked injury to find a great tune, DJs who've given up years of their lives to develop new skills on the decks. Others whose music has been so compelling it's changed the way a generation sees the world. Even the ones who've avoided drama have still put in unholy amounts of effort: amassing music and knowledge in the service of a better party.

There are great stories here. Plenty of drugs, a little sex, a smattering of extreme wealth, and a good deal of rock'n'roll. We had a lot of fun meeting all these people and some of them have become good friends (sadly too few of the ones with the extreme wealth). There are no women here. That's not our fault, that's how history's dealt it so far. And it's certainly not an exhaustive list. There are plenty of significant and amazing DJs waiting for volume II. In particular there's no reggae. Here we hold our hands up, but we'll have a great book next year which will correct this (and in our defence we did once walk the entire length of Brooklyn's Fulton Street to try and doorstep the elusive Clement 'Coxsone' Dodd).

Anyway, enough of our yakking, there are musical obsessives waiting to tell you all about DJing – the behind-the-scenes slog and the behind-the-decks thrills, not least the weird and incomparable excitement of sharing music. As Mr Weatherall puts it, 'I've had the joy of hearing this for the first time, now it's your turn!'

Bill and Frank

Join us on our website **www.djhistory.com**
Listen to our weekly podcast **http://tinyurl.com/chn2sa**

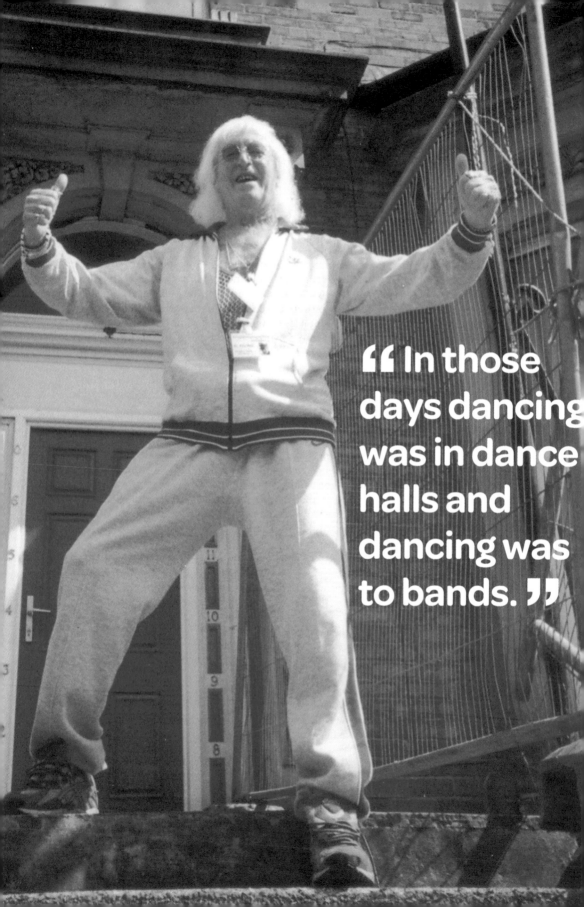

" In those days dancing was in dance halls and dancing was to bands. "

Jimmy Savile
Dance hall disrupter

Interviewed by Frank in Leeds, May 20, 2004

Now then! Now then! Bevan Boy coalminer, professional wrestler, original *Top Of The Pops* frontman and the first superstar DJ, Jimmy Savile is a self-made force of nature. Starting as a tough post-war entrepreneur (his autobiography talks of taking control of Manchester 'below the legal line'), by shaking up the format of Mecca Ballrooms up and down the land, it was Savile more than anyone who moved British nightlife from the dance band to the DJ.

Our interview is in the tower of Leeds General Infirmary, where there's a centre for keyhole surgery supported by Savile's relentless fundraising. It's here he has an office, aided by the angelic Mavis. Bounding through the hospital, Sir Jim says hello to everyone who passes, as if he's compelled to announce his presence. He graciously receives people's smiles in return like a Yorkshire Don Corleone. 'This girl's like a coiled spring,' he jokes to a paramedic snatching a smoke outside. 'I'm glad you bought my chair,' he cracks to a guy rolling past in a wheelchair. 'Morning!' he beams at a wizened Indian lady. She has no clue who he is.

He never uses names, just 'my friend', or 'our pal here'. Effortless, smooth. Before the interview can start he poses for photos with a young boy who's receiving money for treatment from his foundation. There's a short speech and the family are ushered out. He's resplendent in Asics sneakers, a white Nike tracksuit and a ragga-style string vest. There are no cigars, but the trademark jingle-jangle is to the fore: a chunky bracelet, a gold wishbone with diamonds hanging from his neck, and a big gold ring on his thumb that he twists round constantly.

You were effectively working in a nightclub in your teens?
I was born in 1926, right. In 1939 war broke out. And that has a tremendous effect on everybody's life because the basic principle of a human being is whether they're gonna be alive or dead in the morning. Now with the war on you can't guarantee that, especially living in a city like Leeds where we had air raids and all that. And that has an amazing effect on people. It causes them to do things they wouldn't normally do. Or not do things that they should do. Now one of the features was that entertainment was in short supply, because entertainers were in short supply. But from a government point of view they wanted entertainment to keep the workers happy.

Keep the morale up.
And in those days dancing was in dance halls and dancing was to bands. And I'd always thought, even at that age, a record, to me, was quite a fascinating thing. I didn't have any records. I didn't even have a record player – because when you're skint you don't have anything like that – but I used to go round to the lads' houses that had a record player and some records, oh, and they had this amazing music coming out of those speakers. Except they weren't speakers in those days 'cos there was no electric, it was wind-up. No electric motors even.

What kind of music was it?
Well there were the big bands of the time, which were the bands of Ambrose, Joe Loss, Jack Hilton.

....

The radio bands.
Well the radio bands also played in dance halls and hotels, and there were a lot of bands in them days that didn't have a residency, so they gigged all over the place. And all this music was there on the disc. And it never occurred to me that one could dance to a record, 'cos it never occurred to anybody. Now, it's a startling admission that people didn't think you could dance to records, but then nobody even conceived it.

No one danced at home?
You'd play a record at home if you had a record player, but you couldn't be dancing around the carpet 'cos you'd get a bollocking for dancing round the carpet; knacked the carpet up, and things like that. So you could tap your foot, that was about it. But then I heard that this pal of mine had invented this thing: here was this record player, but he'd contrived to make a pick-up so the sound came out of this radio. I rushed round to his house, but by then I was walking on two sticks 'cos I'd been blown up underground in the pits. So I shuffled round to his house and it was an amazing thing.

❝ Now, it's a startling admission that people didn't think you could dance to records, but then nobody even conceived it. ❞

How soon after did you put on your event?
If nothing else in life, at least I've had the ability to recognise an opportunity. I borrowed it there and then. Oh. This is it. A dance! We'll have a dance. And I wrote the tickets out: 'GRAND RECORD DANCE, 1 SHILLING'.

What year is this?
This would be about 1943, '44. And I'd be just 18 at the time. And it was a great night.

Where exactly was it?
The Bellevue branch of the Loyal Order of Shepherds. Up here in Leeds. I think it's offices now. Or flats. 'Cos it was a big house. It was the headquarters of this...

...working men's club?
No, a friendly society. Not a working men's club. They had a room upstairs that they didn't use particularly and my street was literally round the corner from there. And it's wartime, so everybody co-operated with everybody for everything. And they gave me the room for ten bob, fifty pence. Which I didn't have of course. And I never actually got round to paying them.

What was it like?
Even then, as I played the records, and I stood there. I felt this amazing er, power's the wrong word, control's the wrong word. 'Effect' could be nearer. There was this amazing effect: what I was doing was causing 12 people to do something. And I thought, I can make them dance quick. Or slow. Or stop. Or start. And all this was very heady stuff: that one person was doing something to all these people. And that's really the thing that triggered me off and sustained me for the rest of me days.

So that was the moment you realised entertainment was what your life was going to be about?
No. No. I didn't think I was entertaining. What I was doing was, I was creating an atmosphere. An entertainer sings, dances, tells jokes, juggles. I don't do any of that. I was creating. An. Atmosphere. And when I got to the big dance halls and I've got 3,000 people in front of me and I'm on the stage with just the twin decks. And the records playing. My thrill is looking at them, and they're all doing what they're doing because I've just put this thing on. It's a hell of a thing.

How many people at the very first thing you did?
Twelve.

Just 12 people. But you still got that feeling?
Oh yes. 'Cos there were 12 people, six couples, and they were all dancing around to what I was doing. And they weren't even my records.

They were your mate's?
Yes. And they'd all paid a shilling to come in. And somebody said, 'It's a pity there's not many people here.' And I said, 'There's plenty,' because at the time I was only getting 16 shillings a week sick money, so for 12 bob to come in on one night, oh man, wow. And there's seven nights in a week. Oh wow. The only problem was, that nobody agreed with me. Because nobody would turn up to the bloody record dances. Because first of all, the sound left a lot to be desired.

Could you describe the room?
It was like this room [a big living room size] but a bit longer.

Not very big at all. How loud was it?
It was like a small transistor radio. That was the sound.

But it was enough for people to get their groove on. And your mum finished the proceedings on the piano.
She tried to. But it didn't work. Because her music wasn't our music. And she said the burning smell off the top of the piano made her feel ill. 'Cos the thing short-circuited and the wires had burnt the top of the piano.

And can you remember the records you played that night?
They were all band records. Orchestra bands. What we can do is get a taxi and go down there and you can have a look at it. Now that is el scoopo, because nobody knows that that building housed that thing.

The first disco
You're the only one who knows and you're the only one that'll see it. Even Leeds people. It happened in Leeds, and newspapers, television, they've never got round to actually saying, 'Well which one was it?' So we'll grab a cab.

The follow up party was in Otley?
That's right. In Otley there was a café, which was a shop downstairs. And, being inventive, my deal was to suggest that if he gave me the room for nothing I would bring lots of people in and they would buy his tea and cakes and all that. And it sort of worked and it sort of didn't work. Because, again, not many people turned up. And the price of a taxi back to Leeds was £1, 5s – 25 bob. We hadn't taken 25 bob, and the bus fare was ninepence. So there was myself, my dad, who was the cashier, and my brother-in-law, who was the ticket collector and minder. So this poor lady in the café had laid out a load of cups and saucers and cakes and things like that. And only about 20 people turned up, 20, 25 people. And when it came to the interval – 'cos we had intervals in those days – all the punters buggered off to the fish shop, eschewing the lady's tea and cakes. Ah, they've all gone. So. The last bus was 9.30. We had the interval at nine and the dance was supposed to go on till 11. So when they'd gone I packed up my gear and ran to the bus station and caught the bus for ninepence. And when they came back from their fish and chips it was all locked up.

Did you do a few of these?
I did a few, because what happened was, another pal made an electric gramophone turntable and this had a two-and-a-half-inch speaker, so the sound would come out of the speaker. To me, the beauty of that was you could carry it all on one handle. As against having a radio, a record player, a wind-up gramophone, and all that. This: terrific. And so, as long as I set this high enough, so the speaker was level with people's heads. This little two-and-a-half inch speaker. You could put the record like that, turn it up.

Jimmy Savile

··

What was your mate's name?
Dave Dalmour.

And the first guy?
Don't know. I've forgotten his name now. But anyway, what happened was, a girl come and said it's my 21st next week. I can't afford a band. How much? Two pounds ten.

So word had got around?
No. They were all in there, and she thought what a good idea to have music to my birthday party, but they couldn't afford a band. And there was no such thing as a disc jockey because it was unthinkable. And she quite liked the idea of having this jig around to this guy playing records, which in itself was like an amazing gimmick etc etc. And so it went on from there.

You spent some time in France.
The French thing was to do with cycling. Nothing to do with disc jockeying.

It's interesting there was that kind of thing happening in Marseilles and Paris
No. Never saw anything like that. And I doubt if... When I was in France in 1945, I was there within a month of the war finishing. And there were no dances, baby. And there were no discos, and there were no records, and there were no record players. There was bugger all. It was just a bombsite. That's all there was to it. So it wasn't going on in France at all. The only places that ever played records were in cinemas. In between the films. Then they put records on. Now they put adverts on.

Was that your inspiration?
No. I didn't have an outside inspiration. It was recognising an opportunity. And I thought, this is a great band on this record. To dance to this great band would cost a lot of money in London. I've got this here. They can dance to this London band right here. And it was as simple as that. But it didn't take off for ten years. Would you believe it? Ten years, people, but the equipment wasn't right. See.

Were you collecting records?
No.

You were never a record collector.
I've never had a record in my life. People would buy somebody a record for their birthday or Christmas or something like that. People used to play records in their houses. I used to borrow. I only had about 10 records. That's all I needed. And I'd borrow them from anybody.

Were you listening to the radio a lot?
Yes because at the time, because I couldn't walk very well, with my back thing, from getting blown up. I managed to acquire a transistor radio, and by getting a long piece of wire and sticking it in the back and putting the wire through the window and trailing through the window, it was the world's best aerial. I could get all manner of things: American Forces Network. Because in those days during the war AFN was the big thing. There was music there that we never heard of.

Did you try and track any of that down?
No. I heard it. It never occurred to me that I could ever have any. In wartime you were just used to not having anything. So acquisition was just not part of your lexicon. I used to lie for hours listening to this wonderful music, not fastening the two together until I realised that this music, plus room, plus record player, plus some tickets, plus people, could be a way of life. And it was. That was it.

When did you think of getting a second turntable?
This was a great learning curve. I realised I wasn't as clever as I thought. I was about 20, and because I used to put these dance things on I was regarded as a sort of an impresario, and I sort of staggered on, made eight quid here and lost six quid, and then made nine quid there, and lost five quid. So after about two or three years I thought to myself, hang about. If I'm that clever how come I've got no money? Must be something wrong somewhere. And then I

alerted to myself that maybe I didn't know as much as I thought I did, and I wasn't as clever as I thought I was. Now that's quite a profound thing for somebody that age to own up to. So what did I do? I knew that dance halls was my way of life and so by a fluke, in the local Mecca dance hall, the assistant manager had left. So I marched down to the manager and said, 'I'm your new assistant.'

What was the name of the club?
Locarno. The Mecca. The correct title was Mecca Locarno. And I was only an assistant for about seven months, because the governors thought, this guy's got something. Then, when I was about to be the man, the boss, I could do what I wanted. And once again, the record thing raised its head. And now I've got a ballroom and I've got electricians, who could do things. And the company was Westrex, and they looked after the microphones, so I said to them, 'Have you got any record players?'
And they said, 'Yeah, we put them in cinemas.'
So I said, 'Oh, I want one here.'
So they said, 'Okay.'

> ❝ **I've never had a record in my life. I only had about 10 records. That's all I needed. And I'd borrow them from anybody.** ❞

Did they have double ones in the cinemas?
No, just singles. So I came in the afternoon, they were fitting it up, and they were actually up in the light box. Fitting it in the light box. I went what's that then? Well this is where we... No, no, no, no, no it goes on the stage. On the stage? Yes. And, wait a minute, have you got two? And they said yeah, why? I said I want them next to each other. They said you don't need two Jim 'cos these are foolproof, they don't break down. No, no, I says. When this record's playing I want to get this one ready to play. Bloody hell, he says, are they in that much of a hurry? I said, yes my people are.

Nobody ever dreamed of putting two turntables. So I got two turntables together like that. Yet again. Grand record dance. One shilling. Bring your own records. 'Cos I didn't have any records you see. Now the week before we'd had 24 people in. But about 10 to eight we had 600 people turn up. It was like locusts. It was like you couldn't have even dreamed that it could happen. The bloody place was heaving. I was ankle deep in records, on the stage. Of all the bands. Didn't know what the bloody hell they were. If anything worked I played it three times, that's for sure.

But the thing that bugged me was there was 600 people in and they'd all got in for, initially it was free. Initially. And then I got this magic marker, and I put on a 10-inch LP it's called 'The Hucklebuck', which is a jazz tune. A terrific medium tempo. Marvellous. And I put that on, rushed off the stage, went to the poster at the front that said 'ADMISSION FREE' and wrote under 'UNTIL 8PM'. And wrote 'ONE SHILLING'. And another 700 people came and paid a shilling. There was 1300 people in there. It was the most awesome baptism ever.

And from that day on I was the governor. Never looked back. I finished up running 52 dance halls and employing 400 disc jockeys. They made me a director of the company and I left my DJing thing and looked after the whole shebang, the whole of Mecca Ltd.

What was their formula before you arrived?
Dances. All bands. Two bands. Non-stop, no interval. Two bands and it was six nights a week. Didn't used to work on Sundays. But by this time Radio Luxembourg had reared its head and it was overlapping and I was now doing all this for Mecca Ltd and I was on Radio Luxembourg as well. And of course that really made it right that my policy was 100 percent right. I knew it was right. Now everybody knew it was right. Now it was nationally right. And globally right, and I finished up winning the *New Musical Express* award for top DJ for 11 consecutive years.

....

I'd like to talk a little more about those first parties. How did you feel DJing?
I've often thought about it. I've thought about the word 'power' and I've thought about the word 'control', and they are both too harsh. To describe what it was. What it was that I created was an atmosphere. And that is exactly the description. It was the creating of an atmosphere. And the atmosphere would then come back to me and it was total satisfaction. It was also fun.

Like a circuit between you and the people.
Exactly. And they loved the fact that I patently enjoyed being with them. Because I never went onstage as a star or anything like that. It was obvious that I loved what I was doing. it was a tripartite. There was me and the records. There was the venue, and there was the people. And the whole thing was a very terrific worthwhile experience.

> ❝ **I paid the bands *not* to work. No argument. I was taking 50 times more without them than I was taking with them anyway.** ❞

So you were running dance halls for Mecca, and they gave you control over more and more of them.
I brought in record dances and the company realised that suddenly from 24 people they had 1500 people. I was like the guru, the Buddha, I was everything.

You instituted record nights across the whole country
I wasn't a permanent disc jockey anywhere 'cos I was the boss. If they were going to institute a policy in the dance hall I would go and launch the policy. And I used to take two or three disc jockeys with me. And I'd leave them there for a couple of weeks while they train somebody else up. Mecca in London had the Lyceum, The Royal at Tottenham, The Palais at Ilford, The Orchid in South London, Purley. They had about five or six in London. And they all eventually had record nights. Not seven nights a week like I was doing, and obviously it was me that was masterminding what went on, because I was in charge of all the lot. But it was all good fun. Still is.

And you were telling them how to format their nights.
My policy was adhered to strictly by all the disc jockeys.

And what was your policy?
No records over 38 bars a minute [152bpm]. Because what you didn't want was exhibitionist dancers, gyrating about and causing a crowd around them. Everything had to be uniform. No big long sideburns and things like that because they wanted to prove their manliness by cracking somebody. So I made lads wear smart clothes. Because they wouldn't want to roll about on the floor, fighting, with the smart clothes. But they would if I let them in with boots. Or I let them in with jeans. Or as they are today collar, tie, suit. No sideburns. My hair was long but it didn't matter. No sideburns, but if a kid came and his trousers weren't neat and pressed, sorry you can't come in 'cos you look untidy. But if you go home and change you can come back in for nothing. That took the sting away.

What about the DJs?
Now the DJs would stick to my policy. Every hour on the hour was what I called 'smooch time'. All the lights went out and then, bang, we started with the romantic records. But the announcement, the record before smooch time was 'smooch time after this record and it will be a ladies' invitation, as well as the lads'. So the girls knew that if they fancied a lad they could ask him to do the smooch, right. On the hour every hour.
  Bit by bit they would increase the tempo. First of all you'd get a recognisable beat. So you'd finish up with the hardcore smoochers in the middle and the easy boppers on the outside.

Jimmy Savile tells Ben Cree his strange success story. Pt. 1

THE MAN WHO INVENTED THE DISC JOCKEY

"Hi there guys and gals!"

No other way seems really appropriate to introduce a feature on Jimmy Savile, ex-miner turned disc jockey, hospital porter, journalist, charity worker, etc., etc. In fact you name it and the chances are that Jimmy has either done it, is about to do it, or if it's something completely new, will want to do it.

"Dee Jay and Radio Monthly" finally tracked Jimmy down in the lower bowels of Broadcasting House, where each week he records the "links" for his popular Sunday programme "Savile's Travels". We were greeted, however, by a French-speaking Jimmy, who was about half way through a series of ten programmes for the BBC Overseas service – a sort of French "Top of the Pops". In fact Jim's French was very good, and when you consider that he is largely self-taught – "I bought two phrase books which cost me just over a quid, and that's a lot of loot in anyone's eyes!"

– again gives you an insight into the character of the man. Nothing is too much trouble.

But what was it that prompted his interest in becoming a disc-jockey in the first place?

"When I came out of the pits with a broken back and couldn't do any more manual work at that time, like so many people I was looking for work to live. I suddenly decided, because I do things in a left hand sort of way, that instead of looking for a job I would first of all look for the things that I liked, put them all down on paper, and then see if any of the things I enjoyed doing would make me a living.

"It was a very strange sort of list because it comprised things like music, lights, girls, stopping in bed and so on, and it was apparent to me that I could never become an atom scientist or a long distance lorry driver. So my list precluded just about everything the labour exchange had to offer, because

And the hardcore bit got smaller and smaller and smaller and as the tempo increased, so my people would put the lights up just a little bit. Lights up a bit more, so eventually, bang, the lights'd be up, and we'd be back in business with the disco. On the hour, smooch time. In fact so much so that in both Leeds and Manchester and London I've heard people, customers talking, and they'd say, 'Ooh it was foggy, the bus was late. I didn't get in till second smooch.' I took over Greenwich Mean Time, with my policy.

I had four or sometimes five DJs. The new ones would work from seven till half past, when there wasn't too many people in. And that's how they'd learn their trade. And the next one up the rung, half past seven to eight. And as the disc jockeys got better and better, they worked from eight to half past. And I'd usually come on about half past nine. Towards the end, or right at the end. And I always made sure that my lads were more popular than I was. Because I wanted to run my place like a post office, so if I wasn't there I wouldn't be missed. You see. And that's the way it worked, because all my boys were far more popular with the girls ever than I was.

Were they talking between the songs?
Yes, but only what they'd picked up from the governor. One thing I said to them is never fight with your hand. If you're going to say something, say it. And if you're going to play something, play it. But don't try to say it and play it at the same time by turning the volume up, 'cos you're gonna shout over the record – they're not going to hear what you're saying anyway. Even if it's one you've been waiting for: 'The latest from the King'. Bang. But don't fade it up under what you're saying, 'cos it's a bad habit.

What was your patter like in those days? What did you actually say?
I didn't actually say too much, because the early disc jockeys, that was always one of their failings. They thought that the more they talked the better they were. And it was the exact opposite. A record would finish, and instead of saying like a Ministry of Agriculture and Fisheries announcement: 'That was so and so, the next one is so and so.' I'd say 'Ere! As it 'appens...' Now that meant nothing, but it made an impact. I was only saying a few words. As few as possible, which was the exact opposite to the majority of people in those days.

There was a reason for talking a lot on the radio in the early days, in that you were only allowed so much needle time in half an hour. And so if a disc jockey talked or ran a competition or something like that. It would save on needle time. You were only allowed so much needle time. The union would only allow so much in an hour. Or they'd only allow you 40 minutes of needle time.

The union being the Musicians' Union?
Well the Musicians' Union and all the unions that ran that particular business. Radio unions and things like that. So if you could only play 40 minutes worth of records in an hour it means that somebody's got to talk for 20 minutes. It was no good me operating like that because I didn't work like that. On Luxembourg for instance it was the record company bought the time. That was when Luxembourg was at its most successful. EMI'd buy five hours and they would employ a disc jockey to work that five hours.

Yours was Warner Brothers, wasn't it?
My umbrella was the Decca Record Company. They had Warner Brothers, they had London, they had RCA Victor. They had Decca. They had seven or eight labels.

And you'd just be playing records on those labels.
On those labels for those programmes. It was the Warner Brothers show, and the Decca Records show, and all that sort of thing. And so it was just the hard world of ratings. If you were lucky enough to get figures you were Jack the lad. And it didn't matter what you thought, if the figures plummeted, that was you out, finished.

You had a few run-ins with the Musicians' Union, didn't you?
No. I never had a run-in ever. In my dance halls I paid the bands not to work. No argument. I was taking 50 times more without them than I was taking with them anyway.

They didn't even have to show up, or were they standing in the wings?

No. Didn't even have to show up.

Did anyone ever question that?
There was absolutely no problem with it. Because they thought it was marvellous. The band went home and played other gigs. With my blessing. 'Cos it was odd. Even Mecca Ltd said, I'm sure there's something. 'What we paying 'em for?' 'Because we're paying 'em'. They don't come in. And that's it. And of course when they saw the business...

Was it written about? Did the trade press pick up on it? Such a huge leap.
Not really, no. They didn't. They thought it was a mushroom phenomenon... that wouldn't work. And it was like pop music.

> **❝ I've heard people talking, customers, and they'd say, 'Ooh it was foggy, the bus was late. I didn't get in till second smooch.' ❞**

Did any of your protégés become well known?
Two of them are now millionaires.

Who's that?
It's best you don't know. They don't want their names bandying around.

Are they not famous as DJs?
No. But it was disc-jockeying that started them off. They started as disc jockey then got two, three, four more mobile disc jockeys. Put disc jockeys out, allowed them to do other things. As soon as they got a few quid they were able to do that which they wanted. One of them for instance is one of the leading art dealers in Britain.

What was your official title when you were at Mecca?
My official title was General Manager, when I was managing the dance hall. And then I was known then as a 'Working Director' which meant that you had a director status over more than one dance hall. Most had four or five dance halls, but because of this unique record thing, I had all of them, and there were about 52 dance halls at the time. All over Britain.

And what freedom did that give you?
Complete. Complete. Because they didn't argue with me, babe. I won every conceivable award for making money. For them. My hobby is making money. I don't particularly want it for me; I'm alright. I'm OK; but I quite like the idea of making it. When I was with Mecca Ltd they were earning fortunes of money and I was also on Radio Luxembourg, but I still worked for Mecca for a year and a half overlapping the Luxembourg.

So you were earning them fortunes and they were just paying you a salary.
That's all I wanted. I was always odd. They could never understand why I was odd. At Mecca I was earning £60 a week as Mecca manager. And £600 a day on my day off at Radio Luxembourg.

How did Luxembourg approach you?
Somebody came into the dance hall in Leeds. This guy came up to me and said 'I've never seen records played like that before'.
     And I said, 'Really?'
     And he said, 'I'm from Radio Luxembourg do you fancy being on Radio Luxembourg? He said, 'Can you come for an audition?'
     I said, 'No!'
     He said, 'Why not?'
     I said, ' Well you've seen all there is, you either want it or you don't.'
He says, 'You're quite a character, aren't you. Everybody does an audition.' I says, 'Yeah... God bless em.' And he went off and I got a telegram 'Your programme starts next Thursday.'

....

Why were they paying you so much?
I turned a 600,000 audience to 2,300,000 in five weeks. Nobody had ever done that ever. And that was the top, the top thing on Luxembourg. So I ended up with five shows a week. And because I don't have an agent or a manager or anything like that I send me own bills out. And they found that I could actually write commercials. I wrote commercials for Coca Cola, Boots The Chemist, everybody that was anybody, and so I charged them for writing the commercials. And I thought there's got to be another few quid somewhere. So after about three months my bills suddenly included the word 'utterance'. Utterance was £50.

And they said, 'What's utterance?'
And I said, 'Well I'm uttering the commercial.'
'Are you really?'
'Yes, I'm writing it for whatever it is, hundred pound, and I'm uttering it too.' I was quite proud of the utterance because nobody's ever done that before or since. So I was getting £600 a day on my day off. It was wonderful. Great fun.

You were doing very much the same as some of the American DJs, carving a really individual role for yourself. When did you become aware of the American tradition of DJing?
I don't even acknowledge it today that there's an American tradition. All I know is mine. I do what I do. If it matches somebody else that's by coincidence. I'm like the QE2. I go straight ahead. And if you come up against something else: terrific, but I was never influenced by anything, because you don't need to be a brain surgeon to be a disc jockey. It's not the most taxing thing in the world. All you've got to have is instinct.

" I was always odd. I was earning £60 a week as Mecca manager. And £600 a day on my day off at Radio Luxembourg. It was great fun. "

When did you first hear the word 'disco' or 'discotheque'?
The word 'disco' was invented by the French. The first club in London was in Wardour St and it was called La Discothèque, spelt 'T-H-E-Q-U-E'. La Discothèque was unique because instead of having chairs it had half a dozen double beds. And you could go and spag out on the bed, and part of the game was wandering around looking at all the couples on the beds. It were unbelievable. And from a press point of view the fact that a place didn't have chairs as much as it had beds, was like the wildest of the wild. And so that made it notorious. There was no free sex or anything like that. But you were laid down instead of sitting down. And that in itself was such a gimmick, and because the place was called La Discothèque, the name caught on. Before that, everything had been a dance hall, where you could put 3,000 people. Nobody thought of having small places where you'd have 150 people.

So the name disco started being applied to the smaller places.
Yes. For small places. And then society thought it was a good idea. Top London society. So there was the in-place for society people. It would only take about 150 people, and that was called the Saddle Room. And all the horsey-doggy-foxy people went there and they had theirs, and then La Discotheque was there.

In terms of the stardom. I'm sure you took it in your stride. But you were very different from the people you were mixing with. The people at the same level as you were popstars and musicians.
I never thought, to this day, that I was in show business. I created an atmosphere with what I thought was a good idea. It worked, and I just kept going with it. If somebody said to me, you are a star, that would come as quite a cultural shock to me, because I wasn't doing anything that a star did. I was just making a lot of money and giving a lot of people a lot of good times. But I wasn't a star.

You were always flash though, dressed outrageously.

That's different. That's not stardom. Now in the local paper they wrote about a restaurant that has a lot of personalities go in. And it said, 'If you can call Jimmy Savile in a string vest a personality.' It's novel. I've been wearing tracksuits for a million years. Sometimes they're fashionable and sometimes people wouldn't be seen dead in them. I wear trainers all the time. Sometimes they're fashionable and sometimes people wouldn't be seen dead. It's never bothered me. If I'm fashionable it's purely by coincidence. And if I'm unfashionable, hard luck. It's still very convenient. And I've even got an evening dress tracksuit. With silk facings on and things like that.

It sounds a lot of fun in the late '60s, early '70s when it all came together.

Oh, oh. Yeah. You were standing up in front of all these people and it was such a happy fun time that all you wanted to do was have fun. But at nobody else's expense. That was not my nature. But woe betide anybody who came and tried to mess with my people. They lived to regret it. Because there was this responsibility which I felt very keenly: if I knew that something wrong was going down, then I was quite implacable in putting it right. If there was anything untoward, just turn the record off and say 'NO!' The place would go dead quiet. Then turn the record up again and that was it. Nobody asked me to have that concern. It just came naturally.

You must have been a hard man to run all those dance halls.

So they say.

© DJhistory.com

JIMMY SAVILE ORIGINAL 8

CHARLIE BARNETT ORCHESTRA – Skyliner

LOU BUSCH – Zambezi

TOMMY DORSEY – Sunny Side Of The Street

HARRY JAMES – I'm Beginning To See The Light

STAN KENTON – Painted Rhythm

JOE LOSS – Tea For Two Cha Cha

GLENN MILLER – In The Mood

GLENN MILLER – Pennsylvania 6-5000

Compiled by Jimmy Savile

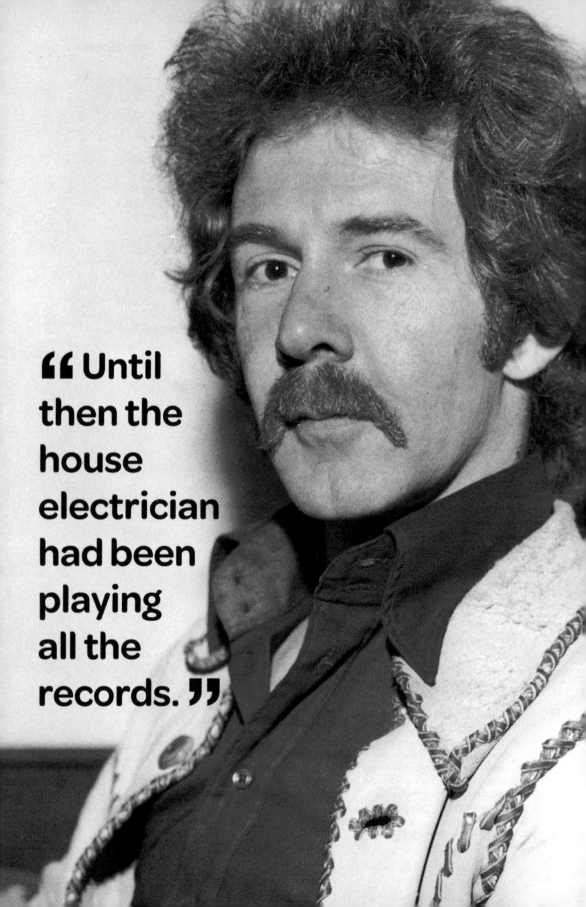

❝ Until then the house electrician had been playing all the records. ❞

Ian Samwell
No. 1 Deejay

Interviewed by Bill online, February 23, 1999

Nifty musician, top songwriter, record producer, all-round smoothie and the man who brought musical sophistication to Britain's discotheques. As well as writing one of the very few credible British rock'n'roll records in 'Move It' by Cliff Richard & The Drifters, Ian Samwell helped transform our swirling post-war ballrooms, venues like the Lyceum in London and the Orchid in Purley, into havens for rhythm and blues music. Thanks to his deal with a New York publisher, Samwell had access to American records well before other people. He worked with The Small Faces, John Mayall, America and Hummingbird, and was the first British songwriter to have a song recorded by an American rhythm and blues act – 'Say You Love Me Too' by The Isley Brothers. Groundbreaking soul writer Dave Godin claimed that the Lyceum was the first proper disco in the UK. It was Ian Samwell who made it that way.

When and how did you start collecting music?
My parents owned a wind-up record player and a selection of pre-war records, so records were always a part of my life. Because I was obliged to do National Service I didn't actually start collecting records until after I got out in the summer of '58. I couldn't afford it. Like everybody else, I listened to Radio Luxembourg and jukeboxes in coffee bars.

I joined the Drifters in April 1958 and Cliff [Richard] had a small record collection, mostly the songs we were performing on stage. I bought a portable battery powered record player with a built-in speaker. I didn't think of myself as starting a collection, I just bought what sounded exciting to me – 'Why Do Fools Fall In Love?', 'Whole Lotta Shakin'', 'Wake Up Little Susie' etc. The Drifters also acquired a number of discards from a jukebox on an American air base. This led to us performing some very R&B material like 'Get A Job' by the Silhouettes and 'Rock'n'Roll Shoes' by Chuck Willis. We didn't know they were race records, we just thought they were rock'n'roll.

You were eventually edged out of the band, but you carried on writing songs for them.
Norrie Paramor [their producer] didn't want The Drifters, he only wanted Cliff. He had a recording contract prepared but didn't get Cliff to sign it until after we had recorded 'Move It' and 'Schoolboy Crush'. It became obvious that Cliff was going to need a better guitarist than I was, so after we got back from Butlin's Holiday Camp, Johnny Foster went to the 2I's and found Hank Marvin. Hank agreed to join if he could bring along his mate Bruce Welch. I traded in my guitar for a bass and set off on tour with the Kalin Twins. On that tour was Jet Harris and he wanted to join and Cliff wanted him so I got fired.

The official story was that I had left to concentrate on songwriting and, in fact, I had been given a five-year contract with a retainer. We were all friends and I stayed around writing songs for a couple of years. I was also a temporary acting unpaid sort of manager-cum-publicist for the Drifters until the time came when they needed someone more experienced in 'The Business'.

How did you get into playing records?
Gradually I 'drifted' away from the Drifters and began writing songs for other artists. I went to

Ian Samwell

....

New York because I was under contract to a subsidiary of an American company, Hill & Range music. I bought or was given a lot of records, which I brought home to England with me.

Back in London I used to hang out in Denmark Street or 'Tin Pan Alley' and I continued to go to the clubs such as the 2i's and The Scene. I was at the 2i's when I first heard of Buddy Holly's death. Times were changing, rock'n'roll was over and pop was the big thing. Most of it didn't appeal much to me and I turned to rhythm and blues: Jackie Wilson, The Coasters, The Isley Brothers...

How did you get the gig at The Lyceum?
I don't know how they found me, I just remember being invited down to The Lyceum one lunchtime. They were looking for someone to spin records for a lunch hour crowd. The house electrician had been playing the records until then. I had never played records as a DJ before. I was broke so I agreed to do it – money for nothin' and chicks for free! I don't know if it was every Tuesday but it might well have been.

Pretty soon it became very popular and I got booked to do Sunday nights as well. I played all the latest records with a few golden oldies thrown in. But I don't remember playing oldies much. There was too much new stuff that I wanted to play. The Lyceum's record collection was pretty pathetic so I started to bring my own records. I played a lot of stuff you couldn't hear on the BBC – mostly rhythm and blues because it was hip and great to dance to.

What made you want to play records in the first place, since it was still a pretty unusual thing to do back then?
It was unusual, to say the least! I'd never heard of anything like it in England. In America they had record hops with DJs from local stations, and sock hops – usually held in gymnasiums. You had to take off your shoes so as not to damage the floor – hence 'sock hops'. But there was nothing like that in England, so far as I knew.

When did you start there?
I think I started the Lyceum in 1962. Mecca made a life-size cut-out photo of me and billed me as 'London's No. 1 Dee-Jay'. Nonsense, of course, I wasn't even on the radio!

What was your next step?
My next project was to run a 'disco' night at Greenwich Town Hall. I did this with Brian Mason, a part-time bouncer at The Lyceum. He took care of the business and I took care of the music. I bought two record players with built in speakers. I placed them next to each other on a table on the stage and placed a house mic in front of each one. The Town Hall had a Tannoy house system I think. The resultant echo spoiled the sound of the records but we had no other choice. People came from all around and packed the place. Eventually we started booking live acts. Some I remember were: The Animals, fresh down from Newcastle and without a record deal. Millie 'My Boy Lollipop' Small, and Sounds Incorporated. I also invited recording artists and gave away promo copies of their latest singles. Jet Harris, Kenny Lynch, Don Charles and Carol Dean were amongst those who graced the stage.

I was eventually given the job at The Orchid Ballroom at Purley which, like The Lyceum, also belonged to Mecca Ballrooms. Occasionally they would send me out of town to do a 'special' night at one of their other places. I gave it up after a while because it was too far to go for too little money. Mecca made a fortune though.

I also played the records at The Flamingo on Wardour Street in Soho. To me, that was the best gig because the audience were either very hip or West Indian and I played nothing but rhythm and blues or bluebeat, which became ska, which became skank, which became the reggae of today. I produced Georgie Fame's first record there, an album called *Rhythm And Blues at the Flamingo*.

It was presumably a blacker soundtrack there. Do you remember specific discs?
The Flamingo was great for James Brown and the Bar-Kays. Stuff like that. Otis Redding, Sam and Dave, Wilson Pickett, Rufus Thomas, Maxine Brown etc, etc, etc. We also played bluebeat records: Prince Buster etc.

There were a lot of black American GIs there. Did they ever introduce you to records?
I don't remember any GIs bringing me records to play. It seems very unlikely that they would be walking around London with a record in their hands.

Tell me about meeting Jeff Dexter?
I first met Jeff at The Lyceum. He was about 16 but looked 14. He was a very sharp dresser, 'The Boy From New York City', he wore mohair suits and button-down shirts from America. He was also the best twister and when he danced all the girls would gather round in a circle to watch him.

> ❝ **There was a tiny basement that sold illegal imports; it was only open for two hours at lunch time. It was all very secretive and exciting.** ❞

You were one of the first people to play 'The Twist'. What kind of impact did it have?
The big record was 'Let's Twist Again' by Chubby Checker. It was enormously influential in terms of introducing American-style dances to Britain. The only previous influence was jive, which was bought over by the Yanks during World War II. Other dances were the locomotion and the mashed potato.

Somebody told me that they heard you play Hank Ballard & the Midnighters' version of 'The Twist' at the Lyceum, which came out earlier.
I don't recall if I was playing Hank Ballard before Chubby Checker. The probability is that I was. Hank's record was released on the B-side of 'Teardrops On Your Letter', which was a pretty big hit in the States. Chubby Checker's 'Twist' came soon after.

Did you talk on the mic?
Yes, I talked on the mic at all the venues. Announcing records (but not before *every* record), and announcing other things like 'dream time', during which we spun the disco ball and played three slow records in a row.

Which clubs were most influential in terms of the music they played?
The key clubs of the early sixties were the Ad Lib, The Scotch of St James, The Cue Club, The Flamingo and, later on, The Speakeasy. There was also Middle Earth, The Scene, The Marquee and the 100 Club on Oxford Street. I've probably forgotten a couple, but those are the ones that come to mind.

Who was your favourite DJ?
I didn't really have a favourite. All the Alan Freemans and the other guys were on the BBC – ''Nuff said', 'Not 'arf!' I've never been a great fan of the in-your-face-type DJ who talks too much and too loudly. For me, it was always about the music and how to present new records and put them together in attractive danceable sequences. Jeff and I both knew how to pack the floor and keep it that way. And we did it without extended dance mixes too! We also had to walk 10 miles through the snow, up-hill, to get our records! These kids today...

You say you were making trips to New York as a songwriter. Where were you sourcing your records?
I used to go to New York at least once or twice a year. Probably five or six visits during my DJ years. I bought records from Sam Goody's as well as the Colony record store. Once someone arranged for me to pick out some records at a One Stop wholesale store.

Do you remember any you brought back from these trips?
I do remember some of the records, notably: Barrett Strong's 'Money' on the Anna label. Berry Gordy's first attempt. Various Stax things, artists like Rufus and Carla Thomas and the first Supremes record 'Baby Love' and Len Barry's 'One, Two, Three'. Most of what I bought

was eventually released in England, but I had them first. Oh, I just remembered – Jackie Ross's 'Selfish One'.

It was really hard to find those kind of records in London at that time.
I mostly just had my own collection. There was a tiny basement on, I think, Lisle Street, not far from the Flamingo. It sold illegal imports and was only open for about two hours at lunch time and only one or two days a week. You really had to be in the know to find your way to it. Everything they had was American rhythm and blues, and blues. It was all very secretive and exciting.

© DJhistory.com

Don Fardon, Carol Deene, Wendy Richards (Pauline Fowler!), little Jeff Dexter, Kenny Lynch, Jet Harris, Doug Sheldon and Ian Samwell pose for an ad for Dougie Millings Tailoring at Greenwich Town Hall, 1962.

LYCEUM 30

RAY STEVENS – Jeremiah Peabody's Poly Unsaturated Quick Dissolving Fast Acting Pleasant Tasting Green And Purple Pills

DEE CLARK – Raindrops

DION – The Wanderer

BARRETT STRONG – Money (That's What I Want)

CHUBBY CHECKER – The Twist

CURTIS LEE – A Night At Daddy Gee's

JOEY DEE AND THE STARLITERS – The Peppermint Twist

U.S. BONDS – Quarter to Three

THE MIRACLES – Shop Around

DEL SHANNON – Runaway

RAY CHARLES – Hit The Road Jack

THE ROOFTOP SINGERS – Walk Right In

ERNIE K-DOE – Mother-In-Law

NEIL SEDAKA – Oh Carol

FREDDY CANNON – Teen Queen Of The Week

THE MARVELETTES – Please Mr Postman

CHRIS KENNER – I Like It Like That

THE ISLEY BROTHERS – Twist And Shout

THE COOKIES – Chains

CAROLE KING – Might As Well Rain Until September

TIMI YURO – Hurt

EYDIE GORME – Blame It On The Bossa Nova

BURL IVES – A Little Bitty Tear Let Me Down

NED MILLER – From A Jack To A King

JOHN D LOUDERMILK – Thou Shalt Not Steal

CHRIS KENNER – Land Of A Thousand Dances

DON GIBSON – Sea Of Heartbreak

GENE CHANDLER – Duke Of Earl

BRUCE CHANNEL – Hey Baby

THE BEATLES – Love Me Do (first ever public play)

Compiled by Jeff Dexter

RECOMMENDED LISTENING

GEORGIE FAME – Rhythm And Blues At the Flamingo

VARIOUS – From Route 66 to the Flamingo

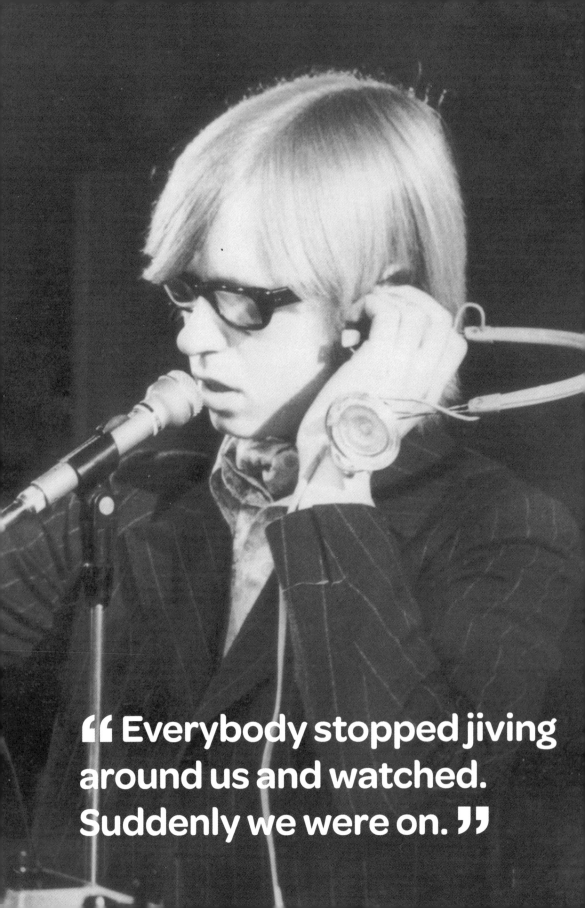

"Everybody stopped jiving around us and watched. Suddenly we were on. "

Jeff Dexter
The modfather

Interviewed by Bill in London, February 18, 1999

All the best DJs start out as dancers. Jeff Dexter was the south London mod who was banned from the Lyceum for dancing the twist and, in the process, liberated British dancefloors from their partnered past. Alongside his mentor Ian Samwell, he became one of the leading DJs in London, playing at mod haven Tiles, a cutting-edge pill palace documented by Tom Wolfe in his story The Noonday Underground. As resident at Middle Earth, Jeff drenched London's dancefloors in acid as the sixties turned psychedelic, as well as being the gun-for-hire at any festival worth its salt, and went on manage several successful bands, America among them. Off-record he can regale you with hilarious stories of the visiting American bands he turned on to the glories of LSD. Jeff is still the nattiest dresser in London Town.

Where did you grow up?
I was born in 1946 in Lambeth Hospital and grew up in the Newington Butts by the Elephant & Castle.

When did you start collecting records?
I've never really collected records. The first record I ever bought was 'Sixteen Tons' by Tennessee Ernie Ford. I just thought it was the coolest song. I bought it in East Street Market from the A1 Records stall and I walked home with it under my arms singing it, thinking I was this big country person digging in the mines. This was 1955 or '56, I think. It was a 78. Not many people had record players to play 45s in those days. I had two friends who lived locally who had gramophones so I could go and play it there. We never had a record player. We had a piano.

So you had an interest in music?
I studied music. I played the piano, I played the flute, I played the trumpet, I did classical. From eight or nine I had a knack of taking off the pop stars of the day: Johnny Ray, at the local mothers' meeting hall. I was never that interested in pop music, as such. I liked the Goons. I liked military music, as well. I'd go anywhere at that age, to see a military band. I liked the uniforms. Unlike most of my friends who were suddenly all besotted by these new images – my brother had become an Elvis fan – I wasn't particularly interested at first, until Buddy Holly.

When did you come across the Lyceum?
I went to youth clubs when I was 13 or 14, and started meeting *teenagers!* down at East Street. I went to a school summer camp when I was 14 down in Godalming, Surrey, and every night the teachers would play records. And a couple of the teachers from other schools brought records that I'd never heard. And I was particularly interested in being with the girls, so I think that was my first bite at really getting into dancing.

I always had a good relationship with girls because I did dressmaking and tailoring and I was the only boy, so I'd heard about places like the Tottenham Royal, and I had a big brother as well. The girls said, 'Oh, when you come back to London you must come to the

Lyceum with us.' 'I can't go to the Lyceum. I'm 14.' And I was four foot eight at the time, and probably looked about 11. How could I go to The Lyceum? I had all the clothes; I had every piece of equipment to look like I was a grown up, but I had this tiny little face and tiny little frame. But I braved it the following Sunday and when I signed the forms I said I was 16 and born in the war in 1944.

And they bought it?
Oh yeah, I already had my front on then.

What was it like when you went in there?
It changed my life in about three minutes. The record club, or Sunday club, opened at three in the afternoon, there'd be records during the afternoon, and then records and bands during the evening. I remember walking up to the top and seeing all the cloakrooms. Huge, I'd never seen big cloakrooms like that. I walked in, up the stairs, down through the gallery and into the ballroom space. And the sound in such a big place just blew me away. It was great.

Did it look like it does now?
Yeah, except it had a level dancefloor. It had a huge, fabulous, multi-coloured dancefloor. Multi-coloured wood. Squares, and gold leaf. And there was Ian 'Sammy' Samwell stood on the stage with his perfect barnet and his mohair suit, who I'd already seen in the foyer with his cardboard cut-out and thought, 'Who is this guy?' I thought he looked really naff.

Really?
Well, he was part of the old school. He was part of what we called the rocker brigade. His hair was slicked back perfectly dark. But there was something about what he was doing on stage and the records he was playing in the afternoon.

There were only a few people who would turn up that early, a few girls, who'd get there early to get their dance steps together. Of course, because the place wasn't full, he was playing records that were new, weren't necessarily out-and-out dance records, until people started to fill the place up. So that first afternoon I heard records I'd never heard before. By 6 o'clock I'd heard a few things and I had to go and find out what they were.

'What music do you call this mate?'

'It's rhythm and blues.'

I'd been watching him, while he was playing and he was singing along to every song he played. He knew every word to every song; and I could barely make out the words.

'How come you know all the words to the songs?'

'I'm a songwriter. I know how they go.'

From that moment we became best friends. I jived my arse off all night with these girls from summer camp.

When was the first time you went?
First week of August, 1961.

Was that the night you got into trouble for obscene dancing?
No that was a couple of months later. That was the end of September when I got barred for obscenity, doing the twist with these two girls.

The twist came over here in about '62 didn't it?
Well, that's when it exploded, early part of '62.

When were you first aware of it?
I knew the song. Sammy had been playing two versions of it. Hank Ballard, which was a B-side of another song. Sammy played rhythm and blues and country; he had a great love of country rock as well. When we got the Chubby Checker version, after about three weekends and Tuesday nights (there was a record club on Tuesday nights) of hearing this 'Twist' I went up and talked to him. 'Oh, it's some new dance they say's happening in America.' In the mailer on the back of the picture sleeve was a diagram of how to do the twist. In three easy diagrams. Place your feet together and pretend you're rubbing your bum with a towel, and gyrate. There was this other girl who'd come the previous week and she talked about some

dance scene she'd seen in New York . New York? It's a million miles away. She attempted to do it on the carpet with this other guy. So I put two and two together and we went and did it. Doing it very carefully at first because you didn't want to make an arse of yourself. And we started going through it, and everybody stopped jiving around us and watched. Suddenly we were on. At the end of it the bouncers came up and removed me from the dancefloor.

Did they give a reason?
'You might start a fight, doing silly things like that.' Then the manager came over and said, 'You can't do obscene dances like that. Out you go!" And I was ejected.

Were you banned?
I think the first time I actually talked myself out of getting thrown out, till later in the evening when Sammy played 'The Twist' again! Of course we did it again and then I got ejected. They said, 'You can't come in the ballroom any more to do that sort of thing.'

How did the press get hold of this?
I tried to go back two weeks later and brave it out. I managed to blag my way in, I'd promised I wouldn't do it again, but the funny thing is the twist had finally made it into the paper; this new dance had been picked up by the Arthur Murray School of Dancing and I think they sent people down to show us how to do it – ha ha ha! And I got captured on film and it got shown around the cinemas on Pathé newsreels. This thing, this obscenity that I'd been ejected for became popular and I got offered a job at the Lyceum. As a dancer! Of course, they didn't know I was still at school and I'd only just turned 15.

" I got barred for obscenity for doing the twist with these two girls. The bouncers came up and removed me from the dancefloor. "

They found out?
Oh yeah. Well I had to tell them. But you could leave school at 15 in those days.

And that's what you did?
Oh yeah. I dropped my tailoring. I dropped my music studies. The thought of being paid to dance with women was just phenomenal!

The twist would be very influential
The twist hadn't really hit anywhere yet and we'd known the record for two months already. It was already a bit passé with us tight-arse mods. We always wanted the next thing. Even though it hadn't exploded. Most people hadn't even attempted it, because they were too busy doing their jive.

What kind of clothes were you wearing? Mod grew out modern jazz didn't it?
It grew of out of the jazz clubs, when all the guys had started coming over in the fifties wearing their Ivy League clothes which were too small for them, and of course, there was the whole thing about the new Italian fashions, which was the box jacket, which the Americans were adopting after their '50s look. The generation who were a little older than me were trying emulate those guys. They'd dumped the drapes and brothel creepers and jumped into this boxy jacket thing.

Were American GIs going to The Lyceum?
Yeah. Not a lot, but there were always Americans there from Ruislip and Hillingdon.

Were there many black GIs?
A few. Not many.

Where were the black kids hanging out?

··

There was a place near where I lived called Clubland, where there were a few black kids, but they kept a fairly low profile when they mixed with the whites. They were only just beginning to mingle with our lot. We had very few black kids who were our friends. But most of them lived in Brixton at that time.

What stuff were they listening to?
Well, down on Atlantic Road, just off the market there, there was a record stall that sold calypso. The black kids that I was meeting, were listening to the pop music of the day. At Clubland, there were black boys there and they just wanted to be part of our culture.

How long were you going to The Lyceum?
Until November '61 when I started off working with the band there. That's how I started off dancing in front of the band. As the twist started to explode there were all of these newspaper articles and television programmes, everyone that had a dance craze of any kind was bringing out a dance record. Any time there was a new dance I had to interpret it in front of 2,000 of my peers... and take a lot of flak.

Where were you finding out how to do them?
In some cases read *Billboard*, or a tip sheet from Sam Goody's record shop in New York which Sammy used to get. And of course, the newspapers of the day and reporters on *Melody Maker* who lived in America and would send reports on what was happening there. If there was no clear indication, I'd just make it up! I was doing nightclubs and cabaret...

❝ It was still pretty new, the idea of record hops. The ballroom scene was where most music happened in those days, so people went there to learn about the music and dances. ❞

So you danced in other clubs?
Yeah. In those days it was either ballrooms or nightclubs in the West End and all the big events at the hotels. Whenever there was a party there, someone rich or something, they'd book a band, Cyril Stapleton's Orchestra, who still had a radio show then.

Was he the Lyceum resident?
He replaced the Johnny Howard Band, who moved up to the Tottenham Royal. Every Mecca ballroom had two bands, they had a big orchestra – a swing/dance band – and a trio or quartet or quintet. The other band at the Tottenham Royal was the Dave Clark Five. We had the Mick Mortimer Quartet at the Lyceum.

How did the nights run then, between records and bands? What was the running order?
There'd be records from about three till six, then the quartet would come on and do a half set, then the stage would turn – all the places had revolving stages – the big band would come on, then there'd be half an hour of records and then another short set from the quartet and another set from the band. Then we'd close the evening with records.

I presume the bands were playing the hits of the day?
Yeah, on those nights in particular they'd only play the pop hits of the day and most of them were the real trashy ones, because they thought that's what the kids wanted. Maaan. Of course, by that time, with all the influx of black imports and rhythm and blues it was a bit different. Cyril Stapleton, I'll give him his due, was very keen to please the younger audience and wanted to know every new record that came out each week. As soon as anything came, that we thought was any good, he'd have the band play it.

Did they use vocalists?

....

Yeah, they used four vocalists and I became one of them as well. I used to do the doo wop bops, and the odd pop song.

Where did Ian Samwell fit into all of this?
The first night he started at the Lyceum was the first night I ever went, which is just one of those beautiful coincidences. I think he'd done a couple of nights replacing people before... The guy who originally played the records at the Lyceum was actually the electrician! I think Jimmy Savile might have done a couple of things before. It was still pretty new, the idea of record hops.

Was Jimmy Savile known at that point?
He had a name as a disc jockey. Maybe he'd just started on Radio Luxembourg as well, along with a guy called Tony Hall. Of course the ballroom scene was where most music happened in those days. All that swing band stuff during the war had introduced people to jives and bunny hops so people went there to learn about the music and dances.

How long did you work Mecca as a dancer?
Until '66. After about 18 months at the Lyceum with Cyril Stapleton, the manager of the Lyceum was asked to move down to a place called the Orchid Ballroom in Purley, which had just been refurbished and was the biggest ballroom in Europe. Biggest dancefloor. Huge, huge dancefloor, four different bars, Chicken & Chicks, as they called it. Fish bar. Chicken bar. They had this big ice igloo where they sold ice cream sodas. And they had a roundabout which was another bar, a revolving bar, all in this wonderful huge, huge building. Now it's a health club, discotheque, bowling alley. Mecca were doing very well at the time. The year preceding that they'd also opened a chain of ice rinks called the Silver Blade ice rinks all around the country. I went to the opening of every Silver Blades ice rink in the country and attempted to dance on the ice!

What DJ equipment did they have at the Mecca places?
At the Mecca clubs we had two Garrard turntables at most of the venues. They weren't 301s. They were integrated systems – all-in-one units. It was semi-pro gear. I think they were direct drive with a volume knob for each deck.

What were the clubs that were regarded as hot?
Le Discothèque in Wardour Street, which was probably the first seedy late night club. And the Flamingo. Late nights at the Flamingo. The Flamingo had more black GIs than anyone else, it also integrated with black London and west London, because it was open late on Friday and Saturday, in fact all night. I worked every night in the ballrooms, and most closed at 11 because of licensing laws. We'd always go to a club afterwards. It might even have been a jazz club.

How late was the Flamingo open?
Well it was usually closed at 12 except on a Friday and Saturday, when they ran all nighters. I think they started running them in 1962.

Were they unlicensed?
They were coca cola bars. But upstairs from the Flamingo, was the Whiskey-A-Go-Go which was licensed.

Is that where the Wag was later, on Wardour Street?
Exactly. The Whiskey was very chic. You'd rather go into the dive below it than the Whiskey, but obviously people who drank would try and go to the Whiskey. There were two other dodgy late night bars in basements in Wardour Street, where you could get a drink if you ordered a steak sandwich for a ridiculous amount of money, like four shillings.

Sammy and I started to do shows at the Flamingo, from '62. Also February '62 we opened a weekly record hop at Greenwich Town Hall, on a Wednesday or Thursday. There was a lack of places to go. Tuesdays and Sundays the place was packed at the Lyceum, and it held 2,000.

The name discotheque never really got used until '62 or '63, really. The only place that used it was Le Discothèque, that's because it had poncey French people running it. It was a great place. It had mattresses all over the floor. So you could go and get sweaty on the

....

dancefloor and come off and flop out on a smelly mattress. And who knows what went on in there?

What did they play?
The pops of the day and a good selection of black records.

What did you think was the best club, in terms of the cutting edge?
Originally, the Flamingo because it was dark and dingy and it had a great cultural mix; it was filled up with a great cultural cross section. You had the Americans, George Fame and people like him. There were a few hot French clubs in town, too. It's really strange because there was this sort of underground set of Frenchies who had properties in London. There was this place called La Poubelle on Poland Street.

The dustbin!
And the French became obsessed with the twist, in fact, they even called it the French twist. And I made a record written by Sammy in early '62 called 'Twistin' Like The French Kids Do'!

What about Le Kilt?
That was very polite French. More middle class. It was where all the au pairs would go to meet rich London men.

What about coffee bars and jukeboxes?
I think every coffee bar I went to in those days had a jukebox.

A good one?
Yeah, fairly good.

Who selected the records that went in them?
There were about two or three guys that ran the jukebox syndicate and went around with the records and punched them out to go into the jukeboxes. I think there was only one major company that supplied the jukeboxes with records in those days. Of course, the Soho ones chose exactly what they wanted though. People like Tom Littlewood, who ran the 2i's, who was in there well early.

Was that so influential?
It was the birthplace of British rock'n'roll. Everybody used to go there and take their bongos. Sammy talked in his memoirs of going to the 2i's with his bongos!

Were you buying records during this period?
I didn't buy records. We had an account at Imhoff's in New Oxford Street, a Mecca account. And every week, from my befriending Sammy, because he lived in south London at the time, we would go up twice a week to Imhoff's and on the release date, read the broadsheet of what was available, take all the records into the booth and listen to one after another. But Sammy also had lots of friends in America sending him records. And there was one little guy that had a basement in Lisle Street, just off Leicester Square. In those days there were a few Chinese restaurants and all the electrical shops were in that street. All the places like in Tottenham Court Road these days. In the basement of one of these shops, every Friday a guy would open up in the morning with a box full of freshly imported records.

What kind of records was he selling?
He was into rhythm and blues in a big way, that was his passion. He would rent this basement on a Friday

So it was only open on a Friday?
Yeah. He'd open up on Friday morning. It wasn't like a shop where you could go in and select, it's just be a big box full of fresh imports. He'd tell you what he had and you'd leave with a handful of records. These were the only records we paid for. All the rest Mecca paid for.

So imports were limited?
Yeah.

Did Imhoff's sell imports?
No.

If you weren't collecting records, did you pool them with Sammy?
We carried four of those old wire racks with the hot selection of that time. Twice a week we'd sit and edit them. Work out which ones we thought were hot, which ones we thought were dead. Plus the ones we would take to the Flamingo, which was always a harder edge, of course. By then bluebeat had just started to happen as well. By '63 or even '62 we started doing a Wednesday record night, then we started doing an all-nighter in the midweek too. We were also doing the late, late shift after Georgie Fame and the other bands had finished playing. Georgie became really popular about '64 when he cut that record *Rhythm And Blues At The Flamingo,* which was produced by Ian Samwell. Sammy was at the cutting edge of all of it.

❛❛ 2i's was the birthplace of British rock'n'roll. Everybody used to go there and take their bongos. ❜❜

Were there any American GIs that brought their records?
They brought records from the bases. There was a good influx of records coming in from all over by that time. There was also another import shop that had opened by that time, on a Saturday morning, in the Haymarket in the basement of a bookshop.

From 1962 we did three and a half years at the Orchid Ballroom in Purley, which was our biggest show. Sammy was the main DJ, I was working with him and still singing and dancing with the band. Every record show was completely packed solid. People would come from all over London. There were shows at Streatham Locarno. We also played records above the Silver Blades ice rink in Streatham. There was a club called the Bali Hai which was for the late night license to get people in who had money, an after hours clubs.

There were other clubs like that opening in London, a place called the Crazy Elephant in Jermyn Street, where all bootmakers used to be. Of course, by that time we had the Scotch and the Ad Lib I guess, by 1964. Those sort of places weren't open to ordinary punters, they were more clubs where you had to be a member.

Were they music industry hangouts?
Music industry, media.

Not as street as the Flamingo?
No, the Flamingo was well street. Great mixing pot. As was the Scene.

Tell me what you know about the Scene?
I don't know when it started exactly, probably '63 or '64. I'd met Guy Stevens [DJ there] a few times buying records. Guy was a collector. He was an obsessive. He was obsessed with the label and everything. He'd been an obsessive before, he'd been a rock'n'roller, he was Jerry Lee Lewis mad as well. He was crazy about Jerry Lee, Little Richard. He already had a collection. They were what I loved, but they were my working tools, I was never a collector.

What was he like?
He was totally enthusiastic about everything, especially about music and clothes. Most of our conversations were spent talking about clothes and music.

Was he a mod at that stage?
Yeah, he was a bit more unusual than everybody else. He had a certain artistic flamboyant air about him. He wasn't that tight-arse mod. Most mods were so into posing around, whereas Guy was a bit more rock'n'roll, a bit looser. But he was totally obsessed with his music. There were a few other people around like Guy, too, like Peter Meaden and Tony Calder and

....

Andrew Oldham. Tony Calder was also a Mecca DJ from '62. He managed to take the job at the Lyceum off of Sammy. A dodgy move. Even if you filled the place with punters, your job wasn't safe in those days and you were probably only being paid nine shillings a set anyway.

But then no-one had any sense of what a DJ was worth in those days though.
Well, everyone thought that anyone can play records...

Was Guy at The Scene from the off?
As far as I remember, yeah. It was a right dodgy place. Seedy. Low ceiling. Bad decoration. Coca Cola bar. That was it. But you could actually get a hit in your Coca Cola. For some reason, it attracted a lot of the lower elements of musicians. It was on the corner of Archer Street, and in those days Archer Street was where all the musicians from the union would meet every Monday and Friday, and all the pluggers and fixers would also meet there and hand out their tickets for the recording jobs. That pub on the corner was where they all met. And when all those pop hits were happening, every musician would go there hoping to get a session.

> **❝ You could go and get a pill off someone, but you could also get a shot of whisky as well. If you were a cool face you would never stand in a pub with a pint of beer in your hand. ❞❞**

You said Coca Cola with a hit. Do you mean they were dropping pills in the Coke?
You could go and get a pill off someone, but you could also get a shot of whisky as well, if you knew how to get a shot of whisky in it. The preferred drink of the day was whisky and coke. If you were a cool face you would never stand in a pub with a pint of beer in your hand. You'd have a coke bottle with a shot of whisky. I think that partly grew out of the fact that Mecca DJs and musicians weren't allowed to drink. Of course, everyone did.

How prevalent were drugs in places like the Scene and the Flamingo?
That's where I first came across marijuana, yeah. It wasn't as obvious as 1964 when the whole thing started to explode.

What sort of drugs were available?
Mainly purple hearts and black bombers. Another favoured drug amongst a certain bunch was amyl nitrate, which you could buy over the counter in those days. If you had a bit of speed and a quick sniff of amyl you could really have a great time dancing. And get higher than a kite. That was before it became a gay drug.

The gay scene must've been very underground back then.
It was very underground. There were two or three little pubs where they would go. There were a few who would come into the bars. No-one wanted to be openly gay, apart from a few musicians and actors.

I imagine the Scene and Flamingo had very primitive DJing equipment?
Very primitive. Guy had two Garrard SP-25s. It was an integrated arm and deck.

How did the mod thing move into psychedelia?
1965, '66, there'd be a new records arriving from America. People like Donovan, who'd gone from this folky thing, were writing strange things, coming back from America wearing different clothes. The Beatles of course. Certain places you could get LSD. There were all kinds of people in pop culture who hadn't been mixing before.

Which clubs captured this interaction best?
UFO [pronounced Yoofo] grew out of the London Free School over in Notting Hill Gate, and

they were actually community based projects like the black housing project, after the riots. It actually grew out of them trying to do good things for the local community over there. Unusually arty things.

Who set up UFO?
Hoppy was a photographer, and he'd been out photographing demonstrations and protests. He worked for the *Melody Maker* at that time, as well, and was seeing other things; other bands. Who else was around then? Andrew King, Peter Jenner, he managed the Pink Floyd. Hoppy, Jim Hayes, Joe Boyd had come into the frame by that time.

What was the template they used for it, because it was obviously different?
They didn't try and copy anything. They were just making their own little thing. Of course, the Acid Tests were coming over. All the underground poets were arriving. There'd also been a couple of alternate shows at the Marquee: mixed-media stuff.

Who performed?
People like the Floyd, poets, lights. Things also happening in Central London Poly in Regent Street, there'd been a couple of alternate events.

When did UFO start?
Christmas '66.

And you played from the start?
There was no DJ as such. There was a guy called Jack Henry Moore who was an American electronics whiz. They had the record player, the amplifiers, the lighting equipment, generators and stuff, and he was a sort of mad boffin and he had TV screens with fuzzy images on them. And he played the records. Just records they had around at the time. I started to go that winter and I was doing all my shows at Tiles then. When I started to go I was well received by Mick Farren who was the doorperson, along with Richard Vickers. And I befriended Jack and I used to bring along all the new records I got every week and tell him which ones were hot for me. And he introduced me to things I was totally unaware of. Really weird American stuff.

So what was the difference between UFO and elsewhere?
It was totally unstructured. It was a free-for-all. There was no presentation as such, it just happened. For me, coming out of the straight world of ballroom showbiz, this was a brave new world. It was just built around the people who were there.

Did people dance?
People did dance, yeah. It wasn't like a ballroom or a club where everyone just rushed in and took their coats off. They spent more time talking to each other and dropping acid, reading books. There was a head shop in UFO where you could buy... strange things! Little sparklers, sparky wheels, defraction gradings, funny glasses that made everything look strange.

I would imagine it looked pretty strange anyway...
It did because there were the light shows. So everything was bathed in a wash of colours.

When did you start DJing there?
I wasn't part of the original set up at all. Lots of people think I was. There was no-one who would announce records. Jack had this sort of scaffolding area where he kept all the electronics and stuff and records would just be popped on to the deck. There was no thought of mixing. He also had loads of stuff on tape: electronic music, stuff like the Grateful Dead. It wasn't just a question of records. And there were bands: Arthur Brown, Soft Machine. It wasn't really a record club.

And you were DJing at Tiles?
From '66 I had a thing Wednesdays at Tiles called the Jeff Dexter Record And Light Show, which was a good crossover of soul, rhythm and blues and bluebeat. And new records of the day, the new psychedelic records.

Where was Tiles?
Opposite the 100 Club. Corner of Chapel Street or Dean Street and Oxford Street. It was

turned into an aquarium after Tiles. The entrance was further along, but Tiles had its own Tiles Street, which was like a mini Carnaby Street. You'd go in the club, it was a huge open space, and one end was a big coffee bar and off to the side was Tiles Street, where they sold clothes and paraphernalia. And also a tiny little record shop. It was an incredible place, Tiles. It was the only place that had its own real PA system. One of the backers of the club was a guy called Jim Marshall who owned Marshall PA and there were something like 40 columns of speakers that ran all along the dancefloor. And they had a proper sound system and proper amplifiers.

So it was pretty impressive sound wise?
The sound was low-fi, it wasn't hi-fi, but it worked incredibly well. It was the only place where things didn't break down as well. Marquee never invested in a proper PA system. In Tiles, everything was laid on, all the equipment was installed by Imhoff's. You had a switch and a volume pot for each deck. And they were vari-speed. That was the last of the Garrard 301 decks. After that same year, '66, they introduced the 401. Tiles was the only club I worked in that invested in it and took it totally seriously and made it work for the DJ. All the other clubs, they had baby hi-fi equipment. A few of them had 301s or 401s, but most of them had smaller Garrard units.

Tiles did an all-nighter on Saturdays. I did the midnight to 6am shift. There were a selection of DJs and styles. Clem Dalton, Mike Quinn, and Sammy as well. Tiles was raided regularly on its all-night sessions. Hundreds of police would come, because it was supposed to be a drug den.

Was it?
Yeah! Well, kids always took pills to dance on didn't they? They came up to London to have a good time, so there were always plenty of pills.

I was still working at Mecca ballrooms. I was doing Hammersmith Palais, Empire Leicester Square. Prior and simultaneously. I got the sack from Mecca, my main gig was still Orchid Ballroom up to the summer of '66, Sammy had gone the year before and I was doing all the shows there. Sammy had gone back into writing and producing. He'd fallen out with the Mecca.

The lunchtime thing at Tiles. What was that all about?
It was a coffee and sandwich bar at Tiles. The doors opened at 12. Taped music would play until 12.25 and then I'd put on my intro record. 12.30 the curtains would open and there I'd be playing to almost a full lunchtime crowd. And of course there were a bunch of kids who never went to work anyway. And we'd spend the next three hours doing this.

What were you playing?
Dance records. Bluebeat, ska, because we had plenty of ska by then. I played all the new records of the day. Bit of psychedelic, but very little at Tiles, because the audience was mainly tight-arse, pill-chewing mod kids. The late-on mods.

What do you mean?
Well, the ones that came to it very late. To me mods died in '62, but obviously there was still that funny culture of Carnaby Street and, of course, there were all those new dandy fashions from the end of '64 that had now crept into the mainstream.

You mean the regency look?
Yeah, it had been around for a few years before but it had gone more mainstream. In fact, by that time, there was a chain of shops called Dandy Fashion.

What was the timescale at Tiles?
1966 to '67. I went on holiday to Majorca in the summer of '66. The Brits had started opening discotheques there. They'd taken this old mill in the centre of town. I was asked to come and open a club called Snoopy's. There was a whole new set of Brits going to do what was happening in London, in the sun. I sent a guy called Pete Sanders in my place. There was too much going on here to spend a summer in Spain. In some ways I wish I'd done it because when I arrived there it was just incredible, because I took with me a bunch of acid. The Animals were there, Tom Jones was there, and in those days Tom was quite acceptable.

What did you find when you got over there?
There was a whole new generation of people who there in Spain at that time. Not only the club entrepreneurs, and the bands, but there was this great influx of British going there for their summer holidays. You could go for a week all-inclusive for £35.

So this was the beginnings of the package holiday?
Yeah.

Were there other nationalities there, too?
Scandinavians in particular. A few Germans, not so many. Mainly Brits and Scandinavians, a few Spanish.

You played at Middle Earth didn't you?
Towards the end of UFO. My main gig at that time was Tiles. I was doing five lunchtimes a

week, and three nights. In 1968 UFO got closed down at Tottenham Court Road and moved to the Roundhouse by early summer. Then moved out to a bingo hall just off Ladbroke Grove, which is where it came to an end at the end of '68.

Then Middle Earth started in Covent Garden. It was originally called the Electric Garden, and tried to do more or less what UFO was doing: bands, poetry... Middle Earth jumped on the back of that. So we set up this thing called Implosion, which would do what UFO intended. Anyone who played there would have to play for the community, they would not get a cut of the door no matter who they were. And they'd all get a fixed fee, which was £20. Of the money we made, half went into keeping the Roundhouse alive, and the other half was donated to needy causes like the Release charity.

> ❝ **Thanks to LSD, people were wandering off in different directions. They were seeing the colours coming out of the speakers!** ❞

In Middle Earth, what was being played?
Well there were the hot bands of the day. John Peel was also DJ. And John hated ska and bluebeat and most of those records that I'd lived on. He thought they were awful. I was totally into what he was doing, but he didn't understand what I was doing. The thing is, people still loved to dance and you really couldn't dance to a lot of the new psychedelic records that were around. They were horrible to dance to. So to keep people moving I had to mix it up a bit.

You came from a club background and he was a radio person.
Yeah. John's records were strictly for listening to. I played to the audience. Any DJ worth his salt knows how put one record on after another so they seem seamless and, although that was becoming less important, and it was something I didn't want to do so much any more, because I wanted people to listen, to me it was still important that, once the place was full, I wanted those people to have a good time. I mixed the two together.

What sort of people were there?
All the bands of the day, various media people. Middle Earth actually attracted more of the younger punters, people from the suburbs who would have normally gone to other clubs. UFO wasn't really for the punters so much.

What bands played?
They were the mainstay of the business. Dantalion's Chariot, The Byrds, Soft Machine, Pink Floyd, the Move, who'd become a psychedelic band by this time. They were brilliant.

How did the Byrds fit into all of that?
They were very psychedelic. Incredibly so. They really psychedelicised the whole folk thing.

Was it more media-oriented?
Not so much media. Alternative.

Early hippies. Heads.
Yeah, but a lot of them didn't want to call themselves hippies. I definitely became a hippie. Peace and love was the most important thing to come out of my mouth. And be nice to each other.

That must have affected the music you played.
Yeah. It became much more gentle. Much more open. And not so restricted to having the beats in the right place at the right time.

Do you think that was because LSD was replacing speed?
Yeah. People were wandering off in different directions. They were seeing the colours coming out of the speakers! It was also the birth of what became known as idiot dancing.

Which is basically middle class flopping about.
That's right. Waving your arms around. There wasn't enough space on the dancefloor to have a real good dance, so you just sort of shake yourself and wave yourself about.

The whole thing had exploded by the late '60s. I ended up running all the shows at the Roundhouse. DJing at all the shows. Doing all the festivals. The summer of '67 was the Festival of the Flower Children at Woburn Abbey. Similar set up to Knebworth. They had a wildlife park there. The following year there was another festival at Woburn.

I presume by that stage, you weren't really playing dance records?
Head music, but there were records that crossed right over. Canned Heat who played boogie. The Lemon Pipers! They had a big hit called 'Green Tambourine', it was bubblegum psychedelic.

What do you mean by bubblegum psychedelic?
Well the pop market had tried to creep in: the Lemon Pipers were one. People danced to the Doors, Creedence Clearwater Revival. There were records that you could dance to and I still mixed the two together, although I was becoming less fond of the black records that were creeping up, on Motown and Stax. To me they'd become plastic. They didn't hold that element of magic and soul that they'd done before.

© DJhistory.com

TILES SOUND & LIGHT 30

THE SOFT MACHINE – Feelin' Reelin' Squeelin'	**THE GAYLORDS** – Lady With The Red Dress On
THE JIMI HENDRIX EXPERIENCE – Stone Free	**PRINCE BUSTER AND THE ALL STARS** – Al Capone
THE SMOKE – My Friend Jack	**DESMOND DEKKER AND THE ACES** – 007
BOB DYLAN – Rainy Day Women Nos. 12 & 35	**FOUR TOPS** – Reach Out I'll Be There
THE PURPLE GANG – Granny Takes a Trip	**WILSON PICKETT** – Mustang Sally
THE PINK FLOYD – Arnold Layne	**DYKE & THE BLAZERS** – Funky Broadway
TRAFFIC – Hole In My Shoe	**ALVIN CASH & THE REGISTERS** – Twine Time
THE BEATLES – Tomorrow Never Knows	**KOKO TAYLOR** – Wang Dang Doodle
TOMORROW – My White Bicycle	**ROY C** – Shotgun Wedding
THE MOVE – I Can Hear The Grass Grow	**THE TEMPTATIONS** – Get Ready
CREAM – I Feel Free	**EDDIE FLOYD** – Knock On Wood
REX GARVIN & THE MIGHTY CRAVERS – Sock It To 'Em JB	**SAM & DAVE** – You Got Me Hummin'
ALVIN ROBINSON – Searchin'	**THE BAR-KAYS** – Soul Finger
THE WAILERS – Put It On	**JOE TEX** – You Better Believe It Baby
ROLANO AL AND THE SOUL BROTHERS – Phoenix City	**Compiled by Jeff Dexter**

RECOMMENDED LISTENING

VARIOUS – The In Crowd (4-CD boxed set)

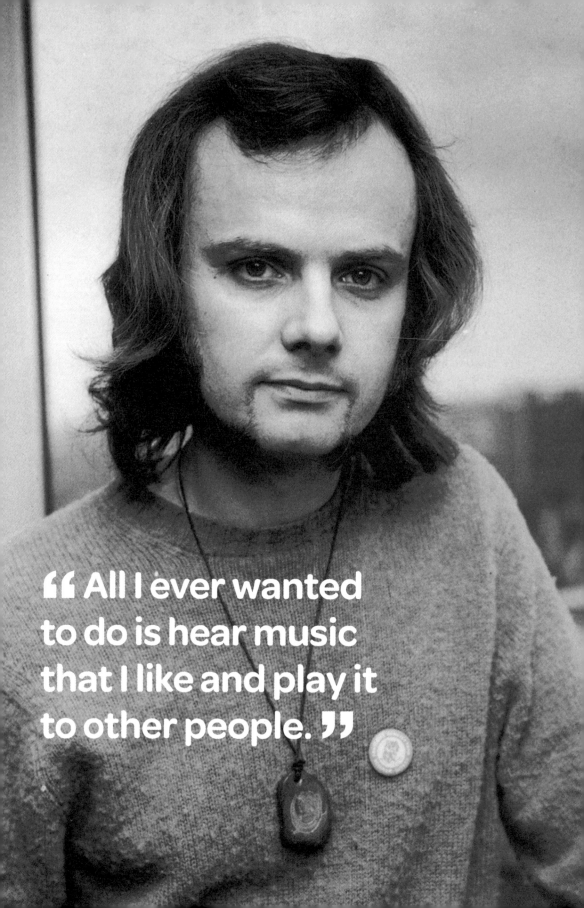

"All I ever wanted to do is hear music that I like and play it to other people."

John Peel
Inspired everybody

Interviewed by Bill in London, April 7, 1999

Lord John. The godfather of modern British music. He shaped the tastes of several generations. In fact, it's hard to avoid the conclusion that John Peel did more than *anyone* in the long history of popular music to expose new sounds, inspire young musicians and encourage radical genres.

He began his broadcasting career as a putative Beatles expert in the United States, before returning back to the UK just in time to surf the final wave of '60s pirate broadcasting. Cast adrift on a ship in the North Sea, Peel hosted a late-night show, The Perfumed Garden, that made a huge impact on the burgeoning hippie scene. When Radio 1 was launched as an answer to the pirates he secured a slot called Top Gear, before embarking on his own long-running show that lasted nearly 30 years until his untimely death in 2004. He championed everything from glam rock, via punk, early hip hop and house, to Napalm Death, Ivor Cutler and, of course, The Fall. He brought to radio a style so unique that Radio One enlisted three DJs to replace him and it still feels like there's a yawning chasm where once was John Peel.

We sit on the terrace of a café round the corner from Radio 1 on a lovely spring afternoon only interrupted the occasional over-zealous bin lorry driver and classic British sports car. Today, John is a bit grumpy.

Did you go over to America as a DJ?
Oh good Lord, no. The DJ didn't exist, as such, when I went over there. I went over in 1960 and there were DJs on Luxembourg like Pete Murray, Alan Freeman and David Jacobs. I had in the back of my mind that it was something I'd like to do. But I went over there really to... because my dad dared me to. My dad didn't know what to do with me. So he said, 'I'll send you to America if you'll go.'

After I'd been there about a year, I got on to a radio station in Dallas playing rhythm and blues, because I had records they didn't have. I was rather excited by it all, but I didn't manage to get back on the radio until the Beatles came along and it became fashionable to be from the Liverpool area. So I was a Beatle expert for KLIF in Dallas and then I got my first full time DJ job at a radio station in Oklahoma City: KOMA. I think it was the end of 1964. I did it for 18 months, followed by 18 months immediately after in San Bernadino in California. I came back in the spring of 1967.

Were you playing album tracks at San Bernadino?
We did actually. Mainly because I had to do a six hour programme at the weekend in order to get a day off. It was actually quite hard work. You didn't just do a short programme and go home and hang out with your famous pop star friends. You had to man the news cruiser, or go to some kind of promotion the station was doing. Myself and a fellow called Johnny Darren, who ended up as musical director of KRLA in Los Angeles, went to the station's management and suggested we ought to have a much more varied format; you know, get away from just playing the platters that mattered. They turned us down. If they'd let us go ahead, we would have been the people who introduced what subsequently became [freeform] FM radio in the States.

John Peel

Wasn't Tom Donahue the first one to do that?
Yeah, he was. We were about six to nine months ahead if we'd been allowed to do it. As it was in the six-hour programme I used to do an entirely fraudulent British chart, which involved LP tracks. But I'm not trying to claim credit for it or anything...

What was it you played on your British chart? Brit boom stuff of the period?
Tracks like John Mayall's Bluesbreakers' first LP. A track by the Yardbirds called 'The Naz Are Blue', which never was released as a single, but nevertheless did extremely well in my fraudulent British chart.

When did you come back to UK?
In spring 1967.

So you must have been on Radio London almost immediately. How did you get the gig?
My mum lived in Notting Hill and next to her there was a chap that did advertising with Radio London, so he suggested I went to see the station manager. Purely on the strength of having recently worked in California. Fortunately they didn't ask for an audition. They must've known they only had a limited time left. So they said, 'Yeah, off you go.'

I went down to the ship and started broadcasting. I had to do a regular daytime programme, but also somebody had to do the late night shift, the midnight to two shift. I quickly realised that no-one on the ship listened to it and started playing the sort of things I wanted to play in California. And got away with it. I dispensed with the format. I didn't run any ads. I didn't run news. I didn't do the weather. I just played lots of records, really.

How did that go down?
Well, the audience liked it. There was an extraordinary response from the audience. The last couple of months of London, I used to get – Keith Skues would confirm this – a prodigious amount of mail. Seven or eight times as much mail as everyone at the station put together. At a time when flower power, hippies and everything were happening in London, well all over the place, it was *their* radio programme. It was called Perfumed Garden. I didn't know there was a saucy book with the same name.

Where did the name come from then?
Daft idea that came into my head.

What type of records were you playing on there?
Well a lot of stuff I'd brought back from California. Almost the entire output of Elektra Records: Love, Doors, Paul Butterfield Blues Band, Incredible String Band, Judy Collins. And then people like Hendrix, Pink Floyd, Cream.

Was Joe Boyd living in London then?
He must've been because I met him. I was amazingly naive. I like to think I still am really. But I was terrifically excited at being able to get into things for nothing, which I rarely managed to do. But at the same time you felt that you were playing a part in something bigger than just doing a radio programme. It was an exciting time, really.

Were the people who ran the station simply in favour of free market capitalism, or was there a more benign agenda?
I don't think there was benign agenda at all. Radio London, as far as I know, was run by Texan businessmen. It was just a money-making operation as far as they were concerned. Caroline sort of affected a slightly more idealistic reason for existing. For them too, though, it was a business. Caroline, you used to have to pay to get records played. Pay-for-play. Radio London didn't do that. It was all about bending the regulations. We were all paid out of the Cayman Islands so we didn't have to pay tax in this country.

What about the attitude of the DJs. Did they have a different agenda?
Not at all, no. They were either Americans that hadn't been able to make it in America or thought it might be amusing. Or people who saw it as a means of getting into another career, possibly getting into television.

This is one of the things that bedevilled Radio 1 when it first started. I suppose, in a way, it's in the back of people's minds now that it is a device by which you can procure a very remunerative outside living. You can do gigs. You can get onto television. Start your own record label. Whatever. In the early days of Radio 1 it was seen as a bit of a disadvantage to take an interest in music. It really was. It sounds like the sort of thing you say for effect, but it was genuinely the case. It was very odd to be interested in music because the BBC believed it made you susceptible to influence from record companies; you know, pluggers and that sort of thing.

Is that why they had a lot of bands playing?
No, that was all to do with needle time. Which was the amount of time during the day to play records. The arrangement they had with the Musicians Union before Radio 1 was allowed to go on the air, was about seven hours of needle time a day. The idea was it compelled the BBC to employ live musicians. But as you say, that would mean the Northern Dance Orchestra, they would do cover versions of the big hits of the day.

At a time when flower power, hippies and everything were happening all over the place, it was *their* radio programme.

Is it true they did a version of 'Purple Haze'?
The Northern Dance Orchestra did a version of 'Purple Haze', which I should love to have had on tape in any medium known to man. It was a very strange system. But the BBC had no choice.

What was it like living on a boat?
You'd do two weeks on and a week off. I quite liked it. I was coming to the end of a very unhappy first marriage. So being away from London for two weeks was pretty neat, really. It was an entirely male establishment. You had a little cabin. I think I shared with Mark Roman when I first went on there.

It was moored off Felixstowe. And Caroline was within view and I remember Johnny Walker and some other geezer rowing over from Caroline to see us every once in a while, which was the buccaneering spirit. Most of the time I just sat there, or got slightly stoned, or listened to music. I was relatively content on there. I watched TV a lot.

Were there any incidents involving being boarded?
Not while I was there, certainly not, no. It was a very ordered kind of existence. A little boat would come out of Felixstowe with the new record releases.

Were the programmes boring during the day?
No they weren't boring, they were exciting daytime programmes. Certainly set against what people were used to. They were boring in comparison with what we'd been doing in California, but in comparison with what people had been doing hitherto, they were really exciting. They played a lot of records. A lot of rather good records, too.

There was a feeling that something was going on. There was a definite excitement in the air, even on the most boring days. And I only wish I could remember more about it to be honest. It wasn't that I was out of my head most of the time, I just don't have a terribly good memory. I was lucky that the weather was never truly dreadful when I was on there. We used to climb down the side and sit on the tyres that were hanging on the side of the boat. We'd sit down and gaze out to sea and think beautiful thoughts.

And how did you get out there?
On this little tender, a tug boat thing. You'd be picked up at the quayside at Felixstowe. It also went back and forwards each day picking up the mail, provisions and replacement DJs.

How did you get on to Radio 1?

....

Obviously when we knew Radio 1 was starting and Radio London was closing down we knew they would have to find their DJs from the pirate stations, so we all wrote greasy job applications, I suppose. For a while I used to believe I hadn't done that and then somebody presented me with the oleaginous letter that I'd written so I could no longer pretend to myself that I hadn't. I was only hired initially for six weeks. In competition with Tommy Vance, Pete Drummond and others.

This was a show called *Top Gear*?
Yeah. You knew eventually someone was going to be the sole presenter. Fortunately, I had the inside track because Bernie Andrews, the producer, wanted me to do it. I have to say in the teeth of opposition from middle management. Much of what went on in the early days of Radio 1 was due to Bernie and a fellow called Bev Phillips, his right hand man and engineer.

Was Top Gear taking what you'd done with Perfumed Garden a step further?
It was a step back in a way. It was that but with certain restrictions placed on it by the BBC. Also, Bernie was very unenthusiastic about playing anything that was more than five or six minutes long. Of course in hippie days that eliminated a lot of stuff. You had to worry about the peculiar sensitivities of the audience, or the imagined sensitivities. So anything that could be possibly presented as a drug song, you had to be wary of. They did ban quite a few records. There was a certain narrowing of focus. But then you were doing it for a national station.

> ❝ **When Radio 1 was starting we knew they would have to find their DJs from the pirate stations, so we all wrote job applications.** ❞

Were you doing club gigs as well?
I did do a few actually. There was a notorious club on Oxford Street called Tiles…

Where Jeff Dexter played?
That's right, yeah. I did the last night in Tiles. Notorious.

A drugs den.
It was certainly not the kind of place where they wanted to hear what I was doing. And there were waves of irate customers coming up over the footlights to try and persuade me to play whatever it was they wanted me to play. Which certainly wasn't the Grateful Dead and Jefferson Airplane and Country Joe and the Fish or whatever I was playing. They didn't like me at all. Then there was another club somewhere, where I played the closing down night. For a while there, I seemed to feel that where my future lay was in finishing places off [laughter]. Administering the coup de grace.

Did you play UFO?
Do you know, I don't know. I used to go there.

What was it like?
Well, it was really good. The only time I took acid deliberately was at UFO because I felt I was kind of safe and I'd be kind of okay. It wasn't like clubbing these days. Rather than dancing around – obviously some people danced about in a fairly idiotic manner – you just lay on the floor and passed out [laughter]. It sounds like fun, doesn't it?
    You'd get people like the Soft Machine and Arthur Brown, Pink Floyd and so on playing there. It's quite nice to go somewhere where you feel that the other people there have essentially the same interests as you do. That's what I felt about UFO. I was very star-struck, and again, still am in a way. People'd say, 'Of course, you know Brian Jones is here.' And I got to know Brian Jones a bit. I was quite awestruck that I knew a Rolling Stone well enough to have his home phone number. I didn't know many famous people. I knew the drummer out of Pink Floyd. I did a lot of gigs with these people. I did several gigs with Hendrix. I did one

with Cream at the Saville Theatre, where Ginger Baker played a 20 minute drum solo and I thought I was going to have to drag him off the stage it was so boring. He was a surprisingly hostile man.

What about Middle Earth? Jeff Dexter said he played with you a few times there.
I think we kind of alternated. I was the radio man, he was the live DJ. He always did the Roundhouse. Lots of Creedence Clearwater Revival records. I did Middle Earth a few times certainly, which meant you were in a box under the stage all night. Which was hard going. Certainly couldn't do it now, and I could barely do it then. But Middle Earth was pretty neat. But it wasn't UFO.

What was the composition of people at UFO?
I don't know. I can't remember that I ever spoke to anybody there. I used to go there on my own and stand there looking probably rather pathetic, I'd have thought. But I certainly wasn't alone in doing that. It was like people going to festivals now; the sense of community was as important as anything. Even if you're not actually communing [laughs]. Just the feeling that the other people feel the same as you.

How did they use the music there? Was it as part of the ambience?
It was the link. It was the most obvious element that people had in common I guess. They weren't the sort of gigs you'd get people coming in casually off the street for. If you did, they'd very quickly leave again. It was a unifying factor. The cement in the lifestyle. I suppose a lot of people, me included, the following morning they'd be different people. They hadn't got the courage to go through the streets full time in beads and bells and expensive hippie gear. Well, I didn't have expensive hippie gear, I just had an awful kaftan that was made from a bedspread, that I paid an insane amount of money for in Carnaby Street. And a pair of appalling trousers that I never had the courage to wear in public. They just hung in a cupboard.

How do you see your role at the BBC over the years. Are you their safety valve?
Well it's possible to see that that was the function in the early days, certainly. If anybody phoned up to complain about the general blandness in those days they could say, 'Well you can always listen to John Peel and his sort of music.' Not the case now, I don't think. There are just so many programmes that are devoted to music rather than to personality.

What changes have you seen. Has it got better?
I think it has. The great beauty of things there is that they've always left me to get on with it; once they've accepted that I know what I'm doing and people quite like it. No interference at all. It's extraordinary and I can't imagine that I'd have had that kind of freedom anywhere else.

That's the paradox of the BBC, though isn't it? Innately conservative, yet freed from the constraints of competition.
That's true. You've got these two great forces pulling against each other at Radio 1. The need to maximise audiences and have high profile presenters. Originally Tony Blackburn, now Zoe Ball. Also this public service remit, where they do have programmes more to do with music than anything.

Has it taken pressure off you having these specialist shows on air. Twenty years ago, your show was the only place you could hear hip hop, electronic music, punk, all sorts.
Yes, it was and I was always aware of that. It wasn't a situation I liked much either. It put a lot of pressure on me that I didn't want. I'd like there to be more programmes like mine, so I'd have something to listen to myself. There are programmes I listen to on Radio 1, but these days they tend to be, by comparison with the station output, quite liberal, but within their own terms, quite conservative.

Having started as a DJ so long ago, DJing has got an awful lot more respect now than it had 20 or even 10 years ago...
It certainly has.

How do you feel about the changes that have happened over the last 15 years?

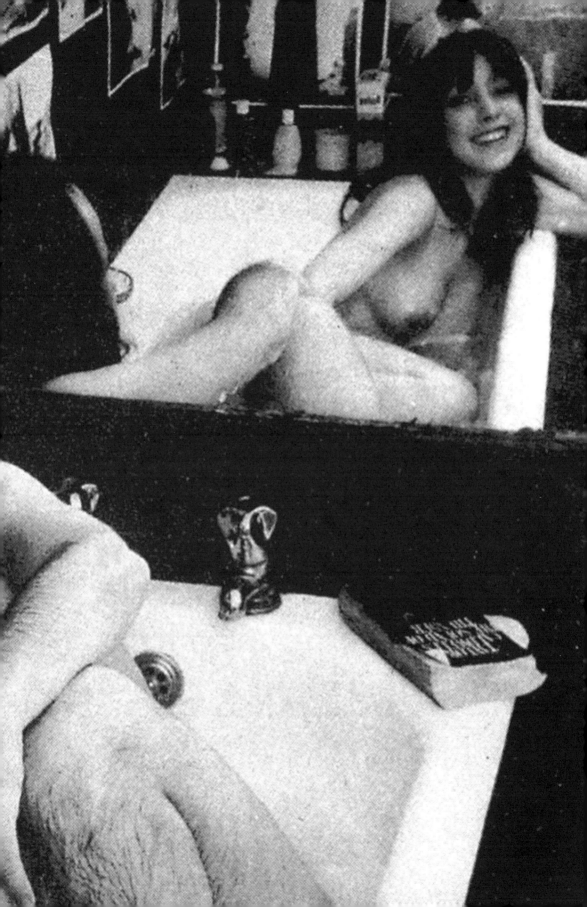

Well, I don't think about them much at all. I don't devote much of my time to, you know, self-analysis or trying to discern my position in society. I don't have time. There's too much to do. I just get on doing what I do. I know that's not a very adequate answer. In fact, it's no answer at all, but it is the truth.

❝ I'm doing what I wanted to do when I was 12: sitting at home and playing records. ❞

Do you ever think that the DJ's status has been overblown, now that he's venerated as a pop star, when he's basically a bloke playing records?
Well, again, there's never been anybody who's been as big as Noel Edmonds, who's achieved the extraordinary status of being famous for being famous. Obviously, he's built a career on it. And good luck to him. If someone said to you what does Noel Edmonds actually do, you'd have to say, 'Fucked if I know.' You know, he's confident and wears brightly coloured clothes. But there's a lot of people like that. In a way, I think DJs tend to be more obscure now than when Radio 1 started. Somebody like Tony Blackburn or Jimmy Young and the audiences they had, a gigantic number of people listened to their programmes. Far fewer listen now, because there's so much other stuff to do.

Do DJs serve a useful function as filters on musical culture?
Well, there are more of them, but there are more radio stations. Unfortunately, a lot of them seem to reflect the worst rather than the best aspects of Radio 1. A lot of them seem to have eliminated all specialist programmes apart from dance music. The DJs just seem to be happy to do what the station wants them to do: supervise idiotic competitions, talk a lot, you know what I mean? It's all rather predictable and dull, frankly.

How do you feel about having influenced DJs and producers?
You're influenced by such a lot of stuff that happens to you, and being part of that influence is kind of... you just feel as though you've helped to feed back into the musical community whatever you've taken from it. You're aware of being part of a vaguely circular motion. What goes around comes around. So if people say they were influenced by listening to my programme, then I'm very flattered, and if it helped and encouraged them to do what they now do then I see that as being quite a useful function.

What do you see your personal role is as a DJ?
I don't really view it as anything! I suppose you could sum it up by saying all I wanted to do from the very start and all I want to do now is go on doing what I'm already doing. I'm entirely without ambitions, beyond doing what I do now.

How would you describe what you do?
Living out in the country, hearing music that I like and playing it to other people. Now I do one show a week from my home and that represents for me an achievement because that's what I wanted to do when I was 12: sit at home and play records I liked for other people to listen to. The fact that they're not in the house is probably a good thing since it's not a very big house... I hope that bloke was waving at me, because it's always embarrassing when you wave back to them and they were waving to somebody else...

© DJhistory.com

THE PERFUMED GARDEN, FINAL BROADCAST

THE BEATLES – Sgt. Peppers' Lonely Hearts Club Band

THE BEATLES – With A Little Help From My Friends

THE ATTACK – Anymore Than I Do

DONOVAN – Guinevere

THE PURPLE GANG – Granny Takes A Trip

JEFFERSON AIRPLANE – White Rabbit

JOHN MAYALL – Dust My Broom

THE BYRDS – Eight Miles High

TIM BUCKLEY – Song Slowly Sung

THE MISUNDERSTOOD – I Can Take You To The Sun

PINK FLOYD – Astronomy Domine

CANNED HEAT – Rollin' And Tumblin'

TYRANNOSAURUS REX – Rings of Fortune

SIMON & GARFUNKEL – At The Zoo

HOWLIN' WOLF – Dust My Broom

THE SYN – 14 Hour Technicolour Dream

THE VELVET UNDERGROUND – Venus In Furs

JEFF BECK – Rock My Plimsoul

BIG BROTHER & THE HOLDING COMPANY – All Is Loneliness

BOB DYLAN – It Takes A Lot To Laugh It Takes A Train To Cry

JON – Is It Love?

THE BEATLES – And Your Bird Can Sing

THE BEATLES – For No One

COUNTRY JOE AND THE FISH – Not So Sweet Martha Lorraine

ORANGE BICYCLE – Hyacinth Threads

MARC BOLAN – Hippy Gumbo

JOHN MAYALL – Double Trouble

TIM HARDING – Hang On To A Dream

THE ELECTRIC PRUNES – Wind Up Toys

DONOVAN – Epistle To Dippy

CREAM – Tales Of Brave Ulysses

GIANT SUNFLOWER – February Sunshine

SHADOWS OF KNIGHT – Light Bulb Blues

ELMORE JAMES – Dust My Broom

THE ROLLING STONES – We Love You

MOBY GRAPE – Changes

GEOFFREY PROWSE – The Perfumed Garden Blues. A poem by Adrian Henri

CAPTAIN BEEFHEART – Abba Zabba

THE JIMI HENDRIX EXPERIENCE – The Burning Of The Midnight Lamp

ROY HARPER – The Sophisticated Beggar

THE PAUL BUTTERFIELD BLUES BAND – Look Over Yonder Wall

THE GRATEFUL DEAD – Cold Rain And Snow

LOVE – The Castle

MARC BOLAN – The Wizard

THE INCREDIBLE STRING BAND – The Mad Hatter's Song

TRAFFIC – Coloured Rain

JACKSON C FRANK – Milk And Honey

TOMORROW – My White Bicycle

THE MISUNDERSTOOD – You Don't Have To Go Out

BIG BROTHER AND THE HOLDING COMPANY – Call On Me

ORANGE BICYCLE – Amy Peat

JOHN RENBOURNE – Another Monday

SIMON & GARFUNKEL – Fakin' It

THE WHO – Run Run Run

DAVID BLUE – The Street

THE BEATLES – Getting Better

THE BEATLES – Fixing A Hole

THE BEATLES – Lucy In The Sky With Diamonds

JUDY COLLINS – Liverpool Lullaby

THE JIMI HENDRIX EXPERIENCE – I Don't Live Today

DONOVAN – Sunny Googe Street

TYRANNOSAURUS REX – Highways

THE SEEDS – Mr Farmer

THE MOTHERS OF INVENTION – Plastic People

THE MOTHERS OF INVENTION – Duke of Prunes

THE MOTHERS OF INVENTION – Call Any Vegetable

ZODIAC (COSMIC HOUNDS) – Aquarius The Lover of Life

JOHN'S CHILDREN – Desdemona

THE BLUES PROJECT – Flute Thing

DONOVAN – Sand And Foam

THE VELVET UNDERGROUND – Sunday Morning

JOHN MAYALL – Crawling On Top Of The Hill

PINK FLOYD – Matilda Mother

THE SYN – Flower Man

CAPTAIN BEEFHEART – Sure 'Nuff N' Yes I Do

SHAWN PHILLIPS – Cold Tattoo

Two poems by ROGER MCGOUGH – John's Children, Sarah Crazy Child

THE BEATLES – The Word

BOB DYLAN – On The Road Again

THE MISUNDERSTOOD – I Can Take You To The Sun

DONOVAN – Writer In The Sun

SIMON AND GARFUNKEL – The Sparrow

The final Perfumed Garden on Radio London broadcast August 14, 1967

RECOMMENDED LISTENING

VARIOUS – John Peel and Sheila – The Pig's Big 78s, A Beginner's Guide

VARIOUS – John Peel Sampler

VARIOUS – FabricLive 07 (DJ mix)

" I didn't want people to know that the song had changed. "

Terry Noel
Original mixer

Interviewed by Bill in New York, September 30, 1998

Terry Noel was the first DJ to mix records. At a time when nightclubs were essentially jet-set hangouts for the famous and wealthy, this former dancer lived with Jim Morrison and hung out (and strung out) with Jimi Hendrix. In his 1960s pomp, he was the man who brought seamless mixing to New York dancefloors, firstly at Arthur, Sybil Burton's swinging discotheque (named after Ringo Starr's haircut), and then at Salvation and Salvation II, where the scene was so debauched that its repentant owner Bradley Pierce ran off to become a priest. Terry was the man from whom Francis Grasso took his cue (and job).

Still as dapper and flamboyant, these days he is to be found painting in his Greenwich Village apartment. Given a chance to share his memories, Terry takes great delight in re-enacting the highlights of his career in dramatic fashion, his face animated and alive, with energised sweeps of the arm for emphasis. For an afternoon, Terry is back on the dancefloor at Arthur as if it were yesterday.

How did you come to be in New York. Are you from there?
I grew up in Syracuse and I was going to Syracuse University, but I hated it because it was so gung-ho. I transferred down to Pratt Institute in Brooklyn. This was 1960. In 1961 I entered a dance contest at the Peppermint Lounge and won, so they hired me.

What was Peppermint Lounge at that stage? A supper club?
No. They started twisting in there, so celebrities started mobbing the place. It only held about 140 people. It was a hustler bar, a gay hustler bar on 45th Street, right off Times Square. Then it got very chic. They had this big contest with celebrity judges and I won. I said, 'To hell with this school.' I fell in love with the whole thing because I was in the middle of every celebrity in the world.

So you ended up working there.
I had redesigned the place so we had a stage, which we didn't have until that point. We knocked out the columns and made it twice as big, put in dressing rooms, all kinds of lights. In fact, I was the first person to use black lights and strobelights in the show. At the end of the show we did 'Shout' and we would cut off the lights, put on the black lights and all the gloves on the girls' palms would turn pink and they'd stand there with a fringe on going like that. Then we'd put on what was called the Lobster Scope; it was a wheel with a bright light behind with like a lobster claw in the wheel. And the wheel would turn fast and it would be like a strobelight.

Was it motorised?
Yeah, it had a motor on it. It was the original strobe light. The Wild Ones were working there at this time and Sybil Burton comes in – and she had just divorced Richard Burton, which was a big scandal – and she picked the Wild Ones to be the opening band for Arthur.

Who were the Wild Ones?
They were just a group. They never had a hit or anything; but their big song was 'Wild Thing'. Of course, Jordan the lead singer was gorgeous. He was my room-mate. It comes to

opening night at Arthur and I wanted in on this real bad. So I snuck in to the opening and Sybil was dancing with someone so I tapped her on the shoulder and said, 'You know, the music sucks. This is horrible. Do you now who I am, by the way?'

She says, 'Yeah, aren't you the dancer from the Peppermint Lounge?'

'Yeah, my name's Terry Noel. Jordan knows me.'

She didn't even know Jordan at that stage, but she ended up marrying him. So I said, 'I'll knock your socks off. I'll show you music. It's not working right. I know what your concept is.'

At Arthur, they didn't have any special lighting. They didn't even have pin-spots then, just little white lights over the top of the stage. There were these little bars that came down from the ceiling, like track-lighting. They had these little bulbs: green, blue, yellow, blue. They didn't blink or anything. It was black, except for smoke-tinted mirrors around the entire room, with banquettes going around and little tables with stools. Every drink came in a goblet, no matter what you got, which I thought was the coolest thing. Sybil took care of every detail. I was just very impressed with it. Then, of course, every celebrity in the world came. So she hired me on the spot and said, 'You come in tomorrow at 9 o'clock.' I said, 'I'll bring in records.' I worked on the first night.

66 John Wayne asks me for Yellow Rose of Texas. I go – snap! – 'Oh, it's broken,' and I threw it on the dancefloor. He goes, 'You faggot!' His toupee was falling off his head! 99

So you were a record collector already?
Oh yeah. All my life. I got records in storage downstairs: original Buddy Holly 45s, Ricky Nelson, everybody. I had tons of albums. Then I started knowing what I was doing and began blending the music and she just fell in love with it. And she said, 'I love this this; it's just what I always wanted.' So I said, 'I told you I could do it.'

What kind of stuff were you playing?
At that time soul was very big. WWRL, up in Harlem, was the big station and that's where I would get most of my music from.

Any DJ from there that sticks in your mind?
Frankie Crocker. He's been around a long time. WWRL was it. It's been through loads of stages and now it's back to what it was originally, playing stuff from the '60s. I would start out slow, and then I would build the pace, and build the pace until it was totally frantic. Then I'd make everybody sit down and order a drink. Then start building again. The idea was, I felt, to make people buy drinks. Today you don't have to do that, I don't think. Then, you really did. I used to write down every song that I played. The time, the date, everything. There used to be a guy called Jerry Love, he was the biggest record distributor in the city. He'd bring me 20-30 records a week. Then I'd start going over to his warehouse: 'What's this?'

'Oh, I don't know.'

'Lemme try it.'

I'd just pull out all these records, any I wanted, and take them home in a cab and listen to every one of them. I'd only listen to them for a few seconds and, if it sounded really interesting I'd throw it on in the middle, then if it was *really* interesting, the end. I'd go through hundreds of albums and singles a week. Hundreds. Then Berry Gordy and Smokey Robinson would come in and bring metal discs. I've still got 'Don't Mess With Bill'.

One night Murray Drucker, one of the owners, had cut me off and said I couldn't have any drinks. I said, 'Bring me a drink.'

'Murray cut you off, he says you're drinking too much.'

So I say, 'Oh, okay, no problem.'

So Murray comes in and the place is packed and there's not one person dancing. Normally, he'd come in and the dancefloor's mobbed. And he walks over and says, 'What's going on?'

I said, 'What do you mean?'

'There's nobody dancing.'

'Would you like to see some people dancing?'

'Of course!'

I put up my glass of Coca Cola and said, 'There's nothing in the this glass of Coca Cola.'

'Well, you've been drinking too much.'

'So do you wanna see people dance?' I took the needle, threw it, landed on the record and boom! It was Frank Sinatra. Because I knew the crowd that was in there would feel okay getting up there slow dancing to Frank Sinatra. Straight after that I went into the Mamas and Papas, then something else until it got hotter and hotter and these people who wouldn't be caught dead on the dancefloor are now going wild. 'Anything he wants! Anything he wants!' says Murray

John Wayne used to come in and he asks me for 'Yellow Rose of Texas'. I said, 'Gee, I happen to have it.' And the booth was not isolated like they are now; I was right on the floor, just one foot up. He's standing there, slightly looking down and I go – snap! – 'Oh, it's broken,' and I threw it on the dancefloor. He goes, 'You faggot!' His toupee was falling off his head! Sybil was sitting behind where he was, Judy Garland was sitting beside her and Lauren Bacall next to her. And they're watching this whole scene and they go, 'Teeerrrry!' They loved it, because they hated him, you know.

Terry and a well-known mop-top beat combo (that's him between John and Ringo).

What kind of equipment did you use?
Technics turntables. They were wonderful, except I kept breaking the rubber band on them. I didn't like anything they had, really. For a mixer I had a dial for turntable one, and a dial for turntable two, and you'd just blend them in one from the other.

I thought that I wasn't getting everything I wanted out of it. We had four major column speakers in the room. I said that we were getting vibrating noises when the bass gets up too high, so I said to [legendary production manager] Chip Monck, who became quite famous with Woodstock, 'I wanna be able to get separate controls for each speaker, and separate bass and treble controls too. I wanna be able to swing the sound around so that – boom! when the full song comes in I put it through all the speakers with dynamic bass, and the hi-ends and lows.' He did all that for me. He changed everything for me. Six months after I was there I realised that I couldn't excite these people the way that I wanted to excite them. I wanna thrill. I want them to feel like they've never felt in their life before. I'd watch people's heads on the dancefloor going, 'Wow! What was that?' It's like those movie theatres today where you hear the gunshot behind you. It was the same with me. Except I was doing it in the '60s.

What were you doing in terms of the mixing?
Sometimes I'd have to put the needle on the exact spot where I'd want it, and I used to have a felt mat instead of a rubber one, so that the turntable wouldn't hold if I held the record. I knew what I was coming in with, and I knew what I was going out with. I didn't wanna lose a beat. I didn't want people to even know that the song changed. Many people would come up to me and say, 'I was listening to the Mamas and Papas and now I'm listening to the Stones, and I didn't even know.' I used to try some of the wildest changes without losing a beat. I used to get people coming in who wouldn't even dance, they'd just come in to listen to the songs. I wasn't at Arthur the last year, the gangsters started coming there; they had a shooting, so I was like, 'I can't take this any more.' And then I left and went to California for a year.

> **❝ I'm good friends with Hendrix, we'd hang out – sometimes two days at a time. I mixed the Beatles with 'Foxy Lady'. Jimi turned round, gave me the finger and walked out. ❞**

You came back to New York to play at Ondine. Tell me about it.
Bradley Pierce owned it. I told him about these bands: the Buffalo Springfield, the Jefferson Airplane and the Doors, because I was living with Jim Morrison out in California. I said, 'You gotta bring them.' Ondine was on 59th Street, underneath the 59th Street bridge. Little place again.

People like Andy [Warhol] started coming in; Jim started getting wilder and wilder. In LA he used to stand in the corner at the back of the stage and do the whole set there; he wouldn't come out front. He was so shy. Then he got here and saw Andy and his superstars all whipping each other in black leather on the stage, and he started getting a bit loose. Then next thing you know he's got black leather pants on; he's into all this stuff. I said, 'Jim, you're going the wrong way. If you're with him, you're not with me. That's it.' The last time I heard from him, he and his manager came over to apologise to me and they rang my doorbell. I just said, 'I don't wanna talk to you.'

Prior to me being there, Jimi Hendrix was a busboy. He used to sit there and play his guitar with his teeth at Ondine and Bradley said, 'I don't know what to do with you. It's like a freak act.' Then we opened Salvation at 1 Sheridan Square and we get in touch with Jimi, and he's a big star now and asked him if he wanted to play at the club, so he comes over. Ondine wasn't about the records, it was about the bands, because we had all the greatest bands in there. I don't remember a lot about it, for many reasons.

ARTHUR

EATS

EGG & BACON CROQUETTES, FRESH TOMATO SAUCE
& FRENCH BREAD 2.50

SCOTCH SALMON, THIN BROWN BREAD,
BUTTER, LEMON, CAPERS 6.50

HAMBURGER
2.50

ARTHUR PLATTER, CHICKEN LIVERS WRAPPED IN BACON,
SPARE RIBS, SAUSAGE IN PASTRY BLANKET AND MEAT BALLS
FOR TWO 5.00

POTATOE PANCAKES, ARTHUR APPLESAUCE 2.50

WHISTLER'S MOTHER'S SANDWICH 3.00

STEAK SANDWICH, ON FRENCH BREAD 4.50

DEVONSHIRE TEA, ENGLISH SCONES, THICK CREAM & JAM
2.00

Was Arthur mainly drinking or were there drugs?
Oh yes there were. But it was very very subtle. There was nothing blatant anywhere; you'd never know anything was going on.

What kinds of drugs?
Amphetamine was the number one: crystal meth. Coke. And acid of course. I had my first trip at Arthur. We had these people, the teenyboppers, that they'd let in for free. The mob would be out there, but we'd let these in for free, and they'd get free Cokes just to dance on the floor and look gorgeous. They were all after me, because I was gorgeous then. And I'd say, 'No, I'm not taking any drugs.' I'd take maybe a toke on a joint once in a while, or something. Before I left, I gave in. When I went to California I met Owsley. Do you know him? Owsley acid. He invented the purest acid in the world. Well forget about it. I'd never take acid today. I haven't taken it in 20 years because it's not real, it's all pumped up with things that make you hyper. If you ever had real acid you'd know

Anyway, Salvation was very about the records. That was when I went into three turntables. I was really into it. Soul. The Chambers Brothers' 'Time' was the theme song to Salvation. I'd build up to that and everybody would know it was coming. I'd turn off all the lights and you'd hear – *thud, thud, thud*. We were so primitive then, we had this ball that had a light inside it and it shot out little rays of light and it actually had a string on it and I would pull it to make it rock across the dancefloor. 'Time has come today...' I'm doing lights, I'm pulling strings, I was like the Wizard of Oz. I had great lighting, I was in control of the whole thing.

This is a play. You're directing a play. It's very dramatic. It has to be dramatic, and no automatic programming is ever going be any use, because it's different every night and every time you play the record. Prior to Salvation, there weren't any lighting effects. Once I'd started to lose control of the lights, I couldn't build the drama the way I wanted, where I'm going with this particular audience. That's another thing: I don't understand how these guys in their bullet-proof glass booths five floors above the dancefloor can ever comprehend what's going on. You gotta feel the people.

I'd take my earphones off and I'm looking to see who's there tonight. I know the crowd, I know the people who are coming in. Possibly it's too intimate. Sometimes, of course, you'd hold out on them, because you knew what they'd want next. But you tease them. But some of these people... they don't tease them. I used to say, 'I know what you want and you're not going to fucking have it!' So sometimes I'd hold out for two or three songs, play some new ones, because I know they know that song is coming that they want. I'd slip in a new song and they'd be, 'Whoah, yeah.' The next night, they'd be asking for that song.

> **You're directing a play. It has to be dramatic, and no automatic programming is ever going be any use, because it's different every night and every time you play the record.**

How did the three deck thing come about?
I got to the point where I would play two records at the same time. I'd mix them. You'd be hearing like 'Foxy Lady' by Hendrix, and you'd hear the lyrics from the Beatles. I went to Salvation II and I'm good friends with Hendrix and we'd hang out together, sometimes two days at a time. Jimi walked in one night and I did exactly that mix. He turned around, gave me the finger and walked out. I was part owner of this club and my partner Larry Buckner comes and says, 'Terry, you've just chased Jimi Hendrix out of the club!'

'Don't worry he'll be back.'

Around closing time he came back and we go back to my loft and hang out for a day. In fact, I called in that night, couldn't come in, and we were up two days.

At Salvation, it was set up like an amphitheatre with seats going up and a sunken dancefloor and there were people who would just come in and sit there. A lot of them were on acid. And they'd just listen to my music. I didn't know this at the time; I met people subsequently who told me this. I did care about what I did and I did have some mastermixes that were wonderful, but I usually tried to be incredibly creative so I wouldn't do the same thing. So I'd try mixing this with that, bring that into there and slide another one on top of that with the third turntable. So you've got a beat going perfectly, and I'd throw a little riff or something from the other turntable. By that time I had controls for everything. I wished I was an octopus, I just didn't have enough hands to do everything, along with working the lights.

So *Magical Mystery Tour* was coming out and we had a party at Salvation. The Beatles were flying over from England. I put out a flyer with 'Terry Noel Invites People To A Surprise Party For Two'. I didn't even know what the surprise was going to be. Sid Bernstein calls me and says, 'I've got *Magical Mystery Tour*, the film, would you like to show it?' I'm saved!

Jerry Love is there and he goes out the back and makes some acid punch. I start playing 'Fool On The Hill' and then bring down the lights and start the movie. Everyone just sits down. After the film, everyone just stands up like zombies and files out of the place like the Living Dead. Brad says, 'Terry, it's not even 2 o'clock.'

So I said, 'The whole club took off, flew out into the universe, came back and landed. You gotta go home at that point. Everyone was exhausted.'

Next night everyone came in: 'Wasn't that unbelievable?!' And everyone had had the same trip: been picked up by a flying saucer, flew out into the universe, circled around and came back down again.

Was Salvation open every night?
Yes.

So you'd DJ seven nights?
Yeah. Nine until four. I was getting beat. At this point, the clubs were starting to get like they are today. It started to change at that point. We were so exclusive. One night the doorman turned away Mick Jagger. He was so proud of it. He said he'd turned away Mick Jagger and

Keith Richard. So I ran down the club, ran out into the street and said, 'Mick Mick, you can come in the back door here with me. Come on.'

So he sits down; he's steaming. Then he says, 'Fuck this,' and walked out. Towards the end of Salvation the Beatles came in and 'Lady Madonna' was out and *Magical Mystery Tour*. I was pissed with them because I felt they were just trying to do *Sergeant Pepper* over again. I went up to Paul, 'What is this stuff? Come on give me a break! It's like *Sergeant Pepper* II.' They dragged me away because he was pissed. They were afraid that once I got on the turntables, I'd start talking to them. Because everyone was aware that I'd talk to you.

What stuff were you playing at Salvation?
Chambers Brothers, definitely soul music. Not a lot of rock. Mamas and Papas were long gone. I would never have used a Frank Sinatra record at Salvation, because it was a much hipper crowd.

I moved to Salvation II because Bradley thought I was getting too outrageous with what I was playing, and that I was getting too personal. He wanted straight music. So his bookkeeper came down there, got turned on to drugs and starts wearing a bandana and makes a deal with someone, and that's when we opened Salvation II. The guys who had muscled in with Bradley down at Salvation, thought they were wiseguys, when they weren't. They find them dead out in Queens, with the ritual bullet through both sides of the temple and one through the centre of the head. Insane. So Bradley immediately runs off becomes a priest. He's still a priest, up in Connecticut.

© DJhistory.com

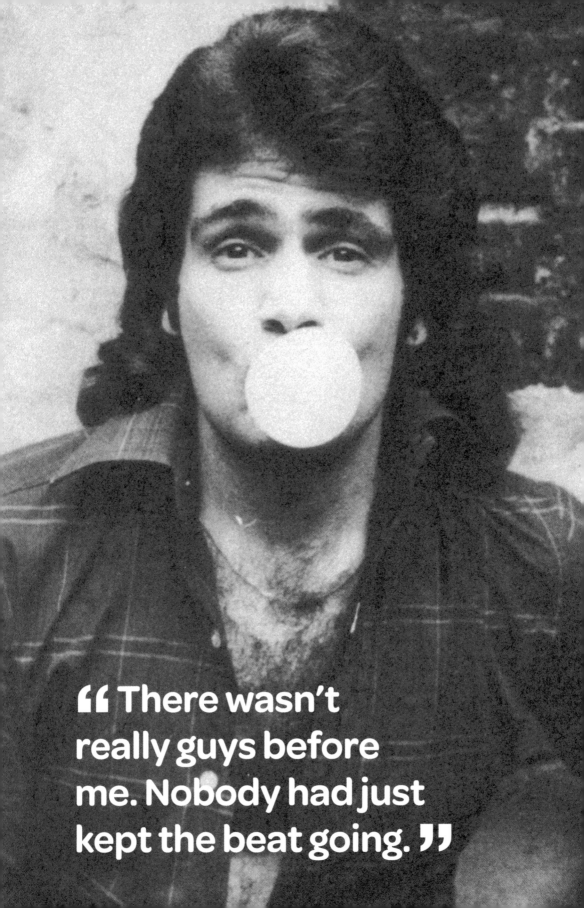

" There wasn't really guys before me. Nobody had just kept the beat going. "

Francis Grasso
The groundbreaker

Interviewed by Frank in Brooklyn, February 4, 1999

We found him in the phone book – the grandaddy, the pioneer, the first DJ to do what DJs do today. Before Francis, disc jockeys were technicians playing records one after another; after him they were performers programming whole nights of music, leading their dancers on a journey, and making them submit to an endless beat. He wasn't the first to mix records, but he made it an essential skill as he stitched rock, soul, Latin and African tracks together for an adoring crowd. The central inspiration for the DJs who would create disco, Francis Grasso founded modern DJing by showing everyone just how much was possible.

The subway ride is a full hour into Brooklyn. The plan was to meet outside the Carvel ice cream store. But what will he look like? His voice on the phone conjured a big fatso bum. Anyone male, white and middle-aged gets the once-over, and then a 50-something groover, skeletally trim, with a brown leather jacket and a mane of long, fuzzy grey hair comes into view. Somehow it's DJ Francis without a doubt. His face is a little skewed from the infamous mob beating, and he is obviously missing a few teeth, with several others in the wrong place altogether. This makes his voice sloppy, nasal and very quiet. Straight into Joe's bar, to interview the godfather of DJing, downing glasses of draft Bud at 10am.

So you're from New York originally?
Brooklyn. Born and bred, lived in many different places.

And you started off dancing, didn't you?
Yep. One of the original Trude Heller go-go boys. Dancing on a little platform with a live band. It was in the Village, Sixth Avenue, on the corner of 9th Street. You had 20 minutes on and 20 minutes off, and you could only move your ass side to side because if you went back and forth you'd bang off the wall and fall right onto the table you were dancing over.

What were you wearing?
Slacks, you know and you'd have a partner, and they'd play 'Cloud Nine' by the Temptations for about 38 minutes [laughs]. It was the most exhausting job I'd ever had in my life. I was beat that night.

What was Trude Heller's like? Was it ritzy?
Kind of. Kind of date-oriented. Couples, very few recorded records. She was just somebody who became famous, had her own nightclub. It was the hardest $20 I ever made in my life. I'm going home, my muscles were killing me. I remember on the train it was...

How did you get into that?
What? Dancing? I got three major motorcycle accidents, so I couldn't co-ordinate my feet and the doctor suggested for therapy that I try dancing.

So it was a therapeutic thing?

Yeah, sort of. Very, very wacky sort of way. I never thought I'd go down that sort of trail, 'cos I'd gone to college for literature.

Where were you at college?
Long Island University.

You studied English Literature
No, I started out in math, I'd gone to a basically math high school: Brooklyn Technical.But I changed into literature. 'cos I had an English literature teacher she said I belonged there.

How did dancing turn into DJing?
Well, I was managing a clothing store on Lexington Avenue between 57th Street and 58th Street. It was upstairs. And the bartenders used to come in from a club called Salvation II, and I'd become familiar with Salvation and [manager] Bradley Pierce. So they said come by. Back then it was couples only. Eight dollars minimum. At that time they wanted to distract from loners, you know somebody who'd dance with the waitress. Because somebody dancing makes people who are a little laid back get off their buns and move. If they had a couple of drinks.

And there was a disc jockey named Terry Noel in Salvation II, and I went there on a Friday night, and he didn't show up for work. Which later I found out why when he showed up at 1.30 and he'd taken acid. It's not a good start to a Friday night! And they so liked me, they asked me if I wanted to try. I was pretty familiar with the music, and I had a ball.

❝ I was at the Haven the night of the Stonewall riot. They locked the doors, the cops were clubbing people, they were throwing bricks and bottles. ❞

What was the set-up? What were the turntables?
It was a Rek-O-Cut fader with two Rek-O-Cut turntables and the fader was just somewhere in the middle of both turntables. They were Rek-O-Cuts, probably not even in existence now, like radio quality at the time, motor driven. Not belt driven.

And all you had was a switch to cut between the two?
No. It was a knob, a fader. It was a fader, so you could do mixes. Sort of. If you knew what you were doing. But this was my first night.

And you took to it like a duck to water?
Basically, yeah.

Do you remember the first record you played?
I don't know, but I had a hell of a good time. And they paid me a lot of money, and I said 'Wow, they paid me this much money,' and I would have paid *them*. I had that much fun. I know when Terry showed up he was fired.

Because he was unreliable and you were the new kid?
Well, I played better too. He used to do really weird things. Like he'd have the whole dancefloor going and then put on Elvis Presley. I kept 'em juiced. He would play bizarre records... He's still bizarre, but anyway. But he showed up at 1.30, which is now Saturday morning, the club closes at 4. It's not the right time to show up for work. And the owners had probably had enough of his attitude.

Can you remember the kind of records you were playing the first few times?
'Proud Mary' [by Creedence Clearwater Revival] was very popular. I played things like '96 Tears' [by ? and the Mysterians], Temptations, Four Tops, Supremes. There was no Jackson 5 then. Umm…

Can you remember the date when you first played?
Ooh no.

You remember the year?
1967 or '68. Then Salvation II closed. So I was out of work. I was doing air conditioning work. And I was at this club in Union Square called Tarots, on 14th Street. And I asked them if they needed a disc jockey one night and they said go. And he just had a switch, he didn't have a fader. You went from one to the other. And back then it was basically the same tunes. 'Knights In White Satin' was very popular.

How long did you play there?
Until the bouncer from the Sanctuary came to the club on a Sunday night. He turned around and said to me, 'You know the guy we've got at The Sanctuary really sucks, so would you like to, you know, audition?' I said sure. And at the time I had Brian Auger & the Trinity and Julie Driscoll. I went there with eight records; I thought if I can't do it in eight I'm not going to do it all night long. And they were practising for a fashion show, with models. And in eight records I had the job. Next thing I knew I was at the Sanctuary.

And they were the wild years.
No. Those were the quieter years. It was when the Sanctuary was straight and it was mostly couples like Salvation II. What was really funny was that the manager of Sanctuary used to be the manager of Trude Heller's. And we all thought the day manager and the night manager hated each other. But in reality they were shacking up, and they took off with like $175,000.

This is from Sanctuary?
The original Sanctuary, the original owners. The one in the church. It's the one that was called the Church first. Open two weeks and the Catholic church got an injunction to close us down. 'Cos we had this mural that I would face that was unbelievably pornographic. And what was interesting about it was the devil, no matter where you stood in the club he was looking at you. Angels were fucking and… So what they did was they changed the name to

the Sanctuary and reprinted the menus, and they stuck plastic fruit in various places, bunch of grapes here, you had red grapes, you had green grapes.

To cover everything up.
Yeah, 'cos it used to be some kind of German protestant church. But because this guy took the $175,000 they had to change hands. So they wanted to make the first gay bar. And they fired everybody, 'cos they didn't want women, 'cos this was after Stonewall, suddenly… Well, it was the first time they'd taken the concept of a gay bar without a jukebox.

And not being secret…
Well, I remember the Stonewall. I was at the Haven the night of the Stonewall riot. I remember seeing the police come in a city bus. It was like wacky. They locked the doors, the cops were clubbing people, they were throwing bricks and bottles. It was a wacked out night that night.

Anyway, at Sanctuary, Shelley and Seymour came in [as new managers]. They had to get a new crew, or at least see who they were gonna keep or let go. So it became evident that I had the job. We used to close Mondays and Tuesdays, now we're open seven days a week. And we're packed.

I remember one time at the Sanctuary, when it was all gay, it was so crowded, and they were passing poppers around. Even if anybody *wanted* to pass out, there was no room. They were literally holding each other up it was so packed. 'Cos then we had a maximum occupancy of 346 people; we stopped counting at 1,600 at the door.

I used to go to the men's room, and customers always tried to pick me up. I remember one time I was in a urinal pissing and this guy was in a business suit, and he said something to me, I said, 'Employer policy is that employees cannot date customers.' Then I started going to the ladies' room 'cos there were no ladies. I remember one time there was a fellow named Alan who used to stand by the door and greet people. And somebody was doing an article and they said, 'Do you get straight people here?' and he went, 'Yeah, there he goes.'

I had such power at that time. Two female friends of mine came to visit. They were just friends. At 2 o'clock in the morning, a weekday night, and I had James Brown *Live At The Apollo* on, 25 minutes and 32 seconds, and I said, 'If you don't let them in, you better get somebody up there to change that record.' So after about five minutes of this stalemate, they let them in.

> **❝ They didn't know how to bring the crowd to a height, and then level them back down, and to bring them back up again. ❞**

Jane Fonda filmed the movie *Klute* there. She had a big argument with Seymour and Shelley because they wouldn't permit lesbians in the club. I'm the disc jockey in the movie, and I had like three weeks work, doing the whole thing. It was fascinating to watch. Only thing is I was doing double duty: I was showing up at the movie set at 7.30, driving home, to Brooklyn, walking my dog, shave and showering, going back to work, till 4 o'clock in the morning. It took its toll.

I bet.
It was summertime and they would have a big table with coffee and bagels and doughnuts and everything you wanted. And then the cops came in, 'cos to get the feel of real hookers they had real hookers. Then they sent the cops in 'cos there was a lot of drug-dealing going on – in between takes! It was a lively crowd.

How was it through those times being the only straight guy?
Occasionally I had… fantasies! They would mistake you smiling hello as an answer back.

But those were good years because I wasn't engaged and I could devote all my time to my work. And I used to lift weights. I would do that every night, before I went to work. And I had my dog.

So you didn't play at the Sanctuary that long?
Oh, about a year.

From what I've read, the Sanctuary was a wild place. Did it change?
It got wilder. In the summertime they were having sex in people's hallways.

What about in the club? Did that go on?
Only me! 'os we were open all night. We're a juice bar now. We lost the liquor license. So they had to be doing something. We were staying open till 12 o'clock in the afternoon – Saturday afternoon, and Sunday afternoon. And they'd be so smashed. In the summertime they'd be in peoples vestibules, in their hallways... It was a very... I have articles on it. *Daily News* used to call it a 'drugs supermarket'.

What drugs were people doing back then?
Back then? The biggest drug people were doing back then was Quaaludes, the small ones, 300 milligrams, the pills. And you had the capsule which was 400 milligrams, and back then they went for $5 apiece. I had a pharmacist friend of mine and he used to get them in a sealed bottle and I'd sell them for a buck a piece, to my friends who came in. Made a lot of swaps for tapes, back in those days.

You would play high?
Oh yeah.

But no-one knew.
No-one knew. The idea was to show up, give yourself a facial, shave, shower. And talk to people like you're a hundred percent normal. They never knew. I remember the first time I came clean with my mother. I said, 'Didn't you ever wonder?' I had bought a house in New Jersey. 'Didn't you ever wonder, how I could come from work, take you someplace in Brooklyn, and drive back to New Jersey and go to work. Didn't you ever wonder how I stayed awake?'

And what did she say?
'Good point.'

And you had quite a following?
I'd get into a club with eight or nine people, didn't pay, drink all night. I'd be out walking my dog, people would scream out my name on the street, in the supermarket. I would do average things, they'd yell 'Francisss'.

That must have been great! Was it people you knew from the clubs?
You'd be surprised. If you put an average of 1,500 people in a room, for however many years I was playing: 17 years, a lot of people are gonna get to see you. I made a lot of fans in New Jersey. I made a lot of fans everywhere.

You were pretty much the first DJ that had that kind of following, but there were guys before you, so what were you doing differently?
There wasn't really guys before me. Nobody had really just kept the beat going. They'd get them to dance then change records, you had to catch the beat again. It never flowed. And they didn't know how to bring the crowd to a height, and then level them back down, and to bring them back up again. It was like an experience, I think that was how someone put it. And the more fun the crowd had, the more fun I had. See I really loved the atmosphere. I just wouldn't have wanted to have been a customer. I loved being in the room, but I couldn't see myself like being amongst one of the customers, being on the dancefloor, because I couldn't handle that. I really hate crowds. But it's fun to absorb it.

And to be in control.

Basically, yeah.

So how did you develop all of that?
I was a dancer! I was a dancer, so it was rhythmically… not hard. And I play a few instruments.

What do you play?
Well, I started on the accordion. I was young then. Then I went to guitar and then drums and saxophone.

Did you play in bands at all?
I played in high school.

You say musically it wasn't a problem, and I can understand that: if you're a dancer you know what you want to dance to. But technically it must have been a real problem… with the equipment you had back then.
Today you've got a disc jockey that puts on a 20-minute 12-inch. I'm changing records every 2 minutes and 12 seconds, on average. These guys don't really work today. Unh-uh. I mean if you're playing mostly 45s… If you're dealing with seconds and minutes you've got to time everything. I had certain bathroom records, certain records you played only when you had to go to the bathroom.

What were they?
James Brown Live At the Apollo, then I used to play the *Befour* album, Brian Auger & the Trinity. I played a lot of English music. I had gotten a lot of imports over my time. I had a deal with the record store where I used to live. He would let me take all the new 45s, go in the back with this little portable Victrola, listen to them. And I'd buy them. And if I didn't buy them I'd put them back. So I had a shot at all the new 45s that came out. Basically that was all there was back then. It had to be really good for me to buy an album. You had Booker T and the MG's, you had Sam and Dave, you had your Memphis sound, had your Detroit sound, the Motown sound. You had to mix it up.

> **❝ I dated Liza Minnelli for a while. I ran into her husband at the Salvation, he was at the urinal and he's like, 'I understand you kept my wife company while I was in Kentucky.' ❞**

You pretty much invented slip-cueing, right? How did that come about?
Well, to tell you the truth, my good friend Bob Lewis was a disc jockey on the radio, at CBS, before they went to oldies, way back when they played rock'n'roll, and his engineer had taught me. But I found with the two slide faders, that I had gotten so good. You see the reflection off the record, you can see the different shades of the black. And I got so good I would just catch it on the run.

You would just drop the needle on it?
No I could catch it in the beat. The record's spinning, you put the needle in it, right into it. And you just practised. I practised live, I guess.

So when did slip-cueing come in with felt pads?
Not till around the disco convention started [1975]. And the Bozak started coming in, the Bozak mixers. But I never liked the knob faders. The Bozak may have technically been more perfect, but you couldn't do what you could do with slide faders. I don't know why. You had to do the thing of turning your whole wrist, as opposed to just moving… With a slide fader one hand could do everything.

How did you programme the records?

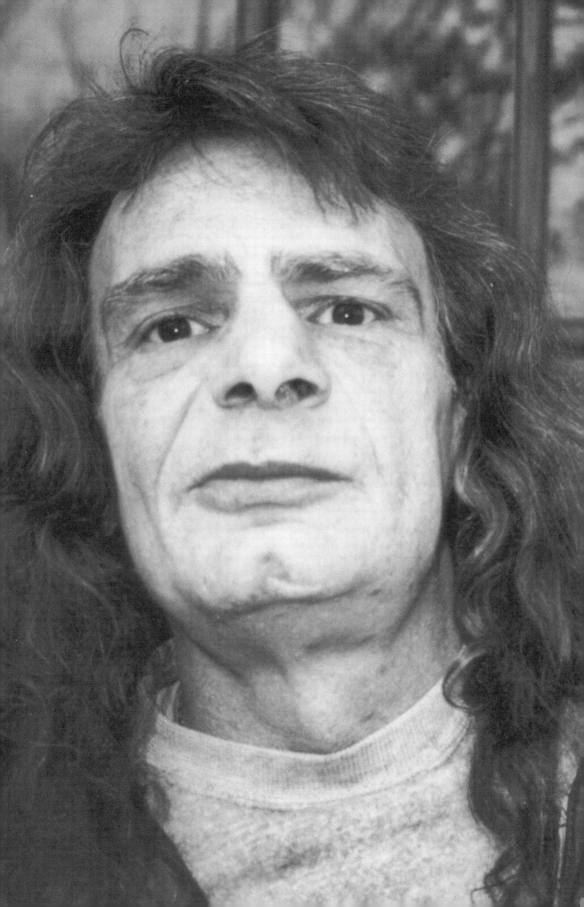

Francis Grasso

....

You can't be shocking in any way with sound. You can't be overpowering, 'cos then too many people would notice. You start out with records like, say, The Staple Singers' 'I'll Take You There', now that's a slow beat, and you build slowly and slowly, till you get them dancing fast. Like I used to play 'Immigrant Song' by Led Zeppelin, I loved playing that. I discovered a lot of records too: Abaco Dream, which was really Sly And The Family Stone, their tune called 'Life And Death In G&A' was a biggie. I discovered James Brown's 'Sex Machine'.

So what year were you able to beatmix, and completely segue?
I was able to beatmix right away.

That must have been so difficult with the records back then.
It was very difficult.

Did you have to remember exactly what tempo they were all at?
Well I know I had a basic variety of certain records in stacks. You bumped them into stacks; certain stacks would play a certain beat, like 2:4 beat, 4:4 beat, and you'd increase it. And when the drugs kicked in you just got crazy and the crowd got crazy.

So which club was the craziest?
I can't really single out one.

They were all pretty wild?
Yeah. When I was at The Machine I really couldn't see what was going on, 'cos it was like a stadium, the seating was on the left and right of me, and I was up there in my booth, and with the lighting in the booth over the turntables, I couldn't see what they were doing, but the bouncers would tell me what they were doing: fucking and sucking, all that shit. Compared to these days, back then people were doing it a lot older. They were flaunting it, and carrying it around.

You mean the drugs.
And sexually and everything else.

What were your peak records?
'You're The One' by Little sister, which was also Sly And The Family Stone. 'Hot Pants' was very big, by James Brown, when it came out.

How long were you at the Haven?
From '69 to er… I can't remember. Things were starting to happen. People were approaching me with business deals and stuff, always wanting to make a dollar quick. And I would make a deal with them, that they invest it in equipment, 'cos I had always believed I was only as good as my equipment. The only limitations I would put on myself was the equipment I was working with.

Who were you working with equipment wise, Alex Rosner?
At first it was Alex Rosner, then it was Dick Long. Not Bob Casey that much; he came in later on. Richard Long used to be Alex Rosner's fix-it man. If something happened during the night, he'd send Dick Long out. Then they had some kind of disagreement or whatever and Richard, he outbid him, he outperformed him, and he out-equipment-wised him. Dick and I used to have some really serious conversations about sound. Dick was into perfecting it and making it more and more reliable. 'Cos you know if you have nothing [in back up], and it goes, you're screwed. I didn't even have a tape recorder back then.

Alex Rosner built you the 'Rosie' at the Haven, didn't he. The prototype DJ mixer in a nightclub. What did Richard Long build for you?
I would say the first one was the one I had in my apartment. It was called Disco Associates; it had a triple volume control, single headset. Richard was really on the cutting edge. And gave me separate microphone input, and he was always toying with improving it.

When did you first have cueing?
I had that at Salvation II, but Tarot was sheer luck. They just had a switch. You didn't have a fader so you couldn't hear it coming in.

Was it a celebrity scene at Sanctuary? Did famous people come in?
Oh yeah, all the time. I dated Liza Minnelli for a while. When it's people like that you'd just nod hello. Recognition is like... people think it's really cool to say hi, but a lot of times it isn't 'cos you're expected to be always on. My second fiancée took a picture of me once, waking up. My hair was like this, you know. She's caught me in the middle of a yawn. And she went, 'This is the real Francis.' Because I was so vain and my hair always had to be impeccable. Even my dungarees had a crease. I'm serious.

That's what you wore in the booth.
At Sanctuary? No, I wore dress clothes. But at the Haven I made dungarees popular. The 501 Levis. Button fly.

" I was caught so many times getting oral sex in the booth it was disgusting. I would tell the girls, 'Bet you can't make me miss a beat.' "

How did you meet Liza Minnelli?
In Salvation II, when I was starting out. She left me for a coke dealer. Her husband at the time was playing in a piano bar in Kentucky, Peter Allen, and I ran into him at the Salvation, and he was at the urinal – people like to discuss things at urinals... I don't know. He's like leaning over my shoulder, he's like, 'I understand you kept my wife company while I was in Kentucky.' Back then I didn't snort anything. Back then a wild night to me was a wine and a little 7-Up in a glass.

I knew a lot of famous people. Knew Jimi Hendrix very well. In fact when he died, his main old lady, after she flew his body back to Seattle, when she came back to New York, she moved in with me. She wasn't a fiancée, a little off the wall for my taste! Not too stable. But nobody was stable back then.

I remember one time I ran into Jimi in the mens room at Salvation II. He was so stoned, he had his dick out and he couldn't remember what to do with it after he'd finished peeing. It wasn't a very large bathroom, so I said 'Jimi, it's Francis, what are you doing?' 'Trying to wash my hands.' I said, 'don't you want to put something away first?'

That's when he started hanging out with Buddy Miles, got into that heroin shit. Buddy Miles had the gang with the dark sunglasses at night, the long leather coats, the hoodlum look. People like Jimi they get run out of the way, over the deep end. I remember a time he was playing in Houston, and going over to the stadium he took five tabs of sunshine acid. And *to him* he sounded good. They booed him like crazy.

Were you able to see your influence on other DJs?
Yeah. I taught two of the most prominent: Michael Cappello and Steve D'Acquisto.

How did you meet up with them?
Hanging out. From them coming in as customers. I basically needed somebody reliable and who knew what they were doing, at least had an idea. I had to teach somebody. I was teaching in secret because it was really hard to do what I do. I may teach you the basic moves, but it's your interpretation that makes or breaks you.

Steve D'Acquisto has stories of the three of you staying up for three or four days.
Just three or four? [laughs]. I remember the first time they replaced me. Of course I had to teach somebody, when I had the walking pneumonia, in Sanctuary. And I went to work that Sunday night. I was in another room, I was so sick. The family doctor came to my bachelor apartment, and he said, 'You got walking pneumonia, you can't go to work.'

Oh shit!
That's what I said. But having a dog always kept me, you know, stable. Responsibility! I'd

never stay out and party. Go home. Probably why I'm still alive today.

Wasn't there a story that you got really badly beaten up? What was that?
That was opening up Club Francis. It had to be around '73, '74. Over the old Cafe Wha. My nose has been broken about 12 times. Least that's when I stopped counting.

Was it another club behind it?
Yeah, the Machine.

Because you were so successful.
Yeah, they didn't want me to leave. And they had the Mafia sit-down. The guy in the corner had instructions not to hit me, but to scare me. Only the guy they sent got carried away.

Shit! How bad was it?

> ## Michael would constantly scratch my records. He'd pass out on Tuinols on the turntable; we had to get another copy.

Bad. Kept me home for three months. I remember sitting in St. Vincent's hospital. I told the cops that I had went out to get a breath of fresh air, from the club, and these guys were coming up MacDougal Street, and they hit me with beer bottles. And I remember, these two doctors, in the emergency room of St Vincent's hospital in Manhattan, they said, 'Shame, must have been a good looking guy.' I had to reinvent myself so to speak, sitting at home for three months. And really when I walked my dog people thought I was Frankenstein. I was a teenage Frankenstein, with the bandages the whole bit.

Was that the end of Club Francis?
No that was the beginning. That was the first night of Club Francis.

You must have been pretty discouraged
Well, I broke up with my fiancé. I was gonna get married. Broke up with her.

That was fiancé number...?
Well, we never quite got it, we just sort of eloped one night actually. My cousin walked into Club Francis and he was with this ex-nun. And I said, 'Dierdra, let's get married.'

She was an ex-nun?
No, my cousin's girlfriend was an ex-nun. Dierdra was a Playboy bunny; she worked in the gift shop. And she said, 'Are you serious?' and I said, 'Yeah.'

So where did you play after Club Francis?
I went back to the Sanctuary. And they were starving, they were dying. It had become a juice bar. When I left it had had alcohol, they were open til like seven in the morning.

It was still a gay place?
Basically, but they had more women there. 'Cos they were harder up for money. It was like a dungeon: depressing. And I just turned it back on again. This is '72, '73 maybe. Like I say I went back and forth to Sanctuary a lot.

And were they the real wild years?
Oh, I was caught so many times getting oral sex in the booth it was disgusting.

While you were playing?
I would tell the girls, 'Bet you can't make me miss a beat.' Gave them a little challenge and away they go! In fact in the Sanctuary one time the manager walked in. He walks into the disc jockey booth, and he sees this girl on her knees, chick's head's going up and down,

and I says, 'Don't bother me now. If you're gonna yell, yell later.' I had such an amazing experience with women over the years.

What were the other rewards? You got pretty well paid?
Oh I was making a lot of money. I think my drug bill was – at that time drugs were a lot cheaper – was about 250 a week. And that was for what I'd give away. I'd go to work I'd have 20 joints. I'd buy pot by the pound, bring 20 joints to work with me. Buy an ounce of speed.

What kind of kick did you get out of DJing personally?
It was just feeling, the excitement, the electricity that was in the air. It was just phenomenal. I would have paid *them*. It was that much fun.

What were you aiming for when you were playing?
That high. People should have the same amount of fun I'm having.

Did you practise a lot.
I never felt that I'd done a good job. I always felt I could have done it better. I still do that today. Always doubting myself. There's always room for improvement. It wasn't until I moved to this neighbourhood that I didn't have a disc jockey set up. I built a booth in my living room.

What were the best times?
I try to learn something from everything. Even after the beating I tried to learn something from it. Taught me a lot of lessons in life – for what use I have no idea.

Did you feel like you were really connected with the dancers?
For years. For years I felt like that. Then that line dancing shit started. And that syncopated sound. They put everything to a disco beat. Like 'What A Difference A Day Makes', they had some great tunes, but making disco out of it, it just didn't work. It didn't have the real live sound. And in my opinion today's musicians are nowhere near as good as my generation's musicians. I mean back then it was magic. It was great until the middle '70s when everybody got into disco and *Saturday Night Fever,* and then it became so routine and mundane, and everybody wanted to be a disc jockey. Like, hey, everybody's a disc jockey. Everybody and their mother's a disc jockey actually.

You made mixing an important part of DJing. Can you tell me some of the records you were mixing together?
I had been known to make mixes like Chicago Transit Authority's 'I'm A Man', the Latin part, into 'Whole Lotta Love' by Led Zeppelin. I played a lot of African music. I started African music in nightclubs. Michael Olatunji's 'Drums Of Passion'. It bothered me when Santana came out because they didn't give Michael Olatunji credit for 'Jingo', and it's not even pronounced that way. It's pronounced J-I-N-L-O-B-A and in Santana's album it's J-I-N-G-O, and it wasn't until the third release of their album that they put M. Olatunji credit for 'Jingo'. Probably the best thing Santana's ever done.

What were some of the other big mixes you would do?
I was responsible for bringing Osibisa's 'Music For Gong Gong', Earth Wind And Fire, 'Sweet Sweetback's Badaaaasssss Song'. Mitch Ryder went with the Memphis sound. Mitch Ryder and the Detroit Wheels went to Memphis and it was called the Mitch Ryder Experiment, which was very good. I would lay down say 'Soul Sacrifice' by Santana, and then put the live Woodstock version on top of it. And extend it, and go back and forth. The Woodstock version is just a little bit faster.

You would totally overlay the two things? How did that sound?
Phenomenal! It was actually the first reverb anybody had ever heard of. But it wasn't. And the owner had these wooden discs coming out of the wall, where I would hang my 45s, 'cos back then you played 45s.

This is where?
The Haven. I used to have junk records, you know, so whenever I'd throw a temper tantrum

I'd take a record, and the wall was brick, and I'd throw it and break it off the wall: 'See what I think of that idea?' It was a good effect. He didn't know they were junk records.

Did you ever use two copies of the same things and extend things?
'You're The One' [by Little Sister] was similar, with part one and part two on the other side.

So how would you work that?
Well, you always get two copies, 'cos you only had like two minutes.

You had two copies of everything?
Mostly. If they were really big, like James Brown's 'Hot Pants', that was big, 'cos people wanted to dance, it's summertime, the tube tops were in, no bras, the whole bit.

If you had two copies, how long would you work it?
I'd never push it more than three times. On Little Sister's 'You're The One', part one ended musically, part two would begin with a scream, so you could blend right into the scream, and then go back to '...You're the one...' Or the scream twice. Play it twice, part two, flip it over and play it, twice. They didn't know I was playing two 45s.

But you didn't cut it up any more. You didn't say, 'Right I'm gonna play the intro, then another intro,' that kind of thing. Did you do that?
Occasionally. It would depend. I just basically tried everything there was to try.

Did you get any interest from the record companies recognising the promotional value of what you did?
Yeah, some, but back then everyone was caught up in their own thing. It was like, I'm doing my thing, leave me alone.

Did you know any of the producers or the musicians?
I was an upstart. I went to Colony Records just like everybody else, and I bought my records and then I went to work.

There was no way you could tell the labels: why don't you extend things or make it like this…?
I told them: the manager of the radio station, CBS FM; I said 'What you need is to stop putting commercials between records, and tie records together.' I made a tape for CBS, of what I could do. And they did adopt that idea, but then the station changed to oldies. But I did have my own radio show.

When was that?
1968 '69?

On CBS?
No, WHBI. Michael used to come with me…

Michael Cappello?
Yeah. We broadcast from Jersey City, but we used the Empire State Building transmitter. So I'd have to go through the Holland Tunnel, it was a couple of blocks from there. That was pretty interesting, couple of times I brought my great dane in the booth, you could hear the rustling of the dog under the table. I'd say things and I didn't realise the mic was on, and I was on the air. Got a letter from the FCC. I wrote back on the inside cover of a pack of rolling papers. A quote about freedom.

And you never got into remixing or production work?
I sort of did that live! You know they went to 16 tracks, then to 32. Equipment, technologically, things were going just so fast, leaps and bounds on the nightclub scene.

What were the big changes in the booth, technologically?
You had the crossover network separating the midrange, treble and bass.

Did you play with that?
Oh yeah.

When did that come in?
I was doing that way in the beginning. They just didn't know I was doing it.

You had crossovers back then?
Not crossovers, I'd just play with the treble. If a song was poorly recorded, and needed treble, just crank it up, and lower down the bass a bit. 'Cos back then a lot of 45s were poorly recorded.

It was funny because I'd listen to dance music when I got home. I listened to the Moody Blues, or King Crimson, Yes, Zeppelin. I discovered this record Andwella, 'Hold Onto Your Mind'. I always felt that if you had a little bit of a Latin beat it made it easier to dance to. It catches the audience's ear. Andwella was like that. Colony Records didn't even know they had it in the basement.

And the club had the records at that time; they didn't belong to the DJ?
The club had the records. For a long time that was the way it always was.

So you changed that.
I changed that.

That meant you were more independent then, because you had your own collection.
I also had a friend that worked at Colony. He charged me a dollar a piece. 'Cos Michael would constantly scratch my records. He'd pass out on Tuinols on the turntable; we had to get another copy. If you fall on top of the needle you're gonna gouge out the grooves of the record. One record I got through seven copies. Jimi Hendrix and Buddy Miles, the first album they did together at the Fillmore, had a lot of copies of that.

So what happened to your records then?
They were stolen when I was in hospital. And my equipment.

Do you think that was connected?
It was my next door neighbour. He convinced my family he was gonna hold onto them for me. He didn't tell anybody he was moving.

That must have been heartbreaking.
Well, considering I took such care of my records.

And you had so many
Yeah, over the years you get quite a collection.

Have you built it back up.
I just mix cassettes now and again. I really don't listen to dance music.

" Back then if you met somebody at 3 o'clock in the morning, they were a freak like me. Now they're just a degenerate. "

You don't have the old records you used to play?
Not that much. I remember... When Barry White came out I said he's the poor man's Isaac Hayes. Saw him a lot. Used to see – I forgot his name – from Blood Sweat and Tears, used to meet him in the Village. Back then if you met somebody at 3 o'clock in the morning, they were a freak like me. Now they're just a degenerate. And they're looking to rob you.

When did you call it a day?
1980, '81.

And that was because...?
I didn't quit 'cos it was a money issue; it just wasn't the same any more. It became work. I

got disgusted… this bullshit. And the people had changed. As it turns out I was lucky to get out, 'cos it was just the advent of AIDS and I had always thought that AIDS would develop into a heterosexual disease. And Richard Long died of AIDS. I lost 38 friends. Then I found out Richard Long died, made it 39, all of AIDS.

What's your greatest memory behind the booth?
I remember when I was working at the Haven, the Sanctuary manager, Michael Crennan, called me up and said somebody's been fooling around with the cartridge in the back. And could I take a look. I said I could stop up there before I go down to the Haven to work. And when I walked in and the customers saw me behind in the booth, they all applauded; there was this big cheer. People stood up, the house lights were all on. I'm like [shrugs] I'm not staying.

Did you sell tapes back then, mix tapes?
Well people didn't want to spend the money. They'd want to buy a reel-to-reel. If you had to buy the records, it'd cost you 500 dollars. Without my talent. People were interested, they just weren't into the money.

Did you ever make tapes and sell them?
I traded. For clothing. I'd make like cassettes for clothing and things like that. But as far as going into making a tape, I'd do it for friends. If somebody… Albert Goldman had a 4th of July party one time; I made a tape, reel-to-reel that he played at his party.

You were friends with him?
Yeah.

Did he get it right in his book *Disco?* Is that all correct?
Basically he got it right. The *Penthouse* article that it was taken from, my mother went out and bought so many copies. She framed the picture of me. Its like a centrefold, they took the staples out. So you see this naked broad Ginger and then the next page is me.

How did you meet up with him.
He called me up. And he came to work one night and sat in the booth, and he said, 'Now I see what they mean.' He said he'd spoken to a lot of disc jockeys and nobody could exactly explain what they did, and I was the only one that was able to… that made sense.

How come you never wrote a book about it all?
It's not over yet. My life is an adventure.

What do you think makes a great DJ?
A lot of persistence. And a lot of being aware of your surroundings, and you gotta have a natural feel for rhythm.

What makes a bad DJ then?
[laughs] The wrong records.

© DJhistory.com

FRANCIS GRASSO 26

IRON BUTTERFLY - In-A-Gadda-Da-Vida
RARE EARTH - Get Ready
FOUR TOPS – Don't Bring Back Memories
LITTLE SISTER – You're The One
CHICAGO TRANSIT AUTHORITY – I'm A Man
FOUR TOPS – Still Water
OLATUNJI - Jin-Go-Lo-Ba (Drums Of Passion)
BOOKER T & THE MG'S – Melting Pot
TEMPTATIONS – Ball Of Confusion
ANDWELA – Hold On To Your Mind
ABACO DREAM – Life And Death In G&A
OSIBISA – Music For Gong Gong
JAMES BROWN – Hot Pants
MITCH RYDER & THE DETROIT WHEELS – Liberty
BRIAN AUGER, JULIE DRISCOL & TRINITY – Indian Ropeman
SANTANA – Soul Sacrifice (live)
CAT MOTHER & THE ALL-NIGHT NEWSBOYS – Track In 'A' (Nebraska Night)
THE MARKETTS – Out Of Limits
TIMEBOX – Beggin'
ELEPHANT'S MEMORY – Mongoose
THE DOORS – The End
CREEDENCE CLEARWATER REVIVAL – Proud Mary
? & THE MYSTERIANS – 96 Tears
LED ZEPPELIN – Whole Lotta Love
MOODY BLUES – Knights In White Satin
TEMPTATIONS – Law Of The Land

"We'd play them covered up so people wouldn't know what they were."

'Farmer' Carl Dene
Treasure seeker

Interviewed by Bill by phone, March 28,1999

Before there was northern soul and before there were £15,000 records, there was Carl Woodroffe, aka 'Farmer' Carl Dene. An original mod, Dene travelled all over the country to all-nighters like Manchester's Twisted Wheel and the Mojo in Sheffield, before taking up spinning himself. A rare soul collector, he's the antecedent of northern soul pioneers like Ian Levine, Kev Roberts and Richard Searling, and his residency at the Catacombs in Wolverhampton was a crucial proving ground for the nascent northern sound. By emphasising collecting and connoisseurship he set the tone for the vinyl obsessives who followed. He also alerted the sleepy UK music industry to the possibilities of hit records emerging from the dancefloor. One of the first soul records to be crossed over from the clubs rather than radio was 'Hey Girl Don't Bother Me' by The Tams, which came from the crates of 'Farmer' Carl.

Where are you from?
I was born in Birmingham in 1945.

How did you get into collecting records, especially black records?
It all started when I first went to the Twisted Wheel, which was at the end of 1964. The sort of music being played at the Wheel you really couldn't hear on the radio and in the ordinary clubs.

How did you find out about the Wheel?
It was just word of mouth. And the fact that there was a similar club going on at the same time in Birmingham called the Whiskey-A-Go-Go. People used to know it in Birmingham as Laura Dixon's Dance School, because that's where it was held. It was an all-nighter like the Wheel, with no alcohol for sale. They played similar music. There were a number of disc jockeys there. They were mainly collectors, but there was no main disc jockey.

What was your impression of the Wheel the first time you went?
It was different to anything else I'd been to before. And, obviously, the atmosphere, because it was an all-nighter. There weren't many all-nighters going on then, maybe a couple down in London, the one in Birmingham.

Wasn't there also the Mojo in Sheffield? People say that was important.
Well, it was. The Mojo was a counterpart to the Wheel. I only went once to the Mojo, during a holiday weekend. Somebody introduced me to Peter Stringfellow who was DJ there at the

time, and I think he'd heard of me. He probably wouldn't remember me. I was playing at the time. The Mojo wasn't so much a club-type atmosphere. It was more like a dance hall. You had lots of rooms at the Twisted Wheel, both upstairs and downstairs, and the room where the groups would play. The Mojo wasn't like that. It was bigger. It therefore hadn't got quite the atmosphere, but that wasn't the fault of the records. I tend to think that the Mojo grew out of the Wheel to be quite honest with you. But it was certainly a very very good place.

He had good taste then, even if he hasn't now!
He certainly was the DJ. I met him when he was standing behind the record decks.

So tell me about the Wheel?
The Wheel in Brazenose Street was quite unique because it had that quite compartmentalised feel to it, with the various rooms.

Do you know when they moved to Whitworth Street?
About 1967 I think. I went every week from about 1965 to 1966. They'd have a major name on one week then a local band on the next. But the atmosphere was still there no matter, and what you got was an opportunity to listen to different kinds of records. Certainly in Brazenose Street, the band would be on in one part and the records would continue to be played in another. I remember seeing Georgie Fame there. You would get quite regular USA visitors.

> **❝ It was unusual to buy records like that in those days; you wouldn't see people walking around with a box of records. ❞**

What kind of music of was being played? Roger Eagle said he was dictated to by the pills that were being taken, so the tempo became faster.
The records that were popular around the time I was there would have been 'Call On Me' by Bobby Bland, 'Sweet Thing' by The Spinners, Earl Van Dyke's 'All For You', 'It Keeps Rainin'' by Fats Domino, 'The Jerk' with The Larks, 'Why You Wanna Make Me Blue' and 'The Way You Do The Things You Do' by The Temptations. And three that always followed each other: Fanny Mae 'Buster Brown' on Melodisc, Wayne Fontana 'Something Keeps Calling Me Back', which was the B-side to 'Pamela Pamela' and 'I Need Someone To Love Me' by Errol Dixon. They always used to be played one after the other. Then of course, there are the more well known ones now like 'What's Wrong With Me Baby' by The Invitations and 'Scratchy' by Travis Wammack, which was an instrumental.

Did that kick off that instrumental thing, I thought 'Six By Six' by Earl Van Dyke was an early one?
No that was later, that was more 1969. It was a follow up to 'All For You'. What other ones were there? 'Picture Me Gone' by Evie Sands. There was one that Roger Eagle used to play regularly and I actually bought it off him. 'I'm Not Going To Work Today' which was originally by Clyde McPhatter, but done by Boot Hog Pefferly and the Loafers. That was a good mid-tempo one, sort of like the Drifters. A real one-off. It really hit me that one, so I bought it off him for £1/10s, which was a lot of money then!

It was unusual to buy records like that in those days; you wouldn't see people walking around with a box of records. The DJ would have records, and there would be the odd collector like Brian Phillips. I used to write to him about records. He was more of a collector than a DJ, though he did become well known shortly afterwards as a DJ at the Wheel.

Anyway, the old Wheel used to be on until about seven in the morning. And eventually they threw people out a little earlier, and it changed to 6 o'clock and people would be wondering what the hell to do with themselves. But that club was rife with pills. People would bring them in with them. And the comment we always used to hear from the police was, 'Well, what's the point of raiding the place when we know where all the villains are?'

They didn't want to spread the problem around the city! The atmosphere there was quite incredible though.

There were other places to go on a Sunday morning after the Wheel closed. There was a club in Bolton, I can't quite remember the name, but it used to open at 12 o'clock. I used to come back from the Wheel, sleep for about three or four hours and then go down to the Chateau Impney in Droitwich which was a Sunday afternoon club on from four till seven. People used to travel from all over the midlands to go there. Same sort of music. I worked there for a good year or two. This was after the new Wheel, in 1968. That was a well-known venue. It was there that I was headhunted for the Catacombs.

Do you remember any records that you introduced to the new Wheel?
I don't know whether I introduced it, but it wasn't played very often and it became very popular: 'Tired Of Being Lonely' by the Sharpees on Stateside. A big sound up there that was probably started at the Catacombs was Gene Chandler and Barbara Acklin 'From The Teacher To The Preacher' on Brunswick. Another record that was very popular at the Chateau that I think I introduced to the new Wheel was 'I'll Do Anything' by Doris Troy. Then there was my own discovery 'Baby Reconsider' [by Leon Haywood] which found its way there through one of my Gloucester collector friends, either Froggy or Docker, I can't remember which. I bought it from a shop called Moores in Leighton Buzzard who were importing records at the time.

When did the Catacombs open?
It was in about 1969. The owner came round and asked me if I would do a couple of bookings at the Catacombs. The DJ at the time was new on the scene and he didn't have the records that I'd got. The DJ at the time it first opened was Alan S [Smith]. They were looking for the more specialist tunes that I had. And Wolverhampton had a very big northern – or 'rhythm & soul' as we used to call it – following at that time.

How did you get your nickname?
Everybody was choosing names that were different. At the time there was a guy called Roger 'Twiggy' Day, who was on Radio Caroline. I used wear a hat and somebody said, 'Have you got your farmer's hat on today?' So then it became Farmer Carl. The Dene sounded a bit like people like Carl (Wayne), who was in the Move, although at that time he was in Carl Wayne & the Vikings.

Where were you getting your records from?
In 1964 and '65, there was no-one importing records. The other records that were being played at the Wheel were not imports. They were UK issues. In '64 and '65, there were very few imports. They started coming in 1966 when shops were starting to import them. I think Dave Godin started to import them. There was a shop in Manchester, there was a shop in London. I used to go to a record shop called the Diskery. Most of the DJs used to go there, because they would have a lot of stuff. If you went into another shop and asked for the Impressions, they would say, 'What are you talking about?' But Diskery would have all the stuff on Stateside, on Motown. It was a real goldmine for records.

Where did you find out about new releases?
Well, in 1964 and '65, the only place we found out was from the Diskery. There weren't any magazines to speak of.

Were was the first place you DJed?
Le Metro club in Birmingham, in a converted railway arch. It was actually where they filmed one episode of the '60s soap opera United. They came and filmed the club, but it was a very very good club, and well designed too. I worked there for three years, twice a week.

When you started at the Catacombs you had records that they didn't have at the Wheel. Did you bring up stuff to them?
Yes I did. Well, because I'd been buying records since the early '60s, when the new Wheel came about, because I'd accrued these records, a lot of which had never been played in a club, and I'd bought them off the shelf, I'd introduce them as my own inventions. We used to play them covered up so people wouldn't know what they were. Do you know about this?

Yeah, there was a guy called Count Suckle in '63 at the Roaring Twenties in London who did the same. When did you say you were doing it?
He was doing it before me. I was doing it from about 1965.

> **❝ It was so unique. You wouldn't hear it on the radio. You wouldn't hear it in a regular nightclub. You'd have to go to a chosen place. ❞**

Were you inventing names for them as well?
What we used to do was we'd get a record we didn't want and cut out the centre and stick it on top of the record. And because it already had a name on the label that would throw people. So you put it on top of whatever record you were playing at the time and it would cover up the record.

Do you remember some of the records that you did cover up?
Yes. 'Darkest Days' Jackie Lee, and more recently Carl Douglas; another thing we used to cover up was Donald Height's 'She Blew A Good Thing', a cover version of the American Poets tune which was a big one at the Wheel.

My main claim to fame, which I forgot, is I broke 'Hey Girl Don't Bother Me' by the Tams. We used to play that in the George Hotel in Walsall. Although it came out in 1964, we were playing it around 1968. We also used to play it at the Chateau. We didn't cover it up. And everybody, particularly the girls, went absolutely wild about it. And they would all go to their local record shops and ask for this record. The shops would ask the reps, who would tell them that it was deleted. The number of requests they were getting for that record must have far outweighed anything they'd had before. The company reissued it. I remember at that time Peter Powell, who was from Stourbridge, near to the Chateau in Droitwich, he'd heard it and played it on to the radio. He'd heard about the clamour for the record.

What station was he on then?
Radio 1.

Do you remember any other records like the Tams that crossed over?
'Just A Little Misunderstanding' by the Contours, one of the best dancing records of all time, which was popular at the new Wheel and everywhere else. You really can't go without mentioning it. Classic sound. That came out originally in 1966. The A-side was called 'Determination', so this was the B-side. 'These Things Will Keep Me Loving You' by the Velvelettes. Issued in 1966.

Were these ones that broke out generally from a number of clubs?
I think they were. It would be wrong for me to claim any kind of responsibility for those. I did my fair share, there's no doubt about it though. The one that was the biggest after 'Hey Girl Don't Bother Me' was probably Mary Wells' 'What's Easy For Two Is So Hard For One'.

How long did the Catacombs last for?
It went from 1968, but it ran through to 1974 or '75, but its heyday was 1969 to 1970. It was on Temple Street, an industrial premises that had been converted. Not a big club, only 500 or 600 people maximum. It was open from eight till 12. Not all-nighters, they brought them in in the early '70s.

Which ones do you regard as the big Catacombs records?
'Breakout' by Mitch Ryder and the Detroit Wheels, 'At The Top Of The Stairs' by the Formations, 'Let The Good Times Roll' by Bunny Sigler, 'Right Track' by Billy Butler, 'Wade In The Water' by Marlena Shaw, 'Candy' by The Astors and 'Walking Up A One Way Street' by Willie Tee, 'Fife Piper' the Dynatones, which were both big at the new Wheel too.

A special discotheque was held at the Gladstone Liberal Club, Dudley, on Saturday, in aid of the newly-formed Dudley Liberal football club. Guest of honour, Jeff Astle, here tries his hand as a disc jockey with help from the resident D.J., Carl Dene.

POPULAR Albion centre-forward, Jeff Astle, was the guest at Dudley Liberal Club's weekly discotheque on Saturday.

Interviewed by D.J. Carl Dene, Jeff answered questions about England's World Cup activities in Mexico, and was given a tremendous reception by the 200 members.

All proceeds on Saturday will go towards the formation of a football team at the club, which will compete in Division II of the Brierley Hill League next season.

Mr. Arthur Lewis, a director of the X'Newm agency that promotes the discotheque, said that a lot of work had been put in by the club's entertainments secretary, Mr. D. Raybould.

The football team's manager will be Mr. Jack Jukes and Mr. Bill Beasley will be looking after the secretarial work.

th win

'Farmer' Carl Dene

....

Did you play any of the records that later became known as funk, such as James Brown?
Oh yes! For James Brown you've got to go back to the old Wheel. There was stuff – again very popular at the old Wheel – at the top of any list: 'Night Train' and 'Out Of Sight' were some of the big ones, another one was 'Tell Me What You Gonna Do'. Then of course, there were later James Brown records like 'It's A Man's Man's World', which were more pop-soul rather than soul-rhythm and blues. Yes, I did play him certainly. In the late sixties red Atlantic was very popular and most DJs then were playing it. The Arthur Conleys, stuff like that. I played my fair share of it, but it was the rare soul, the more sophisticated stuff, that I liked playing personally.

Why did that rare soul thing grow? Where did it come from?
I think it was because you couldn't head it anywhere else. It was so unique. You wouldn't hear it on the radio. You wouldn't hear it in a regular nightclub. You'd have to go to a chosen place, and there were only a handful of those around. Part of the enjoyment was actually travelling there. Looking forward to going. The motorways didn't really exist then as they do now. The M6 for example, didn't start until you went north of Cannock to go to Manchester. Likewise, the M1 to London, you would have to go down to the A45 to Coventry and join the M1 from there. It was a holiday going to Manchester or Birmingham or London.

Did you go to any of the clubs in London?
No, I didn't. Some of the people from the Whiskey-A-Go-Go went. I always preferred Manchester to be quite honest. Having been there, you don't tend to change your habits; like watching a football team. Certainly the travelling, and the uniqueness was key. It was a day out. You'd go out with a change of clothes. One of the things that we did do in Birmingham was take up mohair suits to the Twisted Wheel. People used to go in casual clothes so we would wear mohair suits and ties, shirts. And you'd try to get up there with your suit in pristine condition. The looks we used to get, from people who were dressed casually, were amazing! You'd go up with your jeans on and change into your suit for the all-nighter. And then change back into your casual clothes to come home.

What other clothes were people wearing at the old Wheel?
Mohair suits, smart. Just smart clothes of the day. You'd be wearing your mohair suit, shirt and tie in a stifling atmosphere with the heat. You'd be wringing wet with sweat but still wearing your suit when you came out of the club! It was always a good way of endearing yourself to the women. It went down well, that.

How far and wide were people travelling from?
Well, the Wheel you'd have people travelling from the east, places like Yorkshire, Sheffield, Huddersfield, coming from places like, there was a guy that used to come from Scunthorpe, Grimsby...

Why do you think it was that in London they got caught up in psychedelia, while in the north they remained unaffected by it?
I can't explain that at all, but I think it's probably largely due to tastes developing separately, because they never intermingled. Most people in the north of England didn't bother to go down to London. Most people in London didn't bother going north of Watford.

© DJhistory.com

CHATEAU IMPNEY / CATACOMBS 60

MARY WELLS – What's Easy For Two Is So Hard For One
THE O'JAYS – I Dig Your Act
MITCH RYDER – Break Out
THE SPINNERS – Sweet Thing
BOBBY SHEEN – Dr Love
LEON HAYWOOD – Baby Reconsider
KIM WESTON – Helpless
THE ELGINS – Heaven Must have Sent You
BOBBY MCLURE – You Got Me Baby
MARVIN SMITH – Have More Time
DOBIE GRAY – Out On The Floor
THE CONTOURS – Just A Little Misunderstanding
THE INCREDIBLES – There's Nothing Else To Say
THE INVITATIONS – What's Wrong With Me Baby
DEAN PARRISH – Determination
CHUCK JACKSON – Chains Of Love
RONNIE MILSAP – Ain't No Soul In (Left In These Old Shoes)
ROSCOE ROBINSON – That's Enough
CHUBBY CHECKER – You Just Don't Know (What You Do To Me)
JAMES CARR – That's What I Want To Know
THE ASTORS – Candy
LITTLE ANTHONY – Gonna Fix You Good (Every Time You're Bad)
THE VELVELETTES – These Things Will Keep Me Loving You
LINDA LYNDELL – Bring Your Love Back To Me
DORIS TROY – I'll Do Anything (He Wants Me To Do)
THE AMERICAN POETS – She Blew A Good Thing
THE FASCINATIONS – Girls Are Out To Get You
EARL VAN DYKE – All For You
WILLIE TEE – Walking Up A One Way Street
MAJOR LANCE – Everybody Loves A Good Time

THE TYMES – Here She Comes
MARLENA SHAW – Let's Wade in the Water
THE TAMS – Hey Girl Don't Bother Me
THE SPINNERS – I'll Always Love You
JACKIE DAY – Before It's Too Late
PERCY SLEDGE – Baby Help Me
BOBBY BLAND – Call On Me
THE VIRGINIA WOLVES – Stay
LITTLE HANK – Mr Bang Bang Man
THE DYNATONES – The Fife Piper
DARRELL BANKS – Our Love (Is In The Pocket)
THE TEMPTATIONS – The Way You Do The Things You Do
BUNNY SIGLER – Let The Good Times Roll
THE IMPRESSIONS – You Ought To Be In Heaven
FRANKIE VALLI – You're Ready Now
DANNY WHITE – Keep My Woman Home
RODGER COLLINS – She's Looking Good
TOMMY NEAL – Goin' To A Happening
CHRIS JACKSON – I'll Never Forget You
BILLY BUTLER – The Right Track/Boston Monkey
WILLE MITCHELL – Secret Home
WILLIE MITCHELL – Everything is Gonna Be Alright
BOB KUBAN AND THE IN-MEN – The Cheater
RUFUS LUMLEY – I'm Standing
THE FORMATIONS – At The Top Of The Stairs
BARBARA RANDOLPH – I Got A Feeling
ART FREEMAN – Can't Get You Out Of My Mind / Slipping Around
FRANCES NERO – Keep On Lovin' Me
FIVE STAIRSTEPS & CUBIE – Stay Close To Me
GENE CHANDLER/BARBARA ACKLIN – From The Teacher To The Preacher

Compiled by Carl Woodroffe

RECOMMENDED LISTENING

VARIOUS - Chartbusters USA (vinyl only)
MAJOR LANCE - The Rhythm Of Major Lance (vinyl only)

CATACOMBS
temple street · wolverhampton

Tonight - (Saturday)
From the Revolution Club, London

THE RAVING SOUL SOUNDS OF FEARN'S BRASS FOUNDRY

Disco by Farmer Karl
8.0 p.m. to 11.30 p.m.
Admission 7/6

“ I discovered the greatest haul of northern soul records ever to be discovered. ”

Ian Levine
Soul adventurer

Interviewed by Bill in London, March 2, 1999

Iconoclastic and confrontational, few DJs have broken as many records as Ian Levine did at his Blackpool Highland Rooms residency during northern soul's 1970s apex. Alongside Colin Curtis, he debuted new discoveries weekly, exploiting his wealthy background to make regular transatlantic record-buying trips (his parents owned a casino on Blackpool's Golden Mile). His stateside excursions eventually drew him to lead the northern scene out of its obsession with oldies and into a new era of disco and jazz-funk, a move that led to fatal fissures within. As a regular visitor to New York's Saint and resident at the newly opened Heaven in London, Levine also pioneered hi-NRG – the sound of gay dancefloors worldwide that was later co-opted by Stock, Aitken & Waterman and sold on as pre-teen pop. Levine went on to produce various boy bands including Bad Boys Inc and Take That (he's currently working with another one, Injustice).

The interview takes place in Ian's rambling post-Edwardian house somewhere on the road between Acton and Ealing in west London. We head for his sitting room where he reclines in an armchair next to an original Doctor Who dalek, as a young lad brings him a plate piled high with bacon sandwiches (Ian is larger than life in so many ways). He has an incredible recall for music, reeling off an endless succession of artists and titles, all delivered with the bombast and self-assurance of someone used to getting his own way.

Tell me a little about your background.
I was born in 1953 in Blackpool and started collecting Motown records as early as 13 years old. Really intensely by the time I was 14. I set out to get every Motown record ever released in the UK. The guy who claims he was the first ever rare record dealer, Gary Wilde – records were six shillings. in those days and he charged £5 for these rare Motown and northern things – had a cigarette kiosk in Blackpool town centre in Victoria Street. He sold cigarettes and rare records, and all the mods would congregate outside his kiosk. He was a real pioneer of this. This was 1967 and '68. And by the time I was 15 I was going with my parents on holiday to America and finding very rare Detroit records in these record shops.

Whereabouts?
Miami, mainly. As far back as 1970 we went to New Orleans and I found those Ric-Tic records: JJ Barnes, San Remo Golden Strings, things had never been discovered by anybody and I found them in a joke shop in 110 degrees heat in New Orleans. I had a little battery-operated Discotron I'd borrowed. I put this JJ Barnes record on and this Motown-type drum started and a wonderful Marvin Gaye meets the Four Tops fabulous stomping sound came out of it. I freaked and my life changed from that moment on. JJ Barnes got me into northern soul.

There was a kid called Stuart Bremner who was older than me and I looked up to him. He had DJed at the Twisted Wheel and the Blackpool Wheel. The Twisted Wheel was the first all nighter where northern soul grew out of. And he was DJing down there and going down with his mates, all these cool mods, '60s, you know.

I couldn't go to the Wheel until I was 17, until 1970, just before it closed. Went down and saw that I had a load of records with the same beat that people were dancing to that no-one had discovered yet, and I brought them down. 'Hit And Run' by Rose Patrice, which is a real Detroit record. I just blew everyone's mind by having these records that no-one else had got.

It was an embryonic scene. The Twisted Wheel was a club in Manchester that had been playing the Motown sound, but some of them had a more earthy Memphis sound. And the northern scene moved away from the earthiness and into the very slick, smooth, orchestrated sound of the Supremes and Four Tops. Except it wasn't; it was by other artists on other labels that had flopped. The more that a record had a Motown-y sound to it and was inaccessible. So people stopped playing the Supremes and the Temptations and started playing records like 'Baby Reconsider' by Leon Haywood and 'More Of Your Love' by Bob Brady and the Concords, which was a cover of a Smokey Robinson song; 'Darkest Days' by Jackie Lee and Sandi Sheldon's 'You're Gonna Make Me Love You'. Those four records were super-rare, and literally were £50 each, because everybody wanted them and no-one could get them.

This guy from Gloucester called Docker came to the Twisted Wheel with the Leon Haywood record and there was only one copy known of in the whole England, on a tiny little label called Fat Fish. Although Leon went on to have hits in the seventies, this record was super, super rare. Everybody would crowd round him just to have a look at this record because it was legendary and so rare.

The main pioneer of that scene was a guy called Rob Bellars who DJed at the Twisted Wheel. People were fed up with the same old songs, like Franki Valli's 'Are You Ready Now' and Earl Van Dyke's 'Six By Six' that had been played at the Wheel for years. There was a hungry crowd at the all-nighters, pilled out of their heads on amphetamines who wanted to dance to fast Motown-style records with a new beat and new sound.

When I say new it's as in undiscovered, and it was '60s records, because by 1970 and '71 America was making funky records like James Brown and Lyn Collins. Funky stuff. So instead of looking for new records as they had in the past, they had to hunt for records that were four or five years old. And that hunt led to an obsession with rare records.

When the Wheel closed in the last week of January '71, a couple of other smaller nighters got raided by the police, so everything then got focused on Blackpool Mecca because it was the one place in the country that played this kind of music. You had 1,000 people congregating in the Highland Room every Saturday to hear these exclusive records. Tony Jebb was DJing there with a couple of pop wankers called Stewart Freeman and Bill The Kid, but Tony soon ousted them, because the crowd wanted to hear rare soul and I was the godfather, pulling the strings. I'd said, 'Get Les Cokell.' But Les couldn't keep up with the records, he was using all mine and one time when he was ill the crowd said, 'Come on, you can DJ,' so I did.

By '72, I'd got this huge reputation for finding and playing rare records. Big all-nighter in Stoke called the Torch, Tony defected there, with Colin Curtis, Keith Minshull, Martin Ellis and Alan Day. Leaving me at Blackpool with Les. We'd go down to Stoke and get there at three or four in the morning, after we'd finished playing. And I wanted to do the Torch, and Tony Jebb persuaded Chris Burton [the promoter] to get me on there. So Blackpool closed down for a few months, because Les couldn't do it on his own.

The Torch had a lot of trouble with drugs and the police closed it down after a year of all-nighters there. It was the forerunner of Wigan Casino. It was the first big northern soul all-nighter, in a converted cinema with an oval-shaped dancefloor, a gutted-out cinema with balconies on top. It held about 1,600.

It was in the middle of nowhere wasn't it? Tunstall?

Yeah. The Wheel had been a small clique. It had been the ultimate underground club. It held about 5-600 people, all the legendary artists from the Drifters to Ike & Tina Turner, to the more esoteric ones like the Vibrations and James & Bobby Purify and Edwin Starr. They'd all appeared at the Wheel.

The Torch was fantastic. And Major Lance was an iconic artist. He'd had a run of hits in the '60s, although they hadn't been hits in America, they had this absolutely quintessential northern soul sound, with the vibes, the strings and the right beat.

Didn't he record a live album at the Torch?

That's what I'm coming to. Because he'd had more hit 45s than anyone else – bar perhaps Jackie Wilson – that had been big on the northern scene, he built up this legendary reputation. If there was anyone that people on the northern scene wanted to see, it was Major Lance. Chris Burton pulled off the amazing coup of finding him in Chicago, and getting him to come along just to perform at the Torch.

That night was the first night I DJed there and it was the most electrifying night of my whole career. You could not have squeezed one more person in that club. They were hanging off the rafters. It must've been 120 degrees. It was so hot and packed, the sweat was rising off people's bodies as condensation and dripping back on to them from the ceiling. He sang with the worst band you've ever heard. It was some British band who had no concept of what northern soul was, and they went through all of his hits. 'The Beats', 'Monkey Time', 'Ain't No Soul In These Old Shoes'. Because everyone loved it so much, we – John Abbey from *Blues & Soul,* Chris Burton and me – decided to bring him back to do a live album at the Torch. The guy had never seen anything like it.

❝ I went to Miami that summer and brought back 4,000 singles I picked up in old Salvation Army places for 5¢ each. ❞

What happened with the Torch was firstly Colin Curtis and Keith Minshull dropped out because they'd heard it was going to close, so they went to the Top Rank in Hanley. Tony Jebb got busted for drugs. It was just me and Martin Ellis left. I went from being the last of six, to being the number one. They closed it down and Colin and Keith, very craftily, had got Blackpool Mecca back. They lived in Stoke, I was living in Blackpool.

When the Torch closed, Chris Burton took over the Top Rank in Hanley, so I was going from Blackpool to Hanley and Colin and Keith were going from Stoke to Blackpool to do their gig. I wasn't very happy about it. Keith Minshull wasn't really pulling the crowds in. And Colin was very hungry for the records I was discovering.

I went to Miami that summer and brought back 4,000 singles I picked up in old Salvation Army places for 5¢ each. I discovered the greatest haul of northern soul records ever to be discovered. By then Radio 1 had interviewed me about it all. I was a name on the northern soul scene. I could look at the producer, arranger or singer and tell straight away whether it was going to be a ballad or northern soul record. In fact, we burnt it out too quick.

One time when I was in Miami I heard a record on a radio station by the Carstairs. They'd had a big record on Okeh called 'He Who Picks The Rose' and they had this new record, 'It Really Hurts Me Girl', and it blew my mind because it had this very throaty northern soul vocal, and a northern soul feel but a slightly shuffly beat. Not as modern as the Philly disco stuff, but just a bit modern, a bit dangerous for the northern soul scene. Anyway, I tried to buy this record, but couldn't find it. No-one had heard of it. I went to the radio station and they said they'd been sent a demo from the record company. Here's the number. I phoned the record company Red Coach, Gene Redd's label, distributed by Chess, and they'd lost their distributor and the record had not been released. It was shelved. I bugged the radio station, said I'd give them anything they wanted. They refused because they liked it as well. So I was fucked.

Back in England I found this dealer called John Anderson who'd moved from Scotland to Kings Lynn. I told him I wanted this Carstairs record and he'd just had a shipment in from America of 100,000 demo records from radio stations. We went through this collection, me, Andy Hanley, and Bernie Golding, and we found three copies of the Carstairs record. Went back to Blackpool, played the record and changed the whole scene.

Blackpool Mecca suddenly became the home of this new northern soul sound. I would've heard this record in 1973, when it was supposedly released, but not obtained it until 1974. After the Carstairs came this record by Marvin Holmes called 'You Better Keep Her', Bobby Franklin's 'The Ladies Choice', Don Thomas's 'Come On Train' and 'I've Got The Vibes' by Jay Armstead. This new wave of shuffly, hypnotic rhythms, as opposed to the stompiness of the '60s stuff. It was wonderful for while. Wigan hated it and carried on playing the '60s stompers. But when things like the Carstairs got played the floor was much busier than when some of the stompers were played. What had happened was the bootleggers had killed it off for us, because every record that we found – 'I Never Knew' [by Eddie Foster], 'I Worship You Baby' [by The Glories], 'I'm In A World Of Trouble' [by The Sweet Things] – every time, four or five weeks after they'd started to break they were bootlegging.

Our rule at Blackpool was as soon as a record was bootlegged we dropped it like a hot potato. If three or four bootlegs were coming in every week, which they were at that time, three or four records got dropped from the playlist and three or four had to be found to replace them. The quality of the sounds started to deteriorate. What was happening in 1975 was the floor was packing to the more modern stuff and the crowd were dictating which way it went.

> **❝ The concept of northern soul was that people could travel 200 miles on a Saturday night to hear records they couldn't hear anywhere else. ❞**

Wigan was the complete opposite. They were looking for anything they could find with a beat, so all they could find at that time were pop records, like Gary Lewis & the Playboys' 'My Heart's Symphony'. They were playing some good soul records, but a lot of white pop was getting played. Muriel Day 'Nine Times Out Of Ten', Lorraine Silver 'Lost Summer Love' and 'The Joker Went Wild' by Brian Hyland.

Then it got worse. It got to 'Hawaii 5-0' by the Ventures and even to 'Joe 90'. The soul fans started to desert Wigan. At the same time, Dave McAleer was releasing these records on Disco Demand by Wigan's Chosen Few. They had these horrible pop novelty hits that were masquerading as northern soul. So whereas the diehards hated it and quit Wigan, thousands of new people would see these dancers on *Top Of The Pops* with their badges and singlets and think oh, this is the new thing, let's get into this.

A new crowd descended on Wigan, who stayed for a while, but were really like sightseers and tourists who'd got into northern soul through the TV exposure it got. Blackpool Mecca was much more for purists. There was a huge war between Russ Winstanley and myself at that time. And the records that I had begun producing like the Exciters were banned from Wigan. There were two feuds going on that split the scene. The one between Blackpool and

Ian Levine, Barbara Pennington and friends, Neil Rushton

Wigan, or between me and Russ – funnily enough I get on great with him now. And the most bitter feud of all was between Dave Godin, who had championed northern soul in *Blues & Soul* for a long time and Tony Cummings at *Black Music*.

How did you meet Kev Roberts [collector and Wigan Casino DJ]?
Through Jack Bonnington. The two of them came up from Nottingham every week, got into northern soul about '73. He was very shrewd and good, and I clicked with him. He'd come early and bring a box of records and sell them as a dealer. He'd be the first person here at 8 o'clock and I'd be playing the new discoveries, and he'd give his opinion. He took a real interest in it all. Kev and Richard were great, but Kev fell out with Russ very early on. But it was Kev, Russ and Richard who took Wigan to great heights. Kev went about '75. There was some major row between them.

Tell me about Farmer Carl from the Catacombs.
'Farmer' Carl Dene was the one who discovered the records that were taken up to the Wheel. He was the one they all thought of as a god. Catacombs was a tiny little club in Wolverhampton, upstairs rather than downstairs like the Wheel. Long and narrow. The Wheel's policy of playing rare records was influenced by the Catacombs, who went out of their way to play them. They found this record by Richard Temple called 'That Beating Rhythm' on Mirwood Records. Nobody even believed it existed. You had to go to the Catacombs to hear it. That's

Ian Levine, Belinda Levine, Michael Jackson, Jackie Jackson

how come that guy from Gloucester got the copy of 'Baby Reconsider' and took it to the Wheel. The Catacombs could find them but weren't in a position to break them wide open. The Wheel, because of its prominence and crowd, was. So they were both equally influential.

Can we talk about Cleethorpes a little bit?
I was about to come to that. They played new stuff like Black Nasty 'Cut Your Motor Off', 'Summer In The Parks' [by East Coast Connection]. That grew out of Dave Godin's attention to them. It did. It was better music than Wigan.

I see it as mixture between Mecca and Casino...
Yeah, that's what they've all said on the interviews I've done for this documentary. Got nothing against it in retrospect, but I was annoyed at the time because it was just Dave Godin using it to sink his teeth into something and be ornery.

Can we talk about the crossover records – the ones that alerted the industry to what was happening?
The first acclaimed northern soul record was 'Hey Girl Don't Bother Me' by the Tams, which was played at the Wheel and got in the pop charts. But it was certainly the wrong sort of sound. It was not the northern soul sound. It was the earthy sound of the Wheel. The first record to break out of Blackpool Mecca was Archie Bell & The Drells' 'Here I Go Again'. Records that were modern, but had a '60s sound, were complete throwbacks: Archie Bell and Esther Phillips' 'Catch Me I'm Falling'. 'Here I Go Again' was so big at the Mecca that Atlantic reissued it due to the demand and it got in the pop charts. But that had been a recent release so I suppose it could have been a hit anyway. But the super definitive northern soul record, that was only released because of its demand from Blackpool Mecca, was Robert Knight's 'Love On A Mountain Top'. It caused a furore. There was no other excuse because it was at least five years old. Massive radio record. Everyone started getting interested in northern soul records then. Motown issued 'There's A Ghost In My House'.

Who played it originally?
Yours truly I'm afraid. I got it out of my Motown collection. There were a couple of rare Motown records we played: the Dalton Boys' 'I've Been Cheated', R. Dean Taylor and the

Isley Brothers' 'Tell Me It's Just A Rumour'. In the Tony Jebb early period of the Highland Rooms, they had all been northern soul records. R. Dean Taylor, really, is a nasty white pop record on Motown, I suppose I should be ashamed of it.

Not really, it's a good record.
But it doesn't sound black.

So what?
For all my sins, I broke the R. Dean Taylor. It had been on a *Motown Memories* compilation in the '60s. It had originally been on the VIP label. It had been available in some form. There weren't many Motown records played, really.

But wasn't that simply because so many crossed over in the first place?
Yeah, they were considered too commercial.

How do you see Motown, because even though there weren't many Motown tunes played, it sort of defines the whole sound doesn't it?
Motown was my be-all and end-all. It drove my whole life. I was obsessed with Motown to the extent that I ploughed all the money I'd made from 'So Many Men' [by Miquel Brown] into my Motown reunion and lost it. My love of northern soul grew out of my love of Motown. For me they had to be good enough to play, they had to have that wonderful slickness of the Motown sound. If you look at the classics of northern soul at that time: Sandi Sheldon 'You're Gonna Make Me Love You', Jackie Lee 'Do The Temptation Walk', Bobby Hebb 'Love Love Love' and 'You Want To Change Me', The Glories 'I'll Worship You Baby' and 'Blow My Mind To Pieces' by Bob Relf. There are so many great records, and they still make the hair on the back of your neck stand on end. They're every bit as good as the classic Motown productions.

Northern soul was a slightly blacker, slighter rarer version of the Motown sound on obscure labels, but it all comes back to Motown. The thing that's keeping the scene alive now is this vault of undiscovered Motown songs that Chris King and Pete Lowry have found Patrice Holloway 'It Keeps On Rolling', Brenda Holloway 'Trapped', 'Baby A-Go-Go' by Barbara McNeir, Frank Wilson 'My Sugar Baby', Jimmy Ruffin 'He Who Picks The Rose'. As good as anything we've ever heard and they're all unreleased Motown masters.

> **❝ Northern soul was a slightly blacker, slighter rarer version of the Motown sound on obscure labels, but it all comes back to Motown. ❞**

Tell me more about the splits that were happening around this time.
It all crystallised at the Ritz. Neil Rushton was running these all-dayers at the Ritz. Everybody came. It was a huge success. 1,500 to 2,000 every Sunday. It was crammed. All the Blackpool crowd came because me and Colin played, and all the Wigan crowd came because Richard Searling DJed. At that time we were playing all this modern disco stuff that we'd been playing at the Mecca: Doctor Buzzard's Original Savannah Band, Tavares, 'Car Wash', 'Jaws' by Lalo Schifrin. And they were playing anything with a stomping beat.

It was like two football crowds: Manchester City and Manchester United. It didn't work. All of these Wiganites with their singlets and baggy pants were shouting, 'Fuck off! Get off! Play some stompers!' They went for me and one of the Blackpool guys, Steve Naylor, stepped in to defend me and got his glasses smashed. They started wearing these 'LEVINE MUST GO' badges and one Saturday night Pete King from Wolverhampton and Shelvo from Leicester had got an 11 foot. banner that said 'LEVINE MUST GO' and walked through the Highland Room with it. It was all getting quite nasty because they hated the change in the music from the stompers to the modern stuff.

What do you think about all that, looking back from the perspective of today?

I'll go on record here and say we went too far. The northern soul scene was very special. But I've never been one to be told what to do. I was a soul rebel at 14. The concept of northern soul was that people could travel 200 miles on a Saturday night to hear records they couldn't hear anywhere else. And when we started with the Carstairs and Marvin Holmes, they were equally rare but more modern. Then we're playing Tavares, Crown Heights Affair and Kool & the Gang, even. And suddenly, you weren't hearing anything that you couldn't hear anywhere else. It had no uniqueness about it.

We should've stopped it before it went too far. Because what we did was split that scene into two with an axe. Wigan Casino, in retaliation to what we were doing, went so far the other way and played pathetic jokes for records like Hawaii 5-0. And for us to be playing Sylvester 'Mighty Real', or Colin Curtis got as far as playing Parliament and Funkadelic. Nothing to do with northern soul. The fact of the matter is that northern soul never died it just shrunk down. We all left it and it survived for 15 years and now suddenly blossomed out again.

© DJhistory.com

BLACKPOOL MECCA 100

FRANK BEVERLEY & THE BUTLERS – If That's What You Wanted

BOBBY HEBB – Love, Love, Love

THE O'JAYS – I Love Music

ANN SEXTON – You've Been Gone Too Long

DEODATO – Whistle Bump

WORLD COLUMN – So Is The Sun

INSTANT FUNK – I Got My Mind Made Up

FRANKIE (LOVE MAN) CROCKER – Ton Of Dynamite

CAMEO – Find My Way

GIL SCOTT-HERON/BRIAN JACKSON – The Bottle

SKULLSNAPS – I'm Your Pimp

TEDDY PENDERGRASS – You Cant Hide From Yourself

DR.BUZZARD'S ORIGINAL SAVANNAH BAND – I'll Play The Fool

SAVADORS – Stick By Me Baby

TOMANGOES – I Really Love You

MONTCLAIRS – Hung Up On Your Love

CARSTAIRS – It Really Hurts Me Girl

VOICES OF EAST HARLEM – Cashing In

BOBBY HUTTON – Lend A Hand

BO KIRKLAND AND RUTH DAVIS – You're Gonna Get Next To Me

DIANE JENKINS – Tow-A-Way Zone

PRINCE GEORGE – Wrong Crowd

EULA COOPER – Let Our Love Grow Higher

BILLY WOODS – Let Me Make You Happy

CROWN HEIGHTS AFFAIR – Dreaming A Dream

AL HUDSON – Spread Love

LENNY WILLIAMS – Choosing You

EVELYN 'CHAMPAGNE' KING – Shame

TAVARES – Heaven Must Be Missing An Angel

ELOISE LAWS – Love Factory

ANDERSON BROTHERS – I Can See Him Loving You

COMMODORES – The Human Zoo

MOMENTS – I've Got The Need

ThE NATURAL FOUR – I Thought You Were Mine

ESTHER PHILLIPS – What A Difference A Day Makes

LAMONT DOZIER – Going Back To My Roots

THE EXCITERS – Reaching For The Best

JODI MATHIS – Don't You Care Any More

JAMES FOUNTAIN – Seven Day Lover

ARCHIE BELL AND THE DRELLS – Soul City Walk

SISTER SLEDGE – Love Don't You Go Through No Changes On Me

BETTY WRIGHT – Where Is The Love

DOUBLE EXPOSURE – Ten Percent

THE NITE-LITERS – K-Jee

LARRY SAUNDERS – On The Real Side

CREATIVE SOURCE – Don't Be Afraid (Take My Love)

BILL HARRIS – Am I Hot, Am I Cold

JACKIE MOORE – This Time Baby

BRAINSTORM – Lovin' Is Really My Game

COFFEE – Casanova

LINDA CLIFFORD – Runaway Love

BESSIE BANKS – Don't You Worry Baby The Best Is Yet To Come

SIDE EFFECT – Always There

JOBELL & THE ORCHESTRA DE SALSA – Never Gonna Let You Go

AQUARIAN DREAM – Phoenix

PETE WARNER – I Just Want To Spend My Life With You

NORMAN CONNORS – Once I've Been There

MARVIN HOLMES & JUSTICE – You Better Keep Her

YOUNG-HOLT UNLIMITED – California Montage

JOE BATAAN – The Bottle (La Botella)

MEL BRITT – She'll Come Running Back

DETROIT EXECUTIVES – Cool Off

DON THOMAS – Come On Train

HOSANNA – Hipit

THE FULLER BROTHERS – Time's A Wasting

JOHNNY CASWELL – You Don't Love Me Anymore

ROSE BATISTE – Hit And Run

OSCAR PERRY & THE LOVE GENERATORS – I Got What You Need

BARBARA PENNINGTON – 24 Hours A Day

CHARLES EARLAND – Let The Music Play

ALVIN CASH – Ali Shuffle

ODYSSEY – Native New Yorker

ROY AYERS – Running Away

FAT LARRY'S BAND – Center City

FRANCINE MCGEE – Delirium

LYNN VERNADO – Wash And Wear Love

ROCK CANDY – Alone With No Love

KENNY SMITH – Lord What's Happening To The People

THE BROTHERS – Are You Ready For This

EPITOME OF SOUND – You Don't Love Me

TONY CLARKE – Landslide

ARCHIE BELL & THE DRELLS – Here I Go Again

JERRY WILLIAMS – If You Ask Me (Because I Love You)

ISLEY BROTHERS – Tell Me It's Just A Rumour Baby

BOB RELF – Blowing My Mind To Pieces

THE COASTERS – Crazy Baby

EDDIE FOSTER – I Never Knew

EARL WRIGHT & HIS ORCHESTRA – Thumb A Ride

MORRIS CHESTNUT – Too Darn Soulful

PHILADELPHIA INTERNATIONAL ALL-STARS – Let's Clean Up The Ghetto

D.C. LARUE – Cathedrals

ASHFORD & SIMPSON – Bourgie Bourgie

CHANTAL CURTIS – Get Another Love

VICKIE SUE ROBINSON – Turn The Beat Around

PATRICE RUSHEN – Haven't You Heard

THE CROW – Your Autumn Of Tomorrow

SHALAMAR – Take That To The Bank

THELMA HOUSTON – I Ain't Going Nowhere

FOUR BELOW ZERO – My Baby's Got E.S.P.

LADA EDMUND JR. – The Larue

CLOUD ONE – Atmosphere Strutt

Compiled by Pete Haigh

RECOMMENDED LISTENING

VARIOUS – On The Real Side – The Modern End of Northern Soul

VARIOUS – The Northern Soul Story Vol. 3: Blackpool Mecca

"The minibus crew said, 'We're going to the new all-nighter in Wigan.'"

Kev Roberts
Casino royal

Interviewed by Bill in Worksop, September 21, 1998

The Wigan Casino was Britain's first superclub. In an age when people rarely went further than the pub for their entertainment, the Casino attracted dancers by the busload from up and down the country. With a closing time of 8 am it was the end-up spot of choice for the nation's northern soul fans, including a sizeable contingent who would travel down from Blackpool after the Mecca shut for the night. Billboard voted it the best club in the world in 1978, a year before giving the same accolade to New York's Paradise Garage.

Given the club's vast size, steering it was tricky, especially given its amphetamine-fuelled taste for 'stompers', and many of its DJs resorted to crowd-pleasing. So, just like later superclubs, its most famous DJs were not necessarily its best. While there are other Wigan DJs that more people may remember, we think Kev Roberts' taste and collection puts him up there with the best.

An early collector of northern soul and dancer at the Torch, the teenage Roberts got his big break when he chanced upon copies of rarer-than-rare 'Take Away The Pain Stain' by Patti Austin and 'World Without Sunshine' by Sandra Phillips. He was thrust into the Premier League, securing a Casino residency. He was later instrumental in the scene's stylistic evolution when he brought new disco records from New York for Ian Levine. Roberts has stayed true to northern soul, organising regular events and weekenders and issuing many excellent compilations through the Goldmine label. Frozen drizzle clings to the car as we zoom towards Worksop where Kev now lives, on the next leg on our northern soul odyssey. It's one of those 1970s throwback days where the echoes of the north's soul cling damply in the air.

How did you get into soul in the first place?
The first people I ever bought records from were Brian Selby and John Bratton. Both of them worked for a very good independent record shop in Mansfield called Syd Booth's. A legendary record store, in fact. One of the biggest indies in the north. Brian and John were obviously soul boys. They'd got access to the tunes of the day: the Direction label, the Stateside label. I wouldn't say northern at that time I think because that was just coming into its own at the Wheel. I was far too young for that. I was certainly buying 'Everyday People' by Sly & The Family Stone as a new release. I bought 'Sixty Minutes Of Your Love', Homer Banks, on Minit. Standard records in that particular shop. I think the reason is that in '68 I wasn't going to clubs, but by '69 I was sneaking past the bouncer to the local dance hall.

Local as in Nottingham?
Mansfield first, then into Nottingham.

Was Mansfield more happening?
Well Mansfield is a very large town that happened to have a lot of club action going on. It was interesting in the north midlands, because you found those kind of scenes there. Yes, they were playing pop music like Love Affair too, but like a lot of other good working class towns, they were also playing Homer Banks and James Carr and they were playing ska and soul mixed in.

A very good friend of mine had a brother who used to go to the Wheel, so by 1969 my taste had moved from early Tamla to Stax and Atlantic, then suddenly discovering the Artistics, Billy Stewart, Tony Clark, these kind of people. And really, natural progression. Also, Brian and John left Syd Booth's and opened a record store in Nottingham: Selectadisc. Legendary record shop. They had a soul cellar downstairs so you ended up just discovering things in the cheap boxes. And of course if you're a collector and it's cheap you buy it regardless of whether you know it.

Especially, if you already recognise a name you like on the label, like the producer...
That's right. And if you get it home and it's good, it's even better. That's pretty much what I was doing. I was buying a lot of records that I didn't know, and come 1971 I'd amassed quite a few. My entire earnings were spent on records. Not super-rarities, but lots of £3 and £4 sounds. I didn't become aware of the northern scene until early '72. Up The Junction in Crewe was my first nighter, with the Selectadisc crew. One of the guys who worked in Selectadisc was Alan Day, who was a big DJ at the time and he took me under his wing. But I got a severe bollocking from my mum and dad for staying out all night and not telling them. Quite right, too, because I was 15. But the next one was to the Torch in Stoke. And I absolutely loved it. I lived for that particular club.

❝ I'd never come across so many unknown records in my life. And every one of them was a stonker. All fast, furious, great vocals. ❞

Tell me about the Torch.
This incarnation was was only open for a year in 1972; before it had been a rhythm and blues club, which was very well-known in the mid-'60s – if you wanted to go see the Graham Bond Organization or the Beatstalkers. The residents were Alan Day, Colin Curtis, Keith Minshull, Tony Jebb and Martyn Ellis. I thought it was terrific, because that was the first place that had an abundance of American 45s. I never went to the Wheel, but I think there was an awful lot of British stuff and rhythm and blues and other factions, like mod music. By the time the Torch came it was US stuff. By 1972 it turned into an all-nighter, much to the dismay of a lot of the locals, I might add.

Why?
I think when you're in a parochial place, they find out-of-towners suddenly coming into their patch a little hard to swallow. I don't mean that disrespectfully, I think it's just the way it is. For me though, it was terrific. I'd never come across so many unknown records in my life. And every one of them was a stonker. They were all fast, furious, great vocals. Girl groups. Odd labels. Obscurities on the Okeh label. I'd only ever seen that label with Major Lance and suddenly I was hearing Sandi Sheldon's 'You're Gonna Make Me Love You' and Larry Williams, Johnny Taylor, Billy Butler. They were great. And I loved the way it was laid out which was like a ranch.

What did it look like from the outside?
Outside it looked like a social club in the middle of a terraced street. It was on Hove Street in Tunstall. Tunstall is the end of the world for any venue. How can I describe it? You're from Grimsby, right? It's like going to Humberstone and finding an all-nighter. It was five miles out of the way. There was no railway station. You had to go to Longport, which was on the Stoke to Crewe line. And you had to walk a mile up a great big bank to get to it. But once you were inside it was absolutely terrific.

The Wheel had a lot of credibility because it was playing really black records at the time, stuff like Bobby Bland. By the time it got to the Torch, the DJs had unearthed a series of very obscure American singles that had to be bloomin' good to sing to, to dance to and to do backflips to. 'A

World Of Trouble' by The Sweet Things, 'I Worship You Baby' by the Glories, 'Our Love Is In The Pocket' JJ Barnes. They all had incredible Motown-type choruses. It surprises me even to this day why they couldn't get major airplay in the States at the time because they all had that knockout punch that every hit record needs. Yet here were 50 or 60 brand new discoveries all being played at a new all-nighter, all of them fantastic.

Did the DJs playing have previous track records?
Well yes and no. I think they were all collectors who were on the fringe of the nighter scene. They didn't work at the Wheel, they hadn't been inherited from other clubs. Keith Minshull was local. Colin Curtis was local. I think these were guys who were plotting their course. Buying records. I'm sure they all went to the Wheel.

One other thing that was surprising at the Torch, and it might seem a bit cheesy now with the credibility factor that hangs around northern soul, I actually think they were playing new releases, 'Sliced Tomatoes' by Just Brothers, 'Scrub-Board', the instrumental version of 'Hold Back The Night' by the Trammps. That was out three years before the Trammps recorded the vocals. They were playing 'Stop What You're Doing' by the Playthings, 'A Man Like Me' by Jimmy James, and 'This Is The House Where Love Died' by First Choice. New singles being played at an all-nighter. Unheard of really. Again, they worked a treat. The song element was very important at the Torch. The record had to have some substance to it.

When did you start DJing?
I started DJing in January of '73, about a month after I'd first been to the Torch. I'd bought a few records at the Torch. Most of them were £15-£20 and I couldn't afford those, but there were a few at the cheaper end: The Shalamars' 'Stop And Take A Look At Yourself' and the Tymes' 'What Would I Do?' which were played constantly and were only about £3 each. So I amassed a few of those – the cheaper end of the Torch playlist and I got a job at the Britannia Boat Club, the Brit as they called it, in Nottingham, which was part of a row of boat clubs in West Bridgeford.

I used to take my records down there, just hoping that one day I might get that opportunity to put records on. The manager was going to start a Saturday night and the other guys already had other gigs. So he said, do you fancy it? It went fairly well. And then I think because the Friday night was costing him a fair bit in DJs, he lost a couple of DJs, and so I ended up there on a Friday and Saturday. I went from having a day time job earning 20 quid a week, to doing two nights and earning 40 quid, much to my mother and father's dismay. So I invested my entire salary on better records. I was suddenly being able to afford at least one £10 single a week. By the time summer arrived in '73, the Torch had closed and I decided to go to Blackpool Mecca. Nine till two session.

Was that when Tony Jebb was still there?
No. He'd gone. It was Colin Curtis and Keith Minshull originally. Keith left and Ian Levine came back into play. He was originally at the Mecca and came back. Playing strictly '60s northern there. They hadn't quite moved on to the modern thing yet. Even what I call the northern modern sounds, like 'Seven Day Lover' [by James Fountain]. So from the Brit, after I'd finished. It was only on till 11 and I got someone to cover for me the last hour. I'd get to Blackpool at 11.30 quarter to twelve, just for the last two hours. Then come back. Just for two hours in Blackpool. But it was just the place.

At this stage who was the key DJ there?
Ian Levine. Definitely. He was the most innovative. Because he didn't listen to the whys and wherefores of any other DJ. He found records and if he liked them he'd play them. And he'd play them 10 times a night till people danced to them. And if they didn't dance to them – NEXT! – and he was on to the next one. That for me was a creative DJ. I didn't particularly rate him as a DJ by the way, in terms of ability. But he could break records. Anyhow, through Selectadisc circles I met Simon Soussan.

It's alleged he stole the Frank Wilson record.

Debatable whether he stole it, but I'll tell you what I know. He was a French-Moroccan character who came to England in the '60s, went to the Wheel, loved northern soul. He was a tailor for Burton's at their head office in Leeds. Incredibly intelligent guy. But slippery. The first guy really to go to the States, find records and put lists out. Some people got the records. Some people didn't. So he developed an 'unreliable' tag. However, he found absolutely fantastic records. A lot of the Torch stuff came from him.

He then moved on to become a record company type guy. He wanted to reissue these in-demand records. So he got in bed with Selectadisc who were definitely the biggest retailer of northern soul in Britain. One night they brought him to the Brit and he had a look in my box, probably laughed at some of the five pound sounds there. But one thing he liked: he had a deep passion for British labels. Out of my box, I had a good few British records: Kenny Bernard 'What Love Brings', which was an emerging sound and it was only on English Pye. And he wanted all of them.

He showed me a box of absolutely top notch winners. Some I'd heard of and some first time evers, like 'World Without Sunshine' by Sandra Phillips and 'Take Away The Pain Stain' by Patti Austin. I was the first person ever. I mean, Ian Levine didn't even have them. We did a trade and I started to play them. My reputation went like WOW! Suddenly I was getting gigs from all over the place. Really, my reputation grew over the course of four weeks. From August 1973 onwards. That was it for me. I was suddenly getting calls. We went to the Mecca, I showed Ian Levine some records. He was going out of his mind at some of the stuff I'd got. So of course I was a giant ego. On September 30th 1973, we'd been at the Mecca and the minibus – I'd taken my records with me, as I did everywhere...

On the off chance?
Well... Yes and no. I would never have taken my records to Blackpool Mecca because I would never have been worthy. It was more for credibility. In those days it was a macho thing. You'd got your box, people have a look and you got the seal of approval. 'Bloody hell, have you seen what he's got in there?'

The mini-bus crew said: 'Change of direction. We're not going home. We're going to the new all-nighter in Wigan.' All right. Okay. Went down. Paid our money to get in. There I was with my box. We walked in and I distinctly remember it. The first thing: there weren't many DJs on. And secondly: the music was crap. Actually, it wasn't crap, but the records were easily available. You could buy them from Selectadisc. And there wasn't much I didn't know. So to me the night was an anti-climax after the Mecca because they did have records that I didn't have. Lots of them. So my mates were really uptight about it. One of them went up to the resident disc jockey Russ Winstanley. 'Have you got Sandra Phillips? Have you got 'Pain Stain?'

'Er no. What are these?'

'You want to get 'im on! Kev Roberts from Nottingham.'

'Who's he? I've never heard of him...'

It was a strange all-nighter in that it was the only one where nobody knew the DJ names. Ordinarily, if you'd got a big room and a big all-nighter the first thing you'd do was book Ian Levine, Colin Curtis or Keith Minshull. But for some unknown reason Russ Winstanley didn't go down that road. Himself and a guy called Ian Fishwick, just a local pop DJ from Wigan, had decided to play northern soul with nobody else on. So I became the next man in line.

I went on. I played an hour's worth of my top tunes and they went down a storm. They loved them. I was up there absolutely petrified. It was a massive room. And Russ came up to me and said, 'Great. Do you wanna work here every week? Ten pounds.' There I went. Really from that moment on, northern soul took over. I got bookings everywhere, the phone never stopped ringing. Chris Burton in Stoke, in particular, had recognised that northern soul was very popular, phoned local Mecca dancehalls and on a Monday to Thursday night he'd make sure there was a northern soul night and I'd be sent there to do a job. There'd be a pop DJ playing hits of the day: the Sweet, Gary Glitter. Then I'd come on and play 'There's A Ghost In My House'. The Sweet crowd would sit down and the baggy trouser brigade would get up. It was bizarre. But it taught me a lot about being a DJ. That's when I really had to start thinking seriously about being a disc jockey.

Can we talk about the rivalries that developed between Wigan and Blackpool?

I think as Russ grew in stature with Wigan Casino, the Casino developed its own crowd. Very different to the Mecca. So Ian Levine was king of his castle and Russ Winstanley was king of his. The two didn't mix. Ian Levine was playing his own sounds. He wasn't interested in Wigan. He wasn't interested or influenced by what they were playing. But neither was Russ Winstanley either. He might have thought he needed Ian at some stage, but he had a bigger venue. By Christmas of 1973 – no disrespect to Blackpool Mecca – but they were running second. There were 2,000 people at Wigan. Why would Russ even have to listen to what Ian had to say? Even though Ian Levine was the most creative, he was the most innovative, he had the best records; it didn't make any difference. With Russ, myself and, by January '74, Richard Searling, whatever we played we had an even bigger dancefloor.

Was Russ more of crowd-pleaser than Ian?

Well, Russ was nowhere near as intelligent or innovative as Ian Levine. I think Russ would be the first to agree with that. But I wouldn't say that he played only to the crowd. The problem was that Wigan had an awfully big dancefloor. I remember playing a record that I love to this day called 'Do You Love Me Baby' by the Masqueraders. I had the first copy in the country. When I first got it I thought this is going to be a monster and I played it about six times over three weeks but it was a disaster. It cleared the floor. It probably wouldn't have cleared the floor at Blackpool, but on that massive dancefloor unless the tempo was really kicking immediately the record was a no-no. And the crowd didn't like it.

It was heartbreaking when early white label copies of 'Goodbye Nothing To Say' by Javells were being touted and Russ first played it – and myself, I might add. I didn't like it, but, wearing my DJ hat, I found myself with a new pop record that had just been recorded for the Pye label filling the dancefloor and my great soul record from 1967, the Masqueraders, a disaster. That was the difference between Wigan Casino and the Mecca. The tempo was absolutely critical because of the size of the venue.

> ❝ **Wigan was 95 percent drugs. If a person is swallowing by 12 and speeding by three, you'd best be ready with something fast.** ❞

Was there a difference in the drug consumption of Wigan and Blackpool?

Oh yes. Absolutely. Wigan was 95 percent drugs. Blackpool was more like 30 percent. If a person is swallowing by 12 and speeding by three, you'd best be ready with something fast, because anything slower is not going to happen. Wigan Casino had the fastest tempo of any all-nighter.

Your love of northern soul eventually took you to the States. How did that happen?

I first went to New York in 1975. I found northern soul records by scouring through the Yellow Pages, as per usual for someone who'd never been before. I was oblivious to bad areas. If someone said, 'Hey I know a soul shop in Spanish Harlem,' there could be gun fire passing my nose but I didn't care less. All I knew was that shop on 122nd Street and Eighth Avenue had got soul and I was going. This opened my eyes to a different sound, because the Mecca was now playing what I call modern soul. They weren't playing disco though. They were playing 'Cashing In' [by The Voices Of East Harlem], 'Seven Day Lover' and a few other modern ones.

I always remember going to a store called Downstairs Records in New York. Still open to this day. Run by Nick and I was Nick's first supplier of 12-inch British singles. Nick and a guy called Roy, they'd originally worked at Greenline in Queens, both '50s doo-wop collectors. They'd recognised the disco scene was developing. So they opened a shop selling oldies and new stuff. I saw piles and piles of guys wandering in and they'd just go in listen at the counter. Stuff on Scepter, Roulette and Wand. They were piling 12-inch singles up and walking out with them. So I started to take a few back.

....

Didn't you take him Southshore Commission?
Yeah, but the one record that really changed it for me was the O'Jays' 'I Love Music', because I had the first copy. I met this guy Tony Gioe who was the DJ at Peppermint Lounge and also the A&R man for Midland International. He was the guy that licensed Silver Convention and he had the only copy of 'I Love Music' because Kenny Gamble had given it to him. I came back off this trip and told Ian Levine I'd heard this fantastic record by the O'Jays. He said, 'Great,' thinking it'd be out shortly. A month later it started to get to him. He said, 'I've tried everywhere and no-one knows anything about it.' Next time I went Tony was still playing it and I persuaded him to give me the record.

I think the Ritz all-dayers had just started in Manchester, so a slightly different crowd was developing. The Ritz had a northern soul crowd, but it also had a bit of a dance crowd. 'I Love Music' really opened the doors, I think, to new singles. It made dance records acceptable to the northern crowd. It paved the way for things like 'Heaven Must Be Missing An Angel', which was a northern soul monster. Absolutely. 'Young Hearts Run Free', another perfect for a northern crowd.

Was this when the 'split' was happening?
Yeah. Some records escalated the split. I can picture the face of someone hearing 'I Love Music'. They'd be saying, 'It's a bit of a new one, this isn't it? But it's a good un.' In the middle of those three I've mentioned which we're acceptable was another one: 'Turn The Beat Around' by Vickie Sue Robinson. A record hated by the hardcore. But a monster to everybody else.

❝ Ian made a pact with himself to say northern is unofficially dead. And he went completely into the disco thing. ❞

Who started playing it?
Undoubtedly Ian Levine. From the moment 'I Love Music' had been accepted, Ian made a pact with himself to say northern is unofficially dead. And he went completely into the disco thing. In some quarters it worked a treat, and he captured a different audience. But some of the hustle-type records he was playing were not well received in northern soul terms.

Did he alienate his traditional crowd? Did he attract a new crowd?
Both. The alienated went down to Wigan and stayed there. He brought a new crowd in. Manchester people.

What was the difference in crowd composition?
It was a slicker, more smartly dressed, trendier crowd. More club oriented. City people. Undoubtedly the group that broke the mould for the Mecca was Brass Construction. When they started playing 'Movin'' by Brass Construction that brought in a different level of person altogether. It was a funkier groove. It was a new tempo for people north of Watford to get into. It was the time when the Chris Hill, Robbie Vincent thing moved up north. Around 1979 was when the north and south were coming together for the first time. That was the progressive movement of Blackpool Mecca, Levine and Curtis. More so, Colin Curtis for the funkier kind of groove.

Yeah, I see Levine being more of a Southshore Commission guy.
Yeah. Colin liked the look of the James Brown thing and got into that.

Why do you think the scene died. I know Wigan lost its license, but was it on its way out anyway?
No doubt about it. People were growing up, getting married. End of an era.

Can we move on to cover-ups [DJs covering up their secret weapons with fake labels]?

BLUES & SOUL: 162

31

It was an interesting quirky thing started by Ian Levine, I think. He was protective. It was great when they were playing Freddy Jones 'My Heart's Wide Open' for about six months. It turned out to be by the Coasters on Atco. But I wasn't really a fan of it and I don't ever remember covering up records myself.

Do you think people took it seriously?
Yeah, they did. But that was at the tail-end of the Wigan Casino when I think northern soul was going crazy. Credibility-wise, northern soul had two big disasters. Disaster one, late '74 the record companies clocked on to what was happening and started infiltrating northern sounds and won over Russ Winstanley and persuaded him that this is where it was at. And Russ started playing 'Goodbye Nothing To Say'. Then he extended it to 'Hawaii 5-O' and the 'Theme from Police Story' and hideous, stupid pop records that were neither anything. They became popular, because they were odd stompers, but they didn't have any substance.

Hawaii 5-0?
By the Ventures. Russ played it and it was massive. That very much swayed me against Wigan. I was still playing there, this would be late 75, but I did not like that at all.

The next big mistake was 1978. For some unknown reason, there was an abundance of good northern soul records being played by Richard Searling, but I think the problem was Richard had become the new Ian Levine. He'd got the cover-ups, he'd got the unknowns, he'd got the good sources. Russ totally went against that and created his own dancefloor. I'm not saying Richard Searling packed the dancefloor any more than Russ. But Russ suddenly went a million miles down the road and started to find pop stompers that were worse than the first lot. I'll give you an example. He used to play 'Theme From Joe 90' by the Ron Grainer Orchestra. Obscure pop records: 'Nine Times Out Of Ten' by Muriel Day. 'Optimistic Fool' which was the other side of an Irish Eurovision entry. Just bizarre. Dusty Springfield. American obscurities with almost Dolly Parton type vocals.

That was the kiss of death. The real soul fans were getting off on what Richard was trying to do – find good American soul records, but I think he was on his own. The northern scene was shrinking. And if you went to a local disco in Warrington it would be 'Nine Times Out Of Ten' you'd hear not Richard's stuff. And home made stuff, because he was working for Casino Classics who were re-recording stuff, 'Skiing In The Snow'.

....

What was Richard playing?
In the early part of the Casino Richard brought 'Tainted Love' Gloria Jones, and lots of credible stuff. By later stage there was only Richard and Russ left as residents because I'd left, and you liked either one or the other, because what they played was so different. Casino Classics came from Spark and Barry Kingston. They had a few hits, like 'Three Before Eight'. They then went crazy and started issuing bizarre records like 'Theme From Joe 90'. How did that come about? Richard stuck to his guns and started to introduce records like Cecil Washington's 'I Don't Like To Lose', obscure American 45s.

All this talk of cover-ups brings me to the tale of 'Do I Love You'. For years you owned the only copy in existence, didn't you?
By Frank Wilson. I'll tell you the story of Frank Wilson. It was a disc unearthed by a guy who's no longer with us called Tom dePierro. Tom was an archivist who was employed by Motown to reactivate the Motown Yesteryear series. Tom didn't manage to get many fantastic records released at that time, but he did manage to put some other stuff out. On a chance meeting with Simon Soussan, Tom loaned Simon some records and in there was the Frank Wilson disc. Simon Soussan heard it and did some research and it turns out that nobody had ever seen or heard it. He subsequently covered it over, sent some acetates to England, notably to Russ Winstanley, who was definitely the first person to play it – he called it 'Do I Love You' by Eddie Foster. Eddie Foster incidentally, was already someone who'd had a northern soul hit, so he chose this pseudonym to make people believe it was him. The record was instantly massive.

Simon Soussan quickly pressed up copies which sold like wildfire. Soussan then decided to sell his record collection and a guy called Les McCutcheon, who discovered Shakatak, acquired the disc reputedly for $500, which was a lot of money back then. The record then left Les's hands to a guy called Jonathan Woodliffe. I bought the record from Jonathan for a load of albums and 12-inches worth £350, an unearthly sum then. I remember very clearly the minute I bought it quite a few people – because northern was dying then it was '79, '80 – said to me, 'Oh, it's by Frank Wilson and it's on a Tamla Motown subsidiary. £350? There's loads of them around.' So I kept it, never thought any more about it.

Slowly, over the eighties I'd get the odd call every six months: 'Have you got the Frank Wilson record? Do wanna sell it? I'll give you £700 for it.' Anyway, got to about 1987 and suddenly I was being offered a grand for it. The upshot of it was I kept it till 1991 and Tim Brown offered me £5,000 for it. So I sold it. Here's the rub. Our partner in Goldmine, Martin Koppell, bought a Motown collection from a guy called Ron Murphy in Detroit, and a second copy was unearthed in the early nineties. And that copy has just been sold to a collector in Scotland for £15,000! So there are two copies now. The first ever copy is with Tim Brown and the second copy which is in better condition is with this guy in Scotland.

There have been a bunch of revivals over the years, how do you feel about it all now?
Well, there was only one golden era of northern soul. There was only one definitive playlist. Now, you can argue how many records were on that playlist, but really it's no more than about 200. I'm talking 'Landslide' [by Tony Clarke], 'There's A Ghost In My House', 'Tainted Love' and so on. The absolutely stonking mega dancefloor fillers.

© DJhistory.com

WIGAN CASINO 20

THE TOMANGOES – I Really Love You

THE SALVADORS – Stick By Me Baby

YVONNE BAKER – You Didn't Say A Word

THE CASUALEERS – Dance, Dance, Dance

THE VELVETS - I Got To Find Me Somebody

EDDIE FOSTER – I Never Knew

LORRAINE CHANDLER – I Can't Change

RUBIN – You've Been Away

MICKIE CHAMPION – What Good Am I

BERNIE WILLIAMS – Ever Again

SHANE MARTIN – I Need You

THE COASTERS – Crazy Baby

DANA VALERY – You Don't Know Where Your Interest Lies

THE MYLESTONES – The Joker

THE VAN DYKES – Save My Love For A Rainy Day

THE POPPIES – There's A Pain In My Heart

VICKIE BAINES – Country Girl

LEE ROYE – Tears

MORRIS CHESTNUT – Too Darn Soulful

ADAM'S APPLES – Don't Take It Out On This World

Compiled by Kev Roberts

RECOMMENDED LISTENING

VARIOUS – Wigan Casino Story

VARIOUS – Wigan Casino Monsters

VARIOUS – Mastercuts Northern Soul

"Northern soul was like an eighth wonder of the world."

Ian Dewhirst
A northern soul

Interviewed by Bill in London, April 2, 1999

Ian Dewhirst is the Zelig of dance music. As a northern soul ingenue DJing under the name 'Frank' (he bore a passing resemblance to footballer Frank Worthington), he cut his teeth playing in Sheffield, Wigan and Cleethorpes, establishing himself as one of the northern circuit's more forward-thinking jocks. Subsequent to that, he put together the group Shalamar, did his first line of coke with George Clinton, created the groundbreaking compilation series Mastercuts and got himself involved in every major dancefloor trend from jazz-funk to house. During the northern years, Ian guested across the country, but is best remembered for his residency at the Winter Gardens in Cleethorpes. As horizontal rain lashed in from Denmark, he'd spin immaculate soul a hundred yards out over the north sea.

We meet at his offices in Simply Vinyl near Bond Street, before repairing to the pub, where he regales us with increasingly outlandish tales, lubricated by increasingly outlandish amounts of lager. The tape runs out before the stories do, so we arrange to meet again. Dewhirst is one the great raconteurs of British dance music and an encyclopedia of American soul.

How did you get into black music?
I got into soul when I got my first transistor radio and I used to listen to Tony Prince and Mike Raven on Luxembourg and Dave Simons' rhythm and blues show on Radio 1. I started hearing things on the radio that you wouldn't hear under any other circumstances, and it was the Motown thing that got me. The school I went to was a grammar school and everyone was into heavy rock; I was the only one into soul. But I started finding this sort of little crowd that were into Motown, the youth club crowd essentially. When I was 15 I got a job at a clothes shop in Bradford and there used to be a market stall called Bostock's, and they did 20 records for a quid, American imports, with no centres in. I used to buy records, even if I didn't know what they were. Anything on Motown basically. Every Saturday for about a year I used to go to Bostock's in my lunch hour come back with a bag of 40 records.

The next move, for my 15th birthday, I found this DJ who wanted to get rid of his records, which he had in this big case. There were things in there like 'He's Got The Whole World In His Hands' by the Isley Brothers, James Carr 'Freedom Train', 'Free For All' by Philip Mitchell, 'Slippin' Around' by Art Freeman on red Atlantic. I paid £25 for the collection, which at the time was a lot of money, and my dad always reminds me that I never paid him back! Together with the stuff I was buying in Bradford market, I probably had about 1,000-1,500 records just before I was 16.

I went to a pub in Cleckheaton that had a Motown night and I saw these blokes in blazers with this symbol – The Torch – so I said to them, 'What's this thing?' And they were like, 'It's a soul club, mate. They have an all-nighter every Saturday.' And he started telling me about it. So we carried on talking and I said, 'Well, I'm into that stuff, too.' So he says, 'No, you won't know this stuff. This is northern soul. But there's a place in Leeds on a Friday night and we go down there. It's called the Central.'

So I went down with them, and it was like everything I'd been looking for. All of a sudden, this sort of underground, secret world. I didn't know 95 percent of the records, but they all sounded fantastic. It had this elite feeling to it; there were some nice looking, well-dressed girls, and the guys looked pretty smooth. The DJ had played a couple of records I had in my collection and, though I knew what they were, I didn't realise the significance of them. One of them was Earl Wright's 'Thumb A Ride'. Third week I went, he played it and the guy who was DJing was called Tony Banks, so I went up to where he was playing and said, 'I've got this at home.' And Tony says, 'No, mate, you haven't got this' – he was playing an emidisc [an acetate] – 'There's only one of these in the country and Tony Jebb's got that.'

'No no, I've got it. It's called 'Thumb A Ride' by Earl Wright and it's on Capitol.

So the next week, I brought it with me to show him and of course it caused this massive flutter because at that point there was only one known copy in the UK, and this wally, who'd only been going down there two or three weeks, had one. All these guys were offering me money and swaps for it, but I wasn't really into letting anything go.

I had a few others similar that I didn't think anyone knew about, so I started bringing those down. A lot of stuff that came from Bradford market: 'You Hit Me' by Alice Clark, The Shalamars, the Triumphs, The United Four's 'She's Putting You On', The Younghearts. I had lots of things that were northern, but I didn't realise that they were. Like lots of early Wheel or early Torch sounds, but there was a lot that actually weren't known.

Banksy starting borrowing my records and within a few weeks they started becoming popular. Every week before I left, he'd say are you going to bring your records down next week. One week I was going to go on holiday the following week and Banksy said, 'Can you leave your records with me?' I didn't really like the sound of that, but anyway, I agreed to leave the records with him if he'd let me do the warm-up DJing when I got back. Came back and started playing between nine and 10 o'clock on a Friday when there was hardly anybody in, then he'd come on at 10 o'clock and go all the way through to two. That's the point when I really started collecting. I started going to the Torch. It was just at the point when everything was just starting to get good.

❝ Imagine a kid from Mirfield, never been further than 20 miles outside of Huddersfield, to be getting in a car with all these hardened soul boys. It was like a dream. ❞

When was the first time you went to the Torch?

I went with the mob from Huddersfield. It was towards the end of the Torch, maybe about '73. I was about eighteen.

Describe it.

Just like nothing else I'd ever seen. You've got to imagine a kid from Mirfield, never been further than 20 miles outside of Dewsbury and Huddersfield, to be getting in a car with all of these hardened soulboys, going down, stopping at Knutsford services. There was an air of expectation going in there. It was like a dream. Like suddenly knowing you're home.

The first DJ I saw was Martin Ellis, who was really good on the mic, he actually used to get people going. And this wonderful feeling of togetherness. All these other enthusiasts, misfits, nutters that had travelled from all over the place. It was just a really little, elite, very tight scene. Funnily enough I didn't take drugs at that time.

Describe what it looked like.

Well, you're pushing there. I only went twice. I could describe Wigan to a tee. I can describe the atmosphere: electric. I can remember some of the records; I remember hearing 'Countdown', 'Crying Over You' by Duke Browner, 'Just Ask Me' by Lenis Guess, and 'Catwalk' by Gerry and Paul. The first time I went to the Mecca the thing that stood out for me there was 'Nothing But Love' by the Tartans. There's three versions: John Rhys and the Lively Set, the Tartans and the Kadoo Strings. I ended up buying an emidisc of it.

That whole period when I was first venturing out was like a learning period for me. At the time, I think I was restricted to when I could go because of school and exams. It used to be a pain in the arse, explaining to my parents that I was going to this all-nighter. Then I got a motor and that started making things easier. I then became one of the few with a car. There wasn't too much happening on the east side of the country at that time, it was mostly Stoke and Manchester. I remember going to the Heavy Steam Machine at Hanley. I think at this point the Torch had shut and the Mecca was the place where you'd go every Saturday. There was Va Va's in Bolton with Richard Searling. But that always had a weird vibe to it.

When did you start playing at Wigan?
Within four weeks of it opening. We all went to the opening night. I remember Russ had this record called 'Cool Off' by Detroit Executives, fucking brilliant record, and Levine had been hammering it for about six weeks and it turned into the number one record at the Mecca. And it was the record everyone wanted. Russ had just got a load of records sent by his so-called uncle in Miami [possibly Simon Soussan-.

You used to DJ as 'Frank', where was that from?
After the Huddersfield Town footballer Frank Worthington. I used to DJ with a guy called Twink, so it was Frank & Twink, and we were the residents at the Central, we used to hang around together 'cos we were also mates and we'd go to the Mecca every Saturday, then on to Wigan. And Russ just said, 'Well, do you guys wanna do a spot?' So we did a spot and, bang, that was it.

Did you have a regular slot?
Well, I used to roll up there about 3.30am; it was a better time to get there, I always felt. But that's how I met Mary Chapman [who ran the Cleethorpes all-nighters]. I was coming back from Wigan, we stopped at Woolley Edge services on the M62, and this elder woman sat next to us, started talking. I thought they were some dysfunctional couple who had accidentally stumbled into Wigan Casino. But they turned out to be soul fans. I ended up having a chat with them because they were really nice and from that point on, I said, 'You should come to Samantha's on a Friday.'

Friday night I was doing three gigs: Leeds Central 10 till 12, then I'd go over to Huddersfield do the Starlight from half 12 till half one, then I used to drive over the Pennines to Sheffield, get to Samantha's about half two and stay till eight in the morning. It was a good kick-off to the weekend.

Quite often, I'd then drive off down to Kings Lynn in Norfolk, to Soul Bowl. Jon Anderson was the guy who used to get records in. He'd go to the States every four weeks. His list always had interesting stuff on it, but once he got on the northern thing, he'd go over and find stuff. The main thing was trying to pin him down the day he got back from the States, because whoever got there first, got the first pick. Once out of every four or six weeks, I'd leave Sheffield after Samantha's drive all the way to Kings Lynn for about 10 in the morning, get all the records bought, finally crash out for a couple of hours in the car in the afternoon and quite often I'd try and dovetail that with doing a gig on the east coast, especially if I was doing a gig in Cleethorpes as well. Quite often they'd have gigs in Louth, occasionally I'd do Burton-on-Trent. At that point I was doing both Wigan and Cleethorpes, and Russ got funny about Cleethorpes so he said it's either one or the other. But Cleethorpes, at that point, had a different vibe about it to Wigan and so I thought: Cleethorpes I'd been with literally from the word go, and Wigan can be a bit wanky if they've got the wrong guys on, so I stuck with Cleethorpes.

Where you there the first night?
It was a really influential spot that. The scene was governed by traditional old northern soul. Levine always had a bit more eclectic and – dare I say it – better taste. It would be Levine that would champion a record like Jody Mathis' 'Don't You Care Anymore'. A lot of the real soulful ones, Levine would generally find them. There were a million and one fast stompers with a white vocal, that seemed to lean towards the Wigan. Soul Sam, that's kind of all he played; and Russ; and John Vincent did. I had this little bit of a snobby attitude: it had

CLEETHORPES IS BACK WITH A

BANG

This Sunday: August 13
12 NOON–11p.m.

With an explosive mixture of
NORTHERN and FUNK
and the very best ever Deejay line up
MAIN HALL:
100% STOMPING NORTHERN SOUL
DJs: SOUL SAM ★ NEV WHERRY ★ POKE ★
RICK SCOTT ★ JOHN MANSHIP and BUB
UPSTAIRS:
100% SUPERGOOD SUPERRARE FUNK
With the best Funky DJs:
IAN 'FRANK' DEWHIRST ★ PAUL SCHOFIELD
★ & POKE (Soul Bowl)
Licensed Bar (Drinks at normal bar prices)
Admission: £1.50 (includes both rooms)

to have a black vocal to it, male or female. I'd occasionally let a white one through if it was a Dean Parrish or Paul Anka. What happened was Levine would go to Miami to stay with his parents once or twice a year. They had a casino in Blackpool and a house in Miami. So Levine from a young age was in every warehouse in Florida and, of course, discovering incredible stuff and bringing it back.

Now, there was a point after one trip when he came back with Gil Scott-Heron's 'In The Bottle', a terrible record called 'Shake 'N' Bump' by Snoopy Dean, and 'Cochise' by Paul Humphrey. Now Cochise was an immediate monster. Nobody knew it at the time, but it was a new release, but it might as well have been brand new northern. And so this modern influence drifted in. Previously when that had happened it was records like Millie Jackson's 'My Man Is A Sweet Man', which by accident was a stomper. It was about that time that he brought in 'Music Maker' by King Sporty, 'Seven Day Lover' by James Fountain, 'I Can See Him Loving You' by The Anderson Brothers and the Carstairs' 'It Really Hurts Me Girl' – my favourite record of all time. And Levine, gradually, was bringing in more and more modern ones in.

Then what happened was he stopped going to Miami, and when he was 16 he went to New York, still looking for northern records, but by this time he was hanging out in a lot of the sort of big underground gay clubs. I think the one he went to at the time was the Anvil. He started bringing back this stuff. If you look at the early disco stuff, like 'Free Man' by Southshore Commission – a big Mecca record – was the same pace as northern, but just a more modern recording. 'Super Ship' by George Benson was one of the biggest northern records, even though it was a new release. If I hadn't been down to the Mecca on a week that Levine got back to the States, I'd ring round on the Sunday and ask what he brought back.

'The fucking biggest record of the night was 'Super Ship' by George Benson.'

Then I'd get the record, put it on, and yeah it all made sense. The scene hadn't yet split, but if you went to the Mecca you'd have Levine leaning much more and more on to the newer stuff, but you'd still have Colin Curtis, who was into one-offs like Youilla Cooper's 'Let Our Love Grow Higher' or 'No One Else Can Take Your Place' by The Inspirations.

Curtis used to like stompers, but also quite liked some of the new stuff, and Levine would bring doubles back for him. You used to get a real balance of these new records which were essentially early disco, dovetailed with the northern stuff. Russ, for instance, banned new records. I can remember Levine getting his first spot at Wigan and he put on 'Shake 'N' Bump', which isn't my favourite record anyway, 'cos it was quite funky and it didn't really dovetail with what you'd call northern soul. But Russ made a thing of saying 'I don't want Snoopy Dean and I don't want Ladies' Choice by Boby Franklin'. There were some records that were more funky than others and Levine could get away with them at Blackpool, but Russ wasn't having them at Wigan. Cleethorpes was a melting pot for it all.

I was doing Cleethorpes every week, but I was getting disillusioned with what I was having to pay for rare records. The top DJs would be Levine, Curtis, Searling, Soul Sam, me, Russ, there'd be about 10 of us. And if we wanted a record, whoever sold us it knew we'd only have to play it three weeks and it would be worth 10 times what we paid for it. So, by that point I was being asked to pay a lot of money for unknowns. I was getting in bidding wars with people. The best example I can give is a track called 'Ever Again' by Bernie Williams, because Colin had the only copy on Bell. It wasn't a normal northern record, but it was just one that Colin would play in the last hour at the Mecca. The last hour at the Mecca used to have this tradition: that's when they'd try out the new records. Every week Colin kept playing this Bernie Williams record and it had a small group of followers. And it really got under my skin; I really liked it and I thought I can definitely break that at Cleethorpes. I remember ringing Colin and asking him whether he was going to do anything with that Bernie Williams record: 'I could really use it. You're too late mate, I've just done a deal with Jack Bollington in Derby.'

Jack always struck a hard bargain if he knew you wanted something. He said, 'I don't really wanna get rid of it, what've you got?'

'Well, World Column' – of which there were only four copies.

He wanted £50, the World Column 'So Is The Sun' on Tower and Susan Barratt on RCA. It doesn't sound a lot now, but it was a fuck of a lot of money. I was earning a bit from the gigs, but the records, previously, you could get them for £10-£20. So anyway, I went down to Cleethorpes on the Saturday and you know the coffee bar at the side? That's where all the deals used to go on. At that point Johnny Manship from Melton Mowbray had leapt into the DJ equation, suddenly started collecting records and bit by bit started getting some good ones, managed to get some spots at Cleethorpes. Johnny had a good contact in San Francisco called Bob Cattaneo and he used to get most of the good records from him. So anyway, he says, 'Have you got any good records this week?'

> ## " Cleethorpes Pier about four in the morning and all you'd hear was this STOMP! STOMP! STOMP! from about a mile and a half away, and it'd be the dancing. "

'Yeah, I've got one I've been after for ages, Bernie Williams, 'Never Again'.'

'Never heard of it.'

'Yeah, it's the only one in the country, Colin's played it but only between one and two and I'm gonna bust it right open.'

So I'm just telling all this thinking the deal's sealed and I get back home on the Sunday and I get a call from Jack Bollington: 'Look I don't think I can do that deal any more.'

'What are you talking about? The deal's done, we've agreed on it.'

'Yeah, but Manship's rung and offered me a fucking fortune.'

I said, 'You've got to be joking! He doesn't even know the fucking record.'

Then we had a bidding war, bit by bit it was edging up until my final bid was £100 in cash and four records, which would have taken it up to about £160. And Manship rang him and offered virtually the same four records and £150. And at that point I thought I can get gazumped here by any kid who's got more money than I have. Whether they know the record or not. Next time I saw Johnny I said, 'You're a cunt you are. You didn't even know the fucking record.'

'No, but a few people had told me about it. You weren't the only one.'

I only got my revenge four weeks later when he got the Anderson Brothers' 'I Can See Him Loving You' on GSF, which he didn't realise was my most wanted record of all time, and I managed to get it off him for about £50. And bang! it suddenly shot up to £200.

What sticks in your mind most about Cleethorpes?

I used to get to Cleethorpes Pier about four in the morning and by that point all you'd hear was this STOMP! STOMP! STOMP! from about a mile and a half away, and it'd be the dancing. It was surreal; there's this place jutting out into the sea and it's four in the morning and all you can hear is STOMP! Multiplied times a thousand.

What was the Mecca like?

If you were a serious collector, the only place you could conceive of going was Blackpool Mecca. Levine was there, and Levine was the arbiter of taste. He always had the most breathtaking array of records. You might not know them all, but you'd know they'd all be good. And he would take chances. You'd never have heard 'Seven Day Lover' by James Fountain at Wigan. I have to give him respect, even though he's pretty obnoxious to be around a lot of the time. He was the guy who brought back 'There's A Ghost In My House' by R. Dean Taylor. It was a VIP single. Levine comes back from the States and of course I'm on the phone on the Saturday afternoon. And he says, 'I've got the greatest northern soul record ever.' But he used to say this all the time.

'It's on VIP, it's written by Holland, Dozier and Holland and it's by a well-known singer. It's 'There's A Ghost In My House' by R. Dean Taylor.'

So I'm like, 'Fuck off! It must be around, it can't be that rare.'

That night he played it about six times and by the third time everybody realised that, yes, it *is* the greatest record ever. Overnight it's the most wanted record in the country. The buzz spread. He's done it again, he's found a killer.

So the next day everybody's on to their contacts in the States, saying come on you must be able to find this, it's easy: R. Dean Taylor. We all went for it and everybody came up with a blank. We just couldn't believe it was that rare. This went on for about six weeks and the pressure for everybody to get this record was ridiculous. The thirst for this record was huge. Then the weirdest thing happened. Someone was coming back from Wigan Casino and went into a motorway service station and was bending down to get a Sunday paper and there was a rack of those old Music For Pleasure budget LP racks. And there was an R. Dean Taylor compilation called *Indiana Wants Me*. Track three, side two, there it was: 'There's A Ghost In My House'. So it's in every record shop in the country and we all fucking missed it! Of course, the game was up, within about a week I'd found about 50 copies and I was knocking them out at a fiver each!

> ## " Suddenly my gig rate shot up because I was the only one outside Blackpool who had that record. "

Do you remember the northern crossover records?
Previously, there'd been 'Hey Girl Don't Bother Me' by the Tams, which I think was one of the early examples of something that had been rare and crossed over. By all accounts it had been a Wheel record. Barry Tasker, I think, was playing it. 'You Sexy Sugar Plum' by Rodger Collins was another one. 'You Sexy Sugar Plum' came from this guy in San Francisco, Bob Cattaneo, otherwise known as 'Disco Bob' to collectors. He had this record by Rodger Collins on Fantasy, and he'd already had a big Wheel record called 'She's Looking Good' on Galaxy, then there'd been this gap. Disco Bob was sending out lists and we were all looking for the most wanted records like the Carstairs, the Inspirations. And on the list is this 'Sexy Sugar Plum' for four quid. Can't be any good, we thought, because it was cheap and new. And of course somewhere along the line someone got it and then there was a feeding frenzy for it. It was a must-have record.

The Esther Phillips ['What A Difference A Day Makes'] was Levine coming back from New York. These records coming from New York at that time were new, but it was taking them six weeks to come through to England. Like the Paul Humphrey record, 'Cochise', it was a new record. Another example is 'Love Factory' by Eloise Laws. A couple of dozen records came through to the UK and that was it, it disappeared. Two or three years later, bang. I think it came out in '73 and '75-'76 it became huge. It didn't feel like it was rare because it was on Music Merchant and you used to see loads of crappy Music Merchant records – but never the Eloise Laws.

It's happened a few times that I've had records within my grasp and they haven't felt that sexy so I've dismissed them, maybe because they're on a label that's not that rare. I did it with Billy Woods' 'Let Me Make You Happy' which is one of the greatest records ever made, purely because it was on Sussex. You used to fall over Sussex stuff everywhere, I just couldn't imagine that there was a rare record on Sussex and it turns out to be one of the rarest records of all time.

Why was Cleethorpes different?
It almost the naiveté of the people who ran it, Mary and Colin Chapman. It has to be one of the greatest venues ever, as far as mystique goes. The weird thing is as soon as they nailed it they rang me up and they said, 'Look we've got a venue to do this all-nighter,' and there was no precedent for doing an all-nighter anywhere east in the country. So there was a good contingent from Yorkshire and Humberside. What was brilliant about Cleethorpes was that it offered an alternative. Credit where credit's due, they didn't go for that headhunting of top names, I was the nearest to a top name, and Kev Roberts did a few. They let the local lads coming through have a chance like Rick Scott from Scunthorpe, and Poke.

I took it really seriously; I did seven till eight and generally I'd do a spot between three or four. The point when I did Cleethorpes was when I was riding high. I had a box full of records that were guaranteed floorfillers. I had the Four Perfections' 'I'm Not Strong Enough', 'I Can't Change' by Lorraine Chandler, The Carstairs which only Levine and myself had. Suddenly my gig rate shot up because I was the only one outside Blackpool who had that record. The Carstairs had had a huge record at the Torch, 'He Who Picks A Rose' and then 'It Really Hurts Me Girl' came out on Red Coach in 1973 and nobody could find it. I had the luckiest break with it, too. I was at an all-dayer at the Heavy Steam Machine at Hanley and got to this gig at four in the afternoon. This guy Dave from London was leaving and he had a record box, and I knew he always had odd records, so I said, 'Can I have a quick look through your box?' Flicking all the way through and the last two records are the Carstairs' 'It Really Hurts Me Girl' and Dena Barnes' 'If You Ever Walk Out Of My Life'. The two biggest records in the country and he's got them at the back of his box in paper sleeves. So I asked him how much he wanted for them and he said 15 quid apiece. And I had about 20 quid so I bought the Carstairs, but I didn't have enough for the Dena Barnes and Keith Minshull walks up wondering what I'm buying, sees the Dena Barnes record and asks how much. Fifteen quid, so he gets it.

So for the next two years, only me and Levine had it. The Carstairs used to be on that label Okeh. Then they turn up on a subsidiary of De-Lite, the Kool and the Gang label, and you put the needle on the record... Jesus Christ, man, if you want everything on one record, then this record's got it. The most passionate vocal, scintillating beat, brilliant strings, produced by George Kerr, the fucking archdeacon of northern soul! Everything compressed into this one record. I spent almost a week looking at the label. There are very few records where there are one or two-offs; usually someone, somewhere will dig more up.

Okay, so let's talk about the Wigan Casino.
One of the best things was the anticipation of going there, because you always knew what to expect; you always knew you'd meet pals from all over the place, so there was that whole exodus thing. And Wigan, in those days, was a pretty depressing place to be going to. Miles and miles of terraced housing. A lot of the fun was the people you were with, because nine times out of ten, there'd be two or three speedheads in the car, who were vibing everything up. I was the music person, so as soon as I got in I'd be looking in boxes of records and talking to DJs. We'd pull up. And there'd always be a mass of coaches and cars and this build up of atmosphere. Eventually we got sophisticated and used to get down about 3.30 or four. So you'd spend three or four hours at the Mecca, doing the Mecca thing, and then it'd be about 45 to 50 minutes to Wigan.

But there was this tangible excitement in the air, because you knew you were going to be walking into a cauldron of activity and energy. The entrance to the Casino was really tatty. Zero money spent on maintenance. It was almost a dump. If it was a really busy night, there would be steam coming out of the entrance. I've seen that happen to cellar clubs a lot, but for a building that big... but there was a lot of energy being expended there. As soon as you walked in, this whole thing hits you. You're aware there's a really fast record playing, clouds of condensation hit you in the face, you hear the handclaps; it's almost like a drug. At its height, it was a real buzz. You know some clubs get it right. The right club at the right time with the right DJ; all the ingredients are right. And that's how it was with Wigan.

You had to have membership to get in. It was that sense of community as well. It's like going to Glastonbury these days, except it was every Saturday night. You were part of this select, exciting scene. When you look at most of the market towns, the height of the week would be going to Tiffanies in Bradford until 2 o'clock. Being drunk in the taxi queue. Getting a curry. Then there were all these kids, dressing really differently, and getting in a car and driving hundreds of miles. You had the nutters of course, who were 'chemically motivated'.

Apparently loads of chemists used to get knocked off on the way to Wigan....
It happened every week! Certainly wouldn't have been me that did it, because I never did anything then, believe it or not. I was Mr. Straight in those days. My induction into all of that came when I took a line off George Clinton – when I was there during the recording of 'Flashlight'.

What would happen with the chemist shops then?
Somewhere along the line, some of the bad lads must've reconnoitred all the different ways into Wigan and looked at the chemist shops that didn't look like they had the greatest security. There used to be bunches from all around the country and you'd have people like Psycho from Leeds, whoever the nutter was from Nottingham. And whichever way they came in you could almost bet your life that a chemist would be broken into and done. I always kept one step removed from it.

The other thing is a lot of the records that took off had drug references in them. That was another peculiar side to the northern soul scene. Records like 'Blowing My Mind To Pieces', 'Blowing My Mind', 'Cracking Up', 'Ten Miles High'.

And the Invitations as well?
Yeah: 'Gotta get my gear out, ready for winter's near'. When I'd be going to these places with Rod and Sid and Smithy and Scotty, that's all they'd talk about. They'd be as high as kites. Those were the parts of the records they'd sing: 'Gotta get my gear out!' It was all part of the journey there.

What was it like DJing at Wigan?
The first gig we got at Wigan, that was quite a big step. I'd done all the smaller gigs. At this point I was starting to get some great records together. The problem at Wigan was that you had 2-3,000 kids there and you had to keep that energy level. There was no such thing as blowing a spot at Wigan. You couldn't afford to. If you can imagine the collective downer if two records on a row bombed out... the atmosphere would palpably slump, and I've seen it slump for certain people. And all of sudden it's a drag.

So Wigan was less adventurous in terms of breaking records. I always like DJs who had exclusives that were great records, but didn't try and break new material to the detriment of the atmosphere. That's quite a balancing act, especially with 2,000 people. It's one thing that I've been very conscious of ever since: programming is dead important.

Imagine: there are two decks on a stage, and you. It's not that different from playing a concert. These aren't normal people. They've worked their balls off all week. And they've come here to have a great Saturday night. All night. It really makes you keep your programming together. And Wigan was stomper-friendly. It was not the environment to be playing nice sweet Philly things. Do you remember 'Afternoon Of The Rhino'?

Mike Post Coalition?
Yeah. Boy! What a record. That's a real crowd-peaking record. Every one of those you played, you had to have a killer mid-tempo tune to keep them on the floor. So pacing was really all-important.

What did it feel like to play a record that took the roof off at Wigan?
Incredibly fulfilling. Especially if it was something that you wanted to see break, and maybe it's taken a bit of time. There were some really weird records. I didn't find this, but I was instrumental in Tobi Legend's 'Time Will Pass You By'. Do you know that record?

It's one of the Three Before Eight [the end-of-the-night tunes].

Yeah. I found Gerri Grainger's 'I Go To Pieces'. It wasn't my type of record at all. I played it because the girls seemed to like it. 'I'm On My Way' by Dean Parrish was another. Did I tell you about Kegsy, the guy who discovered that?

Kegsy's this guy from Bradford. Completely off his nut. He'd be walking around bombed all weekend. You'd arrive at Bolton or Wigan at three in the morning, and Kegsy would generally be hanging about outside. And you'd be, 'Hiya Kegsy. Alright?'

'Well, yeah, I set off from Bradford last night with 12p and a Mars Bar and I've got £23 in my pocket and a bunch of records!' That was the joke with this guy, he'd always end up with money and records. Kegsy would go all over the place and he'd always go on about these records. And he came to the Central one Friday night with the Dean Parrish which was on Laurie. And Laurie was a bit of a crappy label.

Kegsy could be quite powerful. And he came up, all sweaty and hardly able to speak, saying, 'Play this it's fucking brilliant!' I put it on in the cans and all I can hear is this horrible guitar at the start. I honestly thought Kegsy had gone mad. 'All you've gotta do is play it,' he says. Anyway, he's at Va Va's sticking it in Searling's face, then at the Mecca he's doing the same to Levine! Then he's at Wigan, on the stage, and the funny thing about this guy, he had a tooth missing and looked a bit of a thug, but he's got the record in Russ Winstanley's face. And the thing about Russ is he'd cave in to pressure and also he'd give things a try, he had a nice democratic attitude about records. So Russ played it, and the rest is history! The poor guy's plugging it for 36 hours before anyone plays it.

❝ I saw a guy die once, doing an aeroplane spin. He couldn't stop doing them. They twirl round faster than the eye can see. ❞

What's your best memory of DJing at the all-nighter?
I suppose the best thing about DJing was seeing your vision confirmed. It must've been the same for a musician. If a musician writes a song, and it gets accepted, it must be a gas playing it. It's the same with finding an unknown record. You listen to it at home and wonder whether it will work. It's like seeing a baby suddenly mature. Suddenly it's a hot one. And seeing an unknown record go from zero value to being valuable. It was almost like a stock market.

Where and who were the best dancers?
The legendary dancer from the Torch was a guy called Frankie Booper. Every scene has a king, and Frankie Booper was the number one dancer. Everyone would get out of his way, and he knew it. He was one of those guys who had a strong physique, and he would run up to the wall and do backflips off it. He'd do things of such astounding athleticism. Frankie was the king at the Torch. I did notice in the Wigan period, you'd always get the ones doing aeroplane spins. In fact, I saw a guy die once, doing an aeroplane spin. He couldn't stop doing them. They twirl round faster than the eye can see. I once saw a guy at Cleethorpes get locked into doing one. And when he came to a standstill, blood was coming from his eyes, his nose, his mouth, his ears. He blew up. It was upsetting because it was right in front of the DJ stand.

Is it true promoters would book certain DJs just because they had a particular record?
Oh, yeah. I mean if you wanted 'The Laws Of Love' by the Volcanoes, another early Trammps record or Mel Britt's 'She'll Come Running Back', you had to book Richard Searling because he was the only that had them. You knew who had which records and what exclusives. That's why we used to go to the Mecca every week, because, between them, Curtis and Levine probably had three or four dozen records that only they had. The quality of an all-nighter was generally dictated by the quality of DJ. One of the problems of Wigan was that you had Richard Searling, who was what you'd call a good-taste DJ, and then you had Russ Winstanley, who really would play some pap. It was one of the things used to wind me up about him. Here he is, he's got this great club, it's packed to capacity

with kids, and we've got all of this incredible music at our disposal, so why is he playing 'Good Little You' by Joey Dee & the Starliters?

Do you remember any records that crossed over as a result of Wigan?
'There's A Ghost In My House', 'You Sexy Sugar Plum'. That started off on a list. You couldn't get it because it was in San Francisco. There's a record called 'The Flasher' by Lloyd Michael and Mistura that became a novelty pop hit.

What about 'The Night'? Was that a big Wigan record?
Mammoth. It didn't do shit when it came out. Some of those records burned out quite quickly.

Why was that? Because they were pop?
Yeah, we'd drop them a long, long, long time before they were in the charts.

So does no-one ever play 'There's A Ghost In My House' now then?
No. It's a shame, it's a good record.

> ❝ **When the whole rave thing went ballistic, to me, it felt like northern soul 20 years on. Lots of people getting off their heads, dancing to fast music and this love attitude.** ❞

Tell me the Tainted Love story.
Marc Almond used to be cloakroom boy in the Warehouse. We booked the Q Tips to play on the Tuesday and Wednesday night. I thought, 'Great, I'll pull some soul stuff out.' I brought the more accessible northern stuff out, so I could play it as people came in. I put 'Tainted Love' on and this guy who I'd conspicuously avoided for nine months – he was always getting in fights with women or something – he came rushing up in the middle of Gloria Jones. 'What's this record? I've got to know what this record is!'

'It's Gloria Jones with "Tainted Love".'

'I've got to have a tape of it!'

He'd done an EP called 'Mutant Moments' which was doodly electronic stuff that I couldn't play. He'd done something on a Some Bizarre compilation and 'Memorabilia'. Anyway, the upshot of it was he ended up coming round my house. I remember it because he's allergic to dogs. I put Gloria Jones and a load of other stuff on tape for him. Probably even Judy Street, though I can't be certain of that.

What about the use of microphones in northern clubs. Rob Bellars says they never used a mic at the Twisted Wheel. Were they talking at the Torch?
Yeah, Martyn Ellis was the king of the microphone. Most northern DJs can't use the microphone. I can remember all sorts of funny incidents with Levine on the mic. Levine on the mic is very much what he's like when you're talking to him [adopts Levine accent] 'And now the most incredible record from the Carstairs. It's the third time I've played this tonight, but it deserves to be played 10 times a night.' He could never get his head around the equipment side of things. So he'd come in the Mecca and arrange his gut on to the DJ stand. Often he'd go, 'And that was the brilliant sound of the Just Brothers and now we're... oh... what's?... What's happening here?... This is broken.... Where's Colin?....HELP!' And he'd be doing this on the microphone and there'd be 1,500 people thinking what the hell is going on!

What do you think is the legacy of northern soul?
The northern soul thing to me was almost like an eighth wonder of the world. You're looking at the depressed north of England where there wasn't a great deal there apart from steelworks and coalmines. So you had people doing this boring repetitive work during the

week, and hard work, too. And when they went out on a weekend, they really wanted to go out. Just going out to 12 o'clock to the local pub wasn't going to be good enough.

That ethos of exclusivity has pretty much continued. Those drum and bass guys have to have everything on acetate now. When the whole rave thing went ballistic, to me, it felt like northern soul 20 years on. Lots of people getting off their heads, dancing to fast music and this love attitude. This is this generation's version of northern soul. What was so revolutionary about northern soul was there was no antecedent for it.

© DJhistory.com

CLEETHORPES WINTER GARDENS 50

THE CARSTAIRS – It Really Hurts Me Girl

BOBBY HUTTON – Lend A Hand

GIL SCOTT-HERON/BRIAN JACKSON – The Bottle

THE VOICES OF EAST HARLEM – Cashing In

JAMES FOUNTAIN – Seven Day Lover

THE TRAMMPS – Hold Back The Night

THE POINTER SISTERS – Send Him Back

MARVIN HOLMES & JUSTICE – You'd Better Keep Her

FRANKIE 'LOVEMAN' CROCKER – Ton Of Dynamite

DON THOMAS – Come On Train

THE MOMENTS – I Got The Need

BABE RUTH – Elusive

THE ANDERSON BROTHERS – I Can See Him Loving You

KENNY SMITH – Lord, What's Happening To Your People

MEL BRITT – She'll Come Running Back

BITS 'N' PIECES – Keep On Running Away

THE MONTCLAIRS – Hung Up On Your Love

BILLY WOODS – Let Me Make You Happy

REGGIE GARNER – Hot Line

THE WORLD COLUMN – So Is The Sun

LOU PRIDE – I'm Com'un Home In The Morn'un

RODGER COLLINS – You Sexy Sugar Plum

MAURICE WILLIAMS – Being Without You

YVONNE BAKER – You Didn't Say A Word

THE FOUR PERFECTIONS – I'm Not Strong Enough

THE DEL-LARKS – Job Opening (Pt. 1)

THE MATTA BABY – Do The Pearl Girl

PRINCE GEORGE – Wrong Crowd

THE DETROIT EXECUTIVES – Cool Off

KEANYA COLLINS – Barnabus Collins – Love Bandit

THE RIMSHOTS – Do What You Feel

BLACK NASTY – Cut Your Motor Off

THE BROTHERS – Are You Ready For This

THE BOOGIE MAN ORCHESTRA – Lady, Lady, Lady

LORRAINE CHANDLER – I Can't Change

JOHNNY BRAGG – They're Talking About Me

PORGY & THE MONARCHS – My Heart Cries For You

TOWANDA BARNES – You Don't Mean It

THE TEMPREES – At Last

BETTY WRIGHT – Where Is The Love

EAST COAST CONNECTION – Summer In The Parks

CROWN HEIGHTS AFFAIR – Dreaming a Dream

TODAY'S PEOPLE – S.O.S.

THE MODERN REDCAPS – You're Never Too Young (To Fall In Love)

JOE MATHEWS – Ain't Nothing You Can Do

SAM AMBROSE – They'll Be Coming

LOU EDWARDS & TODAY'S PEOPLE – Talkin' About Poor Folks

RAW SOUL – The Gig

JACKIE BEAVERS – Trying To Get Back To You Girl

ILA VANN – You Made Me This Way

Compiled by Ian Dewhirst

RECOMMENDED LISTENING

VARIOUS – The Cleethorpes Story

VARIOUS – Classic Jazz-Funk Mastercuts Vols. 1-3

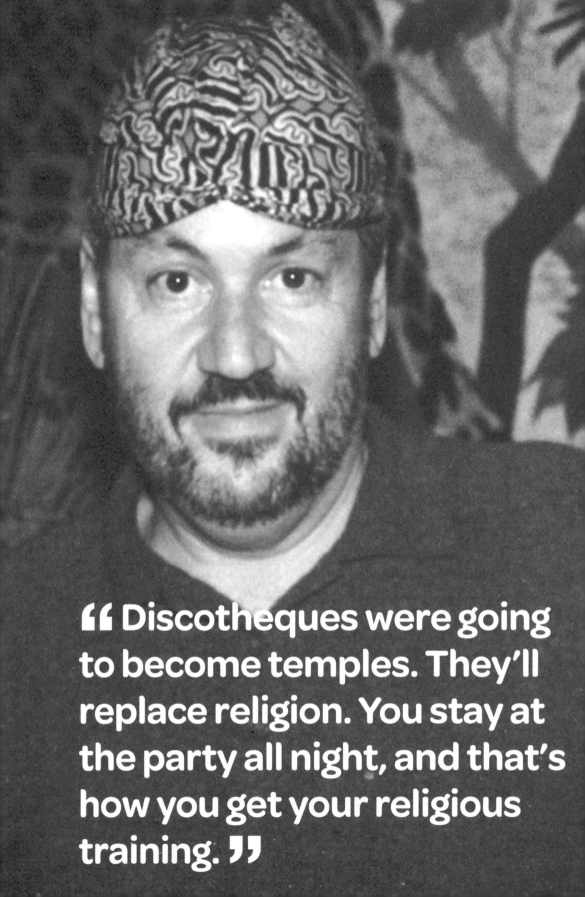

"Discotheques were going to become temples. They'll replace religion. You stay at the party all night, and that's how you get your religious training."

Steve D'Acquisto
Disco's radical

Interviewed by Bill in Manhattan, October 5, 1998

Steve D'Acquisto was disco's firebrand, a revolutionary who saw it as much as a movement as it was a style of music. Steve saw a DJ booth in place of the soapbox and found his own Communist Manifesto in the lyrics of Gamble and Huff. He is from the very first generation, a sparring partner of Francis Grasso and Michael Cappello. Although he built a reputation as a great DJ at places like The Haven and Tamburlaine, it's as a facilitator and cheerleader that he will be remembered, nurturing and helping DJs and artists like David Mancuso and Arthur Russell, with whom he made the Loose Joints records for West End.

Sadly, Steve died of a brain tumour in 2001. He played what was probably his last ever gig at the New York launch party for our book *Last Night A DJ Saved My Life*, an incredible honour, not least because his mother had passed away a day or two earlier. With a beautiful set of fragile, poignant disco, he made the music a tribute to her.

Our paths first crossed in 1996 at a convention in Chicago where, despite his greying hair, he had an incredible enthusiasm for music. The second time we meet is in New York in Charlie Grappone's Vinylmania store on a beautiful fall morning. He's tall, with spiky hair and a gentle yet distinct New York accent. Although he's very laidback, you can still feel a personality coming through that's as spiky as his hair, and indeed down the years his militancy has alienated some and pissed off plenty. Today is Steve's 55th birthday.

Tell me little about your background.
I was born in Brooklyn, my dad would be 102 years old if he were alive today and he had quite a record collection. A lot of Italian music and waltzes. He was born and raised in Sicily. He was a merchant seaman. He bought gramophones. I have an older brother and sister and they also loved music. I was born in 1953. I'm 55 today actually. My brother bought me an old Traveler Victrola which was electric as opposed to crank up. My parents told me that by the age of three they had a party trick where they would ask me to put on a record and I would. I was born before TV, so I listened to radio dramas and comedy shows.

So I started collecting records as a kid. Other kids would ask for toys on their birthday. I asked for records. When I was eight, nine, 10 I could name what was going to be number one. I had an ear for public taste. I have 6,000 78s. I can't even count the 45s.

Tell me about the radio DJs you listened to.
The first one was Martin Block. This was before rock'n'roll. He was an institution here in New York. He was on WNAW-AM. He was also influential in terms of live broadcasts of swing bands and one of the first people to start playing records on radio, as opposed to live music. Because of Alan Freed I fell in love with Elvis. But I was also buying Doris Day. I heard 'I Want You, I Need You, I Love You' by Elvis, which blew me away. That was the last 78 I bought. And the first 45 I bought was 'Let The Good Times Roll' by Shirley and Lee, which was also an Alan Freed record. Ultimately it got banned because of the lyrics. It's a great party tune. It's all about sex and fucking. But those things existed on records before, like Bessie Smith's

'Nobody In Town Can Bake A Sweet Jelly Roll Like Mine'. That's all about getting fucked. Fats Waller's 'Hold Tight' is all about cunnilingus. 'Hold tight I want some seafood mama.'

I had Little Richard records. The Platters. All the doo-wop comes from what the Ink Spots and Mills Brothers were doing. Penguins, Cleftones, Orioles. Alan Freed took us into a whole new world. Subsequently, there was Peter Tripp. When Alan Freed left, or got fired, which we thought was bizarre, Murray the K came in and took over from Freed.

Do you think Freed was persecuted because he championed black music?
Yes. Absolutely. No question about it. They went after him because he was ruining the youth of America. He was taking their children and turning them on to this bizarre music, because at that point in time it was considered the devil's music. I saw an Alan Freed show at the Brooklyn Fox on Fulton Street – now torn down – with Fats Domino, Everly Brothers, Joanne Campbell, The Platters and Little Richard. The crowd was mostly black. That is etched in my memory. They were trying to kill it, but it just wouldn't go away.

Where did you hear Symphony Sid?
He was on the fifteens on the AM dial. At that point I was into Billie Holiday. We would listen to it at a friend's house. I'd already started to collect Billie Holiday and Bessie Smith records. The first album I bought of Billie Holiday was *The Golden Years*, a two-record set on Decca. She said on the liner notes her influence was Bessie Smith, so I went and sought out those records, too. Here I was going between jazz, rock'n'roll and pop.

What we're you doing for living after you left high school?
I'm a licensed funeral director. At 17 a friend from childhood had a father who was opening up a funeral parlour a couple of blocks from my house. His father took a liking to me and I was there for seven years. Then in the '60s I took LSD and that completely changed my life.

> ❝ I was driving my cab and taking amphetamines so that I could drive 12 hours straight. People had to get in the car while it was still moving; that's how fast I was moving! ❞

When did you first take that?
In 1966 or '67. At that point we were listening to Rosko on WNEW [not to be confused with Emperor Rosko] and Scott Muni early on. Roskoe was the most influential of the '60s DJs. He played rhythm and blues, long tracks, really WNEW was the first station to start playing album tracks rather than just the singles. You started hearing five, six and even ten minute tracks. 'In-A-Gadda-Da-Vida' by Iron Butterfly was probably the longest record to be on the radio; 'MacArthur Park' was another one [by Richard Harris]; 'Get Ready' by Rare Earth. Ultimately, we would end up playing these records in clubs. Early on we played 'In-A-Gadda-Da-Vida'; we played 'Get Ready'.

Before I go on I should go back to Francis [Grasso].

So here I was, infatuated with LSD and marijuana. Smoking and dropping acid all the time. Started to go out to clubs, gay bars like Stonewall. So I was around when the Stonewall riot happened. I was there a few nights before, but not on the night. I was on blue cheer LSD that night; beautiful colour, beautiful colours as well.

While I was waiting for my license I went out and drove a cab. I didn't want to do embalming, but my parents had spent all this money. I was driving my cab and taking amphetamines so that I could drive 12 hours straight. I was the highest cab driver at the company. People had to get in the car while it was still moving; that's how fast I was moving! I dropped somebody off at the Haven, at 1 Sheridan Square, which I later found out was where Café Society was, where Billie Holiday had her biggest successes.

....

So what did this guy say when you were dropping him off?
I asked him, 'Where you going?'
  He said, 'Oh, it's an after-hours.'
  It was an illegal after-hours, because they used to sell alcohol. Didn't have a license. Mmm, wonder what this is all about? So I went down there...

Was this after Stonewall?
I believe it was. Or around the time of Stonewall. It was late '68, early '69. I had long hair right down my back at this point. So they let me in, figuring I was some kind of freak. And I met Francis, who was the disc jockey there, and it was a whole new world to me. Here was this guy, playing records, mixing records, doing all these great things that had never happened before. On radio, basically the fade would come and the new one would come in. Francis had a lot of records, but I had more. And we used to chat, and we got friendly. By that point I'd be going every night. I'd book the cab till 3am, didn't have to bring the cab till 5.30 or 6, so for two hours I'd go hang out with Francis. And we'd speed together. He was a speed-freak as well, loved speed. I always had good drugs, he always had good drugs and we became very friendly to the point where I was doing lights.
  For six months that went on. One night I was at Francis's house and he'd been playing for two weeks straight and his alternate hadn't showed. They called Francis and told him he had to come in; it was a Monday night and Monday and Tuesday were the off nights. So Francis says, 'I can't do this.' You have to remember these weren't six-hour nights, they were 12-, 14-hour nights and it would depend on how high people were as to how late the club stayed open. He looked at me and said,]Do you wanna go play some records? Just make believe you're me.' So I did and I liked it.

What equipment did they have there?
They had two Rek-O-Kut turntables, two piggy-back Dynaco amps and they also had these giant speakers that belonged to Felix Pappalardi, who was one of the producers of the band Mountain. Somehow or other, Nicky Di Martino, who was the owner of the club, was owed money from someone, or whatever, ended up with these giant speakers. Great-sounding things. So we were actually using high-end, hi-fi amps.

Did you have a mixer?
No, it was two integrated amps, literally on top of each other: piggy-back. They had bass and treble controls and volume controls. Both connected to that same set of speakers. No cueing system. You had no clue about the record coming in. You had to listen over the record that was playing, so you could hear. You could actually hear over the PA what was happening. You really had to know your records. Because a lot of these things had long intros, which you didn't want to have, like some of these Gladys Knight records, if you listen to 'You Need Love Like I Do', there's a long intro before it comes in. We used to use the downbeats where the record came in to actually introduce it. I guessed we worked for about a year-and-a-half without headphones. We were always trying emulate radio DJs, listening to the radio, Francis and I.
  Michael Cappello started a few weeks after I did. Michael was a patron at the Haven. Michael was a fabulous person, extraordinarily handsome and just a good buddy. Michael and I were brothers for years and years. I met Michael sitting on a stoop over on Jones Street; he was completely whacked out of his mind on speed and LSD, and I was stoned. I'd seen him at the club and we started to chat, and I found out that he had a lot of records as well. And Francis was moving, and I was taking over the Haven, so I said to Michael, 'Come and play records.' That was when Francis moved to the Sanctuary. Michael ultimately went to the Sanctuary. I ultimately went to the Sanctuary. We were all moving back and forth. The three of us running clubs in the city.

Francis is straight isn't he?
Yes, Francis is straight. Although everyone used to think about it. But he is straight, though I think he would have gone to bed with Michael Cappello at some point. He was going with a woman at the time; she was taking care of him. He was really handsome and had such sex

appeal it was scary. He handled it pretty well. Michael was just a kid. He was like 16 years old when he was playing records, and as far as I'm concerned Michael Cappello was the best DJ who ever did his thing. I could listen to Michael hour after hour, night after night and he never bored me. Always inventive, always genius, extremely clever.

Although he was young he was very worldly. He'd been hanging out in the city a long time and because he was so beautiful and handsome, girls would take advantage of him when he was 12 or 13 years old. By the time he was 16, he'd seen a lot. Women, staying out all night, moving in with women at 14 or 15. Francis was also his senior but not as old as me. But Michael was just phenomenal. He was a great DJ and a spectacular entertainer and a terrific head for music. He discovered some things: 'Give It Up Turn It Loose' was one of Michael's. We would all go out looking for records together.

Where were you getting your records from?
Well, Francis used to have this place on Church Avenue and Flatbush avenue in Brooklyn, where he used to buy a lot of his records, and at that point this was a transitional period where it was becoming a more black neighbourhood. This guy had a lot of good stuff: Dyke & The Blazers, original Kool & The Gang stuff on De-Lite like 'Funky Man', Lou Courtney's 'Hot Butter 'N All' and 'The Chicken' by Jackie Lee. All these funk obscurities. And all these album cuts too. We would all go there. Then we started going to Downstairs Records on 42nd Street, where Nicky worked. Nicky was just a great guy, and he turned us on to a lot of good music. We'd go to Dayton which was on Broadway and Twelfth, and find albums there.

Where you still playing some of the psychedelic rock stuff, too?
We sure were. We were playing Rolling Stones' 'Sympathy For The Devil'. From *Let It Bleed* we'd play 'Live With Me' and 'Gimme Shelter', we'd play Led Zeppelin like crazy: 'Whole Lotta Love'. The Doors' 'Peace Frog'. 'The End' was the closing record for years.

At the Haven?
At the Haven, the Sanctuary and all kinds of places. It was a tremendous record, really long and people would just... come down. At least come down enough to go to the next place! There were other after-hours joints that started at eight in the morning. The 220 on Houston Street was one.

Were these primarily gay?
All the freaks. You'd have gangsters, drag-queens, there were absolutely no barriers. I come from an era where men couldn't dance with each other. There would be a light system which I ultimately introduced to the Loft when we were having trouble with the police in the mid-'70s. They would flip a light into the back rooms because all these places had bars and they had dancing jukeboxes in the back and listening jukeboxes in the front. So they would just turn the lights on and you knew you'd have to stop dancing with each other. And they would pipe in the music from the front jukebox and stop the music from the back jukebox. And we used to put money in the jukebox to dance. This was called the Magic Touch in Long Island, in Oceanside. Gay people used to find these friends, men, women, whatever, and say come with me to this bar and there would be 20 of us in the bar and the straight guys would accept us and it would be a cool experience.

So when did Fire Island start to happen?
Fire Island happened when I was at Tamburlaine. I remember Bobby DJ turning me on to 'Shaft'. He was the first person to play 'Shaft' and he was playing at the Monster and other places on Fire Island, like Ice Palace. Before the transition to mostly black music, when rock'n'roll started to peter out there wasn't really a radio station where you could listen to all of these odd records that we were finding. We would sit at Nicky's place [Downstairs Records] for hours on end and just play records. We'd be speeding. Sometime, Michael, Francis and I wouldn't sleep for three or four days at a time. Go on and on, snorting speed and crystal meth. We were very serious about our speed! We had to though: we were playing 12 or 15 hours in a night, every single night. We all hung out together: Francis at Sanctuary, Michael and I at the Haven.

Did you go to the Sanctuary or were you working?
If I got off early, or Michael was playing I would go to Sanctuary. Go back, listen to Michael. Life was a club, 24 hours a day.

Describe the Sanctuary.
Sanctuary was the most incredible of all the places in its appearance and the structure. The DJ booth was on the altar, so it was a real ego trip. And they had these four giant speakers hanging from the rafters. It was a peaked roof and these four big speakers facing down on to the dancefloor. Then it had, on both sides, these balconies with tables and chairs. Then the bar, you'd have to walk through these two big archways. So you'd come in, you'd go through the bar, go through the two archways and there would be the dancefloor. And at the very end, there would be the DJ booth. That was the first time we had cueing systems.

Who came up with the idea?
Francis I guess, but I really don't remember. The first time there were speakers in the booth, like they have now, was through Alex Rosner.

What was the composition of the crowd?
Sanctuary was mixed again, because Francis took some of the crowd from the Haven; and Sanctuary had its own people from before – I think Don Findlay was DJing there, maybe even while Francis was still happening. Don was an alternate. Don was very handsome man, loved records, and I have some Don Findlay tapes that I treasure.

> ❝ **Sometimes, Michael, Francis and I wouldn't sleep for three or four days at a time. We all hung out together. We were playing 12 or 15 hours in a night, every single night.** ❞

Do you have any tapes of your sets?
Yeah, but I don't know... We were so busy making cassettes, but the cassettes only go back to Le Jardin really. Never really made tapes at Sanctuary or Haven, we didn't have the facilities. When some of these clubs got cassette recorders in, they started making tapes. I don't believe I have a tape of Tamburlaine. Michael has a lot of tapes. John Addison [owner of Le Jardin] used to sell our tapes. We never got a penny from it. We weren't making any money.

Was the crowd at Sanctuary quite druggy?
All the crowds were druggy. Drugs and alcohol. Speed the drug of choice, LSD second, downers – Tuinal, Seconal – third. There were these Lotusites, god they make you do things; extraordinary pills. Slim, oblong, purple pills.

Musically, what was Sanctuary about?
Originally, it was like Haven, but it became more black.

Incorporating some of the early funk you mentioned earlier?
Yeah. We still played some rock'n'roll there. I can remember doing 'Ain't No Mountain High Enough' at Sanctuary. Drag shows with Princess doing Diana Ross. That was later on, when it became a juice bar, after it lost its license. When Shelley got murdered. They shot one of the quasi-owners. They were the owners, but they were also involved with the...

Mob?
Yeah. He got shot, I guess, because he was holding back money or something. Then it was fuck you, you're dead.

And that's when they lost the license?
They lost the license because he was murdered on the premises.

....

Oh shit. Pretty scary.
Very scary. I was at Tambourine one night when one of the bouncers got shot and they lay him across my feet. I used to have a booth at Tambourine which was elevated slightly. They laid him across my feet with his legs dangling on the floor. I put on *James Brown Live At The Apollo*, collected my records and left. Never worked there any more. We were living in a very... Cocaine had just started getting fashionable then, and cocaine is a terrible ego drug. I hate cocaine. I only did cocaine twice in my life and each time I hated what it did to me. I highly opposed it whenever I saw people doing it. I used to turn people on to LSD when I saw them doing coke. Straighten them out, you know. Have some of this!

Tamburlaine was where it all started to come to the forefront. At Tamburlaine it became popular for the intelligentsia to go to clubs. They weren't going to Sanctuary or Haven, these were still very underground things. At Tamburlaine, because it was an east side location, it wasn't a very big place – 300 capacity; 2,000 in Sanctuary. You had people like Peter Max, Truman Capote, Jackie Kennedy, Andy Warhol, Keith Moon. Rock'n'rollers started to come. It was the precursor to what Studio 54 became, but on a smaller scale. People still talk about Tamburlaine. I think it was the high point of my career as a disc jockey.

> **" You had politics, you had funk, you had love. You had all these different subject matters to go through. I'd also try to be intelligent, I'd try to be sophisticated. But it was all about the music. "**

What kind of stuff were you playing?
Anything that people could dance to.

Which was?
Everything. It didn't matter to me what my sources were. In fact, I had rock'n'roll records which I thought were amazing. 'Rock The Boat', that was a good record, but it was considered a bubblegum record. I also had a bit of an immature streak in me; still do. So my music was always youthful. We'd play 'Looking For A Brand New Game' by The Eight Minutes or 'Streetdance' by Fatback Band. I was a freak and a hippie, but I was also a radical. So I'd play these you know. I used to try to tell stories, that was my gig. I used to try and talk with the music. It changed from one story to another: I love you; I need you; you're hurting me; I'm going to leave; But I want you back again. Then it would be: The Government is going to kill us!

Explain how you would tell a political story?
'Law Of The Land' by the Temptations is extremely political. 'Papa Was A Rolling Stone' is actually a political record. Jesus, 'Sympathy For The Devil' is a political record. But you were also trying to create an atmosphere with the music, too. 'Black Skinned, Blue Eyed Boys' by the Equals. That was extremely political. You had politics, you had funk, you had love. You had all these different subject matters to go through. I'd also try to be intelligent, I'd try to be sophisticated. But it was all about the music.

When I stopped playing records in the mid-'80s, it bored me, because I found that people were paying so much attention to the mix that they weren't paying attention to the music. Some of these guys had these books with beats-per-minute and they'd match the songs with the bpm without figuring out that these two records had nothing to say together. Not a shred of a link apart from a tempo. They'd speed up and slow down records which we never did. We always tried to play them at the speed they were recorded. If you wanted to get fast, you played an uptempo record.

How did you come across David Mancuso?
David met me at... I guess it was at Tamburlaine or Tambourine. He introduced himself

to me and gave me one of his cards and said, 'I have parties, I love your club, why don't you come down one night.' I went there on my own one night and I walked into a whole other world. I walked into a world of unbelievable sound. Tremendous beauty. Just special as can be. There was nothing like the Loft. The Loft was a small little place. But it was just unbelievable. The appearance of it: it had this mirrored ball, when we didn't have them. The whole lighting thing was much more theatre than the clubs were. The clubs were a whole lot of blinking and flashing.

That's what Terry Noel told me.
Well, Terry was really the very first of all of them. Terry's the guy that Francis got it from. Anyway going back to the Loft... I went to this place and it's only black people. It wasn't mixed at all, mostly all-black. Maybe six or seven white people out of total of 200. It used to go on to 7 am; that's when the party stopped. The law in New York was bars could stay open till 4 am, every night except Saturday, when they had to close at 3 am. So at 3 am we'd rush down to the Loft. Ultimately, from there I took Nicky Siano and a bunch of other people. If the Loft became famous it's because of the people I brought there. The way he operated the place was always the same. You had to have an invitation or be invited by a guest. But then people started wanting cards, so he expanded into the next loft.

What do you think separated him from the others?
David took not only the music, he knew the sonics of the records. So he'd not only match music, he'd match sonics. Because of his very sophisticated sound system. He had a really great home hi-fi, the ultimate home hi-fi: huge. But he wasn't mixing when I met him. He had two turntables, but when one was stopping the other was starting. He'll tell you. He did mix eventually, for a lot of years. The most popular years of the Loft where when he mixed. I said to him, you should never let the music stop and he took my advice. He had a cueing system, but he mixed like we were mixing years ago. I could always work on his hi-fi because I didn't need to have the earphones. We got very friendly. David and I are soul brothers.

Do you think the Loft has been the most influential club then?
I think the Loft has been – absolutely and completely – the most influential club ever to see the light of day. Larry Levan, Nicky Siano, Richard Long, all these people basically wanted to duplicate what the Loft was doing, but they didn't realise that they weren't David. They were too stupid and to egotistical to realise that the Loft was David Mancuso playing the records, and David Mancuso creating an atmosphere. His whole head, his sophistication, worldliness, they just didn't have it.

What did you do after the Tamburlaine?
I went to a place called Tambourine. From there, I went to Canada for a few months in 1972 because the same person who ran Tamburlaine and Tambourine ran a place called the Ginza, but I didn't wanna work for him any more. He slapped me around. Strong-arm tactics. So I thought fuck this, and I went away. I was never attached to money or anything but playing records. I went to Montreal and worked in a place there called the Limelight, which became a huge club. Owned by George Cucuzzella, who now runs Unidisc. I walked into the club and some guys recognised me – they'd been down to Le Jardin or somewhere – and they asked me whether I wanted to work there. I can remember bringing them 'The Love I Lost'

which they'd never heard before. They gave me 'The Mexican' by Babe Ruth. I brought that back here. Rob Ouimet gave it to me. I worked with him in a place called Love on Route D. I was Rob's alternate. That was the mid-seventies, then I went back to Le Jardin. The Loft. We started the Record Pool.

David's?

David and I, you mean. Let's get the chronology straight. Judy Weinstein had nothing to do with the origination of the record pool. She didn't come until about a year-and-a-half later. I've got the incorporation papers at home. I basically organised it. David put up the Loft as a space to organise it. I got the people together. Michael Cappello and I would go to the record companies trying to get promotional records. Bobby DJ's the one who wised us up to that. Bobby was the first person I know to get promotional records. Bobby was very clever. Clever about the record business. So I was pretty well-known as a DJ; Michael, too. We were both at Le Jardin, because I replaced Bobby DJ at Le Jardin. David and I started the Record Pool. Please get that straight.

I was already gone by then. Twenty years later it's still running and still pretty influential. David and I had had a bit of a disagreement. Judy came about long after I'd gone. We were such radicals! We thought we were Thomas Jefferson, George Washington, Benjamin Franklin. The reason pools came about... Tony Serafino who used to work for Kudu Records which was part of Creed Taylor's CRT had this record, 'What A Difference A Day Makes' by Esther Phillips. He wouldn't give me a copy of a test pressing, because he said I wasn't big enough. That outraged my friends. Certain companies would set up these times when you could pick up your records and these times were not conducive to the way we ran our lives. We were out till six in the morning, we didn't wanna be going and picking records up at 11. There was this big meeting at Hollywood, Sharon Haywood ran it, which degenerated into this big screaming match. And in the middle of it, David turned round and said, Why don't we start a record pool?' We chatted amongst ourselves and I stood up and invited everybody down to the Loft. This was all the DJs.

Who?

Everybody. Richie Kaczor, Joey Palmentieri, Nicky Siano. I said it was pointless arguing here. We needed to get our act together. Suddenly we were standing up for ourselves. And we had this DJ meeting and we wrote this declaration of intent. I still think they're a good idea, although record companies were supposed to contribute money to keep the pool going, but then what happens is that all turned around and they start asking for dues.

How did you get involved in production?

Through DC LaRue. I was working at Le Jardin and DC LaRue came in. I was the hot DJ at the time. Anyway, DC invited me into the studio when he was doing *Cathedrals*. The tempo of *Cathedrals*, and the conga track are my doing with Aram Schefrin. I got a credit on the second album, but I should've got one on *Cathedrals*. But I loved it. Then I got a job working at Pyramid Records, which was part of Roulette, which released *Cathedrals*.

Was Morris Levy still there?
Morris Levy was still the owner. They gave me a job doing promotion. Walter Gibbons had started doing these wonderful mixes. I worked for Roulette for a while. I started being DC LaRue's buddy.

What was Morris Levy like?
He was a gentleman.

Because he's had a bad rap hasn't he?
He was a nice guy. He gave a lot of people breaks when they didn't stand a chance. I'm sure he did some bad things as well, but I had no privy to that. So we had Whirlwind on Roulette. Roy B was the in-house guy, and I did promotions. I was approached to do a mix by H&O Records. They wanted me to do promotion for them and do a mix of a Sandy Mercer record. So I asked Walter Gibbons to go along. I played him the track. I like to collaborate. I wanted to work with someone I admire. So I asked Walter. We worked on this Sandy Mercer record, 'You Are My Love' and 'Play With Me' which was an even better record, but no-one ever got on it. Then I met Corey Robbins at one of these disco conventions. He was cute. He was working at MCA Publishing. Anyway, he invited me to work with this guy, Joe, who did Gary's Gang.

Eric Matthew?
Yeah, except his name isn't Eric Matthew, it's Joe Tucci. Italian guy, with a studio in his garage in Queens. So I'm driving out there one night, and in the car this 'love dancing' thing comes into my head. You know, 'Can you see the expression on my face?' So I go to everyone, I'm supposed to be working on something else and I say, 'I got this great idea, let's do this.'

And he's like, 'Love dancing? What you talking about, it's bullshit.'

Couple of months later, there's this record by Gary's Gang called 'Let's Lovedance Tonight' produced by Eric Matthew. So I told Arthur Russell who I'd met at the Gallery. I told Arthur this story. A couple of nights later, Arthur comes back and says, 'We've written a song.'

So we wrote some more words to it, and there's a whole other part, another verse, that you won't have heard. So one night at the Loft, there's this back room we used, and Arthur brings his guitar and plays these songs. I said, 'Look I can get money for this.'

So Mel Cheren [of West End Records] gave us money. He gave us $10,000, and then he gave us another. We spent $20,000. We did 14 reels of two-inch tape. We made a two record set. I said to him we were working on the equivalent of the *White Album*. It was all with really fine musicians. David Van Tieghem was on those tapes. Peter Gordon, the sax player. The four Ingram brothers, who I found.

> **❝ Even before singing, there was dancing, just moving your body to rhythms. It's one of the closest things to God. The whole experience was almost religious, we used to feel that way. ❞**

Who sang the vocals?
Three people from the Loft that I picked off the dancefloor. Robert Green, Melvina Woods, Leon McElroy. In one night we laid down 'Is It All Over My Face', 'The Only Usefulness', 'Dawn Sunny', and 'No Heart Free'. Then we cut 'I Wanna Tell You Today', 'The Only Usefulness' and a couple of others. I was supposed to be a partner in Sleeping Bag Records. We met Will Socolov at the Loft. His dad was a lawyer. That's later on. Arthur went along with him, I didn't like Will's dad. Arthur, who was constantly the starving artist, went wherever the money was. And because we had such a poor relationship with Mel Cheren...

....

Why?
Because he never paid us! We never had a royalty statement from West End Records, and that record's been selling all over the world. Whatever. He keeps promising that he'll give me my tapes back. Then he was going to make us partners in the new West End, me, Kent Nix and all these guys that he fucked over all of these years. He's got 'Love Dancing Part 2' and 'Pop Your Funk'. Actually, 'Go Bang' and all those sessions are the Loose Joints band. That's why Loose Joints is so enduring though, because that shit's all live. It was made like jazz. It's some of the great dance music of all time. It was cut in the studio with good musicians; it wasn't structured, it wasn't planned. I wanted to be John Hammond, which is another reason I sought out Arthur, because Arthur was recorded by John Hammond.

CBS's John Hammond [legendary A&R man]
Yeah. John loved him, I've got a couple of reel-to-reel tapes with John talking to Arthur and everything. Arthur taught Allen Ginsberg how to play guitar. And Allen was a friend of John Hammond. He was playing with Ernie Brooks of the Modern Lovers, all those guys. Arthur used to think David Byrne stole his style from him. Arthur played on Laurie Anderson records, Philip Glass. He's been the greatest thing I've known in my life. Even more so than the Loft. He had this energy and the beauty of his music: the strength, the tenderness, the visuals. He was an abstract painter, really.

What do you think the legacy is that you've left as a DJ?
I wrote this thing in the early '70s for [disco fanzine] *Mastermix* that basically said that discotheques were going to become the temples of the '80s. They'll replace religion. You stay at the party all night; and that's how you get your religious training: from the spiritual aspects of music. The spiritual aspect of music was very important to us. 'What's Going On' [by Marvin Gaye], that was political. So much politics in music, and we were very committed to it. We knew that some people were just coming up and they were getting their education from what we were doing. That they weren't going to church, they weren't going to a temple. They were learning from us. All of us thought that dancing was the first form of expression. Even before singing, there was dancing, just moving your body to rhythms. And then we found our voice. It's one of the closest things to God. There was never a fight at the Loft, or any club I played in. The whole experience was almost religious, we used to feel that way.

© DJhistory.com

STEVE D'ACQUISTO SELECTED DISCOGRAPHY

PHILLLY CREAM – Motown Review (producer)
LOOSE JOINTS – Is It All Over Your Face? (producer)
LOOSE JOINTS – Pop Your Funk (producer)
LOOSE JOINTS – Tell You Today (producer)
ARTHUR RUSSELL – In The Light Of A Miracle (producer)
BILLY NICHOLLS – Give Your Body Up To The Music (producer)
SANDY MERCER – Play With Me (remixer)
DEPT. OF SUNSHINE – Rude Boys (producer)
DC LARUE – Cathedrals (uncredited production)

RECOMMENDED LISTENING

VARIOUS – Original Soundtrack from the documentary 'Gay Sex In The '70s' (CD only)
VARIOUS – David Mancuso Presents The Loft

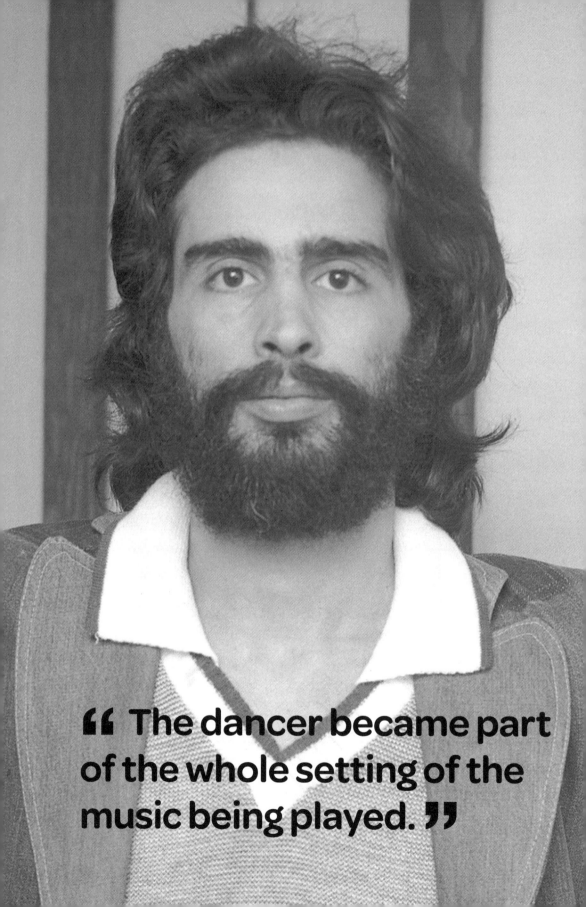

"The dancer became part of the whole setting of the music being played."

David Mancuso
Party messiah

Interviewed by Bill and Frank in New York, October 3, 1998

A softly spoken mystic, it's easy to imagine David Mancuso inspiring devoted followers. Talking to this shy man sipping minestrone in an ancient East Village diner it's harder, however, to picture him as the most influential figure in nightlife history. Mancuso's club, The Loft, lit the fuse on the kind of clubbing we enjoy today and certainly on the places we go to do it. Its importance lies in what it was not. The Loft was the antithesis of the '60s jet-set nightclubs that preceded it. It wasn't commercially motivated, it was in a private apartment, no alcohol was served and beyond having a friend who danced there, there were no restrictions on who could join. Instead, it was here that the notion of dancefloor inclusivity blossomed into life, to be copied, consciously or not, by almost every nightclub that followed, and all this at the same time as the era's musical soup was bubbling into what would become disco.

Mancuso discovered and championed scores of classic dance records, he inspired a whole generation of DJs, he completely raised the game as far as club sound reproduction is concerned, and most enduringly he took nightclubs from places for elitist chit-chat to somewhere where music was the focus. Enthralled by the communal and spiritual power of music, David Mancuso has devoted his life to creating the transcendent dancefloor experience.

Give us some biographical details.
Born October 20th 1944 in Utica, New York state. I came to New York just as I was turning 18, during the Cuban missile crisis. I had a very strange upbringing. My mother had some difficulties when I was born so I was in an orphanage. Which I don't like to talk about. A kid I used to play with – I didn't remember him, but he remembered me... Way down the line, 20 years down the line, he wants to finds the nun that changed his diapers. We were infants. There were 18 kids. That nun handled 18 of us. It took him about five or six years to track me down. Eventually he found me. He went to New York for our first meeting. He had found the nun, Sister Alicia. And she had pictures: he brings these pictures that she had took of us since we were about four, five years old.

She would get this record changer and a stack of 45s on a great big radiogram and some juice from the refrigerator. There were these little tables where all the kids used to sit around. I don't know if you've ever seen my invitations, but there's all these kids sitting around the table. She would find *any* excuse to have a party. So I have a feeling that part of my influence, why it's communal, why I do it the way I wanna do it: it has to be do with back then.

What's her name?
Sister Alicia... 'I Want To Thank You'.

Is she still alive?
Yeah.

Did she ever come to one of your parties?
No, she's very old now, but I believe that she would enjoy it. I was 36 and she was 35 years

older when I made contact with her. She's a religious lady. What do I do? So I called her Christmas week. I said, 'Sister Alicia.' She knew I was going to call, my friend had told her I would. 'Do you remember me, Sister Alicia?' Then I heard her voice, and very softly she says, 'I remember you like it was yesterday.'

When did you start throwing parties?
I started on a regular basis in 1970, on Valentine's. But I was doing parties from '68, '67. I had found a loft in downtown New York. I'd lived there a few years and one day I decided to throw a couple of parties and they turned out good.

Where did you get the sound system from?
I had it before. I was always into audio. I'd been building it up since I was a kid. Literally. I used to have those old radios that had a 12-inch woofer. Short-wave, everything.

And when did you start amassing your record collection?
From when I was a teenager. From 14 years old, I was very fortunate enough to be around people who liked music and knew music and liked to party, so, at the age of 15 I was already living on my own. I had more freedom than most kids.

What we're you doing?
Shining shoes. In Utica. Me and my best friend decided to go to New York City. We came on Labor Day weekend, September, I was here three days and I was awed by it. Thirty-one days later, I was back. I met some people, so I could stay with them. And I did. I had $2.15 in my pocket. Got a job. And New York has been very good to me.

What did you do to make your way the first few years?
I did a lot of waiting. I worked in a publishing company. Then I worked in a health food store. Then I became a personnel manager for a restaurant chain. That was my last nine-to-five. There wasn't much difference between collecting unemployment and being a disc jockey. So that would be up until about 1967. I travelled a lot. I stayed in Chiswick for three months, but I haven't been back recently.

> ❝ I went through the '60s, the psychedelic movement, civil rights. As far as the music goes, I'm a very communal minded person. ❞

What was the inspiration for the first parties?
I used to love to go out dancing at parties. Also I went through the '60s, with the whole psychedelic movement, the civil rights thing. As far as the music goes, I'm a very communal minded person.

I had certain things I wanted to do to send a message, and it had more to do with social progress, because you had mixed economical groups. Now that I was very interested in. You had people from all sorts of different backgrounds, cultures, whatever. No matter how much money you had in your pocket or how much you didn't have in your pocket, when you paid that $3, paid that $5, to get in, you got the same as anybody else. Overall it was the break-even. I just wanted to break even.

I met a lot of people. And they all interacted with each other. Anyway, I knew a lot of different people, a lot of different names. I had this space. 647 Broadway. Now what I used to do were these rent parties: 50¢. And, if you use that money to pay your rent in New York, it's legal. So you could have a party in your apartment so long as you don't break the law or anything. You can actually charge admission. I was in a commercial loft. There were sprinklers and everything. So I decided to do rent parties. I sent out 36 invitations. But it took about six months to get going.

How often were you doing them?

Every two weeks. It would start at midnight. And in those days the bars were only open till 3am and if anything was open after three, you could be pretty sure it was gambling, or liquor and I wasn't into any of that. I didn't want to be into any of that. I wanted it to be private. And the loft was also were I slept, where I dreamt, everything. But after six months it started really taking off.

What was the composition of the people who were coming?
Everybody. Gay, straight, bi, black, Asian. There were a lot of different people and they were my friends. And I keep my friends, so they brought their friends. You would have really the whole spectrum, and there was never a problem with fighting or anything.

What music were you playing?
In those days Motown, because Motown was the hottest label. And Stax. rhythm and blues. Hendrix, Stones, Doobie Brothers, it was a mix. We decorated it with balloons. Very simple. The vibes were good. It was clean and it doesn't take much to make the place comfortable. After six months, it opened up every week. When you came in, everything was included in the contribution. It was an invitation. You were not a member. It was not a club. I didn't want to be in that category. It meant different things to me. I wanted to keep it as close to a party as possible. It was like $2.50, and for that you'd get your coat checked, food, and the music.

What drinks were there?
We used to squeeze fresh orange juice and organic nuts and raisins. We did it up. Everything was quality. Everyone used to come there: Patti Labelle, Divine, all of them. As people, because everybody that came there was able to relax. And of course you would not get into this space unless you had an invitation.

Who named it The Loft?
The Loft is a given name. That was hippie dippy stuff, like 'What do you call this?' 'Oh call it whatever you want!' So it became a given name. It's sacred to me. I've never used it for commercial purposes as far as promoting it. I remember the first time I got in the media. Little did I realise, I was on the front page of the *New York Times*.

When was that?
'72. Around about '72 and a half, the first place opened up that was similar to what I was doing, and that was the Gallery – actually, Tenth Floor might have been a little bit before that.

The Gallery was Nicky Siano.
Nicky was coming into my place when he was 14 years old. He started going right back to the beginning. He opened his place up on Fridays. Then the Soho opened up, which was Richard Long. Then Reade Street opened. And that became the Garage. Then the Gallery moved. The Flamingo was right around the corner from me. But basically, my whole situation grew from very close friends of mine and stayed that way. So I wasn't really bothered that those places opened. I was glad they were doing it.

Why were you glad?
Because there are eight million people here. A lot of people want to party. It's a positive thing. And the more people partying the better it is. The more you can get through the week. There were enough people around. Why not? It was like the civil rights movement: the more people you had marching the better it was.

How did the music develop; where were you finding records?
Okay, I was in Broadway; left there in 1972 and went to Soho [99 Prince Street]. Soho, nothing was happening there at that time. I went from 500 square feet to 10,000 square feet. Two floors. I didn't want to do it. At that time there were already a lot of places going on. The city was scrutinising and seeing if we had exits and all that stuff. I always had exits, but at my first place I didn't have what they call a Certificate of Occupancy. There was a lot of stuff in a music magazine, and so the city became a lot more aware of what was going on.

David Mancuso

And you go to know some of the city's leading DJs.
I went to Sanctuary. I liked Francis [Grasso]. Francis was good. It started with Steve D'Acquisto. He worked at – I don't know which came first out of Tambourine or Tamburlaine – but anyway he worked at one. And I liked the way he was doing things. So I walk over to him and say, 'You know, I really like the music. Look, I have this place it's downtown. It's my place, it's a private party. Do you wanna bring a friend?' And he did. That's how I met Michael Cappello and Francis.

So you were going out to other clubs?
I was more into parties. I wasn't too much into clubs. I didn't even start drinking until I was 26. When I did go it would be purely for the music, not anything else. But mostly, I went to rent parties and house parties, that was my thing.

It was a time when DJs were becoming important
When the disc jockey got two turntables and was in a club using recorded music a new menu was started because the dancer was part of the performance. You'd have your live musicians, where you'd have go some place and listen to them play. Or your home, where you'd sit on your couch and listen to records. Well, the disc jockeys got into between this and created something new... where the dancer became part of the whole setting of the music being played. That was the difference. You'd have one foot on the dancefloor and one in the booth. The disc jockey was able to create this whole new format: between the performance and the listener.

Were you mixing records to achieve this?
It wasn't mixing, this was before. I used to make tapes and I'd put a sound effect. When I threw a couple of parties, in '67, '68, I did a tape. I didn't know about mixers then. I didn't even know if they existed. So just as a record ended, I would put a sound effect right there. I'd take these from sound effects albums. So there was always a continuance.

Did you record these on reel-to-reel?
Yeah. I wanted the music to be continued, with no blank spots, but I also wanted to play the records as the musician intended. I got into mixing for a while and then I stopped, because the mixes were all about the musicians. You try to have a flow, but I really try not to disturb the recording – from the beginning to the end. [When I used to mix records] I would go from one record to another, chopping them up. And then one day I just said to myself, what am I doing? It's like having a painting on the wall. I shouldn't change the colours, I should leave as it was intended, let it stand on its own.

You're gearing up for your mix, and your intentions are good, but you end up being judged by the mix rather than the record. And the record should be more important than the mix! The mix is two or three seconds, and the musician makes the mix. Maybe that's too philosophical. I thought we were getting further away from the message of the music. Personally, I keep coming back to, 'Let the song play'. I don't think that mixing is wrong. But once in a while let the song be its own self. Just like your own child that you raised, at some point, that child has to stand on its own.

You're saying the DJ shouldn't try to be an artist?
No, no, no. I'm not saying that! The disc jockey *is* an artist. He is shedding his ego. If he's gaining an ego he's not going to be an artist, and he's not going to be there for music. He's going to be gone. I believe there's a third ear. And you look at the big picture: you're painting something. I'm not saying the other ideas are not valid, but this is what I found after many, many years.

What style of music were you playing after you stopped mixing?
Same thing, but I just stopped mixing. I played from the beginning to the end. With mixing it became like the audience were preferring this mix over that. But don't worry about that. The music came before the word; music is a gift from the gods.

Without a mixer, the sound signal can be purer too.
Yes, for sonic purposes, too, because the less equipment you have down the line, the more open the sound is. So that was another consideration.

You took incredible efforts over your sound system
About my 11th year. About '79. That's when I started getting into heavy equipment. I started getting $3,000 cartridges. I wanted it to be as pure as it can be. Music has a life energy.

Klipschorns [loudspeakers] were built by a man that simply followed fundamentals of physics. If you do that, you will come up with an amplifier that also follows the fundamentals of physics. Follow the Yellow Brick Road, so to speak. You put one watt in, you get one dB back. Once that fluctuates, the music is affected. So anything that I used was mathematically correct.

Take a turntable. A turntable is only a thing that turns around. Has nothing to do with the foundation. Has nothing to do with the arm. Commercial turntables come with all this stuff, but basically the foundation is one piece. Richard Long did the bass, the foundation of it. The bass develops a lot of energy. And if the slightest goes back in, the sound's no longer clean. There will be a couple of percent, believe me. Once you hear it you can't go back.

> **❝ I started getting into heavy equipment, $3,000 cartridges. I wanted it to be as pure as it can be. Music has a life energy. ❞**

How heavy is it?
It's very heavy [laughter]. The point is that it's also in the tone arm, it's also in the cartridge. The cartridge is made in onyx; the case is in stone. Room acoustics is rule number one. Concert hall level is 80dB. If you're listening to more than 90dB sound levels for more than 45 minutes straight, you start to develop ear fatigue.

You started the first record pool, tell us about that.
When I was at Prince Street, while I was fixing it up, that was the birth of the first record pool. There were 26, 27 disc jockeys; we all knew each other. And we always connected about records, very natural. This is how we bonded. In those days it was very much like that: you shared.

The idea was to straighten out how DJs received records from the labels?
Right. There was a meeting once in Club Hollywood: the record companies and disc jockeys got together for the first time. It was a total disaster. And so I asked Steve D'Acquisto to make an announcement, 'cos I don't like doing any of that stuff. I'm a background person, a behind-the-camera person. And Steve likes to talk, so... I invited the disc jockeys back to my place. I knew a lot of them. And at that meeting I proposed the pool.

Judy Weinstein [who went on to found the Def Mix production company] helped run the pool; how did you meet her?
She worked for me. I met her through Vince Aletti [leading disco diarist]. The Loft and the Record Pool were at the same place. Vince Aletti knew someone who needed some work.

How did you know Vince?
When we started the pool, we had these meetings. The record companies would come and some media people would come. I believe that's how I met Vince. He would take a tiny record player and invite me around to his house to listen to records. He would listen to records on this and then write about them. The guy's incredible.

So how did the pool work?
The disc jockeys would get the records and they'd fill out a feedback sheet; they would give the personal reaction and the floor reaction. And that information, based on the test pressings, would go back to the record company and they would adjust certain things or whatever. There was a lot of communication and organisation and *sanity* regarding the whole scene.

And the record companies saw they could gain advantage from it as well?
Well, the *accountants* in the record companies, not the promoters. They had different days you could go get records. For record companies it came to the bottom line: it was cheaper to send the records to a central distributor, through the pool. So the music got out.

We didn't get involved in the problems between individual disc jockeys or record companies. We did not distribute a record unless we could give it to everybody. We had up to 275 disc jockeys. I mean there's not as many clubs about today, but if you had even 50 clubs, the amount of people that would come dancing is the same as a small radio station. So records were starting to break before radio.

❝ The condition that disc jockeys used to work in... I know some that got electrocuted. That's why we started the Record Pool. ❞

The companies liked it because they were getting better feedback?
Twenty-seven disc jockeys. We designed all that. We just wanted to collaborate. Little did we know we were working out a system between the record companies and the disc jockeys. It was the only pool for a long time. And it worked very well. But the accountants saw it being cheaper. A lot of record promoters thought that they would lose their jobs through this, because they thought they wouldn't be needed any more. Not true.

When did you form the pool?
1974. We'd list 10 records, not in any order, and we'd have a library section so we'd list everything there. Another thing is, the condition that disc jockeys used to work in; I know some that got electrocuted. Someone else could come in and they'd lose their job, and this and that. That's how, when we started the Record Pool, it helped change a lot of things.

So informally it was a bit like a union?
Yeah, a natural brothers and sisters union. Absolutely. Keep those politics too.

How much did the DJs pay you?
It was non-profit.

Did the record companies try and pervert the system and hype records?
They really couldn't. We needed each other's cooperation, and we wanted to give it to them because we loved the music. Like Denise Chapman, she used to work with Salsoul, but she used to hang out. A lot of people hung out together. A lot of these people came to my place on Broadway, before they ever got into the business.

I suppose there were so many good records by the mid-'70s they were falling on your lap?
The music that came out when we had the Record Pool was in existence was the best. The music between '75 and '80. Most of the classics are right there. A slow week would be three to five good records. I mean *really* good shit. Now, it's difficult.

How did you find records like Barrabas?
Barrabas 'Woman' – I brought that one in. I was in Amsterdam looking for some records. I found it. I'd never, never heard it, I just liked the information that was on it; it looked interesting – I would buy records like that. I brought it back, checked it out and there were a couple of good things on it. So I called the record company. And they went by the box and it was $2.70, postage, record everything. So I ordered them, and I'd sell them to other disc jockeys.

Where else did you go looking for records?
London. I would go there for the vinyl. Better pressings. 1972 I was in Chiswick. I knew this family, and I was very close to them. The mother had cancer and he took his whole family and I was invited over.

What was The Choice?
I took a sabbatical. I got this building on 3rd St. between [Avenues] D & C in 1982. That was when Alphabet City was the worst neighbourhood in the entire United States. I knew some of the grandmothers. I shut down. It was so bad over there. Business was tough. I wanted to rent out the Loft. It was in the loft, but it was called Choice. So I decided to just take a break. It was very hard. People were dying, dropping like flies – a lot of friends. I decided to rent the place to someone, and took some time off and stay at my house up near Woodstock for about two years. 1980 was when I bought the building, '84 was when I moved over there, '88 was when I maybe rented it out, '90 was when I went back.

When was it open?
From '88 to '90 I think. Almost two years.

You influenced so many people: DJs who became famous, people who started labels, they got their inspiration from the Loft.
There were two things. There were a lot of people I directly helped in finding locations or connecting them with things or whatever.

But a lot of people were also inspired to copy the idea of the Loft, its spirit, the way it operated. Who do you think took the idea and got it right; who are you most proud of?
Nicky Siano was probably the closest. I won't say I have objections, but there are things I wouldn't have done that he's done. But he was the closest. He didn't sell membership cards. He was private. Basically, they had food...
    The one thing the Loft did do was set a standard: getting your money's worth. A decent sound system: I wanna hear the music. Once you hear the sound system that means you're getting ear damage, ear fatigue. So you want music, not the system. Same with lighting. You don't want fatigue. Anyway, Nicky was about the closest. But hey: do it anyway you wanna. Some of them deviated much more. Others, like the Garage. Larry, I got him his first job.

And you fought hard to establish the legal right to throw your kind of parties. You were taken to court over it weren't you?
No, I took them. They closed me down once when I was on Broadway, because it was an unlicensed cabaret. The case was thrown out. When I went over to Prince Street, and I had two floors, more space, I didn't want that to happen. This had to be established. So in 1974 I had the longest hearing in the history of consumer affairs. I *was not* a cabaret, because I did not sell food and drink directly or indirectly to the public. I wanted to establish that. The city was so upset. They were holding me up about paying rent. This established for all the places that had opened up as long as you were private. That was in '74. Had to be theend of September. I have a copy of the ruling if you want it.
    I actually had a very good track record with the police department and fire department. Never a police problem. Never a fire or safety problem. The fireman and policemen would come to hang out. I thought that was great for everybody.

Which records have you most enjoyed playing there over the years?
'Starchild' [by Level 42], 'Love Is The Message' [by MFSB], 'Walking In Rhythm' by Blackbyrds, Ashford & Simpson 'Stay Free', 'Roots'...

What do you think made your parties so special?
It was the times. And if drugs were being used by people, they were more in the recreational side. At first everybody was together. Then it became like the same with any business. They gotta start splitting up the nights between straight, gay, black, white. Slowly, but surely...

When did that start to happen?
I don't want to mention a place. I really don't. Let's say around '79, '80.

Isn't that a natural process, that people would want to party with similar people?
Yeah, but why take a place that's already open and people are together and start splitting it up?

So people implemented things like door policies?
The Garage did it. I respected Michael [Brody] and everything, but they started splitting

things. When you filled out an application it was, 'Are you straight or are you gay?' And that was the night you got a card for. If you can mix the economic groups of people together then you have social progress.

How do you see the role of the DJ?
Maybe not by his choice, but on the negative side he could be like a short-order cook. But certainly as a humble person, who sheds their ego and respects music and is there to keep the flow going, to participate. It is a unique situation. It is a very humbling experience.

But it's also a controlling experience?
What do you mean? Talk to me.

In terms of controlling the party.
This has been my experience. I'm sure you can relate to this. When the music's starting to flow... I got into the sound being more open and that sonic trail, the artist, the nuances, everything. It's very important. There's lot of music in those nuances.

I would take requests. And play the requests in the order that they were given to me, because I wanted people to participate. Then what started to happen was someone would ask, 'David could you play...?' And I just happened to have it in my hand. I'm ready to push the button. You get to a psychic level. You know what I mean. You can't explain it. There's a higher level, a higher power. Not preaching or anything, this is about music.

❝ Sometimes for minutes, sometimes for hours. You just feel good. You have your life energy raised. ❞

Is this about oneness on the dancefloor?
It can happen.

Any notable occasions you remember?
Yeah, many times, but I can't say... sometimes it happens. Sometimes for minutes, sometimes for hours. You just feel good. You have your life energy raised. I can't have mine raised unless yours is raised. And vice versa. But each one of us has a role. It's all about music.

What is the ideal relationship between you and the people on the dancefloor?
That we all play in the same band. All characters in the same play.

Can you say what was the best night?
Each party I have learnt something one way or another, especially in the early '70s. A lot of music was anti-war music; a lot of music had to do with the economical situation, it had a message about the people, or about romance and about this. I can't categorise individual parties and say one was better than the other. Some parties are more intense than others, but I've always come away feeling better about the world, better about myself, better about people; I always felt something good from it.

If you go to the hot springs you'll always come back feeling better. Maybe some days more than others, because maybe you didn't need it as much, but it's always cleansing.

LOFT 100

BARRABAS – Woman

CENTRAL LINE – Walking Into Sunshine

CODE 718 – Equinox

CROWN HEIGHTS AFFAIR – Say A Prayer For Two

BLACK RASCALS – Keeping My Mind

MANU DIBANGO – Soul Makossa

DINOSAUR L – Go Bang!

D TRAIN – Keep On

JOE GIBBS – Chapter 3

EDDY GRANT – Living On The Frontline

JOHNNY HAMMOND – Los Conquistadores Chocolates

BRASS CONSTRUCTION – Music Makes You Feel Like Dancing

JAMES BROWN – Give It Up And Turn It Loose

ASHFORD & SIMPSON – Stay Free

DOUBLE EXPOSURE – My Love Is Free

EASY GOING – Baby I Love You

FINGERS INC – Mystery Of Love

FIRST CHOICE – Doctor Love

FORRRCE – Keep On Dancing

THE GAP BAND – Yearning For Your Love

WAR – City Country City

FRED WESLEY – House Party

THE WHISPERS – And The Beat Goes On

LENNY WHITE – Fancy Dancer

DAVID WILLIAMS – Come On Down Boogie People

WINNERS – Get Ready For The Future

EDGAR WINTER – Above & Beyond

JAH WOBBLE, HOLGER CZUKAY, JAKI LIEBEZEIT – How Much Are They?

IDRIS MUHAMMAD – Could Heaven Ever Be Like This

NICODEMUS – Boneman Connection

NIGHTLIFE UNLIMITED – The Love Is In You (No. 2)

NUYORICAN SOUL – Nervous Track

ODYSSEY – Inside Out

RISCO CONNECTION – Ain't No Stopping Us Now

DEMIS ROUSSOS – L.O.V.E. Got A Hold On Me

SANDEE – Notice Me

BUNNY SIGLER – By The Way You Dance

SLICK – Space Bass

LONNIE LISTON SMITH – Expansions

SOFT HOUSE COMPANY – A Little Piano

THE O'JAYS – Message In Our Music

BABATUNDE OLATUNJI – Jingo-Bah

LARRY SPINOZA – So Good

SYLVESTER – Over And Over

THE O'JAYS – Love Train

ONE WAY WITH AL HUDSON – Music

THE ORB – Little Fluffy Clouds

OZO – Anambra

PATTI LABELLE – The Spirit's In It

LIL LOUIS – Music Saved My Life

ATMOSFEAR – Dancing In Outer Space

DAMON HARRIS – It's Music

EDNAH HOLT – Serious Sirius Space Party

DON RAY – Standing In The Rain

BABE RUTH – The Mexican

LUNA – I Wanna Be Free

RINDER & LEWIS – Lust

DEEP VIBES – A Brand New Day

ALFREDO DE LA FE – My Favourite Things

MFSB – Love Is The Message

ANDWELLA – Hold On To Your Mind

DOROTHY MORRISON – Rain

ARCHIE BELL & THE DRELLS – Let's Groove

BLACKBYRDS – Walking In Rhythm

CANDIDO – Thousand Finger Man

CASSIO – Baby Love

NICK STRAKER BAND – A Little Bit Of Jazz

SUN PALACE – Rude Movements

VAN MORRISON – Astral Weeks

THIRD WORLD – Now That We Found Love

TAMIKO JONES – Can't Live Without Your Love

HOLY GHOST – Walk On Air (Sun & Moon mix)

FRANK HOOKER & THE POSITIVE PEOPLE – This Feeling

INSTANT HOUSE – Lost Horizons

KAT MANDU – Don't Stop Keep On

EDDIE KENDRICKS – Girl You Need A Change Of Mind

GLADYS KNIGHT – Friendship Train

BO KOOL – Money No Love

DEXTER WANSEL – Life On Mars

EARTH WIND & FIRE – The Way Of The World

PAL JOEY – Spend The Night

MICHAEL WYCOFF – Diamond Real

IAN DURY – Spasticus Autisticus

POWERLINE – Double Journey

PLEASURE – Take A Chance

GEORGE DUKE – Brazilian Love Affair

THE TRAMMPS – Where The Happy People Go

280 WEST FEATURING DIAMOND TEMPLE – Love's Masquerade

TEN CITY – Devotion

MAN FRIDAY – Love Honey Love Heartache

JANICE MCCLAIN – Smack Dab In The Middle

CHUCK MANGIONE WITH HAMILTON PHILHARMONIC – Land Of Make Believe

RITA MARLEY – One Draw

HAROLD MELVIN & THE BLUENOTES – Wake Up Everybody

MIROSLAV VITOUS – New York City

LAMONT DOZIER – Going Back To My Roots

PSYCHOTROPIC – Only For The Headstrong

RESONANCE – Yellow Train

STEVIE WONDER – All I Do

PRINCE – Sexy Dancer

Compiled by David Mancuso & DJ Cosmo

RECOMMENDED LISTENING

VARIOUS – David Mancuso Presents The Loft

VARIOUS – David Mancuso Presents The Loft Vol. 2

"Essentially, I was trying to make hit records longer."

Tom Moulton
Father of remixing

Interviewed by Bill in New York, September 30, 1998

It's still hard to square the tall, handsome and impeccably dressed man before us as the inventor of the modern remix. He looks more like an executive from a multinational advertising agency than the visionary who transformed dance music's landscape. During the '70s Tom Moulton singlehandedly developed the disco remix, reasoning that extended versions of singles were precisely what was missing from the DJ's armoury. He tested his theory with a painstakingly crafted reel-to-reel which seguéd the hits of the moment into an inescapable whole. After this set Fire Island ablaze, he applied the theory to vinyl. In doing this he created scores of disco classics and secured the phrase 'A TOM MOULTON MIX' a unique place in DJs' hearts.

He then gave us the 12-inch single on which to play those classics. Before this, most dance singles were halved across two sides of a 7-inch. Forced to stamp a test pressing onto an album-sized blank, Moulton inadvertantly created the DJ's most enduring format. Tom also wrote the influential disco column in *Billboard* for much of the era.

The walls of his apartment are stacked with neatly arrayed shelving, all filled with perfectly catalogued DAT tapes, cassettes and CDs, the product of a lifetime spent working with music. The interview is occasionally interrupted by Tom leaping up to play yet another incredible unreleased mix of the Trammps or BT Express.

Tell me a little about where you were born and grew up.
I grew up in Schenectady in upstate New York. I moved to Philadelphia. After two years, I struck out on my own and moved to California. Fudged my age a little bit, because you could there. You could get a driver's license without a birth certificate.

When did you start collecting records?
Before you were born. The first record I asked my mother to buy me was 'One O'clock Jump' by Count Basie. I was five years old. That was 1945.

A 78?
Oh absolutely. It was ten-inch 78, one of the big ones.

Were you into collecting straight away?
Absolutely. I always felt like a music sponge. Things that seemed to turn me on, seemed to turn most people on. I couldn't tell you what it was, but if I liked it I would play it over and over again. In a way almost trying to rid myself of this attraction to it because it was so overwhelming, like I could never get enough of it. And it would only increase the intensity of attraction for it. I realised then the power that music had.

Originally, I wanted to be a disc jockey; I wanted to be someone who exposed people to this music. I felt it was my calling, being in a position to play this for people. I envisioned myself as being the next Alan Freed. Then the payola scandal hit and that kind of killed it forever wanting to be on radio. It upset me, the idea of taking money for playing a record. I thought they did it because they loved it. Even when I became a promotion man I never had to pay anyone for playing a record. My respect would have gone so far down for them. I'm doing a job, and you're doing a job to play records, so you do your job and I'll do mine, that's how I looked at it.

I got a job working as an assistant buyer for Seeburg, the jukebox people. I had such a good time doing that, because I used to buy all the 45s for them and I felt like Mr. Powerful. You would buy these records and in those days, we were effectively a one-stop, even though we made jukeboxes. We wanted our jukebox operators to be able to go to one place for their records rather than this distributor and that distributor. They paid 3¢ more for a record, but they had the convenience of a one-stop.

In those days, when a record would come out, I'd listen it, and the first crack you would have at it, if you ordered 500, you would get 150 free. This is before it was on radio, so you were taking a chance, because you couldn't return it either. I was very lucky, because most things I picked were very successful. Two of the things I picked – and I almost lost my job over it, because I took 1,000 of each one – one was 'I Fall To Pieces' by Patsy Cline. It bombed: nothing happened. Then, of course, about seven months later it hit and we had it, when no-one else did. The other song was 'Mother In Law' by a guy named Ernie K. Doe. That was another record that was a sleeper then became a number one record. But that was almost a year later.

> ❝ **It was mostly 45s that were three minutes long. It was a shame the records weren't longer so people could really start getting off.** ❞

There was a guy down there called Madman Muntz, who used to make Muntz TV. He bought the patent on an eight-track tape machine, where really it was two-track, but played four different tracks in stereo. This was in late '59. And he had this idea to have stereo in the car and of course stereo was just starting then. I was fascinated with the sound: two ears, two speakers. It just opened up so many possibilities for music, and anything that would help people turn on to music I wanted to be a part of. So I started working for them. They were in it for the money and I was into educating people. After I worked for Madman Muntz, I worked for King as a promotion man.

James Brown's label?
That's the one. I loved it. Freddy King was starting to get very popular out in San José, which is why he made that record 'San José'. It was a tribute to the city. 'Hideaway' was a pop record there, the white kids loved Freddy King. Elsewhere it was Freddy Who?

Who else was on the roster?
James Brown, Little Willie John, Hank Ballard and the Midniters, Nina Simone. We were doin' all right. Then there was an illness in the family, so I moved back east. I had the idea to go back to retail. One weekend I went to Boston and I was in this store and all these people were asking for different records and this clerk kept saying, 'Just a moment I'll look it up for you.'

So I said, 'Listen, do you mind, this is ridiculous. What else you looking for?'

I was spitting the answers out left, right and centre. Finally the guy says, 'You really know your music don't you. Do you wanna job?'

So I went to work for Crays in Boston. I took the job on the condition that if a job came up in promotion I could take it. I worked for Crays for a couple of years, but I was getting angry at the way it was going because I was ordering stereo things and they would have a fit. The owner would say, why are you buying this crap? We sell 95 percent mono and 5 percent stereo. I said, OK, we'll change that. But it cost more: $3.98 for stereo, $2.98 for mono. People would come for a record and I'd say, 'Mono or stereo?'

They'd say, 'Which is cheaper?'

So I'd say, 'Excuse me? You have two speakers. Let me show you: this is what you're getting. Here's the mono. Now listen to this one.'

'Oh my god it sounds so alive,' they'd say.

'Ah-ah, spending $2.98 is like having nothing, so by spending one dollar more you can have the whole world.'

It was in *Billboard* that year how one store had reversed the trend from mono to stereo. This was in the early '60s. Finally we got this new record on a label called Motown and it was the Supremes. It was called 'Where Did Our Love Go'. I ordered it in stereo and the distributor said you're going to have to take a box. Fred had a fit. I played it and naturally we sold it. People didn't know, but they wanted to learn.

Then I got a job at RCA in '66, '67. I was gung-ho for stereo. I was a salesman for the company. I had the account for Jordan Marsh, the big downtown dept. store in Boston. And they had the stereograms right next to the record department, so I asked if they could play this album on their stereos and put a card on it saying what was playing. Well, we sold 7,000 copies in a month. It was by Hugo Montenegro The Music From *A Fistful of Dollars And For A Few Dollars More*. I just felt I was meant to get into promotion.

Eventually though, I got completely out of the business because of all the bullshit. Then somebody invited me out to Fire Island, and I'd heard so many negative things about Fire Island. I thought it was all drug dealers, low-lifes. I thought Sodom and Gomorrah here we go. But I went. This was 1971. But it was fascinating. I was a model, so I was using my body instead of my brain. The guy who was at the same agency as me owned a place called the Botel out in Fire Island and they had thing called a tea dance where people would come back from the beach and they would dance. I was so fascinated, especially seeing all these white people dancing to black music. I thought, 'Hey, these are my kind of people.' It was nothing to do with the colour, it was just good soul music they were dancing to.

I was so thrilled. I asked John, 'You have a tape machine? I have this idea. Would you play it if I did it?' The reason I wanted to make this tape was I was watching people dance and, at that time, it was mostly 45s that were three minutes long. They'd really start to get off on it and all of a sudden another song would come in on top of it and the people would be... And he was a terrible DJ, too. It was a shame that the records weren't longer so people could really start getting off. I came home and tried it and it took forever.

What were you doing, just recording 45s on reel-to-reel?

Yeah, but I had sound-on-sound so I would back it up. In other words I would get the record playing out and bring the other record in on the over-hang, just for two or three seconds, so they would flow. I watched how people got off the floor and they always got off the floor on the one. Now that's interesting. Let me try and start a record that's before the one. So that way, if they go to leave, they're already dancing to the next record. That was the hardest. I made one side of 45 minutes and it took me 80 hours. I thought this is ridiculous.

Where you splicing tape?

No, I was doing it with sound-on-sound. It was an interesting concept. I didn't want people going what the hell's going on here? So I had a vari-speed on my turntable and I would listen to the next record I was going to do and I would mark it with a pen, then I would work out where the record playing would have to go and I'd mark that with the pen and gradually speed it up. I think it might have been an Empire turntable.

So what happened was I gave him the tape. And he said, 'Don't give up your day job.' I was so hurt. I was absolutely destroyed by this. I was waiting by the dock to get the boat back to Long Island. So this guy, who was the doorman at the next club, says, 'What's the matter you look like you've lost your best friend?'

I said, 'It's worse than that.' I told him the story.

He said, 'Don't worry that guy's a jerk anyway. You're probably doing something he can't do, so why would he give you a start? Look, I don't have much to do with it, but my partner is the one who handles the music. If you want I'll take the tape and let him hear it.'

Anyway, about two weeks later I get a phone call on a Friday. 'Oh they hate it,' he says.

'They don't know the music.' But he calls me soon after at 1.30 in the morning and I can't hear him because the music's so loud. He says, 'They're going crazy over your tape!' So he calls me the next day and says, 'Can you make me a tape every week?'

'In your dreams,' I say.

'I'll give you $500 if you can make a tape.'

'It has nothing to do with the money,' I say, 'it's the amount of hours.'

'Can you give us one for Memorial Day? An hour and a half. Then can you give us one 4th July? And Labor Day?

So I said, 'Okay.'

So I went scrambling round to some of the record companies asking them if they had any instrumentals, stuff like that, because I've gotta make these things longer or I'm never gonna be able to pull this off. A couple of people gave me some tracks and I was able to make them longer and I did them in such a way that they thought, wow it's like a long version of this particular song. Then someone asked me to try and do the same in a studio. So I went in there, despite not knowing anything about studios, and told 'em what I wanted and went over to Bellsound and they said, 'Oh, it's too long to make into a 45.'

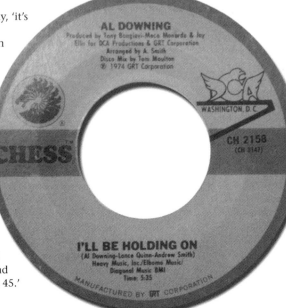

I said, 'What's wrong, what's the problem?'

'There's too much low-end in it'

'Is that all?'

So we went back to the studio and re-EQ'd everything, so it apparently had a lot of low-end, but it didn't. And that was 'Do It Till You're Satisfied' on Scepter. That was 1973.

Wasn't Mel Cheren at Scepter?
Yeah, that's how I met Mel. I was introduced to him through May James who was National Promotion Director and Mel was in A&R. That's how it started.

How much did you increase it by?
5.35, that magic number, from three minutes. They hated it. The band absolutely hated it. We had a station here called WBLS and they played the long version, not the short version. And it became a number one record and they were on *Soul Train*. And Don Cornelius interviewed the band and asked them about the length: 'Oh yeah, that's the way we recorded it.' I was so fucking mad.

Any time I did a record after that, I said I want to talk to the producer first. I want him to know exactly what I'm doing so there are no problems. Essentially, I was trying to make hit records longer. If I heard a record that had some magic on it, I would want to get my hands on it. Sometimes the people concerned would not even know it was a big record, but I could feel it. I wasn't right all of the time, but a lot of the time I was. It was a big thrill for me, especially when everyone else thought it was a great record. Then they'd get a long version of it and they'd go wow, but I'd always do a short version of it too. I always wanted to make sure that the short version was chopped up from the long version, but it was actually just the opposite.

When was the next time in the studio? Almost immediately?
Yeah. 'Dream World' by Don Downing. That's where I met Tony Bongiovi and Meco Menardo and they were thinking of doing a Gloria Gaynor thing. I had this idea, to make this medley, because the disc jockeys would play it, because then they could go to the bathroom and it would be 18 minutes long; one song straight into another. It would be perfect. Sure enough,

the *Never Can Say...* album came out and that's what it was: three songs all put together ['Honey Bee', 'Never Can Say Goodbye' and 'Reach Out']. And considering it was three two-and-a-half-minute songs, that was quite a feat. I remember sitting in the office and Gloria hearing it and the first thing out of her mouth – I'll never forget it – 'I don't sing much.' I felt so hurt over that.

Every album after that I had to use that same concept, but I had only wanted to do it for her. I liked the idea of working with the same artist, so we would grow together. I had to be careful though, because at this stage people were really starting to make a lot of money and I was just charging my fee plus one point on a record. I wanted everybody to pay the same price and everybody to be able to afford me.

Had you been DJing at any point?
I never was a DJ! This friend of mine Barry Lederer said, but you've played at Sandpiper. And I said, 'But I'm not even a DJ!' It got me. I want to be better than a DJ. I want to capture what I call a suite. Start here, and for 45 minutes I would literally have them. Control them. So you could peel them off the walls by the time that 45 minutes was up. Screaming and yelling. I wanted them to get off on the music like I got off on it.

You did the column in *Billboard* didn't you?
Yeah, but only because who else knew the disco? They contacted me. I didn't want to write about my own records, but they said no. So I would try to be objective but it's almost impossible. But then I would never write anything negative about anything. I was trying to build disco not tear it down.

You mainly worked at Sigma didn't you?
I had Studio A locked-out four nights a week for 10 years straight. Monday, Tuesday, Wednesday, Thursday. I had that studio at night.

How many studios did they have?
Three. Joe Tarsia, who owned Sigma, to me, he's the greatest engineer that ever lived. Bar none. I can't think of anyone who has had more influence on music and putting class into music than Joe. First off he started Cameo-Parkway. He did a lot of 'Expressway To Your Heart' [by Margo Thunder], all the Jerry Butler stuff. All those big hits that Gamble and Huff did, all of them, Joe did. The Spinners, the Delfonics, the Stylistics. It goes on and on. There are so many gold records at Sigma. And he did 'em all. Even on the O'Jay's 'Money', that was his idea: to flip the tape over and use the backward echo. I learned a lot from him. I learned that if you want to do something right, you take your time.

❝ The 7-inch blanks, they were out of them. So he had to give me a 12-inch. And I said, 'Heugh, that's ridiculous.' ❞

What's the story of the 12-inch single?
Well, I take the credit for that. It's a shame because most good things happen by accident. I think most things are created that way. It's a mistake, a negative that turns into a positive. I José Rodriguez, my mastering engineer, ran out of 7-inch blanks. I used to do work at Media Sound on Fridays – that's where we did Gloria Gaynor – and I wanted to have the Trammps record cut. This was the first Trammps record on Atlantic, so I asked Dominic, the mastering engineer if he could do it and it was Friday. He said he couldn't do it. He was going away that weekend.

'Ask me Monday,' he said.
'I gotta get some refs cut.'
He said, 'Well, I can't help you. And I said what about your assistant?'
He said, 'You mean the Puerto Rican sweeper?' I went crazy.

But I said to José, 'Aren't you learning to master?'

'Oh yes.'

'Fine,' I said. 'I'll be the ears, but you make it work.'

'It's called "That's Where The Happy People Go". I want you to cut me ref dubs.' I liked it so much I said, 'I'm gonna do you a big favour. I'm gonna put your name on that record.' I did it mainly because I was so mad at Dominic for calling him a Puerto Rican sweeper. It was such a lousy thing to say. But that wasn't the first 12-inch. The first 12-inch was 'I'll Be Holding On' by Al Downing. It was never commercially available. The 7-inch blanks, they were out of them. So he had to give me a 12-inch. And I said, 'Heugh, that's ridiculous.'

So they said, 'I know what we'll do: we'll spread the grooves and make it louder.'

And of course, when I heard it I almost died. And at that time there only about seven or eight disc jockeys around and I used to see them on Fridays and I would give them acetates.

Who did you take it to?

Oh, let's see. There was Richie Kaczor, David Rodriguez, Steve D'Acquisto, Bobby DJ, Walter Gibbons. A lot of fun back then. And so many of them are dead now. It's sad. Especially because these guys, they all loved music, they really did. They would rather be admired by their peers than be super-successful.

Do you not think that's the same in any profession?

Well, the thing is you want to be successful. What's wrong with being commercially successful. I always wanted disco to appeal to the masses because it's not going to do anything if it only appeals to the select few. But if you can get the masses, then you have power. Why not?

❝ He'd take the microphone: 'Okay, I'm in a bad mood, it's gonna be a down night. So if you wanna go somewhere else, you'd better go now.' ❞

What was your first commercial success?

'Do It Till You're Satisfied'.

What other ones subsequently?

Well, 'Hold Back The Night' by the Trammps. And that was something that was in the can and never came out.

How long had that been around then?

A couple of years. Because I had the idea of coming out with the *Legendary Zing* album. But there was no such thing as a *Legendary Zing* Album, because it never existed. So I had the idea to do this thing. So they gave me a couple of things that were in the can, and 'Hold Back The Night' was one of them. I slowed it down that's why Jimmy sounds so funny. Because it was recorded a lot faster than that.

Did you think it would be a hit straight away?

Oh, the minute I heard it. It was that groove. It just had that groove. Even they were surprised it was such a big hit. That was one of the biggest hits they'd had until, of course, 'Disco Inferno'.

What relationship did you have with DJs?

I liked people who liked what I do. And then some of them wanted to start getting into mixing. So I said, 'Okay, but it's rough, there's a lot to have to learn.' This is my approach to it. You can't let people intimidate you just because they know more than you. But you've gotta go in with a basic idea. You have to have a goal.

Jim Burgess wanted to get involved in mixing. I said, 'Let me see if I can throw anything your way.' I went over to see Rick Stephens at Polydor one day. He played me this song and

I hated it. It was Alicia Bridges' 'I Love The Nightlife'. I hate it to this day. I just said, 'Jim Burgess is the one to mix this.' I was just doing Isaac Hayes ['Moonlight Lovin']. Anyway, Jim got the record and it became a big hit.

Did you go to Infinity? What was it like?
Crazy. Spectacular. I liked the mood of it. Of course, nothing compared to the Garage. People went to Infinity because it was a great place to go. But when you went to the Garage you were the serious party dancer people. One of my favourite places was 12 West, because I loved the DJ there. His name was Jimmy Stuard. Jimmy was really something. We introduced Grace Jones there. But then I realised that they were the only ones who weren't inhibited. Most people hear a new song, they walk off the dancefloor, because they don't wanna be taken some place if they've never been there before. They want to be familiar with it. They're very self-conscious about their dancing. In the gay club, if it's good they wanna move, you know? I guess they trust the DJ.

Do you think it was to do with the restrictions placed on them outside. That this was their territory, so they could relax more?
I never thought of it that way. Well, I noticed that when something became very commercially successful, they moved on. I was more fascinated with the fact that they liked black music, the roots of black music. It just loosens something in you, shakes you up. It's like Walter Gibbons. He played in a black club and he was as white as can be. But when it came to black music he'd give you a run for your money. He's Mr Soul when it comes to deep deep black. He knows his stuff.

At Galaxy 21?
Yeah. It was mainly black. And it was dark. And David Rodriguez, I wish more DJs were like him. He was probably the most aggressive DJ that I've ever known. I think if he were around today, I think music would still be a predominant force. He never let what other people played influence him. He'd take the microphone and say 'Okay, I'm in a bad mood, it's gonna be a down night. So if you wanna go somewhere else, you'd better go now.' This was at a place called the Limelight on Sixth Avenue in the Village. Oh my God.

Time: 5:52

Disco
Remix:
Tom
Moulton

SCE-12395
(SCE-12395BS)

DO IT
('TIL YOU'RE SATISFIED-PART II)
(B. Nichols)
B. T. EXPRESS
Produced by Jeff Lane & Dock Productions
for "O" Productions, Inc. Strings
Arranged by Trade Martin
℗ 1974 Scepter
Records Inc.

At that time there was a song that everybody liked called 'A Date With The Rain' by Eddie Kendricks. And everybody kept saying, 'Play ...Rain, play ...Rain.'

So he said, 'Not till you dance to this.' And he played 'Make This A Happy Home' by Gladys Knight & The Pips, which was a kind of uptempo ballad. Nobody would dance.

'You're gonna hear it all night then.' The owners are banging on the glass. He plays it over and over again. Finally, he says, 'I'm serious. Unless you get up here and dance, this is all you're gonna hear, so you better leave.' So they get up and dance.

And he says, 'Okay, one more time with a little more enthusiasm.' Then he played 15 minutes of these crashing sound effects and all of a sudden you could hear 'the rain... the rain' through the noise. And they started screaming and yelling. It was unbelievable. But David played what he wanted to play when he wanted to play it. He never worried what other people thought.

A few of the guys thought like that. The guys today, 'Oh I can't do this, we need the beats in the beginning; we need the beats here.' You take away all of their creativity. Absolutely. It's like castrating everybody. Fine. But just remember you guys did it to them. By giving them what they want, you're taking away their creativity. How do you think it was for us to play a record and it had no intro? But if you loved it enough, you'd figure out a way to play it. But once you make it easy for everybody, it's just another one of those easy records to get in and out of. You're killing the thing that you want to preserve by making it easy for them.

Do you still keep all of your records?
No. I finally got rid of them. People started stealing them from me, so I gave them to a friend.

You mentioned the Garage earlier on. What are your memories?
The thing I liked about the Garage was that it was really Larry Levan's club. People went there because Larry always managed to put on a good show. He always, but always, delivered a good evening. You never went there thinking, 'Oh it might be a good night, or it might be a bad night.' It was always a good night. He never came out and said it to me, but I believe he always wanted to please the people, to give them a night to remember. But he was very clever, very creative and I think he really cared about the people that came there, he really did. And I can't say that about many guys, because not many people felt like that. Everyone had their club and Larry had his, and Larry never compared himself to anyone else, because you couldn't. Larry always played good music that made you wanna move.

It's like when they had the Studio 54 movie. I said, 'Oh well at least they'll have "I Will Survive" on there.' Oh, no they're not going to put it on. Well, then it can't be about Studio 54 then. I remember when Richie first played that record. It's the B-side of 'Substitute'. Everyone walked off the floor. He kept right on playing and finally turned it over. Became his biggest record. But that was Richie Kaczor. People always try to change history. The minute I think of Richie I always think of that song. He used to spin at a place called Hollywood. Oh, I loved Hollywood. That was on 46th Street. And Le Jardin was where Bobby DJ….

What happened to him?
He died. I used to be so friendly with these guys, but I certainly wasn't into a lot of their lifestyles which were a little beyond my comprehension. A lot of them, these creative little enhancements. I'd gone beyond that, age-wise. People would go around with these things of pills, and they'd be like, 'Do you want some?'

I'd be like, 'Do you think I'm stupid?'

And then I found out that another DJ was selling drugs on the Island. I was really annoyed over that. He said, 'Sometimes I can't make enough money playing.'

I said, 'I know, but how can you sell stuff like that?'

I dunno, it bothered me a great deal.

What's the thing you're most proud of?
I thought if we can make this disco thing work and we can get people to buy a record when it's not actually on the radio, we could influence radio stations so much that they would have to play things. That would be amazing. 'Never Can Say Goodbye' was proof of that. That record was selling 20,000 copies a week in New York and no radio station was playing it.

© DJhistory.com

TOM MOULTON SELECTED DISCOGRAPHY

BT EXPRESS – Do It (Till You're Satisfied) (remixer)
DAWSON SMITH – I Don't Know If I Can Make It (remixer)
AL DOWNING – I'll Be Holding On (remixer)
THE CARSTAIRS – It Really Hurts Me Girl (remixer)
SOUTH SHORE COMMISSION – Free Man (remixer)
GLORIA GAYNOR – Never Can Say Goodbye (remixer)
THE TRAMMPS – That's Where The Happy People Go (remixer)
MELBA MOORE – Make Me Believe In You (remixer)
PEOPLE'S CHOICE – Jam Jam Jam (All Night Long) (remixer)
FANTASTIC FOUR – I Got To Have Your Love (remixer)
THE TRAMMPS – Disco Inferno (remixer)
PAPA JOHN CREACH & THE MIDNIGHT SUN – Joyce (remixer)
GRACE JONES – La Vie En Rose (producer)
FIRST CHOICE – Doctor Love (remixer)
CAMOUFLAGE – You've Got The Power (remixer)
TONY VALOR SOUNDS ORCHESTRA – Love Has Come My Way (producer)
CLAUDJA BARRY – Love For The Sake Of Love (mixer)
EDGAR WINTER – Above & Beyond (Instrumental) (remixer/producer)
SALSOUL ORCHESTRA – 212 North 12th (remixer)
LOLEATTA HOLLOWAY – Love Sensation (remixer)
TJM – I Don't Need No Music (producer)
LOOSE CHANGE – Straight From The Heart (producer)
MFSB – Love Is The Message (remixer)

RECOMMENDED LISTENING

VARIOUS – Disco Gold (vinyl only)
VARIOUS – Disco Gold Vol. 2 (vinyl only)
VARIOUS – A Tom Moulton Mix (CD and vinyl)

" If I saw
the dancefloor
getting out of hand
I'd think, 'Show me
how I can go further.' **"**

Nicky Siano
Wild man of disco

Interviewed by Bill in Brooklyn, October 7, 1998

They were a crazy bunch, those early New York DJs, filling their nights with music and drugs, and burning their days with more of the same. And by most people's reckoning (his own included) Nicky Siano was one of the craziest. A wild, excitable teenager blessed with smarts and ambition and the financial wherewithal to follow his dreams, he took David Mancuso's Loft blueprint and launched it into the public sphere. Siano's Gallery took the same pains with sound and decor, but encouraged a wholly more abandoned atmosphere. Mancuso was inviting you to enter his home, Nicky wanted to take you up up and away.

He was one of the first of the city's DJs to move into production, and as disco progressed he was chosen to fill the booth at the new Studio 54, but a few months later achieved the impressive feat of being fired from this palace of drug-taking for being too strung out. A long period of recovery followed.

Frankie Knuckles and Larry Levan started their club careers at the Gallery, preparing the place for take-off, and it's fair to say Siano was the DJ conduit between Mancuso's family function and the large-scale dance devotions of Levan's Garage and Knuckles' Warehouse. It's intriguing to ponder where Nicky would have taken things if he hadn't passed the baton quite so early. We meet in his Brooklyn apartment where he's generous with his stories and keen to share photos and memorabilia. There's a serenity to the place, but from the animated anecdotes and the twinkle in his eyes, the wildness is still there, waiting for the next night behind the decks.

How did you get into records?
From going out dancing. I met someone in high school who took me to the Village; the first club I ever went to, which was the Firehouse. Immediately, I really dug the music.

How old where you went there?
Fifteen.

What year was that?
Do we have to discuss that? [Laughter] 1970. About a year later, I was dancing around with my brother's girlfriend and she said, 'If you really like dancing you've gotta come to the Loft.' She took me to the Loft and that was it. I was in total awe. I was hooked on the whole experience. The Loft was such a controlled environment, as well as the sound.

Describe it to me.
First of all, I'm not talking about Prince Street, I'm talking about Broadway. It was only 2,000 square feet, with 500 square feet of DJ booth. It was tiny. First of all, the Klipschorns; he put them in a way that they put out the sound and they reflected the sound. So they covered the whole area and exaggerated the sound. His room was perfect to do this with. He used to be on the dancefloor and the lights would go out, there would be these little lamps in the corner and the tweeters would come on and the lamps would go out. It was freaky deaky. I knew I was gay from a very young age, I was going out with men, but I met this girl from

high school and we started going out together. She convinced this club owner to let me play records. It was called the Round Table. I played every night for $15 a night.

Had you started collecting records when you were in high school?
Yeah, I used to drag my girlfriend round the city looking for them. But there was really only one record store that was carrying these records: Colony.

How did you go from being a dancer to playing records?
I wanted to play records more than anything else in the world. I mean I was possessed by it. I had a little hi-fi, and a stereo and I would mix records back and forth between these two separate units. I had to do it. All I could think of was records. I remember I heard 'Rain' by Dorothy Morrison, I could not get it out of my head until I could get it in my hand, but not many record stores had it. I just searched and searched until I found it.

What kind of stuff where you playing at Round Table?
I guess stuff like 'A Little Bit Of Love' by Brenda and the Tabulations, War 'City Country City', 'Girl You Need A Change Of Mind' [by Eddie Kendricks]. Listen, if you remember everything, you really didn't have a good time! [Laughter].

Had you come across some of the other DJs like Steve D'Acquisto and Francis Grasso?
I never came across Francis. And I never heard Steve D'Acquisto play. Steve played at Tamburlaine and Tamburlaine burnt down, Christmas Eve I think, right before I turned 17. I remember we went that night and we watched it burn down, Robin and I. Then we went to a club called the Tambourine, but Steve wasn't playing there; it was Michael Cappello, at least as far as I remember. Now Michael and David Rodriguez, those were the people I'd go hear all the time.

Why were you attracted to those as DJs?
Well you know, Michael was so easy to look at.

I have heard this.
Oh my God. He was so easy to look at. Michael used to go out to dinner with us and he would take a Coke bottle and put the whole fucking thing down his throat. He did that so well. Michael was not a very talkative kind of person, but he was just really good at playing records. One of the things I really remember was that his mixes were really really smooth.

At that time, they had the Thorens – the TT125, not the direct drive. They were really old and were built into a casing which they would float in. I used them at the Gallery because the DJ booth was on the floor and when people jumped up and down the records would skip. It was very hard to cue records though, because they were belt-driven, so if you put your hands on the turntable, it would stop the record. You had to be really light with your touch.

Anyway, they used to speed the records up a little bit to make them more exciting. Neither David nor Michael were into changing the speed of records. They said to me: 'Well, they didn't record it that way, so why should we play it that way?' They had a purist attitude to playing records, which I think people should heed a little bit more.

Michael played at the Limelight which was more of a bar. I dug his music but, you know, everyone basically played the same records back then. It was just how people put them together. Some people would play what I would call a filler record, and then a good record and then a filler record and then a good record... But my style was to link the fillers and let them build and then go into the good ones and just go off, on an hour of good ones until people were screaming so loud they couldn't stand it any more, and then go back. David Rodriguez was more like that. He played at Limelight too. But Michael would peak the crowd.

So he would take it up and down...
No he would take it up and it would stay up, and it would go up and up and up and up, beyond where you'd feel you could go. It was great.

So tell me about David Rodgriguez.
David Rodriguez was the funniest person on earth. He could be very cruel. Sometimes the cruelty got to you. So then she'd take another Tuinal and take it even further. We used to

call the Tuinal gorilla biscuits. I got so mad at him one night. I was playing records. I didn't need to fall on the turntables any more than I already did. Well, she's standing next to me doing ethyl chloride. I don't know whether you know what this stuff is, but they spray it on you, it's like a local anaesthetic; it freezes your skin when you're getting a shot. Anyway, you used to spray it on a rag and stuff it in your mouth and inhale it. You'd get this buzzed out feeling, and you could pass out from it.

So anyway, he's standing there with a rag in his mouth and he's just spraying this shit – you're supposed to spray the rag, put it in your mouth, get a little buzz and try it again. Well, he's got the rag stuffed in his mouth, and he's got the bottle in front of the rag and he's just spraying the rag, and spraying the rag and inhaling. All of a sudden – BOOM! – right on the turntables. Everyone turns and looks at me. You got 600 people all turning around looking at you and I just looked at him: 'You fat fucking bastard!' I pulled him by the hair, threw him on the floor and started kicking him. It was really sad because I was so mad and really I should've been concerned but I wasn't, I was like, 'You did this on purpose you fat fuck!' He cut his head on one of the milk crates in the booth and he had to get three stitches.

❝ My style was to just go off – until people were screaming so loud they couldn't stand it any more. ❞

How was his style?
Honestly, his music didn't move me to craziness, but he is the person who influenced me most. He was the person who came into my booth and said, 'Don't cut off the words, blend it here...' He really stayed with me a lot and he was just a wonderful friend. He really helped me launch my career.

He probably discovered more records than anyone else. He was out there looking for new records all the time and would turn other people onto them. But of the five that he discovered that week, two were really good. He would turn us onto the same five and Michael [Cappello] and I would look at each other and we'd both pick the same two that were good, and then we'd play the same two over and over and really get the crowd going. Now at his night he would play all five and never really left an impression on you, but he took more risks in playing new music than anyone else back then. He was a real innovator.

Is David still alive?
No. He was one of the first people who died of AIDS.

When did you get Gallery going?
My brother and my girlfriend Robin were going to the Loft, and they were like, 'Let's do one of these, because there's only one of them around. And let's open it for a straight crowd, because this one already has a gay crowd.' Coincidentally a friend of ours had just gotten this accident settlement $10,000. So we borrowed $5,000 more and built the Gallery. And then David [Mancuso] went away that summer and immediately people came. Alex Rosner did the sound system. It was awesome from day one. I think Gallery on Mercer Street surpassed anything at that time because of the lighting system. It was like Studio 54 in 1973. We had the simplest lights going, built on three tiers, so it looked like it was going up into the ceiling.

Did you do that yourselves?
My brother is an architectural engineer, so I told him what we wanted and he did it. I designed it and sort of did the structure of the building. And we had an electrician come in and do the wiring. It was really very simple, we had three different light colours on three levels, but they moved up in a triangle. If you looked up, the lighting would go up into the ceiling and that structure itself would be decorated, so you wouldn't see the actual lights, you'd just see the colours.

And you modelled it very much on the Loft?

Yes, but you know David's place was his house and you can't ever recreate that in a club or compare it. Ours was like a more commercial club version of David's, but that feeling and atmosphere was there. I mean when I played a record it was played everywhere. When David played a record, someone heard about it, and then if they played it was… It was more underground and it remained that way, although he had a tremendous influence on a lot of people, including myself.

What crowd did you have?

Unlike a lot of clubs, the Gallery was a place to dance. Although people met there and went home with each other and stuff like that, that's not why they came. There was always acid, that was the big drug. At the old Gallery, it was very intense, because it was much more similar to the Loft, because there was only a very small area. The sound was intense. I remember someone having an epileptic fit one night because they were just driving themself so hard.

After about 15, 20 months, we got closed. All the clubs got closed for having improper fire exits. We moved. We went from a homely, close atmosphere to a club environment. A lot of the clubs were very kind of homey, slapped together places and this really had a hi-tech look. We had all this track lighting at the front area. There was a balcony that overlooked the dancefloor where people would hang out. Again, people did a lot of acid and I was doing a lot of drugs. The opening night was packed; you could not move. 1,500 people.

> **❝ If there was a break on a record, I would extend it back and forth. Or if the beginning was hot I would play the beginning over and over. ❞**

Do you remember any of the great nights at the Gallery?

I think great is an understatement for nights at the Gallery. I think extraordinary. People got really out of control. I mean, there are points when the music was taking people so far out and getting so peaked out, that collectively people would be chanting, 'TURN THIS MOTHERFUCKER OUT.' That started at the Gallery. Can you imagine 700 people doing that? They're blowin' whistles and screaming, 'Yeah yeah yeah yeah!' Then I'd turn the bass horns and the lights would flash and go out and everyone would screeeam so loud you couldn't hear the music for a second. They would be dancing so hard that if you went downstairs you would see the wood floor moving.

What was the soundtrack to the second Gallery?

I remember the songs I played at the opening night: 'What Can You Do For Me?' by Labelle was really really big, 'Love Is The Message' [by MFSB], which was really my theme song; I had been the first one to really work that record. David and Michael had been the first ones with 'TSOP' and then I turned the record over and fell in love with 'Love Is The Message'. I had heard it some place else before, Le Jardin, I think. But then I ran with it.

I was with David Rodriguez and he went up to CBS and it was the CBS Christmas party and LaVerne Perry was our contact there and she played us 'TSOP' and I said, 'Oh, I gotta have this.'

She said, 'Well, I only have one.'

I said, 'LaVerne, honey, we play at two different clubs, you gotta give us two copies.'

Meanwhile, there was another copy sitting right there with her other records. She wouldn't give it up, so we just took the one. We walked off, she went back to the Christmas party and David went back and stole the other one. And then he took this big picture of the Three Degrees off the wall and put it under his jacket and walked out. I mean, it was huge. It had to be eight by six feet! Had it hanging on his wall for years. Yeah, those were big ones at the Gallery: 'Dirty Ol' Man' [by Three Degrees], 'The Love I Lost' [by Harold Melvin and the Bluenotes], 'Brothers Gonna Work It Out' [by Willie Hutch].

....

So you were into the Philly sound?!
I loved the Philly sound, but then everyone did. They made great records. Early Trammps: 'Love Epidemic', 'Zing Went The Strings Of My Heart'.

What would you do with a record?
Well, this whole third turntable thing. I had a dream one night that I was playing 'Girl You Need A Change Of Mind' and then I brought in 'Love Is The Message' and I used to have this jet plane sound effect that I would play on 'Love Is The Message', and I had a dream that I was playing all of these together. So I brought in my turntable from my house and I hooked it up. No-one else was doing stuff like that. I had vision and creativity. There's creativity about the music and then there's creativity in the big picture. You know, noticing the lighting, noticing the decorations, noticing the way the sound sounds, and then taking the music beyond what it is and making it something better.

Did you use two copies of the same record to do your own mixes and things?
Well actually, Richie Kaczor was playing in Hollywood and he did this thing one night with 'Girl You Need A Change Of Mind'. He offset two copies so it was going, 'Girl you need a change, girl you need a change…' It was in perfect time and sync. It was just fabulous, it was incredible. But one of the things I would always do, was if there was a break on a record, I would extend it back and forth. Or if the beginning was hot I would play the beginning over and over, and then bring in the song.

What was the crowd, was it all drawn from people you knew?
Do you know Stephen Burroughs?

No.
Okay. Stephen Burroughs was a fashion designer. Willie Smith, very famous fashion designer. Calvin Klein. I mean these were people who came when they weren't really big. I mean we had at one point Mick Jagger and David Bowie there one night, Patti Labelle. But it wasn't a club that was about celebrity. They were 'off' if they were there that night.
Right. They were looking for a really hot spot to dance and people said go to the Gallery.

I heard a story about you dressing up in the stars and stripes.
The Bicentennial was the first time I did it. It was the Fourth of July and we had a big party and we made this flag of our logo and I dressed up as the Statue of Liberty making these faces as they read the new Declaration of Independence according to the Gallery, where everyone has the right to dance and party as they choose. As we unfolded the flag everyone screamed and all the lights went out and I had this crown on and it lit up. And one of my friends started screaming, 'They're electrocuting him!' She was tripping her tits off and they were like, 'Calm down Monica.'

How long did Gallery go?
Till '77.

And you were there the whole time?
Yeah, I partially owned it. The beginning of 1978 our lease renewal came up and my brother said, 'You know, you are totally strung out on drugs,' – which I was – 'and I feel you're killing yourself and I can't watch this. Are you gonna clean up, or we gonna close the club?' I was an arrogant little drug addict, I just said: 'Close it! I don't give a shit.' And he did. Then I went over to Buttermilk Bottom for a year. I went to Europe and when I came back I had lost my following. Then again, I was still on drugs and still all fucked up.

Tell me about your studio work. You were one of the first DJs to move into the studio.
Well, Kiss Me Again [by Dinosaur]. What other DJ did a record in 1977? No-one. There were no DJs producing or mixing then.

So how did that come about?
Arthur Russell used to come to my club and he came up to me one day and he said, 'We should do a record.' I was like, 'Get the fuck out, leave me alone.' Then I started to think well this is a good idea, and I went into the studio but I didn't know anything, and he basically did everything. By the end I might have worked on a mix more than the recording process.

So what was he looking to get from you?
You know, now that I look back on it, it was just financing! [Laughs] I financed the project. But I think he wanted to get from me, input on creating an exciting dance song.

So it was your knowledge of the dancefloor and how they would react?
Right, right right. And what happened was I ended up really pushing the record, too, and actually this record would have gone much further than it did, had it not been for Ray Caviano who took over all promotions for Atlantic when my record came out. He hated it and it had sold 100,000 copies already. Records today don't sell that but back then they did.

Did that lead to more remixing and production?
Well, they picked up our option on Sire, and this is how drugged out I was, I was sick from drugs so I went to California to recover and meanwhile they're waiting for the next record and I was like, 'What record?' A couple of years passed and I got clean, and that's when I started doing one record after another. That's when I did 'Pick It Up' [by Sofonda C], and all those other records. That's really when I did my major body of work. 'Tiger Stripes'. Honey I have a version of 'Tiger Stripes' [by Felix] that is killer!

Frankie Knuckles and Larry Levan got their start at the Gallery. How did you meet?
Robin came to me and said, 'This guy Frankie wants to work for us.' I said there are 600 people here and we don't have anyone working for us, maybe it's a good idea. And then Frankie came to me one week and said, 'I know this kid. He's a little crazy but he's very talented, could I bring him?' I said, 'Sure.'

That was Larry. I was very close with Larry. We lived together; we were lovers for a while. I just loved him as a person. We would just roll down laughing sometimes. He did the decorations and he worked the lights and we would go on the off nights and play some records. I would tell him what David Rodriguez taught me: don't cut off the lyrics on a song, try to make the tempo match, and so on. I still think the selection is more important than the mix. I don't know where all these people think every record has to match. I think that is the most retarded thing I've heard of.

Why do you think Larry's myth grew so potent?
Do you want me to say the politically correct thing?

No I want you to say the truth. He was very much your protégé, wasn't he?
That's it. You said it. I didn't.

What I didn't realise until recently was that he had the ear of Frankie Crocker, who was looking to him to suggest records he could break on the radio.
And why did that happen? He was the only really successful black DJ. They became friends, I think, because of the race issue. But you know I don't know. You can't do this body of work and not be talented. I mean, just look at his mixes alone: 'Can't Play Around' [by Lace], 'Nothin' Going On But The Rent' [by Gwen Guthrie], 'Is it All Over My Face' [by Loose Joints]… Some of these records are classic forever. Incredible work. There are certain things he did – 'Heartbeat' [by Taana Gardner] – that will live forever. You can't not be talented and do stuff like that.

Did a Garage night ever compare to a night at the Gallery?
I certainly don't think so. I mean it was just a whole different vibe than it was later on. I mean a night at The Gallery, people went insane. They lost their fuckin' minds. I mean there wasn't anything that wasn't off limits. People at the Garage were very controlled…

Really?
Oh yeah. They were screaming but not like Gallery. Larry was a very controlling person. If I saw it getting out of hand on the dancefloor, I would think, 'Oh this is cool, show me how I can go further than this, 'cos this is out of control.' That would scare Larry. He would try to bring it back.

66 Studio 54 fucked the whole thing up. It was about the body, it was about the look, it was about sex. It was so self-centred. 99

How did you first meet Steve Rubell?
First I met him at Enchanted Hellhole.

You mean Enchanted Garden, in Queens?
Yeah. Billy Smith, who was a promotion man at 20th Century Records, invited me out to Enchanted Garden which is in Queen's. But when we get out there, it's got a golf course, and it's beautiful. And the thing was, from there, you could see Manhattan, a great view, and it was wonderful. Steve Rubell comes to the table and introduces himself and says, 'This is my fiancée, Heather.'
I'm like, 'Fiancée! You have a fiancée?'
I was very confused at that point.
Then Steve asks [adopts hilarious Rubell accent]: 'Would you consider playing here?'
'Okay.'
But I asked for $150 a night, when everyone else was getting $75.
So after the evening was over he gave me a lift back home. After that he was at the Gallery every Saturday night. A year later I finally couldn't take travelling out to Queen's every week. They were offering me coke and stuff, but by that stage I wanted heroin. I tell you though, honey, Steve Rubell was no longer straight when I got done with him. That fiancée? Fell to the curb shortly after.
But then he opened Studio 54 which was a total atmosphere. Like the Loft. The thing is they added this other dimension: it was about the body; it was about the look; it was about the drugs; it was about sex. Clubs before that, it wasn't really the raison d'etre. And it fucked the whole thing up. It was so self-centred. All these things on Studio 54 recently, and not one of them has talked about the DJs. Never mentioned Richie Kaczor. I only played there for the three or four months, but I was so strung out on heroin, and I was only playing during the week. Richie took it over at weekends. He was a fabulous DJ. 'I Will Survive'? He

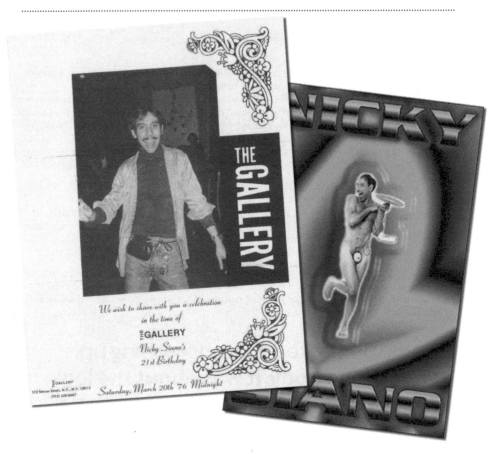

made a hit out of it. One of the reasons Studio happened was because he was so incredible and they never even mention him.

A lot of people said that Studio 54 was kind of the Antichrist...
It could have been me.

But there were good things about it as well, there was a lot of money spent on the lights and the sound...
Steve didn't start out that way. He started out with a very pure motive, he was into the music. But then it all got fucked up. I mean 'cos he started doing a lot of drugs, but I think what fucks you up most is the fact that you set your goals and then you attain everything immediately, and where do you go from there? It's like at 16 I wanted to be a DJ and I wanted to be the best, and at 17 here I am owning my own club and where do you go from there? So the first year was the most fabulous year. That movie is about the *last* year. And it's very dark and kinda...

After it all imploded?
Right. And Studio wasn't like that, it was bright, it was white, in the beginning. You coulda been outside in the sun. It was bright light in there. It wasn't dark. The guns went off and you'd collect confetti, you'd be able to put your hand on the floor like this and pick up an inch-worth of confetti and glitter and everybody had glitter all over their hair and it'd be sticking to people's skin. It was really incredible. But he changed and the club changed.

You had fun there right?
I had a ball. But I only played the first four or five months.

It epitomised everything people didn't like about disco.
It just made everything so commercial and out there.

With the Disco Sucks thing and *Saturday Night Fever* being released and everyone hates Studio because they can't get in. Did it feel like the party was over?
The party *was* over. I mean in the beginning there was no word 'disco'. If you were going to David's you were going to the party, if you were going to Tamburlaine or Limelight you were going to the club. I hate the word 'disco' to this day. Studio 54 opening brought what was an underground incredible party into the mainstream and basically ruined it.

And I guess the sad thing was the party's over and people started dying. That was round about the same time.
The reality of HIV. That's right. And people didn't have time to go out dancing. People were very concerned with taking care of their friends.

Was it something that suddenly came into view?
All within like two years. It was like, 'Oh my God.'

© DJhistory.com

GALLERY 50

FIRST CHOICE – Doctor Love	**DIANA ROSS** – Love Hangover
THE O'JAYS – For The Love Of Money	**ZULEMA** – Giving Up
HAROLD MELVIN & THE BLUENOTES – The Love I Lost	**EDDIE KENDRICKS** – Date With The Rain
HAROLD MELVIN & THE BLUENOTES – Bad Luck	**LABELLE** – What Can I Do For You
	GLORIA SPENCER – I Got It
THE TRAMMPS – Love Epidemic	**TEMPTATIONS** – Law Of The Land
BETTY WRIGHT – Where Is The Love	**TRAFFIC** – Gimme Some Loving (live)
LYNN COLLINS – Think	**DINOSAUR** – Kiss Me Again
SYLVESTER – Mighty Real	**BONNIE BRAMLETT** – Crazy 'Bout My Baby
UNDISPUTED TRUTH – Law Of The Land	**JEANNIE BROWN** – Can't Stop Talking
MARTHA VELEZ – Aggravation	**MARGIE JOSEPH** – Prophecy
WAR – City Country City	**EDDIE KENDRICKS** – Girl You Need A Change Of Mind
LOLEATTA HOLLOWAY – Dreamin'	**JAMES BROWN** – Give It Up And Turn It Loose
SOUTHSHORE COMMISSION – Free Man	**LABELLE** – Messin' With My Mind
THE SUPREMES – Up The Ladder To The Roof	**BARRABAS** – Woman
LOLEATTA HOLLOWAY – We're Getting Stronger	**MFSB** – Love Is The Message
ISLEY BROTHERS – Get Into Something	**DOCTOR BUZZARD'S ORIGINAL SAVANNAH BAND** – Cherchez La Femme
THE JACKSONS – Forever Came Today	**MFSB** – TSOP
LOLEATTA HOLLOWAY – Hit And Run	**MIDNIGHT MOVERS** – Follow The Wind
THE SUPREMES – Let My Heart Do The Walking	**THE B-52'S** – Dance This Mess Around
TEDDY PENDERGRASS – You Can't Hide	**THE B-52'S** – Rock Lobster
DOUBLE EXPOSURE – Ten Percent	**BLUE MAGIC** – Look Me Up
DOUBLE EXPOSURE – My Love Is Free	**MIGHTY CLOUDS OF JOY** – Mighty High
THE TRAMMPS – Disco Party	**DOROTHY MORRISON** – Rain
THE TRAMMPS – That's Where The Happy People Go	**FANTASTIC JOHNNY C** – Waiting For The Rain
REALISTICS – How Can I Forget	Compiled by Nicky Siano

RECOMMENDED LISTENING

VARIOUS – Nicky Siano's Legendary 'The Gallery'

" Because of my musical background, I was always into experimenting. "

François Kevorkian
Disco dubmaster

Interviewed by Bill in Manhattan, October 6, 1998

The man who put the dub into disco. Frenchman François came over to New York to receive drum tuition from the city's leading jazz men, but was soon thrust into the emerging disco scene after securing a gig at Walter Gibbons' club Galaxy 21. François was positioned in the middle of the dancefloor, playing drums to Gibbon's incendiary percussion-heavy disco. People recall that Gibbons played like the hip hop DJs who came later, with lightning live edits, flawlesly executed. François challenged himself to keep up; no doubt this was the perfect education for a career in remixing.

As A&R man at Prelude Records, his mixes became legendary, as he explored the sonic possibilities of the artform, incorporating ideas from Jamaican dub to create something truly unique. Later he opened the mothership of New York recording facilities, Axis Studios, in the building above what was once Studio 54.

After retiring from DJing in the 1980s, François began spinning again in the '90s and – alongside Joe Clausell and Danny Krivit – was responsible for Body & Soul, one of the most successful parties in recent New York history. As if to confound anyone who would pigeonhole him, he can also be heard playing dark nights of tough techno, played with a soul and bounce so often missing from the genre. He still runs his label Wave Music and has a weekly party, Deep Space, in Manhattan. Interviewing François is a detailed journey through a life in dance music. Reflecting the refined structure of his mixes, he tells great stories and delivers them in elegant whole paragraphs.

Give me some biographical details.
I was born in 1954 in Odez in the South of France, very beautiful. I grew up in the suburbs of Paris. Instead of becoming a good college student I decided to do music and join bands. Just get myself involved in situations. I became frustrated with the scene in France and in 1975 I decided to quit, came to New York.

Did you have a purpose in mind when you came here?
Yeah, to play music.

What sort of bands were you into to at that stage?
Jazz-funk. I was into Herbie Hancock, Miles Davis, all the electric period of jazz. They were all being made here, so I thought why why wait for the records to come. There's not a chance in hell that if you stay in France you're gonna get something like that going on. So I came here. I became a student of Tony Williams who was Miles Davis' drummer, but at the time he had his own thing, Tony Williams' Lifetime. I started playing with whatever little band I could get a gig with. Really really rough.

In the process of doing that I got a gig at this club where a DJ was playing. The DJ was Walter Gibbons. I didn't know at the time, but it was a big club, Galaxy 21, and my job was to sit on a little dancefloor with my drums, playing along with the music the whole night. There were a lot of songs I knew, but a lot I didn't. Through that I became involved in the whole early disco scene which was very underground at the time, very downtown, very black, Latino, and quite a bit gay, too.

However much skill and practice and how many hours per day I had to do to be a drummer, it seemed to me that the DJ's job was very basic. And being that I quite liked the music they were playing in those clubs, I figured, well, instead of struggling so hard to be a drummer and make money, why don't I do what these guys do and get some DJ gigs. So I just listened to the radio non-stop, 24-hours a day until I knew every possible song on WBLS. I was already starting to make audition tapes to give to club managers.

What was Walter like as a DJ?
Walter was so fierce, nobody even understood how fierce he was. Nobody saw what he was physically doing with records. He was just outrageous. He had an amazing instinct for drum breaks, creating drama with little bits of records, just like a hip hop DJ, but he was incredibly fast at cutting up records. So smooth and seamless that you couldn't even tell that he was mixing records. You thought the version he played was actually on the record, but in fact he was taking little 10-second pieces on the vinyl with two turntables.

You know the whole thing: his selection, his mixing technique, his pace, sense of drama, sense of excitement. And he was featuring all these big drum breaks that nobody else was really using. He was really into drums. But by the time Walter had turned into that whole religion thing, he had stopped playing a whole section of music and only concentrated on songs with a message. Unfortunately, it mainly fell on deaf ears.

> **❝ However much skill and practice I had to do to be a drummer, it seemed to me that the DJ's job was very basic. I figured, why don't I do what these guys do and get some DJ gigs. ❞**

So you started buying the records by then, too?
Yeah, I only had 30 or 40 but I had enough to make a really good tape. Eventually, I got to stand-in for the DJ at a club called Experiment 4, and his name was Jellybean. He called in sick one day and I was the only person they knew who could possibly do the music and so they said, 'Well, why don't you do it?' So of course I did. From then on I got more gigs at that club, as well as trying to audition at other clubs.

While this was going on I had gotten a situation where I was taking care of someone's house and they had a reel-to-reel tape deck. I started teaching myself how to edit, using scissors and scotch tape. I started making acetates, and dubplates of my own edits. The first one I made was called 'Happy Song' [by Rare Earth] which was just a copy of what Walter used to do live with it. I had made all these little dubplates which were concentrated energy; it was difficult for a DJ to do all these fancy moves all the time all night so my dubplates were really a kind of greatest hits formula. Nobody had these dubplates; they were mine, but later on the guy that was making them ended up wanting to let other DJs have them, because he could see they were a really hot item.

Then I got a job at the Chase Gallery which, by this time, had rented out the Flamingo during the summer of 1977, because when Fire Island starts on Memorial Day the whole white gay population migrates, so the Flamingo closed for the summer. We had this incredible club and just around the corner from us was Nicky Siano's Gallery. From there I decided to audition for a big disco just opening called New York New York. And I got the job doing the main Saturday night party.

Was that one of the Studio 54 rivals?
Well, yeah. It was made by the same people that did Le Jardin, John Addison. It was not really per se a rival when they built it, but it became so because they were obviously vying for the same crowd. I ended up doing sometimes five or six nights a week. It was just a way to make money. I was happy just being able to play records and make money at it rather than a

'straight' job. However, the problem was that it was more the straight, *Saturday Night Fever* circuit. But while all this was happening, we all discovered the Garage, where they were then having 'construction' parties.

When was the first time you were at the Loft?
Either late 1977 or early '78. The first time I ever went to the Loft was when it was on Prince Street. I never went to the Broadway one. I did not know any of the crowd that hung there, like Steve D'Acquisto, Michael Cappello, those people. I really don't consider myself one of those early guys in that sense. Because I was not there. In that sense, I came after the big bang had already occurred in New York.

What was your impression of the Loft the first time you went?
It was so magical, so incredible. However much the Garage was impressive, because of its size and the system and because Larry was so fierce, the Loft had a more delicate quality about it. If you went to the Loft I think you felt that, I better not bother this person because he's having a good time, or he's busy dancing. The Loft was not the kind of place where you'd go to find a date or something. You would feel so awkward. You'd just be there to feel part of the group, to be there with people. Everybody was so into the music and they'd be calling the names of the records, screaming. You could hear people's voices at any time because the music was much lower. It was something more deep and spiritual, touching you not just through the body, but the mind, too. He was also playing stuff that nobody else played.

Such as?
Well, David always had records that he was the only one playing. That was maybe a bit later down the line, but he was always championing Eddy Grant. David was playing Eddy Grant for years before other people caught on to it, including Larry. 'Living On The Frontline', 'Walking On Sunshine', 'Nobody's Got Time', those were David records that you only heard at the Loft. Until a year or two later, when we were like, 'This stuff is incredible.' Although 'Nobody's Got Time' and 'Time Warp' became huge Garage records, I don't think 'Living On The Frontline' ever did. 'Macho City' [by Steve Miller Band] you had to hear at the Loft to understand.

There was a real evolution to the way David played. In the earlier part I remember David playing things were a lot more mainstream, or experimental, or rock. In the later part I think he defined the style as being the more spacey, trippy, movie kind of records. I remember hearing the Bee Gees' 'More Than A Woman' where, I think, it had a special meaning. It was not the same record that was being played on dancefloors uptown. He would play all the big records, whether it was 'Love Is The Message' [by MFSB], but he played it in his own way, which was from beginning to end without mixing. I saw him when he was still mixing. It was really funny, he had little speakers – he didn't use the headphones – and from the turntables, you could heard him cueing up, *ktcheh, ktcheh*. He would never really mix on beat; he had no interest whatsoever. The Loft was a place unto itself, you really had the sense immediately, that this was a place so special.

What were your impressions of the Garage when you went? Was this the first time you'd seen Larry play?
The first time was in the backroom at the 'construction' parties.

But you knew about him already?
No. I was so new to all of this. I was literally propelled into the scene overnight. When you did get to see Larry, especially in the early days, the music was so mad. So intense. He obviously studied from David and Nicky, so he had his pile of Nicky records, he had his pile of David records. He really took from them all these good ideas, and I think really the Garage was just an over-sized version of the Loft. He basically copied the Loft's sound system and made it much bigger, much more powerful. He understood everything about what these places did, but very quickly took it beyond all that into his own domain. I think what Larry did was nothing short of absolutely astounding.

He started to influence people. The Garage became so strong that it became a focal point, and everything started revolving around it. It created gravity, became a planet, and it had other planets gravitating around. There's nothing else that will remotely compare to what the Garage was. Being that it was downtown, black, Latin gay club, a lot of people never even knew it existed. Because that culture, especially in the late seventies, was not really admitting that such things would exist. After *Saturday Night Fever* and the disco backlash, well let's forget about disco, now it's punk; let's go to our little *nyahh nyahh nyahh* guitars and suburban white dreams. But the Garage was forging ahead with a cultural evolution that was so ahead of its time that those people didn't get it. Most people that went there sort of got it, but I remember some people hating the Garage and thinking it was really a bad club.

Why do you think they thought that?
Because it was too much. It was an assault on their senses. It was a kind of tribalistic ritual, that I don't think they could relate to it. They'd never been prepared. If they'd been watching Bob Newhart or Johnny Carson or whatever else they'd been spoon-fed, as Americans, it did not prepare them for that experience.

Do you think it might be to do with a club like that expecting them to invest their intellect into it?
No, I think that it's more that, for you to enjoy these clubs, you have let yourself go to a basic level where you can be free. And not cling on to any preconceived notions. You just have to accept it and see how beautiful the dance is. A lot of people are not ready to do that. They go to a club to be seen, show off their clothes, find a date, get drunk.

You have to remember that a lot of these people that were with the DJs were picking the records. No offence to David, but there were a whole crew of people like Steve D'Acquisto and others, who were really record pickers for David. I'm not privy to how that would happen, but I could see when I went to the Loft that they were showing him, you know, 'Play this. Here's a new record. This is good.' And of course, David was the opposite. After he trusted you, if you brought him a record he would not even listen to it, he would just put it on. So next time if you were gonna bring a record to David, you got so scared. Because if you brought a bad record to the Loft, he would play it. And you would be so embarrassed because everybody knew that it was your record. So nobody would ever dream of bringing a bad record to the Loft. In all fairness, I have to say David DePino told Larry a lot of times, or Judy Weinstein, told Larry what to play. Because they were probably sometimes more up on records than he was. Certainly Judy Weinstein, having the pool, was uniquely placed to get access to music before anybody else got it, including Larry. She would hear about things before they were even made.

Tell me how you got into production with Musique?
I didn't have access to two turntables and a mixer. I had access to one turntable and a tape machine. Because of my musical background, I was always into experimenting, doing a lot of my drum recording with microphones, tape delays and special effects, flanging, phasers etc.

Was this is at home?
Yeah. Then I started doing those edits. I would bring my crazy scotch-taped edits reel to this place called Sunshine Sound, a mastering place, which was in the same building as Strictly Rhythm used to be in. Sunshine Sound was a place where all the DJs would go to get their acetates cut. Bring a tape in mono, and Frank Tremarco, the owner, to make an acetate for $10. This was in 1976.

And were these acetates of people's own edits?
Sometimes, yeah. But he would also sell the best ones. There was one called 'Hollywood Medley' that was very famous at the time; it was like a cut-up of that year's greatest hits. Like 'Stars On 45' [in fact, Stars On 45 just copied those medleys]. Anyway, for whatever reason, he caught on to my stuff. From the first time I brought in that 'Happy Song' he was like, 'Wow! This is cool.' I started doing more of my little edits and he approached me and asked me whether we could make a deal: 'I want to have your stuff; I want to make it available to other DJs, but I'll pay you every time I sell an acetate.' Of course this was not very legal, but it was on such a small scale, it was more to disseminate and propagate the music. So there were certain things I did which became very popular.

Such as?

'Happy Song', which is now a bootleg. I did 'Do What You Wanna Do' by T-Connection; 'Erucu' by Jermaine Jackson, which is an early Walter Gibbons tune. After that, Frank started getting more friendly and he asked me, 'You know, there's this record that's really good that a lot of DJs are asking me about. Why don't you take the record and make an edit of it?' That was Cymande's 'Bra'. So I did a very early edit of 'Bra' which was very basic. Repeated the break three times. That was it.

All these little things were helping me to get into the component parts of the music. I started doing quite elaborate medleys where I would overlay things on top of each other. Almost like pre-sampling. I was working at New York New York non-stop at that stage, and I got to meet these people at Prelude because we were doing the rounds of record labels. I was with this guy Rene Hewitt, and Prelude had just moved into this office and they wanted to play us a couple of tapes. They asked Rene for his comments, then they asked me for mine. 'Thank you very much. Okay, Rene, you can leave, but could you stay?' And on the spot, they offered me a position doing A&R.

> ❝ **My first record becomes a huge hit. They put me in the studio night and day. It would not end. Two or three records a week. It became like an assembly line.** ❞

Who were the people you met?

Marv Schlachter and Stan Hoffman. I started the following week and they put me in the studio to do this record they needed remixing. It was busting out in the New York marketplace: 'In The Bush'. It was my first experience in a proper recording studio, so I would go in the studio, do a listening session and take a tape home of the individual tracks that were on the multi-track. And I would listen to each individual track and make a song map, so by the time I came back to the studio I would know exactly what was on each track.

When I went back in I was with this engineer, Bob Blank, who was quite a talent. He would get all the sounds, then I would tell him what I wanted. So we did a whole pass with different sections and then cut it together to make it work. The record just blew out. I mean, it exploded. Anywhere you would go in the summer of '78, they were playing that fucking record. I brought it to the Garage and Larry loved it. He would not stop playing it. It went gold.

So my first record becomes a huge hit. They put me in the studio night and day. It would not end. I got to pick whatever I wanted. I ended up doing a lot of records for Prelude. Two or three records a week on average. It became like an assembly line. I went to France and started signing records of my own. Things I have to take credit for would be 'Disco Circus' by Martin Circus and I signed this other thing that Tee Scott and Larry used to play forever, called 'Body Music' by the Strikers. The problem was you could not get that record. There were only 100 copies made on Cesaree Records up in Harlem somewhere. You could not get a copy of it.

So for six months that record was getting played at Better Days and the Garage and nobody knew nothing. I finally made a connection with the people that had the record. So I brought it to Marvin and said, 'You've gotta sign this.' And by that time I was really close to Larry so I asked him to come in the studio with me and we did the mix together.

You said in an interview once that Funk Masters was a very influential record for you.

The Champagne Records gold cover remix. That was the first record I heard that used dub techniqes that was not a dub reggae record. I had not been exposed to King Tubby at the time. But when I heard a dance music thing with all those big reverbs, those stops, those crazy effects where a piano comes in, cuts off and decays. To me that was a revelation. Oh, you can do that?

Immediately, I started searching out those sounds. Then I started going in the studio and playing with tape delays and all kinds of crazy regeneration effects. You can hear the result of that – and some heavy-duty editing – with D-Train's 'You're The One For Me (Reprise)', the short one that was only on the album. Because people already knew the original version, when I played that it was like insane. People would go mad at the energy of it. There was that element of wildness that I really think I picked up from Larry. I think I was the first person to play Funk Masters at the Garage and when the remix came out after we'd been playing the original for a while, to me, it was really was mind-blowing. It opened me up to this whole reggae, dub thing.

> ❝ **In early 1990 I decided become a DJ again, so I would call people and say, 'Hey, can I come and DJ at your party?'** ❞

At that time I also got to play in this club AM-PM which was a very very crappy dirty after-hours club which went from three in the morning until 10 or 11. It was all illegal. John Belushi would be there all the time. Billy Idol would be lying on the floor half-drunk. I had to play ska, punk, reggae, disco, electro, whatever. They wanted to hear the Go-Go's mixed with Bob Marley and James Brown. They didn't want to hear a lot of anything. I was not too much into the punk, but I had to play it. It also opened me up to a whole bunch of other records besides the Funk Masters, that had a real different attitude. There were certain dubs that starting coming out in the early '80s, British, rocky kind of bands. Who was it that did a remake of 'Shack Up'?

A Certain Ratio.
Well, those were the bands that I'm talking about. British bands that had a certain punky sound, but were really just recycled disco. The British were obviously much more aware of that dub reggae thing, because there were all these reggae engineers working there. So sometimes some of them would do a B-side version that would have the heavy effects. Then I became aware of Jah Wobble, Public Image. Suddenly, I had all these points of reference that gave me ideas to go into the studio and do things that were a lot more experimental. I started going outside of the mainstream; it gave me very rich matter to draw from. Of course, there's a matter of conscious choice that I'd rather work on an Arthur Russell track than some commercial thing.

By 1982, I'd started taking a lot of freelance things, although sometimes I couldn't get credit for it, because Prelude were starting to get increasingly unhappy with the fact that I was doing these records. I did Yazoo's 'Situation', which was a mega-hit here and I did 'Go Bang' [by Dinosaur L] so it got to the point where it was like, 'Look François, it's okay, but it's cutting into the things we're asking you to do.' So some of them I had to do anonymously. I helped Larry do the edit on 'Is It All Over My Face?' [by Loose Joints], but I never got the credit for it.

Did the outside remixes come as a result of your name credits on Prelude releases?
You've gotta understand that I had the most number ones on the dance chart in 1982: D-Train, Dinosaur L, Strikers, Sharon Redd, Yazoo etc. Everybody in the world was trying to get me. I would suddenly start getting calls from London. Prelude got kind of pissed off when one day CBS, our UK licensee, came up with an album that said *François K's Best Mixes*.

Do you not think that that was fairly significant though, the fact that the label had noticed that it was your mixes that were the selling point?
Honestly, I don't think it would've made any difference to how big a hit D-Train would've had. Maybe I helped some. Maybe in the clubs, some of the versions I did like, say, that special

dub I did of 'Keep On'. That was very much a defining thing where a lot of people copied that stripped down style. But overall, I would like to feel that I'm not so much a part of it.

How do you think house changed things?
Machines. That was the end of live playing. The most significant thing to me about house, you didn't have live musicians any more. You had people programming boxes. So it had a sound of its own. When it came out it was so special, so raw. Primitive, yet very compelling. It was the start of that refining process where, instead of music having all these flourishes, you just had raw, to-the-bone, simplistic, dancefloor-only oriented music. The people that made house music weren't interested in anything other than having the maximum amount of impact on the dancefloor. Retrospectively, I think the more significant thing than house was Detroit.

Why?
Because what was really interesting about Detroit was that they really vibed on all these Kraftwerk and Depeche Mode, early electronic records. And they made it into a sound that was more abstract. Maybe I shouldn't say it's more important. Historically, you might say it has more far reaching implications.

Was that because they were isolated and less driven by the dancefloor?
Yeah, it's possible. I play fewer Detroit records than I play early house. There's always a couple of old house records in my crates. I don't have that many Detroit. But I think that over the course of time, I think it perhaps had a more profound influence on some of the European things. I'm not sure. Commercially, it might be that house is much more successful, because it's spawned all these genres. Also in Europe it's done incredibly well on a pop level. Let me re-phrase that, I think they were equally significant.

How did that alter your approach to studio work?
It didn't really. I quit DJing in 1983. I was producing rock bands like Midnight Oil or working with Mick Jagger. Doing things that had a lot more to do with pop and R&B than to do with hardcore dance music. What did I do that year? 1986 or '87? I mixed 'Solid' which was Ashford and Simpson's biggest hit ever. I was working on Kraftwerk's new album. I didn't have a lot of connections with that stuff. I was more into making music. I had sort of graduated from being a dance remixer to being an at-large kind of guy. I was very aware of 'Jack Your Body' [by Steve Silk Hurley] and 'House Music Anthem' [by Marshall Jefferson]. I was still going out a lot. I went skating every week in Central Park, where they had the sound systems. I was going to the Garage still.

As far as being in the studio, I can't say that I really wanted to copy Chicago house. I was excited to work on a Mick Jagger record because Herbie Hancock and Jeff Beck and Sly & Robbie were playing on it. That, to me, was a lot more meaningful. Working with Kraftwerk was something that was very satisfying. That's where my head was at.

When you eventually started doing house, it was still different, but very you.
What happened was I started DJing again in early 1990. I decided to become a DJ again, so I would call people and say, 'Hey, can I come and DJ at your party?' I started trying to get DJ gigs because I just missed it so much. From there it became a lot more apparent that because I was spending so much time in the clubs it was changing what sound I had when I was in the studio working on records. Quite honestly though, in the early '90s, I didn't get much work at all, mixing or anything at all.

What I was really into in the early '90s was the more experimental end of things: Deee-Lite, LFO, A Guy Called Gerald. The truth is, most of what I was into and doing was not getting signed. But I had Axis Studios which, at its peak, was a major facility with 20 employees. So I said, 'Fuck it, I'll put it out on my own.' Since nobody wanted to release what I liked, I figured I might as well just put it out myself. Also, not only for my own things, but out there listening to things that were really good and not getting signed. I thought it was the right time to start a label. We really haven't had a lot of releases, but we seem to have had a good reaction so far.

With the fragmentation of dance music in the '90s, where do you think that has left DJing as an artform? Is it too easy now?

Well, it's a different vibe. It used to be that we had landscapes, with little hills and gentle valleys, and now they've just taken a bulldozer and made everything flat. Perhaps for the short run that flat landscape suits certain people, because they might have boring lives and desires and listen to very boring music because nobody's inspiring them to have that diversity and that rich textural contrast. I feel that most people have completely misunderstood and taken the easy path to making records. They're never really trying to get in touch with the magical aspect of making music.

How did Body & Soul start?

We started this party in July of 1996. This Englishman John Davis, who was doing a couple of Sunday afternoon parties in London, came over to the States and wanted to do something here. He went to this club Vinyl and they steered him towards using me as the quote unquote main DJ. I told him that if we were going to be doing something then basically I had to be musical director. If it wasn't going to be like that then I really wasn't interested because I had been kicking around the idea of doing a Sunday party myself. So he hired me and then his funding and partnership fell apart in the next week, as we were starting the party. So he asked me if I wanted to be his partner for us to continue the party. I thought that was a reasonable thing to do.

> **❝ An important part of what those early DJs were doing is mixing a lot of things that were not made to be together. ❞**

On the music part, I wanted to explore the possibility of a team effort, where you could be drawing on the talents of various people to present an afternoon's worth of music that was really special. I just decided to call the two people I felt were the most talented people I could think of for doing that in a team context. Meaning that it's not about this guy plays for an hour, that guy plays for an hour. We are actually playing together as a team, at the same time. So we can very easily be in each other's way, but so far it hasn't been like that. We've managed to find a harmonious way to work together.

In essence, we try to provide people with a safe and low-key environment where you could come on a Sunday afternoon and have a party with your friends. More like a family vibe. As far as the music, we want it to be very eclectic and I chose to get Joe Claussell and Danny Krivit as my buddies and we haven't really changed much since we started. The only thing that's changed is from 40 people the first week we started, we now have a big living room; a crowded living room at that. Over the time that the party has existed I think it's started to form its own little culture and now we're providing the soundtrack for a scene that has evolved on its own. Danny, Joe and myself are providing a backdrop for the people who come every week to really express themselves.

The reason I got into this Body & Soul thing is because I wanted to expose people to a variety of music, some of which you would call house, some of which not. And make them peacefully co-exist, and bring a crowd that appreciate that variety. I think there's a whole element of that's lost out there of how grand a party can be. What drama and what can really happen when somebody plays music that is not just a succession of beats, or a collection of this week's new releases, but is actually an inspired reading; it's a message, it's a telling. I can just forget that those things have been. I don't know what your take on it is, but I see today however big that house culture is getting on a commercial level internationally, it's also become very bland, predictable and having very little to do with the original spirit.

I'm fighting to show people right now that you can have a vast variety of music, the majority of the flavour may be this or that, but we put enough of a variety of things that it will create different things. When you go back to the early roots of what those people, those pioneers like David Mancuso, where there was a message, where there was a conscious purpose to playing songs together.

Where is that Garage today? At least in New York. Where is it in London? I feel an important part of what those early DJs were doing is mixing a lot of things that were not made to be together. That was the magic of what they were doing. They were able to pick all these quirky little pop records. All these funny B-side instrumentals. All those early electronic experiments. And all those rock records that really didn't even know they were funky. The DJs put these things together and made it into something that was like creating a new world.

I specifically remember an incident at the Garage when Larry decided to play a movie at the end of the night. He played *Altered States*. What're you gonnna do? There's 2,500 people there and you suddenly play *Altered States*. That's the kind of freedom that I think people need to know exists.

It's interesting that, some of these places like the Loft and the Garage, or some of the people, Like David Mancuso and Walter Gibbons, are becoming icons. And people who never even knew them or saw them, are suddenly admiring them. Obviously there is a significance to all this. It's taken a very long time for some of this to surface, but you can see how strong, dense and rich it was, because it's finally getting understood.

© DJhistory.com

FRANÇOIS K SELECTED DISCOGRAPHY

MUSIQUE – In The Bush (remixer)

SHARON REDD – Can You Handle It? (remixer)

D-TRAIN – You're The One For Me (Reprise) (remixer)

RAFAEL CAMERON – Boogie's Gonna Get Ya (Instrumental) (remixer)

THE STRIKERS – Body Music (remixer)

GUY CUEVAS – Obssession (remixer)

JAH WOBBLE, THE EDGE, HOLGER CZUKAY – Snake Charmer (co-writer/producer)

D-TRAIN – D-Train (Dub) (remixer)

YAZOO – Situation (remixer)

WIDE BOY AWAKE – Set Fighter (producer)

WUF TICKET – The Key (remixer)

KRAFTWERK – Tour De France (remixer)

ASHFORD & SIMPSON – Solid (remixer)

FLASH & THE PAN – Midnight Man (remixer)

DINOSAUR L – Go Bang #5 (remixer)

TERENCE TRENT D'ARBY – Wishing Well (remixer)

FRANÇOIS K – FK-EP (producer)

FLOPPY SOUNDS – Ultrasong (remixer)

MALAWI ROCKS FT. DIHANNE MOORE – Something To Smile About (François K Dub) (remixer)

HERBEST MOON – Blow Your Body (remixer)

RECOMMENDED LISTENING

Various – Prelude's Greatest Hits (vinyl only)

François K – Essential Mix (DJ mix) (CD only)

Various – Deep Space NYC Vol. 1 (DJ mix) (CD only)

François K – Masterpiece (DJ mix) (CD only)

> **I said let me put a couple of these records together, that got breaks in them. Place went berserk.**

Kool Herc
Father of hip hop

Interviewed by Frank in the Bronx, September 30, 1998

Given what the world created from his unique party style of DJing, Clive Campbell, aka DJ Kool Herc is a truly mythic figure. By stringing a series of funk breaks together back to back, rather than playing the records in full, he was the DJ who gave birth to hip hop. His other masterstroke was to play for young kids rather than their parents, tapping in to the moves of the era's teenage breakdancers. Born in Trenchtown, Herc came to the US bringing memories of Jamaican sound system culture to bear on a west Bronx bubbling with energy.

Herc arrives in a beat-up black Lincoln Town Car that looks like a Brooklyn dollar cab. His passenger Rodney Cee, now missing a few front teeth but once one of Herc's rap crew, is waiting for a ride to Harlem. Herc walks back from the payphone, he's huge, maybe six foot eight and has trouble squeezing his legs in under the steering wheel. Almost right away he talks about how he never got either recognition or money from his innovations. His accent still has a lilt of Jamaica. Perhaps he should be a little more publicity friendly; today few people even know he's alive. He argues with this, then agrees. Driving up the West Side Highway, through Harlem and then up Jerome Avenue in the Bronx, the interview turns into a mystery tour of the clubs he rocked in his youth. Curiously though, the first thing on his mind is how drum and bass style dancing keeps you from getting nasty with the ladies.

Not all that jumpin' around, hoppin' around. I can't fuck with it. The closest I can come to it would be the bounce. I hate to see a good piece of ass and I can't get near it. My music, I keep the freak alive with me. I would dance with four or five different girls in one record. Till I find that motherfucker and I spin that ass around on me. But you know what? I hear undertones in that music. I hear some of my music.

Because it's breakbeats, fast breakbeats.
There it is! Exactly. Exactly, you see. I should be around it, to where I can put my spin on it.

You should try and work with some of these guys.
I would like to. I could stay there [in the UK] a good fuckin' six months man. With some shows lined up so I'm payin' my own way. I got crazy shit man. Nobody would fuck with me.

There's a lot of people that would work with you but they don't know you're around.
I know. Queen Latifah, when I met her, she said, 'I heard you died.'

You did do some work with the Chemical Brothers.
I'm on their album, but they muffled my shit on there. But it's me. I was up in England. I was on the Tim Westwood show, and he was acting all funny.

What year did you come to New York?
I came here in '67. I was 13.

So you remember your time in Jamaica?
Oh yeah, Very well. I remember Jamaican independence. I remember when the Queen Mother came. I remember when Emperor Haile Salassie came there.

How was that?

Lovely, lovely. All the rastas came out of the hills. They never seen so much rastas in all their fuckin' life in Jamaica. Camped out, ran on the tarmac. Met the plane. When Selassie came to the plane window he turned back in and started cryin'. He didn't know people was worshipping him like that.

How did he deal with it?

He tried his best. He didn't speak too much English either.

Where did you live in Jamaica?

I was young, my first neighbourhood I live in is Trenchtown. Bob Marley used to live there. He used to live on First Street. I lived on Second Street around by a theatre called the Ambassador Theatre. Right now they say grass grows in the streets there.

Do you go back there?

I haven't been back in years. My father died and it took something out of me.

He was still in Jamaica?

No he came here but he was going back and forth. He caught a seizure in the water and people didn't rescue him out of the water.

What did he used to do?

Top notch mechanic. In Jamaica used to work in this Newport West, fixed the high lifts, the fork lifts. When he came here he started to work at Clarks equipment company, out in Queens.

So do you remember the sound systems out in Jamaica?

Yeah. There was a dancehall near where I lived, up in Franklyn town. We used to be playing at marbles and riding our skateboards, used to see the guys bringing the big boxes inside of the handcarts. And before that a guy used to put up watercolour signs on lightposts, let people know there's going to be a dance coming. And the whole yard would be concrete, and there'd be a high fence. So you can't see in.

Which were the sounds that played where you were?

I didn't know the name of the sound system. I wasn't too much into it. But this guy named George. Used to call him King George or Big George, used to bring his set there.

Do you remember any of the parties in particular?

I couldn't get in. Couldn't get in. I was 10, 11 years old.

They don't let kids in?

Nah nah. It's a liquor thing. And guys burning weed there and shit. If I was 17, 18, I would have definitely been up in it.

So what are the kids doing? Hanging out?

Hanging Out. We on our skateboards, skating round, you know, and you saw the little gangster kids, and they knew who's who from the gangs, the bad bwoys. And they see all the big reputation people come through. We're little kids, but their reputation, precedes them. So the dance would bring them out. And we sit on the side and watch, 'Oh shit, that's such and such.' Little did I know that would be a big influence on me.

Did you ever think you'd end up doing that?

No. But when I got here I see a lot of abandoned cars and TVs. And I set up all in it and I take out the speakers and make my own little boxes for my room. Yeah, you know and it just started to progress from there.

So you were making your own equipment?

Yeah, my own little boxes. I start to get involved more with a working lifestyle. At the time people couldn't understand what I was saying 'cos I had a heavy Jamaican accent. I was on the 'Yeh man, Yeh man.' And they was places called Murphy Projects, which is like a recreation room where they used to give parties once a month. Right by the Cross Bronx Expressway. About a block off Third Avenue.

These were parties you used to go to?
Yeah, go to see how the kids dance, see how they talked.

What were the parties like?
They were playing contemporary stuff. Kool and The Gang, Isley Brothers stuff.

So what year is that?
We talking about say '69. 1969.

When did you start to get involved?
I started to get involved in it right after my house got burnt down. And I was going to parties back then, see. A place called The Puzzle. That was the first Bronx disco. Right on 161st St up near the train station there. This was the first disco I used to party at, called The Puzzle.

" People was dancing, but they wasn't calling it B-boying. There was just the break, and people would go off. "

Who was the DJ?
Never saw him. They was in a room. Used to have me, guys like Phase II, Stay High, Sweet Duke, Lionel 163, all the early graffiti writers used to come through here. This is where we used to meet up and party at: The Puzzle and The Tunnel. That was back – say '69, '70. Then years later, down the block from it, this club right here, was called Disco Fever. Disco Fever used to be right here on 167th and Jerome.

That was where it was? Now it's a shoe store. Who DJed at Disco Fever?
Right there. Junebug and a guy named Sweet G.

What happened to those guys?
Junebug got killed. He was murdered. After that, a guy named Starchild, had the contract of playing up in there. I played up there once, for Junebug's birthday.

So back then you still weren't playing?
I was dancin', I was partying. I was partying. Right around '70…

That was when B-boying was starting!
Yeah, people was dancing, but they wasn't calling it B-boying. There was just the break, and people would go off. The term B-boying came in after I started to play, and I called them B-boys. Guys used to just breakdance, used to break it down.

When did you start playing. What made you start playing records?
This guy John Brown used to play at The Tunnel. Used to play music and I'm dancing with this girl trying to get my shit off, and he used to fuck up. And the whole party, they be like, 'Y'ahhh, what the fuck is that…? Why you took it off there? The shit was about to explode. I was about to bust a nut'. You know. And the girl be like, 'Damn, what the fuck is wrong?' And I'm hearing his mistakes and I'm griping too. 'Cos he's fucking my groove up.

The DJ was taking the song off at the wrong place?
Yeah, yeah, you know. So that stayed in my head. You know, I'm a dance person. I like to party. I used to come home and my whole clothes was soaking wet. I had to tell my mother… 'Where you going with my towel?' And I be, 'Ma, It gets like that up in there!' Sweat Box. Down.

That was what the atmosphere was like, Everyone just getting down?
Partying partying.

What were the clubs like inside?
Huge. Probably gonna hold a good 4-500 hundred people.

Decorations?

Not too much. Not too much disco lights. All they had was a strobe light, and the little exit lights where you come in from the door. It's dark! Not too dark. It's light but it was a low-key light.

When did you start playing?

My stink started to kick up in '71. When I started playing is say 1970, late '70, early '71. That's when the gangs rolled in, the gangs popped up and them. Start fucking people up, going to parties, start robbin' them, fuckin' with their girls and shit.

That wasn't happening before then?

No.

> ❝ **After I who have entered through this door, and certain places such as the Executive Playhouse should be known as a car park... So it is, baby!** ❞

How come that started happening?

Gangs man, they need a place to belong. See what I'm sayin. Punks get into gangs to be a part of something. Some people just ain't shit without being in a crowd. Some guys in the gang are serious about their shit. This is the place called The Executive Playhouse. Years later I played here.

This empty lot?

This empty lot. As I was saying [he delivers this as a booming pronouncement]: After I who have entered through this door and certain places such as the Executive Playhouse should be known as a car park... So it is, baby! After I who have entered through this door, DJ Kool Herc, no-one else shall enter, certain places like the Hevalo, should remain a car lot, so it is baby!

That's how it is. This is Jerome Avenue. Right here off the Cross Bronx Expressway at Mount Eden, this was the Executive Playhouse. This was the spot that gave me a lot of playing time when I was first started playing a room.

This is where you first played?

No. This ain't where I first played.

Where was that?

Over on Sedgwick Avenue.

You remember how it happened?

Yeah. Oh yeah. My sister had a Youth Corps job and she was going back to school and she wanted her some clothes money, she wanted to invest some of her money on more money and she gave a party. And she asked me to play the music. And I was there into my graffiti work, and that's where I graduated from the walls to the turntables.

And you'd been buying records anyway?

Yeah, I had records. I had records.

And how was the night, Do you remember?

Lovely Lovely. Charged 25¢ for girls, 50¢ for fellas, 50¢ for sodas, 75¢ for franks. And beer, beer was a dollar.

And what did she buy with it?

She bought clothes. She went back to school fly.

So you got a taste of it.
Oh yeah.

You loved it.
Oh yeah. This is me at the helm now. I had the attitude of the dancefloor behind the turntables. Come up from the peoples' choice.

Because you're a dancer.
Exactly. You know.

Where were you doing parties?
Recreation room. Back in the recreation room. Till I got too big. Then, up the block.

Where was the recreation room?
1520 Sedgwick Avenue. It was for people in the building, downstairs, for anybody having a birthday party, wedding reception, tenant meeting and all that. You could rent it out for $25.

Kool Herc

How long did you do those parties.
Off and on. It wasn't an everyday thing. It wasn't an every weekend thing, They weren't having it. Once a month or once every two months.

And what are you doing the rest of the time?
Going to school. Going to school.

1970 you were in highschool?
Coming into high school.

So you're real young to be DJing
Oh yeah, oh yeah.

So how were you playing back then. You said you were pissed off with the way other DJs treated the records?
I would give people what I know they wanted to hear. I'd give it to 'em. And introducing them to new music. At the same time playing some slow music for a while. A lot of guys like to get their shit on. I'm a guy that plays slow music. I don't give a fuck how hard the party's rockin', I'll slow it down. I have my shit in stages. I play music in stages.

What were your big records back then?
My big record back then, and nobody had it then, was James Brown, 'Give It Up And Turnit A Loose'. And a couple of records I used to play from the other clubs and as it went on I got 'The Mexican' [by Babe Ruth], I got 'Bongo Rock' [by Incredible Bongo Band], you name them, 'It's Just Begun' [by Jimmy Castor Bunch]. They used to rock that at the Tunnel and The Puzzle.
    Then I gave a block party, and we couldn't come back to the recreation room. So I found a place over here called the Twilight Zone. This was my first place of mass production. Giving parties. Away from the recreation room, was right here on Jerome Avenue, between Tremont and Burnside. The Twilight Zone.

And what was that like?
Lovely. I used to show fights up in there. I had a super-8 projector, and I'd show fights and little movies. And up the block was a place called Soulsville, but they changed the name to the Hevalo. And that was an established club. That club gave me my first break of playing week after week. 'Cos Twilight Zone I only could rent it once in a while.
    [Herc parks the car again and walks into an open doorway. He climbs up some rickety stairs, with metal plates holding the beat-up wood together. It's a factory where 'no habla Ingles' Spanish guys are putting new covers on stained old mattresses. Mattresses old and 'new' are stacked to the ceiling.] ...the Zodiac

This was a club? The Zodiac?
Right, yeah. [A nostalgic Herc asks permission from the owner to look around] Who the boss? Hi, how you doing sir. I used to play upstairs many years ago as a club. [The lady says some Spanish… Bossman shakes his head. She translates: 'He says it's just a store upstairs.'] We just want to look. [more Spanish: 'For what?'] I used to be the DJ many years ago. [She translates and it's okay.]

Some ghosts in here then?
Some ghosts gonna be up here right. [Smoochy Puerto Rican music plays, Herc says to one of the mattress-workers:] A long time ago I used to play music in here. Habla Ingles? This was a club, man.

Where was the booth?
You can't see it, it was in the back. This was the dancefloor.

And now every mattress in New York is here.
This was it. [Back in the street he points out all the clubs in spitting distance of each other.]

This whole street must have been rocking!
This block, Jerome Avenue. This is Herc Avenue really. I dominated this. This, this was the Hevalo. Now it's a car park.

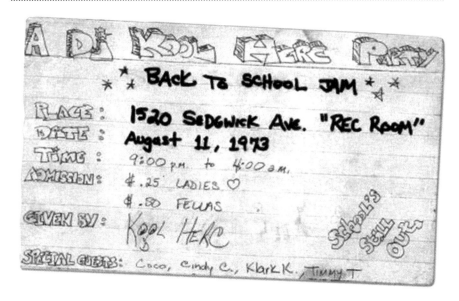

What year did you start playing here?
The good old year here was '75, '76.

When did you start?
'74, '75. I was still doing my shit down here, and then late '74, late '74 and '75 I started playing between here and the Executive Playhouse. I got off the train with my girlfriend to see a sign 'Under New Management' I said shit, let's find what's going on. So I went in I said 'I'm a DJ and I want to play up in here.' And they got a guy used to call himself the Amazing Bert. This guy had some monster stuff. He had good equipment, but he had no skills. I had skills but I had no equipment. But he disappeared and I started buying his equipment.

Back then a DJ brought his own sound equipment to a club?
Yeah. They used to have bands. Around when I started was when the elimination of bands started. Why give a band $600 if you could give a guy $150? You would have to pay seven guys and seven guys might want $100 a head. And how much they gonna drink? All of that. So they called me and I was just building my equipment but they didn't know I had a reputation. I already got experience for playing for kids; now I'm playing for adults.

It was really different?
Oh yeah.

What would you play for the kids?
Most of the James Brown, Jimmy Castor, they would... [he's dancing breaker style in the street] ...you're not gonna have 35, 40 year-old people doing that. Whole different rotation. So I'm playing for them and rockin' their ass. Some bands still used to come up in there now, and I'd play intermission, in the break. But when they didn't have a band I used to play all night.

Then this place burnt down and I started giving parties back over here, at The Twilight Zone. And every time I would play out somewhere else I would come back and I'd bought another piece of the guy's equipment. And it was top-notch shit.

So you bought all this guy's equipment?
I'm building my shit there. I'm rolling with the big Mac. The big Mac, that cost like say $1600. A McIntosh amplifier, a 2300 Mac, the biggest there is, the top of the line. He had a GLI mixer, he had the disco fours, and he had not one McIntosh 2300, he had two of them. And he had two Voice of the Theaters. This system sounded like a band. People used to come just to hear the sound, they didn't give a fuck what he was playing. What was coming through. It was crisp, you was hearing it. You could be on the Expressway and be hearing this shit.

Kool Herc

What turntables did you use?
The Thorens was still top of the line but I didn't like the Thorens turntable. The Technics was just coming out. My model, the 1100A just came out. So I went Technic. I went 1100A. But that turntable, they stopped making it. It wasn't that it was no good, just too expensive. So they pulled it off and put something more durable, and inexpensive with the 1200 shit. I don't fuck with the 1200s. I still got my 1100As, and I wish they would bring them back.

What's the difference?
They got a higher pitch. So spinning back is more easier for me. And weight.

So you'd been doing parties all over the place, and you started to get a name for yourself.
Oh yes. We running this fucking Bronx. You couldn't throw a party on my night. I had guys had to change their dates if they found out I'm throwing a party on the same night.

What year is this?
I'm at the height right now, '75, '76. You can't fuck with us. You can't, you just got to deal with us.

When did you start playing the breaks?
Different people come there and dance to different types of music. I'm catering to each and every set of people there. Well the break thing happened because I was seeing everybody on the sidelines waiting for particular breaks in the records.

People used to do that?
Yeah. People used to wait. I'm observing them. I wasn't just thinking about my technical shit. I'm watching the crowd. Seeing who's up in my place, watching if there's a argument that could escalate into a fight. I gotta see if things running smooth. I said let me put a couple of these records together, that got breaks in them. I did it. *boom bom-bom-bom.* I try to make it sound like a record. Place went berserk. Loved it.

What was the record?
'Funky Music Is The Thing' by the Dynamic Corvettes, the 'Clap your hands, stomp your feet' part of James Brown's 'Give It Up And Turnit A Loose', part of The Isley Brothers' 'Get Into Something' and 'Bra' by Cymande. Took off!

What was your inspiration?
From watching the crowd. Remember, that's where I come from. I come from the dancehall, I can't let them down. I can't fool around and play no wack shit. I'm watching them: the more they're having fun, the more I get busy. I told em: 'I'm a put some things together and I want y'all to check it out.' And I'm a call it the Merry Go Round. See I got to hop on. Once I hear it, I'm not comin' back. I'm gonna go forward. And so I did it, and they loved it.

So how would your set be. You'd play regular records and then a section of breaks?
Yeah. There's some records everybody's gonna get with. So I'd get the crowd going with that. Then I'd just go into cool out music. Then they got the guys that just wanna sit back, they might be doing their little drugs and shit, they don't want too much screaming music in their ears. Play some mellow shit for them. Do what you gotta do. Play it cool. I'd play break music, then slow dance, then go right back to what everybody wanted to hear. The contemporary stuff. Shit that's on the radio. So everybody was okay cool.

So you're playing the whole break and then you'd play it again...?
Two of them, two of them.

But how long would you play each one?
Not too long. 'Bout four times.

And how much time would you give each one?
I'm not givin it too much time for the floor to be bored with it. 'Cos I got to move on. You can't do nothin' that they gonna be bored with, man.

And which breaks from which songs went down the best?
All of them, man. All of them. I don't play wack shit. It don't stay in the crate.

So when you started playing breaks, which year is this?
1974

And that was in the Hevalo?
Yeah. It was earlier than that too, because I had funky music before I even came up into the Hevalo. It was earlier than that. I used to play it but I never really put a lot of emphasis into it.

> **❝ The more they're having fun, the more I get busy. I told em, 'I'm a put some things together and I want y'all to check it out. ❞**

When did people start calling it breakbeats?
They started to do that in the '80s. That's when they do that. They call it breakbeats.

Was anybody else doing anything similar?
No. There was guys were trying to battle me, but I wasn't fucking with them. There was a guy called Smoky, he was coming up, he was on Webster Avenue, had a group called the Masterplan Bunch. Soon Flash was in the cuts. He was making noise and shit. But early on I had no competition.

Who tried to copy you, tried to use your idea?
I never knew. I never went to their parties. I'm doing my shit, I ain't got time to go other places. Saturday, I'm not in your party, I'm in my shit. I ain't got time to check other people out. I didn't hear no name to go check out. What would I do, if they're trying to impress by playing my shit. That's not too impressive.

Tell me about your system.
I called my system the Herculords. People thought I was calling my crew the Herculords. the Herculords is not my crew, it's the name of my sound system. The second sound system I built I called it 'Not Responsible'. Every time you play that set somewhere, some shit always jump off, some dispute, so I call it 'Not Responsible'.

We just used to crank it, let people know, 'Yo! if you wanna come fuck with us, this is what you have to deal with.' I remember one time Flash came to our party, at the Executive Playhouse. I'd just got the Mac then, and he came and I said, 'Yeah I want you to feel the high, I want you to listen to the high, I want you to check out the midrange, I want the bass to walk the place.' And I think I said, 'Flash can you deal with it?' He ran out the spot. He said that was the only time I embarrassed him.

He used to have a sound system called the Gladiators. And Kidd Creole, I'll never forget, he said, 'Yeah, it's a known fact: the Herculords might cause a disaster, but there only could be one Grandmaster.' A-ight motherfucker. It was cool, stood alongside them. Where the fuck we all at with that? So we just left it like that, man. We never battled.

> **❝ Downtown was bourgois to me. My shit was elementary. Up here you could do your thing. Wear your sneakers, wear your jeans. ❞**

Did you rhyme over the records?
No, I just was saying a few little words. If the party rockin' I'd say, 'Yeah, right about now I'm rocking with the rockers, I'm jammin' with the jammers. Young ladies, don't hurt nobody. So remember it ain't no fun unless we all get some. Rock on y'all. Rock, rock and don't stop.' And when 'Bongo Rock' used to come, we'd say 'And you rock, and don't stop. And rock. And don't stop'. And that's the only part. And I used to say, 'Yeah, I like that'. Along the way, as the years go by, little short sayings became right into a full verse.

You just kept it like the Jamaican way of toasting.
Exactly.

Is that in your mind when you were doing it?
Exactly. I'd say: 'Yo you never heard it like this before. And you're back for more. And more, and more, and this year rock this y'all. Her-Herc.' Or this: 'Yes yes y'all. I see you comin' down to check I, Her-Herc.' Or if I'm playing something I'd say: 'Yes this is through the inspiration of I, Her-Herc y'all. Check this out.' And just go into the music, yunno. Took it nice through those raps to cover my mix, so it come on nice and smooth, 'cos I didn't have the luxury of a headphone. I mixed over the music.

Did you ever play reggae?
A few, a few. I never played too much reggae. I never had the audience for it and people wasn't feelin' reggae at the time.

Is that how you started?
I played a few at the beginning but it wasn't catching. I'm in Rome, I got to do what the Romans do. I'm here. I got to get with the groove that's here. So I introduced similar music in a funky way. I find out what y'all in the Bronx like in your music. So this is your funky music to me. And it's similar for what I was trying to do for reggae music. And apply it. So a lot of my music is about bass.

So you're thinking, I want to make it like a sound system in Kingston?
Yeah.

How much of an inspiration was Jamaica to the way you played music?
An inspiration to me, my father knew good music. He loved music and he taught me what was good music. [Jamaican accent] 'That's a good boonce. That's a good boonce.' So I know what a good bounce is.

He didn't play an instrument?
He was a Nat King Cole Man, Johnny Ace, all the classical old blues, rhythm and blues singers. Louis Armstrong all those people. Sarah Vaughan, Ella Fitzgerald. That's his type of music. I knew what good music was, he trained my ears to it.

What was your favourite ever party?
My favourite party was my first boat ride I played for my high school, Taft, in '74. The boat left from

Battery Park, up to Rye Playland. And at the time, 'Rock The Boat' [by Hues Corporation] had just come out, this record. And the boat got ready to dock and the water got kind of rough. And then the boat is rocking like this and I put on 'Rock The Boat'. [sings] 'If you'd like to know it, you got the notion, Rock the boat, don't stop...' and everybody starts running from side to side to rock this fuckin' boat. The captain, the teachers said 'Yo! take it off. Take that goddam record off!' And that shit made the school newspaper.

You never got into making records. How come?
I just, at the time, people got older, having responsibilities, and then narcotics came in, I started medicating myself. My father died, that put me in a slump. I got stabbed up, '77. Drew me back into a little shell.

Why did you get stabbed?
A misunderstanding, shit. Kids come up in there, drunk. I was getting ready to play. I just changed my clothes, walked in the door, and walked into a discrepancy and I got stabbed.

You never played downtown?
No, never did. Downtown was bourgeois to me. My shit was elementary. You had to go through me and go on. It stayed up here. People couldn't... Not only that, downtown you couldn't wear no sneakers. You can't wear what you want to wear down there. Up here you could do your thing. Wear your sneakers, wear your jeans. Downtown you had to be dressed different, yunno. Different style.

And when you started DJing, did you carry on B-boying, going dancing?
I danced behind the turntable. I got my little moves behind the turntable. Cos I got to be into it. I got to be feeling I'm into it. If I'm playing, if I'm throwin' it on and I'm dancing, I know I'm making other people dance.

Me and my friend used to play chess... on the turntables. Me and Coke, my partner, Coke La Rock. 'Cos sometimes egotism was to take both of us at the same time. You want to play and I want to play. So how we gonna straighten this out? okay, cool, no problem, we had a game: this turntable's mine, that turntable's yours. Match me. And the first person who play a record that the crowd say 'Ahh' and walk off...

What's the best thing you got out of it all?
Out of playing music? Until this day, hearing the oohs and the ahhs. Hearin the Ooohs and the Ahhs. People having fun, the mere fact that people enjoying themself, man.

What do you think is the power of the DJ?
The power? Of the DJ? It's to motivate the crowd, man. It's to have the insight to motivate the crowd. To have the crowd at your fingertips. To control the crowd, that's the best fuckin' power, man.

© DJhistory.com

RECOMMENDED LISTENING

VARIOUS – Ultimate Breaks And Beats (bootleg series, vinyl only)
VARIOUS – DJ Pogo presents The Breaks
VARIOUS – DJ Pogo Presents Block Party Breaks

" If I take the most climactic part of these records and string 'em together, on time, back to back to back. . . "

Grandmaster Flash
Scientist of the mix

Interviewed by Frank in Long Island, October 10, 1998

Flash made hip hop possible. He took Kool Herc's idea of playing a string of breaks and turned it from an explosive but haphazard party trick into a precise and astonishing DJ technique. In the process he revolutionised DJing because he showed how a DJ could use records to make new records. So as well as laying the foundations of a world-sweeping genre, he shattered the notions of what it is to be a musician and what it is to make original music.

The task was clear to him: work out a way of playing just the funkiest few bars from a record, then repeat that little chunk, and repeat it, and repeat it, all the time keeping the beat. In other words, manually sample a section of music and loop it into an unshakeable backing rhythm, the perfect soundbed for breakdancers to go wild to, or for rappers to rhyme over.

What makes Flash's achievement even more astonishing is that it was no accident. He knew what he wanted to achieve without having any idea if it was possible, and then locked himself away like a scientist experimenting with potential solutions. With his cautious unemotional delivery, you can't deny there's a strong element of scientist in Flash. His resulting Quick Mix technique works like this: take two copies of the same record and stick a marker on each so you can see where the break starts. While one's playing you're rewinding the other one. Now cut from one record to the other using the mark to start them in exactly the right place, bang on the start of the beat. Practise every waking moment for about a year and you'll have it nailed.

These days the turntablists have made it a martial art, slicing vinyl into ever tinier slivers and cutting Flash's speed into tenths. But what they rarely have is expression. Hear Flash and it's all about poise and pause, as he uses the cleverest slips of time and rhythm to give everything life and bounce.

You got into music by sneaking records from your dad's collection?
Yeah, that's probably where it all started. I have to say I was pretty fortunate. My father was into primarily jazz, like Glenn Miller, Artie Shaw, Miles Davis, Stan Kenton, people like that. One of my sisters was into the Latin thing: Tito Puente, Eddie Palmieri, Joe Cuba. Then I had a sister who was into the Motown sound, Jackson 5, Sly and the Family Stone, Martha and the Vandellas, Supremes. So I been pretty fortunate to grow up in a household where I heard all this. Most of my stealing came from my father's collection. But I would also go steal my sisters' records. And I was mostly in my room being a scientist, but on the times when I did date, I would date women whose mother, or brother, had records in their house.

So there was an ulterior motive.
Yeah, there was always a motive. If I met a person, if I met a female, in a club or whatever, and I went to meet up and go to her house, and meet her people, I'd look around. Or I'd enquire, ''Scuse me do you have any records?' 'Oh these old things? I been trying to get rid of them for years.' And they'd open the closet and it'd be a goldmine in there, and I'd be, 'OK this person has to be my girlfriend for a minute.'

Grandmaster Flash

....

When did you start buying records?
I started buying records when I started getting my head knocked off by my father. Because he was getting pissed off that I would take his records while he was at work. And my sisters would beef about me taking their records. If I had a girlfriend and she found out what I was doing she'd cut me off. I thought, screw this, I'm gonna buy my own records.

At this time I was going to a school that catered to electronics: Samuel Gompers Vocational and Technical High School. Now in school we were taught what mono was and what stereo was. I think the first record that I bought was this Barry White record: 'I'm Gonna Love You Just A Little Bit More'. And what was interesting about it was I really got to hear – like we learned on the blackboard – what stereo was, and to hear how the cellos were in the left speaker, and the drums up in the middle, and the guitars was on the right. I was like: this is some shit.

That's what propelled me to get deeper into electronics. And start getting in my sister's room and tearing up her radio and finding out how it worked and why. And going into the backyards and looking for electronics stuff, and looking for burned out cars, and looking for capacitors and resistors.

Where were you growing up?
South Bronx. 163rd and Fox, on Fox street.

What made you want to be a DJ?
I was gonna be a breakdancer, right. But when I tried to learn it I did some moves and landed on my back and hurt it a whole lot. I tried the breakdancing thing; I was kinda wack at that. But when I see Mr Clive Cambell, Kool Herc, sit up on his podium, heavily guarded, and all these people around enjoying themselves, from five years old to age 50, in one park, for a certain amount of hours, I said, 'I want to do that, I wanna be that, I wanna do that.' So with my electronic knowledge, and my ability to take what was considered junk and sort of jury-rig it together, I started to put together some sort of makeshift sound system. And it was a piece of shit, but it was mines.

At the time Herc had this pair of Shure Vocal Master columns, and these two black bass bottoms. He was always up high on a platform so you couldn't see what he was playing. His music, some of it my sisters had in their collection, some of it I never heard before. But it had such a great feel to it.

Was he the first DJ you saw doing block parties?
He was the first, and what intrigued me about Herc was, he was playing the music that I loved, and he was playing duplicate copies of a record, he was repeating these sections, but I noticed the crowd: if they were into a record they would have to wait until he mixed it, because it was never on time. And I didn't understand what he was doing, at the point, because I could see the audience in unison, then in disarray, then in unison, then in disarray. I said, 'I like what he's playing but he's not playing it right.'

So it was more his music than his technique?
I didn't find the way he played exciting. It was *what* he was playing. The music of the time was disco: like Trammps, Donna Summer, the Gibbs brothers. Herc didn't play that kind of music, he played the songs that weren't considered hits. The obscure records. I found that quite exciting.

What was he playing?
What was I hearing? Like 'Shack Up' by Banbarra. He'd play [James Brown] 'Funky Drummer', or 'The Mexican' [by Babe Ruth], a certain section, but you could see the crowd: unison, disarray, unison, disarray, unison, disarray. So the thought was to not have disarray, to have as little disarray as possible. But I didn't know how I was gonna do it.

And there was another DJ who had a big influence on you...
Yeah, Pete DJ Jones.

And he was a disco DJ?
He was a disco DJ. What I liked about his style is that he kept the music continuous. He didn't take out a certain section of the record or continuously go back and forth, but I just

liked the way he just kept everything going. A lot of DJs at that time would just let the record play, let it end, and then bring in the next song, with no regards of beats per minute.

So he was very much programming things and building up the tempo?
Yeah.

And you became friends
When I got a chance to see his sound system, I was quite nervous. But he was very nice. Herc wouldn't let me get close to him. But Pete DJ Jones and I became real good friends.

Were there other DJs who impressed you?
I had one chance one time to see a DJ by name of Flowers, Grandmaster Flowers. There was a DJ by the name of Ron Plummer. But my inspiration was Kool Herc and Pete DJ Jones.

And your masterstroke was to combine their two styles
How I created my style is watching Pete blend one record into another, versus Herc, who played, I call it the hit and miss factor. Timing wasn't a factor with him, but the type of music he was playing I was quite interested in.

" A lot of DJs at that time would just let the record play, let it end, and then bring in the next song, with no regards of beats per minute. "

And Herc was already playing sections where he'd repeat breaks over and over?
He was taking a part of it, but his timing was not a factor. He would play a record that was maybe 90 beats a minute, and then he would play another one that was 110. He would play records and it would never be on time.

With the two different styles that Herc and Pete had, I sat there thinking about it, I said to myself there's got to be a way to keep it on time, to take just a part of the record and keep it on time. That's where that theory started. My thing was basically, to take a combination of both and create a style out of it.

I had to go into my room and figure out how can I make the music that I love the most seamless? So I would listen to records and I would notice something: wow the breaks on these records are really short. Like, either they were short or they were at the end of the song. Or it was a problem where the best part is really great, but it would go into a wack passage after. I could never allow myself to go into a wack passage or go off. So I had to create something that would allow me to pre-hear the track prior. That's when I came up with something, I called it the peekaboo system.

This is something you got from Pete Jones.
Because I knew he had headphones, I guessed that he was hearing the track before, and that's why he had no disarray. So what I had to do was build a peekaboo system. Peekaboo system consisted of a cueing system as we know it today, where I was able to pre-hear. With my electronic knowledge I was able to tap into the cartridges of both sides, run it through an amplifier, put a single-pole-double-throw switch up the middle and just split the two signals. In the centre position it would be off. Click it to the right and you'd hear the right turntable, two clicks to the left, this is where you'd hear the other one. I had to Krazy Glue it to the top.

You built your own cueing system from scratch?
Basically, yeah.

Once you had cueing, you locked yourself away. How long?
Two years.

From when?
Maybe early '74.

So straight after you'd heard Herc and Pete Jones you're like, 'I got to figure this out.'
Yeah. I got to go away now.

And you totally stopped going out?
No. I didn't play at all. I just stopped. Maybe for like a year or two. I basically didn't have no childhood. No girlfriends, no basketball, no hanging out, straight to my room.

You were working as a messenger?
Yeah, I was working as a messenger at Crantex Fabrics. So between my allowance and my mother and my allotment for my clothing...

> **" I had to figure out how to manually edit these records so that people wouldn't even know that I had took a section that was maybe 15 seconds and made it five minutes. "**

By this time you had decks? What kind, pretty basic?
SL20s, Technics.

That's the belt drive?
I would go through the backyards and rip out the turntables in the old floor-model stereos. I tried those and put 'em in wooden cases. I tried to do that. Of course they were horrible. I even tried Fisher Price, which is a toy company, they came up with this thing called a Close and Play.

That little briefcase thing?
Yeah. I tried that, and that was wack of course. But there was a club around the corner from my house called the Hunts Point Palace. And in this club that I was not able to go to because I was too young, the word on the street is that the sound system in there was incredible. They had the very best of amplifiers, very best of mixers, very best. And I was told by the thieves in my neighbourhood, 'Yo Flash, I can get you a pair of turntables, that's like the best in the world.' I'm like, 'Whatever, whatever,' but I said, 'Find out what they are.' So they found out, they wrote it down and brought it to me – I'm into research! I found out that they were the Thorens TD-125Cs. Turntables around that time were around $1,000. They had the swinging weights and the gimbals on the back of tone arm.

So when I said I want them, they went and got them, and they brought them to my house. And I looked at my turntables and I looked at their turntables and I was like, okay now I can continue my science.

Did you just lock yourself in a room and just practice and practice?
Yeah. A lot of my friends... I had a best friend by the name of Truman, had a best friend by the name of Easy Mike who later became one of my boys and DJed with me. I had a best friend by the name of Gordon. And that's how I came up with my name Flash. And these friends of mines used to come to my house and say, 'C'mon, let's go to the park, let's go hang with girls.' I'm like, 'Naw man, I can't do that. I'm working on something.'

I didn't know what I was working on, didn't have a clue. All I know is that with each obstacle there came an excitement on how to figure it out. How to get past it. How to get past it, how to get past it.

You knew what you were trying to do technically, but what was your goal in terms of the music and the crowd?
I'm watching Pete and watching Herc, when the song got to the climactic part, which was later to be called the break, I watched what the audience did: they got a little more physical. I'm like, 'Oh, okay.' So that was what the feeling was. If I could go right to the meat of the

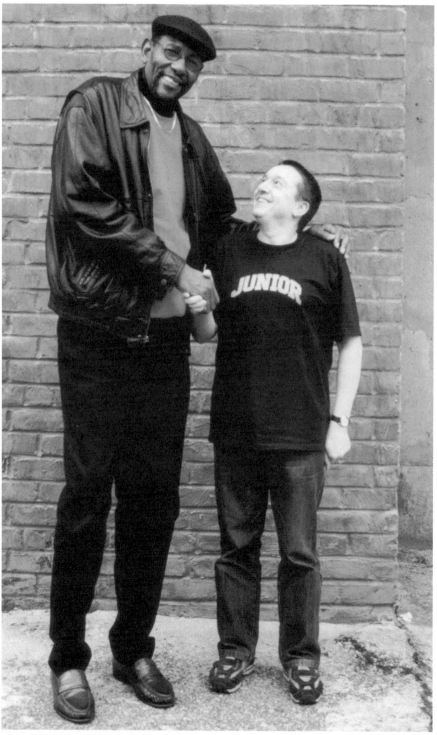

Bill realises why Flash looked up to Pete DJ Jones so much.

....

sandwich, if I could get right there... But timing was a factor, because a lot of these dancers were really good, they did their moves on time. Timing was really a factor.

So I said to myself: I got to be able to go to just the section of the record, just the break, and extend that. So these people that danced, they could just dance as long as they wanted. I got to find a way to do this. I had to figure out how to take these records and take these sections and manually edit them so that the person in front of me wouldn't even know that I had took a section that was maybe 15 seconds and made it five minutes.

And I started to run into so many obstacles. The type of needle: I discovered that elliptical, which is built like a backwards 'J', although it sounded better, would not stay inside the groove. Conical, which is shaped more like a nail, although it didn't sound as good as an elliptical, it would stay inside the grooves, and it would do damage to a record, but that's part of the territory.

Then I had to figure out how to recapture the beginning of the break without picking up the needle. Because I tried doing it that way and I wasn't very good at it. And that's how I came up with the Clock Theory, and that's what DJs do today, they mark a section of the record. And then you gotta just count how many revolutions went by. I called it the Clock Theory because you can put it at 12 o'clock, 1 o'clock, 2 o'clock, whatever, and all you do is count in reverse, how many times it passed, did it pass my cartridge, that's my marking point. And that's how many times I would bring it back, whether I would use what I call the Dog Paddle, which is spinning it back [fingers on the edge of the record], or what I call the Phone Dial Theory, where you would get it from the inner [fingers on the label of the record] and then bring it back. Once I figured that out, it was just a case of getting breaks. No matter how long...

Which records were the first that you were doing this with?
The early ones? Oh boy, there were so many... 'Do It' by Billy Sha-Rae, early Barry White records, because his joints had drums in the middle. Erm, one that probably stands out the most to me. It wasn't an early one, but it was 'Lowdown', Boz Scaggs.

That wasn't when you were first starting?
No that was later. But that was my standard. What else? 'Funky Drummer' [James Brown]. Actually 'Funky Drummer' was... It's like a person who works out. Sometimes he's using 40lbs and some days he wants to push 100lbs. 'Funky Drummer' was like 100lbs. But you had to really be in the mood. Because the way this record is, the drummer played for two bars, then the record would be off.

So if 'Funky Frummer' was a 100lbs, what was an easy one, when you wanted to do a lot of reps?
Ummm Barry White. 'I'm Going To Love You Just A Little Bit More'. The break went forever, so you didn't have so much rush. Another one that was pretty easy is, 'Mardi Gras' Bob James. 'Pussy Footer' [by Jackie Robinson], those were the easy ones.

What about the other hard ones.
'Rock Steady' [Aretha Franklin] was another one that was really a pain in the ass. That song, 'cos it went 'rock... uh-uh-uh... steady... uh-uh-uh...' then it went into that wackness. So you had to really be ready.

Any others in the Flash gymnasium?
Ace Spectrum did a song we called the piano song. It was like [hums a low pitched breakbeat rhythm] and that was it, then it went into some other piano wackness, and you had to get out of that real quick. You had to be in a real good frame of mind.

What was your schedule, you would just get up in the morning and do this?
I guess I would walk Caesar, my miniature doberman pinscher. I'd walk him, that was my best friend, Caesar. Walk him. Then I'd come in, that's it. If it was a school week I would go to school and come right back. If I had to go to work I'd go to work and come right back. There wasn't too much playtime, because whenever I would run into an obstacle it would nag me so much so I had to go back to it. So if I had to go to school, if I had to go to work I would immediately come back, because it was something undone.

You were approaching this whole thing in a really scientific way. What's amazing is that you had this vision. You were so sure that if you worked out this new style, when you came out people would be amazed?
Yes.

How come you were so certain?
Because I seen people gathered from miles around just for one individual, playing music. And I seen what we used to call the 'get-down part' [the break]. I seen Herc play the get-down part of a record and see an audience lose their mind, but it was always unison, disarray, unison, disarray. And then when I seen Pete and his style I seen the people that followed him, I seen them lose their minds. So I knew that if I could just come up with the formula in between I would have something.

> ❝ It was quiet, almost like a speaking engagement. I was quite disenchanted. I was quite sad. I cried for a couple of days. What did I do wrong? What's going wrong? ❞

And eventually you did exactly that.
I called my style Quick Mix Theory, which is taking a section of music and cutting it on time, back to back; in 30 seconds or less. And do that over and over, which has now become the style of DJing.

That's the standard...
That's the standard now. It's my creation. This is my contribution to hip hop, to the DJing aspect, is to take a particular passage of music and rearrange the arrangement. Rearrange the arrangement by way of rubbing the record back and forth or cutting the record, or back-spinning the record. And that's where cutting, which was later to be called scratching, came about.

When did you first play that way in public
After maybe a year I didn't have the science down, but I had enough to go test. I was able to test on a audience. The first person I tried to show was my partner Disco B, but he didn't quite understand it. Next person I tried to show was a gentleman by the name of Gene Livingstone, which was later to be called Mean Gene. We hooked up together and made a crew, a DJ thing.

What I said to myself is, if I take the most climactic part of these records and just string 'em together and play 'em on time, back to back to back, I'm going to have them totally excited. If I play the get-down part of 10 records in succession and keep em on time, I'm gonna have the audience in this total uproar. I'm gonna be the man. I'm gonna beat Kool Herc. But when I went outside, it was totally quiet.

Really?
Almost like a speaking engagement. I was quite disenchanted. I was quite sad. I... you know, I cried for a couple of days. I'm like, what did I do wrong? What's going wrong?

What were the records that you played that time?
'Johnny The Fox' Thin Lizzy, Billy Squier 'Big Beat', 'I Can't Stop' John Davis and the Monster Orchestra, 'Disco Flight '78', and I was on time with these things.

Were you playing a set of records first to warm them up?
No I went straight in. Playing one behind another.

So maybe they were just shell-shocked.
Maybe. They just didn't dance. And that amazed me, and it saddened me.

How did you win them over?
At first I tried to talk – wack! wack! wack! wack! wack! Once I knew I was wack, I couldn't do that at the same time. Cut, and talk. Too wack.

That's what Herc would do.
But if I did it the break would go into the wack part.

> **❝ 'Flash is on the beatbox!' The first time we did it, we didn't get screams and yells; it was 'Oh shit! Flash got this new toy. Flash is making music – drum beats – with no turntable.' ❞**

So you got other people to rhyme for you instead?
I will put a microphone on the other side of the table and see if anyone could vocalise to this rearrangement of an arrangement. And nobody could, until Keith grabbed the mic. Keith Wiggins, who was known as Cowboy. And he wasn't technically good, like he wouldn't go into any thesaurical, dictionarial, heavy words; he was simple. And he was more like the ringleader of a circus. So it kind of averted the attention away from me, 'cos that's what I didn't like. Although I was in the park physically, mentally I could go in my room because nobody's paying me any attention. So now I could set up 290 records, back to back.

And that's where Disco B came in, because now the problem was I can't play and look for the record at the same time. So that's where the pass came in. I called it the pancake factor, because its like flying pancakes. 'Okay I'm done with this,' bam! 'I'll throw you this, you throw me that, I'll pass you this one, you slide me this onto the turntables,' and it was me and B doing this passing thing. So physically to see it was some thing. And with Cowboy saying the things that he did, he made it credible.

And then you had Theodore
Theodore was the icing to the cake. That not only could a teenager [Flash] do it, but so could a little kid.

How did he learn?
The system was in Gene's room, his mother's stereo was in the living room, and it was this little kid that... Where I would repeat a record by spinning it back, and repeating, spinning it back, he would pick up the needle and just repeat it with one turntable. He would just pick it up, and go right to the beginning of the break, and it was quite amazing.

And how about scratching. Because between you and Theodore it's a little fuzzy as to who started it and who popularised it?
Well the way I see it is, if I didn't create the style, there wouldn't be no style. You can only invent something one time. You can always put an extension on it. I think I'd have to say, rearranging a passage of music is mines. Which meant cutting, rubbing the record back and forth. But Theodore, he put another rhythm on it. Just like between Cash Money and DJ Jazzy Jeff, somebody put another rhythm on it, which is transforming [using the volume faders to cut up a scratch sound]. So it's actually taking a record and moving it back and forth, that's where it basically starts, but then it's a matter of the rhythm and how do you work the fader.

How you want to draw the conclusion, that's up to you, but this thing, on a whole I created on my own. There was no blueprint, no draft, it was nobody else doing it. Period. End of story. There was a little kid on the living room who I invited in against my partner's wishes, to learn this. If I had kept that room closed, and kept it shut, he might not have learned it. I would give Theodore credit. I would rub it, I might go *zuh-uh, zuh-uh*. He might have went *zuh-huh, uh-huh, uh-huh*. So...

It's one of those things. You're hearing the scratch in the headphones, you're going to think, 'Oh that's a good noise'.

It's just my theory, that you can only invent the car one time. You could make a round car, a square car, a car with jets. A car with two engines…

How about the beatbox?

It's my invention. There was a drummer that I knew. At the time it was sort of, not really a battle, I don't use that word too much. It was basically for who had the most showmanship between Bam, Herc and Flash. Bam had the records, Herc had the sound system. My sound system was pretty cheesy, so I knew I had to constantly keep adding things and innovating just to please my audience. Because once they'd go to hear a Herc sound, then heard my sound – eurggh! It was OK.

So, there was this drummer, who lived on 149th Street and Jackson. I think his name was Dennis. He had this machine, this manually operated drum machine, a Vox percussion box. Whenever he didn't feel like hooking up his drums in his room, he would practise on this machine. It was manually operated. You couldn't just press a button and it played, you had to know how to play it. And he would use it for fingering. It had a bass key, a snare key, a hi-hat key, a castanet key, it had a, erm, timbale key. And I would always ask him if he ever wanted to get rid of it I would buy it off him. He sold it to me and I gave it a title: Beatbox. My flyer person at the time, my agent at that time, which was Ray Chandler, put this on the flyer: 'GRANDMASTER FLASH INTRODUCES THE BEATBOX. MUSIC WITH NO TURNTABLES!' As a drawing attraction.

When was that?

I think maybe '74, '75. Once I learnt how to play it, I stayed in my room for a month. And myself and my MCs became a routine, 'Flash is on the beatbox!' So the first time we did it, we didn't get screams and yells and whatever; it was 'Oh shit! Flash got this new toy.' It probably got back to Bam, it probably got back to Herc: Flash is making music – drum beats – with no turntable.

Did you play records over the top?

No, what I would do is play it, play it, play it, play it, stop. DJ. So like [a little rhythm] *doomm ah da-da uh-hah*. Stop, zoom play in a record. So it was like I had both of them ready and I would just kinda like, while the MCs was MCin', where you would fade the beat out for a minute, I might switch back to the turntables. Or I would fade that out and the MCs would be doing a routine and I would go back to the beatbox. It was a real high part of our performance. A real high point.

And there was a lot of competition for records, too.

Herc and Bam and me. That's what separated us; that's what made us the shit for a minute: who had that record, who had that real special record. Like Herc had the Incredible Bongo Band, 'The Rock' ['Bongo Rock']. Grandmaster Flash had Bob James. Bam might have the *Pink Panther* with a drum beat.

Amongst the three of us – matter of fact there was even one more, which was DJ Breakout, and the Funky Four, which was way, way, way uptown. We were in a mad scramble for that song that would just get 'em going. I would never forget, me and Herc… Herc wouldn't show me 'Bongo Rock' for a long time. But then he wanted to know 'Sound Of A Drum' by Ralph McDonald. And I wouldn't show him that.

Which were the other ones you had first?

I don't know, My Ralph McDonald, 'Sound Of A Drum', which I called 'Crackerjacks', Bob James 'The Bells' ['Take Me To The Mardi Gras'], actually I bumped into that from a friend that was a friend of mines, I got 'Big Beat' from DJ Breakout which was Billy Squier. I couldn't get too much from Bam because Bam's shit was so deep and so powerful I just didn't know where he got it. A lot of shit I just got on my own. Or I got 'The Mexican' from Kool Herc.

Where did your name Grandmaster come from?

Came from a fellow that used to come to my club. Fellow by the name of Joe Kidd. Said to me you need to call yourself a Grandmaster by the way you do things on the turntables that nobody else could do. It sounded good, but I wasn't going to do anything that didn't mean something. Flash was my favourite cartoon. I liked things that moved fast.

Flyer text:

MR. G in association with CELEBRITY CLUB 125 & 5th Ave.

A CHRISTMAS EVE SUPER DISCO

GRANDMASTER FLASH & THE FURIOUS 5

COWBOY, KID KREOLE MELE MEL, RAHIEM, MR. NESS.

GRANDWIZARD THEODORE /FANTASTIC 5

DOT A ROCK, RUBIE DEE KEVIE KEV, WHIPPER WHIP, ROBIE ROB,

PLUS Enjoy Recording Artists TREACHEROUS THREE

Flash will do thier Super Rap "FREEDOM" and The TREACH will do "ROCK THE BODY ROCK"

Chiefrocker Busy Bee

WED. DEC. 24, 1980

$7 With flyer $8 Without 10 until

GUARANTEED TO PERFORM

When did you start being called Flash, before you started playing records?

My buddy Gordon gave me Flash. And that's way before I started DJing. So I became Grandmaster in 1975, January 1st. Actually it was '74 maybe. It connected with Bruce Lee which was the leading box office draw for movies at the time, and it connected to this guy that played chess, and these guys were very good at their craft. I felt I was very good at my craft. I found it fitting: Grandmaster. Flash. Grandmaster Flash. And that's when it became Grandmaster Flash, Scientist of the Mix. And that was my tag.

How did you feel when the first records came out? For a long time people didn't even think this was something you could put on a record.

I was asked. I was asked before anybody. And I was like, 'Who would want to hear a record which I was spinning re-recorded, with MCing on it?' I told these record companies, these small mom-and-pop record companies, just leave me alone. I'm not interested

What changed your mind?
I guess it wasn't until I heard this song: 'What you hear is not a plate I'm rapping to the beat.'

Sugarhill Gang.
Yeah.

People never heard of them.
Never heard of them. They didn't pay no dues at all. Like if they're not from any of the five boroughs, where are they from? One of the members was a bouncer for Kool Herc, at one of his clubs. So he was able to get a real close look at this rhyming thing.

They pretty much took all the rhymes that were going around.
Yeah basically. He was able to see Cas from the Cold Crush Brothers, he was able to hear Melle Mel, he was able to hear Coke La Rock. He was able to hear the best, do this. And he was working in a pizza shop out in Englewood [New Jersey], and he was asked to be a part of the group, and he was kind of asked can he do that stuff, and he said sure. It was somebody else's stuff but he was able to do it. And that's how he became part of the group.

What was your reaction when you saw that someone had made a record?
I was like, 'Damn I coulda been there first.' I didn't know. I didn't know the gun was loaded like that. Blew up. It was a huge record for them. It was okay though. 'Cos we were gonna come later. We had the talent, and they didn't.

" Joe Kidd said to me you need to call yourself a Grandmaster by the way you do things on the turntables that nobody else could do. "

You did make records pretty early on. How did 'Superrappin'' come about? Was it a version of what you would play in the clubs?
It was more like our added attraction into our act. At that time [DJ] Hollywood did something to the industry, instead of taking a sound system to a building and playing from 10 till four, Hollywood would be on four flyers in one night, make four or five times the money. So eventually all of us put away our sound systems so we would do two to three parties a night. We could do this: if we went to Staten Island, then we might go to Manhattan, then we might go to the Bronx. So what we would do is our normal party thing but then we would perform 'Superrappin'' as an added bonus.

The record is...
Tyrone Thomas and the Whole Darn Family 'Seven Minutes Of Funk'. It's the beat that we used as a backing, and when Bobby Robinson said can you make a record...

It was made with a session band?
Yeah. It was a band.

You asked them to cover the record the way you would play it as a DJ?
Yeah we showed them what it was and they played it over. That was it. And that was our extra added bonus, to go round and do two or three extra parties. Not only were we doing what everybody else was doing, but we had a record.

How did you feel when you're a DJ and you get offered the chance to make a record and you have very little to do with it?
Quite frankly, once I walked into this huge room and seen how it was made, I was like okay, well maybe that's how it was done. Because I knew the end result, when they pressed it I was gonna be the one that set it off anyway. So it didn't really threaten me. I didn't even know better enough to really be angry. And that's what I seen on both occasions. At Enjoy, they

had a great house band, and at Sugarhill. Had a great house band so I was like okay that's how it's done.

I knew that eventually when it became wax I would get special versions of it that only I had, that we would perform. Live. No vocals. No nothing. Raw track. And we would do it live. And that's what I would have. And that's what we did. We also made a show where they would disappear for a while, go off into the wings and I would do my thing. It was a show. A show.

> **❝ Hip hop is not perfect. That's what makes it dope, the imperfections. It's strategically where it's placed that makes it hot, makes it fat. ❞**

Did you suggest making those early records from records instead?
I think at the time I was trying to show Sylvia how you would take it directly from the record but she wasn't with it. And it would have been a long laborious process, because it would have been: record 30 seconds, hold the tape, then punch, then segué... It would have been a long process just to get it on tape. Especially if it was a short 15-second break and you needed five minutes, that's like maybe 80 takes, 100 takes, 200 takes, and who was to say they were gonna be on time? She didn't want to do that.

Because of the studio time
Yeah. Didn't want that deal. She preferred to have it recreated by a band. And the band was excellent though. I wasn't too mad at that.

Did you feel, 'That's taken my role away'?
Basically I did. I did feel that way, but at the time it was my group, my concept. I was part of the group. It was cool.

But eventually you made 'Adventures On The Wheels Of Steel', which is a totally different thing, because it's actually a snapshot of you as a DJ. How did it come about?
I spoke about it with Sylvia quite a few times. And then eventually Mel and I talked to her about it, and then she agreed to take a shot with it. We came up with the compilation of records we wanted to use. You know, all the hit records of that time. And with some of the Sugarhill product. And we did it.

How did you put it together?
It took me three hours. I had to do it live. And whenever I'd mess up I would just refuse to punch. I would just go back to the beginning.

So how many takes?
It was a few. Because now it was a matter of no mess-ups allowed. Timing was critically a factor. 'Cos this was going on a record. So I dunno, 10, 15 takes to get it precise.

How many decks did you have set up?
Three. Three decks, two mixers.

Can you remember how you felt when you heard the playback?
I was scared. I didn't think anyone was gonna get it. I thought they might understand this. DJs'll probably love it because at that time, this style, my style of what I do on turntables was not fully saturated. People still didn't know what I did, or knew who I was, or thought I was a rapper, or whatever. So, to put the record out, it did okay. It didn't take too well in America, because people could not quite understand what it was I was doing. Frankie Crocker used to play it on WBLS quite a bit. So in New York I had gotten some small recognition for it. But in Europe the record was huge.

It did demand that I do it live. I'll never forget that. Sometimes I would be so nervous that

I would mess up, and I'd stop and say, 'Can I try it one more time?' and the crowd would say 'Yeahh.' Cos it was like three decks, two mixers, there was some shit to do. The precise passing of the records, everything had to be where it had to be. Records had to be off. Shit was just flying. It was cool though.

You're very much a perfectionist.
Yeah, sometimes that hurts me.

Why do you say that?
Because hip hop is not perfect. That's what makes it dope, the imperfections. It's strategically where it's placed that makes it hot, makes it fat.

What's the thrill you get from playing to a live audience?
The adrenalin flow. I guess. The screams, the yells.

What do you think when you see these turntablist guys and they've taken what you started and run with it? I mean Roc Raida, someone like that?
I love it. I love it. Just to see them break it down and do some of that crazy shit. In between the beat, in between the fly's ass. I love it, it's fucking great. I love it.

And that's all from your idea.
I like to remain modest about this accomplishment that I did, but there seems to be so much confusion about who started what and who did whatever. This is my contribution to this.

Without a doubt.
Nobody from old school or wherever can take this from me. It's three years of my life that I took to do this. You see, this is what's important to me. I don't care who's better, who's worse… First! My contribution is first. Because first is forever.

© DJhistory.com

GRANDMASTER FLASH SELECTED DISCOGRAPHY

GRANDMASTER FLASH & THE FURIOUS FIVE – Superrappin' (writer)
GRANDMASTER FLASH & THE FURIOUS FIVE – Adventures On The Wheels Of Steel (architect)
GRANDMASTER FLASH – Flash To The Beat (writer)
GRANDMASTER FLASH & THE FURIOUS FIVE – It's Nasty (writer)
GRANDMASTER FLASH & THE FURIOUS FIVE – Scorpio (writer)
GRANDMASTER FLASH & THE FURIOUS FIVE – Black Man (writer)
GRANDMASTER FLASH & THE FURIOUS FIVE – Fly Girl (remixer)
MICHAEL VINER'S INCREDIBLE BONGO BAND – Apache (remixer)
GRANDMASTER FLASH & THE FURIOUS FIVE – Gold (producer/writer/scratching)
GRANDMASTER FLASH – Larry's Dance Theme (producer/writer)
DOOM – Shake Your Body Down (producer)

RECOMMENDED LISTENING

VARIOUS – Grandmaster Flash: Essential Mix Classic Edition (CD-only)
VARIOUS – Grandmaster Flash Presents Salsoul Jam 2000
GRANDMASTER FLASH – The Official Adventures of Grandmaster Flash

**" I had a vision.
I said we just
got to make
this move. "**

Afrika Bambaataa
Zulu king of the Bronx

Interviewed by Frank in the south Bronx, October 6, 1998

The third of hip hop's trio of founding fathers, Afrika Bambaataa was its most adventurous musical explorer and most colourful cultural figurehead. As 'Master of Records', he was a voracious DJ, searching for danceable breaks in the most unlikely of tunes, and eagerly devouring any source of new music, the downtown disco scene included. His vision of combining funk and electronic music brought us 'Planet Rock', one of the most influential dance records ever. A charismatic kid who'd been swept into the dying days of the great Bronx gangs left over from the '60s, he turned his experience as lieutenant in the Black Spades to more peaceful means when, as founder of the Zulu Nation, he helped cement rap music, graffiti and breakdancing together as a unified culture.

Exiting the subway at Hunts Point Avenue, the south Bronx provides a welcome in the form of a nearby gunshot. This aside, it's not as intimidating as its legend – a busy, mostly Hispanic neighbourhood. The Point is a well-cared-for community centre, with a guy who who says Bam will be along any minute. After chasing his dust in vain through his recent visit to Europe, it's a relief to find the soft-spoken giant waiting patiently. In some comfy armchairs the talking starts, the only distraction the centre's inquisitive dog and a middle-aged guy intent on using a bandsaw to finish some carving he's doing in the next-door crafts workshop. Bam is happy to talk in detail about his career, and thankfully the conversation stays largely on DJing and away from talk of aliens, spirituality and the omnivorous philosophies of the Zulu Nation.

What were your very first parties like?
We would give parties in the community centre, and I would bring my house system down and we would bring out flashlights and you have the lights off and you have your flashlight, choosing which records you want, so when you put on one record – you might put on say 'Dance To The Music' by Sly and the Family Stone – then when you know that it's finishing somebody might put on James Brown 'It's a New Day' on the other side…

So you synchronise it with the flashlights?
Right, with the flashlights, and that's the time when it wasn't really mixing, it's just playin' the records. People just wait for the next song to come on, or if you want to keep it going, before we ever had systems, when the flashlight goes on, to the other side, the guy knows to already start his record off while the other one, you hear it going down.

This is when you're real young?
Yeah, real young. Say about 11, 12, something like that.

When did you get serious about throwing parties?
'73 is when it really started getting massive with super-big parties, with larger centres, then movin' into schools and all that. We started off in the old centre which could fit maybe 200 people. That was on 174th Street and Bronx River, between Manor and Stratford Avenue. The Bronx River Center, the big centre, had a large gym that could fit, you know,

1,000 people. And then when we moved into there, that's when we started seeing a large people following us.

And what kind of music were you playing?
We was playin' everything, everything that was funky. Records which was just comin' out, and the disco music of the time. We would play oldies-but-goodies, lot of the soul and funk songs of the late '60s, early '70s, some rock records.

Who else was playing around the same time?
At that time, you had Kool DJ D...

He was down with you, right?
We was down with him at first. You had [Ron] Plummer, Flowers from Brooklyn. You had Maboya from Brooklyn, Pete DJ Jones, this is the disco type DJs of this time.

And what was their style?
It was mainly disco at first, a lot of disco beats, and breaks, and they was rockin' with the disco style of rappin', you know, like you would hear on a radio station DJ.

So they were rhyming?
It wasn't really rhyming it was more, 'Come on one time, get down baby doll,' Something like Jocko, or Gary Byrd, who was doing his style of rhyming and rapping, with his GB Experience on WWIL and WLIB, and you had stuff from the '60s, Murray the K when he used to do his radio station and Cousin Brucie on WABC. Rap was always here, but it was in a different form. Where you got to the heavy rhymin' and the funk under the hip hop culture, was after Kool Herc, myself, Flash and all the other pioneers started comin' out... Furious Five, Soulsonic Force...

❝ I had a crazy record collection, more than all of them. ❞

So you were inspired by these disco DJs who'd been going a long time?
I was more inspired between Kool DJ D and Kool Herc. The disco DJs I just used to listen to them 'cos that was what you listened to on the radio.

So what were Kool D and Kool Herc doing that was so different?
Kool D was the first out of the street gang we was in – the Black Spades – to get a whole component set, what they call a coffin, which had the turntables, the mixer, a little echo chamber and all that stuff in there. And then Kool Herc, comin out with the funky breaks that he brought out.

What made you think you could make it?
I had a crazy record collection, more than all of them, so I just decided, I had this vision, I want to make this happen, and incorporate an organisation of people into this new thing I was starting, The Zulu Nation.

So it was at about the same time as you were starting the Zulu Nation?
Right. This is when the street gang era was starting to die out, fade out, and I was trying to transfer people from this other group that I had started – The Organisation – to the Zulu Nation. It started in the black and Latino community, and then it started spreading out to the different communities, throughout the tri-state area, and then throughout the United States, and then throughout the world.

When you started the Zulu Nation, at first it was a breaking crew, right?
Yeah. It was a B-boy, male and female crew. You had the Zulu Kings and the Zulu Queens, and the Shaka Kings and the Shaka Queens. And they were really tearing shit up. Nobody was really beating them, and they started winning contests and breakdance shows throughout the city.

Which year is this?
That was '70s – '74, '75, '76, '77.

Where are your parents from? Are they from the Caribbean?
My parents are from New York, but my roots is from the Caribbean. From Jamaica and Barbados.

So were there elements of Jamaican culture in your family
Always. Jamaica and Barbados. My family and Herc's family and Grandmaster Flash's family.

How much were you aware of Jamaican sound system culture.
Oh, all the time. I'm one of the first. In fact I am the one in hip hop who started playing all the Jamaican music in the hip hop parties. More than Kool Herc and Grandmaster Flash. Even though Herc is from the islands he was focussed more on America, on funky stuff.

Did you ever go to big Jamaican sound system parties in New York?
No, I just knew of them when we did block parties, and after a while when the Jamaicans started bringing they systems outside. We used to have sound systems up in the Valley Park, up in the Baychester area of the Bronx.

Was that an inspiration, seeing sound systems Jamaican style.
Naw, I'd say more the inspiration came from the disco DJs and Herc, when he came out. It was more his inspiration, 'cos he came straight from the islands. Mine was straight from seeing the systems of the disco DJs.

Did you really win a trip to Africa when you were at high school?
Yeah, I went to Africa, way before. It was in high school year, it was '75.

How did that come about?
Well in '74, there was a thing with UNICEF, and people had to write an essay on why they would want to go visit, at that time it was India. So I won the essay to go to India, but when it was time for me to meet the decision staff, I was out giving out flyers for one of my parties I was havin'. So I missed that trip to India. So the next year was a trip to Africa, so I really bust my ass on the essay for that one and I won it.

Can you remember what you wrote?
No, I can't remember. I told them why I need to go to Africa. And then I won and then I went. I went to Africa and Europe. Africa for two weeks and Europe for one week. I was in Ivory Coast, Nigeria, and Guinea Bissau.

And was that a big inspiration?
That was a big inspiration, seeing black people controlling their own destiny, seeing them get up and go to their own work. Seeing their own farmers and agricultures, it was very interesting, when you were seeing all the negativity that you were seeing as a young cat in America, and all the stuff just coming out of the '60s with the civil rights and human rights, so it was very inspirational seeing this.

It must have been a big part of the inspiration for the Zulu Nation.
I always had visions, and always felt I was sent to do a job or something. For the creator. So that was always on my mind, to start this organisation and to do things, especially when we started getting into the knowledge and we got out of the negativity and into the positivity and I started getting into the teachings of the most Honorable Elijah Mohammad, Minister Farrakhan, Malcolm X, Black Panthers... I started incorporating a lot of that and then checking out stuff that I learned from when I was a Christian, and all these other grooves, and then hanging with all these black, white and Catholic schools, then just start incorporating that into the Zulu Nation, start speaking to people in all walks of life. Especially when I started travelling and seeing the world more.

Were you deep into gangs before that?
Yeah, heavy into gangs. Back in the early days. I'd probably be dead if it wasn't for getting straight into hip hop culture, and making a culture out of it, and bringing a lot of my people

from that type of way. 'Cos I never had a problem in poolin' a large army or crowd. So when we shifted right into the DJ thing I already had a packed house.

So that was starting from gang days. And then at high school with the Organisation. What were your aims for that?
We had the saying: 'This is not a gang. We are family. Do not start trouble, let trouble come to you, and then fight like hell.' We used to carry our little cards around and stuff. That's when gangs were starting to die down. And then the Organisation became the Zulu Nation; that's when we was getting more into the music side of things. And then it went to the Almighty Zulu Nation, and then it went to the Universal Zulu Nation once we started incorporating all people from the planet Earth.

Do you remember hearing Herc play breakbeats for the first time?
Herc is not really the first time I heard breakbeats, but it was the first time that someone really pushed it.

Was Herc the first or was there someone else?
No, Herc was the first to push it in the culture, but breakbeats had been around since disco, since James Brown, all the little breaks between records.

But in terms of just playing the breaks? In terms of a DJ who just played the breaks?
Oh yeah, it was definitely Kool Herc.

And do you remember when you first heard him do that?
Hmm, it's a while back. Early '70s. When I first heard it I went, hmm, he playin' some of the stuff I got in my house. I got a lot of that stuff. I thought, that's funky. That's more funky than the way these disco DJs were playing they records.

So you liked the way he was cutting it up?
Yeah. I liked the way he was mixing the records. Like he would say one word and use the echo chamber, and by the time the echo chamber finished it was switched to another record. 'cos he wasn't heavy into all that cutting. All that cutting and scratchin' came along with Grand Wizard Theodore and Flash and all them.

But your thing was more about having records no-one else knew about.
Yeah. We was bringing out more of the funky music and mixing in the funky breaks. The other DJs, they might bring out certain breakbeat records, but the Zulu Nation was more progressive minded, and their audiences. If we played a certain rock record then everyone else would jump on it, because a lot of the other people's audiences wasn't so open like ours. They know our DJs were crazy motherfuckers, just play all crazy type of shit. They even would stop in the middle of a party and throw on a commercial, you know, from some of the TV shows we thought was just bugged and funky for the people to hear.

Where were you buying your music?
Well I had a large record collection, starting with what my mother bought. She probably bought the first 200 records in the house and I bought the other crazy thousands. I started at a very early young age and I was heavy into the Motown, the Stax sound and all them, the Sly, James Brown sound. I was a radio fanatic nut. So I would switch from WABC to WWIL, to WLIB, you know, WCBS…

So where were you hearing records like Yellow Magic Orchestra and Kraftwerk and stuff like that?
Well once I started getting into the record pools, at a young age. I was in the Rock Pool, I was in a pool called Sure Record Pool, I was in IDIC, can't remember all the damn pools I been in.

So you joined them all?
Yeah I joined a lot of pools and when I was risin' up and powering and people's hearing the wild stuff that I was playing, and getting all the records there and plus I was a record collector anyway, and then when I started travelling throughout the tri-state and checking what was in the record stores. I used to look for weird covers; I might have seen Yellow

Magic Orchestra and thought, that's a weird lookin' cover, let me pick this up. Then it was something called 'Firecracker'. I said Hmm, I could play with this...

What were the other tunes you discovered that way?
'Trans Europe Express'.

How did you discover Kraftwerk, do you remember?
It was from some record store downtown, in the Village.

What did you think?
I thought it was some weird shit. Some funky mechanical crazy shit. And more and more as I kept listening to it, I said, they some funky white guys. Where they from? Start reading all the... I always read labels yunno, want to see what it says on the back, who wrote what. I went digging more into their history so I got into *Autobahn*, their dub album, and once I got into Rock Pool, and they told me other things to check out, and I was checking *Radioactivity*, and the more stuff I was checking and playing to my audience.

> ## " I was heavy into gangs. Back in the early days. I'd probably be dead if it wasn't for getting straight into hip hop culture "

You played a lot of crazy stuff.
I got into Hugo Montenegro, looking for *The Godfather* theme, which was a break, then they had another one, Dick Hyman who did a more electronic type of James Brown groove. Then I got into Gary Numan, couple of other things, and mixing their stuff up with the funk, and James and Sly. It was a interesting mix for our audience. They were bugging out when we got into 'Cars', and 'Metal', and you see the audience waits, wants to hear the beginning of 'Metal', the synthesiser and the beat just claps and stuff...

How did they react?
At first it was a bugged reaction. Certain records that when I played, some people were, 'What the fuck is this?' They stopped, but I keep repeatin' it, over, I come back with something else, and then come back with that record again.

What records took a while...
I had a record from the Philippines called 'Ego Trippin'' with this group called Please, and I kept playing just the breakbeat, just to get people going. It used to go, 'Hey, you, stop, freaking freaking.' And the break keep hitting and the louder you hear it, the funk was hittin', and then I started playing the whole record after a while. People was gettin' into that.

You'd be looking for records all over.
We would go diggin' in stores and I would take a posse, walk all over from the Village to stores in the Bronx, to stores in Brooklyn and just look for obscure stuff. I just was finding music from all over the place. Then from my travels, 'cos that's when we started travelling to different cities in the tri-state area.

Your records were what gave you the advantage.
We just was comin' out with crazy breaks. Like other DJs would play they great records for 15, 20 minutes, we was changing ours every minute or two. I couldn't have no breakbeat go longer than a minute or two. Unless it's real crazy funky that we just want the crowd to get off.

Who gave you the title Master of Records?
I gave my own self that, because I knew no-one could mess with me 'cos I was a crazy record collector. I had stores like Downstairs Records, if I was playin' certain records they'd bootleg it up and sell them $50, $40, $100. Or other people might see me buying a Hare Krishna record and they're like, 'Oh give me five of them.' They was buggin', I told them, 'Don't buy

that because it's not what you think it is. It's not breakbeats or nothin'.' And they're, 'Aw, you're just tryin to keep it secret.' Thinking I'm fronting on them. And they go home and hear it and they be mad.

Did you ever get acetates pressed up from albums and things?
Many times. I started all that. I learned that from the disco DJs, of getting acetates and plates, made up. I used to make little mix things with the pause of a cassette tape, where you press it and it comes right on cue. Then we make up a mix song.

So you'd make up mixes ready for the parties?
I did it for parties or for when we having battles. Other DJs used to bug out when they hear me play, 'People get up, get up, clap your hands, get down down-down-down, du du du du,' How the hell he got a record like that? Or I might have a commercial from the Addams family, have it pressed up.

When did you start doing that?
Like '76, '77. Mid '70s. It was on the breakbeat time of trying to get beats, to out-do the other DJ.

Did you have MCs?
We had MCs straight from the early parts. Even in our disco era we always had some type of MC. We had about 11 MCs, or 12. Which after that became the Soulsonic Force, the Jazzy Five, the Cosmic Force.

❝ Flash was in the south Bronx, we was in the south-east Bronx, and you have Herc in the west Bronx. ❞

It was really competitive between you and Herc and Flash
Each DJ had they own respective crowds, they posse. Herc would have have his pack, Flash could have his pack and I could have mine.

And was that by area as well?
Yeah. Flash in the south Bronx, we was in the south-east Bronx, and you have Herc in the west Bronx. And then when DJ Breakout came, he had the North Bronx. And AJ. And then when Harlem started getting into it, Treacherous Three and all them.

Tell me about the battles. They were pretty civilised mostly?
It started, you play your system, I play my system: a bunch of noise going at the same time. You out-louded the next person, and then a member might get mad and go there and knock the turntable or something, and it leads into a rumble. So then we started having it agreed where we play an hour, you play an hour, and this way the audience decides, and it got more peaceful. Because at the early stages it definitely could have led into a lot of beatdowns and killings and fightings.

Herc tells a story of the battle at the Police Athletic League in 1977.
Yeah he had a big loud system. We let them do they thing. Then we did our thing. At the battle we funked them up with our music so much that when we left, the whole crowd left with us too. He had a louder system but when it came to the music they couldn't fuck around.

DJ Breakout had the Sasquatch. DJ Herc and them had the Herculords. After a while we started building our system. Jazzy Jay, he was a wizard at building sets, him and Superman, and they were building up our system which we called the Earthquake system.

One time Grandmaster Flash had this big battle against one of our other brothers at the time, Disco King Mario, and this should've been a movie. It was in James Monroe High School, and Flash came in with this whole nice little wall of speakers, Disco King Mario had nice big speakers that was going this way, but then he sent out for help, so I came with my system, then another guy named DJ Tex came with his system, and we put our stuff together and it looked like a whole big wall of Jericho, and it became a battle with Flash's people against us and Grand Wizard Theodore.

It was just going crazy, crazy, and I gave Theodore some of my records to play, but he didn't know them, so I just punched the spot and Theodore hit the spots just tearin' it up against Flash and them, and then Flash came under the ropes and starts screaming, 'I know you gave him your records, I know you gave him your records.'

What year was that?
Might have been '76. James Monroe High School.

Talking with other people, it seems the Zulu Nation was very separate from the scene at the Disco Fever and the Hevalo.
We played with Herc there at certain places, but when a lot of them were playin' in these little clubs, we were playin' in big centres. Myself and Disco King Mario had big control over the south-east Bronx. So we was the first area to play in schools. He was in the Chuck City Crew, but he was part of our family, it was like two crews. I used to play on his system a lot too, before I got my own system. And we had crazy control in our area of the South Bronx, so anyone wanted to come to that area had to come to us first to play in that area or play anywhere in the Bronx River area.

But you never went to Disco Fever?
No, Fever never grabbed me. Some people went to the Fever, it was their type of thing. They could be cool, get into the drugs and all that. I wasn't into all that shit.

Most of your parties were in community centres or parks?
Parks was only on the outside. Mostly it was in community centres in the beginning and in high school gyms and junior high school gymnasiums. And once we stepped into all the gyms we started bringing all the other DJs in and others started getting chances. 'Cos people see how much control the Zulu Nation had in their parties.

So you didn't play in clubs until you went downtown?
I played in clubs. I played in Sparkles, Hevalo, all that, with Herc. I played in some of the little spots that they had.

So you were pretty tight with Herc?
Yeah. When we first came out we had disagreements and he was like a guardian angel looking over where we go, because he knew we were definitely rising up powerful and had control on our side. And then we became real close and stuff and knew about our West Indian background and we started doing parties together. And Flash crew was also part of our family too. They was the Casanova crew.

There was the three of you, how did it divide up?
Well the three of us had our respective areas.

So it was very geographical.
Yeah, Flash was always in the Black Door or in 23 Park in the summertime. Herc was in the Hevalo, and Sedgwick Avenue Park. I was always in the Bronx River Center, or in high schools or junior high school gyms in the south-ast Bronx. So then sometimes we would coincide and give things at the Audubon Ballroom in Harlem. I had control of the T-Connection uptown which was a strong spot, and everyone was comin' there to play. But we respect each other. You could play in your spot, you could play in my spot.

How come it stayed in the Bronx for so long without people knowing about it downtown?
Basically because we probably wanted it like that. Then when we started travelling – I believe we were the first to really start travelling to all of Connecticut, and Jersey.

You always had the ambition to take it worldwide.
Yeah, 'cos I was always a person who just likes to move around. I just had a vision. I said we just got to make this move.

Afrika Bambaataa

How did you meet Lady Blue [promoter of the famous Roxy nights]?
Met her through [video-maker] Michael Holman, who was one of the first people that brought us to the downtown scene. When we started playing clubs like Negril, and then Lady Blue came in and started doing functions too, at the Negril, with Michael Holman, and then Michael Holman faded out of the scene, they fell out, and Blue was still doing it and we would travel everywhere, into the Negril. Also Fab 5 Freddy brought me down to play clubs like The Jefferson, the Mudd Club…

What was the very first downtown gig you played?
It was probably the Jefferson and the Mudd club.

And that was for Freddy?
Yeah, and the head of the rock pool at the time, I forget his name.

How did you feel about that, 'cos it's a totally different audience?
Oh, they were funky, they got loose. They liked the shit I was playing, Ohio Players, Kool and the Gang, 'Jungle Boogie', all that stuff, mixed with the breakbeats and the disco stuff. Once I was getting more into the Rock Pool and hearing a lot of punk rock records I started playing a lot of their stuff. Flying Lizards and all that other type of things that I might think that would get over there. And that's when my following started happening. 'I want you at Jefferson.' 'I want you at the Mudd Club.' 'I want you at Danceteria.' 'I need you at the…'

Where was Jefferson?
It was down from the Palladium. It was a big old movie house. And they had these romantic parties upstairs, when they used to come dressing like pirates, looking like Adam Ant. Then you had other scenes where they looked like vampires. It was definitely a weird scene. After a while you started getting used to it and it was on. Then when they started coming up to our places, it was very fun and interesting. Especially when we was shutting up the mouths of the press. The media would be saying, 'Oh there's gonna be racial fights,' and all this shit, but then it was just people partying, hanging, taking pictures, cooling out. Lines with black, white all in 'em waiting to get in. And we give much props to the punk rockers, 'cos they was some of the most fair to just come out and party along with the people, for the music. Like Uncle George Clinton used to say: one nation under a groove.

Once we started playing downtown, once it started getting towards the late '70s early '80s you start seeing the white punk rockers started coming to the black and Latino areas to hear the music. They would come to the Bronx. People were scared at first, you know you had the media said 'Oh there's gonna be race violence,' which we showed them was a bunch of shit.

And at first people was buggin', when they first seen them. Blacks and Latino looked at them like they crazy. They had the spikes and the hair, and the colours and all the different clothing, but then when that music hit, you just see everybody tearing they ass up. And then the punk rockers developed a dance which they used to do, and this became a black and Latino dance called the punk rock. You see the punk rockers learning the black dances and the blacks and Latinos learning the punk rockers' dances that they was doing. And then the parties just was killing.

And once we started stretching into Negril, Danceteria and then eventually the Roxy, which became the world club, it just blew up from there, punk rock and hip hop, and got them all to start coming up to the Bronx.

How did you get into making your own records, 'cos for a long time people didn't think it could be captured on records?
We got into it after Sugarhill and all them, and Fatback came out with King Tim III. At first everybody was against that because they thought it was gonna kill our sound system. And seeing as it was a way to make money, I was one who stood away longer. Flash and all them jumped on the scene, and a couple of other people joined with Bobby Robinson's label Enjoy. I stood more watching.

You thought it would kill the scene?
Yeah, I thought it would kill the scene in a way, and then I asked them how it was they

get along with their companies and stuff, and a lot of them told me the problems they was having. And then I tried it out with Paul Winley label, which I didn't like very much working with him. And that's when Tom Silverman came to visit us.

How did you meet him?
He came along with Arthur Baker, 'cos I had met Arthur and them first. And I met John Robie, he came to my house, he was trying to shop a record. He knew about me from my interesting list that I used to put in *Dance Music Report,* or in the Rock Pool list. People were like, 'Oh this guy plays a lot of wild shit.'

> ❝ **Blacks and Latinos looked at the punks like they crazy. But then when that music hit, you just see everybody tearing they ass up** ❞

So a lot of music business people knew you.
Yeah they knew me, and a lot of the organisations, the record pools and stuff, was hearin' about this black guy that was playin' to a large black and Latino audience, all this type of wild rock funk hip hop soul type dance music, so they all started to visit the different places I was playing: the Bronx or wherever I was playing in Manhattan, Harlem, or they would read the list of records that I would pick. And some of the recording artists that made these records even started checkin' us out. That was when Malcolm McLaren came down, to the block party, and he invited us to come play with Bow Wow Wow.

How did Jazzy Sensation come about?
Tom Silverman [Tommy Boy boss] came to check us out. I had made a record with him called 'Let's Vote', with a guy named Nuri.

You produced it?
No we just fixing it and pushing it out for him. Then he came with a girl group called Cotton Candy, which was our first recording for his label. He put Soulsonic on there with a little disco-type rapping. Then we came with my group the Jazzy Five with 'Jazzy Sensation'. We had Arthur Baker do the music with that, and that took off. And then I was deciding to come off with this electro sound I'd been working on for a while. And me and Tom was working on it, and that became the 'Planet Rock'.

'Planet Rock' changed music, but what were your ideas working up to it. What did you want it to be?
I wanted it to be the first black electronic group. After Kraftwerk put 'Numbers' out, and I always was into 'Trans Europe Express', I said I wonder if I can combine them two and make something real funky with a hard bass and beat. So we combined them. But I didn't want people to think it was just Kraftwerk, so we added a track called 'Super Sperm', by Captain Sky. The breakdown as the synthesisers going up, that's the 'Super Sperm' beat. And then we added 'The Mexican' by Babe Ruth, another rock group, and we speeded it up.

Were these records that you would mix like that in the parties?
Yeah, these were records I would play at the parties.

But would you actually mix them together in the same way as you did on the record?
No. I just thought of how they would sound mixed together. I had this thing of pulling different records together and replaying them and stuff. A lot of people think we sampled Kraftwerk but it's just not true. John Robie was a bad-ass synthesiser player, so he was just so good in playing stuff, that it sounded like they sampled the record. At that time there was no such thing as sampling. Sampling came more out when we did 'Looking For The Perfect Beat,' that's when the Emulator machine came out. There was none of these little sampling machines that we got today.

Can you remember how long it took to put together?

We started in Tom Silverman's father's house up in White Plains. We had a bassline taken from BT Express at first, but that didn't grab us and after a while we got Arthur Baker involved and Tom left the project to me, Arthur and John Robie, and shit started falling into place. Commissioned my group to make up this lyric, to where we was talking about the planet rock, 'All Planets are made of rock, but our planet Earth is a planet rock.' And it just took off. With the elements of the Kraftwerk sound and then the hard funk bass, and a beat underneath it. And I decided the name of this sound is the electrofunk sound.

When you first heard it, did you think it would be as important and influential as it was?

Not at first. When I made it I was trying to grab the black market and the punk rock market. I wanted to grab them two together. So that's all I was thinking of. I wasn't thinking of the world and the rest of that. But then when I start seeing Chinese get into it and all these other peoples was dancing and going crazy on the record and people started saying, 'Oh you've got to go to Germany.' To Germany? And I start having to tour countries and cities and small, little clubs, and that's how we started building it up overseas. Whereas a lot of other groups wasn't really travelling, they didn't really care about it as long as they knew it was happening in America.

We were doing a lot of shows with a lot of funk singers and stars, 'cos at that time it was just me and Flash and Sugarhill that was travelling. And we was going against a lot of funk groups. There wasn't really a lot of rap groups so that's why we came with all the wild clothes, 'cos you had to dress wild to deal with the Bar-Kays, and Cameo, and groups like that. We was blowing a lot of people off the stage too, 'cos it was their first time seeing just electronic instruments. One place we got chased off in DC because it was straight up band-land with the go-go. When they didn't see no whole band they booed us off.

❝ There's a lot of fun when you're DJing. Seeing people dance, seeing what records can make them get frenzied and let the God spirit out of their body. ❞

When you're DJing, what's the thrill?

There's a lot of fun when you're DJing. Seeing people dance, seeing what records can make them get frenzied and let the God spirit out of their body and just travel out, and what could bring that calm spirit back into they bodies, where they just mellow out and cool, and then you make them get frenzied again. Or playing other records that makes them think, or makes them just shake their booty. It's the thrill of just controlling the music and seeing the people on the dancefloor partying.

What do you mean makes them think?

If you play certain records, like James Brown, 'Say It Loud'. And the crowd would yell 'I'm black and I'm proud,' and they'd get off on that. Or you might play Sly's 'Stand', and they just waiting for that break part to come, and when that breakbeat come in they just go crazy. So it was different records, like 'Thank You (Falettin Me Be Mice Elf Agin)'

Messages really.

Yeah, messages. 'How many of y'all thank you for bein' yourself?' 'How many of y'all love your mamas? Say yeahh.' 'Cos we were one of the first to add messages, telling the MCs to say more than just throw your hands in the air, how many people smoke the reefer? 'Cos you had a lot of rappers who was all about themself: how many women they can get, but we start getting into message things, political things. Raise money for sickle cell anemia, raise money for our community centre, to get games and TVs and sound systems.

You used to get a kick out of playing things that people wouldn't normally dance to.
Yeah, obscure things. I play stuff where people talk about 'I don't like Latin,' so I play a Latin artist, and get them movin'. I'm a play a rock artist, say 'I ain't into heavy metal,' so I play something like Led Zeppelin, or Foghat or something, then move into that.

Which Led Zeppelin?
'House of the Rising Sun'. I also used to play 'Whole Lotta Love' and 'Black Dog'.

Which Foghat?
'Slow Ride' 'Take it easy...' 'Tom Sawyer', we played 'Honky Tonk Woman', 'Miss You', 'Hot Stuff', all they funky type of songs. Billy Squier 'Big Beat', Eddie Money 'Baby Hold On'. I used to play all sort of shit.

Through it all, what do you remember as the best time?
I think the early hip hop was when it was more fun. It was some parts dangerous, but it was more fun and it was more lovin' and it was just for the music, and people comin' together really to party. Than where it's more now just gangsters want to kill each other and all that type of mess. But I know things go in cycles so you have different feels of time where people have different feelings in the music of hip hop. But they definitely were the best, the '70s and early '80s. Especially through the electrofunk era. I think the electrofunk style of hip hop brought more people round the world together than all the other styles put together.

Looking back, what are you most proud of?
Bringing people together. Settling their differences and spreading the hip hop culture all around the world.

Kind of like a musical preacher?
Yeah, to bring the message of the music and also to get people to be thinkers. You know, especially in this day and age, to stop the foolishness and lies that's been taught through this century and let's get on with truth. We want right knowledge, right wisdom, right overstanding and right-sound reason. Like telling us Columbus discovered America, or Greece is the mother and father of western civilisation, when they got all their knowledge from Egypt and Africa. Let's tell the truth about what black people, brown people, red people, white people, yellow people has did to better civilisation, on this planet so-called Earth.

And let's get into the universal thing that's going on with our planets and galaxies and stuff, because we're shitting on mother Earth and mother Earth is getting tired of this shit, and she's spitting out humours left and right.

Do you ever think it's strange that you're going through life now, spreading this knowledge and visiting different countries and all that comes from just being a DJ and playing records?
Oh definitely. The power does come from being a DJ, but it really comes from the creative force, who is the source. We allow people to take credit all they want but it definitely is a force that's out there which is the source of all. We don't care what name you call it: Allah-Jehova-Yahweh-Elaheem-Jah-Rah-Anu-God, but we know there's definitely a force and it's dumb or blind for people to think that we as humans are the only beings in this whole universe, on the planet Earth.

In Zulu Nation we always told them that there's 12 planets in our galaxy and a 13th one that comes every 26,000 years. They thought we were crazy, but they only found the ninth planet in 1930. It's gonna get up to 12, you know, watch. Because the Sumerians, the Aztecs, the Incas, the Dogons, all them, the Egyptians, all knew about this science and stuff, and all these Hindus talked about the beings in the flying ships...

So when you're DJing, do you feel like it's not just you. It's this power...
It's a spiritual thing. It's definitely a aura or something that hits you. Because I never really rehearse or practise. When you hear me, you always hearin' me fresh and new. I ain't got no time to really sit down and mix this record or this one go with that one. I'm just thinking real quick.

You definitely kept that hip hop attitude: play any kind of music as long as it's funky.

I could go to any country and feel comfortable. When I'm in Bulgaria: 'Let me hear your funk.' 'I ain't got no funk' 'Trust me, you got funk!' Then you find certain records: 'That's funky,' find another: 'You could dance reggae to that,' and go to another place and hear another sound…

It's an international language.
It is, definitely is. It crosses those barriers. And then you catch those people who say 'I don't like Latin, 'I don't like rock.' And you go in their collection, 'Well what's this Rolling Stones doing here? What's that Tito Puente record doing there?' It's all out there. People just get caught up in the categories and like labelising, but music is music. It's just that too many of these radio stations they're caught up in the apartheid of the music. I say just play it all, let the people decide if they like it or not.

© DJhistory.com

ROXY 100

FRIEND AND LOVER – Reach Out In The Darkness

'FUSION MIX': MOHAWKS – Champ, **JAMES BROWN** – Get Up, Get Into It, Get Involved, **DYKE & THE BLAZERS** – Let A Woman Be A Woman, Let A Man Be A Man

EDDY GRANT – California Style

GRAND FUNK RAILROAD – Inside Looking Out

SHIRLEY ELLIS – The Clapping Song

ESG – Moody

FAB 5 FREDDY – Change The Beat

HERBIE HANCOCK – Rockit

HASHIM – Al Naafiysh (The Soul)

THE INCREDIBLE BONGO BAND – Apache

JOAN JETT – I Love Rock'n'Roll

ABACO DREAM – Life And Death In G & A

JACKSON 5 – Dancing Machine

AFRIKA BAMBAATAA & THE SOUL SONIC FORCE – Planet Rock

AFRIKA BAMBAATAA & THE SOUL SONIC FORCE – Renegades Of Funk

AFRIKA BAMBAATAA AND FAMILY – Bambaataa's Theme

GRANDMASTER FLASH & THE FURIOUS FIVE – The Message

GRANDMASTER FLASH – Larry Love

FALCO – Der Kommissar

LYN COLLINS – Think

CULTURE CLUB – Time

DEAD OR ALIVE – You Spin Me Round (Like A Record)

DEFUNKT – Razor's Edge

MANU DIBANGO – Soul Makossa

FOREIGNER – Urgent

BABE RUTH – The Mexican

LIQUID LIQUID – Cavern

THE MIRACLES – Mickey's Monkey

BLONDIE – Rapture

KURTIS BLOW – The Breaks

ARETHA FRANKLIN – Rock Steady

FREEZE – I.O.U.

CHUCK BROWN & THE SOUL SEARCHERS – Bustin' Loose

CHIC – Good Times

JAMES BROWN – Papa Don't Take No Mess

TYRONE BRUNSON – The Smurf

THE BUS BOYS – Did You See Me

HALL & OATES – I Can't Go For That

THE ALEEMS – Release Yourself

ART OF NOISE – Beat Box

THE CLASH – Rock The Casbah

GEORGE CLINTON – Loopzilla

DOMINATRIX – The Dominatrix Sleeps Tonight

PETER GABRIEL – Shock The Monkey

GRAHAM CENTRAL STATION – Now Do U Wanna Dance

THE B-52'S – Mesopotamia

MALCOLM MCLAREN – Buffalo Girls

GEORGE CLINTON – Atomic Dog

PHASE 2 – The Roxy

BOBBY BYRD – I Know You Got Soul

SISTER NANCY – Bam Bam

CAMEO – Flirt

GRACE JONES – My Jamaican Guy

HERMAN KELLY – Dance To The Drummer's Beat

KOOL & THE GANG – Jungle Jazz

TALKING HEADS – Once In A Lifetime

TOM TOM CLUB – Genius Of Love

THE O'JAYS – Money

KRAFTWERK – Numbers

JIMMY SPICER – Bubble Bunch

GARY NUMAN – Cars

POINTER SISTERS – Automatic

LISA LISA & THE CULT JAM – Head To Toe

YAZOO – Situation

KRAFTWERK – Trans Europe Express

MICHAEL JACKSON – PYT

RICK JAMES – Superfreak

MADONNA – Everybody

YELLOWMAN – Zuzuzangzang

LL COOL J – Rock The Bells

RUN DMC – It's Like That

THE SEQUENCE – Funk You Up

SHALAMAR – A Night To Remember

STEPPENWOLF – Magic Carpet Ride

ZAPP – More Bounce To The Ounce

SHANNON – Let The Music Play

SOS BAND – Just Be Good To Me

QUEEN – We Will Rock You

RAM JAM – Black Betty

ROCK STEADY CREW – Hey You Rock Steady Crew

ROLLING STONES – Start Me Up

NEW EDITION – Candy Girls

NICODEMUS – Boneman Connection

TREACHEROUS THREE – Yes We Can Can

TROUBLE FUNK – Trouble Funk Express

MAN PARRISH – Hip Hop Bebop

LITTLE SISTER – You're The One

STRAFE – Set It Off

SUGAR HILL GANG – Rappers' Delight

DONNA SUMMER – I Feel Love

WEST STREET MOB – Breakdance

VAUGHAN MASON – Bounce Rock Skate

MICHIGAN & SMILEY – Diseases

PRINCE – Controversy

SLY & THE FAMILY STONE – Family Affair

GEORGE KRANZ – Din Da Da

FELA RANSOME KUTI – Shakara

CYNDI LAUPER – Girls Just Wanna Have Fun

SHANGO – Zulu Groove

YELLOW MAGIC ORCHESTRA – Firecracker

Compiled by Afrika Bambaataa & Kool Lady Blue

" The night we cut 'Planet Rock' I said to my wife, 'We've just made musical history.' "

Arthur Baker
Maestro electro

Interviewed by Bill and Frank in Camden Town, January 25, 1999

Arthur Baker laid the studio foundations for today's electronic dance music. As a producer whose inspiration came firmly from the dancefloor, in an age when technology opened up a vista of new possibilities, he pioneered recording techniques so influential they founded whole genres. 'Planet Rock', the record he made with Afrika Bambaataa, was the basis of electro, the vanguard of the second wave of hip hop, and one of the first records to show how much sampling was going to shake things up, even before digital samplers had come of age. He brought drum machines crashing into the street styles of rap, and in his work with New Order played a major role in the electronic rebirth of danceable rock. He's been behind classic mixes like The Rolling Stones' 'Too Much Blood' and Fleetwood Mac's 'Big Love', and has produced everyone from Tom Tom Club to Bob Dylan.

For many years he's made his home in London and we meet at his flat over the Regent's Canal in Camden. Although he can occasionally be spotted behind the decks, his enduring success comes from a love of dance music combined with little desire to play records. Arthur Baker is a failed DJ with an acutely successful ear for the dancefloor.

This is the history of the DJ?

Yeah.
Well, I was never really a DJ. Actually, I was probably one of the worst disc jockeys ever. No, I was. Because if I didn't get a good reaction on a record, I'd just rip it off, break it up and throw it on the dancefloor. And that was before I took drugs.

So let's get started
Okay, so I was born in Boston, Mass. April 22nd 1955. I grew up in Boston until I moved to New York in '81.

How did you get into dance music then?
I worked in record stores over the Christmas season when I was 12 or 13. We'd get free records but we wouldn't get paid. The first promo I ever got – and I got the last pick out of the records – was Al Green. That was when I started getting into soul music: Jackson 5, Temptations, Sam & Dave. Before that I was into rock'n'roll.

When I was 16 I started working in a record store in Boston and it opened me up to a lot of music because anything new that came in I'd get to open up and listen to. That was '71 or '72. It was the golden era of Philly. As far as I'm concerned, '72 was the best year in black music ever. From the O'Jays and Spinners, to the Stylistics and Intruders.

Around that time I'd started going to clubs a bit. Like I'd go to the Sugar Shack, which was a black club where all those groups would play live. Since I worked at the record store I'd get free tickets to go to the gigs. I got to see James Brown, Bob Marley, Roy Ayers. I went to college in '73 – Hampshire College in Amherst – and about that time I got involved with people putting on parties and I DJed, because I had the best collection. At that time it would've been Stevie Wonder, Average White Band, Tower of Power. A lot of my friends were Puerto Rican and we started going down to New York. We'd come back with all the 45s.

....

That's when I started getting into a more underground sort of disco thing, because we would go to Downstairs Records.

Did you go to any clubs at that time?
In '73 we pulled this scam where a friend of mine met some kid whose father was defence minister or something and he took his father's jet and we all went to New York. One night a friend of mine, Apache Rainbows, comes by and he says, 'Yo, man there's this guy and he says he's got a jet and he wants to go to New York and he wants us all to come with him.' So the next day this guy calls us up and we all get into a van, go to Springfield and there's a Learjet waiting for us. So we get in and we're flown to New York and a Bentley picks us up, stocked with champagne. None of us had any money, but I had the keys to my father's friend's apartment. There were like eight guys and a couple of girls. We went to the Barefoot Boy and a few other clubs. My friends were all Hispanic and they were telling all the girls that they were Santana, so they flew back first and took some girls with them. Then they sent the jet back and I left with some other guys. It was great. That was my first club experience in New York.

And then – a footnote to the story – we see on the TV the guy had gotten arrested because although it was his father's jet, he was using it without his father's knowledge, and he'd had him arrested.

> **❝ A friend of mine met some kid whose father was defence minister or something and he took his father's jet and we all went to New York. ❞**

After the first year at college I got a gig at this club called Rasheed's which was owned by an Arab guy, the only club in Amherst. I quit school after '75 and I went to Boston and started DJing at this place called KD's and another one called Sadie's. Real Mafia places. But I got into the Boston record pool, which was run by John Luongo, who was a real influence to me. He was probably technically the best DJ I ever saw.

Who were the big DJs on Boston at the time?
The big five were Danae Jacovidis, Jimmy Stuard, John Luongo, Cosmo Wyatt and Joey Carvello. I wasn't really a good DJ, but I was getting into record production.

What was your first record as a producer?
The first record I did was 'Losing You' by the Hearts of Stone. I produced it, and John Luongo did a mix, and Joey Carvello and Danae had their names on it. This was around 1977, '76? I ended up selling it to Disco One in Canada, which was run by this guy Pat Deserio, who was also involved with those groups there like Kebekelektrik.

Then at that time I started going to New York a lot and I went to the first *Billboard* Disco Convention, which was run by this guy Bill Wardlow, who was supposedly the godfather of disco. I used to go to record companies and blag records even though I wasn't playing anywhere major. And the people I got into see were DJs working in promotion like David Todd, who became a really good friend, and Doug Riddick at Atlantic. I met Richie Kaczor because he was involved in the first disco magazine. Luongo did a magazine in Boston called *Nightfall*, which I started writing for.

Then I did some records under the name Northend. The first one was 'Kind Of Life' on West End in 1979. Luongo mixed it and Jimmy Maynard did the percussion. And Larry [Levan] used to play that record. That was probably the first record I made that he played at the Garage.

And I did all these Philly influenced tracks. Tom Moulton and his brother Jerry came through, because they were both from Boston, and gave me a horrible deal, and I sold them all the tracks. They came out on Casablanca as TJM. One of them, 'I Don't Need No Music', was on the *Record World* chart. That was when I met [music journalists] Brian Chin and Nelson George. I met all those guys through going to the disco conventions. Then I made that record 'Rap-O Clap-O' with Joe Bataan for London. Then London went bust so it went on to Salsoul.

What made you get into production rather than DJing?
Because I was a shit DJ.

Were you a musician?
No, I just had ideas about what I wanted to do with music.

But you were obviously influenced by DJs, weren't you?
Yeah, I was a DJ, I just wasn't a good one. I wanted to make music, I didn't want to play records. Put it this way: I knew the power of the DJ. I was friendly with all the good DJs. I'd go and hang out in other clubs when I wasn't playing. I'd sit in the booth with Danae or Jimmy Stuard or John Luongo, who was a genius. He could take two records – the thing that became famous with hip hop – two 45s. John would extend intros, and he would just do it on the fly. He'd really mix a 12-inch version out of 45s. He was really quick. He used to play at a black club called Rhinoceros.

In Boston the straight clubs were nothing. It was either the black clubs or the gay clubs. Danae played at Champs, Jimmy was playing at the 1270. You'd go to those clubs and watch. When I went to New York David Todd would introduce me to people. He took me to Galaxy 21 and there was this record which just seemed endless with all of these cuts in it. It was amazing. I was like 'How is he doing this, he must be so quick?' I went up the booth and it was one record. It was 'Ten Percent' [by Double Exposure]. Then I'd hang out at Scepter, that's how I met Mel Cheren. There was a real small group of people, so you could talk your way into seeing people.

Going from being a DJ to producing was quite an new idea then though.
Yeah, it was. John Luongo was a DJ who was doing remixes. Jimmy Burgess was a DJ doing remixes. But they were all big name DJs. No-one was going to give me a remix. I had to do it from the other way. I had to make my own records, and that's how I got to be able to remix records: by having hits. After I did 'Planet Rock', 'I.O.U.' and 'Walking On Sunshine', that's when I got remixes. Before that, I never remixed a record.

Where did you learn how to make records?
I was a real student of records. Back then, it wasn't easy. Now you can take a sampler. Back then it was all live. All those records were live. For instance, when I did 'Happy Days' in '79, we had to work five hours to get that drum sound. It was all live musicians. You know: make what you're able to hear. I loved Gamble and Huff, so you'd get a musician in and say, 'Listen to Earl Young and try and play as good as he does.' I'd write songs. I'd find a keyboard player and go in and write songs together.

On Northend, I had these guys Tony Carbone and a drummer Russell Presta, who got murdered right after we'd had a couple of records out. He was a really good DJ too. If he'd have lived he would definitely have done big things. There was this other guy, a keyboard player Andre Booth. He produced 'This Beat Is Mine' [by Vicki D]. Him and his guitarist Charlie Street played on 'Happy Days'. No-one said you couldn't do it, but no-one gave me money. I had to raise the money to make a record. But the first thing I made came out.

And when 'Happy Days' happened Larry used to play the shit out of 'Tee's Happy' [the B-side]. I moved to New York right after that.

Was that the spur to you moving there?
That and the fact that my wife at the time was a lawyer and she got a job in New York. When I moved to New York I met Tee Scott and I had him mix 'Happy Days'. I really loved the sound coming out of Better Days. I met Shep [Pettibone], I'd heard some of his stuff on the radio. The next record I did was 'Jazzy Sensation', which was on Tommy Boy, and Shep had played his edit of the original 'Funky Sensation' [by Gwen McCrae] on Kiss and I really liked what he'd done, so I called him up and said, 'Why don't you come in and add some of those overdubs on to my rap version?' So he did that and I think he did a re-edit. That might have been his first credit on a record, maybe his second. After that, when I did 'Walking

On Sunshine', I brought in Jellybean. So I was going to all the clubs and meeting DJs and bringing them in. Whether they added all that much at that point I'm not really sure. I just wanted to have that connection and input.

How did you come to do Jazzy Sensation?

I had been writing reviews for *Dance Music Report,* which was owned by Tom Silverman and he was starting up a label. The first record he did was 'Let's Vote', by this guy Erik Nuri from Boston. And I was the only producer that Tom knew. We went into the studio with Andre Booth, Charlie, this bass player. It was basically Andre Booth and his rhythm section. We went in and we were either going to do a 'Genius Of Love' rap version or a rap version of 'Funky Sensation'. But a bunch of people had gone in and done 'Genius Of Love', so we did 'Funky Sensation'. And that did really well and sold 30,000 records.

So Tom says, 'Well, you did pretty well on that, do you wanna do another one?' Bambaataa was with the Jazzy Five and he said 'Do another record, but with Bambaataa. Here's another group: Soulsonic Force.' And I'd been into Kraftwerk, and Bam was into Kraftwerk, and we just had the idea of merging the two Kraftwerk songs together.

How much did those two Kraftwerk songs have to do with what Bambaataa was doing as a DJ?

I used to hear 'Trans-Europe Express' all over the place. In playgrounds, clubs everywhere. At that time, when I moved to New York, I worked at a record distributor Cardinal One-Stop. When I had lunch I'd sit in the park and there'd be guys with the big beat-box breakdancing. So I'd hear it all over the place. Then 'Numbers' came out. And I used to hang out at a record store in Brooklyn called Music Factory, and the guys who later became Rockers Revenge – Donnie and Dwight – worked there, and they turned me on to things. I came in and heard 'Numbers' and they said, 'Oh man, it's flyin' out of the store.' So me and Bam decided to mix the two together.

What you were doing was very much like sampling without a sampler.

Definitely. Yeah.

Was that a new thing?

Well, people would do cover records. Black music has always had cover records. What I was trying to do was mix in the DJ bits of other records. It was a conscious thing. It was almost like a medley, but not really, because you only used little bits of things. I tried to create what a DJ would do with records.

How much were you influenced by the Loft and the Garage? Rockers Revenge sounded like a Peech Boys-style record when it came out.

Oh yeah. I tried to make it sound like a Peech Boys record! I'd go to the Garage and I was able to get into the booth because I knew people there. And Larry loved 'Tee's Happy'. He used to really love the break in it. There was a bass-synth line in it that he used to call 'The Pig' – *boww-boww-b-boww* – and he used to love that. He would let me in the booth and I'd hang out with him. We'd talk music. I was obviously influenced by the Peech Boys record. Everyone was influenced by the Peech Boys record. When those handclaps started whipping around the place...

I'd go to the Loft a lot, too; the Loft was a great experience, but hearing a record in the Garage... there was no comparison. The Loft might have had the vibe and everything and the system was good. But the Garage was just so loud and punchier. If you heard a record on that system, you remembered it. When records like Ashford & Simpson's 'No-one Gets The Prize' and Diana Ross's 'The Boss' came on...

The first time I heard 'Rapper's Delight' [by Sugarhill Gang] was at the Paradise Garage. I mean, you'd go there and he'd always pull out two or three records which would just blow you away. Obviously, the Garage was a major influence. 'Walking On Sunshine' was specifically made for the Paradise Garage.

Did it get played there?

Oh shit, yeah. He used to play the fuck out of that. He was playing a lot of my records at that time. He even played 'Planet Rock'. Larry was really open. He was playing Imagination, he was playing Level 42, he was playing the Clash, He would play anything, so you knew whatever you did he'd give it a fair listen. His taste was weird though. Sometimes you'd do a record that you'd think he'd love and he'd hate it. Then there'd be this thing that you wouldn't think anything of and he'd play it. So you couldn't really promote a record to Larry.

He'd do this a lot too: you'd wait for him to play your record, and he wouldn't play it. Then you'd go home and the next day someone like [record promoter] Bobby Shaw would call and say, 'He played it three times after you left!' That happened a lot.

66 You'd wait for Larry to play your record, and he wouldn't play it. Then you'd go home and the next day someone would call and say, 'He played it three times after you left!' 99

So you would go into the studio and say I'm going to make a record for this particular club?
Well what I would do is go to a club and then the next day go into the studio all inspired and make a record. Same thing with the Funhouse. 'I.O.U.' was definitely a Funhouse record. 'Confusion' [by New Order] was a Funhouse record. You knew those weren't Larry's kind of records.

How did you come across Jellybean?
'Planet Rock' had come out and Tom Silverman wanted a 7-inch edit of it, but he didn't want to pay. And he knew Jellybean had a quarter-inch tape machine. So we did the edit of 'Planet Rock' at Jellybean's house. I think that's how I met him. We hit it off really well.

Then when I did 'Walking On Sunshine' Jellybean came in and helped me mix it a bit. That was at Blank Tapes studio. It was really funny, because his contribution was hitting the reverb button on the explosions on the snare! For a long time that was his major trick he got from me. He helped with 'I.O.U.' and he's on the record for 'Confusion', but I don't think he was there when we did the final mix. But Jellybean would play all those records at the Funhouse. He would play anything Larry would play, plus he could play even more, because he was playing the more freestyle and hip hop things. I don't think 'Confusion' got played at the Garage, but it was definitely a Funhouse record.

How did the New Order thing come about, because I know that they were very influenced by New York.
They approached me because they had been a fan of 'Planet Rock', and they also liked the story of how we settled with Kraftwerk.

What was the story?
After 'Planet Rock' we owed Kraftwerk a lot of money, so to compensate for the fact we raised the list price of the record. Silverman raised the price of the 12-inch so that it raised the amount of money they owed. So New Order sent me an album, *Power Corruption and Lies* and the only thing I really liked was '586' which was an instrumental that became the basis of 'Blue Monday'. Then they came to me and said they wanted to work with me and we did 'Confusion' and 'Thieves Like Us'.

In the 'Confusion' video you go into the Funhouse with a reel-to-reel tape. Did you really do that?
Oh we always did. That's where we got the idea. I'd tell them, 'We'll finish it and we'll go to the Funhouse so Jellybean can play it right away.' Jellybean was one of the first people – as well as Larry – who had a tape machine.

How did the band react?

··

They loved it. They loved the idea that I could just take the tape down there and it would get played. That's why they did the Haçienda, because they wanted their own club.

Didn't you guess 'Planet Rock' might bring Kraftwerk knocking?
Yeah, in fact that's how 'Play At Your Own Risk' came about. We were worried we'd have problems, so we did an alternate melody line. And I had wanted this D-Train/Strikers sounding clavinet part on it. So we had all these extra parts. But when we went to mix it, Tom said, 'Oh just use the Kraftwerk melody.'

But afterwards I said, 'Listen, there's another record here. This could be a big record.' I thought the clav and the other melody were even hipper than 'Planet Rock', and this is what ended up as 'Play At Your Own Risk'. I had a rough mix of it and Jellybean was playing the instrumental of it. That record was number one at the Funhouse six months before it ever came out. People would freak out. They'd hear the orchestra hit – 'Planet Rock' had been the first with that on I think – and there'd be this different music. But it was the same beat. We knew it would be a hit. I knew these singers from a group called the Ambitions: Bobby Howard, Herb Jackson. I even got François in to do a mix, but we didn't end up using it. He was into his percussion phase. It just didn't work.

> ❝ **On 'Planet Rock' we didn't have an 808, but there was an ad in the *Village Voice*: 'Man with drum machine $20 a session'.** ❞

How did you originally meet up with Bam?
Through Silverman. That was how I hooked with [John] Robie, too. There used to be a remix service called Disconet and Robie had had some song on it that Bam liked. I think Bam had had a record on it, too.

Do you remember the first time you saw hip hop being played?
Oh yeah, Joe Bataan brought me up in '78 or '77. It was before there had been a [hip hop] record out. He brought me up around 129th Street, because he was from there. And he said, 'Check this out! There's these kids talkin' over records.' He said, 'Someone's gonna make a million dollars out of this.' No, he did, he really did! We went in and used 'To Be Real' [by Cheryl Lynn] and did 'Rap-O Clap-O', and Jocelyn Brown sang on it and I think that was the first or second record she sang on.

Jellybean was the first superstar DJ wasn't he?
He got in that position pretty much for one reason: because he was going out with Madonna. I mean the Funhouse was a good club, but then the fact that he was Madonna's boyfriend really helped.

It was still pretty early in Madonna's career, though, wasn't it?
Yeah, but Madonna blew up in New York after her first record. I'm trying to think what made him different from other DJs, because Larry did lots of remixes, too. The superstar DJs in New York doing remixes were Shep, Larry, Jellybean, François, Tee Scott to an extent. It was really those four that were the big names. And Jellybean was the only straight one. Well, François was straight, too, but I'm just saying... I think that made a bit of a difference. There are a lot of reasons. He was really smart. He was a good businessman. He was more of a businessman than the others.

Funhouse was a really straight club too wasn't it, so it was more accepting of hip hop, freestyle and the like.
Well it was a street club. It was the only mixed straight club.

You mean racially mixed?
Yeah. I remember sometimes black kids having a problem getting in and we'd have to go out and help them get in. It was a Mafia club.

Where was it?

Near Sound Factory, on 26th. Right around the corner from the Tunnel. He was mixing Hall & Oates. He'd mix all the big names. In the beginning he was getting a lot of mixes. For instance, 'Girls Just Wanna Have Fun' [by Cyndi Lauper]. He did the first mix. Then she didn't like it, so I did one which they ended up using. So I was just behind him. He was making his name by mixing records that I had produced. 'Planet Rock' was on his résumé and he had only done the single edit! So anything he got near he was using on his résumé. I mean, he was smart. Looking back now he never struck me as being into the drug thing as much as others. He wasn't as druggy. He was more motivated by money. He was always a little businessman. Always.

He must have been the first DJ to get a solo deal.

Yeah. But he got that because of Madonna. Definitely. Because she was going to sing 'Sidewalk Talk' and she only ended up doing backgrounds. He had done Madonna's record. He had done 'Holiday'. He was a really great DJ.

What made him good?

He really mixed well. He mixed between records really well. I mean, Larry wasn't a great mixer between records. He'd let a record end and he'd throw another one on. But Jellybean could really mix. And he just picked the right records. 'Slang Teacher'.

By Wide Boy Awake?

Yeah. He'd play records like 'Was Dog A Doughnut' [by Cat Stevens], 'The Mexican'. He came from a hip hop mentality, where he'd play things that weren't supposed to be played. But Larry would do that, too. He would play 'Rapper's Delight'. He played that when it first came out. He played that five times a night. Jellybean had a very commercial sensibility when he made his own records. He didn't make earth-breaking records or mixes.

Can we take you back to Bambaataa. How much was he involved and how much was he more the inspiration?

More of an inspiration really. When we did 'Planet Rock' he brought Captain Sky 'Super Sperm'. He said: 'This beat here. Let's use that.' So we had that break in 'Planet Rock'. He definitely had influence. Bam definitely had really eclectic tastes. Flash did too. But he didn't know about the studio.

But it wasn't the first time a DJ came in with no knowledge of the studio and a pile of records and said, 'Here, make me this record.'

Nah. Sugarhill did that before we did, so I don't think it was the first. It may have been the most interesting and different but I don't think it was the first. It was in the vicinity. It might have been the first rap record with a drum machine because all the Sugarhill records were played live. After 'Planet Rock' people started using drum machines.

When did you record it?

1981. We didn't have it that long before it was on record. I remember going to For The Record or one of the record pool parties at Christmas and I put on the acetate and people went mad. Then it came out a little after that in 1982, and it was a big hit in the summer.

How quick was it to make?
It was pretty quick to make because we didn't have much money. We'd get downtime, night-time sessions. The guy who owned the studio gave us a deal. Maybe it was three all-night sessions. We did all the music in one session and a bit of the rap. Then we did the rap. Then we mixed it.

Were you aware it was a historic record?
I knew before we even mixed it. I knew before there was even a rap on it. I went home the night we cut the track and brought the tape home and I said to my wife at the time, 'We've just made musical history'. Oh, I knew.

❝ All we used was the explosion and the orchestra hit. The Fairlight was a $100,000 waste of space. ❞

Did you feel that you were documenting or transferring that live hip hop feel on to record?
I don't think I did that. I think Def Jam did. I missed out a bit on that. When we did *Beat Street,* we started to have Jazzy Jay doing cuts live. On 'Breaker's Revenge' I did all the cuts on that but I don't think that came out till '83 or '84. After 'Planet Rock' came out everyone was doing that. And me and my programmer John Robie didn't want to do another one like that.

Instead we did 'Looking For The Perfect Beat', which took forever to do, I came up with the concept of 'looking for the perfect beat'. And 'beat this'. I came up with that, too. It was almost a taunt at Sylvia because there was definitely competition between us and Sugarhill. So when it went 'beat dis' and we threw one beat on. It was like a challenge.

What was your first experience with a sampler?
The very first time was the Emulator 1. First time I heard that was at Unique. They had an Emulator 1 with lots of samples, like Three Stooges, Tarzan, stupid vocal things.

What was it like?
It was a keyboard. The first sampler I used was the orchestra hit on 'Planet Rock'. That was a sample from a Fairlight. Then when we did 'I.O.U.'

So you had access to a Fairlight when you did 'Planet Rock'?
Yeah. But all we used was the explosion and the orchestra hit. The Fairlight was a $100,000 waste of space.

They just had pre-programmed sounds in them?
Yeah, there was a really hard-to-programme sequence. It would take forever. On 'Planet Rock' we didn't have an 808 and I wanted to use one, and there was an ad in the Village Voice: 'Man with drum machine $20 a session'. I don't even remember the guy's name or anything. So I got him for $20 and said: 'Programme this'. But the first time we ever used an Emulator to really make a difference in a song was the solo on 'I.O.U.' Jellybean was saying 'You should do A-E-I-O-U'. That was the first time we did that. Then after that everyone used the Emulator on those stupid voices. For three years there were the orchestra hits, the 808 and the Emulator. Then later on it was the multiple edits...

You did lots of rock mixes in the '80s, how did that compare with the dance stuff?
I don't think I ever clicked with a rock group because I like to do my own thing. I don't really like to serve someone else and when you do a rock thing, you're someone else's servant. And I hated that. As a producer, I came from rhythm and blues, Gamble & Huff, where they wrote the song...

Very much producer-led...
Yeah. Which is what dance music is. To then go to rock music... If I got offered a group and

I didn't like the songs, then I'd go, 'Fuck I'm not gonna sit around for eight months'. The Chili Peppers I was supposed to do an album, but I turned it down. The Mondays, I turned them down.

You did *Empire Burlesque* with Dylan in 1985? What was he like to work with?
Well, he didn't like the studio all that much. I was basically hired to arrange and mix it, but I ended up cutting three tracks with him and doing tons of overdubs. He was like a rummy at the time. He was drinking lots of rum. I was doing lots of coke.

Rum and coke! A perfect combination!
He'd want to start at five at night. And he'd work for three hours and then leave. And I'd be up all night doing drugs and working on the record. He was an idol so it was pretty nerve-wracking. He wanted me to do his next record, but I didn't want to do it because the songs weren't as good as before.

So what was the main difference between your rock remixes and dance productions?
All my dance productions starting '80 to '81 were all programmed. When I started doing mixes it was Bruce Springsteen, it was Rolling Stones, it was General Public, and those mixes were all live, so it was really different. They'd want you to do what you did, but the technology wasn't really there to do it, you know? There was the technology to put a click track on: you'd have to use the snare and the kick from the live track and you'd trigger the click from that. But it was really imprecise, because the drumming was all over the place. So you'd try to make a click that went all over the place but that the sequencer could follow. For instance, the Emulator had an internal trigger, so at least you could trigger their snare off the Emulator.

This guy Chris Lord-Alge was really good at doing a click track because he was a drummer. He did 'Dancing In The Dark' [by Bruce Springsteen], 'Swept Away' by Diana Ross. He was the engineer on a lot of that stuff. I think 'Dancing In the Dark' might have had a drum machine. That was really tight. But a lot of my other remixes, like 'Too Much Blood', which people still play, I'd just change the bassline. My theory always was that if you had a really groovy bassline the drums don't have to be a straight kick, because people dance to the bassline. So when I did Living In A Box, which was one of my first big remixes here, and also Fine Young Cannibals' 'Ever Fallen In Love', I would change the bassline for like a Norman Whitfield bass approach. Then the band would call up: 'You didn't make the chord changes; you didn't do this and you didn't do that'. And I'd go: 'Well, listen to Norman Whitfield. His basslines never change'.

I remember Lindsey Buckingham [of Fleetwood Mac] calling me back after I did 'Family Man', being all upset, and 'Big Love'. I would start by redoing the bass live. I had this bass player Brian Rock and he would play dubby bass, like on 'Too Much Blood', 'Cover Me' [by Bruce Springsteen]. Then I'd have Bashiri Johnson come in and do percussion. Then, if I could, I'd somehow play the kick drum in. Chris usually did pretty well on that. But the technology was not really there to sync it up.

How time consuming was it? How long did it take to do 'Too Much Blood' for example?
The edits would take so long. And I was so coked out of my brain. So between me being coked up and my engineer being coked up, we'd spend three days on the mix. I had 20 reels of 'Too Much Blood', and we'd go into the editing suite and there'd be so much, the Latin Rascals would just look at it and say, 'What the fuck are you doin' to us, man?' It would take weeks. Junior [Vasquez] used to edit for me. Juan Cato used to edit for me. Benji Candelario. Cevin Fisher. Victor Simonelli. Lenny Dee. These were all editors that worked at Shakedown.

It's a good job they weren't doing as many drugs as you!
They couldn't afford it! Until they started editing for me, and then they could definitely afford it. They used to make so much money, it was $20-30 an hour.

In general how do you think the DJ's sensibility affected the way records were made?
Well, I mean if you're making dance records you want DJs to play 'em. A lot of record producers didn't realise that, so they'd have to get DJs to go and remix them. I would get DJs to go in and remix it with me, but I never gave the track to a DJ because I knew what I wanted. I wanted it to be credible with the DJs, so I knew having a DJs name on it would help. But also because the DJ could also add a little something. And that could make the difference. When I was really hitting, I don't think any of the records were made in the mix. They were made in the conception.

So do you think the DJs affected the conception then?
Oh yes, definitely. If I hadn't been a DJ I wouldn't have known what to listen for. When I did the mix of 'Living In A Box' I would have all these dropouts where I would have the bass keep going and there'd be an explosion and the drums would come back. And they were saying 'You can't do that. You took the drums out. People won't know how to dance to it.'

Why didn't he understand it?
I don't know. He didn't. He hadn't been to New York yet. He moved to New York after that record. I'd been to the Garage I knew you could drop things out. From listening to Larry and seeing how he would drop acappellas in, that really influenced my mixing. In mixes, I think I was one of the first to drop things out – except for the vocal – but that's having the confidence to do that. 'Dancing In The Dark': BOOM! 'This gun's for hire' (sings) BOOM back in. DJs would pick up on that and use the acappellas on records to do quick cuts. 'Don't Make Me Wait' started with the acappella and then the claps would come in.

Were you consciously taking ideas from dub?
No. I was taking ideas from the Garage. I can't say I was into dub. I like dub, but I'm not going to say I was listening to dub. I know François said he did but he was more international.

Where did you get the ideas for using decay, reverb etc.?
Well, from Norman Whitfield. Rare Earth records. They always had these wild delays. Rock records used to use a lot of delays. 'I'm Losing You' [a Rare Earth and Temptations song]. It wasn't new. I don't think even Jamaicans came up with it. It was on rhythm and blues records. Motown records. But Rare Earth records specifically. But it was going to the Garage. I'm not going to deny that. Larry would use delays on the handclaps, everyone would go wild and I'd say 'Hey, sounds good to me!'

How much influence have DJs and dance music had on popular music?
I think it's limited to dance music in a way.

© DJhistory.com

Tom Silverman of Tommy Boy and Arthur Baker.

ARTHUR BAKER SELECTED DISCOGRAPHY

NORTH END – Happy Days (producer)
TJM – Small Circle of Friends (arranger)
AFRIKA BAMBAATAA & THE JAZZY 5 – Jazzy Sensation (producer)
CUBA GOODING – Happiness Is Just Around The Bend (producer/mixer)
TOUCHDOWN – Ease Your Mind (remixer)
AFRIKA BAMBAATAA & SOULSONIC FORCE – Planet Rock (producer/mixer)
PLANET PATROL – Play At Your Own Risk (producer/mixer)
ROCKERS REVENGE – Walking On Sunshine (producer/mixer)
FREEEZ – I.O.U. (co-writer/producer/mixer)
NEW EDITION – Candy Girl (producer)
NEW ORDER – Confusion (writer/producer/remixer)
LOLEATTA HOLLOWAY – Crash Goes Love (producer/mixer)
BRUCE SPRINGSTEEN – Dancing In The Dark (remixer)
FLEETWOOD MAC – Big Love (remixer)
ARTHUR BAKER – Breaker's Revenge (producer)
ROLLING STONES – Too Much Blood (remixer)
CRIMINAL ELEMENT ORCHESTRA – Put The Needle To The Record (writer/producer/mixer)
BLIND TRUTH – Boombaata (writer/producer)
WALLY JUMP JR & THE CRIMINAL ELEMENT – Jump-Back (producer/remixer)
JACKIE 60 – The Jackie Hustle (producer/mixer)
DIANA BROWN – Love In Return (producer/mixer)

RECOMMENDED LISTENING

VARIOUS – Tommy Boy Story Vol. 01
VARIOUS – Best of Minimal Records – Rough House Vol. 1
VARIOUS – The Freestyle Compilation – The Best Of Criminal Records

" As a musician already, I started using my music skills to manipulate the turntables. "

Grand Mixer D.ST
Turntable virtuoso

Interviewed by Frank in Harlem, October 10, 1998

D.ST is the grandaddy of all turntablists. While scratching was first brought to life by Flash and his protégé Theodore, it was D.ST (born Derek Showard, now called DXT) who gave it wings and inspired kids all over the world to stay in their rooms flicking their wrists and wearing out crossfaders.

D.ST was the first DJ to win a Grammy. He stepped up to receive the award as part of Herbie Hancock's band for the 1983 single 'Rockit', a track which for most of the world was the first time they'd heard scratching. D.ST was the soloist pulling a wealth of itchy sounds from a copy of Fab 5 Freddy's record 'Change The Beat'. To a video of high-heeled robot legs, he showed that in skilled hands a turntable could not only lay down scratched rhythms but could also make improvised tones – musical notes. Jazz keyboardist Hancock, ever one to experiment, added him to his touring band.

We meet at his girlfriend's place, a spacious ground floor flat in Harlem's East 140s. He shows off the home studio he's built for her, including some 'fifteen grand' piece of equipment he's just brought in with him. The TV is on without sound throughout, and KD, his enthusiastic sidekick sits patiently listening. After the interview D.ST heads over to his studio in Jersey, dropping his girl at her job in a midtown fashion store. We barrel through Central Park in his jeep talking about playground games.

Where were you growing up?
In the Bronx.

How did you get into music?
I'm from a musical family. My mother sings. She still does. Blues and pop, Billie Holiday kind of stuff. And my sister is a professional dancer. So my whole family was in showbusiness.

How about you?
I always enjoyed music. I used to sleep in the living room on the floor by the radio. I would just spend a day listening, changing from station to station. As far as playing music, I started off as a drummer. I had my first drum set, I had to be four, five, maybe younger. It had one of them British rock groups on the bass skin, like the Beatles or something.

It was always percussion?
When I got into school I learnt how to play the clarinet. And I noticed something about playing the horn: it's a feeling. You can actually play it if you feel like playing it. If you feel what it feels like to get those sounds out – that's how I did it.

Instinctive?
Yeah. It's an instinctive thing. I played drums for a long time, and in my neighbourhood all the musicians were older guys, and they all played jazz, and I would always want to play some of the more hip stuff that was on 99X radio station.

What was that like?
Rock, pop. It was a real radio station, not like what we're listening to today; they had a

....

variety of stuff. But I would only be allowed to play with these guys if I was gonna calm down and just play some shuffle beats.

What year is this?
1973, '74. Right around '74 I was playing jazz in the summertime, in parks all around the Bronx. In my neighbourhood we'd set up outside, and just play, they'd bring out the amps. By that time, my drum set, I had beat it to death. My mother couldn't afford to buy me a new kit. So now I'm borrowing pieces. I got pieces of everybody's drums.

So what inspired you to try DJing?
I became a roadie for a band called the Funkmaster's Gang. This was a complete cover song band, from Mount Vernon. I was their first and only roadie. I used to use the vacuum cleaner to blow the dry ice on the stage. We did a party at a Latin club and there was a DJ there when the band wasn't onstage. And just the way he was playing, I thought it was pretty impressive. And to this day I don't know who he was; he wasn't a Kool Herc or none of that, but that was the first time I saw a DJ. He was just playing some old classics: like Bobby Byrd, 'Keep On Doing It'. But when it came on the whole crowd got up and everybody got into it.

And Kool Herc was a big inspiration too.
A friend of mine, James White, I called Jazzy. He was telling me, 'Kool Herc's doing a party. Yo man we gotta go.' I went to see Kool Herc and I realised that he has the same kind of pull that the bands have, the local bands. People go see him just to see him, and I just stood there and watched him DJ and I was amazed. He didn't cut on time or nothing like that, he just... his variety of music, the songs that he had, it was very clever. And it moved the crowd. It was a combination of the old and new.

Where was this?
I went to see him at The Executive Playhouse, in 1974.

Was he playing breaks by then?
He was playing them but he wasn't cutting. Kool Herc never cut. To this day, he don't cut. When the break would come up he would just move it on. He would just pan the fader over; it would be all off-beat or whatever.

So he would play the breaks just fading between them?
Yeah. He would play the breaks without being synchronised.

Was he playing two copies of the same record?
Yeah, yeah. So he's actually the first guy who... But Flash made it to the point where he would cut them so it's more of an edit.

On beat.
Yeah. I stood there, and at the time I was a B-boy, so you know I was ready to breakdance at the drop of a dime. So I'm listening, checking out people doing the hustle, and I'm waiting for 'Apache' to come on, so I could B-boy. And I'm checking out Herc. And I'm also in there breakdancing. So now there's a place, there's a guy I can go, to his party and practise my moves. Whereas anywhere else you'd just be waiting for the breaks.

So would you just be standing on the side?
Most B-boys would be like this [arms folded tight under his chin]. That's where that came from. Just waiting. Not from trying to be cool.

You're just waiting for the break.
Yeah, you're just standing there waiting, you know... while the hustlers are doing the hustle.

And then the breaks come on and then, bang!
Yeah. There was a bunch of guys, waiting around for Kool Herc to play the beats. And sometimes he played the disco for the disco crowd, then all of a sudden he would play the beats and it's B-boy time. And some of the best hustlers were some of the best breakdancers too. And back then it was still into, you know, asking a woman to dance. With some class. And then you can impress her by doing a spin on the floor. So it was a great time, man. So

that was it. I became a fan, instantly, of Kool Herc.

Just how legendary was he at that stage, in the Bronx?
I mean, these guys were famous, man. They were incredible. And in my neighbourhood I was like the Kool Herc guy, cos I was the only guy with all those records. My mother had all them records so I started stealing all her records. And making little tapes and stuff and blasting my music into the neighbourhood.

'Cos all that time I was making pause button tapes. Everyone had one of my pause button tapes. I was one of the biggest pause button guys. And back then they didn't even have pause buttons. Nah, I would just cut with the record button halfway down...

> **❝ I was a B-boy, so I was ready to breakdance at the drop of a dime. I'm listening, checking out people doing the hustle, and I'm waiting for 'Apache' to come on, so I could B-boy. ❞**

Did you sell the tapes or just give them away?
I was just giving them away. Sometimes five bucks. Then when I got a pause button I was off the hook! Then we started making plates, acetate plates.

It took me a while to get a pair of turntables. I think it was '77, I hooked up with some guys who had turntables. But since I was a drummer already I knew about synchronising time. That helped me a lot whilst I made the transition: I already had that skill. Plus as a drummer, I knew I could not allow the rhythm to fall off. For me it was so clear that it had to be on time.

In 1976, the bicentennial year, I was hooked up with two other guys and they happened to have two Garrard turntables and a mic mixer that had four knobs. And we started putting our records and stuff together and doing house parties. And we would literally have to be in a room so quiet, so we can hear the record, 'cos there were no headphones. To cue up the next record we would put our ear to the record, to the needle while it was playing. Like, 'Shhh, be quiet.' and you could just hear the *ch ch chsh chush...*

You'd be mixing from another room?
Yeah, we'd be in another room. And then we'd turn the four knobs, and mix. And what was ironic was that people were already calling me D.ST, which stood for D Street. and these two guys, one guy's name was Shevin and the other guy's name was Timmy and they called me D, so D. S. T. – Derek, Shevin and Timmy. It just went together that way.

Where did the name D.ST come from?
I got that name cos I used to hang out on Delancey Street downtown, and people called Delancey Street D Street.

But then those guys got with this other guy, one of the neighbourhood thugs, who had the most equipment, 'cos he was trying to DJ too. And I just wasn't into the rough guy scene so I started doing parties myself. Another friend had a pair of Technic turntables, and there was a mixer, so I ended up going up there every day. Working on my craft.

Then I started going to these parties up in Mount Vernon. My cousin Todd would take us, and I got popular up there, from breakdancing. So this one guy, who was one of the big DJs up there, DJ Rob The Gold – his brother was DJ Smoke, from the Kool Herc crowd. I got down with his crew. And another guy named City Boy. They had big 18-inch woofer cabinets, and so I'm really playing on a real set now. They had 1800 turntables, the Technics, the real big heavy ones.

And up there they didn't know nothing about Grandmaster Flash, Afrika Bambaataa, or Kool Herc; they were still straight up disco. I went up there. I got these beats. So I'm like

Kool Herc now. When I'd get on I'd start playing these crazy records, and people would be like, 'What are you doing?'

They didn't get it?
I would clear the dancefloor.

How long did it take for them to figure it out?
Took a summer. By the end of the summer it was like all the girls… Once the women get into it, that's where the guys are gonna go.

" All of a sudden I was doing all this insane stuff. And people started realising that you could do all this shit with the record on the needle. "

When did you start thinking about what you were doing, playing records, maybe you could take it another step further?
Once I left DJ Rob and City Boy and decided to start my own crew, cos these groups started coming up, like Furious Five. So I said I gotta get some MCs now. I had Baby T and Baby Ace, two girl MCs, then I had Baby T, Half Pint, Kool Out, Infinity. Then Al B, who became a gangster. He left, and by this time, now I was in high school. And I met this guy Shaheim, and he was saying rhymes. Raheim from Furious Five, he was there, all of us was in the same school, so he'd come up and we would just make these tapes, of us cutting and rhyming.
And then I had a guy named Little Quick, he was my understudy. And we had this little, little white kid named Joe. He was like nine or 10, and he was no joke. I used to stand him on a milk crate to DJ. So it was the three of us, the three DJs, and Kool Aid, who was the 'Master of Beats', 'cos he would read album covers and he would look for specific percussionists, specific drummers and he knew how they played.
I would spend eight to 10 hours a day in my house, in my room, driving my mother crazy. I went from the drums, she went, 'Good, he's got rid of them drums, now I could get some sleep,' and now I had some turntables, finally.
I had my whole entourage, it was Kool Aid, Master of Beats, Little Quick, Big Joe, Infinity Four, Masters of Ceremony, which was Shaheim, Baron, Kimba and Mike Nice, and Jaheim, who was the programme director, so to speak. He would keep all the records in order. He's the guy who would pass me my records.
And we had a whole synchronised thing. I would never look backwards. And I was so fast at it. It was a whole synchronised set of how we got down. We had a little rock'n'roll light rig with us so each MC had their own colour, and just that little change was enough to add more to the show. And we also was the first to put four mic stands out. Nobody did that. And everybody was like, 'Damn, they gonna do a show!' And I was so synchronised that, the timing, you would not know that I changed the record, and I would do crazy tricks.

Your style was just beats?
I had the traditional disco DJ blending skills. You start there, you have to have that. But then the more radical things were the most demanding, so you practised them more.

And you ended up playing at The Roxy
I was the DJ at the Roxy, which was the biggest scene in New York, and I would start out by playing the typical stuff that you hear on the radio, and some of the club stuff. And then all of a sudden I'd just twist the whole club. I'd throw on 'Stop The Love You Save' by the Jackson 5, from the beginning [does the drum and horn intro], and the whole club would go, 'Oh shit.' and then from that point I'd go left, completely go fucked up.
And that's what makes hip hop so special, because it's a combination of everything. I mean we would throw on Elvis, 'Love my baby, and my baby loves me' ['C'mon Everybody'] that's a hip hop classic. And 3-6-9, the goose drank wine ['The Clapping Song'] and 'The

Name Game' [both by Shirley Ellis] and all these old songs. These are songs that you'd play in a hip hop club.

It's the way you'd combine them.
Yeah, you know you could be playing 'Don't You Want Me Baby' [Human League], all of a sudden you'd throw on 'Shoe shine boy, shoe shine boy, been all day shining shoes, da da da da da' [Eddie Kendricks 'Shoeshine Boy] and the club would go crazy.

What about scratching. How did that come about?
That was Flash and Theodore, and another guy who doesn't get no credit: DJ Tyrone... Cool DJ D, his hip hop DJ was a kid named Tyrone. And he used to take 'Apache' [by Incredible Bongo Band] and he would go *dmm-zmm, dmm-zmm, dmm-zmm* [ie just scratch back and forth]. That's all he would do. But it was so dope because nobody ever did it before. And then he would let it play, then [catch it again for another little scratch]. That's all he did, but it was enough to go 'Ohhhh shit!'

And then Theodore, who was phenomenal, and he was a prodigy. He was so skilled so young, it was ridiculous. It was effortless, his cutting ability. I mean, he was faster than Flash. Flash will deny that, but he was faster than Flash. And he was articulate with the shit, physically, you know.

What do you mean?
He expressed it. Without opening his mouth, he was articulate. He was physically articulate, in his gestures, and in his ability to be so precise, and synchronise – 'cos Flash was good. And Flash was a definite technician, but there was something about Theodore that made him different.

And remember he was a student of Flash. He had this knack for speed, and to be on time with the speed. And he expressed it, the way he would physically move. It was an expression. What I mean is, articulate for me, 'cos I'm a DJ and it was a language that I understood.

How did things progress?
As a musician already, I started using my music skills to manipulate the turntables. And so I started forcing the whole threshold of the concept of being a turntablist. I moved it because all of a sudden I was doing all this insane stuff. And people were like [amazed], 'He did *that* with the turntable?' And people started really, really focussing on it and realising that you could do all this shit with the record on the needle.

What kind of things were you doing?
Like needle-dropping: it almost doesn't happen no more, but the most talented, the best DJs are the ones who can needle-drop, on cue, at will. Theodore... There was only about four or five of us that mastered it. And believe it or not, Little Quick mastered it; it's just that he didn't get the recognition. But he was one of the best too. Flash was not one of the best needle-droppers. That's why he started the Clock Theory, spinning records back, 'cos he couldn't drop.

There was me, Theodore and Imperial JC, who were the best needle-droppers. JC was also the fastest cutting, out of everybody. Out of *everybody*. JC was the first person to go 'Good, good, good, good, ' with 'Good Times' [by Chic]. 'Cos I got this fast: 'Good times, good times, good times, good times,' I mean precise, 'cos everybody said that when JC did it the shit was all crazy and out of time. I remember the first night I seen him do that and I went [sharp intake of breath] 'I gotta go home and practise.' And he did it on Herc's turntables. That's when he was spinning for Herc.

And that was the whole thing about the hip hop culture. Every time you went to one of the parties, you never knew what to expect from one of the real premier DJs 'cos they was always home. Just like these new battles, these DJ battles, same thing, 'cos every time I go, now it's off the hook. And I look at these guys and I think: we started that shit. It's incredible these guys what they took from us and there's no end to it.

I love to go there and see these guys. Me and Flash at the DMC [DJ mixing competition], we was sitting there going 'Yo man, look what we did. Look at this, man, this is ridiculous.' To actually know that you have inspired a genre, a whole movement, and we just in the projects, doing that, with no money, man, just for the love of it.

Were you playing that style of scratching already?
By that time I was off the hook. I was doing all kinds of crazy tricks and stunts. I did everything but blow up the turntable. I was running around the place coming back and cutting on beat with no headphones on. Breakdancing, kicking the mixer, everything.

Scratching means it's not about the record, the record isn't important. I'm just using the record to make notes. When did you start doing that?
When we were just doing *chzzum-chm, chzzum-chm*, the simple stuff, it was just a matter of time before we'd want to do that more intricate... As a musical person I decided that I can play rhythms, because I'm a drummer. So I was listening to rhythms. But the idea of getting certain sounds, like the record backwards, and a little bit more staccato than just *chzzum-chm, chzzum-chm*, that was an accident. One day I was doing my thing and I fucked up and Shaheim was like, 'Yo, yo, that was dope.' I was like, 'What? It was a accident.' 'Well do it again.' So I did it again, and it was dope, so I just started practising doing it.

> ❝ **Quincy Jones took a chair, spun it around backwards and sat in front of me like this: 'Go ahead, play.' Then he gave me a bear hug.** ❞

What exactly was it that you did that time?
It was *drit dru drit... drit dru drit* where before it was just *drit, drit, drit* [the difference is we're now hearing the pullback noise as well as the choppy forward scratch]. And so now it had more life to it and I started to practise that, [imitates a complex scratch which makes a breakbeat rhythm], and I'm thinking, [more complex drum patterns], and now I'm humming it. So once I realised that there was something there, my musical skill kicked in and I started singing these phrases And I started practising whatever I sang. I just applied my drum skills to the turntables.

When did you first feel like a musician rather than a DJ?
Took me a while. You know when I really felt it, when Quincy Jones came and sat in front of me, took a chair, spun it around backwards and sat in front of me like this [chin on folded arms]: 'Go ahead, play.' Just like that. And when I finished he picked me up and gave me a bear hug, and walked the fuck out. Then it was official for me. When Quincy said, 'Yo man, that shit is dope. That's some dope shit you doin'; that shit is so bad, it's incredible.'
He said 'You playin' triplets. You playin' a lot of triplets.'

When did you meet Quincy Jones?
When I was with Herbie Hancock and the 'Rockit' band.

How did you hook up together?
Playing at the Roxy. I met a guy named Jean Karakos who owned a French label called Celluloid.

What record did you use to scratch on 'Rockit'?
I started recording my first single with this label Celluloid, and Fab 5 Freddy did a record with them called 'Change The Beat'. And of course at the end it has '...this stuff is really fressshhh.' When we were doing 'Rockit' I was going through a bunch of records to find the sounds that I wanted. We're all in the studio and I'm doing my rhythms, and I used fresh *wisht wshht* and everyone went, 'Woah. That's it, that's it, roll the tape!' and I just did my part. I just did whatever I felt.

Did you right away think 'I've made the turntable into an instrument'?
Yeah. By the time I got to the 'Rockit' band I realised there was something special, with the turntables, and it was growing. And like I say I didn't really feel the respect from the band yet. They kind of looked at me like, 'Can't have a turntable... in a band, man.'

They thought it was a gimmick.
But when Herbie saw it, because Herbie he's totally into that. Because it's new, it's clever, it's technical. So he was totally into it.

He was open-minded enough to say, yeah, I'm gonna make a record with you?
Yeah. So, we did it and made history with that record. That was a great experience. That was my introduction to mainstream showbiz, and to be introduced on that magnitude, is incredible. Boom! hit record, world tours, grammies. It happens so fast that you don't enjoy it. 'What happened?' 'Yo man, you got a hit record.' Like I never saw the effect that the record had in the United States, I never saw it 'cos I was gone.

You were touring, supporting it?
I never was in my neighbourhood to see how people responded to it.

People must have told you though.
In those neighbourhoods people are poor, so they think you've made it, so now you can't talk to nobody, so everything gets real funny. But I wasn't in my community when that record blew up like that. I became so busy, that your life just changes.

How long were you on tour?
I did from '84 to '88. And that band ended and I was in the Headhunters also. I was playing keys, and singing lead by that time. And turntables. So I took the ride, you know.

What made the band finally respect you as a musician?
It was a song we were working on; there was some trouble at rehearsal, and they were asking Herbie – they were saying 'Hey Herbie, this part?' And he said 'Yo man, don't ask me, ask him, he did the damn song.'

© DJhistory.com

GRAND MIXER D.ST SELECTED DISCOGRAPHY

PHASE II – The Roxy (scratches)

INFINITY & GRANDMIXER D.ST – Grandmixer Cuts It Up! (writer/producer/scratches)

RAMMELLZEE & SHOCK DEE WITH GRAND MIXER DST – Rammellzee & Shockdell At The Amphitheatre (scratches)

GRANDMIXER D.ST – Crazy Cuts (producer/turntables/synthesizer)

GIL SCOTT-HERON – Re-Ron (backing vocals)

D.ST & JALALUDIN M. NURIDDIN – Mean Machine (Dub) (producer/writer)

D.ST – Megamix II: Why Is It Fresh? (producer/arranger/writer)

HERBIE HANCOCK – Rockit (scratches)

DST – Home Of Hip Hop (producer/writer)

GINGER BAKER – Satou (scratches)

HERBIE HANCOCK – Metal Beat (turntables)

BILL LASWELL FT. DXT – Black Hole Universe (scratches)

APC – Magnetic D. Street (scratches)

RECOMMENDED LISTENING

VARIOUS – The Celluloid Years – 12"es And More

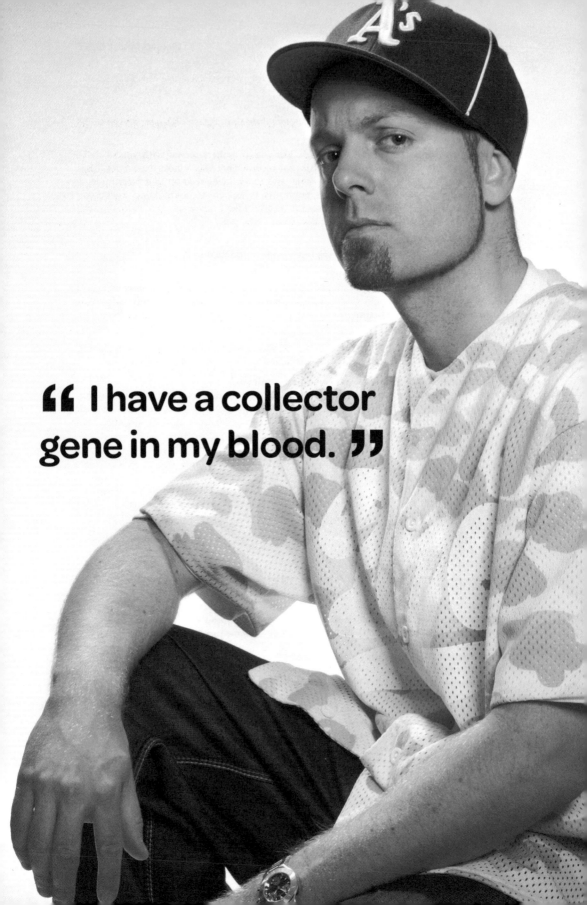

" I have a collector gene in my blood. "

DJ Shadow
Vinyl resurrectionist

Interviewed by Bill by phone to San Francisco, July 7, 2005

The trainspotter's trainspotter, Shadow is as likely to be found in a damp basement rescuing records from floodwater as in a comfortable studio crafting beats from his latest treasures. In a world of ones and zeros, MP3s and WAVs, he epitomises many DJs' undying thirst for vinyl. His missionary ardour for discovery hits right at the heart of what the best DJs do: unearth killer records.

Having long mined the seam of forgotten American funk and soul, Shadow left these more conventional hunting grounds to move like a ghost through obscure scenes and ignored territories. When even Abyssinian go-go and Lebanese prog had given up their secrets he took digging into the impossibly obscure world of private press – one-off records cut by hopeful bands and crooning Valentines. And even here, thanks to the antennae he keeps hidden from earthlings, he found gold.

Shadow's digging has helped resurrect the careers of artists like David Axelrod. He has been responsible for some brilliant records of his own, too, both under his own name and behind the collaborative moniker of UNKLE. *Endtroducing* is still regarded as one of the landmark sample-based albums of the '90s (as well as providing meat on the bones for that dreaded genre 'trip hop'). We catch up with him over the phone from London to San Francisco. He regales us at length with talk about his archaeologist craft and associated obsessions.

When did you start collecting?
I had always been a collector. I collected baseball cards as a little kid and then when I was about eight I started collecting comic books. Then I started getting into hip hop in about '82, you know, on the radio, listening to 'The Message' [by Grandmaster Flash and the Furious Five] and going to the store with my allowance and buying 12-inches and the few albums that existed then. From the moment I started buying vinyl, I was a collector. I mean the first 70 records I owned, I'd put a little sticker on them denoting the chronology of when I bought them. The first album I bought was *Street Beats Vol. 2* which was a Sugarhill Records compilation and I bought it because it was good value.

Anyone who was into that culture kinda gravitated towards one another and in my school there was perhaps only a dozen or so that were really into it. I remember this one kid who used to go to Sacramento quite a lot, which was the nearest major city to where I lived. He had access to some records that we weren't able to find locally and when he decided to sell his collection I bought all his stuff, so I was always out there fiending.

Then I started buying older stuff around '87, because I started being obsessed about sampling and the samples that people were using, and what they were; from my dad's record collection I was able to start spotting certain samples. He had some Isaac Hayes records and some other jazz stuff like Clifford Coulter, jazz artists with semi-funky cuts on them. I remember the first time I went to a store with the intent of looking for breaks and samples, which was about 1987 and I bought The Payback by James Brown, the second Soul Searchers album and 'Dance To The Drummer's Beat' by Herman Kelly. At that time that stuff was plentiful and cheap and nobody cared. At least not where I was and that really was the case for another eight or nine years.

I didn't get into 45s until about late 1989. The impetus for that was this cat was staying in town, which was a college town, and he was the first guy I knew who had an SP1200 [sampler]. He was from New York and he claimed to have some sort of ties to the Bomb Squad, Public Enemy's production company. He had a big stack of 45s and I was looking through going, 'What's the point of these?' I always thought 45s were just shorter versions of things you could find on albums or 12-inches. He said, 'No no man, 45s are where it's at.' He proceeded to play me some and I remember General Crook's 'Gimme Some' was one of them. I remember staring at the label.

Yellow and red label?
That's right. So I thought, 'Whoah, better start paying attention to 45s.'

What was it about vinyl collecting that got you?
I have a collector gene in my blood. Aside from the fact the music was everything to me, it satisfied multiple dimensions. It was tactile in the way that comic books are tactile. And yet, they spoke to you sonically as well. I was a collector, but I was never a collector that wanted to find everything in pristine condition, or trying to find the rare versions of things, until probably the mid '90s.

But I guess if you're into scratching you have to have a slightly throwaway attitude towards the records...
Yeah. Also I never thought of rap as being worth anything to anybody other than me. I was fiending for it on an educational basis more than anything. Also rap didn't circulate back into the used market until the early '90s anyway, so you couldn't really go to shops, nobody knew where to put this stuff and nobody was buying it anyway. It was marginal music.

> **❝ I have this fear that one day I won't be able to bring records in to the door. I want to make sure I'm not caught playing the last record. ❞**

Now you've accumulated this music what do you see your role as, curator, archaeologist, or just a DJ?
I have a close circle of friends who, when they come over, we geek out for a few hours on the stuff I don't let out of my sight, the one-of-a-kinds or whatever. But for the most part my records are stacked and they're not in any order. I need a lot of stuff coming through the door, one for inspiration, two for DJ use, three for sample searching... there's so many reasons I buy this stuff.

I suppose in some ways, it's obsessive-compulsive, but I have this fear that one day I won't be able to bring records in to the door any more. You know used record stores are closing down. So I want to make sure I'm not caught playing the last record, you know, I don't have any more new records to play. There are obviously things I bought 10 years ago that I never thought I'd listen to again, and now they're quite interesting. As far as what I consider my role to be, I don't have any grand illusions about what I'm doing, even though I know on a personal collection basis, it's pretty large. But I don't have a precious attitude about it.

Yes, but at the same time you did help exhume people's careers, so even though it might not be the motivating force it is a by-product of it.
I overheard a phrase about eight or nine years ago: urban archaeology. And sometimes when it's all clicking, in a unique environment, looking through records you've never looked through before, in a unique place in the country or in the world, there is an electrical charge that I get and I'm sure other people who dig get, when they feel like they are doing something noble, in a way. Even though they're probably not.

It's almost like digging for bones in Egypt. There is that parallel.
Yeah. I mean there've been basements where there are rats running around, water seeping in from the Michigan River and you're knee deep in it and you're just sitting there thinking, 'Shit, this is my one shot to get in here and rescue some stuff'. Possibly for the purpose of putting them on to a compilation, reissuing things, or putting them on a mix so people appreciate and look for them. In its most noble form, and there are a lot of aspects of record collecting in which there is nothing noble, a lot of scummy people that engage in it.

How does it feel to help someone like David Axelrod have his career started again?
It's really very little to do with me. I remember somebody was interviewing him and he applied this term to me. Forgetting the term was about me, I just thought it was a great phrase: he called me a 'gateway' for people to listen to music. I love exposing music I like, whether it's a dirty south group from Tennessee or a garage rock band from '66, I love telling people what I'm into, in the hope they will be into it and something will happen with those people. It's really satisfying. I know David Axelrod pretty well and it's not like I say, 'Hey man, you owe me a huge debt here!'

Does your constant digging spoil your enjoyment of music itself?
I don't think so. No. What hip hop taught me really early on – and I always have to go back to hip hop because hip hop is what got me digging, and hip hop is what got me appreciating other types of music – I didn't have any respect for conventional rock'n'roll until I listened to what was being sampled in hip hop records. People sampling Black Sabbath breaks, Led Zeppelin. I hated the Beatles because I thought that was my parents' trip. Growing up I loved music but I had a real resentment for anything that I felt was being shoved down my throat. I remember in about 1986 all those baby boomer acts like Stevie Winwood, George Harrison, Travelling Wilburys, Grateful Dead, Jefferson Starship were making really atrocious pop music and it was all really successful because my parents were buying it [laughs]. I just despised all that stuff. okay, so you can't hear any rap, but all you hear is this rehashed tripe. So it was only slowly that I began to appreciate and allow myself to appreciate other types of music and it was all through looking for samples and adopting the hip hop aesthetic that anything can be applied. Kraftwerk are a text-book example.

Is that a liberating way to approach music, because the rock critic mode of musical appreciation is all about the 'rock canon' or the 'soul canon' and there is no room for those accidents of genius that occur all the time?
It's definitely liberating. I was reflecting this morning on how I always have a problem in interviews when they ask me, 'So what are the 10 records people should check out right now?' because I've never been trendy as a music consumer. Hip hop was never trendy when I was buying every single thing that came out. I have a real resistance to anything being pushed on me. As a result what I was listening to lately was a group from the Bay Area called The Phantom Limbs, kind of forgotten hip hop album by Black Male from 1990, Goldfrapp's *Felt Mountain* for no apparent reason. None of these records are what you consider of the moment, when I should, I suppose, be listening to TV On The Radio or…

DFA?
Exactly. Although maybe in two years' time I might be interested in checking out the entire catalogue. So it's ironic that I was once on Mo' Wax which was a very tastemaker or of the moment thing. To us it wasn't though, it was just us rehashing our influences.

Does looking for samples or breaks change your aesthetic approach to digging?
In 1992 I met Automator. And as someone who was about five years' older than me, had already been going to New York a lot, and was going to legendary places like Lenny's Record Shop and Downstairs Records where people like Large Professor were buying their breaks from. So he had a knowledge that I was impressed with when I first met him, and also there were very few people in California who understood the New York breaking culture as well as he did. We were able to speak the same language and there weren't too many people like that out of my immediate clique or whatever. He was the first person I knew who had a portable turntable. Danny B who runs ADD Records in Berkeley also had one. I looked up

....

to these guys because they were out doing it and if they had a portable, hey, why didn't I think of that?

So I got myself one and you're right, it was all about finding breaks, though if I found myself a killer loop or a track that was just undeniable I'd pick that up too. But over the years I'd carry the portable with me, then suddenly it stopped being about the portable and I'd leave the portable at home. And that's when I started just going off instinct. When you've looked at hundreds of thousands of records in your lifetime you start to get a feel of what you haven't seen before and you start to realise that that's the stuff you should be picking up. I still hear people say they just don't look at 45s because they're intimidated by that world. 45s, to me, were the crack cocaine of record collecting. It was the final frontier of collecting. Talk about your out-there labels and out-there records! That was really the 12-inch before the 12-inch. For hip hop if you don't collect 12-inches you're nowhere. And I quickly learned that was true with soul and funk and for that matter garage and punk or any other music that existed during the 45 era. There are about 300 must-have funk albums, and that's tops. And when I say 300 I'm including the James Brown family. But for 45s it's endless. The genre is not represented on album. Hip hop is five or ten times more prolific than that era.

Do you think sampling had become a little complacent before you arrived?
Well, it's funny because a lot of people are sampling again. When I listen to KMEL a lot of records by people like Kanye West are sampling soul again. There's obviously the Neptunes type stuff but even on labels like Cash Money you certainly hear samples. It's a weird and interesting moment right now, because sampling itself is almost nostalgic. Like you hear people sampling classic breaks because it takes you back, you know? You had the New York hegemony. You know if you read *Source* magazine it was generally accepted that anything outside New York just wasn't good. Being in California I knew that wasn't the case, so I think I had a broader view than even people living in New York, as would've someone in London or Tokyo for that matter.

But obviously the big shift was when *The Chronic* came out and then Snoop Dogg's album. Even though there were some samples, it was an interesting combination of them with synthesisers and a broader palette. That was what really set it off. And concurrently what was happening in the south was really bedroom, and people didn't really have a lot of cultural attachment; there was just the music. So they didn't think, 'We need to further the tradition'. There was a sense that this was a way to be heard. People buying their own regional sounds. I'm battling to say that I think all of this contributed to non-sampling. I don't think it has honestly anything to with people getting tired of giving away publishing, which I'm always reading about. Kanye West is still sampling.

Well, Dre had voiced this before.
Well for some people, they don't know anything else at this point. I wouldn't put Dre in that category, obviously. Someone like Manny Fresh. But then he's old school. David Banner is old school. I guess what they're doing is just trying to make something that is hot. And what's hot are the 36 Mafia Beats, Scarface beats, that's the blueprint for a lot of these dudes.

Do you think your level of digging has forced other people to dig harder? Like I got the impression that Kenny Dope was pretty impressed by Keb's extremes of digging.
That may apply to Kenny Dope but that man has been digging since before it was cool to do it, and he's been producing hip hop records since 1988 and house records since about that time, so far be it from me to say anything on his behalf. The only person I knew who collected funk was my good partner 8th Wonder, that was his graffiti name, we got into it a big way, but we start to do these big road trips. There was no reference point. There was no book to tell us what to do. There was no website that told us what to look for. There was nothing. So we listened to everything.

So you just turned up and looked in the Yellow Pages?
Yeah, old school, nothing scientific. We would only go 200 miles or so. We were not driving cross country. My first cross country trip was 1993. So 1991 and '92 we were getting into all kinds of records, some of which are still considered rare today, some of which we liked but

aren't considered rare at all. Then I came to England and I was at Mr Bongo and there was guy in there saying, 'Do you have any of these funk 45s?'

And I remember Hugh saying, 'No, but you might wanna try Soul Jazz.'

So I said, 'Can I see that list?'

Anyway, to make a long story short, it was Malcolm Catto [funk collector Heliocentrics drummer] . He'd be saying, 'You've got 'Spitting Image' [by JB's Latin]? Who are you?' Post rare groove there wasn't a funk scene. So I was intrigued by this person with this list, because I had some but there were others I didn't. Our first trade was for 'Spitting Image' I think, because that was a Californian record and I had a few of them. Then I met Keb down at Camden Lock market when he had a stall there.

Did you go and visit guys like [record dealer] John Anderson at Soul Bowl?
No I didn't get connected with him till a few years later. He's obviously someone who's one of the prime reasons there's a soul scene in England.

Do you regard your music as hip hop?
That's almost unanswerable. Hip hop is what got me interested in music as a career, hip hop is the paradigm through which I view everything. It was like my religion for lack of a better word – and I really don't like the word at all. It was the screen through which I saw everything, be it politics, history or anything; it's where I learned a lot, it's what taught me most things about my life. So when I make music there's a lot of good listening coming out through me, and I've spent over 20 years listening to this stuff, so it's hard for me to imagine that what I make isn't hip hop, but at the same time I'm at the age where I'm not interested in restricting myself to one style or one scene or genre. I feel like I've learned more than that would allow me to do. I've moved beyond being just a purist.

❝ To me sampling was the secret knowledge that only a select few DJs in New York had. I was really intrigued and tantalised. ❞

How do you feel about the price inflation when you've sampled a tune or used it on a mix?
Well, when I do see it, it's usually the same three or four records that were always easy to find. It's not like anybody's pulling out this incredible break on this record that still nobody knows about. It's the same three or four and trying to squeeze every last penny out of their lame record. It was sort of amusing at first, but now it doesn't even register any more.

When you started making records only using other people's records was that an aesthetic decision?
Yeah. What first got me into rap was the music. I heard 'The Message' and 'Planet Rock' almost at the same time and 'Planet Rock' was being played as an instrumental on the radio for some reason. 'The Message' was all about the lyrics. My favourite era in hip hop coincides with a very fertile moment in anybody's musical listening, which is the 13-16 year bracket when your brain is like a sponge. I tried to dress like my idols, I put their records on my wall, started trying to go to concerts. During that era it was all about sampling. To me sampling was the secret knowledge that only a select few DJs in New York had. I was really intrigued and tantalised by that.

On the rare occasion that a nugget of wisdom was divulged, like in *Rap Attack* or in in *Breakin'* where's there's a scene where you can see two of the records spinning. Any little moment where you can somehow grab some article. I used to buy the *NME*, *Melody Maker* and *Soul Underground*, because there was a newsstand that specialised in European magazines so I'd buy *Melody Maker* and there'd be Sweet Tee on the cover or *NME* with a five page feature on Just Ice. That just did not exist in the States. You could not get that here, not in *Rolling Stone* or *Spin*. You couldn't read about hip hop. There was no *Source* magazine. There was no internet.

None of the black magazines supported rap.

Did that make you feel part of a secret society?
I'm sure I would've been thrilled if it had been easier to assimilate for me and easier to learn about, but all I had to go on were the few odd moments where hip hop was able to poke through into the mainstream. I didn't live in New York, so maybe in *Village Voice* they had stuff.

I also remember reading a big thing about sampling in the *NME* or *Melody Maker* with a big interview with Mantronix, who was one of my heroes, talking about different beats. I remember it saying 'Blag Blag Blag' on the cover. 'NORMAN COOK'S TOP TEN BREAKS', with Elvis Costello. All of that stuff I was writing down in a ring binder and going down to my local record store and looking for them. Incredible Bongo Band? Okay, check. 'Ashley's Roachclip' [by The Soul Searchers]? Check. That's when I was stymied by things I could never find, either because they were on 45s or like 'Synthetic Substitution' [by Melvin Bliss]. It was all very gradual. My parents had gotten divorced when I was young so when I visited my dad in San Jose, he'd take me round the record store or I'd be listening to the mixes on Friday and Saturday night and then the next day in the store begging and pleading for a couple of the 12-inches that they would play.

> **❝ I generally tend to wear people out. Not trying to say I'm some crazy digger. But I tend to be the one that goes the extra length. ❞**

So when you're in a studio, is it just a bag of samples, a sampler and you?
Well, yeah, but nowadays it's mostly Pro-Tools-based because it's so much more flexible. I got tired of the rigidity of the way you have to use an MPC. I was in London last month working, but I didn't have any records with me, I'd gotten the tracks to a certain place and I wanted some percussion on one track... The first two albums were all about me wanting to make a statement about sampling. I'm not really fussed now about whether I'm allowed to put a bass guitar on it. It's not an aesthetic decision anymore. It used to be, because it was valuable to make those points and it may be again at some time but right now I feel really liberated being able to do whatever suits the track.

Are you still discovering funk 45s?
Yeah.

What was the last one?
Creative Movement 'Junky Man' on Asphma Records.

Where and when did you find that?
I found that in the north of England about four weeks ago.

Really? On a British label?
No. A guy that used to come to the States buying records and is not really a funk guy per se.

How about digging for non-indigenous music?
The best way to answer to that is the breakbeat at the end of 'The Number Song'. That comes from a South Korean record that somehow made its way to California. If you're attentive when you're looking for records and a lot of records made it to the States, Israeli, Turkish etc. Not in abundance, but you do see them. I bought Demon Fuzz *[Afreaka!]* from the UK in 1990 not because I knew what it was but I stumbled across it. I don't think it's ever entered my mind that this is what I'm going to swing into. I'm aware that worldwide there have all been bands who said, 'Ooh now we must do the funky thing!' and do a funky track. I don't have a terrible affinity for a lot of European funk, jazz or anything because it doesn't resonate with me. I'm much more likely to sample a traditional Turkish record than a wacky record that record dealers try and hype up as Turkish funk.

Who's the most obsessed digger you've ever met?

I generally tend to wear people out who I'm with. Not trying to say I'm like some crazy digger or cool in any way. But usually I tend to be the one that goes the extra length. Or wake up extra early, or stay extra late, or venture somewhere where I shouldn't be venturing. But, really, I don't think I'm as obsessive as a lot of northern soul guys. In different stages of my life, I've had different people I've done trips with. I don't have the overriding compelling need to do trips anymore. I like having the company, but I used do trips by myself quite a lot. I find when I'm with somebody I quickly learnt that you spur each other on. Saying all that, what I was gonna say there are people I met when funk became a big thing in the States, a lot of really greedy unscrupulous guys came into it in about 1999. Those people were obsessive, but not about digging or music, they had a love for cash.

What's the most trouble or danger you've gone through to get a record?

In the gatefold of *Endtroducing* you'll see a picture of a gatefold cover and it says 'Blackout'. It's got these guys in costumes with a blue sky behind them. That's a high school record from Oklahoma. Lyrics Born, who's also been known to dig, but goes off on his own tangents, he was the first guy I ever talked about high school records with. He had this thing and I didn't have it. He got it at a swap-meet in Oakland. So when I was in Oklahoma, right after *Endtroducing* came out, I went to Oklahoma to find this thing. I went with B+ who did the album cover; Chief Xcel from Blackalicious. It snowed one night. I was going through the phone book calling people trying to crack this thing. Went to a music store and guy says, 'Yeah, I went to Douglas High, I might be able to get my hands on some of those in the morning.' B+ was driving and the streets were icy. When we woke up in the morning he was really unhappy about the situation. 'Dude, I don't know, this is messy.' So we get in the car and cars are sliding all over the road. Eventually we slid hard into the kerb. He said, 'Look this is madness.' I was in the backseat. 'OK well I'm going,' and started walking… I wasn't going to be deterred.

© DJhistory.com

DJ SHADOW SELECTED DISCOGRAPHY

SHADOW – Lesson 4 (mixer)

DJ SHADOW – In/Flux (writer/producer/mixer)

DJ SHADOW – What Does Your Soul Look Like (writer/producer)

DJ SHADOW – 89.9 Megamix (scratches/mixer)

DJ SHADOW – The Number Song (writer/producer/mixer)

DJ SHADOW – Organ Donor (extended overhaul) (writer/producer/remixer)

DJ SHADOW – Dark Days (writer/producer)

DJ SHADOW – 6 Days (producer/mixer)

UNKLE – Unreal (writer/producer)

UNKLE – Chaos (producer)

UNKLE – Rabbit In Your Headlights (writer/producer)

MASSIVE ATTACK – Karmacoma (remixer)

LATRYX – Lady Don't Tek No (writer/producer)

DJ KRUSH – Meiso (remixer)

DEPECHE MODE – Painkiller (remixer)

POETS OF RHYTHM WITH LYRICS BORN – I Changed My Mind (mixer)

STINA NORDENSTAM – People Are Strange (remixer)

DJ SHADOW – GDMFSOB (writer/producer)

DJ SHADOW – This Time (mixer/arranger)

RECOMMENDED LISTENING

DJ SHADOW – Endtroducing

DJ SHADOW & CUT CHEMIST – Brainfreeze

DJ SHADOW & CUT CHEMIST – Product Placement

" When they declared disco is dead, I had to start changing things in order to keep feeding my dancefloor "

....

Frankie Knuckles
Godfather of house

Interviewed by Frank in New York, February 27, 1995

....

Anyone with even a passing knowledge of dancefloor history knows Frankie Knuckles respectfully as the 'Godfather of House'. In truth, the creators of house music were the electronics manufacturers who made the first cheap synths and drum machines, and the clubbers who put them to immediate use, turning out raucous primitive rhythm tracks that were as effective as they were basic. Frankie's role had been to inspire Chicago, to create an underground, and show the city how much creativity was possible for a DJ. As disco dried up he began playing edits of older songs in an effort to keep his dancefloor moving, and it was this aesthetic that guided the emerging style. So 'Godfather' is apt – as well as a career making some of the most sublime records in house, he raised the genre under his roof and gave it spiritual guidance throughout.

Frankie entered clubland with his childhood friend Larry Levan, running wild on the early disco scene: his first job was blowing up balloons and spiking the punch at Nicky Siano's Gallery. Transplanted to Chicago after a residency at the bacchanal of New York's Continental Baths, it was his sets of ballsy older disco at the Warehouse that ignited this polite midwestern city and gave house music its name. This interview took place just after the shock closure of New York's Sound Factory, another great room that Mr Nicholls had (briefly) made his own.

When did you get into DJing?

I started spinning at the Continental baths in July 1972. As well as the club area, there was an Olympic-size swimming pool and a TV room at the very end. Alongside the pool was a sauna and a shower room, then there were boutiques and restaurants and bars, and back into an area where there was apartments and private rooms.

I was scheduled to play Mondays and Tuesdays, and Larry [Levan] played from Wednesday to Sunday, and on the nights he played I found myself playing at the beginning of the evening, or playing before he woke up... *if* he woke up. I mean Fridays and Saturdays he was generally okay, but Wednesdays and Thursdays he wouldn't get started till very late.

I played different other clubs around the city, this one after-hours called Tomorrow. Larry eventually left Continental and went to work at a club called Soho, which was owned by Richard Long, who was the premier sound engineer, he was the one who taught us everything about sound.

The Continental went bankrupt and closed in '76. I worked a couple of other places here in the city, but I was looking for something a little bit more than just a job. I figured I'd already put five years in one club and it had gone bankrupt, so if I was to go and work at a particular club at this point I wanted more of an incentive. If you give me a piece of what's going on then I wouldn't have a problem applying myself and working hard to make everything work. Or else to me it just wasn't worth it. To just go and play records and collect a pay cheque.

Originally they wanted Larry in Chicago, but Larry didn't want to leave New York, and besides, the club Soho was beginning to take off – no, as a matter of fact, he had left Soho and they were already at Reade Street which was what Paradise Garage came from. They

....

were already building that and he didn't see himself leaving. They had pretty much already had their ideas for what they wanted to do with that. He had no intention of leaving the city, so they came to me second and asked me to do it. I went out to play for the opening and I was there for about two weeks, and I really liked the city a lot. I only played twice because the club was only open one day a week: on a Saturday. But on both those nights it worked really, really well.

They offered me the job at that particular point and I gave them my terms, how I felt about it. They offered me a piece of the business. So at that point I realised I had to think about what I wanted to do. If I really wanted to uproot from New York City and move there. Then actually when I looked at it I didn't have anything holding me here. I figured what the hell. I gave myself five years and if I couldn't make it in five years then I could always come back home.

Describe walking into the Warehouse
It's such a long time ago. I look at a lot of different parties and stuff that I play for, when we go out on the road like the Def Mix tour, playing over in England and things like that, and I look at the energy of the crowd and the stuff like that, and the energy is the same. The energy is most definitely the same. The feeling, the feedback that you get from the room, from the people in the room, is very, very spiritual. The Warehouse was a lot like that. For most of the people that went there it was church for them. It only happened one day a week: Saturday night, Sunday morning, Sunday afternoon.

Was that the first time you'd experienced that sort of energy?
No, because it was the same thing here. I mean you know a lot of these kids that are hanging out and doing all these parties and running around all these different clubs in England — not so much here in the United States because it's a much more surefire thing in England I guess it's pop so that's the reason why — A lot of them think what they're doing and the type of fun they're having in clubs is something new. It's not. I'm here to tell them that it's not. This is something that's been going on a very long time. What they're doing is actually nothing new, what they're doing is carrying on a tradition. Which I think is great.

The Warehouse: It was predominantly black, predominantly gay, age probably between 18 and maybe 35. Very soulful, very spiritual – which is amazing in the mid-west because you have those corn-fed mid-western folk that are very down to earth. Their hearts are always in the right place, even though their minds might not always be. Their hearts are definitely in the right place. And I think those type of parties we were having at The Warehouse, I know they were something completely new to them, and they didn't know exactly what to expect. So it took them a few minutes to grow into it, but once they latched onto it, it spread like wildfire through the city.

And in the early days, between '77 and '80, '81 the parties were very intense – they were always intense – but the feeling that was going on, I think, was very pure. And a lot of that changed between '82 and '83, which is why I left there. There was a lot more hard-edged straight kids that were trying to infiltrate what was going on there, and for the most part they didn't have any respect for what was going on.

So it was a black gay scene?
Yes.

Who else was involved?
Just a lot of outsiders.

Some people have said there was quite a merging of the alternative, punk scene.
Not with what we were doing. When punk came about they had other clubs like Neo's, places like that where those punk kids went to.

Chicago, believe me, it was very segregated, very much like it is now. The white kids didn't party with the black kids. What really tripped me out was when I first moved there... growing up in New York City, all kinds of people grow up around each other, it's pretty much like you see it, to me here it's not that big of a deal, race and colour is not that big of a deal. When I got to Chicago, it was. You had the black folks living on the southside of Chicago, and on the immediate west of the city. And the only place where you find different coloured people living together, was on the north side of Chicago like Newtown, that type of area, which is where I lived at. It bothered me at first, when I didn't see enough white or other races on the dancefloor at the beginning, and then I realised I had my job cut out for me because I had to set out and try and change that.

And then when I found that the black gay kids didn't want to party with the white gay kids, and the white gay kids weren't gonna let the black gay kids hang out in their clubs, I was like, everybody's rocking in the same boat but nobody wants to... everybody wants to play this game and it made no sense to me. We're all living the same lifestyle here. We're rocking in the same boat but you don't want me playing in your clubs because you don't want my crowd following me in. It made no sense to me. When you go out in the gay clubs in Chicago now, it's changed a lot. But while I was there it didn't change at all.

What were the drugs that were driving the scene at the time?
Probably a lot of acid. A lot of acid.

What was the club scene like when you arrived in Chicago?
By the time I got to Chicago the disco craze had pretty much already kicked in. The difference between what was happening with music then and music now is that songs lasted a lot longer then than they do now. I don't mean as far as length-wise, but songs lived in people's consciousness a lot longer than they do now. So a lot of the stuff that came out in the early '70s on Philly International. I was playing a lot of stuff like that, that was still working pretty strong, in '77 when I moved to Chicago. And a lot of the popular R&B club stuff and dance stuff that was, disco records that were coming out then: Salsoul stuff, Philly International.

> ## ❝ The Warehouse was very soulful, very spiritual – which is amazing in the mid-west because you have those corn-fed mid-western folk that are very down to earth. ❞

When did you start doing edits?
I didn't actually start doing things like that until like 1980, '81. A lot of the stuff I was doing early on I didn't even bother playing in the club, because I was busy trying to get my feet wet and just learn the craft. But by '81 when they had declared that disco is dead, all the record labels were getting rid of their dance departments, or their disco departments, so there was no more uptempo dance records, everything was downtempo. That's when I realised I had to start changing certain things in order to keep feeding my dancefloor. Or else we would have had to end up closing the club. So I would take different records like 'Walk The Night' by the Skatt Brothers or...stuff like 'A Little Bit Of Jazz' by Nick Straker, 'Double Journey' [by Powerline] and things like that, and just completely re-edit them. To make them work better for my dancefloor. Even stuff like 'I'm Every Woman' by Chaka Khan, and 'Ain't Nobody', just things like that, completely re-edit them, to give my dancefloor an extra boost. I'd re-arrange them, extend them and re-arrange them.

Was that a revolutionary thing to do?
No, it had been done. It was already being done before I moved to Chicago. When I was still in New York there were people that were doing it here. But to my audience it was revolutionary. It was just a matter of time before I could learn how to do it myself.

And it was all on reel-to-reel.
Yes. And by the time I did get to around to start doing it. It might not have been revolutionary to anyone else within the industry, from the DJ side of it, but as far as the crowd in Chicago, it was revolutionary to them because they had never heard it before. They went for it immediately. And they would rush to the record stores the next day looking for that particular version. And never find it. It used to drive the record stores crazy.

Did you ever do the same things live?
That's how I used to do it before I started editing. Once I learnt how to edit, and I started changing things around like that it wasn't necessary for me to play like that in a club any more. I could do it all ahead of time and pre-record it.

What about extra beats laid over songs. When did that start to happen?
The first time I started doing some of that might have been in '83 because I had a rhythm maker then.

A what?
A rhythm maker is what they have with organs – *chik chik chok ka ka*. You just set what particular rhythm you want. I would just set the rhythm that way and play it underneath what ever I was doing.

Had anyone done that before?
I don't know. I didn't finally get my first drum machine until 1984. I got it from Derrick May. A Roland TR-909. Somehow he had two of them, and he called me from Detroit to tell me he was coming down. At this point I was at the Power Plant, I had my own club open. I left the Warehouse in spring of '83. I opened the Power Plant in the fall of '83. Anyhow, he had called me up and said he had these two drum machines and he wanted to sell me one. And I told him I didn't know the first thing about programming them. He said, 'It's easy, I'll show you.' So he came down that weekend and he brought it.

The first time I used it, I used it on a version of 'Your Love' that I did with Jamie Principle. And I would use it live in the club. I would program different patterns into it throughout the week, and then use it throughout the course of a night, running it live, depending on the song and playing it underneath, or using it to segué between something.

> **❝ They would come and hear me play and then they started putting together their own beat tracks. Which is OK but I've never been one to sit back and play a bunch of beat tracks. ❞**

Jesse Saunders is credited with making the first beat track...
Well they would come and hear me play and then go back to their club, The Playground, and they would do the same thing. And they started putting together their own beat tracks. Which is okay but I've never been one to sit back and play a bunch of beat tracks. They called themselves having the same kind of parties at The Playground that we were having at the Warehouse or the Power Plant, but they really weren't. Because they were into playing a lot of beat tracks all night long, and to me that's all they were, were a bunch of beat tracks.

And they didn't overlay them with songs?
No not necessarily, no. They would play a bunch of beat tracks all night. And the type of crowd I played for was much more sophisticated than that. They wanted to hear songs. Granted, I can break it up here and there a little bit, but for the most part they wanted to hear songs. And if I didn't play enough of them then they had a problem. The audience I had were very true, very loyal and they would never come down on me about it, but I knew exactly what they wanted. I could read them really, really well. I couldn't stand there and play beat tracks all night long.

What were the other differences between the clubs?
The Music Box was a heavy drug crowd. And they were more into like the angel dust, those dark scary drugs. I'm not saying they didn't do drugs at the Power Plant because they did, but the kind of drugs the kids did at The Power Plant were more like MDA and ecstasy.

How important was ecstasy to the scene?

Ecstasy wasn't around. I mean it was but it was MDA. But I don't want you to say that it was revolving around the drugs, whatever they were, because the main focus was the music and the dancefloor. The drugs that people took, recreationally, or why ever they took them. I mean I know why: they took them because it was a part of the evening. But I didn't have people walking out of there and years later ending up in rehab. It wasn't like that at all. The audience that I had was a working-class crowd, and on the weekend this is what they did, to hang out, it was part of their evening.

But were there enough people taking MDA, with its empathetic qualities, for it to make a difference to the atmosphere?

Yeah, there was enough that it made a difference. Yeah sure. But then you had that other half of people on the outskirts of the crowd, that was doing stuff like cocaine. When they can't... those people that wanted to smoke Sherman sticks, or happy sticks, or dust, as in angel dust. Sherman sticks were Sherman cigarettes dipped in something like formaldehyde. I mean I wouldn't allow those type of things to happen in my club. But the crowd that went to The Music Box they got into that.

How was the music different over there?

Ronnie was doing a lot of his own edits as well, and a lot of his edits were very repetitious. Very high energy and very repetitious. He would take a song and take a certain part of the song, and he'd run that for 10 minutes, before the song even played. And then he'd go into the song or go back to another 10 minutes and just play one particular part. But The Music Box, the whole atmosphere was a lot darker than what we had.

What was the Power Plant like physically?

It was about 9000 square feet. You first came into it you came up these stairs and there was a big lobby area where we had like our kitchen set up and coatroom area. Couches and banquette seats where people can actually sit back, and chill, things like that. Nice Venetian blinds on the windows, that whole thing. And you came around this corner into where the dancefloor was, this big open area. And at the end the booth was slightly raised at the back. I guess it was kind of a T-shaped room. We kept the colour scheme of the place very muted: charcoal grey, exposed wood floors, and we really just concentrated on the sound. The sound to me was the most important.

When did people realise that they were creating something new; that this music was something that wasn't just old soulful underground disco?

They didn't. They didn't know what they had until it was gone. As much as I loved the Power Plant and as much as I tried to give it, I was also beginning to move into production. And all of a sudden the crowd began to change a bit, and then it began to slack off. And for me, I looked at it as a blessing in disguise. Things slacked off, I can close the club down. This'll give me more time to do the things I want to do, for me.

I closed it in September of '86. And there were all sorts of rumours flying around: that we were busted by the city because of drugs, which wasn't true, that the IRS shut me down for tax evasion, which was not true. Just all kinds of weird rumours. And these rumours got started by people from the Music Box. There was no competition. The Music Box is what the Warehouse turned into after I left it. See there was no competition. I had already been there. I had already worked that room.

So it was the Warehouse crowd that moved on to the Music Box

No it had changed. It had changed drastically. It was a completely different crowd. I mean the first time a marathon was played at the Warehouse, I did that, I instrumented that. Ron Hardy was still in LA. He didn't know what the fuck that was. By the time I was leaving there they were trying to get him to come over there and play.

He came to me and asked me how did I feel about it. I told him I really think you should go ahead and do it. But go in there with your eyes open and your mind sharp, and don't let them offer you things you can get yourself. Go in there, make sure that when it comes to everything it takes to make you comfortable in there they give you. Don't work with a half-assed sound system. Don't have them offer you drugs and this that and the other when you can just as easily go out and buy your own. Tell them this is what you want and this is how much money you want and this is what you need in order to do your job here. This was my advice to Ron, so they would never have him in a position where they can have him over a barrel. I saw that happen to too many friends of mine.

Who else was important to the scene in '84, '85? How important was the radio, the Hot Mix 5?
Well okay, I was a part of the Hot Mix 5 too, and I didn't necessarily like it. I was with them for about a year. Everybody that was on that team, they had egos beyond, beyond out-there. It was ridiculous. Everybody's head was so big. And it was alright. I mean, they were all riding around in their fancy cars and they had their gold jewels dripped all over them and all of this. And that's fine.

They wanted me to be a part of the team that in all actuality I had nothing in common with. I mean the four of them Farley and Julian [Perez], Frankie 'Hollywood' Rodriguez, and who else? not Ralphi [Rosario], but... But anyway I had nothing in common with them. I had probably the most successful underground club in the city; the only underground club in the city, to be honest with you, and it was the most successful. And with me being a part of that team and making tapes and being on the radio, it lent a lot of credibility to the show.

Was it easier to break records from the radio or from the club?
It's easier to break them from the club, but anybody who's making records wanted their song to be on the radio. So automatically with those guys, they played all these one-off gigs all over the city, and with the exposure from the radio station, there was always a lot of hype behind those guys wherever they go. So it drew a lot of people out there. I wasn't interested in that. I had the Warehouse, I had the Power Plant. I had my own club, so anytime I would get booked out to play anywhere else it would usually bring out more people than anyone expected. But I didn't run myself around like that all the time.

So I used to get accused of not being a team player. And when I broke it down to them I said, 'Look I don't have anything in common with you guys.' I mean plus out of all of them being the only one that's gay, didn't help matters any. But none of them would attack me to my face. None of them were man enough to attack me to my face. They would say stuff behind my back about my lifestyle and my being gay, but they'd never come to me and say it.

In your opinion what were the things that came together to create house music?
I'm not exactly sure. And I'm being absolutely sincere: I'm not exactly sure. Because when it looked like things were about to take off, I guess in '85, '86 I came here to New York with Rocky Jones and the whole DJ International thing, for that New Music Seminar that summer. And there were a lot of British press that were here, trying to chase down the story of the whole house music boom. And my name kept popping up. And when I came here that summer for the conference all of a sudden I was being chased down by all these journalists. They said, 'Well we know you got the right story.'

It really freaked me out at first and I wouldn't talk to that many people. So eventually what happened was they followed us back to Chicago. They got in town and I would take them out and show them around, show them everywhere and what was happening and who was doing what. Whereas everybody else wasn't that readily interested or available. And that was Rocky's game plan, to try and keep some kind of mystique, or some type of mystery. Oh, please!

When they came up to Chicago I would take them round, show them where the Warehouse was, and they'd come to the Power Plant and hang out. I took them to the Music Box. I took them everywhere. But there was always a lot of conflict going on. You had people like Rocky Jones and Larry Sherman, who was capitalising on the music of all these young kids, and not giving them a cent.

When I was working with Jamie [Principle], his whole thing was to have something out there quick. I knew producing would do the right thing for me, but I also knew we had to take our time if we wanted to do this. Because see I'm not in this for the moment, I'm in this for the long haul, and if you don't have the patience to sit there and wait well you should just go ahead and do what you gotta do.

And then what eventually happened was, with all the stuff that I worked on with him, he eventually just kind of jumped ship with me and ran and got together with this management company, and they filled his head with all kinds of foolishness: that I was out to use him, and take advantage of him, and not do anything to help him. And he believed all that. Him and Stevie Hurley, and all the rest of them. Which is how he managed to suck all of them in.

But I happened to see how they were dealing with all the artists. I saw how they used Marshall Jefferson and On The House, after those guys had been on tour for like three months, and gave them not a dime. They were out there working every night and he gave them not a dime.

Now that's not gonna happen to me. So they caught themselves trying to blacklist me in Chicago, and tell me that I will never play in Chicago again. This is the end of '86, beginning of '87. I was like, 'You people don't have the power to do that. You can believe it if you want but you don't have the power to do that.' You can tell people what the hell you want to tell them. I know who my crowd is.

66 There was a sign that said 'WE PLAY HOUSE MUSIC'. I asked this friend of mine, 'Now what is that all about?' 99

What was your best night in Chicago?
I had a lot of them.

Describe a really incredible night at the Power Plant.
That's really hard to do because I get completely immersed in what I do. And what I'm doing, when it comes to having to play for my crowd. And every night was spectacular. All these nights would run about 12 hours each, it's hard to pick out any particular moment. It's not like someone onstage performing. I'm so involved in what I'm doing that not every night was perfect, but I'd say that 98 percent of them was as smooth as glass.

When did people start using the word 'house'?
I think in '80, '81.

As early as that?
Yes.

And where did that come from?
The kids that were hanging out at the Warehouse. Some of the new kids that had begun to discover what the Warehouse was all about: Farley, Jesse Saunders, Chip E, and all the rest of them. I would see them around I didn't know who they were. And they started having different parties on their own in these different taverns and bars in Chicago. And when they'd call them that they had a lot of success with it.

One day I was going out south to see my god-daughter, and we were sitting at a stop light, and on the corner there was a tavern, and in the window it had a sign that said 'WE PLAY HOUSE MUSIC'. I asked this friend of mine 'Now what is that all about?' and she says, 'It's the same stuff that you play at The Warehouse.'

What about 'jack'?
That was the kids at the Warehouse. That was round about when I first moved there in '77.

What came together to create the music?
People like Steve Hurley and Jamie Principle. Farley Keith even. There were so many people that were making music back then, and I remember being interviewed by a journalist in '86 where did I see this all going, and what did I think was going to happen. And I remember telling her this music's gonna be around for a while. It's gonna take it a long time for it to get to where it needs to be at, but it'll be around for a long time. The only shame about it –

because there were so many people making music, and some of them were good – but their intentions were wrong. They were in it for the fame and the notoriety. And I told her it was a shame because not all these guys were gonna survive.

I knew I was gonna survive, because I know what I'm doing. I'm not in that much of a rush to get there. I think timing is everything about anything that's worth having or worth doing. I wouldn't say I necessarily had a game-plan, but this is a growth process. Moving back to New York City and joining Def Mix and working with the different guys that I've been able to work with over the past seven years I've been back here. Being able to gain the studio knowledge that I have, and all of the remix knowledge that I learnt in Chicago before I came back here. I made no money off the music I worked on in Chicago, not a dime, but I learnt a lot about moving around a studio. Plus all of those underground records that I had worked on, they were big records in New York, but they were nothing in Chicago. I mean stuff like 'Your Love' and 'Baby Wants To Ride', and stuff that I did with Marshall Jefferson. They were bigger here and they were bigger in England.

When I moved back here and joined Def Mix I already had a name here and didn't even know it. So timing was perfect. The market was really opening up, and people were beginning to look at house. This is '87, '88. I was really at that point where I felt there was nothing else I could do in Chicago. I was having parties and playing for different people. But I needed to broaden my own horizons and do something for me. Probably if I was going to succeed as a producer I needed to be here. I had a choice of moving here or moving to London. So I came back to New York and began playing The World.

Tell me about the Roxy.
In the beginning working there I thought it was wonderful, that those guys wanted me to come over there and play for that crowd in that room. That was like the premier gay crowd in the city. I figure if I can capture this crowd then I'm in there. I started in about 1991. So within that first six months to a year it was fine. But they weren't fixing things and it became more work than pleasure.

❝ Sound Factory was the last great room of that calibre. There's not gonna be anywhere like that again. ❞

When did you play the Sound Factory?
1990 to '91. I played for a year. Junior had left, there was some type of dispute about ownership. And the rumour was going around that he quit and then they pulled me in there afterwards. And there was another rumour saying I had taken his job. Nothing could be further from the truth. Because Junior owned part of that building. When he walked out that was on him. There's no way I could take his job.

What memories do you have from that time?
I think that was probably one of the best years I've ever had playing records. For one for hooking up with Phil Smith [Sound Factory co-owner] the person that brought me in there. He has his own sound company, so the sound system came from his company, the sound system belonged to them, him and Steve Nash. We chatted and hung out for about a year, and he never let on to me that they were having problems with Junior or Junior was gonna leave. It was all of a sudden he called me and I was in the studio working on my first album, and he called me on Monday. 'I need to talk to you. Junior just left. And he's not coming back. Are you available to play?' And I was like yes, 'cos all I had been doing was playing around the world.

It gave me an opportunity to show New York City exactly what I could do. When you have a room that size, and you have a sound system that enormous, and that pristine, my first thought was going in to play on the first night: you're only gonna get one chance to do this right. Either it's gonna work for you or it's gonna work against you.

Phil and his partners loved the way I handled the sound system, the music I played over it, and the crowd really got off on it. The first time I played there I think was the first time I played 'The Whistle Song' for anybody. And the room really got off on it. I went in there with a number of different things working in my favour, and it turned out really really well.

How do you feel about the club's passing?
I think it's sad. It's really sad. I stopped hanging out at the Sound Factory, once I stopped working there. I would drop by on Junior's birthday or something like that. But it's really amazing because the night that they closed, I was there. And I got there about four, 4.30 in the morning and I hung out there until eight. But there was no word. Apparently they told him at around 11 or 12 o'clock in the morning. It seemed like normal. I feel really, really bad about it because even though his music didn't reflect the old school, that was the last great room of that calibre. Of the old school calibre, that was left in the city. And there's not gonna be anywhere like that again.

© DJhistory.com

WAREHOUSE 50

SPARQUE – Let's Go Dancing	**ROY AYERS** – Running Away
KAT MANDU – The Break	**PETER BROWN** – Do You Wanna Get Funky With Me
DON ARMANDO'S SECOND AVENUE RHUMBA BAND – Deputy Of Love	**ESG** – Moody
ECSTASY, PASSION AND PAIN – Touch And Go	**POWERLINE** – Double Journey
TAANA GARDNER – Work That Body	**SLAVE** – Party Lights
GIORGIO MORODER – E=MC2	**GINO SOCCIO** – Dancer
GWEN GUTHRIE – It Should Have Been You	**HARRY THUMANN** – Underwater
DINOSAUR L – Go Bang!	**TWO MAN SOUND** – Que Tal America
THE ORIGINALS – Down To Love Town	**UNLIMITED TOUCH** – In The Middle
DONALD BYRD – Love Has Come Around	**PAUL SIMPSON CONNECTION** – Use Me, Lose Me
CANDIDO – Thousand Finger Man	**KLEIN & MBO** – Dirty Talk
POSITIVE FORCE – We Got The Funk	**PATTI LABELLE** – Music Is My Way Of Life
SKATT BROTHERS – Walk The Night	**LOOSE JOINTS** – Is It All Over My Face?
INDEEP – Last Night A DJ Saved My Life	**MACHINE** – There But For The Grace Of God Go I
HOWARD JOHNSON – So Fine	**CHANGE** – Paradise
DAVID JOSEPH – You Can't Hide Your Love	**THE CLASH** – Magnificent Dance
PRINCE – Sexy Dancer	**GWEN MCCRAE** – Funky Sensation
DIANA ROSS – The Boss	**SERGIO MENDES** – I'll Tell You
CHAKA KHAN – I'm Every Woman	**TONY COOK & THE PARTY PEOPLE** – On The Floor
YELLO – Bostich	
EDDY GRANT – Timewarp	**INNER LIFE** – Caught Up (In A One Night Love Affair)
NICK STRAKER BAND – A Little Bit Of Jazz	
TANTRA – Mother Africa	**GERALDINE HUNT** – Can't Fake The Feeling
MFSB – Love Is The Message	**IMAGINATION** – Burning Up
CHAKA KHAN – Ain't Nobody	**JIMMY BO HORN** – Spank
PHREEK – Weekend	
ASHFORD & SIMPSON – It Seems To Hang On	Compiled by the Committee

RECOMMENDED LISTENING

VARIOUS – Frankie Knuckles Presents	**VARIOUS** – United DJs Of The World: Frankie Knuckles (DJ mix)
VARIOUS – Choice: A Collection Of Classics	

❝ I took a drum machine to clubs. I could play any rhythm track and people would go crazy. ❞

Chip E
Chicago architect

Interviewed by Bill and Frank in Knightsbridge, May 5, 2005

Known to his mum as Irwin Larry Eberhart II, Chip E is one of the founding fathers of Chicago house music. He was among the first to produce records for the scene, releasing an album called *Jack Trax* on Gotta Dance records as early as 1985, as well as co-producing Frankie Knuckles on his cover of 'You Can't Hide From Yourself'. As a pioneer bedroom producer taking advantage of cheap electronics, Chip's tracks were some of the first anywhere to show how the future of dance music would be built from cheeky samples of older records. A promising early career brought him club hits in the UK, but he was mired in a legal wrangle with DJ International that prevented him recording for anyone else, which allowed his production career to peter out.

We meet in London in a pub in Knightsbridge. Chip has been shopping with his missus and there are a few bags to be accommodated at the table. He has a great perspective on the whole Chicago scene, and in recent years has taken up the role of house historian and, as the architect behind the documentary *The UnUsual Suspects – Once Upon A Time In House Music.*

First of all tell us a little of your background.
I was born in Chicago in 1966. Grew up on the southside of Chicago. Most of the guys who started house music grew up on the southside. For a while I went to school in LA, which opened my eyes up to the new wave sound. I came back to Chicago where I guess it was more disco and such. My parents were eclectic and listened to all sorts of things – a lot of bossa nova! I studied marketing and music at college and I worked in a music shop, Imports Etc and I also DJed. So if you put that together, the music shop, the DJing and the marketing, I had a good sense of the business of it, as well as what people wanted on the floor.

When I started in high school, DJing was new and cool. All my friends would cut class to go to a guy's house to play records. I thought I was mixing, but really I was just doing train wrecks. But I was fortunate because I had a friend who introduced me to Imports Etc. And since I had all the good music, they always asked me to come by. I was doing train wrecks for a long time until finally there was a guy at Imports called Brett Wilcox, he listened to one of my tapes and he said, 'You know, this sucks, but I can teach you how to mix. You know, I taught Frankie?' 'Really? You taught Frankie?' 'Yeah and I got his old decks' They were a pair of old Technics 1100s. I came over and within about 20 minutes I went from knowing nothing about mixing except these are two decks and this is a mixer, to actually understanding phrases and segues etc. It was a big eye-opener.

What kind of places were you DJing?
Mostly high school parties. Sock hops we would call them, in high school gymnasiums. I started playing small places. There's a place called the Candy Store, The Playground. That was where Jesse and Farley started DJing.

What age group would go there?
I guess it was mostly 13 to 18. When I was about 11 I went to this place called the Loft as an assignment for a city-wide high-school newspaper. There was a guy there, Eric Bradshaw,

he had a group called Vertigo and he threw parties at the Loft, which was on 14th and Michigan. Their preferred DJs were the Chosen Few, who were essentially Wayne Williams, Tony Hatchett, Jesse Saunders and Alan King. Later they added Andrew Hatchett. I was 11 or 12 the first night. He got me in, because I had no business being in there. Everybody there was 15-18. I remember it just like it was yesterday. It was packed full of people, it was a proper loft, the floor was moving up and down because there were way too many people in there. The music's pounding and they're playing Martin Circus 'Disco Circus', and Alan King was on the decks. There was all these people sweating and dancing and having fun and I thought, 'Wow, this is something I really wanna be a part of.' From that point on I was hooked.

" Here I'm gonna blow all the myths, because really house music has very little to do with the Warehouse. House music came at least two years after the Warehouse closed down. "

Tell us about the Warehouse and the origins of house music.
Here I'm gonna blow all the myths, because really house music has very little to do with the Warehouse. It's *related* to the Warehouse but you have to realise that house music came at least two years *after* the Warehouse closed down. Frankie played R&B, disco, funk, soul at the Warehouse, he even played country and western, but he never played house music.

The way the term 'house' came into being was through Imports Etc. I was one of the buyers there at the time. Kids were coming in looking for the older disco music, they'd say, 'I want some of that music played at the Warehouse,' and this was referring to disco. And we found that if we put up signs that said, 'As Heard At The Warehouse', the records would fly out the racks. Eventually that got cut down to just 'The 'House'. That became the vernacular – but we were talking about disco records.

Basically myself, Farley [Farley Keith, aka Farley Jackmaster Funk], Steve Hurley and Jesse Saunders all said, 'You know what, all you gotta do is make a record and put 'house' on it and it's gonna fly off the shelves. So why don't we make some new music and call it house'. That's essentially what we did.

The others were older than me, Steve, Jesse and Farley have probably three years on me, so they would've had the opportunities to go to the Warehouse, but they avoided it because they were very homophobic at the time and the Warehouse was known as a very gay place. We weren't gay so, you know, we didn't go. But we understood the power of marketing. We understood the power of using that word 'house'. We all gravitated towards making our own music.

And Jesse's record 'On & On' was the first?
True enough, Jesse made one of the first records he calls house music, but I kinda think it's not 'cos it was 'On & On', which was a remake of a bootleg.

Supposedly it was his theme tune, which he used to open his sets, but someone stole it so he reconstructed it.
Yeah, see I get mixed stories on that. Wayne Williams, Jesse's half-brother, is really important to the story. Wayne *did* go to the Warehouse and Den One and these places.

Wayne was going to the Warehouse and bringing the music back to the southside and the straight clubs.
Exactly. Also he was helping out guys on the radio, like Herb Kent. So he was introducing it to an even broader audience, this disco music.

Wayne told me this bootleg 'On & On' was actually *his* record and Jesse would play it and Wayne eventually said, 'You know what, you can't play it any more,' so Jesse said, 'That's okay,

I'll *make* it!' So he went away got a drum machine, ran into Vince Lawrence – and Vince's father was already in the record business so they had all the connections. They ran into Larry Sherman [of Trax records] and he can press the records. I can't say whether Jesse was inventor of house music but he was certainly one of the pioneers, and he was pretty integral to starting the scene in Chicago where people were making their own music in their own houses.

And because he was from Chicago when people heard his record on the radio, everyone thought, 'Shit we can do this.' It might not have been good, it might not have been house, but it was made by someone in Chicago in their bedroom by someone they all knew.
Yeah, exactly. It was definitely an inspiration. You just put one and two together.

What about Jamie Principle then, he was making stuff early on. Wasn't he before Jesse?
It was about the same time. Jesse's record came out first then we heard Jamie's music at the Power Plant. For years and years played off tape.

That's one of the controversies, isn't it, how much Frankie had to do with it?
There should be no controversy, Jamie did it all himself. Jamie is a musical genius. Jamie was a big Prince fan. One of Prince's name was Jamie Starr and Principle is from Prince…
Jamie's music wasn't really influenced by the Warehouse or the Power Plant because he didn't go to those clubs either. He came from a pretty conservative and religious family so he wasn't allowed to do those things, it was a friend who took them to Frankie. So Frankie really had nothing to do with Jamie's music.

So Jamie never heard his music played in clubs?
Not for a long time.

How was Frankie received when he arrived? The story that's always told is that Chicago's scene wasn't as sophisticated as New York so straight away he was a star. Is that true?
No. It was the venue, it was the venue, really. It's not that Frankie wasn't a good DJ, but he wasn't really mixing back then. He was kind of playing records like David Mancuso. There was no segueing, no beat matching at all. Robert Williams [Warehouse owner] came from New York and he tried to bring the New York scene in via the Warehouse.

Didn't it move around different venues?
Yes, it was in different lofts and warehouses, so the Warehouse was really a nickname, its official name was actually US Studios. All the flyers would say 'US Studios' but everyone would call it the Warehouse.

Who were the big DJs before Frankie came to Chicago?
Herb Kent. Herb Kent was huge on the radio. He played disco and a lot of new wave.

Were there other DJs playing the same stuff as Frankie?
No.

So he was pretty unique then?
Oh yeah.

So what do you think needs telling then, what's the truth?
We were all either in our late teens or early twenties when the press first came to find out the story of house music. So we said, you know… Frankie… The Warehouse… etc. Well, it's really the Power Plant. The Warehouse is where it takes its name, but it's the Music Box and Power Plant where house music got played. More than anything I guess it's about electronic equipment becoming affordable.

I think it was about 1983. Disco had died out around '81, but you still had the Italo disco, Claudio Simonetti, Doctor's Cat, Klein & MBO. They were taking disco and turning it into electronic music. So what we did was take it to the next phase, so it's disco, Italo-disco and then house.

In about '83 everyone jumped all over the Roland drum machines, the Roland sampler, and around the same time was the Ensoniq. As far as sampling was concerned you had Trevor Horn who was using the Fairlight and then you had the Kurzweil keyboard, which was still thousands of dollars. Then the Synclavier which was expensive. But for under $2,000 you had the Ensoniq Mirage, a polyphonic sampling keyboard, and for under $200 you had the Boss sampling pedal, which was my first introduction to sampling. They actually made it for guitar players, but it had about eight milliseconds of sampling on it, which was enough to do 'Like This' [as in Chip E's 'Like This']. Later Joe Smooth, who was a frequent customer at Imports Etc, he had this prototype which was the Ensoniq Mirage. So we said, 'Why don't you come in the studio with us and make a record?' That was how that happened.

And Frankie was making New York style edits for the Power Plant.
Again that was primarily this guy Erasmo Rivera. Erasmo did a lot of tape edits for Frankie, a lot of reel to reel tape edits. They didn't do any new production on it, they didn't do any new vocals, they just took the existing music and did tape edits of it. Then you take Jamie's music and Frankie didn't have anything to do with that other than playing it. So at this point, to say Frankie invented house music is like saying Dick Clark invented rock'n'roll. He *played* it, but he didn't invent it.

His importance was more as a catalyst.
Oh yeah. I just wanted to clarify his position, because it was not as a musician or producer. His first production was a remix of First Choice 'Let No Man Put Asunder', which came about because Paul Weissberg, who was the owner of Imports, had a good relationship with Salsoul because he bought a lot of their product. So he arranged, as a birthday present for Frankie, to do a remix. His first actual record didn't come out until 1987 and that was 'You Can't Hide'. And I actually produced that for him.

'Godfather of House' is apt, because it doesn't say he created it, but he was an overseer.
Yeah. I think that's fair.

When did you start working at Imports Etc?
Late '82, early '83.

Was it opened specifically as an import store?
Yeah. It started off as a record pool. Paul Weissberg had a record pool called IRS. Independent Record Services. Eventually he saw a business opportunity, so he thought he could sell these records to the general public. Can't remember the name of the guy but the company was called C.A.P. Exports.

When did he open it?
About '81. Gramaphone had been established earlier. They didn't move into the dance music arena till later.

Why was Italo-disco so big in Chicago?
Well, because of the Hot Mix 5, who were some of the first DJs in the country beatmatching, and the Italo disco records, because they were so synthesised, they were really easy to mix. Anything that came out, it was almost like a system, you'd put them on the decks and they just worked. Instead of trying to mix disco records, they're all over the place.

Larry Sherman at Trax and Rocky Jones at DJ International pretty much had the city sewn up in terms of putting out records. What was the attitude to them early on?
Well, you know, we were young and these guys had cheque-books. We didn't look at them as villains, we looked at them as saviours. Here they were giving us a way to exploit our music, to *some* extent.

What sort of advances were they offering back then?
Between $500-$1,500.

Pretty small, then. Did you ever see any royalties?
Beyond advances, no.

What about when they were licensed to London Records over here?
Never.

Did you ever challenge them?
Not really…

Did you sign a contract or was it all done on the back of a cigarette packet?
It was done on a licensing agreement. It was challengeable, but I don't know if you know JB Ross. Have you heard this name? He was a solicitor. Basically Rocky or Larry would come up with a contract, Jay would write them. They'd say, Go over to Jay, he'll help you sort out the contract.' You didn't understand that that was *their* solicitor, who's working on their behalf. But most of the contracts were five or 10 years licenses, and they've all expired.

So you own your own productions now?
Yeah.

Rocky Jones ran a record pool didn't he?
Yeah.

So he was in some way supportive of the scene. You don't run a record pool unless you're into it.
I think he started off to be very genuine in his intentions. I think he was corrupted by the power. All of a sudden he had the capability of finding these artists in Chicago and selling their music all over the world. MIDEM was critical in house becoming worldwide. This was before the internet, it was a way of getting to all the markets at one time.

> ❝ We were young and these guys had cheque-books. We didn't look at them as villains, we looked at them as saviours. ❞

Tell us about the first time you saw Ron Hardy DJ?
Some friends of mine had taken me to the Music Box. I think it was one of the nights that Frankie was hanging out with him. It was very dark and narrow. It just had an incredible sound system, minimal lighting, compared to what contemporary clubs were. It had a couple of Mars lights, a couple of strobes.

Mars lights are like police lights?
Yeah. The music was incredible and the energy in the place was just unbelievable. It reminded me of the Loft [the Chicago Loft]. Pounding music, dancing, sweating, nothing like the other clubs. I called them S&M clubs because people went there to Stand And Model. People would put on their Versace suits and they wanted to look good, they didn't want to sweat.

Even the Power Plant?
It was kind of like that. People wanted to dance and have a good time, but they didn't want to sweat too much. Whereas the Music Box was down and dirty. A lot of times people would carry sweat clothes, and they'd carry towels with them, too.

Do you remember the kind of music Ron Hardy was playing?
He was playing First Choice, Exodus 'Together Forever', MFSB 'Love Is The Message'. He was playing Sylvester 'Don't Stop' and he was playing a version with an edit on the breakdown – it just went on and on forever. The next day was when I discovered Imports Etc. It was like Columbus discovering America, because after I heard that song I asked my friend 'Where do I get music like *this?*' I picked up my two copies of 'Don't Stop'.

And he was pitching tracks right up?
I think that was a lot later. You hear the stories about him being on drugs and pitching things up, that may have come later, but for all the times I was a patron of the club he played everything pretty much at normal speed, or whatever was appropriate to the mix. And he wasn't really doing a lot of drugs. The drugs came later with the popularity and esteem.

Pierre told a story about when he made 'Acid Tracks' he sat on the front for two hours waiting for Ron to turn up. There was that kind of adoration.
Yeah, there was. There was a sense that if you wanted to get a hit, if you wanted to get people to hear your music then you gotta get it played at the Music Box. These were guys who were pretty open, but Frankie not as much as Ronnie. Frankie you really had to be in the inner circle to get something played. I was very fortunate because I worked at Imports Etc so he was one of my customers.

How would you describe the difference between the two of them?
Ronnie was kind of *skinny* and Frankie was kind of *fat*. They really did play similarly, but Ronnie would take more chances. I could go on a Friday night and take a tape to Frankie and he might wait around for two or three hours and listen to it in the headphones and say, 'I think I can fit it in here'. Whereas *Ronnie,* I could take him a tape and within ten to 15 minutes he had it on and was banging it, and then playing it several times a night. He was much more courageous in his style of playing.

Listening to tapes, the edits that Ronnie played were really repetitive and very 'house' compared to Frankie's.
Neither Ronnie nor Frankie did any of their own editing. Erasmo did editing for both of them but there were a lot of people who gave both of them edits of mixes.

The ones Ronnie played are definitely different in style to Frankie's.
I think that was because of his audience. It was a younger crowd. Frankie's crowd had followed him from the Warehouse and went to the Power Plant. They were older. When Robert Williams started the Music Box, he specifically started it for a younger crowd and for a more mixed crowd. You had black, white, Latino, gay, straight whatever.

❝ I took Jesse's 808 and with my drum programming on there we played at clubs. People went crazy. ❞

Did you get to see Ron Hardy during his disco phase. Did you go to Den One?
No, I first came across him in about '83 when the Music Box opened. Robert Williams, he was the owner of the Music Box and the Warehouse. He also had a club called the Music Box in Texas and he would go back and forth between them. Eventually he decided he wanted to open a Music Box in Chicago and he brought Ron Hardy in because he had Frankie Knuckles at the Warehouse, but that was kinda winding down, they had some problems with the building, they weren't able to renew their lease. And then Frankie decided he wanted to move on and do something different and that's when he went on to the Power Plant. And so he found this guy Ron Hardy.

So the Power Plant and Music Box had the same ownership?
People thought they were rivals. But they were really good friends. For instance, they really didn't compete much: Power Plant was a Friday night crowd, Music Box was Saturday. On Friday you might find Ronnie hanging out at the Power Plant and on Saturday Frankie at the Music Box. They were great friends. Everybody else on the outside tried to make them out as rivals.

But that's good for business anyway isn't it?
Yeah.

Hip hop didn't really take off in Chicago for a long time, but that hip hop sensibility was there. There were even battles weren't there?
Oh definitely. From the early '80s, when the Hot Mix 5 first went to the New Music Seminar [in New York], they just took over, because they were the first guys who were really

beatmatching. Farley had an incredible style with scratching and all these tricks of the time, like triples, phasing and back-spinning. For instance on 'Like This', specifically one of the reasons we put at the beginning the 'L-L-L-like this' was because we knew DJs liked little pieces like that that they could manipulate.

How much did the Hot Mix 5 influence taste in Chicago? Were they more important than Knuckles and Hardy because their audience was bigger?
Yeah! Because they were on the radio. The Hot Mix 5, they were big!

They had a mix every lunchtime didn't they?
That was later, but it started off just their *Saturday Night Live* show, Armando Rivera was the host: *Saturday Night Live Ain't No Jive Dance Party*.

So their part was a section in his show?
No it was the whole show on Saturday night. And the *whole* city was tuned into the Hot Mix 5's show and if you had to go out you made sure somebody was taping it for you.

How much were *their* tastes shaped by Hardy and Knuckles?
I would say… not much at first. Farley and Jesse were big followers of the Warehouse… Again I'm working at Imports Etc so I knew what the guys are coming in and looking for, 'cos there was essentially only two record stores. If you were a DJ in Chicago you had to come to Imports Etc. There was no way around it. The Hot Mix 5 were members of the IRS record pool.

So they had an allegiance to the store?
Exactly. So I knew what all the guys were playing. I'd say that four of the five, Kenny Jason, Ralphi Rosario, Scott Sills and Mickey Oliver, those guys weren't too influenced by anything other than what was sold at the store. They were looking for Italo disco. Farley, being the only black member and being the only southside member, was more influenced by and understood the importance of clubs like Music Box, Power Plant, Warehouse. He was the one who would play more of the older disco tunes. The other guys not at all, they would play mainly Italo, some Philly sounds and maybe some New York sound.

Were there records that they played a lot that weren't played in clubs?
Well, initially, everything they played was not played in clubs but within six months it became the club style. They changed the music. Some of the early songs were Capricorn 'I Need Love', also all the Kasso stuff, Doctor's Cat, of course you know that *Mix Your Own Stars* was huge.

What was that?
It was an Italian compilation of rhythm tracks. These were nothing more than drum tracks. The most popular track was one that was called '119' because it was 119 bpm. And the track just went *do-do-doo-chak-chak-chak, do-do-doo-chak-chak-chak* and it was huge. It was just a bass drum, a little snare, some toms and a clap. You could pack a dancefloor just by playing this. It was one of the early inspirations for house music.

It was an achievable sound, too, for budding producers.
Exactly. Not only that but it just fit. All the Italian tracks were using Roland drum machines so it was very easy to mix in and out of, with any record.

What was the inspiration for you personally to start making tracks?
Marketing class. I learnt how you had to create a need for a product first. And from taking a drum machine to clubs and finding out I could play any rhythm track and people would go crazy. I had a Boss Dr Rhythm drum machine and a Casio VL-Tone keyboard, not even a professional, it was a little toy for kids. I made tracks with these two things, put them on reel-to-reel and I remember taking them to Jesse Saunders because he lived down the same street as me, I lived on 77th and King Drive and he lived on 71st and we went to the same grammar school. I took my tracks there and he said, 'I think you should find a new hobby.' That just energised me. I took the track to Ronnie and he played it and people went crazy. 'No, I know people like this stuff'. I would hang out in the basement with Vince [Lawrence]

and Jesse and one day when Jesse wasn't there, Vince said, 'Here, I'll show you how to programme an 808.' Then he said, 'Here, take it home with you.' I took Jesse's 808 and with my drum programming on there we played at clubs. People went crazy. This was '83.

Who was first to do that?
I'd say probably Jesse with an 808, but Farley got a Linn because he wanted to be different. Then, probably Steve and maybe me. My mom spent a lot of time on the west coast because she worked in advertising and when she went, my brother and I would have these little basement parties. We thought we were DJing and this guy Steve Hurley, who didn't live too far away, came by and one of his friends said, 'Can Steve get on the turntables?'

I'm like, 'I'm not letting him get on this is my party.' Anyway he went on and tore it up. He was great and I was really jealous.

What about Marshall, did you know him?
He didn't come along till much later. He didn't come along till about '86 or '87. I actually did the remix for 'Move Your Body' but never got any credit, not even any label credit to this day. But I did the mix on that that put the mix on-beat. I took his song and put it in a way that was DJ friendly. He would go four beats, then two beats, then six. I did all the sampling on the 'rock your body' bit.

But that was the name of the game in Chicago, stealing?
But still a little disappointing. So I decided it was time to make my own records. I sold my turntables to get studio time. I brought a bunch of friends into this little studio Reel To Reel Studio. Dwayne Thamm was the owner and engineer and we made this EP called 'Jack Trax'. We weren't too organised. I had a lot of drum programmes and I had a few ideas of what I wanted to do like stuff with 'house' in it, and jacking was the way the dancing was described so I made this song called 'Time To Jack'. All it said was 'time to jack' and 'jack your body'.

After that we still had studio time left and I'd decided to do a song called 'It's House' and that's all that said. The bassline for it was actually an accident. We didn't have sequencers but Joe Smooth had this Roland RX7 drum machine which had the capability to do MIDI sequencing. We plugged it in and it started playing this rhythm. We didn't even programme it, it just happened. The bassline for 'Time To Jack' was actually 'Jungle DJ' by Kikrokos.

That's one of the famous Ron Hardy edits, wasn't it?
Yes. That's how a lot of house happened. There were lots of records and edits you couldn't get anywhere so we would emulate them. And people were already familiar with the bassline, so by emulating the bassline you were almost assured to have a hit. I remember the first time it was played in a club was at the Mars Bar. Farley slammed it on and people went crazy. When the bassline came in, people lost their minds.

After the *Jack Trax* album I met this guy Lidell Townsell and he was a keyboard player. One of my favourite songs was 'Moody' by ESG and I asked him whether he could play the bassline and he said, 'Yeah, I can play that'. That was 'Like This'. From there, because I understood the equipment and because I was one of the architects of the house sound, I started putting my hand on all the songs that went through DJ International. So basically every song that came through, I was either doing the rhythm or final mixing or the vocals.

How did that work, were you on contract?
Yeah, which was good since I wasn't getting royalties. I was getting advances off every song they did.

You must have had a good relationship with Rocky at that time?
Yeah, I did. I was 18 and I was able to move out of home and into my own place, buy a car, get an apartment. All was good.

When did you realise that all wasn't good?
When I saw other artists being pushed further and deals were coming through, I was like the secret weapon, I made all the tracks but I was pushed in the background. For instance, Full House 'Communicate', which I had my hands on, they were pushed forward because they were the artists whereas I was just the producer.

....

When I tried to go a little more mainstream with the song 'If You Only Knew', it was more radio friendly, it had a potential to be a really big hit, it was the first song to be played on all the major Chicago stations. Timmy Regisford wanted to pick it up for MCA. He wanted to pick me up as an artist. At the time – this was in '87 – Rocky told him that it would be $100,000 to buy the contract. I can say honestly, I don't think I was worth that, but it was a way to thwart me going forward. That's when I opened my eyes and saw all the licensing. So I thought if I can't move forward and grow I'm just gonna stop, so that's what I did in 1989, I stopped recording, period.

The story a lot of people tell is that when the majors came knocking Larry and Rocky weren't interested, they wanted to keep it all for themselves. How quickly did kids in Chicago realise how successful their music was in the UK?
When the English press started coming over. And then when we first started coming over to England, which seemed like almost monthly. The Hippodrome was the first. I can't remember the names of any others. Paradigio in Rimini. Once we started coming over and seeing how big it was… At home house was played in underground clubs and on the radio sometimes, but when we came over here they were playing it on TV, on *Top Of The Pops*.

How did things fade out in Chicago?
It had a lot to do with the press, I think: reporting it as a black gay thing. It put those bookends on house music: house music is a thing for black gay people. That perception definitely limited its capabilities.

Do you think the stigma was linked to disco?
I would say that it was initially that. When New York started doing house music they called it garage so they kind of separated themselves from disco, and it didn't have the stigmatism of being black gay music. New York was a tight-knit community whereas in Chicago there was a lot of stealing and fighting.

Was there any sense when you were working on those records early on that this music would have such a massive impact?
We didn't think it would go on for 20 years. It was something for the moment. When you're young you don't think about the future.

© DJhistory.com

CHIP E SELECTED DISCOGRAPHY

CHIP E – Time To Jack (producer)

CHIP E – It's House (producer)

AUTO BAHN – Do You Like This Beat (writer/producer/mixer)

CHIP E – If You Only Knew (writer/producer)

FRANKIE KNUCKLES – You Can't Hide From Yourself (producer/remixer)

K-JOY – Like This (writer/producer)

THE IT – Donnie (remixer)

CHIP E – No Reason (producer)

BLACK BALLS – Clap Ya Hands (producer/remixer)

RECOMMENDED LISTENING

CHIP E – Jack Trax (vinyl only)

VARIOUS – Chicago Sound: House Music Vol II (vinyl only)

" My friends all said, 'Stupid motherfucker bought all this equipment and don't even know how to play nothin'.' But by the next year, I had records out. "

Marshall Jefferson
Leader of the jack

Interviewed by Frank in Billericay, February 22, 1999

A friend described Marshall Jefferson as someone who's still excited that he's not a postman any more, and sure enough, he seems constantly thrilled that he gets to do things like make music and do interviews and play records for money, bursting out with wild snickering laughter like a naughty kid after school.

As cheap electronic instruments revolutionised music-making, Marshall was one of the first in line for a synthesiser. And as Chicago dancefloors became the testing ground for home-made dance music, stripped-down to the basics, and made by clubbers instead of musicians, he became one of the city's leading producers. With no musical training, in the space of a couple of years or so he'd made classics that had made it round the world to soundtrack Britain's acid house revolution.

Bizarrely we meet in deepest Essex in a tiny Brooksidey close in a little country town that has played host to some of the biggest names in American dance music for the last 10 years. Pierre stays here, so does Tony Humphries and so apparently do loads more DJs from the Windy City, thanks to the fact that the house is owned by a DJ agency. It looks like your mate's just-left-school, boys-only crash-pad. There's a copy of *Playboy* on the sofa and a shelf with every single *Star Trek* episode on video. Serbia's biggest DJ is upstairs in a home studio and some American guy is knocking up health juices in the kitchen.

One thing I can't get is that the name house music...
...Comes from the Warehouse.

But the music that Frankie Knuckles was playing at the Warehouse at that time was pretty much straight-up disco.
Disco, yeah, yeah, yeah.

He was editing it, extending it, but it was disco. So how come the same name was then used for these tracks that everyone started making?
Okay...

How come they didn't call it something else?
Because they ripped off old disco songs. And also, by then they would call anything that was played in that type of club, 'house music', right. Underground music was 'house music' to us. It was house music because of where it was played, not because of what it sounded like. The name house music got its name from Frankie's club. Just like garage got its name from Larry Levan's club, but that doesn't necessarily mean that he was making the music. It's like, Tony Humphries don't make no music, right, but suppose somebody made some music and called it Ministry music. Right, boom, that's it. So that's the thing.

Did the scene feel very special?
Hell yeah, we would hear music that nobody else would hear... in the world!

Did people realise that?

We would walk down the street and see somebody and say [dismissively], 'They don't know what's happening.' We had that pride about our musical taste.

And people would actually say, 'He's house but he's not house'?
Right.

You could tell by what people looked like?
The clothes and the styles, the same thing, you know. You could tell who had a clue and who didn't. Or what they were listening to on the radio. If they were listening to the Gap Band they weren't house [collapses in laughter].

What kind of things were people wearing?
It was hard to explain. You would have to ask somebody else about the fashion aspect. I was automatically house because I was making the hippest records in the city [cackles uncontrollably].

So who started house music as we know it?
Jesse Saunders is behind every thing in your interview. He did the first house record and the significance behind that, right, is, it got non-musicians into making music. Everything came from that. See, Jesse was a DJ. He was one of the top club DJs in the city. And the next step for him was to make records. Vince Lawrence talked him into it.

> **❝ It was Jesse made everybody want to go and get a drum machine and start making records, because... Jesse's shit wasn't that good. ❞**

Making records for his own dancefloor.
Yeah, for his own dancefloor.

That was his track 'On And On'.
Yep. I'm telling you the amount of stuff that comes from Jesse, that you can trace back to Jesse Saunders, is every single thing that's happening now.

So what made him start making music?
He wanted some pussy!

Simple as that?
Him and Vince Lawrence, because Vince Lawrence's dad had the record company, and Jesse Saunders was the star DJ. He was the biggest DJ in Chicago. Jesse Saunders actually put out a record. That's what got me started in house music. That's what got everybody started in house music.

But people were making tracks before they were making records. People were making tracks and bringing the reels straight to the DJ.
Yeah, Jamie Principle. But, the thing is, right, nobody started making music because of it. Jamie's stuff was too good. Nobody thought they could duplicate it. Everybody thought that Jamie was somebody from Europe.

But he was pretty much the first?
Actually, Vince Lawrence was the first 'cos his dad owned the record company. And, if you listened to Vince's first record, 'I Like To Do It In Fast Cars', it sounds like house music, but at the time it wasn't considered house music.

Why not?
Nobody paid attention to it. He wasn't a star DJ. He just put out records.

So Vince made some records that got ignored, and then Jamie Principle started making

tracks and giving them to Frankie Knuckles to play?
Right.

And was that what made everyone suddenly want to go and get a drum machine?
No – it was Jesse made everybody want to go and get a drum machine and start making records, because... Jesse's shit wasn't that good. You know what I'm saying? It made it more accessible. When Jamie's stuff was played in the clubs, everybody was like 'Fuck that's too good! I can't do anything like that.' But when *Jesse* did it everybody says 'Fuck! I could do better than that!' When Jesse did his stuff everybody started making music. You see?

Exactly, you feel 'Well I could have a go.'
That's what got me involved. That's what got everybody involved. You got all these DJs starting to make records.

If it wasn't great music, what was its power to inspire?
Okay, supposing there were no porno movies and then people started making porno movies, and they were all the rage, and you knew the main porn star, right, and your dick was twice as big as his, and he turned out to be a millionaire. Now wouldn't you consider to give it a shot? Hell, you know what I'm saying. That's what's inspiring. Somebody make it big...

...but not be that great.
Yeah. You see what I'm saying?

Exactly, exactly.
And that's how it was. That's what inspired everybody. It gave us hope, man. When Jamie was doing it, nobody thought of making a record. His shit was too good. It's like seeing John Holmes in a porno movie. You know you can't do better than him. But if porno movies were just starting, and you see a guy with a three inch peter, and all the women are swooning all over him and he's a fucking millionaire, you would seriously consider it, wouldn't you?

When Jesse made his first tracks, how was he getting them out there?
Man, Vince Lawrence and Jesse were totally driven by pussy. Now I'm gonna tell you something... [stops his thought] No I'd better not say it.

Jesse's stuff started playing on regular radio in Chicago. He was bigger than Prince in Chicago, man! And next to Jimmy Jam and Terry Lewis, it would sound like bullshit. It would sound like tin cans, man. But, everybody knew Jesse, so it was popular shit. And by the time he finally did 'Real Love', which was one fifth the quality necessary to make the radio – everything else was like one twentieth; that shit came out, it was huge! But none of it left the city. Because Jesse didn't leave the city. If Jesse would have left the city, or if the States had a national radio station, and a female programmer on there... [Laughs fit to bust]

He'd have been off the hook!
Yeah, man, oh it was so fucking exciting, to see, behind the scenes. To see all this shit coming together, and Jesse was, he was the king, man. But nobody knows about Jesse, That's the thing.

Why not? He's in LA, isn't he.
Well see, this is the thing right: everybody started making better house music.

Who was next out of the gate?
Me, Farley 'Jackmaster' Funk, Steve 'Silk' Hurley, Larry Heard and Adonis. When us five came out, all at the same time, house music left Chicago. And that's when Jesse stopped doing house music. For some reason. Well the reason was... he got a major label deal. So he was, 'Aw fuck house music. Been there, done that, I'm gonna start doin some R&B now.' And when all this shit started happening, when everybody started saying 'HOUSE MUSIC, HOUSE MUSIC, HOUSE MUSIC', there was no fuckin' Jesse Saunders.

He'd already left town?
He'd already left town. He was going for the big shit.

Marshall Jefferson

....

He missed all the fun
See that's the thing. Everybody's gonna tell you what they did, and all that shit, but nobody woulda got started without Jesse. Nobody. Jesse Saunders and Vince Lawrence…

Vince's father owned a record company.
Yeah, Mitchbal records. Mitch is still around.

Wasn't that an old soul label?
I don't know what it was but he put out the first house records.

So that was even before Jesse had stuff on vinyl.
Yeah.

How come Vince didn't get any recognition?
Nobody really knew Vince, 'cos Vince didn't sing. Jesse sang on his shit. And Jesse Saunders was a star DJ. Jesse wouldn't have made records if it wasn't for Vince, you see because Vince's dad owned the record label right. Vince, went to Jesse and said 'Hey man we could get a lot of pussy, man, putting out records. We could be fuckin' superstars.'

They were pushing each other forwards.
Well, it was like, Vince pushed, man. Vince was the pusher. Jesse, said okay. Jesse was driven, but nobody was driven like Vince. 'Cos if you meet Vince, he ain't gonna get laid unless he got an edge.

So what about your clubbing days? You went to the Music Box right?
Yeah. I wasn't even into dance music before I went to the Music Box. I was into rock'n'roll. I was a postman. We used to get drunk and stoned after work every day. We would call it a different holiday. 'It's… hmmm… Kiss the Nuns Day', woo-hoo! And we would get drunk and listen to rock'n'roll. We were like 'Disco Sucks!' and all that. I hated dance music 'cos I couldn't dance. The only reason I got into dance music was there was this girl at work, she took me to the Music Box, and I thought dance music was kind of wimpy, until I heard it at Music Box volume.

What was the difference?
The volume, man. The way Ron Hardy played. I had never heard music at that volume since. It was really amazing. And in like 15 years I have not heard a single club that even came close to that volume, and the reason being, there would be loads of lawsuits from damaging your hearing. Because the Music Box was so loud anywhere in the club, not just on the dancefloor, anywhere in the club, the bass would physically move you.

How big was it?
I guess, maximum you could fit up in there would be about 750.

So who took you there the first time?
This girl, her name was Lynn, she's really religious now, but she was a stripper back then. Great body, right, and she liked me, and stuff. I never jumped on her, 'cos she was working at the Post Office right next to me every day. That was a little too close. I wanted to be a bachelor, I wanted to like spread myself around. Anyway, she took me to the Music Box. I just wanted to go 'cos I wanted to see her body in action. She was wild, you know. She would talk about all the stuff she did, it was really wild stuff, so I wanted to go to the wild club she was going to.

What was the crowd like?
It was mostly gays, and you know man, I got in there, I never heard any music like this, I was like, fuck! Damn! This is brilliant, great, and that's when I got into dance music.

You found religion.
Yep.

Did it feel like that?
Yeah, man. One night I got converted to dance music, by Ron Hardy.

Did a lot of people feel that way? You get the impression that it was church for people.
Yeah.

Can you remember the songs he was playing that night?
'Let No Man Put Asunder' [by First Choice], 'I'm Here Again' by Thelma Houston, 'I Can't
Turn Around' by Isaac Hayes. All of those.

> ** ❝ I hated dance music. The only reason I got into it was this girl at work, she took me to the Music Box. I just wanted to go 'cos I wanted to see her body in action. ❞❞**

How would you describe Ron Hardy's style?
Well, I'll tell you sir. There was two distinctly different styles. Frankie played more disco. He
didn't get into the new wavey stuff like Ron Hardy did.

What sort of things?
Well, you know stuff like, 'It's My Life' by Talk Talk, the ABC stuff, Eurythmics, all that shit,
'Frequency 7' by Visage. Frankie wouldn't play none of that shit. Frankie would play like more
straight-up disco, the black disco stuff. But Ron hardy would play it all, man, at really high speeds.

Really?
It was rockin', man. And Hardy was busier with the records, too. He would fuck with the
EQ more. Frankie would just mess with the bass occasionally; Hardy would mess with every
fuckin' thing.

And he would extend everything for ages?
Both of them would extend everything for ages, to tell you the absolute truth. But I would
watch Hardy sometimes, editing songs, man, and he would do it with just a cassette player,
he would play the record, *ssst*, pause and then *whmp* play it again, the same part and pause
whmm then do it again.

He would make loops with a cassette deck?
Yeah. Right on a cassette deck. Then when the party come, he would play the cassettes.

Was he playing a section of disco and a section of new wave, or mixing it all together?
Mixing it all together. Hardy… did every single drug known to man. How the fuck you
gonna programme that? He didn't give a fuck about programming.

He was just for the moment.
Yeah. And when I saw Larry Levan later, I wasn't impressed, because I'd already seen Ron
Hardy. Same type of DJ, but Larry Levan passed out while he was playing. Ron Hardy never
passed out while he was playing. As high as he got, he never passed out, 'cos he was so
pumped up.

Right.
Larry Levan would pass out, fall asleep on the decks, you know all of a sudden you hear a
[needle scratch noise] somebody grab him, move him out of the way, 'okay I'll take over,'
Larry Levan would have on nights, where…

…Where it worked.
Yeah. But he played the records at their proper speeds.

So how fast was Ron Hardy playing them?
Well… Shit man, Hardy would do shit plus six, plus eight, you know, fast as he could play it.

....

Must have been a crazy atmosphere in there.
Yeah, the energy man, the energy. Since Larry Levan played everything at the proper speed, there's no way he could duplicate Ron Hardy's energy.

After Jesse Saunders inspired you, how quickly did you get into making tracks?
I would say after Jesse's first record came out, in about two months, I bought equipment. In two months I started making tracks. I was working at the Post Office; I had a good job. You should see how the sales people in America treat people from the Post Office, because they know it's the closest thing to impossible to get fired from. So I was able to buy the equipment. We went to a music store, me and a friend of mine who played guitar, and this guy at the music store showed us a sequencer. Told me, with this thing you can play keyboards like a real keyboard player. And my friend was like, 'That's bullshit, you gotta take lessons.' And I was like 'No, man, I believe him. I'm gonna buy it.' He said, 'No man, don't buy that shit,' 'cos it cost like $3,000. But since I was working at the Post Office I got instant credit. The only reason I bought it was I thought that must be what Jesse Saunders must be using. I didn't know he had a keyboard player playing all his shit.

❝ Hardy never waited for the record, you gave it to him on cassette. ❞

So I said, man I want to be like Jesse Saunders, 'Okay, I'll take this sequencer'. He said 'Wait a minute, you don't want this sequencer and not have a keyboard to play, do you?' 'Oh yeah, you're right.' So I bought the keyboard too. And he said, 'Hey, you don't want to have this sequencer and this keyboard and not have a drum machine?' I said 'Oh yeah you're right.' He said, 'You don't want to have this sequencer and this keyboard and this drum machine and not have something to hear it all on, do you?' I said, 'Yeah you're right.' So I bought this mixer. 'You don't want to have this sequencer and keyboard and drum machine and mixer and not have something to record it all on, do you?' So I bought this recorder, right. And he said, 'You want to have a good monitor system, and you want to have a second keyboard, and this bassline, this 303. I was like yeah, yeah, yeah. Well I ended up spending about nine grand.

What did you end up with?
A JX-8P keyboard, which I still have. A TB-303, which I think I got for under a hundred dollars; sold it for a thousand to Bam Bam. Sucker! A Korg EX-8000 module, a Roland 707 drum machine, a Roland 909 drum machine, Roland 808 drum machine…

The whole works.
Oh man! I got a Tascam 4-track recorder. I got a whole bunch of shit.

So you took all these goodies home. How long did it take you to start making tracks?
Er, two days. Because that night my friends all gave me grief, they came over and laughed at me, said, 'Stupid motherfucker bought all this shit and don't even know how to play nothin'.' But by the next year, I had records out. 'Move Your Body' came out and all the DJs in the world when they found out about house music, they started hiring keyboard players to play like Marshall Jefferson. So there! [Uproarious laughter]

So how did you do it?
Well 'Move Your Body' was at 122 beats per minute, right. I must've recorded those keyboards at 40, 45 bpm: *Dumm dum DER DER DUM bom-bom-bom.* Then I speeded it up: 'Oh Marshall's jamming! Oh man!' You know.

That wasn't the first track you made?
No man. I made a rhythm tracks album. I made Sleezy D 'I've Lost Control', before that.

Which was the first one that got played in the clubs?
Sleezy D 'I've Lost Control' was huge at The Music Box, man. Yeah, man. 'Cos Hardy could relate to that. Frankie didn't know what the fuck was going on.

He was always in control!
Yeah. You know. He didn't know what to do about that. So he wouldn't play it. When I did 'Move Your Body', he liked that. But 'I've Lost Control', you should have heard it man, they used to go ballistic when that shit came on. 'I've lost control... AAAAArghhhghggghgg!'

And he played it from a reel, or did he wait for the record to come out?
Hardy never waited for the record, you gave it to him on cassette.

On just a regular cassette?
On a cassette, man. I would take the cassette down. I would put it on the DJ booth. Ron Hardy wouldn't even see me come up there. I would just put it there and – whoo – leave. So I had this mysterious thing about me. Plus I had to stop going to the Music Box because they put me on the graveyard shift at work. So my friend Sleezy started taking the tapes to the Music Box. And of course he told everybody down there he did it. Right. So at first everybody thought Sleezy did the stuff until I got my hours changed at the Post Office.

So you didn't even see how people were reacting to it.
No.

What was it like when you walked in and they're playing your track?
The first time I went to the Music Box – and heard my stuff playing? 'Cos I had gone to the Music Box before, that was the inspiration for all of my music...

You were making it thinking of that crowd and that place?
Yeah. That crowd and that place, man! Every record that was coming on they were screaming! He played seven of my records in a row. Seven! And by the time the fifth one got on, it was 'I've Lost Control', and that was the biggest reaction. They ran onto the dancefloor. It was like a stampede, everybody going aaaarghhh, and I was thinking 'Oh man. Yes!' 'Lost Control' wasn't the only song. But it was the biggest hit out of all of all the songs I did. Ron Hardy played all of them.

What were the other ones?
Shit, I don't know man.

They never came out.
Well, they got covered. Illegally. A lot of the Chicago stuff that came out, were like remakes of other people's tracks, or in some cases, the actual track itself.

Dubious ownership.
But you know, I didn't care. Everybody knew I did it anyway, but Sleezy of course told everybody he was doing the tracks... 'cos he was sleazy! So when the record came out we had to call it Sleezy D, 'I've Lost Control'. He was really pissed off about the D.

Why?
Cos he was just Sleezy, man. Everybody called him Sleezy. But at the last minute, guy from Trax Records, Larry Sherman, he put 'Sleezy D' on there because of Chip E. And Sleezy, he hated it, he said, 'Man, I'm just Sleezy,' he said, 'Fuck that D.'

So you've got all these kids running around making tracks and giving them to the DJs to play. Did some people take them to Ron and some to Frankie?
Well, Ron was more accessible than Frankie, because Frankie had Jamie Principle.

He was a little more discerning?
It was better quality than what everybody else was bringing.

You couldn't take him a cassette I'd imagine.
Well, he took a cassette of 'Move Your Body'. See Jamie's stuff was higher quality to everybody, so after that it wasn't too much he would play, but Hardy would play everything. He wouldn't care what kind of quality you were. If it rocked the crowd then he would play it. He was more accessible than Frankie.

Frankie had that aura about him. If you've ever met Frankie he's like a toned-down

....

character. He's really even keel. He doesn't seem that approachable, while Ron Hardy was a screamer. And Ron Hardy would sell his tapes – because he was a drug addict – he would sell his tapes. You'd say [desperate], 'Ron can you make me a tape, Ron, please can you make me a tape.'

He'd say '$50.'

'$50?!'

He'd say, 'It's worth a hundred.' It was so fuckin' funny when I finally got to know Ron Hardy.

So how much of an inspiration was Frankie Knuckles. Him coming to Chicago in '77 and bringing the New York music. Was that important to Chicago?
Frankie Knuckles, yeah man. But you know Ron Hardy was playing in Chicago before Frankie Knuckles.

Yeah, back in the '70s he played at a place called Den One.
Yeah, but then he went off to California.

Do you know why he went?
Who knows, man? But when he came back Frankie was the king. And Frankie went with some other guys and they opened the Power Plant. The owners of the Warehouse on the other hand, opened a new club called the Music Box. Now, of course they're gonna have this rivalry thing right. For somebody to follow Frankie Knuckles, because all of Frankie's people said, 'Oh they're opening a new club but they don't have Frankie.' So for Ron Hardy to make the Music Box like it was, was quite a feat.

To come in after Frankie.
Yeah, to come in after Frankie was something, 'cos he was ruling the roost. They were calling it house music now, and that was because of Frankie. And for Ron Hardy to come in there, and steal Frankie's thunder, was really something. They were competitive: like two gunslingers. The Power Plant closed down, because of the Music Box. The Music Box just took everything; it took the Power Plant's crowd.

Wow, they deserted Frankie?
It wasn't deserted. People still liked Frankie, But it split off into two different crowds. The people that really liked loud, wild-ass music, and they were kids. When you have a situation like that, the kids are always gonna go to the wild-ass shit. You see this in rave music. And Frankie's crowd turned into the people with like a more distinctive, a higher class of musical taste…

So the Music box was younger than the Power Plant.
Yeah, yeah, more energetic. And Frankie opened another club, CODs, right after Power Plant, and that closed down after a few months. Then he went to DJ at the Power House, which was owned by Italians. And before that they got the Music Box closed down.

Mobster stuff?
They didn't want to be bothered.

Radio was really important, too: the Hot Mix 5. We're they playing the same stuff you'd hear in the clubs?
They didn't play the same records. The Hot Mix 5 would play more commercial stuff, a lot more European stuff. Like Falco, and stuff like that, Doctor's Cat 'Feel The Drive', Klein & MBO. Well, Hardy would play Klein & MBO too, but Hot Mix 5 would play shit like Divine. You know, commercial shit. And more vocal stuff. A lot of stuff that came out of England. Hardy would play like your funkier disco stuff, underground stuff. 'Optimo' and 'Cavern' by Liquid Liquid. 'Moody' ESG, Atmosfear: that's the kind of stuff Hardy would play. They wouldn't go near that with the Hot Mix 5. But if you went by straight up mixing ability, the Hot Mix 5 would mix circles around fuckin' Ron Hardy.

Did they play all together with a bunch of turntables, or did they take it in turn?
They would take turns, one of them at a time.

So just two turntables
Yeah just two turntables

A lot of people, like Pierre, said that was the first time they heard mixing.
Yeah.

❝ For Ron Hardy to come in there, and steal Frankie's thunder, was really something. They were competitive: like two gunslingers. ❞

Was there anybody else who was really important but forgotten. Unsung heroes?
Oh shit? Unsung? Wayne Williams. Wayne was actually the guy that brought house music [ie underground disco] to the masses. Because Wayne would go to the Warehouse, and he really liked the stuff that Frankie was playing – the disco music. When Farley and Jesse heard it they were like, 'Oh that's that old fag music. That's that old house music shit.' you know they would joke about it. Jesse went off to college right. When he came back Wayne had made house music big. He brought it to the straight kids, right. And he was a damn fucking good DJ. And powerful minded too, because when he first did it, he used to clear the floor.

Because they dismissed it as fag music?
Yeah, but man he started banging it and banging it and banging it and, wheeeeew.

Where was his club?
He played all over, man.

When people started making records did you just take your masters into the pressing plant and ship things out yourself, and go sell them in the stores?
That's what I tried to do. I don't want to get into that too much...

There was a lot of shady dealing.
Yeah,

So if you wanted to press it up yourself, you still had to go to Larry Sherman at Trax, 'cos he owned the pressing plant.
So he had the option, at any time, to change whatever I brought him, to his record label.

And he had all the masters.
Yeah. And if you notice not a single record came out on my record label. I paid him to press up three fuckin' songs [laughs]. You know.

So you gave him the labels and everything.
Yeah.

You had them printed up.
Yeah. Oh, you know about the labels. We got the labels, Adonis has the labels, of all those records. He saved them all these years.

What about royalties? Did you ever get any royalties from them?
No.

Nobody ever did, right?
No.

Did you know that when you went into...?
I didn't care.

So you'd just get a one-off payment for a track?

I just wanted recognition. And I wanted to get pussy like Jesse and Vince. That's what I wanted out of it.

So people were ready to be ripped off. They didn't really care about money so much?
After me and the first generation got ripped off, the guys that came after us were a lot more wary, and they made sure they got money. For instance, like I talked to Pierre, and he was talking about getting $5,000. $6,000, $7,000 advances from Larry. I was [outraged], 'You got *WHAT?*'

So they benefitted from your mistakes.
Yeah. A lot of stuff I really had to fight to get out out on Trax records. Like Fingers Inc 'Can You Feel It'. Larry didn't want to put it out. Like the 'Virgo' EP and 'I've Lost Control' and even 'Move Your Body'. When I did 'Move Your Body', Larry Sherman said [Elmer Fudd voice], 'That's not house music, house music doesn't have that fuckin' piano in it.' So I called it a house music anthem, you fuckin' weener, you don't know. He don't have a fuckin' clue. [Hilarity ensues] See!

> **❝ I would hear people saying, 'Yeah, I'm a buy me a acid machine so I can make some of that bullshit and make me some money.' ❞**

How did you get into producing tracks for other people?
I was a songwriter, I needed people to sing. And that's when I ran into Byron Stingily, you know I was already working with my friends from the Post Office. Curtis McClain sung 'Move Your Body', but that wasn't really working for other people, he was my buddy.

What happened to him?
I don't know. Curt wasn't really a hard worker. He would always say he could do something but he would never do it. I was the hardest working guy, out of my friends from the Post Office, 'cos there was bout five of us, and we all wanted to make records, but I was the only one that wound up making them.

You helped a lot of people get their music onto record.
I helped everybody. I started everybody. I started damn near everybody off, man. I gave Steve Hurley his first major label remix, and Frankie Knuckles his first major label remix. Lil Louis, I physically did his first record, 'The Video Clash'. DJ Pierre. Man, a lot of the Trax Records guys. Fingers Inc 'Can You Feel It', would have never come out if it wasn't for me. I just knew it was special.

You helped Pierre produce 'Acid Tracks'?
Yeah, yeah. Yeah. That shit wouldn't have come out if it wasn't for me. Pierre gave me a tape, of 'Acid Tracks'. And I called him the next day, I said, 'Okay let's do it.'

You didn't know him before that
Never heard of him.

What did you think of the acid sound?
I liked it when Pierre did it. I didn't like it when everybody else did. I would hear people saying, 'Yeah, I'm a buy me a acid machine so I can make some of that bullshit and make me some money.' It's that attitude.

Was the money because the acid sound had started making it in the UK?
Well, that's what started separating house music. Acid house was the start of them separating it into different things. 'Cos shortly after acid house you had techno, and you had the New Jersey sound, and trance, and all that shit. It split. And before that it was just house music.

When was the first time people in Chicago realised it was hitting in other places?
Shit, when everybody started coming to the city wanting to interview everybody and talking about house music. That's when we knew.

1986?
Yeah. That's when everybody started panicking, tripping over each other, and holding each other back.

What would have happened if there hadn't been any powerful DJs in Chicago. Would kids have still made all these tracks?
No. Definitely not.

It's funny how you say that Jesse was the guy who started it off by inspiring people because his music was so basic.
Jesse changed music, man. Even though I was listening to dance music, I wouldn't have made any of it if it wasn't for Jesse Saunders. I wouldn't have thought that I had the ability, or the chance, to get music out there.

That's what got Todd Terry into it. That's what got Masters t Work into it. That's what got David Morales into it, man. Because they thought, 'Fuck I can do that.' When that shit came out, all them New York guys got into it. Said, 'Fuck, man, I can do this.' And the same thing when it hit London: 'Fuck, I can do this. This is great.'

© DJhistory.com

MARSHALL JEFFERSON SELECTED DISCOGRAPHY

MARSHALL JEFFERSON – Move Your Body (The House Music anthem) (producer/writer)

ON THE HOUSE – Pleasure Control (producer/writer)

VIRGO – R U Hot Enough (producer)

KYM MAZELLE – I'm A Lover (producer)

TEN CITY – Devotion (producer/writer/arranger)

STERLING VOID – It's Alright (producer)

SLEEZY D – I've Lost Control (producer/writer)

ON THE HOUSE WITH MARSHALL JEFFERSON – Ride The Rhythm (producer/writer)

HERCULES – 7 Ways (producer/co-writer)

ON THE HOUSE – Give Me Back The Love (producer/writer)

JUNGLE WONZ – The Jungle (producer/co-writer)

MARSHALL JEFFERSON PRESENTS TRUTH – Open Our Eyes (producer)

JUNGLE WONZ – Time Marches On (producer/co-writer)

TEN CITY – That's The Way Love Is (producer)

JUNGLE WONZ – Bird In A Gilded Cage (producer/co-writer)

TOM TOM CLUB – Oceana (remixer)

TEN CITY – Superficial People (producer)

UMOSIA – We Are Unity (producer)

WHAT IT IS – Do You Believe (producer)

RICHARD ROGERS – Can't Stop Loving You (producer)

DUSTY SPRINGFIELD – Nothing Has Been Proved (remixer)

MARSHALL JEFFERSON VS NOOSA HEADS – Mushrooms (vocals)

RECOMMENDED LISTENING

MARSHALL JEFFERSON – Timeless Classics

VARIOUS – Tribal Gathering '96

VARIOUS – Chicago House 86-91: The Definitive Story

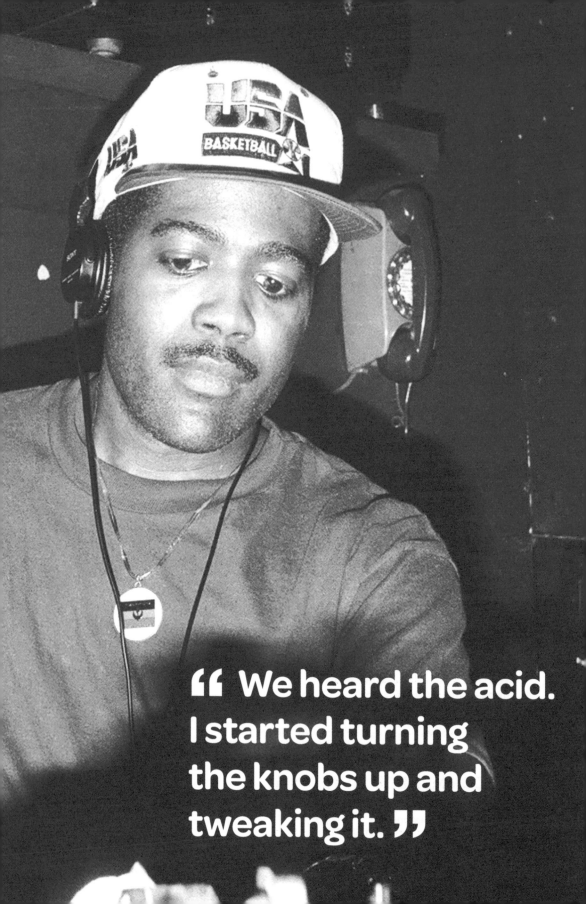

"We heard the acid. I started turning the knobs up and tweaking it."

DJ Pierre
Acid originator

Interviewed by Frank in Kensal Green, February 17, 1999

Pierre staked out his spot in dance history when he and his mate Spanky took an obscure piece of music equipment and tweaked the controls until it squealed for mercy. The Roland TB-303 was designed to provide buskers with basslines, but if you turned everything up to 11 what came out was a bubbling alien scribble. So weird was this sound that a whole new genre could be built from it: acid house. And because the acid records were the most out-there of the new imports, in Britain this phrase grew to cover the dance explosion itself, the whole social movement this music propelled. In truth, acid house records were just a small part of the rave soundtrack. But in spirit they were its revolutionary vanguard.

Emboldened by early success, Pierre has enjoyed a long career as a producer. His wild pitch records were so distinctive they could arguably be another sub-genre in themselves: hypnotic, slow-building epics built from layer upon layer of relentless loops. He moved to New York in 1990 to be near the dance industry, because, as he says, 'house was my life and house was dead in Chicago.'

A knackered Pierre arrives at the west London offices of Strictly Rhythm from Kiss FM where he's just done a review programme. He dumps his records and jumps on the phone to New York. He's got to be at Bar Rumba by 11, time is running out. We walk to the William IV on Harrow Road in the rain and Pierre shows what a gentleman he is by carrying Fran from Strictly's shopping. We get a table in the back. Pierre picks at some chips, saying he'll fill up on gross fast food before his gig. As he relaxes he turns into Cheshire Cat mode, talking through a constant smirk in that tuneful southern accent so many Chicagoans have. He's as generous as ever with his time, and would talk for ages if he didn't have to go off and play some records.

When did you start DJing
I started DJing when I was 13, around '83. I had met Spanky [his partner in Phuture], I had seen him in the neighbourhood. Then everything happened fairly quickly. It wasn't like it was a lot of years. Everything kind of happened '84, '85.

You started playing regularly at Lil Louis parties out in the Bismarck Hotel.
That was the first time that Chicago had heard me. But before then I was playing out in the south suburbs of Chicago, playing in skating rinks and places like that.

What were the Bismarck parties like?
Fuck. 3,000, 4,000, 5,000 people. It was just like... you know how small parties have a lot of energy? It was like a big small party. It wasn't like big parties are normally, with small crowds going off here and there. At the Bismark the *whole crowd* would be going nuts. Everybody would be slam-dancing.

People would slam dance to house?
Oh yeah, that's where it started. The whole crowd would sway this way and then this way.

It was a hotel ballroom?
Yeah.

....

What was the crowd like? Was it just suburban kids?

It was mostly Chicago but suburbs too. They would scream the DJ's name and they'd get really interactive, and you know who was DJing. Not like these days, you wouldn't get anybody yelling a DJ's name.

What kind of music were you playing back then?

At the time I was playing Euro type of house music – like Happy Station 'Fun Fun', lot of stuff like that. Doctor's Cat. You probably don't even know these songs, but that's the kind of stuff I was playing.

Things coming in from Europe? A lot of Italian things?

A lot of Italian house, but Spanky said, 'You got to get off of that.' He said, 'Pierre you got to get with this real house music and you got to start playing these kind of songs.' So he would come to my house and I'd be in the garage practising, he kept bringing all this disco stuff over. And he brought 'Chocolate Chip' by Isaac Hayes.

I was like, 'I can't play this old stuff. I don't even like this. I was trying to mix it.' I said, 'Damn it's going all fast here and slow here. I can't even mix that. I can't do it.'

He was like, 'You just got to go to the Music Box, you'll see the real deal.' I really couldn't get in the club, but Spanky took me down there one night, snuck me in the place, and basically it blew my mind. I heard all that old stuff, and I heard house music, real house tracks, made with drum machines, and after that I was baptised or something. I got goosebumps. Going crazy, dancing, and people were screaming Ron Hardy's name. I had never seen that before. I seen famous DJs playing, they never got that reaction, 'cos they never played that kind of music. I seen how soulful everybody was.

> **❝ People were dancing, jumping up in the air. Doing these twists like they were some modern dance, ballet sort of people. It was amazing. ❞**

What was his style?

He was energetic, real energetic. He played classics and tracks and vocals, all in one set, and everything was real energetic. And when he took you down, it was real moody and soulful. Like you would feel love. People were literally doing the nasty on the dancefloor.

Literally?

Yeah. It was dark. He didn't have all these lights that clubs have now. The only lights he had was strobelights.

And then he switches them off and that's it.

When it wasn't some crazy track and it was just something regular the strobes would just pop slowly: *boop... boop... boop...* and you would see him like that.

Did he play the classics and the tracks mixed up, or did he have a section for one and a section for the other?

Whatever... he wouldn't play a track and then a classic and mix it literally like that. If he was playing tracks he played a certain amount of 'em. He played stuff long. He didn't play no track for no three-four minutes. You got the full shit. Fifteen, 20 minutes.

He'd be extending it and extending it...

Yeah yeah, and he did editing. You know 'Bad Luck' [by Harold Melvin & the Bluenotes]? He would make a part just keep going. You know where it go [sings], 'Hey hey hey hey', he'd loop it, on a reel and keep that part just keep on and on.

He'd loop it on a reel-to-reel?

Yeah. Like 'It's Not Over', he looped that beat, and it would go on a long time, and everybody just be there, just *dmm dmm dmm*, just dancing off that one beat. Then finally, he'll let the rest of the song go, and everybody just explode. I mean stuff like that you just can't do nowadays, 'cos people get bored with it. He would play a beat, like just a couple of bongos or a couple of sounds in it, and that was good enough.

So what were Ron Hardy's biggest records. The records he would play, records that really summed up the Music Box?
'Acid Tracks'. Wow, a lot of Robert Owens tracks. 'Move Your Body'. Damn. I remember when he played that song.

How would he play that?
Man, he had that damn piano part at the beginning, he had that shit going forever. Marshall must have made an extra long beginning, or he edited it and made it longer, but he would do that shit for a long time. And then the vocals would come in. Man, that stuff, I'll tell you, never be like that again, never be like that again.

Were you a real regular?
Yeah, but I only got to go to the Music Box for a short time. Because like I said I stayed in the suburbs.

Can you describe the Music Box. What was it like the first time you went?
A lot of people. It was small. It was really like a hole in the wall, basically.

What was your reaction?
I just looked at it and soaked it all in. You know how you could be somewhere and you can catch the vibe of the people and it just sweeps you in. That's sort of what happened. It was just as much the people's reaction to what he was playing as to what he was playing.

But the music, it grabbed me also. People were dancing, jumping up in the air. Doing these twists like they were some modern dance, ballet sort of people. Like spinning, they could spin around a long time. People can't dance like that now. They'd jump, spread their legs, come down, spin around, go down to the floor, and then come back up. And you'd be like, wow. Just sit there, it was amazing. Nowadays you don't see nobody doing nothing fancy. They would spread their arms out. They would literally do legitimate modern dance ballet moves out there.

Everybody wasn't doing that, but you always had the die-hard Music Box people that was, and everybody else could do a little bit. A guy would actually pick up a girl and start spinning her and stuff. Can you imagine seeing that in a house party? That would fuckin' blow your mind.

And it was a mostly gay club back then?
I guess when it first started. But you know most gay clubs get invaded by straight people. So I really don't know what it was at that time. I didn't really pay it no attention. I mean at that age I didn't even think about that shit.

How did people dress in those days?
To be in house music that meant that you dressed really well. People had on nice Paisley shirts, that's what was in, and a solid colour pair of pants, the slacks, with some shiny shoes. And your shoes had to be slippery, 'cos if they wasn't you couldn't spin. So everybody would have shiny shoes, and you'd put salt on the floor, or powder...

Baby powder?
Yeah, so they could spin real good. And then the pants have to be baggy. And the haircuts were sharp.

Spiky?
Yeah. If they didn't go up in a box, they went up a little bit at the back and then they would tilt up like that. In a fade side. They would wave it up, put some of that holding gel in your hair so it would hold up like that. I'm telling you, that's how it was. Whoever had the longest, the highest – we used to call them 'pumps' [a high-rise flat-top]. People'd be like, 'Damn, look how high his pump is.' Everybody used to talk about how high my hair was. If you look on them records...

DJ Pierre

....

And then Girbauds came out. So everybody started wearing Girbaud jeans, 'cos they were baggy. I mean you had a whole scene that was dressed like that. And everybody would know somebody that was house. 'Cos we be like, 'Ah, they house,' You'd point out somebody that was house music, and say that they were house. 'He's house, she's house. There's some house people.'

I've seen a picture of you with a pretty impressive pump.
But that's not even the highest. When I did 'Time And Time Again' on Jive Records, I had my hair up even higher, and then I had a gold streak up in it. That's how it was.

What year was that style?
Back then! It carried on from '83, all the way up until '88, '89.

What were people into if they weren't into house. Who were the opposition?
Hip hop. Or rap, as it was called.

Hip hop never took off in Chicago until recently.
It never took, well it's took now, it's took all over. But back then it didn't really take; it was kind of underground, like house. People like A Tribe Called Quest, when they first came out they were opening for me. I was the headlining act, not them. It's weird how it switched.

Why did people get into making beat tracks in Chicago? What was their motivation: why did people go out and buy the equipment, to go home and make a track?
I don't really know. Spanky from Phuture, he kept buggin' me, he kept saying, 'I'm gonna buy this drum machine. I want to make some music.' He told me, 'Hear those tracks? You know how they make those, don't you?'
I said, 'How?'
He said, 'They buy this thing called a drum machine and it has those drum sounds in it, you punch a button and they play,'
I said 'They have drum sounds in a *box?*' I just couldn't comprehend.

Were people making them so they could get played in the clubs?
Yeah. They were making them to play in a club. Most of the time when people made those drum beats it wasn't to make a record. It was to play in the clubs. So you wanted to find some DJ that would play it. Spanky would give me his tracks, and he would bring the drum machine to the party. And I would play his drumbeats, and play his acappellas over his drum beats, like 'You Ain't Really Down' [by Status IV], and stuff like that.
Back then they wasn't on records yet. They was mostly on reels. DJs like me would want somebody to make me a beat, so I had a beat no-one else had, and I would play it in a club, and that was all it was for. I never really thought about making any records or nothing like that. Nowadays people make records. They think of that.
Spanky was like, 'Pierre, I want to make some music.' He would give me his tracks, and he would bring the drum machine to the party. And I would play his drumbeats, and play his acapellas over his drum beats, like 'You Ain't Really Down', and stuff like that.

Tell me about when you got into making tracks. You come from a musical family right, and you play some instruments?
Yeah, I play the clarinet and the drums.

What made you want to make drum-beat records and take that direction?
It was just the interest in the equipment. Just being a kid, being excited about what a drum machine did, how it worked. I would just play with it, and I kept making good stuff. Spanky'd be like, 'Oh that's dope, we gonna use it, that's dope.'
The funny thing is that wasn't even my dream. It was Spanky, he was the one that said, 'Oh I gotta do it, I gotta find out how they do that. I wanna make music.' I was just along for the ride. I was only supposed to be a DJ, who played his tracks, 'cos back then a producer found a DJ to play they stuff. And they would be a team. Like: 'Pierre's my DJ, he plays all my tracks.' That's sort of how I went.

Was that the kind of team that a lot of people had?
Yeah. It was a competitive thing. Every DJ had their own people that gave them special

edited tracks or different mixes, just to make them better than the other DJ, and so Spanky was the person that gave me special tracks, and he didn't give them to no other DJs. Once you chose a DJ, it was an unwritten agreement that, okay now you give me your tracks and I'm gonna play 'em at the parties. He would get attention from me playing his tracks, and I would get attention from having tracks that no-one else had.

How come the DJs didn't make the tracks themselves?
I don't know. Later on they started to. Personally I never thought about it. I just wanted to be a DJ.

What originally inspired you to start DJing?
Ever since I went to a party and I seen this guy DJing and I seen him doing something with this record here, moving it back and forth and I didn't hear it. And then I seen him touchin' the other record, and I was like, wait a minute, how come I didn't hear nothing change? 'Cos he was making this one part of the song go longer and longer, he was extending it, he was looping it. The beat was the exact same and he was changing from one record to the next, and I was like damn, how does he do that? I was, about 12. And ever since then I was like I wanna do that. That was my first fascination. It wasn't with making any tracks. It was with being a DJ.

〃 Everybody would know somebody that was house. You'd point out somebody that was house music, and say that they were house. 'He's house, she's house, there's some house people.' 〃

How important was the radio, the Hot Mix 5?
Oh, very instrumental. Because even before I started DJing, I was making mixes. I would hear songs on the radio, tape them, and then I would get the record. Then I'd record it and use the pause button to make a part go more than once. Me and my friends would compare mixes. Listen to what I did!

So you were inspired by hearing the mix shows, people like Farley on the radio. I heard kids would skip lunch to tape it?
Hot Lunch mix. Every day.

And you also had battles like the hip hop DJs in New York
Our competitions had the whole thing. A DJ had to bring his own sound system, his own MC, and bring a big sign with his name on it. And it'd be in a big gymnasium. Then another DJ, he'd bring his sound system, and a third DJ'd bring his sound system. And you had to do your thing for 30 minutes or an hour, and whoever's sound system and DJing skills sounded the best won the competition.

What year was that?
Some time around '84.

And you did that kind of thing?
Yeah. I didn't have no tables or nothin', but my friend, his father was a DJ, and his father let us use his stuff. He brought the stuff down to the gym. And he let us DJ under the banner of his DJ team. So we was like juniors or something.

Who did you battle against?
Two of the other DJs in our area.

No-one who became known?
No.

....

How often did that happen?
It happened all summer. It was always at a school, or a skating rink. I lost a battle because I didn't have 'Time To Jack' [by Chip E]. It was brand new, the buzz was huge on it, and we lived in the suburbs, and you couldn't get the record in a suburban record store. You could only get 'em in the city. Maan, I was winning this battle, and then my toughest competition didn't have the record either. So I was gonna beat him. But then, he borrows the record from somebody else in the competition who wasn't any good. So he plays the record, and he wins 'cos he had that record.

Was this just something the suburban DJs would do or was that happening in the city too?
You know what, I don't know, 'cos all the competitions I knew were in the suburbs. Maybe they did do it in the city. I don't know.

And what was the music like then, this was after the tracks had started coming in.
Yeah, cos 'Time To Jack' was out.

So tell the story of how you came to make 'Acid Tracks'? What happened?
To make a long story short. Spanky bought a 303, him and Herb was messing around with it and heard the acid, they called me over. I heard it and at the time it was just playing straight. And I started turning the knobs up and tweaking it and they were like, 'Yeah, I like it, keep doing what you're doing.' We just did that, made a beat to it, and the rest is history.

> ❝ **When we made 'Acid Tracks' that was an accident. It was just ignorance basically. Not knowing how to work the damn 303.** ❞

What did you want it to sound like?
I wanted my shit to sound like anything I heard in the Music Box, or I heard Farley play. But when we made 'Acid Tracks' that was an accident. This sounds wild and different. It was just ignorance basically. Not knowing how to work the damn 303. And putting a beat behind a track that was already in the 303. We didn't programme that track. When we bought it, it was in it. And whenever the batteries would go dead and you would put new batteries in, it was in it again. It couldn't go away. You could erase it and programme something different, but once the batteries went dead and the memory went away, 'Acid Tracks' was back up in there. It was part of some kind of pre-set noise or something I guess. I don't know. It's in that same 303.

You still have it?
Spanky has it, it was Spanky's 303.

What happened once you'd made the track?
We gave it to Ron Hardy, and if Ron hardy had said he didn't like it, it would have been the end of acid. Because he was the man: if he said he loved something, that was it. If he said 'I don't like it,' we'd have thought, 'Oh well, back to the drawing board.' We'd be tryin' to make something different, and acid may have never been born.

Were you there when he played it the first time?
Hell, yeah.

So what happened?
Fuckin' floor cleared.

Really?
Hell, yeah. And we were like, 'Okay, I guess he won't be playin' that ever again.' But then he waited until the crowd got real full, and he played it again. And the people stayed on the

floor, they thought, it's that track again, okay, whatever. They just danced through it. Then, at peak time, he dropped it again, and then they were like, 'Fuck, what is this damn track?' And they started going off to it a little bit. 'This shit is crazy.' Then... he played it again, like about four in the morning. Then they just went ballistic.

When their drugs had kicked in.
Yeah, I guess. Maybe that's what it was. People were dancing upside down... this guy was on his back kicking his legs in the air. People going crazy. They started slamdancing, knocking people over and just going nuts. And he had the crossover working so it just stopped and all you hear was the high hats going *tss-tss-tss*, then everybody, Aaaagh!, started screaming, Then he went just the bass: *bom, be-bom, be-bom*. Everyone was going crazy.

After that all these rumours started coming out. Everybody was buzzin' about this new track, and we started asking people, 'Whats this new track, whats this new track? And someone said I got it on tape, its called Ron Hardy's 'Acid Tracks', he'd been taping it in the club. And sure enough, we heard the bells: it was our track. He said, 'Man, people are going crazy over this track. Ron Hardy's 'Acid Tracks'.'

So it got its name from the clubbers in the Music Box. You didn't even call it that?
It was called 'In Your Mind', whatever that means. But if everybody's calling it 'Acid Tracks', it would be stupid to come out under a different name. Then the shit just blew up and the name caught on, not just as the name of the track but as the name of the sound.

How come it took a while before the tracks came out on records?
We didn't even know how to make a record. We made 'Acid Tracks' and we was running around trying to ask people, 'How do you make a record? How does a record come out? Who do you go see?'

Marshall was doing 'Move Your Body' at the Power House. He was onstage. I wrote my name and number down: it said 'My name is DJ Pierre, I'm in a group called Phuture, and we did a track called 'Acid Tracks', and Ron Hardy has been playing this track off a reel. Could you help us make a record.' I gave it to [vocalist] Curtis McLain. And he gave it to Marshall, and he called me the next day. That goes to show you how much we knew about making records, let alone getting royalties and stuff like that.

So how long was 'Acid Tracks' made on reel before you made it into a record?
I think it was on reel in '85. And it came out in '86.

What did Marshall do for you? He mastered it, mixed it?
He set the levels on it. We mixed it. But he had a big impact on 'Your Only Friend'. That cocaine song [B-side to 'Acid Tracks']. I wrote the song and I had it in my regular voice, and he was like, 'You know that's cocaine talking. You got to do something with that voice, Pierre. Make it sound scary.' He said, 'Here, we'll put it through this and it'll make it sound real deep and nasty.' And he put it through that machine, that harmoniser, and that voice was born. After that we started using it on every track. So he gave that idea to us, and countless people have been using voices like that ever since.

And it was going real fast too. It was going 130 [bpm], and back then, nobody had tracks going 130. He said, 'Oh that's too fast Pierre. If you want New York to get into it you've got to slow it down to like 120, 117, 118.' He said if the DJs want it faster, let 'em speed it up.

So you were looking to New York already?
He was. We never even thought about New York. Our whole world was Chicago. Chicago, that's it.

Were people aware that they were dancing to a different music than anyone else on the planet?
I don't think people thought about it. I knew the music was big in Chicago, and Detroit. That's it. I didn't really think of anywhere else in the world. And then, even though Marshall had said something about New York, I still didn't think about New York. I heard it all over the radio in Chicago. I never travelled to no other cities. I thought it was like just a Chicago thing. That's how we got ripped off so easily.

We didn't realise that our music was getting outside Chicago, period. The labels did a very good job of keeping it from us. They knew that if we knew the whole world was listening to our music then we would know how much they were cheating us. And we would start travelling and meeting other labels and they would have competition with other labels, and they wanted to oppress us, keep us in Chicago, and keep our horizons not past Chicago.

How did the success of 'Acid Tracks' change things for you?
What's amazing is the confidence you get after you make a track that everybody loves. 'Cos you like what you doin', and if you like it they gonna like it. But we stayed on acid for a while. 'Cos we were the only ones doin' it in the very beginning. But then two or three people came right after that really fast.

How did people figure out how you made the noise?
I dunno. We used to lie. Marshall probably told somebody. But Marshall was already using the 303, and so was Adonis, so they probably already knew. They probably said, 'Shit, they made a track out of that crazy shit that our 303 makes. Shit, he made one, lets make one too.' You know.

And the name 'Acid Tracks' was because of the drugs they'd take in the Music Box?
Probably, but no-one didn't really say. Acid was a big thing in Ron Hardy's club. I never did drugs. But that's probably why they called it that.

So did you get quite close to Ron Hardy?
Naw. No, I mean...

What kind of guy was he?
I went to the Box a lot, but it wasn't like we kicked it, or talked. If I seen him somewhere, like at Trax Records, then we'd talk. He was kind of mild-mannered. It wasn't like he was open to a big conversation, so we'd just say what's up and a couple of words and show some respect and just kind of leave. That's how it was. It wasn't like he wasn't friendly, it just seemed like...

...he was in his own thing.
Yeah, like you, didn't feel like trying to talk to him too much.

Would you give Frankie tracks as well?
Yeah, I did though.

Before or after Ron?
After. I went to his house, he was real cool. Frankie always has been real cool, but I don't know, I'm not real sociable. Besides the people I grew up with – like Felix, Roy, Spanky – I never really teamed up with anybody else.

Let me flip you forward a little and ask you about wild pitch. How did you come up with that sound?
Basically I sampled a popular record and I didn't want no-one to know, so I flipped it backwards. And I just after I flipped it backwards I did the track, I was adding different sounds and the way I built it up real slow...

This is 'Generate Power'.
Yeah. It just had its own kind of feel about it. I called it wild pitch because it was real popular in these Wild Pitch parties that this guy Greg Day used to throw in New York. Greg Day and Nick Jones. He used to DJ at these parties.

And the key to it all was it was backwards.
The key was how it builded, the way it built and break down. So I just started calling stuff wild pitch mixes, and kept making 'em similar to that first mix. If you stick with a name at least its recognisable. People be like, 'Ah, its one of those wild pitch mixes.'

Do people know what the track was that you sampled?
No.

Can I ask you?
I ain't never gonna say; they'd be tryin' to get publishing money.

If I go and play it backwards, can I tell?
Well... [laughter]

Is Chicago still different when you play there?
Even now Chicago is so much in their own world. I played there last year, in October, and I played this beat track, and they just was loving it. Just the beat track. Just had a couple of sounds in it. And that's all it did. I messed with the bass a little bit. They just love it, they feel it. But if I were to play that track out here it wouldn't be good.

> **❝ The DJ's power is like a parent. It's like a president. It's like anybody who the crowd looks to for direction and looks to learn from. ❞**

It's hard to do that these days. People have such short attention spans. I think it's because there are so few real residencies any more. Everyone's used to guest DJs who breeze in and play for a couple of hours.
Yeah. Clubs used to have one DJ and he played the whole damn night.

And he knew the crowd, and he played there every week
And the crowd knew him. The crowd said, 'Fuck it I'm gonna see so and so.' They wouldn't say they wanted to go to the Ministry of Sound. They say they wanna go hear Tony Humphries. How well do you know DJs now? You're not in tune with 'em. You used to be sittin' there listening: 'Bet you any minute he's gonna play that record.' Or if it's going in one direction, you say, 'Ah he's gonna slow it down now, I can't wait.' You don't feel that any more.

....

Today's crowds don't care though. They pay their money, they expect to dance and drink and have a good time, they don't really care about the music.

But how can you care about music that you don't get a grasp of? You don't get a feel for the DJ. You don't get a feel for what each DJ's bringing. If you went to a club and there's one resident, you knew what he was doing, you knew what record he was on. That shit makes people feel like they know the DJ and they feel in touch, and makes them say, 'That's my DJ. I like how he plays and I know when he's gonna do this and do that.' You feel more in touch and you have more of an intimate thing with them. And if he play a new record, you gonna definitely give it a shot. And if he keeps playing that record you're gonna say, 'Fuck, I like that shit.' And of course he has a chance to win the crowd over: he's playing all night.

So he can educate them.

Yeah, 'cos most likely he's gonna play different things. If DJs play for just one hour or two hours, you don't get a chance to really do a lot of different stuff. And that takes the power away from the DJs.

Do you think clubbers' attention spans are getting shorter?

Probably. I think you got to slowly start taking it back, so that people start appreciating something for a little bit longer. People play songs real short. They don't let 'em play no more, they already comin' in with the next song. People get used to that so they're bored if they hear one record for six minutes, they just want you to bring in the next one. A new record comes in and then they get hype for like the first minute.

What for you is the thrill of DJing?

Shit, thrill of DJing is being able to express myself. And I like to express what I'm feeling. So the biggest thing I like is to have a crowd that I can express everything I'm feeling with. Most of the time I get a crowd who I can express the hard side of myself, *grrm grrm,* play some hard tracks. Then I get another crowd I can express some deep house vocals and some disco tracks with them. And then you get a crowd where I can play some classics for 'em.

What is the power of the DJ... when it really works?

The DJ's power is like a parent. It's like a president. It's like anybody who the crowd looks to for direction and looks to learn from. And I think the DJ has a responsibility, because while you're on those turntables, you in a position of power. So when you have an audience you better do the right thing and make sure you educate, and let them know what you're about, and make sure that you're saying something they wanna hear.

© DJhistory.com

DJ PIERRE SELECTED DISCOGRAPHY

PHUTURE – Acid Tracks (writer/co-producer)
PIERRE'S PFANTASY CLUB – G.T.B. (writer/producer)
PHUTURE PFANTASY CLUB – Slam (writer/co-producer)
LISA M – Rock To The Beat (remixer)
PIERRE'S PFANTASY CLUB – Dream Girl (writer/producer)
PHUTURE – WE ARE PHUTURE (co-writer/co-producer)
DJ PIERRE – Muzik Is Life (writer/producer)
PHOTON INC – Generate Power (writer/producer)
JOINT VENTURE – Master Blaster (writer/producer)
PHUTURE SCOPE – What Is House Muzik? (writer/producer)
PHUTURE – Rise From Your Grave (co-writer/producer)
DARKMAN – Annihilitating Rhythm (writer/producer)
DJ PIERRE – Muzik Set You Free (writer/producer)
WAY OUT WEST – Ajare (remixer)
DANELL DIXON – Dance Dance (remixer)
URBAN SOUL – Sex On My Mind (remixer)
YO YO HONEY – Groove On (remixer)
THE DON – The Horn Song (writer/producer/remixer)

RECOMMENDED LISTENING

Various – Hot Wax Volume One (DJ mix) (CD only)
Various – The Essence Files Volume 1 (DJ mix) (CD only)

"To be put on a pedestal for doing something that I love doing naturally, is mindboggling."

David Morales
Hitmaker

Interviewed by Frank in Manhattan, February 4, 1999

High above the hot neon of Times Square David Morales is mixing the Pet Shop Boys in a big fat 48-track studio. We listen to the track pump past a few times as he slides faders here and there, listening to the imperceptible changes he's made.

Morales is one of a select few DJs who made their names in the early '90s as surefire hitmakers. As the music business learnt that it could use remixing as a marketing tool, he was the guy they called when they wanted an indie band or an R&B starlet to reach the ears of the dancefloor. Everyone from Sheena Easton to U2 to Björk to Michael Jackson has rolled through his mixing desk, and at the time of this interview his remixing fees were top of the tree. As a name remixer, he was among the first generation of DJs to have one foot in the club world and another in the music business proper.

He gives good interview. After hearing a few more passes of Neil Tennant we sit in the hospitality room and he lets loose his Latin enthusiasm, offering plenty of poetic insight into the world of a star DJ. The engineer keeps putting his head around the door but Morales ignores him. He's so wrapped up in our conversation that only when it's over does he get round to lighting the cigarette he's been holding for an hour and a half. The Pet Shop Boys track sounds like the Village People.

Let me start by asking you about your background.
Born and raised in Brooklyn, grew up in Flatbush, parents are Puerto Rican. I guess I liked music from when I was really little. I remember taking this record from a friend of my mother's, and the record was 'Spinning Wheel' on RCA Victor, back in the days. I must have been three, four. I always liked black music; I didn't like the Spanish music. There used to be a social club downstairs, and I was free to roam around. It wasn't like today where you don't let your kids go out, once the morning came the door was open. I found myself in the craziest places. As a child you just wander.

What clubs did you go to?
I mean real like ghetto neighbourhood clubs. Like painted black with black glow paint. I mean real primitive shit. And that's when 'Mr Big Stuff' [by Jean Knight] was out, I remember. Maybe '68, '69? I remember 'Want Ads' [by Honey Cone].

How did you get into DJing?
I used to be the one appointed to play the music. We all be hanging out and I be the one hanging out by the stereo. And I be picking the tunes. And this is with just one turntable. It wasn't about two turntables at the time. I never saw that yet.

When did you take it to the next level?
When I was 13 there was a prom, my prom. And this is when 'Ten Percent' came out, it was the first time I saw two turntables, and a guy mixing, and this was outside.

Who was that?
I think the guy's name was Grandmaster Flowers. He was doing black block parties, and I was like, wow! You know: people hanging out in the park and then they be playing music.

Now when I first started mixing with the mixer with the headphones, I was about 13 and 'San Francisco' was out by the Village People. We was in my friend's sister-in-law's apartment and the decks were in the kitchen. Forget about having monitors, the monitors were the speakers that were in the living room way over there.

Who was your first inspiration as a DJ?
His name was Ernie Dunda. And I saw him, I was 15 years old, at a club called the Starship Discovery. I remember I had my nose glued to the bubble that was the DJ booth. That was the first DJ I saw in a real club. I was just like wow! Bozak mixer, proper booth, amazing. I didn't care about meeting chicks I was just glued to that bubble.

After doing house parties I started going to a club called the Loft, on Saturday night, probably like 1980.

> ❝ **The Loft was Saturday nights and a lot of people from my neighbourhood used to go. I used to be there for like 12, 15 hours, dancing. I was one of the last ones to leave.** ❞

What was that like for you?
It was amazing. I guess up to this I was what you'd call a commercial DJ, I bought the hits, I bought the records you bought in the mom and pop shops, that's what I knew. When I went to the Loft I heard all this different music. I thought, wow, I like this. Then it was all about where I could buy these records. That's when I went to Vinylmania. I was already going to Downtown Records since I was 14.

So I was 19, 20, something like that. Started going to the Loft. The Loft was Saturday nights and a lot of people from my neighbourhood used to go. I used to dance. I used to be there for like 12, 15 hours, dancing. I was one of the ones who got there early and I was one of the last ones to leave.

Who did you meet there who went on to be in the industry?
I saw François [Kevorkian], but I never met him at the time. David Mancuso, Steve D'Acquisto. Those are really the people that I remember from the business, 'cos I was going there from such an early stage, that I wasn't in the business.

It was after Frankie and Larry had been hanging out there.
I know Larry would come after the Garage, because the Loft stayed open later. And he used to bring certain records. I went to the Garage a couple of times on a Friday. It was only a couple of times because I started doing my own parties in like 1981.

As a mobile DJ?
No, no, no, as a summer resident DJ. I was a mobile from the minute I started, I went everywhere.

Where were you resident?
I started at a place called the Ozone Layer, that was in Flatbush. I use to do it on Friday nights and it was somewhat based around the way the Loft did stuff: I gave fruits and tried to make it a party. But it was on a Friday and it was a smaller venue. A lot of people in my neighbourhood used to go.

How did you get the gig?
My girlfriend at the time, her girlfriend was going out with one of the owners from the club. So she had asked us to do a party of her own. She asked me to play. I made the invitation too, 'cos I was a graffiti artist, and at the end of the day the people that really came out were my friends, people that I used to invite to house parties. But the house parties were free, whereas this was pay.

So then I approached the owner and asked him to let me do some parties on my own. And I just wanted to play records, so I would get other people to promote the parties, to be co-host. But they wanted to give me some sob story they weren't making money at the bar, at the door, all this kind of nonsense, they give me some bullshit trip.

After going through that a couple of times, some of them had brought some new faces each time, but there was a core audience, and that was my audience. And I started to realise that I didn't need these folks promoting. I could do this, people were coming for *me*, they're coming for my music. So I said I'll run this. So I got it together with my girl. She handled the front, and I played the music.

What kind of music were you playing back then? Very much the same as the Loft?
Yeah, the Loft and the Garage. Plus the new stuff. So it was the underground stuff, at the time. Of course with some other commercial records.

And I know you played a few times at The Garage. How did you that happen?
That's the funniest story. I had been to the Garage five times…

Just to hang out?
Yes. I come dressed… trying to get in, 'Yo get me in, get me in…' and 'cos it was a private club. And I'm always one of the last ones out. Not to mention the kind of stuff I used to do to stay there! But anyway, it was part of growing up like everybody else.

Even before I went to Garage I heard stories: four turntables, the guy's incredible, and all of this, you know. Anyway, I was one of those kids that sat there and looked at the booth and like, 'Oh my god…' just fantasising, like any guy would do. This room was just incredible.

I used to go to the Loft but the Loft wasn't about mixing. He had two decks, but with Mancuso you play the record from beginning to end, the way it was made. And that was his philosophy, that was it. No artificial flavours, no MSG, nothing, and that's the way his sound system was: straight, everything was straight. No processors in between, no crap. Just pure, you know. It's like eating organic food.

Whereas the Garage was the monster system. It was a showcase for Richard Long. It was his room. So anything new that he built it was there; the Garage had a booth unmatched by any booth there's ever been in the world.

Even now?
Even now. He had a carousel, for the record bin that *schwoooo* [acts out spinning it round]. This thing just spun around, with records in it, and drawers… It was his house. I mean… you see pictures of Mick Jagger and Grace Jones up there. Of course I didn't see any of this until I got privileged enough to go up there and work there.

What year did you first go?
I was 20, 21. It's '81, '82?

And he really impressed you, he blew you away?
Naaaah, he didn't. Didn't. I mean, the music was – cha! Incredible. Couldn't say anything about the music, but you know, as a DJ I had this vision: I was gonna hear science. But to me the mixing part, I wasn't impressed by the mixing. At the time I'm young… I was too young to understand at the time, a lot of things, I didn't get the whole picture. There were some mixes that were awesome, when you first hear him do the acappella of 'Love Is The Message', which he was the first one to play, that shit was like… that was the whole…

How did he play that?
Well, that was when they started doing acappellas.

So he would just kill everything and play that?
No, no, no, he had 'Don't Make Me Wait' [by Peech Boys], and he would play 'Love Is The Message' over that. That was it man. That was it. He would play some of his early productions of Peech Boys at early stages, just ideas…
He could be SHIT for seven hours and he could take 15 minutes, and kick the shit out of you, and that made your night! That's what it was about. There was nobody that was able

....

to do that. And he didn't care either. You be like, 'Aww man what is this guy up to today?' I thought I caught him on a bad night. Which was alright. Second time I went I thought, 'Oh, I caught him on two bad nights.'

How did you end up playing there?

So anyway, here comes 1983, I'm in the record pool. I got in because of this DJ Kenny Carpenter. He was playing at a big club called Bonds International, which was a huge club, six, seven thousand people it used to hold, right in Times Square. They used to have people like the Clash, and Planet Patrol, Soulsonic Force, all that shit. And he lived in my neighbourhood. I had met him through a mutual friend, I hung out with Kenny, and Kenny took me to the record pool. And that record pool, that roster of DJs, it was a privilege to be in that pool. Which is For The Record, Judy [Weinstein]'s pool. I mean all the big guys were in that thing at the time. There was a waiting list to get in. So I gave some tapes to the pool director at the time, David Depino, and they were looking for somebody new, so they referred me. I didn't know they had referred me.

How did you hear?

So we're in my house listening to some new records we got from the pool. I'm talking to Kenny Carpenter, and another friend of ours, late friend of mine, Larry Paterson, he used to play at Zanzibar, and Larry Paterson was my mentor. And I get a phone call. I pick up the phone.

'Hi, my name is Mike Brody, I own a club called The Paradise Garage, I'd like you to play my club.'

I'm like 'Yeah rrright.'

And he says, 'You've been highly recommended.' He said – quote – 'Our DJ's been playing like shit lately, and we'd like you to come in and do a spot.' So by now I've sunk to my knees and I'm trying to write with a pen and a piece of paper to tell my friend who it is I'm speaking to. So he says, 'I have two dates available.' He's not even just offering me one date, to see how I do. It's a definite: 'I got two nights for you.' He'd never heard of me, at all.

He heard your tape though?

Didn't hear nothing. Totally recommendation. From Judy and David Depino.

Was she managing you?

Naww. It was her pool, that was it. I was 21 years old. I was working at a restaurant… and doing parties…

An amazing break.

Because to play at the Garage, everybody knows who was playing at the Garage. If you were a guest DJ your name's on the marquee, and you're advertised, and they tell you what club you come from. Do you know what that was for my name to be on that marquee? I had people come to me and say, 'How did you pull that off?' because there were other people that were a lot more worthy of playing in that room, before me, that were incredible DJs.

So anyway they picked me. I play in a sweat-box in Brooklyn, and here all of a sudden I'm playing at the mecca of the greatest club in the world. At 21 years old. And this wasn't about doing two-hour sets, this was about 11-hour sets, beginning to end, 12 to 11. And you had to beg me to stop!

Can you remember how it was the first time?

I had never played for a gay audience, either. And I thought that playing for a gay audience you had to play different music. When I went to Garage I went on straight night. So when he asked me if I wanted to play Friday and Saturday I said I didn't think I could handle the Saturday, I've never played for a gay crowd before. He said, 'Just come here and do what you do best, that's all I want you to do. The rest… You'll love it.' And man, I can't tell you…

And I never played on Thorens turntables, that's another thing. I only used the Technics. The 1200s were out at the time. I said can I put in some 1200s, and they said we'll see what we can do, but no, it wasn't about that, I had to play on the Thorens. This was belt-driven… even though there were a lot of belt-driven turntables then, the Thorens was a whole 'nother beast, altogether.

So I was like, shit, I'm playing at the greatest club, and yet I'm playing on turntables I ain't never played, and you've got to remember, it's like I've been driving a Volkswagen and all of a sudden I'm given a Ferrari. I've got this fuckin' major machine goin' on here, and I remember doing my first mix, and it was like milk.

Can you remember what it was?
It was my first two records, one was 'Encore', I believe, which was Cheryl Lynn and I can't remember the other. I remember going to all my friends saying it was gonna be slamming tonight, 'cos I just felt it. The greatest thing was that I wasn't part of the politics, at all. I was naive to anything. So even the people that didn't like me, as far as the pro-Larry Levan. Because of course his people, you come to hear your favourite DJ, he ain't there, who the fuck is this guy over here? I had people throwing darts behind my back and I had no idea. They just bounced off because I wasn't part of the politics, I didn't care.

❝ So we're in my house listening to some new records And I get a phone call: 'Hi, my name is Mike Brody, I own a club called The Paradise Garage, I'd like you to play my club.' ❞

So how many times did you play there?
About 10 times. I did the Friday and Saturday, October 13th and 14th, I'll never forget it – 1983, I still got the invitation; it's framed. They even asked me who I could pick for my artists to sing on my night. I picked Jocelyn Brown, and Captain Rapp, at the time his track was 'Bad Times'. And then I came back the following February and played two weekends in a row, 'cos Larry was gone for two weeks straight.

What did that lead into?
All of a sudden I was the new kid on the block. There was a new sheriff in town. That kind of effect, so then clubs in New York approached me and I had a residency at a place called the Inferno, with Vito Bruno. It was a straight club, on 31st Street I believe. Right off Sixth Avenue.

And in between you're still playing at Ozone?
No I wasn't. I asked… Kenny Carpenter took over the whole night. After the Inferno I had a residency at Zanzibar. That's where I met Larry Paterson. Zanzibar was like the Garage of Jersey, and Tony [Humphries] was Saturdays. Tough sound system, people went to it. So I had a residency there for about a year. I was doing Fridays and then I had my own night which was Wednesday. And then I started doing Lovelight which was on 33rd street, right after the Garage closed, 1987. And then from there I worked at 1018 which is now the Roxy, and then in 1988 I started working at the World, and I worked at The World for about a year and a half, and after the World I went to the Red Zone, in '89.

And the Red Zone was really your place?
Yeah. The Red Zone was where I really made a statement for the new age. I think the Red Zone was definitely the turning point on the maps for music changing.

Why do you say that? For you personally?
I think for music in New York. I was in New York, and the only person that was really playing different stuff was Mark Kamins, 'cos he used to travel, so Mark would bring these imports and you know.

He was at Danceteria.
He was many years ago, but at that time he would play at Mars, and he would play at Red Zone on other nights, so I had the residency on Saturdays. In 1989 I took my first trip to England, and I brought back a lot of records. I was the first one playing KLF 'What Time Is Love'.

That was one of my biggest records. And people used to run up to the booth, 'What are you playing?' 'Cos I was playing some of the British sound, this whole different sound.

Did you do any remixing before Red Zone?
Yeah, I did a couple of things. In 1987 I did 'Instinctual' by Imagination. I did some more deeper stuff. But when I started doing Red Zone I started branching out away, away from pure soulful. The Red Zone dubs, that's when I stepped away. The core mix had all the soulful stuff, the songs, and then the Red Zone dubs were more on the daring side, going somewhere different.

> ❝ **Three decks, bam! David Cole would come in, play around on keyboards. It was all live: live remixing, did it on the spot.** ❞

What were you trying to do?
It was mostly experimentation, just feeling that I'm in the Red Zone. It was making records for somewhere between here and abroad, which was what the Red Zone represented. We were playing ska and all that stuff. Nobody was playing ska. I was playing 'This Is Ska' [by Longsy D], and 'Ska Train' [by Beatmasters], those records, and they used to lose it.

What was the crowd like?
Very mixed, you know it was a B-crowd, B-list. Mixed with some A-list. It was a dance crowd. It had a great sound system, the lighting was incredible, and we used to put on a show. Sometimes Satoshi Tomiie would come, he'd play keyboards while we were DJing. We used to go off in that place; it was severe. Everybody who got to experience the Red Zone will tell you it was one of the last places of its kind. And then came Sound Factory. The big Sound Factory was the after hours to go to. You went to Red Zone first, and then you went to Sound Factory, that was the idea. 'Cos Red Zone closed like 5 o'clock, 5.30.

Was remixing a natural progression. Not that many DJs were doing mixes at that time?
I made remixes back in 1983, '84, before I even thought about it. I knew guys in the pool, like Steve Thompson, or Bruce Forrest, and they used to come in and say I just mixed the new Madonna, or the new Rolling Stones. Steve Thompson, I think he's producing Metallica now and things like that.

Bruce Forrest was the resident at Better Days. It was five nights, he used to play four and I used to play on a Thursday night. He introduced me to the world of samplers and drum machines and keyboards, 'cos he used to bring them in the booth. And we used to take live remixing to a whole 'nother level.

Back then you were doing it purely for your dancefloor,
Yeah.

There was no commercial thing?
No.

You were doing it in the club, live?
In the club, at the time. Three decks, bam! David Cole would come in, play around on keyboards. At that time it was the Chicago house sound, so it was great for all the synthesiser stuff that was going on. It was all live: live remixing, did it on the spot.

So from my club Ozone in Brooklyn which I had for about four years, I bought myself a keyboard and a drum machine. Even though I couldn't play anything to save my life. Then in 1985 I hired Steve Silk Hurley when they were JM Silk, him and Keith Nunally, and I hired them to spin at the club. That was round about the time when I started to play around with the CZ-101, that was my first keyboard, Casio CZ-101, and I remember Steve Hurley and Keith Nunally performing in front of the decks, that was a little soft spot too.

So anyway Bruce invited me down to the studio. I liked it; it grabbed my eye. Bought myself one or two pieces of equipment, I tried to make my own drum-beats and things like that. I'd work, do as much as I can with what I got. And then I did a record with David Cole and Robert Clivilles called 'Two Puerto Ricans A Black Man And A Dominican', and we cut that at Judy's office. I was basically mixing records, David played keyboards... it was just something we did on the fly, which was very successful. And then David and Robert went and turned it into something else which is a whole 'nother story [C&C Music Factory].

So that was the start of you having a name as a remixer or a producer?
Yeah. When I really got a lot of profile, publicity, was when I did 'Instinctual' by Imagination. That was my first real hit. I remember Larry Levan telling me 'Great, great job.' I was like, 'Wow Larry told me I did a good mix.'

How did it come about?
I was originally an Imagination fan, from 'Just An Illusion', 'Changes', 'Burning Up', we used to play those records. And then when I heard this record that was done by Phil Harding, the PWL crowd, it sounded like a Rick Astley record, I was like, 'Yo dude, I can't play this, this

is not even Imagination, what happened here?' I said let me remix it. Anyway, even though it was off-key with the vocals. Arthur Baker and the group were like, 'You know its off-key?' 'Yeah, sure.' But it worked. Nobody couldn't say anything, because it worked.

And then my second one I did right after that, was Whitney Houston 'Love Will Save The Day', and they rejected it, it was too housey.

Really?
Of course. It wasn't bubble gum enough. And I was traumatised, I was devastated. Because it would have meant so much to my credit at the time.

Do you find there's a compromise when people hire you for a remix? They have a very precise idea of what they want you to make, for commercial reasons, but then you take the song in a completely different direction. How often is there a real conflict?
Well, not too much but sometimes it does happen where they expect a certain style. And sometimes that's not the style I want to give it because I don't want to have one particular style.

And sometimes the song isn't right for that.
Right. What some A&R man hears in his head is totally different from what can actually work. I've had moments when they've said, 'But I wanted this style, I wanted it like this and

....

like that!' Because I don't normally ask them what style do you want, I want to go about it the way I hear it.

Remixing has come a long way. It started as a DJ's tool to feed his dancefloor.
It's totally leftfield now. It's totally in another place. I mean let's not even call it remixing any more. In the beginning of remixing you remixed the original track. You used what was there to create the intro, your body, your break, your tag – the end of the song.

And then it started changing: okay you change the bassline, added percussion, or you added some things, but you still had the song. You still had the artist intact. Let's make it like that. So it was less changing around. So that was cool.

Then it came to the point with the production, when you just got rid of the original music. Now you started to put new music...

So you've just got the vocal track
All you got is the vocal track. So then people expected to hear something totally different. Now the expectancy was: 'Well, did he change it?' Now they wanted to hear something totally different. It's come to a place where now you're changing the music so what you do to it makes the record successful. You're only getting a one-time fee. You're not getting a writer's share, but in reality you're sort of becoming a co-writer.

So that's why the fees went up so much.
When I started remixing there wasn't too many guys who could mix songs [ie vocal tracks], there still aren't that many. Now remixing has crossed over into R&B, which is great. I think remixing in hip hop, in R&B is the most creative, more than the dance remixes.

Why do you say that?
Because they're re-doing the song. They all re-do the song. There's no time-stretching, you understand; they're re-cutting the song. They're adding rappers to it, so they're producing. They're all productions. Which is where I've taken remixing to now: production.

You're actually working with the artist now.
At that time there's the artist and the guy that mixed the record. So you knew at least when the record came out it was close to what it was originally. Now when the time-stretching [altering the tempo without changing the pitch] started, of course it's easier for more mixes to come out, it's less of a challenge to remix a downtempo record. So it made it easier. Now, alright, I believe the reason why I even still get a lot of work is, I do vocals. because I work with the song. You have tons of other guys...

Who just take that much [a pinch].
And not even that. It's gotten to the point that there's no respect for the artist any more. You're selling the remixes, that's who you're selling.

So is that how you approach it, that it's gonna come out recognisably the same song?
Of course. I mean that's what the challenge is. But what guys are doing today is like, you working on a track in your studio, you put a slamming track together. Somebody says, I need a remix of Tori Amos. It's not even a question of I need you to mix the record, or the vocals, you know what I mean, verses, choruses – no fuckin way. It's not going to happen because you never done that. You don't have experience in that. There's no way. So you take a piece of a vocal: 'Bla'. That's a remix ? That represents the artist? That doesn't represent the artist, it represents you.

In reality you're giving up publishing, because you're giving up a whole track. You're giving it to somebody else's name. That really doesn't represent them. That they'll never perform, either! So you know...

Why did it get so out of hand with the money? It got quite crazy a few years ago.
It's still crazy. It's crazier! I don't think it's any less crazy. I mean, I dunno, I can't explain why you can spend so much money on a record and it not do anything, and then there could be something where there's no effort, that's put together in two hours, and for some reason the thing just hits, and that's it! I mean Stardust ['Music Sounds Better With You'], how much work you think went into Stardust?

About an afternoon?
Know what I mean. It's sampled. Whoever went into the sample, that was where the work was. When those musicians made the original, that was where the time was spent. But look how huge that thing was.

❝ So you take a piece of a vocal: 'Bla'. That's a remix? That represents the artist? That doesn't represent the artist, it represents you. ❞

You have the privilege for having the highest fee for any one remix. Michael Jackson 'Scream'.
Probably.

Didn't they fly you over to LA rather than send the tapes etc...
They wouldn't give me the masters. They flew me to LA, flew everybody, money was no object. It was a lot of work. It wasn't like that was my fee for one mix. I must have did three different mixes. I mean I spent a week in Michael Jackson-land. But that was back then, compared to now. Hip hop guys are making that kind of money, regularly.

Do you know who the highest is now?
Probably Puffy. Who knows.

What does he get nowadays?
I don't know. It would be interesting. You can't be surprised at a guy like Puffy, probably wouldn't do it for less than a 100 grand, between 75 and a 100 maybe.

Cos you got 80 for the Michael Jackson, is that right?
Nahh. It was... I can't say.

But did that feel a bit crazy, all that Michael Jackson-ness.
You know what, it was definitely a moment, with Michael Jackson.

Did you meet him?
No I didn't for anything. I should have for all of the security I went through, you would think he was coming. I mean they were guarding those tapes like it was their life. It was the first track off the album.

That's why it was so secret.
Mission Impossible. And I felt that I compromised. I compromised my sound. I went to another place. I took everybody out of the environment, and we tried to recreate that somewhere else and it just didn't work. I feel like I was compromised so I don't feel like my best effort went into 'Scream'. It could have been a much better sounding record...

Do you think the DJ is an artist?
Sure.

What makes him an artist?
The way he puts on music. Not all DJs are artists. It's not something that has to be present all the time. It's something that has to project. But it's like, 'Put on this show,' and you have to pull it from thin air. They don't plan their records, they don't put them in a certain order, say, 'This is gonna be my first, my second...' I take more records than I need, I don't know what the first record is, or my last, or my second.

As great stuff as I have in my studio, I can't turn it on for myself. I can't. I got a great sounding studio, but when I make my show tapes for the radio, I can't turn it on. I don't come up with the creative things that come on when you're playing live to an audience. I can't duplicate it.

What do you get from the audience?
Well, you get the live feedback, and you're working records, you have to present them in

Def Mix: Satoshi Tomiie, Frankie Knuckles and David Morales.

different ways, and its how you present the mixing, the technical aspects of it, its a whole combination of things...

🍷 Ohhhh man, it's like jumping out of my skin. I dance in the booth. I jump up and down. I wave my arms in the air. I can do anything I want. 🍷🍷

How do you feel like when it's going really well?
Ohhhh man, its like jumping out of my skin. I dance in the booth. I jump up and down. I wave my arms in the air. It's that feeling of knowing I'm in full control, I can do anything I want. And the thing is, I like to entertain myself. It's important to me to keep me going this far. I have to get something out of it. I can't just do it for the money. What makes you different and special is that you give it that extra something.

Does it feel sexual or spiritual...
Oh for sure. For me, absolutely.

How does it feel?
Pure sex...

Yeah?
Sex and... oh absolutely. For me it's sex.

Really?
Totally.

So you're having sex with all the audience.
Absolutely. It's spiritual sex – classic, spiritual sex, oh my god. A great night man, sometimes I'm on my knees in the middle of a mix, just feeling it that way, and then when you play a record, you can bring it down, you can just turn everything off and the people going nuts. And you stand back, you just wipe your forehead and, 'Shiit!' Everybody just going nuts and you know that you're right there, you could play whatever you want. *Whatever* you want. You got 'em from there.

You're part of the party; you're participating in the party. I don't spin records I like to play records. There's a difference: spinning you're just spinning them, but playing you're making them talk to each other. When the party is going that great I wouldn't trade that feeling for anything in the world.

Do you still get that thrill?
Absolutely. Nothing beats the energy of a great party: screaming and hands in the air. You can't beat that; nothing in the world. You're making a difference; you're part of something. You're not getting up and being a robot, getting up and doing some generic everyday formula thing. The power to manipulate souls and minds to a frenzy – or to boredom!

And I'm not young. I'm older than a lot of the guys out there. But I actually feel that I'm actually – in all of my years – at the top of my game. I've played at some incredible parties, before the travelling and all of that. I go back to the Ozone to Mirage, to Zanzibar. I got to experience some incredible moments, of music, that have inspired me to carry that on, that a lot of people, the new kids, haven't experienced.

And to me the fundamentals from those days still apply. My experience comes from back then. My experience is not a new generation's experience. My experience is an old school experience. And I do things an old school way. Now I understand records more because I make records. And that just makes you all the more better because you understand.

When you talk to the older guys they say that today records are made so precisely for the dancefloor, so the DJ doesn't have to work as much, whereas in the old days you had to change the record every two minutes.

David Morales

The 45 stage you had to work, and be a lot more creative, because the intro was like this [snaps fingers]. And even when 12-inches came out, the music from that era it was all live. There was no such thing as having blank drums for 16 bars and you got enough time to ride that beat in. Hell no! You had to really be creative, make that shit sound real smooth. You had to be creative and take the night up, down, up.

The way records are made today, it's a system, you can programme it with a computer, man. You really have the technology, it ain't too far from it. You can actually tell, if you have two tracks you know it's 16 bars, okay synch up, what's the tempo of the thing, you punch it in, it synchs up within itself, time-stretches it, whatever the hell it does. It won't be too long before you get some nonsense like that.

Is the DJ's art a dying art then?
Nah, no.

There are always going to be people who put body and soul into it?
Yeah, absolutely. In whatever kind of music. I think the thing about all the best DJs is that they feel it, and that's why they play so well. They have to feel it; they have to believe in the stuff they're playing.

The worst scenario would be playing it for the sake of playing it. It would be like me playing drum and bass or playing something progressive, because hey man I need to make some money to make ends meet, and because I don't have a name, this is what I gotta do.

But the real connoisseur, whether he's working or not, this is what he's doing. Even if he's a bedroom DJ all his life, nobody's gonna take away from him that he loves music. No matter what. So even if I wasn't working I'd still be trying to put some records together. Even if I'm not playing out anywhere I'd still be in my office trying to put some practice tapes together. Because when I started buying records there was no two turntables, there was no clubs. Nobody ever told me that I was gonna get a job as a DJ one day. And I never thought for a moment that that's what I wanted to be.

And then you travel places, and you see that people really love your work; they bring you records to sign and all this. I never realised the kind of impact I really have on people. I mean really, real impact. I've seen genuine tears in their eyes. When they're talking to me. The passion they have for what I do. The happy moments that I've brought to them. Just in general, my music has had a positive effect.

I was doing this video to 'Needing You' in Ibiza and there I was, sitting on a bench and I said to Lou from Manifesto, I said 'I couldn't have life any better right now. I am sitting down on Salinas beach. I am having a Corona, and I'm being paid.' [a high five]

When it all got crazy, what kind of things happened to you?
You mean like handling the whole schedule?

No I mean the kind of reactions you get from people.
One of the most incredible times I had was in Japan one time, a place called Yellow, and they literally wanted to climb over the walls, up to the box. You see people standing around the booth, just like every space, waiting for you to do magic, and you think 'I'm just playing records. I'm not doing anything. You can do this. If you felt it.' It's all here [thumps his heart]. It's here and here [heart and ears]. 'Cos that's what its all about.

For my 40th birthday I took my mother to Ibiza. I took her to Pacha. She knows I make good money and I travel the world, but she remembers me for being a bedroom DJ and telling me to turn the music down! When she finally got to see what it is I do and how people reacted… She was like wow. People coming up to her in the booth saying we love your son, we love his music, he's done so much for us.

Can you remember what it was like travelling to another country to DJ for the first time?
The first time was in Japan in 1988. It was good but it wasn't like it was when I went to England. I went in 1988, and by then I'd made a couple of records, so it was like, wow! And raves had started, so you had Sunrise and Energy, and of course the music that was happening in those days was just incredible. So coming to play over there it was like wow, and places were sold out, packed. I was one of the first Americans coming over.

How do you feel when you go to England and Italy and people treat you like a superstar?
I laugh sometimes. Because the treatment, the honour, the money, the fame… I don't ask for it. My greatest satisfaction is, I'm a DJ first, I ain't talking about the rest of it, because I been playing for years. Even if I stopped making records tomorrow, I'd still keep playing records. I get a lot of passion from it, and to be paid, and to be put on a pedestal for doing something that I love doing naturally, is mindboggling.

© DJhistory.com

RED ZONE 50

UNDERGROUND SOLUTION – Luv Dancin'
MADONNA – Vogue
DOUBLE DEE FT. DANY – Found Love
SHABBA RANKS – Mr. Loverman
CEYBIL – Special
TECHNOTRONIC – Pump Up The Jam
SNAP! – The Power
CE CE PENISTON – Finally
KLF – What Time Is Love
CRYSTAL WATERS – Gypsy Woman
SOUL II SOUL – Keep On Movin'
LONGSY D – This Is Ska
STEVIE V – Dirty Cash
C&C MUSIC FACTORY – Gonna Make You Sweat
FRANKIE KNUCKLES – Tears
ROBERT OWENS – I'll Be Your Friend
STEVIE V – Jealousy
PET SHOP BOYS – So Hard
THE BEATMASTERS – Ska Train
INNER CITY – Good Life
REESE & SANTONIO – Rock To The Beat
LISA STANSFIELD – All Around The World
INNER CITY – Big Fun
MARK THE 45 KING – 909
2 WITHOUT HATS – Try Yazz
EN VOGUE – Hold On

2 IN A ROOM – Wiggle It
SAFIRE – Taste The Bass
BLACK SHEEP – Strobelite Honey
STARPOINT – I Want You
THREE GENERATIONS FT. CHEVELL – Get It Off
TRIBAL HOUSE – Motherland
SHEENA EASTON – 101
KENNY 'DOPE' GONZALEZ – Blood Vibes
MAXI PRIEST – Close To You
TYREE – Acid Crash
FAST EDDIE – Let's Go
MIX MASTERS – In The Mix
PLEZ – I Can't Stop
A TRIBE CALLED QUEST – Bonita Applebaum
LIL LOUIS – French Kiss
D-MOB – We Call It Acieeed
BLACK BOX – Ride On Time
DEEE-LITE – What Is Love/Groove Is In The Heart
JOEY BELTRAM – Energy Flash
LIL LOUIS – Blackout
EL GENERAL – Tu Pum Pum
BLACK BOX – Everybody
GRACE JONES – Love On Top Of Love

Compiled by David Morales

RECOMMENDED LISTENING

DAVID MORALES & THE BAD YARD CLUB – The Program
VARIOUS – Mix The Vibe: David Morales, Past, Present And Future (DJ mix)
VARIOUS – Cream Anthems (DJ mix)

" My partner and I have started this thing called Masters At Work and we're starting to make some records. "

Louie Vega
Master at work

Interviewed by Bill by Skype to Greece, February 20, 2010

His dad was a jazz saxophonist, and his uncle was salsa vocalist Hector Lavoe of the Fania All-Stars, so when 'Little' Louie Vega got behind the decks aged 13 he was just following family tradition. Years later, when he and his Masters At Work production partner Kenny 'Dope' Gonzalez gathered singers and players for their Nuyorican Soul project, it was clear they were outgrowing their earlier house sound and getting ever closer to old-fashioned organic musicianship. And now, with his Elements of Life ensemble, Louie Vega is a fully fledged bandleader. Apart from piano lessons as a kid, he's proud to say that all his songwriting and arranging skills come from playing records.

Louie is one of a generation of New York DJs whose young ears were tuned to the emerging sounds of hip hop and house as much as to the dying rays of disco. Growing up in the Bronx in an era of street jams and block parties he developed an omnivorous musical palette. Meanwhile the city's Latin traditions were merging with hip hop and electronic disco to create freestyle, a sound heard at Jellybean's Funhouse, David Morales' Red Zone and Louie's own residency at The Devil's Nest. His wide-ranging tastes as a DJ were best heard at another long-running residency at the Sound Factory Bar. Here at the Wednesday Underground Network nights the close-knit New York dance music industry would gather. Barbara Tucker would take your money at the door, Louie would be behind the decks joking with one of the many DJs and producers who came down to test out new tracks, and the city's label owners would be on the floor mixing with off-duty professional dancers.

Under a variety of pseudonyms, Louie and Kenny created arguably the most outstanding body of work in house music history. Through the '90s, a Masters At Work remix was a prized addition to any release. The duo joined the list of go-to remixers whose style was distinctive enough to be wielded as an A&R weapon, and as a result they've reworked everyone from Nina Simone to Aaliya. Louie won a Grammy for his remix of Curtis Mayfield's 'Superfly' in 2006 and is currently working on a variety of projects including producing his vocalist wife, Anane.

Do you think it was inevitable you would end up in music given your family background?
Yeah, but I didn't know I was going to get this far. When I started DJing in the neighbourhood, I didn't know that everything was going to be this big. We were in the Bronx playing music, then came to Manhattan. Everybody was just happy there but we didn't realize that from Japan to the UK it was going to become something so big.

When did you first start playing in clubs and what were you playing?
I started at the Devil's Nest in the Bronx in 1985 and I remember having already the first few house releases on Trax: Virgo, Mr Fingers, Marshall Jefferson. So I was always playing house music, freestyle and stuff from the Paradise Garage as well because I'd been going there since I was 14 years old. But I also played a lot of rock music; a lot of the new wave stuff, from Love & Rockets to Book of Love. There was a big variety which is probably the reason why I do records the way I do. Comes from DJing back in those days.

Louie Vega

....

Devil's Nest was a really important club for the freestyle sound in New York. How did you get the gig there?
Well, the Devil's Nest was owned by Fever Records and Disco Fever, the club. Disco Fever in the Bronx was a famous hip hop club for years…

Is that the one that was owned by Sal Abbatiello?
Exactly. They had a huge success with the hip hop scene: Grandmaster Flash, Lovebug Starski… so many great DJs played there. They wanted to do a dance club, so they opened up the Devil's Nest in the Bronx on Webster Avenue.

At the time I was doing a lot of mobile parties with a friend of mine John Rivera. He was a DJ/promoter and I was the DJ. We used to throw our own parties and we were packing them in so I had built this following. So I found this club up in the Bronx and I had done three parties there, which had 800 to 1,000 people and at the last party I hired a Fever Records artist – her name was Nayobi. Sal Abbatiello came down with her producer Andy 'Panda' and they saw the crowds and they said, 'Look we've opened up this new club, maybe you're interested in playing there?' I started on Friday and as soon as I started, all those kids that were following me came to the club. We had over 1,000 people. They were so happy they ended up offering me Saturday nights as well.

Were you playing stuff like Mr Fingers as well?
Yeah, I played Mr Fingers, all the early house, a lot of freestyle stuff… I was playing a lot of disco classics, a lot of breakdancing classics, I would even play rock music as I said before. It was a young flourishing crowd that was really open to a lot of music. The way I played it I made it work and in those days we were doing six to eight hour sets.

Were you influenced by guys like Jellybean?
Very much, of course! I used to go to the Fun House in the early '80s and I remember seeing him and Madonna, and hearing a lot of the stuff that Arthur Baker and John Robie did. That whole school of music was very much the inspiration – with new wave music – for freestyle in '85.

He was playing stuff like Wide Boy Awake ['Slang Teacher'] as well wasn't he?
Yeah, I'm calling it new wave but it just came from the UK. It was just great music and we all played it. I was playing a lot of that music, Wide Boy Awake, 'A Letter From Afar' by B Movie, they were huge records for us and people were freaking out you know 'cos you had all these Puerto Ricans and African-Americans rocking to this music. I was at the Devil's Nest for nine months from April in '85 through to '86. And then after nine months I was offered a gig at Heart Throb, which was the old Fun House where Jellybean played. The place that as a kid I was dreaming…

That you would play there!…
Yeah! And look, I ended up playing in that club, which was amazing. I played early Trax records, DJ International; I remember Farley Jackmaster Funk used to put out beat albums, and I used to play a lot of that: Larry Levan stuff… I was like the bridge in between Jellybean and the freestyle world and then the breakdance world and the Paradise Garage. I was playing that music but to young people.

Yeah, that was kind of the difference between that crowd and the Garage really wasn't it? Ethnically slightly different and younger?
Exactly, I got like the next generation of the Jellybean crowd. We all went to the Fun House too and we were all growing into the next phase but at the same time we loved the Paradise Garage but we were going to both those clubs. 'Cos I mean in the early '80s I used to go from checking out Jellybean in the Fun House to the Paradise Garage, to Zanzibar to see Tony Humphries, all the way out in Jersey. We used to take trips out there just to see Tony Humphries. In the early '80s we would go to the Fun House first, then to Zanzibar. In those days I was hooked on Tony. He was in his prime, and the way he was mixing the records, he would just get all these records so early and a lot of the New Jersey producers and people from all around would give him all this great music. He was the king of mixing and programming music; it was really something else.

How did you come to work with Kenny [Kenny 'Dope' Gonzalez]?
We met through Todd Terry, 'cos Todd used to hang out at Heart Throb. He used to bring me his music and I was probably the first one to ever play Todd's music in front of larger audiences. I don't know why but he first brought me a cassette. I was like 'Yo, Todd, I don't play cassettes! You gotta make me a reel-to-reel.' Ever since then I was playing 'Party People', 'Bango' and all his hits six months before they came out, so the crowd was already primed you know?

I started making house music with Todd Terry before Kenny. Todd was doing so many records at a time he was like, 'Louie, I need help man, can you just mix these records for me and then I'll just kind of give them to you?' [laughs] Next thing there's 20 songs that I have with Todd Terry, like 'And The Beat Goes On' by D.M.S. Todd needed help with everything just to keep flowing because he was moving so fast. He'd make probably 30 records in a week. He was crazy.

Anyway, he introduced me to Kenny because I liked the songs that Kenny did on his label Dope Wax. He had this tune 'A Little Bit Of Salsa' which I was playing and I loved the song so much and it was so big in the clubs I was playing. Todd said, 'He works out in a record store in Brooklyn, he's a DJ and he's making beats and stuff.' I met Kenny and the rest was history.

> **❝ I loved the way Kenny was into hip hop beats but also into club music; he was into old and new music and he collected all kinds of stuff. ❞**

How come you hit it off so well?
I loved the way that Kenny was into hip hop beats but also into club music; he was into old and new music and he collected all kinds of stuff. He came to my place and I said to him, 'I would love to start a production team with you. I think you have a lot of potential, I think you can compliment what I do and I think I can compliment what you do.' We just hit it off and from there we just started creating a lot of music. Then I said we need a name, we need a catchy name, something that people as soon as they hear it they are gonna go, 'Wow! That's them.'

He said, 'Well I've this crew name called Masters at Work that I lent to Todd but I can easily get it back.' It was the perfect name and that was the beginning of Masters at Work.

With a name like that it's a good job you ended up being good!
You know if we weren't that good then the whole Masters At Work thing would have been a bit like, damn. But when we started I don't think we were even thinking like that. By the time we started working together I was working in Studio 54 and Roseland and I decided to stop playing freestyle, because it was getting very violent. Also since I was making so much house music my head was in another place, so I took a year and a half off and in that time, I was working 18 hours a day with Kenny, every single day. I didn't care about anything else apart from working in the studio and creating a lot of great music.

I was also working on an album with Atlantic. A friend, Joey Carvello, approached me to do an album and I needed a singer so I reached out to this young singer that was always at Heart Throb, who had a great voice, called Marc Anthony.

So was that album that gave us 'Ride On The Rhythm'?
Yes. Kenny did a lot of the beats for the album so we started getting acquainted in that time as Kenny and I were in the studio the whole time.

You did some early house records on Cutting for Aldo Marin who I guess you'd known from the freestyle period.
Yes of course, do you remember that song 'Do What You Want' by 2 In A Room? I was on

the B-side of that with 'Take Me Away' which was a pretty big club record. Anyway, I said to Aldo, 'My partner and I have started this thing called Masters At Work and we're starting to make some records. We love hip hop and we love house and we wanna do something where we put a hip hop tune on one side with reggae influences and on the other side some straight up street house.' That became 'The Ha Dance' and 'Blood Vibes'.

When you started making house music you were working with various vocalists and arrangers almost straight away. You seemed to have bigger ambitions than the average house producer.
Yeah. I always wanted to produce. Jellybean had come to me at Heart Throb and said if I ever needed to go to a studio to learn and just sit in the back and check things out, I was more than welcome. Trust me, when anybody invited me to the studio as a kid, I went: Arthur Baker, Latin Rascals, Jellybean Benitez. I learned a lot from them.

When I did the freestyle records I started producing vocalists in the studio. My first backgrounds session which was 'Dancing On The Fire' was with Jocelyn Brown, Cindy Mizelle and Audrey Wheeler, and I still have relationships with those women today; they're still singing on some of my tunes with Elements of Life or Nuyorican Soul. It was always in my blood, I guess it was destined for me to be a producer.

How did your partnership with Kenny work in the studio? Is it true he did the beats and then you did the music? Or was it more collaborative than that?
Basically I'd be on a keyboard and Kenny would be on the drum machine. He may come up with a beat or I may come up with a groove, he'd build a beat on my groove or I'd build the keyboards over his beats. I was playing keyboards in all the early MAW stuff. When you hear a lot more simplified and raw club stuff, that's me playing. I'm not the guy who does the beautiful chord progressions and everything, but I had a nice groove, basslines and little bleepy sounds.

As Kenny started working more and more, he would watch me produce and see the way I was with artists and he came into his own. So Kenny was involved as well in music we were making together. I would be more the guy who was working with the vocalists, in arrangements, with a lot of sounds, that kind of stuf. But Kenny would definitely put in his word here and there, he was definitely involved. And I would ask him as well because as a team it wouldn't be the same if it were just one of us doing it. I think it was important that we both had opinions and we told each other how we felt. It wasn't a problem. If I didn't like something he did, I'd tell him and if he didn't like something I did, he'd tell me. We tried to change it to make it better; we had that relationship.

It's good to have a sounding board as well isn't it?
Yeah, and we had amazing engineers that worked with us for many years like Dave Darlington and Steve Barkan.

So which gives you the biggest kick, DJing or producing?
I love them both. I really love playing music and especially being able to test the music that I make or my friends make in front of people. I think it's a great thing that goes hand in hand. I love producing in the studio, creating albums, coming up with concepts and tailoring an album to an artist, so I love doing all that stuff, too.

They are such different disciplines aren't they? There's a lot of boredom and repetition in a studio and DJing is, I guess, more direct and instant, the fix you get.
Yeah, when you're in a studio, you're listening to a song hundreds of times. When I'm working on a song and working on an album, I live with that thing for a year. I'm listening to the songs over and over and then I have to play them out, so it's not over yet. It's really great working with artists. I've been told that there's something about me that brings out the best in people when I'm in the studio. I really feel that what those artists are going to give you in those five to eight minutes can be history.

Do you think that's down to just your personality? Or the fact that you DJ, does that bring a different quality in the studio?

I think it's everything. It's definitely the personality because you've got to know how to talk to people, how to get the best out of them, how to make them feel good. Of course you have to have the musical side, you've got to know if someone's singing off-key. But I'm talking about when you're in the studio, making those artists feel good, giving them the confidence. Tommy Lipuma, who's one of the greatest producers of all time, said, 'Louie, what you got out of [George] Benson when you did 'You Can Do It', hasn't been heard since 'The World Is A Ghetto', and he produced 'The World Is A Ghetto' so that was the ultimate compliment.

Tell me your memories of Underground Network at the Sound Factory Bar.
Actually before I did that, I got to play at The Choice a couple of times. Richard Vasquez had taken over The Loft and called it The Choice. I was like, 'I can't believe they want me to play at The Loft!'

This was the one of the places I'd dreamed of. He loved this thing I did called Freestyle Orchestra. I'll never forget when I was playing there. Larry Levan came in when I was playing and he said to me, 'Louie I'd like to compliment you on Tito Puente's 'Ran Kan Kan' and I've got to say that you're the only one in this business that could've taken that record where it went.' It was amazing.

For Sound Factory Bar, I was approached by Don Welch who I knew from a record pool I used to work at in 1984, and Barbara Tucker, who I remembered from her time as singer with Harlequin Four's who had played at Heart Throb. Don said, 'Look Louie, I'm thinking of giving this party here every week on a Wednesday?' Are you interested in throwing this party here every week.

I said, 'That sounds great! I'm not really playing anywhere and I've been looking to get back into it and this music is taking me into a different direction.' He said, 'You can invite all your friends, we'll invite all our friends.' And then we came up with this idea of doing an industry party.

The idea was to make it a place where promoters, singers, dancers – even if you're a Broadway dancer or you're a club dancer – you can come and enjoy yourself. If you're an actor or in the entertainment business, but as well, kids in the street from New York City there. We started with about 50 people and from there we just kept working at it, and in just a few months it became a very successful place for about five years. It became the testing ground for a lot of the house music from the '90s – all the other producers would come in. It was like a who's-who, some huge stars were hanging out at the Sound Factory Bar.

> **❝ I don't know if it's going to be a pop hit, but I know when it's a record that people are gonna like. You start getting goosebumps or you get teary-eyed. ❞**

When you're in the studio and you're making a record, do you always know when you've made a hit?
I don't know if it's going to be a pop hit, but I know when it's a record that people are gonna like. You start getting goosebumps or you get teary-eyed – depending on the kind of song it is. I've made records that have really affected all of us in the studio, where we've we felt these records were so big. Barbara Tucker for example. She wanted to cut some records. She was at the club, hosting the night and we were like, 'Imagine if we make a song?'

When we did 'Beautiful People' I had a songwriting team – India, Derek Whittaker, Lem Springsteen – and I came up with this hot track. It's exactly what you hear: the Rhodes with that little groove. They wrote the song and then Barbara Tucker came in and sang the demo. She did one little ad lib and she sang, 'Deep inside, deep deep down inside.' When I heard it, it inspired me to do 'Deep Inside'. I thought, 'Let me use that hook to get Barbara's voice out there.' Like a promotional tool, almost marketing it. It was a great idea to get Barbara's

....

sound into peoples' head. It did an amazing job. It got into the pop charts in the UK, it did pretty well. It was exciting.

How did DJing, especially DJing abroad, change what you did in the studio? Did it affect things?

I'd say DJing helped me in the studio with arrangements. Because I was listening to so much music over the years, I was learning how songs started with verses, bridges would be with choruses, outros and the vamps, I learnt a lot about arrangement through DJing. I also went to piano lessons when I was a kid. I took classical lessons from the age of six to 11. So I did five years of classical. So all that stuff combined to help. But DJing really helped with knowing how songs were arranged. See a lot of disco records, a lot of Quincy Jones stuff, a lot of Stevie Wonder, I would study all that stuff.

What's the most superstar thing to happen to you as a DJ?

Well, I've played at a lot of high profile parties that were incredible. I played for 30,000 people in South Africa. I got an escort from the police, sirens down the highway, 24 hour armed guards. I'd never experienced anything like that. Also I played for the opening of Atlantis, that hotel in the Bahamas. Man, that was the party of parties. I played at the VIP-VIP-VIP party where there was only 300 people in that room. You looked out and there was Denzel Washington, Oprah Winfrey, Leonardo DiCaprio, Grace Jones… it was so star studded, it was amazing. It was beautiful.

Also the wedding of Marc Anthony and Jennifer Lopez. The press was so crazy. Three minutes before they got married there were six helicopters above the mansions, just hovering over, trying to get a picture. I couldn't believe it. It was a beautiful wedding and it was amazing, but those things really surprised me. I'm happy we live under the radar.

It's a nicer way to live. You get your kudos from people but you can walk down to the bodega and get a soda.

Exactly!

What are you most proud of in your music career?

There are three things. One of them is composing a song for Cirque Du Soleil who performed it at the Super Bowl. Also I won a Grammy for Best Remix in 2006 for Curtis Mayfield's 'Superfly'. The third thing is the work I've done with my partner Kenny Dope as Masters At Work. We've just done an amazing body of work that I'm very proud of.

© DJhistory.com

LOUIE VEGA SELECTED DISCOGRAPHY

INFORMATION SOCIETY – Running (remixer)

MAW & COMPANY – Gonna Get Back To You (writer/producer)

MASTERS AT WORK FT. INDIA – I Can't Get No Sleep (writer/producer/mixer)

DOUBLE EXPOSURE – Ten Percent (remixer)

TITO PUENTE – Ran Kan Kan (remixer)

URBANIZED FT. SILVANO – Helpless (I Don't Know What To Do Without You) (remixer)

HARDRIVE – Deep Inside (writer/producer/mixer)

RIVER OCEAN FT. INDIA – Love And Happiness (Yemaya Y Ochun) (writer/producer/mixer)

SOLE FUSION – Bass Tone (writer/producer/mixer)

BARBARA TUCKER – Beautiful People (writer/producer/remixer)

NENEH CHERRY – Buddy X (remixer)

LIL' MO' YIN YANG – Reach (writer/producer)

NUYORICAN SOUL – The Nervous Track (writer/producer/mixer)

JOE T. VANNELLI FT. CSILLA – Play With The Voice (remixer)

INCOGNITO – Jacob's Ladder (remixer)

TOWA TEI – Luv Connection (remixer)

JAMIROQUAI – Emergency On Planet Earth (remixer)

KENLOU – The Bounce (writer/producer/mixer)

MAW – To Be In Love (producer/mixer)

KENLOU – What A Sensation (writer/producer)

RECOMMENDED LISTENING

VARIOUS – Azuli Presents Louie Vega: Choice, A Collection Of Classics (CD and vinyl)

VARIOUS – The Kings Of House (DJ mix) (CD only)

VARIOUS – 20/10 The Southport Dance Music Weekender (DJ mix) (CD only)

" I talked my grandma into buying me a synthesiser. And the rest was kinda history. "

Juan Atkins
Techno rebel

Interviewed by Ben Ferguson by phone to Detroit, April 21, 2010

Given the huge impact he has had on music worldwide, Juan Atkins is possibly the most overlooked black artist in America. Of the fabled Belleville Three (with Kevin Saunderson and Derrick May), Juan is the key to techno, the sound that emerged from this leafy Detroit suburb. Son of a concert promoter, the young Atkins played in high school funk bands and most days was to be found padding around his house with a bass guitar more or less permanently slung round his neck. When his grandma bought him a synth his focus changed completely and he spent days at a time programming beats in the image of the European electronic bands he loved.

Juan began making records with Rik Davis in the early 1980s under the name Cybotron. In another universe it could have been their eerie 'Alleys Of Your Mind', rather than a broadly similar (and slightly later) record called 'Planet Rock' which ignited electro worldwide. His subsequent solo productions as Model 500, although clearly inspired by a European aesthetic, are among the most inspired productions to come out of black America.

While Derrick May wanted to call this music 'high-tech soul', Juan was insistent that it should be 'techno'. At the last minute the compilation which introduced it to the UK – originally to be called *The New* House *Sound Of Detroit* – was renamed along these lines. And techno, of course, went on to conquer the world. If any one person could be said to have started it, it must surely be Juan Atkins.

You moved to Belleville when your parents split. What was surburbia like?
Well actually what happened was, we were about to move to California but then my father's ma, my grandmother, called us at the last minute and said they're building a new house down the road from me. And talked him into it. It was very very different from inner city life. We lived in Detroit before that.

How old were you?
Like 14, 15.

Were you already listening to a lot of music?
Yeah, yeah, I'd always listened to music. In Detroit I was playing in funk bands, garage bands with friends of mine off the street and around the block, and we'd get together and play in the garage. I played bass guitar. Some lead guitar. So we'd all get together and watch people. This was when I was 12, 13.

Who else played in these bands?
A guy named Jimmy Smith, Chris… I can't remember his last name, Keith Jameson, a couple of other people. I can't remember everybody's names.

Did you keep in touch with them after moving?
Not really. When I moved to Belleville it was kind of a wrap for them. When I went to Belleville I started a whole new band.

....

Still playing funk?
Yeah. Well that was the era. It was the funk era – ha! And a little disco. But then funk became disco, then disco became new wave, then new wave and disco became house and techno.

Your dad was a concert promoter wasn't he.
Yeah, he'd run people like Norman Connors, Michael Henderson, Barry White; he did a big Barry White show down at Cobo Hall.

Did you meet any of the stars?
No, we just went to the show and that was it.

But the shows must have been good.
Yeah, I remember Michael Henderson particularly, because I liked 'Wide Receiver'. That was a big track for me in high school so when he ran that definitely it was memorable for that one track.

And did you ever think about stardom of this sort?
You know, we were just having *fuuuun* [southern accent]. We didn't think about stardom or being famous. We were just kids doing what we liked to do. I would have imagined that there was a little bit of that but really we were just stars in the garage. So you know… When you pick up an instrument there's a bit of you that definitely dreams of being a superstar. That goes without saying. But we wouldn't get around in a group discussion and say, 'Hey, let's try be superstars.' I mean, it was just something that was an unspoken rule. Unspoken rule to be famous basically…

Like how nobody is allowed to admit that they want to make money.
Well, not everybody.

And your brother was living with you as well. By the sound of it he made a big impression on Derrick May, especially the day when he rolled up in his Cadillac with Parliament pumping out of the speakers
[Laughs] Well my brother was a year younger than me. He and Derrick were in the same class 'cos Derrick is a year younger than me too. He would prowl around with my brother before we became friends.

How was your relationship with him?
He's my younger brother. I love him, we're one of the same. But the funny thing is back then I'd hang out with an older crowd. We didn't hang out with the same sort of people.

Were these guys much older than you?
Yeah. Mostly neighbourhood friends.

Did they play you stuff you might not have heard if you hung out with kids your age?
Probably, probably, probably.

So it wasn't long before you put down the bass and picked up the synth?
Basically, when I moved to Belleville I started playing the keyboard. My grandmother owned an organ, this hammered old B3 thing. She'd go into the music shop, Brunel's, for this organ. And right at this time they'd introduced the Minimoog, the Korg NS10, these were small, smart monophonic synthesisers. I'd go into the back room and play these synthesisers and eventually I was able to talk her into buying me one. And the rest was kinda history. I was so wrapped up in this sound, with playing around with these synthesisers. I made drum sounds, drum kicks, everything, all on this one synthesiser. And that's how I started doing my demos and my electronic music demos. And by the time I got to college I had full-blown demos that I played for classmates.

How old were you then?
15, 16.

What did your dad make of this?
By this time my father wasn't around too much. He was into the street and wasn't really

paying too much attention to what was happening at home. Whatever I did in my bedroom that's what I did was my own and no one would come in, especially my dad.

Were you not getting on with each other?
No, no, we were great but he was in control of the nightlife and he wasn't at home a lot.

One difference between playing in bands and using a synth is that music can be made alone. All you needed was your bedroom, yourself and the machine.
Yeah. Well the thing is, being in Belleville the next person I could play with was 10 miles away. It was hard for me to get together with other musicians.

Did it feel like you were doing something unusual?
There weren't too many other people doing that. I was very innovative when I was young. I knew I was doing stuff that was not the normal thing to do.

Was this in reaction to anything? The high school parties perhaps?
No. Not a reaction. This wasn't happening in Belleville. Belleville was different to the inner city schools.

Did you go to these parties?
Yeah, of course.

# 	❝ I was very innovative when I was young. I knew I was doing stuff that was not the normal thing to do. ❞

What did you think?
It was great. All the pretty girls were there.

Did you find out about music from there as well?
Well I grew up to funk. But basically on the radio, where Electrifying Mojo was playing a lot of stuff that influenced my early years. Sometimes I'd just go in the record store and buy stuff based what the album looked like.

Electrifying Mojo inspired a lot of people. What made him different?
He owned his own show, he was in control of whatever he wanted to play. He didn't have a format imposed on him by the programme director. He was an individual, a personality. And quite a personality he was. He played a huge variety of music and exposed a people in Detroit to a lot of different things that they probably wouldn't have otherwise heard.

Like what?
He would play a half-hour of James Brown then turn around and play a half-hour of Jimi Hendrix and then turn around a play a half-hour of Peter Frampton, Parliament Funkadelic. You name it. He brought Prince here. First place I heard Kraftwerk. Believe it or not he'd play America, 'A Horse With No Name'.

Really?
Yeah [laughs], he'd place 'A Horse With No Name', stuff like that.

Where did his style come from?
Mojo was on the radio in Vietnam and when you ask him he'd say that's where he got his eclectic format. He had to play a variety of stuff to his soldiers in Vietnam. I can't remember what city he was in but it had something to do with that. In fact, he was in the Philippines. It must have been playing to all soldiers, that's where he got his strong host of Hendrix, Frampton, America.

Another guy who's famously a Vietnam vet is Rik Davis, your bandmate in Cybotron. How did you meet him?

I met him in my first year at community college. In one of my music courses. I brought my electronic demos to school and when I played 'em everybody wanted to hook up with me because they were so different. So wild. So Rik wanted to hook up with me and play music because he was an electronic musician like myself.

Did he play anything to you?
No, it was only at his house that I got to hear his stuff. He was much older than me, like 10 years and didn't bring anything in to college to show.

Did he have all kinds of tales from the war?
Yeah he had a couple of stories. He told me one time that him and a whole brigade went into the bush and he was the only one that survived. He saw stuff like that. All of his friends in the army got killed.

Was there something that made you click with one another?
I'm sure there was. There must have been for us to come together and put Cybotron together but what that thing was I can't quite put my finger on. There was definitely something. I was a kid though – 17. He was like a father figure to me. He taught me a lot. We didn't have so much in common. I was in awe with him. My father was in jail at the time.

> **❝ Jesse Saunders, Chip E, these guys started coming out with records at around the same time as Metroplex started. It was like a cultural exchange between Detroit and Chicago. ❞**

Techno is often seen as white music. Did you and Rik ever talk about race in relation to your music?
No. Why would we do talk about race? We talked about music, and race didn't come into it. I mean we knew we were black, and we were in America. There was nothing to talk about, those were our circumstances. We had a white guy in the band in fact. He played guitar, controlling the synth with his guitar. If you listen to records like 'The Line', 'Industrial Lies' and 'Enter', all of that guitar work was Jon 5. A lot of my core persuasion was funk music. That could be considered to be black music but we never said, 'Hey we're making black music.' No, we were making electronic music.

And then 'Clear' spent nine weeks on the black music chart!
Okay, well we knew we weren't making rock'n'roll. We were playing in someone's church and it wasn't rock'n'roll.

I guess that's where you and Rik went your separate ways, when he wanted to take it in a rock'n'roll direction.
I think that that was where his mind was. He was heavily, heavily Jimi Hendrix-influenced. You could call him Jimi Hendrix on the synthesiser. I think that was where he more wanted to be in that album-orientated rock.

Meanwhile you had these bubbling aspirations for Metroplex.
Yeah. I started Metroplex in order to release my sound. It was a continuation of the more funk, bass, electro-bass tracks.

You knew you were going to do that from a young age.
Yeah.

Did Cybotron help you realise Metroplex?
Yeah, for sure.

Hopping back a little bit, can we talk more about your relationship with Derrick?
Okay, well he came to live with us after high school. After 'Alleys Of Your Mind', 'Cosmic Cars'. Right around that time Derrick was very instrumental in helping me promote the records. I was living in Detroit with my grandmother and Derrick was living with us there.

Tell me how Deep Space came about.
Well it was the label that Rik and I released Cybotron out of, but then Derrick and I took the name and it became the sound company that we did parties under and it worked well for me and Derrick.

So you were back in Detroit. Did the move home effect what you thought about music?
Probably not.

Did it change the way you thought music should be heard? You started putting on parties.
Yeah but I don't think the move to Detroit changed something.

What were your parties like?
It was the same. It was only a couple of years after we were going to the parties; the only difference was we were now spinning the parties. Same mix of people, same crowd but this time we were DJing.

Did you play your own music?
Yeah – we played 'Alleys Of Your Mind', 'Cosmic Cars' and got a great response. Those records were huge. By then Mojo was playing the records, we were famous in Detroit.

How did Mojo get your records?
We gave them to him. He heard the demos of our stuff, and liked the demos and that was what really prompted us to play the records was that Mojo liked them. He was like 'I like it', and we went away and pressed it, took it back and he kept his word and played the records.

And did you think from then on things had changed?
No. But I loved the music, I was very confident but where we were going was a mystery to me. The thing is, Just 'cos I liked it didn't mean that another person on the planet had to like it. So I didn't know. I figured it was going to be good.

I don't think the record got the recognition it should have got. Actually. Because of different radio politics, it was hard to get a record distributed nationally in different cities in the States. It's not like the UK where you've got Radio 1 and everybody hears everything all at the same time. Especially during the early '80s when radio was fragmented. Now it's more across the board, if a record is big in New York it gets passed across the cities. Back then you had more personality style DJs and radio would sound different from city to city, you didn't have one radio station across the country. A record that was popular in Detroit might not necessarily even be heard in Chicago or Cleveland and vice versa. There'd be records that if you went on a road trip and you went to Chicago that you thought. 'Wow I never heard this record,' simply because it never made it to Detroit.

That sounds like another world now.
Yeah, yeah. Even before the internet in the last 10 years, I mean radio has become more centralised but back then it was more fragmented.

Had you ever left Detroit by then?
Well what happened was Derrick's parents had moved to Chicago but he was still in high school so he had to stay here to finish up his high school. But he would go there and he would tell these stories about the clubs and who he met and about the radio. And that was my first introduction to Chicago. By the time I started Metroplex he took some of my first records down there, my first copies of 'No UFO's' – my first release on Metroplex – and took it down there and gave it to Farley Jackmaster Funk and Farley broke that record over there and played it in his mix. Farley made it the biggest record in Chicago; Farley made it bigger than it was in Detroit.

Did you know about Chicago house?
Well, there wasn't any house at that time. There was nobody there making records in Chicago. I honestly believe our record… When Derrick went down there and gave it some of the guys like Jesse Saunders – which was kinda like the first house record – Chip E, these guys more or less started coming out with records at around the same time as Metroplex started. It was like a cultural exchange between Detroit and Chicago.

Clubs in Chicago were playing disco?
Yeah, mainly disco. I mean if you listen to some of the early Hot Mix 5 it was just a continuation of disco. A lot of the Hot Mix 5 mixes were Italo-disco tracks because Italians kept making disco records after 1981, and that was the stuff the Chicago boys were playing. And ultimately after that they started making their own stuff. But when you listened to the Hot Mix 5 mixes 80 percent of it was Italo disco.

So it was way more Italo than in New York?
Well New York was earlier. New York was West End, Prelude, Salsoul. All of that stuff fell to the wayside when disco left. They were the disco kings.

Was there any Italo being played in Detroit?
No. Detroit was a hick town compared to Chicago. We had the social club parties, where we heard a little bit of that. Not on the radio though.

❝ We just wanted to DJ. Our thing was about the music. Even to this day. We haven't hosted that many parties but we definitely wanted to DJ at as many we could. ❞

For people who were making music, were parties the thing to aim for? Did you want to become the tastemakers?
Yeah, but we didn't want to necessarily host our own parties, we just wanted to DJ. We didn't care who hosted the party. You know? Our thing was about the music and it's always been about the music. Even to this day. We haven't hosted that many parties but we definitely wanted to DJ at as many we could.

Ken Collier was the best-known club DJ in Detroit. And there was a party where you guys opened for him.
Yeah, that was very enlightening because he was the king. We learned a lot from Ken.

Did it seem like a big deal?
Yeah, there were stints when he had mixes on the radio during the disco era but when disco died they didn't want mixes anymore. But Ken was a main guy when they did have the mixes. He was an icon. We were honoured to play with him; we were glad that he wanted to play with a couple of unknown DJs.

What happened when you started to focus on producing music as Model 500?
I took a step back from DJing for a while. Derrick continued to DJ because he wasn't making music but when I started Metroplex I did take a step back for a few years. And then records got exported to the UK so I started back up then so I could go to Europe.

So you were inspired by a band from Europe, Kraftwerk, and you then found yourself going back over there.
Yeah. But you gotta remember that the electro thing had kicked of in Europe. 'Clear' and 'Techno City' were included on a set of *Essential Electro* compilations so it wasn't like it was the first time I was exposed to Europe.

Did you think about 'Techno City' as a Detroit export?
No, I had no idea that it was as big in the UK as it was.

Europe was maybe a bit more open to experimental electro. Do you think you added some soul to it?
I guess you could say that.

But is that what you'd say?
Erm, I guess you could say that.

You'd heard a lot of European stuff, like Kraftwerk, obviously, and Manuel Göttsching?
'E2-E4' was a great track. It was more on an ambient vibe. Like a summer breeze.

Not dance music
No.

There was something about your rhythms that turned this style into dance music.
Well my style was always dance music. I think that from the beginning everything I had done was very danceable. My first record 'Alleys Of Your Mind' was very danceable.

Did you always want to make dance music?
That's my forte.

© DJhistory.com

JUAN ATKINS SELECTED DISCOGRAPHY

CYBOTRON – Alleys Of Your Mind (writer/producer)
CYBOTRON – Cosmic Cars (writer/producer)
CYBOTRON – Clear (writer/producer)
CYBOTRON – Techno City (writer/producer)
X-RAY – Let's Go (remixer)
MODEL 500 – No UFO's (writer/producer)
JUAN – Techno Music (writer/producer)
TRIPLE XXX – The Bedroom Scene (producer/mixer)
NASA – Time To Party (Engineer/remixer)
MODEL 500 – Night Drive (Thru Babylon) (writer/producer)
KREEM – Triangle Of Love (writer/producer)
MODEL 500 – Testing 1-2 (writer/producer/mixer)
INNER CITY – Big Fun (remixer)
THE BELOVED – Your Love Takes Me Higher (remixer)
DR ROBERT & KYM MAZELLE – Wait (remixer)
MODEL 500 – Interference (writer/producer)
VISIONS – Is This Real? (producer)
INNER CITY – Good Life (remixer)
3MB FEATURING JUAN ATKINS – Die Kosmischen Kuriere (writer/producer)
JACOB'S OPTICAL STAIRWAY – The Fusion Formula (producer)

RECOMMENDED LISTENING

VARIOUS – Techno! The New Dance Sound Of Detroit
MODEL 500 – Classics

" It's about combining the elements of emotion and technology together. **"**

Derrick May
Hi-tech soul

Interviewed by Bill and Frank in Knightsbridge, Aug 30, 2004

The story of Detroit techno is a tale of dislocation. If you're a stroppy black kid growing up in the soul city of Motown, what better musical rebellion than to fall in love with eerie European synthesisers? Forced to summarise the Belleville Three it would go like this: if Juan is the musician and visionary, and Kevin the traveller (he'd seen New York's dancefloors in action), then Derrick May is the energy source. And he burns bright. Starting as a self-confessed square in thrall to the streetwise Atkins, Derrick was Juan's relentless promoter, driving his records over to Chicago and reporting back on the exciting club scene there. Only after an extended apprenticeship did he turn his hand to production, but when he did the results were phenomenal. After filling up a laundry basket with cassette scribbles, in quick succession he gave us the soaring uplift of 'Strings Of Life', and the chilly angles of 'Nude Photo' which blew away the past with its alien mathematics.

It's Carnival weekend and Derrick is in London to DJ for a Faith boat party. We start by grabbing something to eat. As the Lebanese snacks are gathered to take back to the hotel Derrick offers a commentary on the various female forms that enter his field of vision. Meanwhile, he's having a protracted, often heated conversation with someone in Detroit about the city's techno festival. Girls are never far from his mind and his phone is never far from his ear. Back at the hotel we drink wine in a deserted basement bar, where Derrick provides an epic three hours of energetic conversation.

So Derrick, your life, everything. Are you ready?
Everything? Fuck you! Yeah, I'm ready. Go ahead.

Radio was your biggest influence?
Yeah. We certainly heard the Electrifying Mojo on the radio, which changed our lives. Mojo was on the radio every night. He used to land the mothership, he used to use the intro to *Close Encounters,* and then he'd land the mothership, play some Jimi Hendrix, then he'd bump into Funkadelic, then he'd come out with some Prince. Play whatever. Some psychedelic cool stuff, some funky stuff though. And all these were defining moments in what we did.

When I heard my first really funky records it would be... Kraftwerk, Cameo. The first really strange shit I got attached to was hearing Michael Henderson 'Wide Receiver', The Bar-Kays. Those were the first records that really made me realise that something was different. So radio was definitely important, yes.

Back in your early childhood Detroit was still quite a lively city wasn't it?
When I was a kid I do remember there being a lot more business on all the avenues, in all the local areas. There were small businesses, family businesses, a shoe-store, a fabric store. And people walked on the street a little bit more than they do now. It seems like Detroit had went through the worst in the period during Reaganomics. Apparently not true, because Detroit is going through an even worse stage now.

....

The normal story of a kid growing up in the suburbs is that the city has a real pull. Did Detroit not ever have that for you?
I lived in the city until I was 13. And then we went out to the suburbs for three or four years, then we moved back. Those four years were probably the most defining years of my life. There's always this misconception of where we grew up. I mean we weren't country boys. We weren't from small town Belleville. We moved to Belleville, all for different reasons.

You were black city kids living in a white suburb. What was that like?
It was interesting. I remember the first day of school. We went to sit down for lunch. If you just imagine this massive lunch-room with all these lunch tables. And I had spent all summer long getting to know the kids in my complex, and they were mostly white kids. Troy was my best buddy all summer. I'm right behind him, and I got my lunch, I went and I sat down with Troy. And I'll never forget it, because all the white kids at that table looked at me. They gave me this really strange look. So I noticed it, but Troy didn't. But then a black kid came up, and he looked at me and said, 'Hey man, why you sitting up here with all the honkies?'
    And I looked at him and I said, *'The honkies?!'*
    Then a school teacher came up to me and said, 'You should be sitting back there.'

No! For real?
He said, 'How come you're not sitting back there?' In a nice way. But he asked. The third day one of the black kids was in line, he said, 'Hey man, come sit with us.' So we went and sat with these black kids, in the very back of the lunchroom in the corner. Every single person at these four tables was black. And the other 40 tables were all white kids. And these black kids, they would stand up and throw French fries at each other, and just scream obscenities, back and forth, and it was a culture shock for me. It blew me away. I had never experienced voluntary segregation. And I think that changed me. That was a defining moment in my life, because it put me... it made me feel outside who I thought I was.

> ❝ Juan, myself and Kevin, we come from middle class, upper middle class families, so most of the people we associated with were upper middle class to very rich. ❞

Is it fair to say you were a loner or an outsider?
I was. And I pitied these people. I sat back there with them for the rest of the year with pure disgust. I found myself entertained by my own people. I felt like, 'This is fucked up.' And I made a promise to myself that I was going to be better than that.

How did you meet Kevin [Saunderson]?
We came together through sports. We played together on the teams.

And you and Juan [Atkins] met through music.
Juan and I came together from his brother Aaron. Originally it was because Juan played chess, and I played chess.

How did you bond with Aaron then, if you were friends with him before Juan?
Aaron used to tell me he had a car. I didn't believe him, then one day he shows up, 13 years old, at my front door, with a Fleetwood Cadillac [laughter]. Know what I mean? Big red crushed velvet, Aaron was chillin' man. He had the Funkadelic pumpin' through the sound system, he let the windows down, it was almost like a Cheech and Chong movie: out comes this big thing of weed smoke. And it's, 'We love to funk you Funkenstein, your funk is the best...' I was like, wow! This music, this car, this guy! He took me for a ride and it changed my life.

....

And you met Juan through a cassette tape?
Juan, he was basically an introverted guy. He used to play his bass guitar, without an amp, everywhere he went. Just sitting there in the kitchen, just plucking. Juan never really left the house much. He loved people, but he was really just a quiet guy. He would pluck-pluck and write, pluck-pluck and write. He wrote his lyrics, he wrote his own notes. His dream from the age of 12 was to be a musician. He knew what he was going to be. He told me when he was 16 years old he was going to make a label called Metroplex.

First time we met he looks at me and he instantly doesn't like me. Because I'm a complete square. I mean these guys come from another side of town. They've come up another way. I'm just a square kid who likes to play baseball, watch cartoons. I believe everything my mother tells me. Then some years on we became, not exactly friends, somewhat acquainted through playin' chess and through me coming to the house every day.

I left a cassette tape at Juan's house by mistake, and Juan apparently used it. And I said, 'Can I have my tape back?' And he said to me, 'Well listen man, to be honest with you there's some shit on the tape you're not gonna like. Let me just give you another tape.' But I said, 'No give it back to me I want my tape.' And what was on the tape? Giorgio Moroder, some early Tangerine Dream. It was completely psychedelic. When I went back and told him I liked the music, that's when we became friends. And I became his protégé. From that day on.

How quickly did you two start DJing together?
Immediately. During the next couple of months.

How old were you?
Fifteen. We decided to call our company Deep Space Soundworks. We weren't great. Juan was my teacher and Juan wasn't the greatest DJ in the world.

Where did that name come from? It's quite techno.
Juan. It's his thing. His first record label that they put Cybotron on, was also called Deep Space, in 1980. It was all part of his thought process, where he was at.

Was DJing a serious thing, or just a hobby? Did you get gigs?
Not until we were like about 17. Our first gigs were for local promoters. See in Detroit we had a really developed scene. Unlike any other city. I've never seen it anywhere in the world, the way we did it in Detroit.

The high school parties?
The high school scene was amazing. All the young high school kids would dress really nice, you had guys wearing Polo, and Versace, and all this ridiculous stuff in high school. It was amazing how much money these parties were making. People were charging $25 to get into the parties.

So where were these kids getting their money?
Well, keep in mind, this is important. Juan, myself and Kevin, we come from middle class, upper middle class families, so most of the people we associated with were upper middle class to very rich, black people. There was no abject poverty around us.

So socially these parties were very exclusive?
They were highfalutin'. Teenage kids with money.

And was it racially mixed?
Yes it was. Most of the black kids who would come to our parties were at private schools. Girls from the Mercy school. At that time it was a $10,000-a year school. There was a whole social element involved in it.

It sounds very much like a fashion scene.
It was. It was very posey.

So was the music important or just a soundtrack?
It was very important, because if the mix was not right, if the DJ had a bad mix, they would

not dance. Jeff Mills, myself, Delano Smith, Mike Clark, we all come from that scene. We were all part of that high school scene. Because those kids were our guinea pigs for the music.

What were you playing?
We played anything from Thompson Twins' 'In The Name Of Love' to 'Call Me Mr Telephone' [by Answering Service], to 'Capricorn' by Capricorn. We debuted 'Cosmic Cars', one of Juan's records, at one of those parties. We played Risk 'Loving the Music', 'Feel The Drive' by Doctor's Cat...

So there were all these high school parties with names taken from European fashion magazines: Charivari, Gables. Where did you fit in?
They were the establishment and we were fighting against them. There was a competitive company called Direct Drive, and we hated those motherfuckers. Because they played this prissy disco music. We hated prissy disco music. We were playin' a lot of new wave stuff though, too. You would call it new romantic. We played The Plastics, the Japanese group Diamond Head. We played the B52's. We played that at parties, people would be tripping.

And you and Juan were getting pretty deep about the music you played.
Music was becoming our common denominator. We would just sit in his bedroom and analyse records. We would just put on a piece of music and try to figure out what that person was thinking when they made that record. And this would just be our days: full-blown. We also had a pair of turntables, this crappy mixer that we borrowed, and we would sit in Juan's bedroom, with these few records and just mix them over and over again. Constantly mix the same records.

You were really intellectualising it. You're not hearing records in clubs; you're hearing them on a radio or at home, and talking about them. That must have changed the way you saw music.
That's exactly what it did. It changed the way we saw and felt it. Because for us it wasn't a vocal record we would analyse. It was always an instrumental. And there wasn't that much instrumental shit out back then, so we were really caught up. Like we heard Manuel Göttsching ['E2-E4'], and we just listened to that shit for hours man: days, weeks, to try to like figure out what somebody was thinking.

Did you reach any conclusions?
That that person was deep, or that person was thinking about some politics. I just know it helped me develop a sense of conscience, of direction, of where I thought you needed to be to pull this shit off.

How would you come across records like the Manuel Göttsching?
We only had a cassette of it from the radio. Juan was in New York and he heard some DJ play it on a mix. And he recorded it. We would just talk, until both of us fell asleep. And we did this for years. It was what we did: analyse people's tracks.

Did that connect with your DJing?
Completely. I learned that there's always once upon a time in a record. Make sure the story has a beginning, a middle, and an ending. I listen to music now it's like one long breakdown. It taught me that consciously you have to give this a story. You have to give it some sort of sense of purpose.

What was the pull of instrumental music in particular?
We were just anti-vocal. We just thought the vocals were stupid. Talking about love and gettin' some pussy and you broke my heart [a bored sigh]. Oh, this is ridiculous – nothing political, nothing conscious.

Now Chicago. Chicago was a huge influence, right?
Oh yeah. I used to drive to Chicago. And Juan didn't care for Chicago. He thought the whole Chicago house music scene was gay. Juan was like, not with it, at all.

How did you hear about the scene there?
I drove up to Chicago to visit my mom. My mother had moved there from Belleville – I

moved in with Kevin's family so I could finish the school year out in Belleville. And it was an amazing visit. I remember getting in from the train, and the very first thing I heard on the radio – now this is at midday, mid-fuckin'-day, my mom has the radio on, it's low, casual volume, nothing big – 'Feel The Drive' is playing! I never heard that muhfucker before: 'You must feel the drive' [hums it].

So it was a revelation to hear that kind of music in a mainstream setting.
Yeah, because Juan at that time had already made his Cybotron records, and we were trying to figure out how to get them played. See, there was a period when Juan thought that there was this vast ocean and in it was him, in a rowboat with no oars. And there was no help in sight. He had this creative brilliant idea and there was nobody out there to share it with and no-one would ever understand him. He wouldn't be saved. And when I heard this shit, it was like a beacon. It was like a lifeboat.

How did you discover the Chicago clubs?
My mother lived in a really nice area, so I just started walking, and I found a record shop called Gramaphone. And somebody tells me about another called Imports Etc. and every time you walk in you'd hear a record playing, maybe 'Time To Jack' by Chip E, or Jesse Saunders, and that's how I discovered all this music. And this is how I learned about Frankie Knuckles. People would say, 'Frankie's playing the hell out of this, you gotta have that.' No other description.

And that was enough.
Yeah, booom, outta there. Or Ronnie is playing this, and you must have this. Who is Ronnie? Who is Frankie? Finally the people working there told me where to go to hear them play. And being the young kid that I was I didn't have any friends in Chicago, I just went by myself. I went to the Power Plant.

> **❝ I exploded, I just fucking lost it. I was right there in the Music Box with them kids, jumpin' screaming dancing, every week. I was shirt off, going nuts, grabbing girls. ❞**

What was it like?
It lifted me off my feet. I was elevated. I can't explain to you any better than that. The party would go till dawn. You paid 15 bucks to get in, and you'd hear Frankie Knuckles, and he was nothing like he is now. He was unbelievable. He played Front 242, he played Frankie Goes to Hollywood, he played disco, he played Chip E, he played all this music.

And then I finally heard Ronnie. And this time, I wasn't elevated; this time I was flat-out fuckin' busted down. I was beat up. I couldn't believe it. Frankie was my man, I loved him, he set me up for life, but it was Ronnie that moved me to the ultimate level of knowing that I could do this shit. He is the one who made me realise that my teachings from being around Juan, from growing up in Belleville, from listening to that cassette, from listening to my stepfather's record collection, and learning how to pause button with Juan, and always wondering what the future was, and contemplating people's music, it all came under this one basic raw element that this motherfucker right here had painted on my face. First, he painted it out simply: it's all in your soul. Just whatever you feel, just let it out. And I exploded, I just fucking lost it.

And I was right there in the Music Box with them kids, jumpin' screaming dancing, every week. I was shirt off, going nuts, grabbing girls and freaking with girls. And I brought all my friends there. I brought Kevin Saunderson there. And Kevin made a record called 'Bounce Your Body To The Box'. It just changed everybody's life.

Did you hook up with any of the kids who were producing these tracks?

I actually sold Frankie Knuckles a 909. Everybody was producing music in Chicago, nobody had a 909, I had an extra one. So I took it to Chicago, I needed money, I had two – and I should'na had two to begin with. And Juan said, 'Don't do it!' And this was when they had made their first records. I think Chip E had made 'Time To Jack' and Steve Hurley had made 'Jack Your Body', And Juan said, 'Man, that was the biggest mistake you ever made.'

Did going to the clubs in Chicago give you an impetus for making music?
Going to the clubs in Chicago, and also hanging out with Ken Collier. Ken Collier was easily one of the top DJs I've ever heard in my life. Him and Ron had this similar style of mixing. Ken was a drop mix kind of guy, and to drop a mix is harder than blending. When you drop a mix, that shit has to hit. 'Cos if you fuck it up, it's dry. When you drop a mix it's like an explosion.

When was the first time you saw Ken Collier?
It was our first gig worth anything. We were known as guys who played weird music. But cool music. Now there was a period in Detroit where people had lawn parties, at night. You charge 15 or 20 bucks for people to come in to the house, at affluent houses in affluent neighbourhoods. This one promoter, Darryl Tiggs, he didn't have no nicest houses, he had some fucked-up houses in the middle of nowhere. But he played all kind of crazy music. He called his parties the Pink Poodles.

So basically we solicit Darryl for several months to let us play one of his parties. And he said, 'Okay I'll let you guys warm up for Ken Collier.' So we ended up showing up at this party at a place downtown called Downstairs Pub. The turntable was already set up and we didn't have slipmats, we didn't know what the fuck a slipmat was. We had the rubber mats on. So we're playing shit like 'Trans Europe Express', all this stuff. He had this really black, kinda cool crowd, they're standing around, drinking their drinks, not one fucking person is dancing. We're playing the Bus Boys, and all that kind of shit. Muhfuckers are not dancing.

Ken Collier arrives, and this is the first time we ever met the man. He's about six foot two, husky fellow, had on this big be-bop leather jacket. He walks in with his record crates, he has people carrying them for him, and he takes out a record and he takes our slipmats off, and he puts on a real slipmat. He pops his record on. 'Double Dutch Bus' [by Frankie Smith]. Fuckin' place went off. In ten seconds the whole floor was full.

> **❝ I made about 300 pieces of music. I put them all on cassette. I had this basket, what most people put dirty clothes in, it was all cassettes. To the brim. All these first versions of things. ❞**

Was he getting the same kinds of records as the guys in Chicago?
No, he was just getting records from the record pool. And Ken wasn't really interested. He just had his own sound. He was very much into a gay funky sound. He was very much into ESG, that was his thing. He wasn't into mellow records, he was into uptempo music. He'd look for obscure shit, but it had to be funky. If it had a vocal he was pretty happy with that too. Ken was a big Sylvester fan.

Where do you think Detroit's love for Europe came from. The European clothes, Italian names?
It was really the fact that people were informed at a young age, from like GQ magazine, fashion magazines. It seemed cool. It looked cool – isn't that strange, though?

It's not that hard to understand. It's the same fascination Britain has for black America.
It's what you can't touch. It's what you want to get into.

It's so different from your own experience that it's fascinating.
The difference was, if the kids at Charivari, if they had met people that actually looked like that, if they had gone to Cannes, France, and ran into some guy looking that way, they would have been very disappointed. But it seemed cool, and it gave a lot of these kids another level to reach. The Italian music was also very good. Klein & MBO, all the Capricorn stuff. I was the one who brought it back to Detroit. Nobody had it.

You had to go to Chicago for the Italo stuff?
Yeah. That's what gave me my edge. There was only one store in Detroit: Professional Records. Everyone went to the same shop and bought the same records, basically. And they were all very competitive. I don't think there were too many places in the country at the time that had 15, 16 year old DJs getting paid for it.

There was also a ton of British synth pop in the US charts around 1983.
For us that was sweet. We loved that shit. There was a time when Depeche Mode sold out stadiums the size of Wembley, in the States. I though Ultravox were very important. And there was a record called 'Transdance' from a group called Night Moves, and I'm sure to this day it was David Bowie, just fuckin' around.

But Italy was where it was at. And there was a period when the Italy thing dried up, and that was when we got really serious about music. It was, I think, right between the point where Italy dried up and Farley and those guys made their first records. Farley became king with his first records.

So what pushed you into the studio?
I went back to Detroit, and had a real culture shock, going to high school with black kids again. I had gotten some great offers to run track in university. But I just didn't have discipline. I sort of drifted. I ended up living with my grandfather some days, some days I'd live with Juan and his grandparents, because Juan had also moved back to Detroit. And we had lost contact with Kevin at that time, 'cos he was in Belleville, and there was this period where it was just myself and Juan again. And Juan and I were really close.

Obviously Juan was making records already.
Juan wouldn't let me touch the keyboard. I was like his protégé, basically. Just told me to sit back and watch. I was his promoter, I was his cheerleader, I would go around and support and tell people in record shops. I took the first 45s of 'Alleys Of Your Mind' to record shops and tried to get it played. I got us a meeting with Mojo. That's how Juan's career took off.

So how did you come to break away from Juan and do it yourself?
I didn't really make my first record until 'Nude Photo', because Juan wouldn't let me. I had my keyboards, I had everything, borrowed stuff from him, but I didn't know how to use it, so I had to teach myself. Just ended up spending the next year of my life hibernating, and every single day working until I developed this thing. I didn't turn on the radio. Didn't turn on Mojo at all. I didn't turn on the TV at all. I barely even wore clothes. I ate nothing but cereal, and just basically went inside.

Did you make any tracks along the way?
No, no. I didn't let anybody hear it, I didn't ask anybody's opinion. I made about 300 pieces of music. I put them all on cassette. I had this basket, what most people put dirty clothes in, it was all cassettes. To the brim. All these first versions of things

Finally this kid called Tom Barnett brought me this track he wanted to do, which was terrible. But he had the money to put the record out. So I said leave it with me overnight and I'll come up with something. So what I did is I made 'Nude Photo', and he brought me by something that had a bassline that sounded like New Order 'Blue Monday'. Basically I thought it was wack. So I did 'Nude Photo', and then I did 'The Dance'. I did 'Move It', in one night.

I actually had almost done a complete version of 'Strings Of Life' before I released 'Nude Photo', but I was afraid... First I didn't know how to out a record out. I had to go back to Juan. Secondly, I didn't understand what I had done.

....

In terms of what?
I was… frightened. It scared me, that piece of music.

You knew that it was great from word go? Or were you scared that it wasn't?
All I thought was, 'What have I done?' When it was finished I hit the sequencer and it played, and it was like a carnival [hums the melody], like a real playschool sound. It was reminding me of my childhood. And then I finally added the orchestration to it and it scared me. I listened to it for 24 hours, really low. I slept to it. I woke up to it, because I hadn't finished it. I didn't put the drums or the piano to it yet, just added the orchestration. It freaked me out, so I couldn't finish it.

It took me six months to put out 'Strings of Life'. I had Mike James' weird piano parts to it. He had done his piano a year before, but not for my song. I just ended up running across a piece of it, I chopped it and looped it on top of my orchestration, and it worked perfect. Then, Juan had showed me the fundamentals of editing, but this guy Jay Dixon did the edits. And boy did he do the edits: the kind of edits that make or break a great song. Timely edits, exactly where they should be. That's why I never want to remix it. Because it's not just a song that's been mixed; it's a song that's been *choreographed*.

Why did you want to cut yourself off from other music?
Because Juan and I had always thought the outside influence was the worst influence when you're trying to create something.

But you can never completely escape your history and your influences. And there are certain things that work on the dancefloor and certain things that don't.
I don't think about the dancefloor when I make a track. I don't know if that is obvious or not.

When you made your first record, what was your ambition?
My first ambition was to take it to Chicago. Then get Ron Hardy and Frankie to play it. I thought if those guys played my record, I made it. I'm a hero. And I didn't get a chance to take it to Chicago, so I gave it to my friend Al [Alton] Miller. And I remember Al calling me up. 'Man you're not gonna believe this. Ron Hardy played your records four times in a row.'

Was that 'Strings of Life' or 'Nude Photo'?
I think it was 'The Dance'.

How did you see the music you were making?
Soundtracks to everyday life.

The themes of futurology and the decay of Detroit are big in Juan's first records. Were those ideas in your head as well when you were first making music?
I became completely anti-establishment. I got to the stage where my mother couldn't even talk to me. I became a hater of politics, a hater of anything that was conforming. I hated reactionaries, I hated the whole idea of being a conservative. I hated the whole idea of walking the planet oblivious. Reagan was president, it was a fucked up time. Detroit was all fucked up, depressed, people were out of work, a lot of young black men were in prison for shit they didn't do. I didn't have any money, didn't really have any particular vision or goal. It made me angry. It made me passionate to a point where the shit came out in the music. I tended to see my music more like a political thing. Like a message.

If they had lyrics, what would the message be?
They would have been records about the future, making reference to what kind of future we might have. You know, shit like that, making reference to somehow saving the world.

Did you see it having a link to the Detroit music of the past?
No. I didn't disrespect the Detroit music from the past, but I just never made… In Europe you can hear classics on the radio; in Detroit you never heard Motown music anywhere. You wouldn't go to a bar and hear those old songs. I think the most recent generation of kids don't know anything about Motown. They don't even know that Motown is Detroit.

What did you think when all these UK journalists came knocking, telling you you were great?
Blew me away. Didn't believe it. Didn't quite know how to handle it. We used to read *NME*, we learned about European records from *NME* reviews. And I remember saying it would be a dream to be in this magazine one day.

And when Neil Rushton [of Kool Kat and Network Records] called up about releasing your records in the UK?
Neil called and I couldn't understand him, 'cos he has that strong Brummie accent. He said, 'I'd like to bring you to England to meet some people.'
  'Great!'
  But then he called me back, he said 'I can't pay your way.' So I had to make a decision: was I going to buy my own plane ticket or was I gonna not go at all and possibly miss this opportunity? Juan said don't do it. Kevin said pay for it. So I went.

What was the first time you heard the word 'techno' used for your music?
Juan said it. Stuart Cosgrove asked him what do you call this music? He had just done a massive interview for *the Face* magazine. We were supposed to be the front cover, and they needed a phrase. They spent three days with us. John McCready came over too, writing for the *NME*. This was huge to have those guys fly over.

> ❝ Juan said, 'We call it techno'. I said don't say that. I'd kept begging him for the past year not to call this music techno. To me techno was that bullshit coming from Miami. ❞

This is when the compilation was coming out on Virgin [in 1988]?
Right. We didn't understand how huge it really was. So we had a great time with them. We took them to places, we showed them the city, and they got so emotional about it. They didn't know Detroit was ruined like that. Stuart was making reference to loving Motown; these guys had a true admiration for the city, for what had happened to it, they were shocked. Juan said, 'We call it techno'. I said don't say that. I'd kept begging him for the past year not to call this music techno. He said, 'Naw man, this is techno.' To me techno was that bullshit coming from Miami. I didn't want to be associated with it. I thought it was ugly, some ghetto bullshit. I actually wanted to call this music high-tech soul, from the very beginning. That's what I thought it should have been called. But nobody liked it, so...

Where did Juan get 'techno' it from?
'Technology'

There's an earlier *NME* article where you're happy to be called 'Detroit house'.
Yeah. That must have been the first article I had ever done.

And originally, the album was going to be called *The House Sound Of Detroit*.
We all sat down with Neil and decided what it should be called. Detroit music is not house music.

Was that a way of differentiating yourself from Chicago?
Completely. We respected them and loved them but we also had to identify with us, not them.

It's quite an irony that a lot of your music was recorded on quite low-tech equipment.
Yeah extremely. 'Strings Of Life' was done on a cassette. I never even mastered it to another format. Did it on cassette, up till today. I still have the cassette.

And around the same time you started a club for this music. What was the impetus for doing the Music Institute?
It wasn't my idea. I wanted to do a club but never had enough dedication to pull it off. My

friend George Baker did it, with Alton Miller and Anthony – Chez Damier. When it happened it was unbelievable. We all got involved in it after that. I got this girl from London, Sarah Gregory – she was married to the guy from Heaven 17 – I got her over to do a massive mural on the walls. We put in an amazing sound system in there, pin spots, and just went for it. It was beautiful, man; we had everybody, even Depeche Mode in there one time. It was a juice bar, we had the fresh juices up in the back.

Kevin and myself started travelling back and forth to London, so we're bringing all this music back, plus we had all the Chicago music, and we had the Detroit stuff, so we blew people away.

And you were resident?
Yeah. Friday nights. It was open two nights a week. Anthony played on Saturdays but nobody would come. They played traditional house and disco, Detroit people weren't into that.
I was playin house music: Chicago, London, underground music. I played 'We Call It Acieeed' [by D-Mob] a week after it came out. I made that Friday night historic. I played 'French Kiss' [by Lil Louis] three days off the press. Broke it in Detroit. Played it so much it became plaster on the walls.

> **❝ Techno's not black, as far as the music business is concerned: 'It won't last, it's just a phenomenon, don't worry, it'll go away. I don't think we should waste any time on this.' ❞**

Who were the kids who were coming? Did they have a history from high school days?
Yeah. It was everybody. We had a line around the corner. It was 25 bucks to get in, and we're talking 1988. It was only open a year and a half. People think it was open longer.

Why so short lived?
Because myself and Kevin, we got busy with our work. Inner City [Kevin's band] took off. All of a sudden I started getting offers to come play in Europe. I was getting remixes, stuff like that here. I got infatuated with England; I couldn't leave. The last record to ever get played in the Music Institute was my 'Sueno Latino' remix 'cos it came out that week. I remember people were crying on the dancefloor when the last record was played. In tears, in big tears.

Could you define techno? Is it about the purity of how it's made?
It's about combining the elements of emotion and technology together. Many, many years ago I played a party and I never forget, the boys came to the front. All the lads, every single one of them, and I noticed that the girls got pushed away. And I realised that if this music went in the wrong direction it would be something that only guys would like. I remember the way guys ran to the front, on the first tough-house records, from Todd Terry. Anything that had a synthetic snare or kick-drum sound, anything that wasn't organic, the guys just ran to it, and the girls simply got exed out.

What was your inspiration for putting out your own records? Over here we'd had punk to show the way, but how did Juan go about getting it together.
Juan just decided there was no company, in America especially, and we couldn't see beyond America, he just thought that there was no company in this country that's going to put this music out from a young black artist. And all we could do was imagine it coming out on a major label. We didn't know there was any other process.

By necessity.
Right, so Juan bought the book *This Business Of Music* and we all bought a copy of it and learned the business. Followed Juan's lead. I helped him shift and deliver records, that's the

way I learned. I picked up where he left off. Transmat's still going to this day.

Your music is so intimately connected with Detroit. How did it feel to see it selling mostly in Europe?
Made you angry, pissed off. When we put out our first records we sold thousands in the states. We sold tons of records to Chicago and tons in Detroit. Our record 'Nude Photo' was on the radio, regular FM daytime radio. In Chicago, The Hot Mix 5, if they played your record you sold thousands, period. Now nobody even knows of Hot Mix 5 in Chicago, house music doesn't sell. BMX and GCI play nothing but hip hop and contemporary music all day long. It's like it never happened.

Do you think one of the reasons that radio stations didn't like it is because it's the first black musical form in America that broke with black tradition? If you listen to house you can hear the clear parallels with disco, but with techno, although it was clearly influenced by some black elements, it also was very European as far as the music industry was concerned.
It's not black, as far as the music business is concerned: 'It won't last, it's just a phenomenon, it's just a thing, don't worry, it'll go away. I don't think we should waste any time on this. Let's monitor it and watch what happens' – all of that shit. I think it just got to the point where they realised it was not going away, and they would pick it up on the second wave, which is what they did. They got Moby.

How important has the UK been to you?
Tony Wilson made a comment years ago at the New Music Seminar, he brought his group Happy Mondays with him. I was on the panel with Marshall Jefferson and a couple of other guys. It was full. He said that without England this music never would have happened. And I remember that Marshall stood up and got offended. And people started booing.

What do you think now though?
I believe that without England this music would not have happened – to a degree. The diving board was Detroit, the pool that it dived into would be England.

Definitely Britain first?
Britain is the home of pop culture. The cesspool of that shit.

Seeing the way it was received, did that change the way you approached it?
It gave the music and us market value. Which changed the way we saw the music, and what we saw the music was worth.

Do you think that techno is first and foremost dance music, and secondly it's the other kind of stuff that surrounds it. The techno culture.
An owner of a record shop in Chicago told me, 'I've got people coming in here and I don't know how to describe this music, I don't know if they should dance to it on a dancefloor or if they should take it home and waltz.' It was never really defined as to where it was supposed to go. We never defined it. We didn't know anything. I still think today we don't know what we did. I don't think until we're old men, we're out of the business, we'll sit back and fully understand this whole picture.

....

People make techno all over the world now, in all sorts of different flavours. What marks out the style you started?
Straight up driving Detroit melancholy techno music.

You threw in the word 'melancholy' as if it was a requirement. What do you mean by that?
I used to ride through Detroit in the middle of the night. And I just want to cry when I look at this place. I've always said it's like the Titanic above water. Like this big vessel that's just deteriorated: all these steam pipes against the moon, all these massive factories that were just dormant. Like the guy says, 'Detroit has been demolished by neglect.' I just feel pain for that, man. And it just comes out. It was always my motivation.

© DJhistory.com

DERRICK MAY SELECTED DISCOGRAPHY

RHYTHIM IS RHYTHIM – Nude Photo (writer/mixer)
RHYTHIM IS RHYTHIM – Strings Of Life (writer/producer/mixer)
R-TYME – Illusion (writer/producer)
A GUY CALLED GERALD – FX (remixer)
R-TYME – R Theme (writer/producer)
SUENO LATINO – Sueno Latino (remixer)
ANNETTE – Dream 17 (remixer)
REESE & SANTONIO – Rock To The Beat (remixer)
INNER CITY – Good Life (remixer)
RHYTHIM IS RHYTHIM – It Is It What It Is (producer/mixer)
BANG THE PARTY – Release Your Body (remixer)
DA POSSE – Searchin' Hard (remixer)
RHYTHIM IS RHYTHIM – Beyond The Dance (writer/producer)
RHYTHIM IS RHYTHIM – The Beginning (writer/producer/mixer)
DE-LITE – Wild Times (remixer)
YELLO – The Race (remixer)
CHEZ DAMIER – Can You Feel It (remixer)
RHYTHIM IS RHYTHIM – Kaotic Harmony (writer/producer)
SYSTEM 7 & DERRICK MAY – Mysterious Traveller (producer/mixer)
COSMIC TWINS – Solar Flare (writer/producer)

RECOMMENDED LISTENING

VARIOUS – Relics: A Transmat Compilation
VARIOUS – Mix-Up Volume 5 (DJ mix)
VARIOUS – Heartbeat Presents Mixed by Derrick May (DJ mix)

" I grew up wanting to go beyond the barriers of Detroit. "

Jeff Mills
Detroit wizard

Interviewed by Frank in London, February 17, 2005

'The Wizard' is no exaggeration. The way Jeff Mills plays records is supernatural. With three decks, slipping tracks on and off, playing little snatches, longer grooves, segments, samples, hints. Not flustered and frantic like a turntablist, but smooth, adding momentum, always pushing things forward. The effect is mesmerising. Jeff Mills is known as a second-generation Detroit techno producer, making tracks in the wake of Juan, Derrick and Kevin's first brave records, and releasing quintessential Detroit techno on his labels Axis and Underground Resistance, the militant-minded imprint he launched with long-time collaborator Mike Banks.

Mill's importance to Detroit goes far beyond this, however, as he was a fixture on the city's airwaves as early as 1982. Mills ruled Detroit radio with a blaze of hip hop and other fresh sounds, thrown down in the style of his heroes D.ST, Jazzy Jeff and Cash Money. He stayed at the station all day and would be called into the studio at a moment's notice to whisk up a live remix of the latest club hit. His three-hour show developed to the point where as well as re-editing tracks he made his own music for broadcast. We meet in the wood-panelled bar of a refined London hotel. Drinking just water, he's scrupulous in the way he answers questions, and keeps control of the situation by taping it himself on an iPod he places on the table.

You come from a musical family?
I come from a big family, four sisters and a brother. There's bound to be someone who's going to pick up an instrument.

You played the cornet.
The trumpet, the cornet. It was quite common in Detroit for any family to have some instruments in the house: a guitar or a piano.

Did you get into DJing early on?
Early for Detroit. Compared to New York, reasonably late, but say for the Detroit area, yeah.

How old were you when you got your first set of decks?
About 19 or 20

And very quickly you started playing in clubs?
No. First couple of years it was mainly practising at home and I would offer my services as a DJ for home parties, but I never got hired.

What kind of music were you first playing?
It was funk, dance, more Euro electronic type, electro boogie type of music. And then bass station came from Miami and the west coast. Egyptian Lover and those kind of things. Industrial music, industrial dance, a mixture.

Where were you hearing all this?
On the radio, that was where we got our information about new music. On Mojo's show. There was another station called WLVS and they were the first station to bring in young DJs off the

street, so they had mix shows long before I got on the radio. It was stuff that was happening in New York. Friends of mine that I knew from the street, 14-, 15-year-old kids, were on. A guy named Delano Smith, a guy named Daryl Shannon, Kevin Diezard. They were real successful mobile DJs, they were really, really influential and popular at that time so they used to do mix shows on WLVS. It was them for a short time and then Mojo for most of the time.

So you're getting music from all over.
That was an alternative station playing mix shows and Mojo was on an R&B and funk station, and then the rock stations were playing more derivatives of rock, more dance punk, more electronic stuff like Kraftwerk, B52's, 'Frequency 7' from Visage.

Where were you hearing the real industrial stuff, the Front 242 and Nitzer Ebb?
Generally on rock stations. They weren't playing classic rock, even they were playing grey area type of music.

As a DJ were you looking to New York, to hip hop styles?
Back then there weren't any magazines, so you would hear about what Grandmaster Flash had did the previous weekend, or D.ST, by word of mouth.

So who were your DJ heroes at that time?
Grandmaster Flash, Jazzy Jeff, Cash Money, Red Alert, Marley Marl, Mr Magic.

Were you hearing mix tapes as well?
No. It was really hard to get mix tapes. Unless you could go to New York and tape radio stations like WBLS. It was very much a New York thing. You would hear it from your older brothers and sisters who knew someone who went to New York.

Your friends who got on the radio, were they playing a similar style?
No. By the time I reached the radio the city of Detroit had many different types of DJs. We had hip hop DJs which is what I was mainly known for, playing basically street music, more bass station, hip hop, industrial and all that stuff in between, stuff like 900 Foot Jesus, Section 25, stuff that was really considered new wave or industrial, but hip hop DJs were playing it too. So it was a lot of mixing of genres at that time. I was the youngest of all the DJs. So I was kind of the exception. Most of the DJs that were mixing on the radio were house DJs.

So their influence was coming from Chicago.
We were all influenced by Chicago.

When did you first go over there?
My older sister moved to Chicago so I would go over there frequently to visit her. Go record shopping, so I would tape WBMX.

Hot Mix 5?
Yeah, and go record shopping and bring all that stuff back.

What year did you first go?
Maybe 1979, 1980.

So Chicago was always part of your musical background?
Yeah, from an early point.

Did you get to go to clubs?
No, I was too young.

What about later.
Well, a few times. I don't remember the names. I didn't go to the Power Plant and those places.

Were you going out in Detroit?
Yeah, a club called L'Uomo on Six Mile. Ken Collier used to play there late nights on Saturday.

Was he basically the biggest DJ on that scene?
On the late night scene. There were a couple of other guys. You had the gay crowd, black gay crowd, house parties, really progressive, where Ken Collier used to play. You had that in one

direction, and a lot of my friends used to go because the music was so good. And then there was the more mainstream dance audience where I spent most of my time DJing. Which crossed over into Chicago house as well. And then you had hip hop street music, and I also played in that direction as well.

I've heard a lot about the prep parties. Was that the kind of thing you were going to?
When I was very young. Say between the ages of 10 and 16. It was based around high school, basically varsity.

It sounds like a very affluent scene.
Generally when you're in high school people want to be mature and older and as sophisticated as they possibly can. It had got to the point where people were trying to create this atmosphere. The parties, although they were very young they were very sophisticated, very nice places.

It really broke down into which high school you were from. Some schools were considered academically higher than others; that created a separation between students. Of course that also brought in certain connections: whether you knew about a particular party over someone's house, and whether you could be invited to it. It became a very higher type of consciousness [ie snobby]. Yeah, at these parties the DJs were very carefully picked and the music was exceptional. It was basically the music they were listening to in New York. At the Paradise Garage and places like that.

> ❝ **It really broke down into which high school you were from. At these parties the DJs were very carefully picked and the music was exceptional.** ❞

Did you DJ for them?
I was practising in a basement at the time, I was part of a DJ group but we never got hired. We were called Frequency Sound Systems.

When did you first get to play out then?
Well, my first real gig, my older brother used to be a DJ and he stopped 'cos he got married, he used to work with a group of older DJs and he referred me to them. At the time I knew hip hop tricks but I did not know DJ theory: how to read a crowd, how to pace the crowd, really important things. These older DJs taught me that. I would go every Tuesday, sneak in the back door 'cos I was too young to be in the club, stay up in the booth and they would let me play at certain times to learn how to handle a crowd, and I would move up and they would let me play longer, until I would play the entire night. That's where I learned how to really, really DJ. This is in a club called The Lady. My reputation grew, I got older, got more parties, and I began to do my own residencies, and from there I went to radio.

Where were these residences?
Wow, at one time I had three residencies. One was at a club called UBQ on the east side of Detroit, which was a much rougher situation. It was okay; I had that for a long time. Then Tuesday nights at The Lady, downtown; and then I had a residency at a club called Cheeks, just on the outskirts. It was the most progressive place at the time: Wednesday nights, a really progressive audience.

You could play anything you wanted?
No, but the music was really cutting edge.

In a lot of accounts of Detroit there's a lot made of the fact that there wasn't much of a club scene.

....

No, that's not true. It was massive. You had four or five different parties you could go to on any given night. There was a tremendous amount of people out and about.

So were the high school parties more progressive in terms of music? Is that why people have placed so much emphasis on them?
Yes. We were very hungry to learn more about the music. And it was a very competitive time. DJs had to have the most current material, and we were all young and very heavily influenced, so you could play anything and we'd just eat it up.

Did it feel like experimental times?
We didn't think about it at that time but I suppose it was. We were listening to stuff from brand new Cybotron, from that to B52's to Pink Poodles, to... It was a lot of music.

❝ If I played something in the afternoon, by the time I went out in the evening DJs were playing it. They had went to the record store to buy it. ❞

How were you plucked from here to get a show on the radio?
I was playing at UBQ on the east side and it was Prince week. Prince and the Revolution were in town doing seven shows to promote the *Purple Rain* movie and album. The whole city had basically opened up for Prince. Around the city there were all these Prince parties, and the radio stations were jockeying to do live broadcasts from them. It just so happened they came into the UBQ and they wanted to broadcast at the exact time that it was my time to DJ, so they broadcast what I was doing live, and the day after they found out that the ratings were extremely high at that time. The day after they asked if I could come into the station for an interview and audition.

You must have been tripping.
Yeah, because maybe a year and a half prior to that my brother and I were sending tens of demo tapes to all stations. We had the idea.

And you had friends on the radio
Not at this time, WLVS had stopped. So we knew they were mixing in Chicago, we knew about New York, but there wasn't mixing in Detroit, really. So we were eager, sending demo tapes and they never replied back, so when I got this opportunity to go into audition I was ready.

What was the audition like, hip hop pyrotechnics?
I'm not quite sure how they judged it, probably skill and programming.

What kind of presence did you have on the radio after that?
It was anonymous. No-one knew who I was. I used an alias as The Wizard and the show was called the Wizard.

Why did you want to be anonymous?
I did not. It was the choice of the radio station. It was okay because I could see the reaction from another perspective. I could see from the street how many people were actually listening. I loved it actually. At first it was six days a week; two, maybe three times, sometimes four times a day. The idea of a mix show was so new in Detroit, no-one really knew how it was supposed to be, so basically I stayed at the station all day and when the programme director decided it would be interesting to do something mix-wise I was called into the studio.

On standby.
Yeah. And then at night I had my show, which was three hours, every night. At the weekend it was five hours.

It must have been a dream. Hard work though.
I had complete access to their sound library, plus they gave me money to go and buy any and everything that was new on the streets. I was travelling to Chicago, Toronto, buying everything I could find, and playing it immediately. So you can imagine if you're young and listening to the radio and you go from Madonna to Klein & MBO, and really, really obscure stuff, in normal everyday programming, you're really excited about it.

What can you claim to have brought to Detroit?
Lots of stuff. 'Cooky Puss' by the Beastie Boys, all the early Def Jam stuff, LL cool J, Run DMC, I was the first one to play all that. Lots and lots of hip hop stuff for the first time. Things like 'Boogie Down (Bronx)' by Man Parrish, umm, so much. I brought so much stuff.

You must have been working hard to fill that time.
I was doing residencies. I was kind of at school. If you are a resident at a club you're expected to play five hours, so three was actually quite easy. The station had given me everything I needed to be able to do the show live. Three turntables, a tape machine; in my show I had a request line, an assistant. I was really plugging in to the station.

But you never spoke.
I never spoke. I wanted to say things so I went into the sound library and created each show with a theme based from the sound effects, like for Halloween, and that was how I got into conceptual music.

So that was how you learned production as well.
I learned how to edit tape and all that at the same time.

You say you were aware of your influence, were there any examples where that was made obvious?
Yeah. If I played something in the afternoon, by the time I went out in the evening DJs were playing it. They had went to the record store to buy it. I could very easily see. It was a very powerful influence. I immediately began to be more responsible for the type of music. They weren't sculpting my show. I had complete authority to design the programming. So at a very young age I was deciding what would be on the radio. At prime time. Immediately I became more responsible and began to really think in terms of programming. So there was some method to it.

And that's the germ of making records.
Yeah, especially conceptual music. I had literally mastered by the first year, taking music and shaping it into what I wanted it to do. And then the stations became so competitive, I decided just having records wasn't enough. So I decided to buy equipment and bring it into the station and make music earlier in the day. And then play it as if it were a record. Or do different mixes just so the other station wouldn't have it. And that's how I learned how to programme. I started off dealing with drums. I bought a little Boss drum machine and I would layer records on top of that, just to give it a different feel. and then I bought a Yamaha RX-15 with a slight modification to it, and then I discovered MIDI.

This is what year?
About six months after I got on the radio, 1982 or 1983.

How long were you on the radio?
About eight years. Until 1990.

You must have met a lot of people involved in making music in Detroit.
And nationally. From Public Enemy to LL Cool J, Run DMC, George Clinton, UTFO, everybody, Queen Latifah. And then Juan, Derrick and Kevin used to bring in their music.

So you met them early on in their careers.
Yeah. I was aware of Juan of course because of Cybotron, but I didn't meet Derrick until much, much, much later. Kevin used to bring his records, stuff on his Incognito label, just before he had made 'Big Fun', his Reese and Santonio records, to a club I used to spin at in

....

Ann Arbor, about an hour out of Detroit. It was a really successful residency and I would play his records instantly because I knew he was waiting to see the response. I knew him from that.

What did you think of Juan's music when you first heard it?
It was incredible. The only thing we had to compare it with was Kraftwerk. If you really think about how young Juan was, and his technique of putting the music together, it's mindblowing. Even now, when I listen to it and I think about what we were doing at that time. Juan was so far ahead.

Was that an inspiration to you to make records?
Sure, of course.

When did you first make records, making a track rather than these soundscapes?
It started from radio. I had got into the idea of programming these machines so much that I had literally began making my own compositions, and just playing them in a mix. Not trying to press them up or anything. And that led me to production. I used to belong to an industrial techno group called Final Cut. From radio I learned how to programme enough to be able to put together an album.

Tell me about Final Cut. Was industrial the music you felt closest too?
It was what was happening in Detroit at the time. Techno and industrial. Front 242, Nitzer Ebb, the more danceable things. Shriekback, Love and Rockets. I got together with someone who was more interested in industrial and made two records. We performed once, we were asked to come to Berlin from a label called Interfish which was now called Tresor. They put together a festival. Great Pretty Little One was there, Baby Ford was there, Clock DVA, a couple of others

Why did a place like Detroit take to this European music so much?
Mainly because of radio, what Mojo was doing. Geographically, I think that had something to do with it as well: you're so close to Canada. It's another country! You can see it, just across the river. The history of Detroit has something to do with it. Detroit was a very wealthy place back in the '20s and '30s because of the automobile industry and the army. Planes were built here. So people were quite wealthy and they adopted a more sophisticated, a more progressive way of thinking, and that was handed down through generation and generation. My relatives came from the south to the north to work in the factories. Like many other black people they discovered a whole new world, that was futuristic I suppose. So we grew up wanting to go beyond the barriers of Detroit. It was always there. A lot of us searched out certain things, unique things, to define ourselves. And music was just one of them. Fashion is another. You had this small group of kids who were very heavily influenced by those sort of things.

When did you first hear the word techno?
Probably in 'Musique Non Stop' by Kraftwerk.

But when did you hear it applied to what was happening in Detroit?
Probably through the records of Juan, Derrick and Kevin.

Did the industrial stuff lead naturally into what happened later?
At some stage in Detroit they used to mix: the techno crowd and the industrial crowd used to party together. It's a very segregated city so it didn't last very long. The club owner got threatened that maybe something was going to happen.

The two crowds were very different racially?
The industrial scene was more suburban, more white. The techno scene was predominantly black. We were partying together for a time, so this is where we were integrating, and certain people, certain club owners, certain clubs didn't like it. They cancelled a lot of nights. They didn't like the fact that black guys were walking out of the club with white women, and vice versa.

Simple bigotry?

Yeah. Ritchie Hawtin can attest to that. He used to spin in a club which was predominantly white, and he noticed that there were more black people coming so he started playing more black music, and the club owner told him to stop. Stop playing that music so they would leave. Lots of things like that happened. It didn't last very long so eventually it split in two different directions. Some really interesting things happened in that short time.

What sort of time period is this

This was 1983.

> **❝ It started from radio. I had got into the idea of programming these machines so much that I had literally began making my own compositions, and just playing them in a mix. ❞**

Tell me about how Underground Resistance came about.

Mike Banks was in a band called Members Of The House, a funk, dance band. I used to call him and borrow his keyboards, and he would come over and listen to what Tony and I were doing. One of his band left to go to Los Angeles to be a studio musician, so Mike was left by himself, so that's how we started UR.

We were both frustrated about the industry at the time. We had both tried to work with major labels and it just didn't work out. I had a really bad time with Final Cut, to the point where we had to literally give our music away to get out of bad contracts. It was really ridiculous. I thought, okay if I'm going to make a career out of the music industry I'm going to basically have to do everything myself. And that was the same way Mike was thinking.

And by that time there was the example of Transmat and Metroplex.

They were already up and running. I think by then Kevin had come up with 'Big Fun' and 'Good Life' – big hits, and 'Strings Of Life' was already out, so we had things to refer to and people we could talk to about starting up. We tried to put Underground Resistance material on various labels but there wasn't much response. So that was more incentive to do it ourselves. We first tried it at Metroplex, Juan's label, then we went to Derrick at Transmat, after that we decided to do it ourselves.

There was this radical element: all these manifestos and politics. Just the name alone suggests you're really subversive.

We thought by minimalising the structure, keeping a distance from the audience from a personal standpoint and just focusing on the music, using the music to make contact, we have the ability to be much more profound.

How can non-vocal, non-lyrical music be political in that way? Or carry a message?

We figured there's only so many ways of creating a certain ideology. It was a combination of the label design, the titles of the tracks, the name of the EP itself, and then we would give mostly to distributors just a small paragraph, a few words or some type of image as a supplement to the release, to give them some sort of idea. And then it grew from there.

Getting away from the mythology of the artist?

We just wanted people to know us as Underground Resistance.

What about before that? When they first licensed all those tracks for the Virgin compilation, and that blew up, what was the feeling in Detroit?

The city really had no idea what was going on, but the DJs, we knew that it was something special. We never got magazines or anything like that. We did not know what the world was saying but we knew it was a collection of new music coming from Detroit. It was very forward-thinking.

When did you first feel that Detroit techno was something unique, its own genre?
I could hear it much earlier 'cos I had became accustomed to always listening to everything. So I knew what the unique characteristics were. It was the programming of the drum machines, the type of drum machines we used. The melodic type of sequences, the basslines, were much different from Chicago. The music I always thought was more progressive than Chicago house. It was more difficult to listen to because it was more complex. I think that was because we had a more European appetite.

Do you think the theories that Derrick and Juan came up with to explain their music was to a certain extent post-rationalising?
To a certain extent, maybe, because I'm sure they had no idea, really, what they were doing, at the very beginning. And I think I suppose it happens naturally that way. You see the response of people: what they say and what they think. Yeah, you can fall into that type of agreement, I suppose, and it gradually shapes itself.

How did it feel that your music was strongest as an export market.
It felt great. It was a really great feeling.

But how did it feel that your music was applauded all over the world but not in its home town?
Yeah that's true. Well... yeah, especially when you consider the history of Detroit, the success of Motown. When you think about how Detroit really didn't accept techno, it's really sad. But I realise it's just not one of those places... It's known for making and manufacturing and exporting out. It's just one of those cities.

JEFF MILLS SELECTED DISCOGRAPHY

JEFF MILLS – Changes Of Life (writer/producer/mixer)

JEFF MILLS – Berlin (Mills Mix) (writer/producer/remixer)

MILLSART – Step To Enchantment (Stringent Mix) (writer/producer)

H&M – 88 (producer/arranger)

H&M – Suspense (producer/mixer)

H&M – Drama (Upstage Decision) (producer/mixer)

JEFF MILLS – Condor To Mallorca (producer/mixer/editor)

JEFF MILLS – Untitled (Axis 009ab) (producer/mixer)

X-103 – The Gardens (writer/producer)

JEFF MILLS – Humana (composer/producer/mixer)

JEFF MILLS – Growth (composer/producer/mixer)

JEFF MILLS – Reverting (composer/producer/mixer)

JEFF MILLS – Alarms (First Mix) (producer/mixer)

JEFF MILLS – The Bells (producer)

CYRUS – Enforcement (Mills Mix) (remixer)

DJ HELL – Allerseelen (Jeff Mill Remix) (remixer)

UNDERGROUND RESISTANCE – The Seawolf (writer/producer)

FINAL CUT with TRUE FAITH FT. BRIDGET GRACE – Take Me Away (writer)

MEMBERS OF THE HOUSE – Party Of The Year (writer/arranger)

UNDERGROUND RESISTANCE FT. YOLANDA – Livin' For The Nite (producer/arranger/mixer)

RECOMMENDED LISTENING

VARIOUS – Live@The Liquid Room, Tokyo (DJ mix)

JEFF MILLS – Waveform Transmissions Volume 1

X-102 – Discovers The Rings Of Saturn

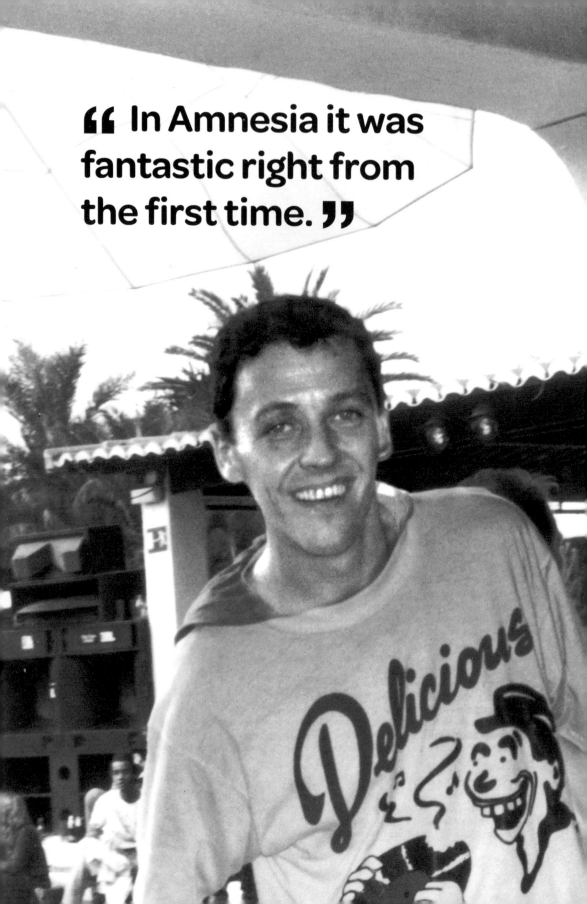

Alfredo
Ibiza's magician

Interviewed by Bill in London on May 31, 2007

Alfredo is an Argentinian exile, driven from his home by the junta, who found peace, love and acid house in Ibiza. Arguably the most influential modern DJ in Europe, it was his eclectic style, with a distinct Latin twist, that provided the catalyst for the wild upheaval of the rave years. His playlist was pored over and rifled through by visiting British DJs, as they filched his template and fired up the clubs of London on premium-grade ecstasy and mad indie records by the Woodentops. Without Alfredo there may never have been an acid house explosion in Great Britain.

Often by necessity, but certainly by design as well, Alfredo combined the most unlikely records into an elegant cascade. The supply of music was limited and there were long hours to fill, so restrictions were pointless. What struck the Brits who heard him, used to the snobberies of rare groove, was the innocent enthusiasm for beautiful music. Forget any preconceptions about an artist, ignore any boundaries of style, if it sounds great with the sun caressing your limbs and the waves sparkling in the distance, then give it a try. Assisted by Ibiza's reputation for hedonism, its beautiful open-air clubs and its glamorous Eurotrash jet-set, the Balearic formula was a winning one.

The sun is shining over the Emirates Stadium, the Arsenal football ground that towers over the surrounding area, including Rob Mello's attic studio. Rob is engineering Alfredo's Ministry Of Sound compilation and we've come to chat about his life and how he changed music. He has the look of someone who has lived a full life and paid the consequences (Alfredo is avowedly anti-drugs these days), but is still full of good humour and a quiet energy.

Why did you move to Ibiza in the first place?
I never meant to go to Ibiza. I left Argentina because the social conditions there were dangerous and horrible for everybody between 20 and 30. I left for Europe in a boat. It took me 22 days. Four-hundred psychotherapists were on the boat. The government were closing universities and psychotherapists were out of work and were persecuted. I was persecuted as a promoter of rock'n'roll groups.

We arrived in October 1976. It was very cold. We went to Paris, then we went to Switzerland. The money ended and I got a letter from a friend from Argentina who was living in Ibiza saying, 'Come and live here, it's fantastic!' I arrived in a boat from Barcelona and within five minutes of setting foot on the island I said, 'Wow, this is the place I want to live!' There was just so much freedom. The climate was like my town in Argentina. We have a hot summer and even the plants reminded me of Argentina. I'd met with other Argentinian friends who were there and I saw I had the chance to live as I wanted to live... as a hippie [chuckles].

Why was it such an attractive place?
The space, the nature, the beaches. On one side you have the climate, the beaches and the nature and then on the other side you've got a population who, when I arrived, the Ibicenco was a very permissive person with a lot of solidarity for young people, something that now is flaking. At the time, I think we respected the Ibicenco much more than they do now,

....

because now they see the young as invaders, I think. I'm thankful to them they gave me the opportunity to re-make my life and my relationship with music came from Ibiza.

What did you do when you first arrived?
Candles. I made them and sold them on a market.

How did you move towards DJing?
That was 1982. Because a friend of mine left his bar to live in Thailand. And in the bar there were turntables, so I start to work as barman and DJ. I'd been running the bar in winter of 1982-83 and he left me the records too.

What sort of music did you play? Was it just the stuff he left you?
Chic Corea, jazz fusion.

How did you progress into clubs from there?
After that I took the decision that I would become a DJ in Amnesia.

Why Amnesia in particular?
It was the most alternative place in Ibiza.

Tell me about your Amnesia audition.
I went Amnesia in 1983 to check with the owner to see if he wants me to play. It was an impossible time because the discotheque never worked. But they decided to take someone else, and I did very well, but they didn't want me to play, so I went to live in Formentera managing a bar. In 1984, the same people decided to take me as resident DJ at Amnesia.

Were there other DJs there?
Just me the whole night. My first year was really difficult. By the end of August 1984, we had not had one person in the club.

" There was no private area at all. The prices were affordable. The public was the most cosmopolitan ever. "

Not one?!
Well maybe some friends of mine. Never more than three people. Then one day we'd been waiting to get paid and some of the people in the club, my work colleagues, asked me to play for them while we waited for the money. The people that came down from Ku [now Privilege], they listen to the music and stay there. Fifty to 60 people. The next day there was 300, the day after 500 and four days later there was 1,000 in the club. Just like that.

Did you stop opening early?
Yeah, we decided to open at 3 o'clock and close at 12.

What sort of music would you have been playing in the summer of 1984?
Pink Floyd, Marvin Gaye, Bob Marley and Italian and Spanish records like Lucio Battisti and Nina, a very famous diva. In the '80s there was a very big movement in Madrid called La Movida. From that movement came Pedro Almodovar, the director. There were many groups who played a sort of rock fusion and one of them was Radio Futura. Alaska [Mexican-Spanish singer] was very good friends of Pedro and the singer of Radio Futura, which I played.

Was this dance music?
Most of the tracks were music to dance to, apart from 'Moments In Love' by Art of Noise, but they used to dance even to 'Moments Of Love' or Malcolm McLaren's 'Madam Butterfly'.

What sort of people came to Amnesia that summer?
Basically people leaving Ku to start with, but by September everybody living on the island.

Many Italians, Germans and French. Not many English. San Antonio was packed with English but not anywhere else.

What was the clientele like?
They were old, young, middle-aged, black, white. The biggest mix I've ever played for.

Were there any drugs around in 1984?
Yeah, but... how can I say this... it wasn't like now where people go to a club and they have to have this or that. It was more free. It was like, 'Okay, if I find something I take it, but if not I enjoy the music and have a drink'. And it wasn't like it is now where you can go to discotheques for 24 hours. The moment we close at 12 o'clock or one in the afternoon, there was nothing else. It was a lot more healthy.

Describe Amnesia to me
Amnesia was like dancing on the patio and garden of an Ibicenco house with a sound system that nowadays would be thought of as shit. Imagine we got a triangle, one bass bin, two middles and one high. There were no lights, no strobe, apart from these three lights that you might get in a funfair, a transparent parachute over the dancefloor, plants all over and completely open air. There was no private area at all. The prices were affordable. The public was the most cosmopolitan ever. Even now, it's hard to find a crowd like that. That's the thing that I miss in the discotheques now. I think there's a big division between the young and old that didn't exist before. An atmosphere of absolute freedom and happiness. This is not hype, it was like that. The drugs weren't the main thing; the people used to go to listen to the music. People went for the dancing, not for the gallery; really dancing.

How did Amnesia progress from that first season?
In 1985 and 1986 it was getting bigger and we became the trendy place in Ibiza. But in 1986 or '87 Space opened. And Space started to send us the police.

There has always been a lot of that going on hasn't there?
Yeah. The owner of Space was the Minister for Foreign Office. And he's the owner of most things here, including the banks. He opened a convention centre for business, then he decided to convert it into a discotheque, which become an after-hours discotheque that opened at six in morning. Obviously we were the rivals. And they tried to send the police. They made us close in 1986 at 10, then at seven. But from '88, there was a big change when these people came from UK, like Paul Oakenfold and Danny Rampling and Nancy Noise.

When did you meet the English guys like Trevor Fung?
I met them in Amnesia, but I never speak English at the time. So our relationship was, 'Hello, how are you?' My biggest relationship was with the girls Lisa Loud and Nancy, because they were more cheeky. Trevor and Paul [Oakenfold] were DJs and you know how DJs are: you're not gonna show that you wanna know which records are playing. So they used to send Nancy [laughs]. I never knew it at the time!

Where were you getting your records from? Was there a record store on the island?
Yes there was a record store on the island, but most of my records came from Germany, because my son was living there, and I used to go to warehouses and distributors in Italy, like Disco Inn and Disco Piu and also in Zurich, but I don't remember the name of the shop.

Where was the first time you heard house music?
The first time I heard house music was in Madrid in 1985. There was a black guy from America who used to bring records over for DJs. There wasn't much importation of records. He used to come with a bag from New York and one time he showed me The It 'Donnie' on DJ International. I went mad for this record. This is fantastic music! The black guy was an American, around 40 at the time, he used to be a basketball player but he got married to a Spanish woman in Madrid and he brought records over. He used to rent a room in a hotel, the DJs would go there to listen to the music and buy the records from him.

Did he supply DJs all over Spain?
No only Madrid. He got business from a military base, there was a massive one near Madrid;

Alfredo

he brought music for them, too.

Where did you find records like 'Jesus On The Payroll' [by Thrashing Doves] and Woodentops? ['Well, Well, Well']?
I bought 'Jesus On The Payroll' in Italy. The Woodentops, Fini Tribe, Residents and Nitzer Ebb I got from Valencia, because at the time in Valencia, it used to have a very strong movement of music Bacalao [Spanish for cod]. They called it Bacalao, because the amphetamine they used to take smelled of fish! Horrible.

Nitzer Ebb, Fini Tribe were quite industrial records, really. What was the attraction?
I'd been really attracted to house music, but we never really had that many. Then in Valencia

in the same period of time, there was a very strong club scene based much more on techno music and I used to buy records in Valencia too. I had quite a big following from Valencia [in Amnesia].

What was the reaction to these records the first time you played them?
In Amnesia it was fantastic right from the first time.

Was Jean-Claude Maury [influential French DJ] anything to do with any of this?
No, he was the DJ of Glory's. To tell you the truth he was the person that influenced me more than anybody. What I did, you could say was a Latin version of what he was doing. He was a French guy working in Brussels at the Mirano, but in Ibiza he had to do what I did: mixing music to bring people together. He had nothing to do with Bacalao, he was much more funky and played more American music. He played things like Johnny Chingas' 'Phone Home'. He was also into Eurythmics, Tears for Fears, David Bowie, and he played a lot of reggae. The people who went to Glory's never went to Pacha.

Did you start incorporating house into your sets straight away?
Yeah.

And did that go over really well?
Yeah. Even with my terrible mixing! There was a record that became massive in Amnesia called 'House Nation', because the people when they heard 'house, ho-ho-house nation' they understood Amnesia. It became massive!

When did you first notice ecstasy in Amnesia?
To tell you the truth the first thing I noticed was people taking mescaline. '85. Ecstasy was for the rich people that used to the private parties. Most of the people used to say, 'Yeah, it's a drug to shag with. You give it to a woman and she opens her legs.' [laughter] Most of them used acid, but you know hippies and post-hippie people, they used to take the drugs more seriously. They wanted an experience that was going to open their mind and ecstasy wasn't that type of thing: it was a pleasure drug.

But it was a factor in Amnesia wasn't it?
No.

Even in 1987?
Yes, in 1987 it was cocaine and ecstasy.

But it wasn't big before 1987, then?
No, ecstasy was big in Ku. In Amnesia they used to take mescaline and acid. They didn't mix things. And once in a while, not every fuckin' day. I had to pay a price because I got into it in a quite big way. I paid a big price for it. I would love you to say this in the interview.

When did you leave Amnesia?
1989.

At the end of the season?
No, I went to work in London and they sacked me. They took my DJ that used to work with me, a guy from Italy who I knew – he wasn't a DJ, but he was a very good guy. But in the end it was alright because Amnesia went down. The last season that was open air was 1989. By 1990 they'd covered it [added a roof]. They year after they offered me the job to run the discotheque. But I was in Pacha and they'd been paying me a lot. They said, 'We pay what you want, but you have to bring the English people in here'! Now it's full of English people.

What's your greatest memory of playing in Amnesia?
There are so many I cannot tell you one. The people that were working there, the colleagues, the bartenders and everything. We went through a very hard first season. And the owners never got money so we have to do the sound ourselves, we had to pool money together. In 1984 we played with no fucking mixer, just two turntables. It was impossible to play. I used to cut the records: one, two, three, four, cut the record. It was another kind of mixing. It was more the feeling of the music than the beat.

❝ When the first people came here, like Pink Floyd and the guys avoiding Vietnam, they found people living in an isolated life. ❞

That's something that's been lost in Ibiza now, hasn't it?
It's been lost all over the world. I don't know. Now we live in a mechanical and electronic world and the pressure is greater than it was 30 years ago. The pressure for money, to live, it's much more great and the music is reflecting the life we live.

How do you feel when you see the huge influence you've had in Europe and the UK?
Different feelings... In a way, I was in the right place, at the right time doing the right thing. It was mostly what the Americans had been doing in America with the house music. But obviously what I was playing was much more European than them, because I was playing the Cure, Pink Floyd and New Order. I used to put acappellas over the first house tracks just to do something different with them. I mixed everything up, black and white, European and American. We know about English history, French history, Italian history, so I mixed it all up!

Why is Ibiza such a party island?
Because Ibicencos... it's not that they are very open-minded, because they are not. But it's a people that live and let live. When the first people came here, like the people from Pink Floyd and the Americans, the guys avoiding going to Vietnam, they found people living an isolated life. They didn't have a connection with the continent: one boat a week or something like that. Tourism wasn't big. And they accept these people. Apparently the first people was good people. Apart from the drugs, they don't steal things, they respect the people. The Ibicencos has been invaded by so many people in the '80s, dance people, clubbers, tourism, they are used to it. Their country has lots of influences from all over. Now they are rejecting it a bit, because – I'm getting into politics – they are conscious that they are destroying the island.

Do you think a lot of people got greedy for all the money they could make?
Of course. Not the first generation. Not the grandfathers. The people that I met was, frankly,

Alfredo

....

fantastic. When I had my son and my ex-wife left the country, when I came back to the same owner of the house and he said, 'Yeah, it's your house forever'. There is a law that if someone is born in the house you cannot evict him from that house until he is 18. They've been very strong on those things. They never charged much for rent. They've never been used to big cars and swimming pools.

The second generation got the problems with drugs; the third generation, this generation, is very greedy. Their ancestors had their own culture and it was enough to live in the island. They knew everything that they had to do to be okay here. But these people now they forgot about their own culture and they don't have a new one.

How would you describe the spirit of Ibiza?
Confused at the moment! [laughter]. I think it's the possibility to have some natural fun to contact people who they would never have met in their own place. That happens even now, even with a crisis. If I were a young person I would say, 'Wow this is fantastic, this is wonderful!' like I did 30 years ago. The rest of the world changed in the last 20 years. It's keeping the same difference as everywhere else.

What did you think when these crazy British people started bringing you to London?
It was like a dream come true. It was incredible. When I arrived they showed me a page in *the Independent* with a note all along the side of the page, all about me, making a new kind of music. Wow, this was incredible. I was never conscious of any of this.

It must have been a thrill though.
Completely surprised. I never thought that people were so much into my music. The first gig I did I had no tunes to play because the DJ before me was playing all my records! He was doing the same mixes, except better because he had been practising. The first ever English gig I got was in Streatham at Project Club which was great until the police came. I played for one hour. Someone parked their car in the middle of the road so a milk float couldn't pass and the police came in and closed it down.

But you came back to Shoom didn't you?
Yeah, I got a residency from Danny Rampling. I used to live in London in the winter.

What was it like playing for a crowd in London compared to Ibiza?
Well, I used to play at the Milk Bar and Velvet Underground. And there was a party with Danny Rampling, and most of the people used to go Ibiza, and I was quite popular at the time. I had a following then. So it wasn't much different.

Why do you think your music had such a big influence on people like Danny Rampling?
I think I showed them DJing wasn't an impossible thing. It had been dominated by older DJs in the UK. They were the untouchables. So I think I opened their minds so they thought, 'Okay, I can do this, too'.

Do you think the incredible mix of people you had at Amnesia affected the atmosphere in any way?
It was a like an alternative European Community, this gathering of these people. It showed you what might be possible in the future. They were all European... apart from the English!

What do you think about what ecstasy has done on the island?
I can only tell you what my doctor told me. He said that massive consumption of ecstasy will send you into depression. That's it. It's a tricky thing and at the moment... I don't know, it's very dangerous.

Did you ever use ecstasy when you were DJing?
Ah, man, you not going to put this in the book! [laughter]

If you don't want to tell me something then don't tell me...
It's true. It's not good to do that [chuckles]. It's not good because you think you play the best gig of your life. And the reality's not the same.

Do you like the music your son plays?

Yes. I think I'm very hard with my son because I teach him and he's been with me since day one. At 14 he was selling the tapes for me in the discotheque – and getting much more money than I used to get! One day some Arab guy asked him to give 10 tapes to the girls who were with him. So Jaime says, 'Okay, each tape is 3,000 pesetas but for you I'll charge 30,000 pesetas!' He has very complete musical knowledge from the past yet he's ashamed to use it, because the fashion of techno and minimal, but anyway I don't wanna disturb the relationship of my son! Technically he's like a Swiss watch, it's amazing.

What does Balearic music mean to you?
Balearic for me is a marketing word. That's it. The other day they interviewed me for a German music magazine. He asked if Balearic music is really just the music you were playing and I nearly agree with that. It was my taste. It was possible to do that because the public bring information for me. They want this in my set, they want their taste represented in your set and I accommodated that. After that, the classification started and I heard Balearic songs that I would never play but it's really just a marketing tool. It sounds good as a term but maybe 'Ibiza music' would be more representative.

Does it make you feel proud that you've had this effect?
It's not good for my ego because it's big enough and I don't want it to control my life. I'm happy that it happened.

© DJhistory.com

AMNESIA 50

MANUEL GÖTTSCHING – E2E4
RADIO FUTURA – Semilla Negra
JOHN LENNON – Imagine
SADE – Smooth Operator
ART OF NOISE – Moments In Love
NINA SIMONE – My Baby Just Care For Me
MIKE POST – Theme From Hill Street Blues
JAMES BROWN – How Do You Stop
ANTENA – Camino Del Sol
ICARUS – Stone Fox Chase
ELKIN AND NELSON – Jibaro
TEN CITY – One Kiss Will Make It Better
TULIO DE PISCOPO – Stop Bajon
ENZO AVITABILE – Blackout
GEORGE KRANZ – Din Da Da
LIAISONS DANGEREUSES – Los Niños Del Parque
DEPECHE MODE – Just Can't Get enough (Live version)
THE WOODENTOPS – Well Well Well
JOE SMOOTH – Promised Land
TALKING HEADS – Slippery People
THRASHING DOVES – Jesus On The Payroll
BOB MARLEY – Could You Be Loved
PRINCE – When Doves Cry
HENRY MANCINI – Theme from the Pink Panther
RICHIE HAVENS – Going Back To My Roots
ORANGE LEMON – The Texican

FINGERS INC FT MARTIN LUTHER KING – Can You Feel It
WILLIAM PITT – City Lights
HERB ALBERT – Rotation
ATAHUALPA 1530 – Andino (Industrial mix)
THE HOUSE MASTER BOYS – Housenation
RICHIE RICH – Salsa House
RUFUS & CHAKA KHAN – Ain't Nobody
KC FLIGHTT – Planet E
THE NIGHTWRITERS – Let The Music Take Control:
BARRY WHITE – It's Ecstasy When You Lay Down Next To Me
GILBERTO GIL – Toda Menina Baiana
IT'S IMMATERIAL – Driving Away From Home
RICKSTER – Night Moves
THE UNKNOWN CASES – Masimba Bele
MALCOM MCLAREN – Madame Butterfly
THE CLASH – The Magnificent Seven
PIL – This Is Not A Love Song
EARTH PEOPLE – Dance
PHUTURE – Acid Tracks
ADAMSKI – N.R.G.
A SPLIT SECOND – Flesh
STEVIE WONDER – Masterblaster
KISSING THE PINK – Big Man Restless
A GUY CALLED GERALD – Voodoo Ray

Compiled by Alfredo

" I was playing more experimental, more jazzy, more quality. "

José Padilla
Smooth operator

Interviewed by Bill in London, March 3, 2005

The man who brought the chill to Ibiza's sunsets, Jose Padilla actually made his name as a straight-up dance DJ at Es Paradis before caressing the Ibizan dusk with Art Of Noise. Padilla's *Café Del Mar* compilation series originally began life as bootleg cassettes sold on hippie markets on the island, turned legitimate and went on to sell four million units worldwide. Jose also claims the first time he saw anyone doing the fabled acid house dance (big fish, little fish, cardboard box) was to 'Music For A Found Harmonium' by the Penguin Café Orchestra.

When were you born and where?
I was born in 1955 in Girona, which is the next town to Barcelona in Catalunya. I grew up in between France and Barcelona. My childhood was in France, south of France, Perpignan. My father was a farmer.

How did you get into music?
Well, my home was always a very musical place. My older brother was a teddy boy, he was into rock, 'The Twist' and all that. I always had a deck in my home with 7-inches from Elvis and Johnny Hallyday. My brother was practising rock'n'roll with his friends.

Did you start collecting records when you were young?
I bought my first record when I was 13 with my own wages. I was living in Barcelona then. Collecting properly, I was 16 or 17 and I was more into rock and symphonic rock; I was a big fan of Genesis, Manfred Mann, German rock, Klaus Schulze, Rolling Stones, of course, and Black Sabbath. When I was about 20 I had to sell my records, because I was in deep trouble. I had about 100.

How did you get into DJing?
The first time I saw a DJ in action, that's what I wanted to do. I was about 16. It was in Lloret de Mar. I was DJing for nothing, really. I was a friend of the main DJ so he was letting me play a few tracks when he went to the toilet or when he was tired. In those days, a DJ played all night long. So when he had a break he let me play a few records. My first wages as a DJ, I was 19, something like that. It was £15 a week. 3,000 pesetas, I always remember. It was good for a 19-year-old guy.

When did you go to Ibiza?
It was 1976. I was 21. It's a long story. When you're that age, I was fighting my family so I was escaping from my family. I didn't want to do the job they wanted me to do. The usual teenage thing. I ended up there and I'm... still there.

Did you go with the intention of DJing?
I wanted to DJ, but in those days you couldn't make a living from DJing in Spain. So I did all kinds of work. I worked as a waiter, I worked in construction, all sorts of different jobs. My first job as a DJ in Ibiza was in a hotel called Bergantin. It was a very little box, with a little room. I was playing Barry White, Abba, Julio Iglesias and all that shit. But, you know,

....

it was decent wages. This was about 1976. Then in 1978, '79 I had the chance to play in Es Paradis, which was the main club in San Antonio, an open air place. In those days, they tested different DJs, so you had to go and prove yourself. I went there and proved myself and got the job.

Was it the sort of job that, once you got it, you played all night every night?
Every night from 10 till six in the morning.

What sort of clientele did it have?
It was cosmopolitan, but there was also the freaky hippie type, you know. It was open air. It was a different vibe. Different people, different drugs. It was more relaxed, put it that way.

What sort of music did you play?
Well, considering I didn't have much choice of records and the disco stuff was really difficult to get hold of it, stuff like Salsoul Orchestra and Chic. I play from rock and reggae to James Brown. I played everything I could. Sometimes I had to repeat records two or three times in a night. We played stuff that had a vibe. In those days, you can make people dance with Pink Floyd. I remember having the dancefloor full with a track from Ultravox called 'Vienna', or funky stuff like Timmy Thomas.

Where did you get your records from?
Wherever I can. There was a very good record store called Flip Music from a French guy, in Ibiza Town. He was the first guy to bring stuff from abroad.

Do you remember any specific records you played when you were playing in Es Paradis?
John Miles' 'Music' was last track of every night, Fischer Z, Supertramp, 'Honky Tonk Woman', Harold Melvin & The Bluenotes, Pink Floyd 'Money'.

But that's a bastard to dance to, it's in a weird time signature!
They loved it!

Really?
Yeah. It was a different crowd, it was more acid and joints. I used to put all the lights out and make it fuckin' black. No music. For a minute. Fuck you! I used to do that. Now you wait. Then they used to start to whistle and scream. Then I start with, I don't know, anything: David Bowie. That's the problem now, they don't have any patience, they don't have imagination.

What other things did you do when you were playing there?
It was really creative. We didn't have CD, we didn't have minidisc, we didn't have DAT. We had two cassette decks and two decks. So I used to put in the cassette decks some birds or some waves or some screaming, you know, sound effects. It was beautiful.

How did it differ from Pacha?
Oh it was really trendy, the hippie jet set.

Which were the good clubs in Ibiza at the time?

At the beginning of the '80s it was Pacha and Ku. There were two Cesars who were DJs. There was a Cesar, who was in Pacha, who was the only guy in Spain who could fly to New York because they have the money and power to do it. Then there was another Cesar, a black guy from New York was playing in Ku. Then there was Glory's, which doesn't exist now. And in Glory's there was Jean-Claude [Maury] from Belgium. And Amnesia was a rock place, it was nothing.

What did you do after Es Paradis? You were there two years?
Three. Then I went to a new club called Manhattan which this guy built with a lot of money. They call it macro-discotheque. It was very fashionable: big, three floors, elevators, swimming pool inside, cinema and all that bullshit. So I went there for money, but it was a big mistake.

> ❝ He was a manic depressive and he shot himself. I tried to keep it going, but when you've got the blood spots in your bar... ❞

Why a mistake?
Because I went for the money. Es Paradis was beautiful during those years, you know? After two years Manhattan burnt down so I lost the job. So then I work in all the discotheques in San Antonio, Playboy, Nitos, Extasis. Then I did a couple of things in Ibiza, played a couple of times in Ku and in Pacha, but only as a guest, I was never resident. Then I opened my own bar on the other side, the Es Vedra side, Cala Vedella. It was called Museo, because it was a museum. It was a lot of work, I put a lot of energy in there and I could play my music. We had paintings and sculptures from artists all over the island. It started in 1986.

What had you been playing up until that point? Had you been playing the chill out stuff you became known for, things like Penguin Café Orchestra?
I tell you what, the first time I heard Penguin Café Orchestra was in Glory's in the '80s and it was this guy from Valencia called Paco who played it. It was the beginning of ecstasy, only a few people were taking it; it was the first time I saw people doing the dancing with that track [mimics acid house type dancing]. I thought, What is this'?

Which tune was it?
'Music For A Found Harmonium'. I used to play that in a club called Nightlife and every time I played it, the owner came up to me and said, 'I'm gonna break your fucking penguin record', because it had penguins on the cover, 'Next time you play it, I break', because everyone left the floor every time I played it. And I loved it. I was trying to break it in San Antonio....

I'm assuming they weren't taking ecstasy in your club!
No, a lot of alcohol.

When was the fist time you saw ecstasy?
Late '80s.

Did you see Alfredo in Amnesia?
Yes. It was at the beginning of the first acid tracks.

What sort of music was he playing?
He played all over, from Tamla Motown, to rock to whatever.

Why do you think DJs in Ibiza have always played this wide mix of music?
Well, I think it was because we were brought up like that, but also there was not much choice. Now you can specialise in Detroit techno or deep house or whatever, then you had to play with what you have. We had to play so many hours we have to play different tracks

to make the session happen. I think that's where it's coming from, really. It's not because in Ibiza we like to play like that. We have to play Talk Talk, we have to play Belgian beat, we have to play rock, we have to play reggae, because we have to fill the space of so many hours.

Do you think that the fact there are lots of tourists and foreign workers affects how music was played or perceived?
Well there was no English DJs in the '80s, there was just one American in Ku and that was it. All the DJs were locals. Of course English people used to bring records. You'd say, 'Oh next time you come bring me a few tunes'. So of course we got influenced by them. We knew some English groups because of records being brought over.

> **❝ In Ibiza we have to play Talk Talk, we have to play Belgian beat, we have to play reggae, because we have to fill the space of so many hours. ❞**

Trevor Fung said he would bring records over and sell them to the DJs.
Yeah. I bought a few records from Trevor, yes. But that was late in the '80s.

So how did your bar go? Now you could play Penguin Café Orchestra without getting threatened with the sack!
Yes! I could play anything I want. I was playing more experimental, more jazzy, more quality, bossa nova... It was my baby.

Was it like Del Mar, lots of people outside etc?
Yes. It was a very nice environment, a big garden, 500 square metres, sculptures, trees, fountain. It held 400-500. But it went wrong, we were three partners, one of them shot himself inside the bar. That was it, then. Heavy shit. We did very well in the summer, then he wanted to open in the winter, but there is nobody there in Cala Vedella, only the drunk people. We didn't make any money. I said, 'Look Frank what are we doing opening in the winter?' He was a manic depressive and he shot himself. I tried to keep it going for another year but when you've got the blood spots in your bar... And he left me with all the bills!

How did the Café Del Mar gig come about?
After the café went down I stopped DJing and started to sell tapes on the hippie market. I was doing my own tapes at home of reggae, soul, whatever. Different styles. I made 20 or 30 of them with nice artwork from a painter friend of mine. First day I went I sell all of them. Next day I did double. I sold them all again. Fuck! I bought another tape machine. Then I speak Alfredo, Pippi, Cesar de Molero, I say, 'Look I got this business in the market, if you make me a master, I'll give you percentage or pay you for the master.'

Really?
So I came home with £3,000! I was sitting on my sofa, with eight machines – boom boom [mimics punching record buttons]. When I was tired my girlfriend would take over. This was 1989. Then people start to copy me. They'd actually buy the tapes from me and make copies of my tapes! It's a big market. That year there was about 10 of them. Then the police start to come. I did that for two years. Then the Café Del Mar guys, who I knew, because I used to live behind it, they said, 'Look if you want to DJ here...'

Who were the owners of Café del Mar?
Pepe, Ramon and Carlos. I started to DJ there. I start to sell tapes. I was selling 100 tapes a day. The wages were like £500 a month. I was working six days a week. I thought I have to do this legally so I came to London and offered it to all the big companies and nothing happened, so I forgot about it for a few years until I saw a friend from Logic, Ceela, he said,

'I've got these friends from React and they're interested.' That's how I did it. First one came out in 1992, I think. When I start to do the CDs I came here for the winter, living in London for three years and two years in Nottingham, and DJing around the country.

They sold a lot didn't they?
First one sold 8,000, second one 30,000. The fifth one sold half a million. The *Best Of* did over a million. We've done between three and four million worldwide now. But I've been in a court case with React for four years, over the trademark for the name.

What's it been like watching Ibiza change over the years?
Actually I'm moving from Ibiza. Ibiza, to me, doesn't mean anything any more. It's for young kids. I've been there 30 years nearly. It's a very unreal place. Go, go, go, party, party. Commercial. There's not too many places you can hang out. It's too fast. Maybe it's because I'm older or because I've changed. Everything is so business-oriented now, there is no spirit or goodwill. It's a big industry. It's a big factory. That's the fucking reality. There are still good DJs there and still some great sets. That doesn't mean it's crap, but that's the way I feel.

In a way, it's the fault of Spanish businessmen being greedy, isn't it?
Yes. Every year there is a big guy, this year it's Timo Maas. He's a brilliant DJ, but it's not me. I prefer to play in Precious Hall in Sapporo, proper fucking club, underground, brilliant sound system, 400-500 beautiful people, play for eight or nine hours, that's where I want to go. I want to have fun and in Ibiza I cannot have fun. Too many chemicals. I think it affects the spirit of the music.

What about all the weird parties on the island like Freddy Mercury's famous birthday?
Still happens. I went to a few. You know what happened with Freddy Mercury, I think his 40th birthday, there was no people. There was supposed to be a jet coming from England with all his friends on but for some reason they don't come. So we send people on the street and say, 'You want to come to Freddy Mercury party?' 'Oh yes!' 'Well you have to bring people with you!'

© DJhistory.com

CAFÉ MAMBO 20

VANGELIS – Love Theme From Blade Runner
ENNIO MORRICONE – Deborah's Theme
ART OF NOISE – Moments in Love
SANTANA – Aqua Marine
WIM MERTENS – Struggle For Pleasure
JOAQUIN RODRIGO – Concierto de Aranjuez
CAMARÓN DE LA ISLA – Nana del Caballo Blanco
STAN GETZ WITH JOAO & ASTRUD GILBERTO – The Girl from Ipanema
AUDIO DELUXE – 60 Seconds
BASSHEADS – All Over The World
PACO DE LUCIA – Entre Dos Aguas.
LEFTFIELD – Fanfare Of Life
DJ SASHA – A Heavenly Trance
MARVIN GAYE – A Funky Space Reincarnation
PROPAGANDA – Dream Within A Dream
WALLY BADAROU – Mambo
PENGUIN CAFE ORCHESTRA – Music for A Found Harmonium
JOHN MARTYN – Sunshine's Better (Talvin Singh Mix)
SILENT POETS – Moment Scale
SABRES OF PARADISE – Smokebelch II (Beatless Mix)

Compiled by José Padilla

"**This record is strange, we'll give it to Baldelli!**"

Daniele Baldelli
Cosmic voyager

Interviewed by Bill in Bologna, April 23, 2004

Daniele Baldelli is the first DJ star to be crowned by the internet. Although the peak of his career came in the early 1980s, he had been swept aside by the house music tidal wave that swamped Italy from the late '80s, confined to back-rooms and distant memories. But as his mixes began to appear online, so his reputation rose, and it's only now we've come to understand how strange and unique his DJing experiments were in the musical Galapagos of Lake Garda nearly 30 years ago.

His record dealer Gianni Zuffa reserved him a copy of every album that came out, knowing there could well be a single track lurking in those far reaches which would fit his tireless explorations. He learnt his craft from two semi-mythical American DJs, Bob Day and Tom Sison, who arrived at a fairy-tale nightclub Baia degli Angeli courtesy of a disco-loving millionaire who'd seen the clubs of New York and wanted one for himself. From a DJ booth in a glass elevator these Americans were probably the first DJs who could mix records in the whole of Europe. Before they returned to the states they taught their craft to Baldelli and his accomplice and sometime rival Claudio 'Mozart' Rispoli.

Baldelli's mixes were exercises in dislocation, filled with incredible unknown music and mixed with the precision and drama of a movie soundtrack. From records played at the wrong speed, to German experimental music re-purposed as disco fodder. Daniele Baldelli is the architect of his own world and sound: cosmic. Despite his claims that his English is not up to the job, he performs manfully throughout our meeting in a Bologna restaurant, helped occasionally by friend and DJ, Liam J. Nabb, and a bottle of Chianti.

Where and when were you born?
1952, Cattolica.

Is that a town or a religion?!
It's a town, near Rimini, on the Adriatic Coast, a tourist resort.

When did you start DJing and where?
1969 in Cattolica. Tana Club was a little club for 300 people, but in Cattolica in that period, there were about seven clubs, because of the tourists. But only two during the winter for the people of Cattolica.

And Tana was one of those clubs?
Yes, it was open all the year.

Had you been collecting records before you started DJing?
When I started I was only 16 and I became DJ... Well not a DJ; when anybody asked what I did I said I put the records on the turntable. In those days, there was no mixer, no headphone, nothing.

Two turntables or one?
Two. Two volume controls, so you turned one off and the other on. It was just important

....

that there was space between one song and another because the people dance, then they stop, then they dance to the other one. When you put the pick up on the 45, you'd hear a little *bzz-bzz-bzz* before the song started, so when I heard that I knew it was ready to turn the volume up.

What kinds of records were you playing?
Mostly rhythm and blues, Aretha Franklin, Ann Peebles, Rufus Thomas, Joe Tex and also the white music, also 7-inches, Atomic Rooster, The Stooges. We used to play five 'shake' records, which is fast music, and then five records for slow dancing. Not like now, all fast music. After six months in Tana Club, then I went to Tabu Cub where I stayed until September 1977.

When did you see the first mixers?
When Baia degli Angeli was born, near Cattolica, two New York DJs come to play in this club: Bob Day and Tom Sison.

When did Baia degli Angeli open? Did they come when the club opened?
Giancarlo Tirotti opened it in 1974 and with these two DJs, because Giancarlo travelled all over the world and so he knew everybody. I was working in my club Saturday night, Sunday afternoon and Sunday night and one afternoon Bob Day and Tom Sison come I was like, 'Oh my God, it's the Baia DJs!' And, at the end, they came up to me and said, 'Hey you are very good. But why don't you take away the rubber from the top of the turntable and replace it?' I said I don't know what you mean. They said, 'Why don't you come to us in Baia and we'll show you.' They used to use a 7-inch with the paper sleeve.

Do you remember when Bob and Tom first came to the club to see you?
1975 I think. Then I became friends with them. In fact, when they left Baia in '76, they recommended me to Giancarlo and they also brought Mozart, so we started together. We were together in Baia from 1977 to '78.

🟫 The crowd was very VIP people, some gay, beautiful women, actresses, people with a lot of money. 🟫

Where did Tom and Bob go?
They went back to the States. We always asked if they were important DJs, but we don't think so. We think they were just two guys who found America in Italy. The important thing was they had a lot of records, that's the important difference. They had records one year before Italians. There was no import/export at this time. It was very difficult to find this music. When they left Italy, they give me a present, the 12-inch of 'Hit & Run' by Loleatta Holloway, with Bob Day and Tom Sison autograph.

What did they look like physically?
Both were gay. Bob Day was white, Tom Sison was mixed race.

Were they boyfriends or friends?
They were just friends.

Did you see them play? What was it like watching them because they were mixing records weren't they?
At that time, watching them was very exciting because of all of the records they played that I didn't know. It was really new and different music from what we had. So that's the first thing. Also to see the mixing at that time was incredible. Now – I have some tapes by them – I realise it was very simple what they did. Just two bits, boom boom, finished. Very short. But to think I could do this with two records then was incredible.

Did the club open all year round?

Daniele Baldelli, Grace Jones, Claudio 'Mozart' Rispoli.

All the year, but only on Saturday night. And in summer for maybe 20 or 30 days in August.

You said Bob and Tom had lots of records that you didn't know. Do you remember what any of them were?
It was the Philadelphia sound. I have all of these records now, but then I did not.

Where were you buying your records?
All over. Another thing: in 1969, all the records we played, the boss bought. But I said to him after two weeks, 'Give me some money and I'll take care of the records because you understand nothing.' So I bought records for myself. Only in Cattolica to start with, then there was a big shop in Rimini, where you could find a lot of albums from America and UK, but you couldn't listen. So you had to look at the cover and think, 'Okay, this could be nice!' [Laughs]. Then somebody told me about a shop in Lugano in Switzerland called Radio Columbia. By 1977 when I was playing in Baia, record shops started to grow and this is when Disco Piu in Rimini opened which was just for DJs.

And every strange record Gianna Zuffa from Disco Piu received he used to say to all the other DJs, 'Oh this record is strange, it's no good. We'll give it to Baldelli!' You know, a lot of the music I played was not really made for clubs, so I played Steve Winwood's 'Spanish Dancer' or I would play Mike Oldfield's 'Foreign Affair' or 'Was Dog A Doughnut' by Cat Stevens. These were not generally people who made music for discos.

It was coincidental that it sounded good in the club?
Exactly.

What was the crowd like in Baia?
Before me, when it was Bob and Tom, the crowd was very VIP people, some gay, beautiful women, actresses, people with a lot of money.

The jet set?
Yes. Because of this, everybody wanted to go to Baia, so it became very popular. In 1977 when I went there, Giancarlo sold the club to somebody else and this new guy made the club more popular for everybody, younger people, not so elegant, regular people. And they

....

wanted to experience Baia because it was a beautiful club. You know, I was DJing in a glass elevator, so it was really something beautiful.

How big was the DJ booth?
Like an elevator!

So quite small then?
Yes, because all we needed was two turntables, a mixer, a little space for records.

When the younger crowd started coming, had the music you were playing changed at all from before?
At that time, we were playing exactly Bob and Tom style. Disco music. Philadelphia. But at the end of the evening I started to play, at 5am, Ravel's 'Bolero', which lasted 12 minutes and I would play Pink Floyd, Jean Luc Ponty, electronic effects or African chant acappellas over the top. I also started to play more electronic in between and songs like Eddy Grant's 'Time Warp'.

When Bob and Tom were playing at Baia, were people doing drugs?
Yes, drugs, but I don't know which kind. I think cocaine.

Was it widespread?
I can tell you when I played what was happening. Everybody talked about cocaine. I didn't know and I didn't care about these things. When I played at Baia, there were two kinds of people: those who smoked hash and a lot of people who took cocaine and maybe speed.

Were there particular records that you started to play there?
For sure some beautiful records that I like very much: 'Ju Ju Man' by Passport. This song was perfect for the club and things like 'New York' by Miroslav Vitous, also and John Forde's 'Don't You Know Who Did It.'

When did you finish playing at Baia?
From September 1977 to end of August '78, because Baia closed because of the drugs. When I was playing in Baia one night, this man called Enzo Longo come to listen to me. He called me in 1979 and said he wanted to open a club in Lake Garda: 'We're going to call it Cosmic and I would like you to come and play.' It opened in April 1979.

Enzo Longo – and his partner Laura Bertozzo – was a dentist. Very young. He was 30 years old when Cosmic opened, but he was from a rich family. His wife had two Fiorucci boutiques. So he was always into fashion and style and music. His idea was to take the logo from Commodores LP to use as the Cosmic logo.

Where in Lake Garda was it?
Lake Garda is 30km from Verona. There were lots of little towns around the lake. Lazise is a little place. A little bit outside, in the country.

What did it look like?
It was very simple: a big room, rectangular, it was really strange for Italy. It was the first club with no place to sit down and no alcohol and it had big sound for Italy. All the amplifiers were McIntosh and all the speakers were JBL. And the dancefloor occupied the whole club, with just a little place to walk around and, like *Saturday Night Fever,* with flashing lights. There were also columns with lights going up and down. In the ceiling there were a lot of neon effects and lasers.

What were the opening hours?
It opened at nine, at 10 it was crowded and at 1 am it finished. The first year, 1979, the music was the same as Baia, funky disco. The first year, it was very nice, nice girls, nice people. It became really popular but in 1980 Verona became a big distribution centre for drugs, especially heroin. So a lot of people that did heroin started to come to Cosmic. At the same time the music changed. Not because the people coming were doing heroin. I stopped playing disco music – it was dying – and I began playing the music I told you about. The beat slowed down; from 90bpm to 105 bpm at the most. A lot of people smoked and a lot of people were doing heroin. So they had to dance slowly, you know! [Laughs]

The pictures of the DJ booth in Cosmic look crazy.
The first booth was like a space helmet with two hands around it, like Thank God It's Friday. Then after two years they built a new booth which was like a spaceship cockpit.

Were you the only DJ there?
I stayed all five years: 1979-84. After one year I called my friend TBC and he played with me for two or three years we fell out. In any case, everybody said that I was the brains because the records were all mine.

When did you start experimenting with playing records at 45 and 33?
I think in 1980. I think this happened accidentally when I put the pick up on the record and played it at the wrong speed. Most of the tracks that I play at 45 were instrumental, of course. Sometimes also with vocals, but the voice was like Mickey Mouse, you know? We didn't care, since Italian people can't understand the words, the voice became just music. This sound – the sound of the voice – became music to me. You know Yellowman? We played all Yellowman's songs at 45 and not 33: 'Strong Mi Strong' and 'Zungguzzuzeng'. But I also played 'Shout' by Depeche Mode at 33 instead of 45.

What happened right after Cosmic closed?
The first thing was it was hard to find work again. I was resident only at this club and because the club was closed because of drugs, the attitude was it is better that promoters don't book Daniele Baldelli because all the people bring drugs with them.

Had it ever been closed because of drugs before it finally closed?
It was closed a couple of times but for minor technical issues, only for one week or so. It was closed for drugs in 1984, but then after one year Enzo won an appeal but decided he didn't want to open because the rules would only be broken again. It never opened again.

What did you do after Cosmic closed?
After Cosmic closed all the commercial clubs started to call us and ask if we could do Afro nights, because they knew people liked this kind of music. Then, in 1988, I went to Baia Imperiale, in the same location as Baia degli Angeli, during the Frankie Knuckles period and I played on one dancefloor, mixing everything up: cosmic, reggae, Brazilian, electronic, etc. My dancefloor was the best so they asked me to play the bigger floor the next year and I started to play some house music. But for me, with my attitude, I kept buying records for the B-side, not realising that the A-side was the one in fashion. I didn't like this. I like the B-side! It didn't work.

❝ The first booth was like a space helmet with two hands around it. ❞

Who were your influences?
Nobody else. Bob And Tom gave me technical inspiration but that is all. Also, when I played at Cosmic, I lived in a little house by myself on the hill all day listening to music. I never went anywhere else to listen to other DJs. I was influenced by myself and without drugs.

Where did you find records like 'Codek' [by Tim Toum] and The Pool?
I found them all in Disco Piu. Because I was looking for different and strange music, when Gianni bought records he would take one copy – no more – of maybe 50 records to test or monitor in the shop. Gianni had this system where any DJ who wanted to order a record they would write their name on the sleeve. A great selling method to young DJs if it had Ralph or Ricky Montanari's name on it!

When you started playing these records did Disco Piu suddenly start selling loads of copies of them?
This happened in Disco Piu, people would play cassettes to Gianni and say, 'What's this?'

Danielle Baldelli

Then Gianni would call me: 'You play this at 45 so I can't understand anything!'

Tell me about your tapes.
I had a lot of trouble over these [bootleg] tapes from the police. People bought a lot of stickers and tapes every Saturday. I sold about 150 tapes each week. And obviously this small amount mutiplied into thousands and thousands. Some fans would come to me and say, 'You see this, my Citroen Pallas? I bought this selling your tapes!' [laughter]

The tapes you sold were they actual recordings?
No most of them I recorded at home, but I reproduced exactly what I was playing at the club. Making mixes with the music of that time was very difficult. It's not like now. Sometimes I would spend all day and night with one record on one turntable and then I'd go through maybe 200 records trying to find the perfect match. It made me crazy. I liked to find the records that synched for a long time so I could make something – a unique feeling. Sometimes you get two records that stay in time but there is no feeling. But sometimes when you hear the violin from this record and the guitar from the other one, you feel this great interaction. So I used to prepare the first hour. But the other two hours were improvised. Some tapes are recorded directly, but most were made in this way.

What was your best memory of playing at Cosmic?
I loved the start of the evening. I always started with effects and strange things. The club would be crowded with people talking and drinking and I'd go into the booth and start to play – *whoosh* – sound effects and the people started to dance! With no rhythm! It was really emotional.

© DJhistory.com

COSMIC CLUB 50

KING SUNNY ADÉ – Ire

AKENDENGUE – Epuguzu

ZAZA – Dschungel Liebe

PAYOLAS – Eyes Of A Stranger (@45)

JIM PEPPER – Ya Na Ho

MONSOON – Wings Of The Dawn

AIRTO MOREIRA – Parana

LOGIC SYSTEM – Unit

GAL COSTA – Pescaria

KOTO – Chinese Revenge

FUHRS & FROHLING – Happiness (@45)

GILBERTO GIL – Toda Menina Baiana

INCREDIBLE BONGO BAND – Let There Be Drums

JEAN MICHAEL JARRE – Magnetic Fields

KILLING JOKE – Requiem

ANTENA – Bye Bye Papaye (@45)

ANTENA – Achilles (@45)

LIAISONS DANGEREUSES – Los Ninos Del Parque

AZYMUTH – Young Embrace

JAN AKKERMAN – Back To The Factory

AREA CODE 615 – Stone Fox Chase

TONY ESPOSITO – Pagaia

KISSING THE PINK – Mr. Blunt (@33)

KOWALSKI – Ultradeterminanten

OSIBISA – Raghupati Raghava Rajaram

TONY BANKS – Charm

BAUTISTA – Vida (@45)

JORGE BEN – Ponta de Lanca Africano

BRIAN BRIGGS – Aeo

FELA KUTI – Zombie

LOVE INTERNATIONAL – Dance On The Groove

CANDIDO – Jingo

CHRIS AND COSEY – This Is Me

TOURE KUNDA – Emma

DEPECHE MODE – Shout (@33)

CAT STEVENS – Was Dog A Doughnut

YELLOWMAN – Zungguzzuzeng (@45)

ZAKA PERCUSSION – Le Serpent

MYTHOS – Terra Incognita (@45)

NAZARE PEREIRA – Chero Da Carolina (@45)

MIKE OLDFIELD – Foreign Affair

OZO – Anambra

PASSPORT – Ju Ju Man

JASPER VAN'T HOF – Pili Pili

RICHARD WAHNFRIED – Time Actor

XTC – It's Nearly Africa

YELLOW MAGIC ORCHESTRA – Computer Game

RAH BAND – Electric Fling

STEEL MIND – Boss Man

TUMBLACK – Invocation

Compiled by Daniele Baldelli

RECOMMENDED LISTENING

VARIOUS – Daniele Baldelli Presents Baia Degli Angeli 1977-1978 (DJ mix)

VARIOUS – Cosmic: The Original

"It wasn't until I went to America that I saw something completely different."

Froggy
Soul Mafia hitman

Interviewed by Bill in Harlesden, September 7, 2004

A natural gift for mixing and an acute understanding of electronics helped Froggy (real name Steve Hewlett) rise from the made-men of the Soul Mafia to become one of the most skilful DJs of his era. The jazz-funk scene in London and the south-east revolved around Mafia capos Chris Hill and Robbie Vincent and a network of suburban clubs like Ilford's Lacy Lady and The Goldmine in Canvey Island. From this extrovert scene came the tradition of dancefloor crews in matching outfits and bonk-fest soul weekenders in seaside holiday camps. What marked Froggy out from the other jocks was an appreciation of American mixing techniques, the first pair of Technics 1200s in the country, and one of the UK's mightiest sound systems, beefy enough to impress even the most unrepentant dub thug. As a result he had the largest black following of any of the Soul Mafia DJs.

Froggy's DJing apprenticeship came as roadshow DJ for Radio 1 DJ Dave Lee Travis (aka 'The Hairy Cornflake'). A heavy gigging schedule brought hard-won dancefloor experience, while an apprenticeship at Plessey in Dagenham gave him his electronic dexterity. He discovered mixing via a trip to New York led by Chris Hill, which he swiftly adopted at his Southgate Royalty residency. Froggy later moved into studio mixing and continued to DJ right up until his sudden death in March 2008.

It's a beautiful early autumn day in Harlesden, north-west London, when we meet at the Lodge on Harrow Road, and we repair to the storeroom-cum-office upstairs with the smudgey sub-bass of disco underfoot to do the interview.

Where were you born and where did you grow up?
I'm a proper Cockney. Born in Whitechapel, by the Bow bells. Born in The Wright Hospital, November 8th. Age I don't talk about. I'm a veteran.

Did you grow up in Whitechapel?
I grew up in Whitechapel, then moved to Rainham between seven and 12, then moved to Ilford. Dad worked at Plessey's at the time, which was a big concern. I couldn't stand school anymore and my dad had influence there and it was hard to get an apprenticeship, and I wanted to do an electronics apprenticeship and in those days you could leave when you were 15, so I left school just after my 15th birthday. Did that till I was 21. Went and got my City & Guilds. Covered all aspects of engineering. My thoughts were always towards the radio, studio equipment and sound systems. Started developing this skill for sound systems and radiograms.

When did you start collecting records?
When I was five. In those days, all you had was wind up record players – clockwork, with a handle on the side. In those days, it was 78s and you had to change the needles after three or four plays. So my pocket money was a box of needles every week, and a record. So they'd lock me in my room and I'd play my records.

What sort of records?
I had a great interest in general melody stuff, things like Guy Mitchell's 'Singin' The Blues',

....

'Rock Around The Clock', I was a big Lonnie Donegan fan. When I started my apprenticeship, you didn't get a lot of money, about a fiver a week. I quickly became the Apprenticeship Association man, which gave me the clout to put a few do's on. Plessey's, at that time, had a social hall. With all my knowledge, I scrounged speakers, an amplifier, and I had a couple of old Garrard decks and started doing little do's for apprentices.

Where you using two decks, then?
There was nothing like mixing in those days. All you had was a big hi-fi amp, a Leek 70 or Quad amplifier, which was the crème de la crème, and both of those had two decks plugs, so you could switch from one to the other. I had a couple of Garrard turntables and an amp and a couple of speakers. And I already had quite a collection and those records were quite appropriate for these do's.

Towards the end of my apprenticeship, I'd saved quite a bit of money, and I went and got two sheets of eight by five and at that time the only 12-inch speaker you could get, associated with Plessey, was a Wharfedale, so I phoned the company up to get the specs and built two cabinets with tweeters in, in my house. These were my first two disco speakers.

Continued with my apprenticeship. I'd heard there was a little place starting up at the Bird's Nest in Chapel Heath. They were Watney's pubs with a little room in each pub and they were interviewing for DJs. So I went along and got it straight away. I did my own night, started with nothing and built it up till it was packed. And it was on a Monday night. So soon as I'd finished my apprenticeship, the day I finished, I jacked it in the next day. I wanted to go professional. To my horror it wasn't as easy as I thought. I bought a little Thames van for £100, put some gear in it. Proudly walked in the next week and told them I was a professional disc jockey. They laughed me all the way out of the door, because you really could not get insured for any kind of entertainment then whether you were a golfer or DJ. I had to go round posing as an electrician. Anyway, got the Bird's Nest going, packed out every Monday night, different promoters started coming in, liked what I did, liked what I played. I was a good entertainer, and good on the mic. So other owners from other places got my number and started booking me. Six months after I'd gone professional I'd managed to sustain a wage from doing it.

❝ Richard Long was fascinated by my interest in sound systems. I was one of the few people that he let up to see what was in the Paradise Garage. ❞

Which other places were you doing?
Bird's Nest was my main one. The Robin Hood in Dagenham on Thursdays. Then one day a guy came to see me at the Bird's Nest, within the first year, and he said I've got a guy who deals with all the bands, manages them, and he was managing Joe Brown who, at the time, was doing quite well. He used to have a venue, and he'd had it for 18 years then. By this time I had a little mobile kit. Couple of speakers, Numan Audio, couple of decks. Anyway, I rang this guy up, George Cooper, who used to put bands in as a package. Two weeks later, I found myself on my way to Scunthorpe, which is probably the hardest ride imaginable. Set off at eight in the morning to get there at five at night to get there in time for the bands. At that time the bands that were big were The Sweet, T Rex, Slade and I had some great fun working with those bands. Only problem was the loneliness going there and back 'cos I only had a Thames van and it was a bloody long drive. There were no motorways then and I used to come home and it did knock the balls out of me.

I did that for four years. First year it was all bands. I realised I didn't have enough equipment to do such a big room, and they were talking to me one day, the manager and

George, and they said, 'Do you know much about any of the radio jocks?' So I said I was a big fan of Emperor Rosko. So they said get him down here. First one they booked was Johnny Walker, then came Rosko, who was my hero and he had this big lorry load of equipment, it was the bollocks and he actually came and sat and spoke to me. He actually let me plug my deck into his system and – boom – I was gone then.

Soon as I got back I started buying every speaker, borrowed money wherever I could, filled the van up with speakers, built up these amplifiers and, next, they booked Dave Lee Travis. The good thing about this night was he commented on how sharp I was. When he looked I always had that awareness so I had a record already cued up, so he'd tell a few gags and entertain. To my amazement at the end of the night he said, 'Could I have a word with you?' We went back to the dressing room. He said, 'Been wanting to do it for a long time but just haven't found the right person. I really enjoyed working with you tonight. There's something about your timing and the music you played. Are you interested in doing some gigs with me?'

I said I'd love to.

He said, 'I want to get together a roadshow.' Within three weeks, I went round to his place, had a talk. He said he wanted to tour and it can be quite hectic. He wanted two dancers, me before and after.

So we got two good dancers, I brushed up the sound equipment and off we went and did our first couple of shows. We didn't have anywhere open after two in those days so we'd do ten till one thirty. So we had the DLT Roadshow with my name in subtitles.

It was so successful we toured the country four or five times. We toured for five years. Dave bought a Winnebago. We had a couple of road crew. Dave was at the peak of his career then, so it opened a lot of doors for me, as you can imagine, and they'd often book me back on my own to do a set on a club night, and that's how I built up my name all over the country.

The Froggy name came from the Bird's Nest because we all had to have nicknames. There was a Scottish DJ called Jock The Jock, and because I was quite wiry it became Frog and then Froggy. I then got asked to do one of the biggest clubs in the country – I'd played there twice as the DLT Roadshow – which was the Southgate Royalty. Just at that time Jeff Young was playing and the manager said, 'Would you come down and do one with your sound system.' By that time I'd built it up into quite a nice system. So I went back and did it on my own, played a lot less commercial stuff, more what Jeff was playing. They said it was great and they offered me a residency. And by that time I'd been touring all the time and I was tired out. I wanted to have a base, so I took it on. Bit of a bumpy ride for six months, because I had to find someone to cover for me with Dave, but eventually I left because I really wanted to stick with the Royalty.

What year did you start doing it?
Years are a bit difficult to quote you. Within the first year I was there, it really built up. I was playing a lot more imports. But I was breaking imports while I was on the road, too. Because I worked at the Royalty, they'd have a bag of tunes for me, literally everything that came in. I'd pick 'em up and pay for them sale or return. In that first year, they did the New Music Seminar in New York. Well, New York was about the biggest place to go, so just inside that year I went over there with a few DJs

That would be 1979?
Yeah. I went over with the Mafia team. Chris Hill, Chris Brown, Sean French, Robbie Vincent, me. I've never experienced anything like it in all my life. It changed my life completely. I'd heard all about it, and I'd heard all about mixing techniques. I was always good at mixing, but not in the way they did it. I always had a good idea of beats and how you could weave music in and out.

The first day meeting everyone I found great. Then we got invited to the Paradise Garage. I never knew nothin' about it. But Chris Hill said to me, 'When you see it, you'll understand what I've been going on about,' because he'd been going on about it for ages. So we left at midnight, we'd all had loads of champagne and everything else. And I'd never seen anything like it. Sound system was the most incredible I'd ever heard. The room was the most

Froggy

....

electrifyin' I'd ever been in. The DJ was just… incredible. The tunes he played were quite fantastic. The two stations then were WBLS and WKTU and BLS was linked with Paradise Garage and was much more streety and WKTU was linked to Studio 54. I experienced this whole night, from 12 till seven listening to this jock and the lighting and the sound was just so incredible, I couldn't believe it.

The following evening we went to Studio 54 and experienced the big queue outside and being picked – we had special passes – and also the Richard Long sound system which was the same as the Garage one. The music was much lighter, but just as entertaining and brilliant. Came back and decided, with all the information I'd got, I spoke to Richard Long quite a lot, who was fascinated by my interest in sound systems, made lots of drawings and notes and came back and got myself in a load of fucking debt. I went out and borrowed every penny I could, bought a lorry and built a big system up. Went to see a mate of mine in Southend and he built these big bins for me and I took two guys on full time. We fitted it into the Royalty every week and people used to come for miles. By this time, I'd had my mixer modified and redesigned.

In terms of the sound, what were you using exactly?
When I was over there, I was one of the few people that Richard Long let up to see what was in the Paradise Garage. He used Thorens decks at the time and they were mounted up from a gimbal in the ceiling. When I had a look at one, they were just too slow for the work I was used to. I needed a quicker start. All the DJs who were doing blend mixing were using the Technics 1200 Mk1 which to my horror, when I brought two back from New York and I just couldn't work with them. I practised on them for two months, then I went to play up north at the Warehouse.

In Leeds?
Yeah, he had guys like Greg Wilson playing up there. When I went up there to play, I fluffed it, couldn't use them; they were too slow, so I flogged them. Anyway, I went over to New York and I'd heard about a new version of the 1200 that they had out, the Mk2, when I went over and played on them, I did a little guest spot, the deck was quick, it had a high-torque motor in it. That changed the whole industry. I bought two back with me.

Was the Mk 1 the one with the little LED screen on it?
No that was the 1500 Mk2. I had the first 1200s in the country. But once I'd got into them: off I went. And the mixing, I studied Larry Levan, Tee Scott, Shep Pettibone, went to KISS FM and watched them. And then adopted it at the Royalty on the Saturday night. Within eight weeks, Chris Hill came up to me and said I was definitely on par with the Americans. So it went on from there.

Were you aware of guys like Greg James at the Embassy?
Yeah, I've got a lot of respect for him. They used these lazy decks which weren't right for what I was doing, but I used to go and watch Greg, he was great. But when the 1200s came out it opened a lot of doors. Also, I'd always had a reel-to-reel, so I started editing. Dave Atkin, from Radio 1, Dave Lee Travis's producer, good friend of mine, taught me. I used to and watch him produce shows, watched him edit singles down for radio. He said, when you get it right, you can have a little mix each week on Peter Powell's show. What I was doing was making the mixes up, but I couldn't edit properly. He taught me to edit properly and I practised and practised. So I'd take him a mix in, have a chat about what was in *Blues & Soul, Record Mirror,* so then I started doing a lot of mixes for radio, 7-inch mixes. Capital heard me and gave me a late night show.

What kind of stuff were you playing when you did Peter Powell?
So you'd read James Hamilton's column in *Record Mirror* and then you'd feature the tracks. We'd ring him up and give him information as to what the big tracks were. *RM* was a bible for the industry and *Blues & Soul* also had a two page segment that Bob Kilbourn wrote.

Within a short space of time, the Mafia, what we played was so upfront they would look up to us to see what to buy. At the Royalty, they'd book Greg Edwards every month, Robbie Vincent, and gradually a team formed to do Caister. I was already doing Caister before the soul ones started. I was doing the 18-30s, great laugh, general music, I did about eight of

....

those. Shagged myself into a coma. Then Robbie Vincent did one of the 18-30s with me and took it back to Showstoppers at the Royalty and said, 'Look why don't we do a soul one?'

In that two and a half years at the Royalty, it opened a lot of doors, I was doing radio, it started to get on top a wee bit. The sound system became expensive to keep running and I took a break at one stage. I put the sound in at Caister and because I'd designed it I was always getting phone calls about it, which just made me too tired. I wasn't concentrating on my work. Then I left it alone for a year and then Brian Rix took it over.

What, the sound system?
No Caister. I came back after a year, had a word with Brian and said, 'Ask the boys if it was okay,' and I came back. I asked him about the sound system, the guy doing it was a friend of mine, and what he put in, I thought I couldn't compete so I left him to it, but at the next Caister, they made me stay in the dressing room until they announced it and I got a bit of a standing ovation for that year I'd taken off.

Do you remember what year that was?
They're a bit of a blur. Anyway, it was a good year and a half I missed. I must admit that, although Brian Rix can be a difficult person to deal with, he runs that event very well and keeps it going, so I do that twice a year.

> **❝ I had the first 1200s in the country. I bought two back with me. The deck was quick, it had a high-torque motor in it. That changed the whole industry. ❞**

Didn't you hire out your system to some of the rare groove guys during the late '80s? I'm sure Norman Jay said he was blown away by Derek B when he saw him in Canning Town and he was using your system.
The problem was there became a lot of jealousy. There are only certain boys that can run a sound system. Where I got a lot of my knowledge from were people like Jah Tubby, Jah Whoosh and those guys. They were telling me about increased costs. You can't just have idiots lugging the gear around, you gotta have a few technicians with you, too. So I started to hire it out and I found I was using it so much to hire it out that I wasn't using it myself. So the last couple of years it has been in storage, so I don't know what to do with it.

But Derek B was using it wasn't it?
Derek B was a protégé of mine. He was like a black version of me. The problem was he got too greedy too quick. I was working with Simon Harris, at the time, doing production work. And Derek B started putting gigs on everywhere saying it was his sound system, so we had a massive row, punch up and everything. Derek B then got a deal with a record company, Simon Harris got a deal and 'Bad Young Brother' was Derek B, so we went our own ways. I did Derek B's first big edit for his album, which he rejected, he then got Simon Harris to do it and he rejected that and the company blew him out. So he got his own in the end.

What sort of records were you playing at the Royalty?
The whole idea of the Paradise Garage was, any good record could be a dance track, which was great. 'Love Injection' [by Trussell], 'We Got The Funk' [by Positive Force], 'Another One Bites The Dust' [by Queen], so I started doing all these little inserts. Pete Tong was so impressed, he was like that's a fucking brilliant idea and that started to influence him a lot. D Train's 'You're The One For Me', 'Can You Handle It' [by Sharon Redd], all the Prelude stuff. One of the biggest labels at that time was West End. They really did have loads of leftfield tracks, there's one that's still getting used now, Loose Joints' 'Is It All Over My Face'. It took me a year to break that track, no one could get into that.

Larry Levan and Froggy

Then on the jazz-funk side you had all the British bands coming up. You had Level 42, I Level… So in your set you'd include Lonnie Liston Smith's 'Expansions', 'Always There' Willie Bobo, then you'd have the jazz stuff to go in there. So jazz-funk included Willie Bobo, you never heard jazz-funk stuff at the Garage, it was all club music. But in this country, you mixed them together. So 'Expansions' you'd play Sharon Redd after it.

What was the crowd composition at the Royalty?
The biggest issue you had was the mixed race thing. To my horror in the first few years I got knocked a lot outside of that for playing black music. The biggest problem was no club owners wanted a heavy – over 50 percent black – so keeping a happy medium was very hard. Very very difficult to keep it predominantly white, as such, because you were playing black music. I did find myself not playing the more leftfield stuff to keep that down a bit. It was heavy.

Did you play any of the electro stuff?
No. I grew to like it quite a lot. At that time, Morgan Khan was doing the jazz-funk and he was on his second album and he wanted a mixed one and there wasn't many jocks around that could mix on reel-to-reel. So I did an electro album for him, me and Simon Harris. So when I did Capital, one of the jocks who did electro before me left, so I would do the electro hour before doing my stuff. Didn't touch the hip hop stuff. 'Planet Rock' and that label it was on…?

Tommy Boy.
Yeah, that was a big concern, did a lot of work for them.

Were you playing any of that stuff in clubs?
No, I never played it out. But on the radio I did editing work and mixing for them. I used to do it incognito, never used to put my name on it much. I didn't want to be associated with it too much. I grew to like it, because I like music in general, but hip hop is not for me, Don't like it at all. Far too heavy. Unfortunately, it's become very big.

❝ The jocks in New York, although technically brilliant, never said a word, though. Combine the two and it gave me something special. ❞

Were there any people who influenced you when you were younger?
Well when I was growing into my teens there was only one radio station. The only one you could get was Radio Luxembourg. Tony Prince was a big name on there, so I used to tune into Tony Prince and Paul Burnett. They were great, a big influence radio-wise. They broke away and did Radio Caroline, which was the forerunner to Radio 1, as you know. As far as live work it was Emperor Rosko, he was always playing live, Johnny Walker for contemporary stuff and clubwise, I didn't really see any DJ in this country who did anything that I couldn't do better myself. It wasn't until I went to America that I saw something completely different. The jocks in New York, although technically brilliant, never said a word, though. Combine the two and it gave me something special. Technically I studied the best jocks in America: Levan, Pettibone and Tee Scott. Those were the ones that did something for me. So then I could mix the tunes *and* rap over the top which became a very good entertainment package.

What was it about Rosko you liked?
I was always a Wolfman Jack fan. He had such a unique style. He used to play to a lot of the campus students. Emperor Rosko was like a British version of him. Basically we became quite close friends, I watched him work live and I was his protégé, no doubt. He had to move back to America because his dad, the famous film director Michael Pasternak died. When he left, my sound system that I built was virtually identical to the one he had, so when he came back to the UK he'd play on my system.

....

I got myself into a lot of debt when he left actually, I borrowed about six grand. I went to Matt Fry, he built all Emperor Rosko's gear and he built mine. I started to admire certain jocks around me, for instance I couldn't help but be fascinated by Chris Hill's entertainment value. He wasn't particularly brilliant technically, but he had this fantastic ear for picking tracks off of albums. The most influential DJ I've ever met. Chris Brown was good, Jeff Young, all the Mafia team.

Did you go to the Lacy Lady and the Goldmine?
I didn't hang out there, because I was very busy. I didn't like the Goldmine much. I didn't like Canvey Island much, but it did have a lot of weight. I preferred the Kings near my hometown. I'd go there as much as I could.

What was the difference in crowd composition between the Goldmine and the Royalty?
No difference at all. Stan eventually sold the Goldmine and they went to another place. They went to some place in the country, but that didn't work that well so they came back to the Seven Kings. So the Lacy Lady carried the name wherever it was held.

> **❝ I remember breaking 'Do You Think I'm Sexy'. No-one had ever heard it before and I dropped it at a Young Farmers' do in the west country and everyone went crazy. ❞**

Why was the Kings good?
It was a lovely room, great acoustics, it had a great atmosphere, the way it was laid out.

Were you doing gigs in the north playing more underground music?
Yeah, well when I was travelling around with Dave Lee Travis, I was still well into my imports. I remember breaking 'Do You Think I'm Sexy'. No-one had ever heard it before and I dropped it at a Young Farmers' do in the west country and everyone went crazy. Out of the maybe 15 singles and one or two albums, I'd select five that would work everywhere. Play them in my set and then play them later in Dave's set because he grew to like them, stuff like 'Love Injection', he featured them on his show when they came out on British labels, and I was able to spread the word around all round the country.

One year, Disco International, to my surprise, rang me up and said I'd won DJ of the Year award. James Hamilton was always interested in what I was playing and what was breaking because I played all over the country. Crown Heights Affair 'Sexy Lady', I played that everywhere. Because you had capacity crowds everywhere you could really work the track. D Train and 'Can You Handle It', instantaneously, they worked. But I didn't overdo it, I'd pick five at a time and work them. All the other Radio 1 jocks who went out and did their roadshows didn't have a fuckin' clue, but Rosko was on the ball and we were. We were the only ones with a two-and-a-half-hour self-contained show. The two of us were the only ones to book.

© DJhistory.com

FROGGY 50

BRASS CONSTRUCTION – Talkin'

LA PRENTUGA – Cameleon

THE BROTHERS JOHNSON – Stomp

PLAYERS ASSOCIATION – The Get Down Mellow Mellow Sound

TRUSSEL – Love Injection

PAULINHO DA COSTA – Déjà Vu

TYZIK – Sweet Nothings

ASHFORD & SIMPSON – It Seems To Hang On

ROBIN BECK – Sweet Talk

JACKIE MOORE – This Time Baby

KINSMAN DAZZ BAND – Love Design

AURRA – When I Come Home (Levan Remix)

SLAVE – Party Lights

KLEEER – Get Tough

MFSB – Mysteries Of The World

MELBA MOORE – Standing Right Here

STARGARD – Wear It Out (Inst)

CAROL WILLIAMS – Can't Get Away

MARK SOSKIN – Walk Tall

CANDIDO – Dancin' & Prancin'

ALICIA MYERS – I Want To Thank You

BABY O – In The Forest

INNER LIFE – Moment Of My Life

CHANGE – You Are My Melody

CHANTAL CURTIS – Get Another Love

CROWN HEIGHTS AFFAIR – Use Your Body And Soul

FRANK HOOKER & POSITVE PEOPLE – This Feelin'

GAYLE ADAMS – Your Love Is A Lifesaver

GQ – Make My Dream A Reality

GREY & HANKS – Dancin'

HEAVEN & EARTH – I Really Love You

HI TENSION – There's A Reason

L.A.X. – All My Love

LINDA CLIFFORD – Runaway Love

LOGG – You've Got That Something

MAN PARRISH – Hip Hop Be Bop (Don't Stop)

NARADA MICHAEL WALDEN – I Shoulda Loved Ya

ONE WAY – Music

PATRICE RUSHEN – Haven't You Heard

PEECH BOYS – Don't Make Me Wait (Dub Mix)

REVELATION – Feel It

SHARON REDD – Never Give You Up

T CONNECTION – At Midnight

THE UNIVERSAL ROBOT BAND – Barely Breaking Even

UNIQUE – What I Got Is What You Need

ROY AYERS – Don't Stop The Feeling

BILL SUMMERS – Straight To The Bank

STARSHINE – All I Need Is You

LENNY WHITE – Didn't Know About Love Till I Found You

B.T. EXPRESS – Give Up The Funk

Compiled by Steve 'Frostie' Frost

RECOMMENDED LISTENING

VARIOUS – Dance Mix: Dance hits Vol. 1 (DJ mix)   **JAMES BROWN** – Froggy Mix

"We broke down a lot of barriers at the beginning of house music."

Danny Rampling
Acid house evangelist

Interviewed by Bill and Frank in London, May 6, 1999

1987 was Year Zero for Danny Rampling. It was the year he recovered from a near-fatal car crash, met his wife Jenni and famously took a trip to Ibiza to celebrate Paul Oakenfold's birthday, in the process discovering the Amnesia alchemist Alfredo. His club Shoom, more than any other, was responsible for transporting the Ibiza vibe back to dank London streets and lighting the fuse on British clubland. DJing there, Danny was as much a partygoer as any of the clubbers, a real departure in an age when DJs were mostly po-faced collectors who refused to make eye contact. With the new intensity a night of house music demanded, the focus was on the DJ as never before, and Shoomers raised Rampling to messianic levels, anticipating the DJ worship of years to come. By popular consensus, it was also Danny who gave acid house its dance. His loping, waving, waggling angles were soon repeated in long-sleeve t-shirts up and down the land.

A long-time pirate broadcaster, Rampling moved from his soul-boy roots to a playlist heavy with house. His show on Kiss FM was transferred to Radio 1 and became the *Lovegroove Dance Party* in 1994 where he remained until 2002. The day we meet, he has just announced his retirement, with plans to move into the catering business and open a restaurant. He has since come back out of retirement.

Tell me about the Ibiza trip and how that changed your life?
When I came back to England I had this new zest for life. There was a dramatic change in my personality and my outlook towards life [he had been badly injured in a car crash]. it was Oakenfold's birthday so we went off to Ibiza on this trip. I'd read about Amnesia and the after hours scene in America so I was already familiar with it when we got there. But Trevor [Fung] was the man who really introduced us to it! I did one [E] first. I certainly wanted to experience the whole thing. I dived in instantly.

The others were monitoring the experience and shortly after, Oakenfold dived in, which I was most surprised at. He struck me as being the most sensible of the crew, but far from it. Then he was followed by Johnny [Walker] and lastly Nicky [Holloway]. We spent that night in Amnesia and it was incredible. I'd never experienced anything like that on the soul scene. Looking back on it, the soul scene was all very normal. Okay, great music, but it was all very provincial. Going to Ibiza was a revelation because it was this international cosmopolitan crowd full of beautiful people. It was a very wild place. Today, Ibiza is still a lot of fun but everything was a lot more natural then because it hadn't had the major exposure it has today. The other exciting thing about it was it was a very word of mouth thing.

What was Alfredo like?
A complete alchemist. The way he weaved music in and out, the styles of music. It was a revelation in terms of the way music was played. Larry Levan was doing that at the Paradise Garage and Alfredo had connections with friends of Larry's. I firmly believe it had an influence on Alfredo and his sound and especially with some of the house records he brought in. They were given to him by a guy connected to the Paradise Garage. But then

....

Alfredo had that natural flair, a very artistic Spanish way of putting records together and telling a story. And every record he played had its own distinctive sound. He picked very unusual records and that made him stand out: The Woodentops, the Residents, Elkin & Nelson. But also his house records: the Nightwriters, House Nation, Ralphi Rosario and then pop things like Mandy Smith. But it was right for the scene going on there. This was his peak time when he was really shining. He had this wonderful audience like all the great clubs. I had it myself at Shoom.

Was he a big influence on what you did at Shoom?
He was my mentor. He was the connector. He really directed me towards that style of being really broad in my musical tastes. I'd grown up with that, listening to punk rock and soul, but you'd never been able to play that in a club.

> **" Shoom was like a house party. If people came and stood around looking boring, I used to ask them to leave. I would be polite and say, 'Well, you can have your money back and go.' "**

When I asked Alfredo why he thought he inspired you so much he said it was because you'd come from the soul boy thing.
He certainly did. But at the same time he had soul and funk and blackness in his music. I come from a black music scene, but he was playing black music alongside white indie music, but even his indie records had funk and that deepness about them. I really admired what he was doing there. He was a leader in Europe. I've always said Alfredo was the Levan of Europe and he had a Paradise Garage at Amnesia. It was a free state where anything went.

When you came back did it feel like you were on a mission?
Yes, a big mission.

What was it that made you feel like that? Did you think it would be enormous in England or just that you wanted some of it here?
Both. It was energy, this driving energy. At the time it was all 105 bpm to 110 bpm, nothing was 120 bpm, except maybe some of the jazz. No dance music was that tempo. The energy wasn't there. Firstly, it was an opportunity to become a DJ. I had a vision that this was music that I wanted to play and came back and completely changed my radio show on Kiss. I wanted to find as many house records as possible.

I decided to start my own club. I played at a guy's engagement party at the Fitness Centre [in Southwark Street]; it was in a part of London that no one cared about and it was left alone by police so you could party all night. Fortunately, I met my wife Jenni at that time and she had management skills, having done fashion management before we started that club. So I'd found this music and also fallen in love all at the same time. 1987 was a brilliant year. She gave me a lot of support and said, 'You've got to do this,' because there was no way in to all the other London clubs.

There were a few places that had tapped into this, like The Jungle and Delirium.
Indeed. That's where we went clubbing, Delirium. But at the time it was only getting about 300-400 people in there. They stopped it just too early, in about October or November '87 just as everything was going to be massive. They didn't recognise what was going on out there. All those people from Amnesia, the English kids, were on that dancefloor at Delirium. Noel's music was fantastic and Maurice even more so, he was brilliant. At the Astoria they were mixing up hip hop and house but it was very rough. But Delirium was great. It had two fantastic DJs there, but it was just slightly ahead of its time.

Jungle was also a favourite club. Colin Faver, who at the time, was my favourite British

DJ. That's why he came to Shoom and played so many dates for me. To me, he was just an amazing, technically brilliant DJ. He had an unusual sound with German influences, Frankfurt stuff mixed in with Detroit. He was very leftfield in terms of his selections. When I first asked him to play he was a little unsure. 'Who's this kid, he's a nobody,' sort of thing. The third or fourth night he agreed to play, then wanted to play every week. In terms of promoting that night it wasn't great clubbing etiquette, but we went out and flyered Delirium, The Jungle and Pyramid. Those three clubs were the ones that we targeted.

How long did it take before it really took off.
The first one, we had this rare groove funky DJ Ian playing with me. Two crowds: half house-heads, Amnesiacs; half Special Branch soulboy lot. He played his music to the rare groove lot and I came on playing house. Carl Cox was there that night. I didn't even know about bpm-ing records at that point. Carl was like, 'That one's 118 and this one's 122; you need to pitch that one up slightly!' So I had to learn pretty quickly. It wasn't about the long mixes all the time, but I was bold enough to try them. That's what happens with the innocence of it and the carefree nature.

People talk about the intensity of feeling in Shoom.
I'd nearly lost my life so I'd had a renewed enthusiasm towards life as a whole and just felt totally reborn. I was so overwhelmed and excited that I was still alive. It happened to be that coincided with house music breaking that particular year, a combination of those elements and also the collection of people that came to the club. And there was also the psychedelic experience to share as well. That certainly played a role in it.

But that also played a role in a sense that the people who were experiencing that started to believe that I was some form of messiah, and that scared me, actually. There was a period at Shoom, where a group of people was trying to hail me as this new messiah and I got a bit worried by it. It quite frightened me because it became so intense.

How did that manifest itself?
I had one guy who opened a page in the Bible and my name was in the Bible in this particular paragraph. He said: 'This is you! This is you! This is what's happening now.' And that completely flipped me out. These people were using a lot of LSD! [Laughter]. I hadn't used it at all during that period, I wasn't really into it. It was a really strange period, but exciting.

Shoom was like a house party, it was opening the doors to everyone that came with a great attitude and wanted to be part of that. If people came and stood around, I used to ask them to leave. If they were looking boring, and they were bored and onlooking, I would be polite and say, 'Well, you can have your money back and go.' We were very aware of what was going on in that club, and made everyone in there – it was a personal thing – feel comfortable. It wasn't just coming into a club: they were part of something.

Were you feeling very evangelical about sharing what you'd experienced?
At that time of my life, yeah, big time. That was very apparent in Shoom. The energy that was in that club. Also sometimes I could go into a trance-state through certain records; through the movement of dance. As with different societies through dance, trance can be obtained. Without the use of drugs, solely through music and the energy and the lighting, and the energy of the people who maybe were on drugs in that room with the spirit of that particular piece of music. An example is Frankie Knuckles' 'Your Love' which induced a trance state on a number of occasions; and the Nightwriters' 'Let The Music Use You'.

It was a wonderful experience. I think it was a combination of everything that was going on at that particular period and the spirit of the human beings that were in those rooms. Everyone was feeling that; everyone was feeling, generally, the same.

How conscious were the parallels with the '60s? Was that accidental?
It was accidental actually, because sometime after Shoom had finished I saw something on TV about Ken Kesey and the Magic Bus and that period in the '60s. Tripping the light fantastic and sharing that with America. Well, we didn't exactly go around the country but we hit Brighton and a couple of other places on the south coast and that was very '60s-induced, but unwittingly. We went off on these bus tours to the country and played out

....

there. There was a connection with that. But there was also a connection with pushing the peace and unity of people.

Also, it was not totally drug-related; that feeling was coming through the music as well. At that particular moment in 1987, there was Ce Ce Rogers and Ten City. They're very spiritual records. All of those records had a big spiritual content through gospel music and R&B and disco. They certainly were meaningful and appropriate for that moment. The whole thing, the synchronicity, was just so well timed. We look at that now and see how major it's gone worldwide. Practically the whole world has been touched by it. Sadly, some of these conflicts that go on in the world... give them house music! Give them more house music, these generations that are not feeling it, because of these fucking awful rulers of countries.

We broke down a lot of barriers at the beginning of house music. It broke everything down. It smashed down the walls. It was a thriving industry in itself. Where a lot of kids didn't have a chance to get a decent job before, they were now getting jobs in the music industry, in the arts, fashion, all kinds of things were opening up. All of this was related to what was going on in that club scene.

With a lot of the stuff you were doing, and the fact that the drugs were illegal, made you sort of outlaws, I suppose. Did you feel like outlaws?
That added to the excitement of it. When the doors were closed, you could do what you wanted. It was our own state of freedom. There were no restrictions in that club, at the beginning, whatsoever. All you wanted to do, that was conducive to that atmosphere, you could do it. Like all of the good clubs that have stood the test of time. So, in a sense, yeah, it was an outlaw period.

Also, the authorities weren't aware of what was going on at the time. Which was great because we were running an illegal party. We could have got hammered for that. But it was a party and, fortunately, the police force were understanding. They could see it was run properly. It was adults running the place and it was efficiently run and safe. It was only when rave went major and it started to attract 25,000 and gangsters, that's when the police slammed into all of us. But those days leading up to that, even leading up to acid house with the warehouse parties, the police generally would let it go on and turn a blind eye. They were cool about it. Unfortunately, that was lost. And then the bloody ridiculous Criminal Justice Bill, which a lot of the clubbers who go to superclubs ignored. They were very ignorant of that bill. It was only the travelling scene and a sprinkling of other clubbers that got behind the protest and were against that bill.

What influence has acid house had on British society and music?
It's had a very positive influence. At the beginning, British youth culture was at the best of times quite divided. Different youth tribes. It did bring a lot of people together, through the music and with ecstasy as well. It did bring a huge proportion of London's youth together.

Everything changed so dramatically. There were parallels between the acid house movement and the '60s. Governments were very repressive, not many opportunities. All of a sudden this came along and the opportunity of the club, and seeing the culture affected through the crowd of people who came in the club, that then had a knock-on effect, with other people in a similar situation to myself who'd been held back. And the message was: Do It Yourself. There were changes politically, but the attitude was, who cares what the government does, we're just gonna get on with it ourselves – from the artistic side of things to the illegal side of things, and most of the opportunities that came along were illegal anyway! It was all black money.

How did that period change you?
It was the happiest period of my adult life. The most fulfilling time. After struggling to be a DJ for seven years and then getting your break, and making the break happen for yourself. For me, I was just eternally grateful that I'd made something happen after all the hardship,

and not getting there as a DJ but still following my passion and belief. It wasn't about the money. It was a fiver to get in. £300 for the sound system, door staff, hire of the building, so there wasn't much left every week. We made £300 on a good night.

Shoom had a very strict door policy didn't it?
It was a space for 250 people, so then people started to get resentful towards to the door policy. It wasn't our intention to keep it to this small dedicated group. It was progressing. There were a lot of underground parties going on. It attracted too much bad media attention. Those three years before that rave scene blew up were incredible. People who lived through the '60s said it was better than the '60s. You could be in a party every night of the week with this wide cross section of people from all walks of society. It was wonderful. One particular party was Hedonism where Soul II Soul were playing and Colin Faver, Justin Berkmann, Norman Jay. I went there to dance one night and it was brilliant.

You did that over a long period of time with Shoom, Pure Sexy and Glam, keeping it intimate. Did you feel protective?
Yeah.

There was a rave at Wembley which a load of Shoomers picketed. They actually tried to stop people going in because they felt it was too commercial, didn't they?
Yes, that was the Shoom militant wing!

When the doors were closed, you could do what you wanted. It was our own state of freedom. So, yeah, it was an outlaw period.

So you felt that this is a special thing and we don't want to ruin it?
Yes it did. That's why the TV crews that came down on occasions were kept at bay because we knew that it was very damaging and destructive to what was going on. And also because it was illegal and it was also rebellious. Why should we embrace them? What had they given us? This was our scene.
Alongside that was the commercialism, people like Colston-Hayter, Dave Roberts and even Oakey, he commercialised it. He'd admit that, he was a businessman right from the start. I didn't treat it as a business. I did it for the love of the party. It was a party every week. I wanted to keep that special. It was perceived as elitist at the time and maybe some of it was. It did feel secretive and special. In Shoom there was a magical mix and that had an effect on those people. There were many times when I wanted to speak out about what was going on but Jenni said, 'No if you do that it will have serious repercussions.' So I didn't say anything when at times I should've. She was worried about the authorities.

It was also where the cult of the DJ first took off in a serious way. You were a bit of a hero to them.
A messiah to some... To some it was a mystical experience and I can understand that, because there was a very unusual energy in there at times. A combination of music and people's mindset and that strong connection between people. I wasn't under the influence when I played there. I had a house to run. So the responsibility of that house was on my shoulders if the authorities turned up. I'd have a couple of scotches before I played to calm my nerves, just with the whole build up to it. Also with the dry ice and white lighting in there, it was trance-inducing. Records like 'Acid Tracks', it was a long hypnotic record, especially in that environment, with all that surging energy and with all the chemicals that were going on in there, a very tribal thing.

Tell me about Pure Sexy and Glam.
That was the clean-up period, really. It was rehab! Everything had become so commercialised.

....

Frightening really. Too much money involved, criminal gangs and a lot of people had let themselves go taking too many drugs. We didn't feel a part of that any longer. Same as happened in the '60s, people had lost control of their lives and lost sight of things. It was a reaction to the dressing down. It was so widespread it had become a uniform. So we moved off into a different direction and were heavily criticised. We closed our club before it closed itself. The last couple of months at Shoom were hard. It had become really sleazy and it wasn't fun. On the last night all of the proceeds were put back into the club and all their champagne was bought and distributed to everyone in the club. Marvellous night!

> **❝ I was doing my show from the 23rd floor. It had this magnificent view all over the whole of London. When house was blowing up, that whole energy and feeling, looking out over the city... ❞**

What were the connections between Shoom and Kiss?
I was doing my show on Friday afternoons between four and six. The best memories were from Cable Street, Hackney. It was at Manasseh's flat, which was on about the 23rd floor. It had this magnificent view all over the whole of London. When house was blowing up, that whole energy and feeling and being 23 floors up looking out over the city and people would be locked into Kiss during that time. It was very popular. That was a very exciting moment for me. I made this transition from playing independent soul to playing this wonderful new musical form that I'd embraced. That just felt amazing.

Was it very much the same records as you played in the club?
Yeah. Also those Balearic records. Which Gordon [Mac, from Kiss], at the time, couldn't get his head around for a moment. Then he came to the club and he saw what was going on and said, 'You're doing the right thing. Just get on with it.' That was a good endorsement.

What was it like being at Radio 1 doing what you were doing?
At the beginning, difficult. I'd felt really at home in London with Kiss, but at that time I was getting a bit disillusioned with them because they'd gone from being a pirate to corporate radio. Lots of suggestions of what you should be playing, lots of new rulings. It felt very stale. Just as I was getting ready to leave Kiss they came and offered me the job at Radio 1. I wasn't sure about the idea initially but Jenni was like, 'This is an incredible opportunity.'

When I first joined it was in the pit at Regent Street, down a tunnel where all these dinosaurs of rock had done their shows. It even had those Smashy and Nicey faders. Very different way of working. First record I played was 'I Get Lifted' by Barbara Tucker. It took me over a year to settle into it before I felt comfortable and I got a lot of flak for it, too. After all the years of playing in the underground.

How do you feel about it now?
The most positive aspect of it was that I was there week in week out sacrificing a great profile on my career internationally to play music that helped a lot of independent labels and artists. I was the black sheep of the family there, didn't play the game. Foolishly, now I look back on it. It taught me a lot about that world and about business. There was a lot of management politics and I got caught in the crossfire.

The best part of it is climbing radio from south London pirate to going national, and global through the internet. Most people who do radio would feel the same, they'd feel made up and accomplished. There were some very good days and there were some very negative days. When I left there I wasn't paid for seven months of work which added insult to injury. To work hard for the company then not get paid it left me very bitter for some time.

Did you think then that the DJ would become a superstar?

Patrick Lilley, who was involved with me, certainly did. He said, 'This is revolutionary in club life and I'd like to take you out on a worldwide tour with what you're doing.' Nowadays, you've got to be technically so brilliant and your concentration level has to be high, so you can't just go berserk in the DJ booth. But Patrick saw something there. He said it was going to be massive.

© DJhistory.com

SHOOM 50

CLS – Can You Feel It?
INNER CITY – Good Life
IT'S IMMATERIAL – Driving Away From Home
ARNOLD JARVIS – Time Out For Lovin'
ADONIS – No Way Back
RALPHI ROSARIO – You Used To Hold Me
PAUL SIMPSON & ADEVA – Musical Freedom
JOYCE SIMS – Come Into My Life
THE CLASH – The Magnificent Dance
ELKIN & NELSON – Jibaro
FALLOUT – The Morning After
FINGERS INC – Distant Planet
GENTRY ICE – Do You Want To Jack
PARIS GREY – Don't Lead Me
RICHIE HAVENS – Going Back To My Roots
TEN CITY – Right Back To You
TAJA SEVILLE – Love Is Contagious
DJ PIERRE'S PFANTASY CLUB – Dream Girl
CODE 6 – Drop The Deal
KENNY JAMMIN' JASON – Can U Dance
MARSHALL JEFFERSON – The House Music Anthem
LAURENT X – Machines
PHUTURE – Acid Tracks
A GUY CALLED GERALD – Voodoo Ray
ADONIS – The Poke
ART OF NOISE – Crusoe

BANG THE PARTY – Release Your Body
PETE WYLIE – Sinful
RICKSTER – Night Move
MFSB – Love Is The Message
RAZE – Break 4 Love
THE RESIDENTS – Kaw Liga
MR FINGERS – Stars
NIGHTWRITERS – Let The Music Use You
PHASE II – Reachin'
S*EXPRESS – Theme From S*Express
MANDY SMITH – I Just Can't Wait
JOE SMOOTH – Promised Land
TODD TERRY – Black Riot
MAC THORNHILL – (Who's Gonna) Ease The Pressure
U2 – I Still Haven't Found What I'm Looking For
RHYTHIM IS RHYTHIM – Strings Of Life
CE CE ROGERS – Someday
ROLLING STONES – Sympathy For The Devil
A SPLIT SECOND – Flesh
BARRY WHITE – It's Ecstasy When You Lay Down Next To Me
THE WOODENTOPS – Why Why Why
WILLIAM PITT – City Lights
JAMIE PRINCIPLE – Baby Wants To Ride
TEN CITY – Devotion

Compiled by Danny Rampling

RECOMMENDED LISTENING

VARIOUS – Mixmag Live Vol. 4 (DJ mix)
VARIOUS – Love Groove Dance Party Vols. 1&2 (DJ mix)
VARIOUS – Danny Rampling: Break For Love

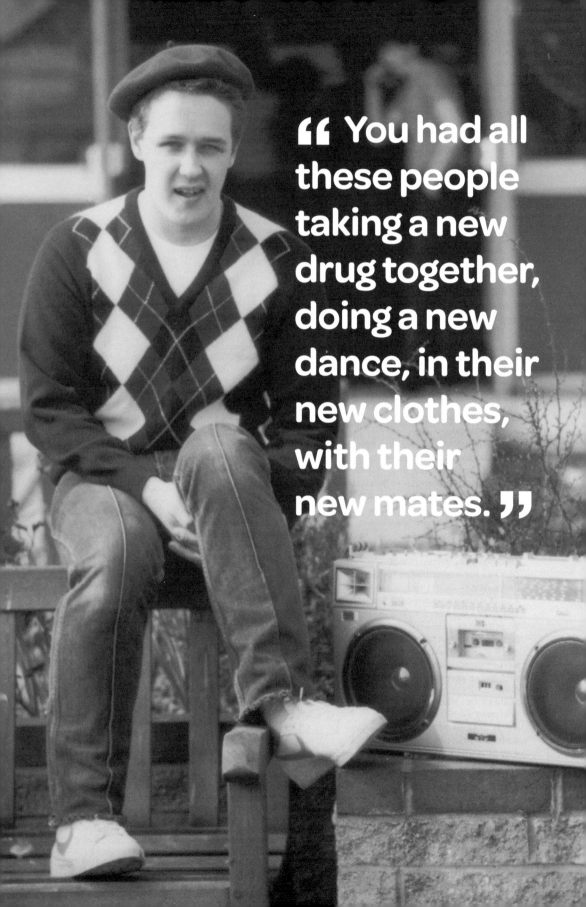

" You had all these people taking a new drug together, doing a new dance, in their new clothes, with their new mates. "

Terry Farley
Cultural hooligan

Interviewed by Bill and Frank at Bill's house, February 23, 2005

'A black gay man trapped in the body of a gas fitter from Slough,' is how fellow DJ and suburbanite Rocky sums up the irascible old soulboy. As a founding member of the Boy's Own collective, Farley led his troops feet first into acid house, converting them overnight from the floppy hats of rare groove to Balearic dungarees. For a short period in 1988, Terry forsook his natural inclination to listen exclusively to black music in order to frequent alien stores such as Rough Trade hunting for Woodentops 12-inches.

The brave new world promised by house music and ecstasy was just the excuse working-class kids like Terry needed to mount an attack on the status quo of London nightlife. For too long, they felt, it had been in the hands of a clique of St Martin's art school graduates. Clued-up suburban clubbers like Terry and his mates were referred to as the 'footsoldiers', a reliable source of bodies to fill a night, but never certain they'd get through the door. With ecstasy the rules changed completely and footy casuals were calling the shots.

The Boy's Own fanzine was the mouthpiece for all this, at the same time a glorious celebration and scurrilous piss-take of the new culture. With Boy's Own Terry also established a reputation for brilliant parties and, when it became a label, for great British house productions (with his long-term partner Pete Heller). The spirit of Boy's Own lives on in the Faith parties which Terry throws with a rogues' gallery of associates. He's one of the most astute observers of British youth culture around and can deduce voting intentions from a stripe on a trainer at 100 yards.

Let's start with a bit of biographical detail.
I was born in 1958 in Latimer Road, London. I lived there till I was about 13, then I moved to Slough.

Did you get moved because of the Westway?
We got moved because they were supposed to be doing a Westway spur. They were supposed to be building another one right down our road and they never did it, but they pulled everyone's houses down. We had an outside toilet and no bathroom. I was 12 and we still had a tin bath. Once I'd moved to Slough, we were on an estate that now looks shit but at the time looked wonderful.

How did you get into music?
Well, I got into music living in London because we were in the white area of north Kensington, but when you got to the bottom of the road you got into Ladbroke Grove and it was very West Indian. I got really into reggae when I was nine or 10. My dad hated it – 'Fuckin' parties all night long!' – we used to love it 'cos it wound him up.

How often were you able to get into the city?
Well, when we moved my mum and dad split so my dad remained in north Kensington, till he died a few years ago, and both my grandparents lived here. I used to come back and see me dad and buy records in places like Dub Vendor in Clapham Junction market and later on

they opened a store just under the bridge, opposite where they are now, in Ladbroke Grove. People in Slough were obsessed with London. Maybe that's why I've always been obsessed with this stuff myself…

When did you start clubbing?
I started going quite late. A few little clubs sprung up in Slough and we were at the front of it all. Then we started coming into London, me and Gary Haisman. We first started going to Crackers, suddenly there was this whole gay thing in your face. There was a lot of people there pretending to be gay 'cos I think a lot of people on that scene had come out of Louise's and Chaguarama's. My dad used to hate Gary Haisman. He used to say to my mum, 'He'll turn him, he'll turn him!' Gary wasn't gay at all, but he was quite effeminate as a kid.

How did you hear about Crackers? Was that the main club you went to?
It was the first club I went to where it was, 'Wow, this is just amazing.' Crackers was the first club for our generation.

The first time a place felt like yours?
I think so. We used to go on a Sunday first. It was on from 7 o'clock till 12, but the last train to Slough went at half 11, so we'd have to leave at half 10. So we'd get there and there'd be no-one in there and just as people started dancing we'd have to leave… it was something like 50 pence to get in and you got sausage and chips! The place stunk of sausage and chips. I think it was licensing laws. I was obsessed. I used to go up on my own and I didn't know anyone in there. It was about 85 percent black.

❝ You couldn't even stand on the dancefloor unless you could dance, because you'd have some guy who was fuckin' amazing come right up in your face and throw all these moves. ❞

What year did you first go?
I dunno. The sort of records they played when I first went were things like Lalo Schifrin's 'Jaws'. It was fuckin' brilliant. I really loved the fact it was like the northern soul thing. It was carpeted, the club, and they had a proper dancefloor, but you couldn't even stand on the dancefloor unless you could dance. White kids, even the ones who could dance, wouldn't go on the dancefloor because you'd have some guy who was fuckin' amazing come right up in your face and throw all these moves and you'd have to walk back… And the first white kid who could dance was Tommy McDonald, he put himself out there. Then Gary Haisman was very good after.

Was the dancing as important as the music?
I think that's probably what got me, it was the dancing. It was funny 'cos you went there and all the black guys in there – Trevor Shakes, Bevis Pink, Jabba from Ealing – the rumour was everyone went to the London Ballet School, but in fact they went to the Pineapple Dance classes in Covent Garden. Everyone started going there. I was working at the gas board and Saturday you'd go along and there'd be these kids getting lessons from someone crap like Arlene Phillips.

Was it a spectator thing?
Well you danced, it was like you had to dance within yourself. If you danced a little bit too energetically, even if it was in a corner, you'd get spotted and someone would come and…

You'd better be good!
Yeah. But then what would happen was people would travel around. There was a club in Dunstable called the Devil's Den which was part of the California Ballrooms. They used to

have big bands playing there like James Brown, Fatback Band. They'd get 6,000 people for some of these big soul concerts. They had a little club in there and you'd get these soul kids from London, and suddenly you realised there were black kids from Reading and Luton. You realised there was a network of these little dancers who were really good and there was a club every night on this circuit.

Was the dancing about battling?
Very much. It did, on many occasions, break out into violence when someone didn't win.

Really?
They danced to the Bee Gees' 'You Should Be Dancing', that's the record they played in the final. There was a guy from Ealing called Jabba who was a really big black man, probably older than everyone. He might have been 25, very muscly. It was very much that someone would dance and everyone would gather round and go, 'Woo woo!' It was the first time I heard people making noises in a club. It was very dark in there because it had a low ceiling. And, especially when George Power took over, it got very intense. You'd hear like Zulu noises in there. It become very intense. These kids were teenage boys from very rough parts of London. Most of the kids who were really good were gawky skinny kids. There certainly weren't no peace or love in there.

If you went to the Royalty or any of those white clubs that Chris Hill was playing it was really friendly. Them clubs weren't like that at all. You could get smacked in the mouth if you stepped on someone's foot. Women losing their handbags. Then they switched it to a Friday lunchtime and it got even younger. You'd come out there with 500 kids running down Oxford Street. There was a shop called Stanley Adams which is where Woodhouse is, and they sold Smith jeans, stuff like that; they'd steam in there, ripping things out, steaming, bag snatching… bad behaviour.

It was quite ghetto?
Yeah, very bad behaviour.

You say when George took over. Who was there first?
Well, when I first went Mark Roman was there. Really cool, older guy. He looked Greek, he wore really nice clothes. We were really into that. We'd go up and say, 'Where did you get your jumper from?' [laughs]. Browns in South Moulton Street was a really trendy shop for older soul boys and everyone was wearing sandals and big baggy jumpers and carpenter jeans. He played really good music, stuff like Bobby Womack's 'Daylight' was massive when I first started going there, 'Let's Do The Latin Hustle' by Eddie Drennon, and 'Bimbo Jet' by El Bimbo. There was lots of people who had maybe been Bowie boys with wedges and girls doing the hustle. It was probably a real mixture, older gay guys, a lot of white kids; the black kids in there were really trendy and good dancers. Then suddenly when George Power come in, it seemed to get really black and BOOM – changed the music. A lot of jazz and jazz funk stuff.

Was it a unique place or were there others?
I think it was unique. Me and Norman Jay talk about this a lot. At the time, 100 Club was on a Saturday afternoon with Greg Edwards. It was pretty much a similar crowd and on a Sunday upstairs at Ronnie Scott's. When you went to another club, like Hemel Hempstead, people'd come up to and go: 'You go to Crackers, don't yer?' Like Shoom was *the* acid house club, Crackers was *the* club.

Did that open any doors outside of the club. Was there a bit of a network going on?
Only to go clubbing, I don't think anything creative came out of it. Maybe it was people's first experience, and first real good experience, that made them do what they do now, but it wasn't like Shoom where suddenly people were opening clothes shops. But that might just have been the age of people, they were very young.

Tell us about George Power.
He was 10 years older than everyone, at least, this Greek guy with terrible clothes. It was really important how you looked. Even the kids who didn't have the right clothes, still did the right dance, so it compensated. But George had everything wrong about him. He used

to use the mic which no one else did. He used to say stuff like, 'Get up, get jazzy!' But he was fantastic. A bit like Tim Westwood. You think, 'Why do these kids accept him, he's so wrong?' Maybe it's the same thing. I never heard anyone saying, 'Let's fuck him off,' and there was a lot of testosterone about. People had a real passion about him.

We're people taking a lot of drugs?
Don't know. I was very naive about what was going on around then. I went to Wigan once, about '76, I didn't even realise that people took drugs there. I was very into all that northern soul stuff and I didn't realise what was going on. I went with a Slough DJ called Alan Sullivan who was a soul DJ and also, apparently, the leader of the Shed! [the football terraces at Chelsea] When I moved to Slough he had a gang called Sulli's boot boys and they said he was the leader of the Shed. He used to DJ and he was a pretty good northern soul dancer.

There were northern parties going on at the Top Rank in Reading. We started going there and he said they were running minibuses up to Wigan. Gary Haisman went, and a couple of black guys from Slough who were treated like absolute royalty. People buying them drinks and shaking their hands. I'd been up north a few times by then, with Chelsea, and it had been disastrous. You'd get the train bricked, you'd get murdered up there, so I couldn't believe how friendly they were at Wigan. Nothing like it was in London.

I think the people at Crackers thought they were the best, because they had the newest records and the best dancers and they were very arrogant about that. I was very much an outsider looking in, but when I went somewhere like Dunstable, I'd be Mr Crackers, you know what I mean? [laughter] And I'd be as gobby and arrogant as they were to me!

So how did you get involved in the all-dayers and stuff?
At Reading they had an upstairs room where they played funk and stuff like that, a lot of black kids, similar records to Crackers. A hundred upstairs, and 1,000 people downstairs dancing to fairly commercial northern soul. Then they did an all-dayer and I think it was Chris Hill who played there. And he led all these people out of the small upstairs room down on to the main dancefloor in front of the DJ and demanded they played funk. It ended up with some funk being played and the northen soulies all standing like this [arms folded, sulking] and then they played a northern soul record and there'd be booing and shouting. When it came round to the next all-dayer, which I think were on bank holidays…

Which year was this?
About 1977 I'd imagine. Suddenly it just flipped. I remember walking in there and there was 300 northern soul fans and 1,000 London-based soul boys. 'Fuckin' hell, where have all these people come from?' Then everywhere, everyone was a soul boy.

Where were the first weekenders you went to?
I went to the first Caister.

1981?
I think so. I went to the next 11 or 12. I've got some funny pictures. When the Malcolm McLaren album was out, *Duck Rock,* in 1982, we was still going to Caister. I've got a picture of Weatherall with a Mohican, Johnny Rocca in full Malcolm McLaren hat, suit, the other people were Cymon Eckel, dressed in full Vivienne Westwood stuff. And the rest of the people were still in fuckin' silk shorts! But, you know, we liked it.

Were people doing drugs or getting pissed?
Pissed. The first time I ever realised people were doing drugs was when I first met Rocca and I was on the production line at Ford's in Langley. I was working on the night shift. There was a guy who used to come in with a portable record player, West Indian guy, he had a box of sevens he used to play. I used to buy reggae records off him. Then this guy says, 'Oh I've seen you go to Scandals.' It was a soul club on a Friday. He said you should come down with me next Friday. They had a half shift at Fords on a Friday, so you went in at two and came out at seven. About three in the afternoon he said, 'You're coming aren't you?'

'Yeah, got me clothes.'

He said, 'Have one of these.'

I said 'What is it?'
'Blues. Everyone takes them at soul things!'
'Do they?' [laughter]
He gave me this tablet, I remember I was putting the tachographs in the cabs. You had a set amount to do and once you'd done them you could finish. I did them in about two hours!

What went wrong with the all-dayers?
It just become enormous. When I first went to Crackers, there were probably only 2-3,000 people in the whole of the south-east of England who were into it. Suddenly, when the all-dayers broke, it was all the kids from where you lived who went. Instead of me going to Crackers with four or five people, it was the whole of Slough. Slough suddenly opened a club and people like Steve Walsh came down.

There was no fun, it was very serious, but it was great because it was your thing. Once the Chris Hill thing came in, they brought fun into it. They marched people down on to that dancefloor. Once that element of fun came in, instead of Mark Roman going, 'Shake your booty,' you've got a guy going, 'Woooah-woooah!' and it becomes shockingly embarrassing. So instead of the soul boys having the best clothes, these people were the worst dressed.

> **I'd been up north a few times with Chelsea, and it had been disastrous. You'd get the train bricked, you'd get murdered, so I couldn't believe how friendly they were at Wigan.**

Did your crowd sack it and look for something else?
Yeah. I got into reggae in a big way again. I was into lovers rock. Went to 100 Club on a Thursday, Prince Far I, Dennis Brown used to play there. Got into the jazz scene, with Paul Murphy at the Horseshoe in Tottenham Court Road. A lot of the dancers who used to go to Crackers moved into that jazz dance scene where that intensity was still going on. Then a lot of my mates got into that indie dance. I personally didn't like it.

Where did you first hear house music?
The first time I thought this is a thing rather than a record, I played at a warehouse party. We used to go to a shop called Demob which was run by Steve Marney and some northern soul people. They had a warehouse in Rosebery Avenue. Being a record collector, I was getting loads of gigs playing backrooms.

Playing reggae?
Not really. I used to play sort of leftfield stuff, early rap, things like that. I'd be playing soul clubs in the back room playing records that people didn't dance to. We used to go in Demob and he asked me if I wanted to play. Big thing for me. Maurice and Noel Watson were playing and I was doing the warm-up. I was playing maybe the sort of stuff that early Jay Strongman would have been playing. They came on and played two hours of records I'd never heard. They were all new New York labels like Sleeping Bag, that real sort of tribally sound. I asked them where they'd got them from and they were like, 'Oh we got them from New York.' That was my first house moment listening to those two play.

What was the response like?
It was good. It was a warehouse with a lot of crazy people in it. It was quite fashion-y. Londoners' negative response to house music wasn't the fact that they didn't like it, it was due to the rare groove scene, which was so enormous and so good. It wasn't they didn't like house, they just didn't need it. Clubbing was probably the best it had been since Crackers. Suddenly the dancing was important again. Even though the clothes were '70s-related, they

were good. It got back to credible again. People going to warehouses. Anthems. There was always another record to find.

Did the warehouses suddenly spring up or were they always happening?
It was part of the rare groove thing. Without the rare groove scene London wouldn't have exploded in the way it did when house came along, because you already had everything there. You had the sound systems, you had the people in the clubs. They just switched the music and, instead of there being a1,000 people, suddenly there was 10,000. It was already there.

So it wasn't house exactly, that the Watson's were playing? It was stuff like Serious Intention's 'You Don't Know'?
Yes, it was. But I remember them specifically playing the dubs of those records, which was quite radical then. And I think they were mixing as well, not well particularly, but in a way that linked the records. The first time I heard house as something different and, 'This is what we're gonna play,' was at the Raid. I used to warm up there and Pete Tong and Oakey were the main DJs. It was just around the time when Tongy was trying to get that thing together with London, and he'd play a half an hour of house and people didn't know how to react to it.

> **❝ Me and Weatherall were on the door, a group of kids come up all Shoomed up and we were like, 'No, you can't come in like that.' A week later I've got dungarees on. ❞**

Did he clear the floor?
Well, people just never danced. Go-go was big at the time. I remember him having two copies of something which he'd cut up and he was pretty good at it. Then things like 'Love Can't Turn Around' [by Farley 'Jackmaster' Funk] would be played and people'd just didn't know how to dance to it. It didn't go with how people were dancing, with the little jazz moves. You could play a Def Jam record next to a go-go record and a James Brown record; but then you played a house record and it was like, 'What am I supposed to do to this?' It didn't fit in with anything else. It only worked when it was only house. It didn't work as part of the tapestry of what was being played

We used to go to Rockley Sands where the music was fantastic, you'd get a good crowd there. You could hear jazz records from the '60s next to Public Enemy. First time I ever seen Danny Rampling was there. He'd been trying to get a gig with Nicky Holloway, who was a mate of his, but he wouldn't let him play. Johnny Walker was playing George Kranz's 'Din Daa Daa' and Rampling jumped on the stage and started doing this Shoom dance. People was going, 'He's took one of them E things! You know them Es? They've got them in Ibiza.' This was in November of 1987 so they must've just come back. They asked him to get off. Holloway was getting the hump. And someone said, 'Look at Chris Butler!' and Chris Butler was in the speaker [laughter].

It was like, 'What's going on?'

They were going, 'If you take one of these Es it lasts all night and tomorrow.'

On Sunday afternoon they were all there dancing, Johnny Walker, Chris Butler, Danny and a couple of little girls. They were going 'Yeah, we took one last night and we're still on it. It's fuckin' great.'

We were like, 'Wow, yeah. Brilliant.'

We all had to have some. It was the first time I'd ever taken an E and known what to do.

Did you go to the early Shooms?
I went in January I think. I missed the first month. My main problem – or my main asset – is when I get into something I go in with two feet and I'm really enthusiastic. The *Boy's*

Own magazine was going, which was totally rare groove. I had the big trousers and the hat. We had pictures of Rockley Sands, pictures of guys in rare groove stuff. Then suddenly – BOOM – there it was. And I was like, 'Right we're changing. This is amazing!' One of these girls, who was one of Chris Butler's lot, did actually say to me, 'You've missed it. It's full of wankers now.'

When?
About the fourth week. The first three were full of the 20 people who'd gone to Amnesia. Suddenly, the people who were in the know started to come in and you could tell even then they were being really defensive about it; they didn't even really want you in there. We were like the first wave and then suddenly, two months later, we were being really defensive about everyone else. Saying to Jenni, 'Don't give any more memberships out.' It was like that.

Why were they like that? They were quite on it with the press.
That was later. First of all it was this wonderful little secret and the people who were there were very much part of that Rockley Sands clique of people. Suddenly people were coming in from outside. Jenni hired a PR company, Victory PR, who were doing the big parties in London. I remember talking to Robert Elms in there and holding Gary Crowley's hand to Joyce Sims' 'Come Into My Life' at the end! All sorts of people in there: Bananarama, Martin Fry, Paul Rutherford, Michael Clark. You could definitely tell there was different levels of people who didn't really get on with each other because everyone thought they were the true Shoomers.

But it was also an end of something and a start of something else, because the Elmses and Bananaramas belonged to the previous generation of elite clubbers.
Well, they tried it. I remember Robert Elms in the mid '80s walking round at the Wag Club in a Gaultier suit and he looked fantastic. Suddenly he's coming up to me in Shoom, in shorts, looking a knob. [laughter].

What were you wearing?
I was into that distressed casual look. The first people who forged that Ibiza thing were kids from this estate called Roundshaw. They were living in Ibiza. That band Natural Life, they were part of it. One of their dads was a bass player. They were all in old Chevignon jackets, Lee dungarees and Converse. That's where that look comes from.

   We did a party at the Raid club underneath this hotel in Marble Arch. Me and Weatherall were on the door dressed up and a group of kids come up and one of them was from football, he was Millwall, and they were all Shoomed up and we were like, 'No, you can't come in like that.' Then Haisman took us there and suddenly I realised all the people in Shoom were the people who I didn't let in six weeks earlier. A week later I've got dungarees on and looking a right pudding! [laughter] That's the way it was.

What about Spectrum?
When Spectrum first started I was playing reggae in the VIP room. The first week there was 100 in there and they give everyone a free E. Oakey played. He played the top 20 Alfredo records. There was people running round with flowers on the dancefloor. It was fuckin' brilliant. Second week, it was brilliant, but only 100 people in there. Third week they were saying they were gonna shut it. I think the fourth or fifth week they were like I can't pay you your £20 wages. Then the last week it was gonna shut, we turned up and there were 400 in the queue. 'Wow, what the fuck's going on here?' Within a month it was however many it holds – 3,000.

What was the difference between Spectrum and say Shoom?
Class, I'd say. Once Shoom was in full swing, it was split between working class, middle class and upper class people, whereas Future was south London and it was quite moody in there. By the time Shoom had kicked off the people at Future were looking down at them. There was a lot of sort of fringe characters who wouldn't have gone in at Shoom, because they wouldn't have gone to the rigmarole of getting the clothes and dancing round to Danny. They were too cool for that. So there were a few plazzy gangsters in there and a few real ones

....

as well. Spectrum, though, was just full of potty kids. Probably the same as the Haçienda and Cream. It was pretty racially mixed for the time, as well, because Shoom wasn't. Future wasn't either.

How did *Boy's Own* start? You were plugged into *The End* in Liverpool weren't you?
Well, I used to write silly letters to them and they'd print them, stuff about football fashion. We met Cymon Eckel and Andy Weatherall and I said I'd like to do a fanzine like *The End* but about London. Weatherall was up for creating this monster and he was very clever. Mine and Steve Mayes' schooling was pretty non-existent, and Andrew, of the first half a dozen magazines, he did nearly everything.

When did it start?
1986. It was a weird time in London. We used to go to football and that whole casual thing was pretty big. To get into the clubs at night we would have to change the way we looked completely.

You'd have to look like something out of *the Face* rather than something off the terraces?
Yeah. Or even something out of London. Ollie who run the door at le Beat Route was Welsh. Chris Sullivan was Welsh. Steve Marney from Demob was Welsh! We all got the hump that we'd go along to these things and they'd let four in but not all of us. We couldn't go straight from football, we had to go home and get changed. It did piss us off. I didn't mind the clothes they were wearing in these places, it didn't bother me, but it was like the inconvenience of being told what to do in your city, by people who were... Welsh. It seemed like the whole club scene was run by a St. Martin's School clique and even the London people like Robert Elms and Graham Ball, they'd all gone to the London School of Economics. I knew as much as they did, I knew loads about records, but I could only come in if I got changed. We hated that scenario.

What did house change?
It meant we didn't have to change clothes! [laughter] I remember talking to Jonathan Richardson [who ran Pop Promotions], I really liked him and I had something tenuously to do with Pop at some stage. I think I might have owned it for a week. I remember talking to him and meeting his friends and he said, 'Yeah, we all met at Cambridge University. Where did you go to school?'
'Er, I went to Broomfield in Slough.'
'What's that?'
'It's a comprehensive.'
Suddenly I realised I didn't know anyone like them. Even when you went to the Wag, you didn't meet people like that because everyone kept to themselves. House was the first time them barriers broke down. Suddenly you were talking to people outside of your class and it didn't matter that they were from up north or what clothes they had on.

House music definitely broke down all kinds of barriers like that. Shoom was very sexually mixed: gays, straights, all sorts of gay palaver going on, which some of the kids in there, who were football hooligans, would never have seen. Michael Clark and a Scottish guy called Sandy, who worked for Vivienne Westwood, they had little real urchin kids from south London who would follow them round like flies. It was almost like they were mesmerised by these Beautiful Creatures. But Danny was all important to that.

Why?
The dance. The whole acid house dance is Danny Rampling. Waving his record while he's playing. Until then DJs used to just put records on. They didn't do anything. During the rare groove thing you wouldn't acknowledge the crowd. They wouldn't even smile at the crowd. The crowd wouldn't smile at the DJ. There was no connection. Suddenly Danny's standing there and he's waving his record around, shouting and people shouting at him and hugging. That was his dance. Then it became the Shoom dance then the Shoom dance became the Spectrum dance, then the whole of the fuckin' country! I'm sure he stole it from Ibiza. I'm sure of it.

That whole movement came pre-packaged. You had the dance, which was so different from everything else. You had the drug. You had a series of records that were totally overlooked by everyone, and they'd already been hits in this club, Amnesia. Rough Trade? Where's that? I'd never been in Rough Trade records. I went in there, 'Have you got this Woodentops record?' First time I met Rocky I was in there trying to buy Nitzer Ebb and the Woodentops! It wasn't a soul boy shop, why would I have gone in there?

It's like you were saying about house, that it was a fresh start.
House only worked when you went, 'Right, this is a house club.' You went there in your house clothes. You did the house dance. You did a totally different drug. So you had all these people taking a new drug together, doing a new dance, in their new clothes with their new mates. I remember really good mates, me, Plug, there was about 10 of us going to Shoom and suddenly all of our really good mates wanted to come and we didn't want them coming. We didn't want these blokes, who we'd hung around with for 10 years, we didn't want them coming. This was our thing.

" We couldn't go straight from football, we had to go home and get changed. It did piss us off. It seemed like the whole club scene was run by a St. Martin's School clique. "

Why is that?
Everyone was like that. This is our thing. This is us.

Were you afraid they wouldn't get it?
We didn't want no-one else to get it. It was so amazing you didn't want anyone else to get it.

But that goes totally against the whole idea of amazing experiences, doesn't it?
Yeah, I know. You went around telling people how good it was, but then you didn't want them coming! [laughter]

Was it obvious that it was gonna be massive when you were stood in Shoom?
No, because you were so in it, so in that fuckin' stew, you never thought about it. I remember me and Sue went on holiday to Portugal in the spring of '88 and I didn't want to go because I didn't want to miss Shoom, because when I came back I thought it might be different. I remember having the headphones on listening to 'City Lights' [by William Pitt] thinking, 'I wish I was at Shoom, I can't believe I'm here, what am I doing here?' No one could say that in a year's time this would still be going on. It was so intense. You thought the police would stop it or something.

There must have been a point where you realised it wasn't going to end?
Not really. Once '89 was over it always seemed to be that the clubs were never quite as good as Shoom or the early *Boy's Own* parties. It felt like you were treading water. Looking back, though, at these clubs, they were brilliant. The one regret I've got about that time is that I wasn't more open. I wish I'd gone to Sunrise.

So you didn't go?
No, in fact, people said, you're not allowed to go. I remember a party at Wembley, I think it was the first ever Biology and there were Shoomers outside and they were saying don't go in.

Like a picket?
Yeah! I think they'd gone down there, found Danny wasn't playing and then stopped people from going in. *Boy's Own* was terribly like that. Once people had become part of that inner clique, it got really cliquey in London. I never went to Confusion, I never to Mr C's club, I never went to High On Hope! We just didn't. It's a shame because we missed out on a lot.

Did house music provide opportunities for people like you? Did you feel you could do things suddenly?

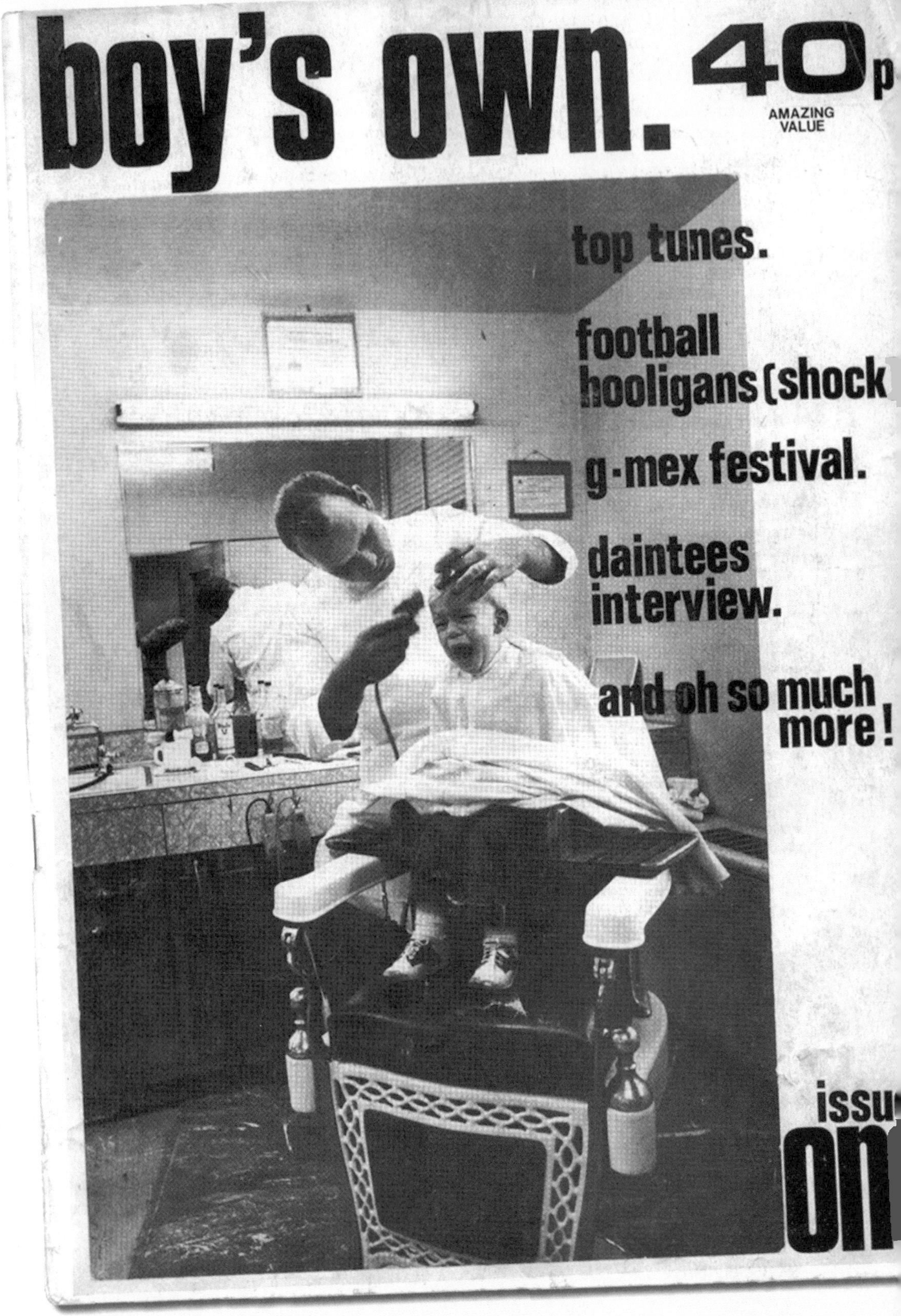

boy's own.

40p

AMAZING VALUE

top tunes.

football hooligans (shock

g·mex festival.

daintees interview.

and oh so much more!

issue

on

Maybe that's ecstasy. I don't think house on its own would have done that. Maybe if it had only been house it would have been another movement like go-go or like rare groove. There were people who opened clothes stores in rare groove times and started to run labels. You had little shoots of creativity. When everyone met at places like Shoom, you thought, 'I could do that.' Maybe they were opening a clothes shop, or selling drugs or starting a label or even making a record, which seemed incredible. No DJs had been making records, not really, till house came along.

❝ All of a sudden all these people started clapping, as though they were acid house geese and we'd trained them. ❞

Where do you think it all went wrong?
I don't think it's gone wrong. There are thousands of people out every Saturday dancing to house music. Or Ibiza.

There are, but it's gotten a lot smaller.
It's got smaller, probably I think because that Bright Bill that was funded by the breweries to get people in their pubs. The breweries suddenly started doing alcopops and cleared the tables and chairs out and put music on. What that meant was instead of there being a club in Hereford playing house, it went back to 30 people in Hereford travelling somewhere else. I think that killed it, the pub chains.

And now they're the ones that are paying for it with a nation of binge-drinking teenagers, when you could have had a nation of E-takers, but not causing any problems. Now they're stuck with every casualty in every major city, with glassings, stabbings and policemen being sorted. No-one got sorted at Sunrise and it's the same kids. Without doubt there was a definite boardroom decision taken. They said, 'We've gotta get them out of these fields and back into our pubs, how we gonna do this?'

There's never been a musical movement that has been so invested in by outside forces as house music.
But also there's never been a music that people have been so passionate about. I don't think there's ever been a movement where you get into something and take drugs for the first time, you've suddenly got thousands of mates.

But if you're 16 now you're never gonna have that experience.
No, but if you were 16 in '94 you didn't have to go to Shoom to have that. If you go out to the End on a Saturday, the majority are 23-30, and they probably had their first experiences when they were 16. There are no rare groove websites. There are no go-go websites. There's no one obsessed about mixes that Chuck Brown did. There are no websites with mixes that Norman Jay did in '82. But I can find Larry Levan, Ron Hardy, it's only house that has that obsession.

What sort of old records got played back then?
I used to play a lot of my old soul records. Anything with the word 'ecstasy' in [laughter]. Jackie Wilson's 'Sweetest Feeling'. I used to play that every week at Spectrum. People would go, 'That record! Fuckin' hell, I never realised this was about E!' [laughter] Loads of records that were obviously about love, suddenly people were hearing all sorts of drug connotations. Especially the word 'ecstasy', like the Barry White.

How did you start the *Boy's Own* parties?
We did a few small ones before acid house. But early on in '88 we said we wanted to do a party and we asked Danny to play. We found a guy who owned a big house in Guildford. He had a really small barn about twice the size of this room [a living room] and a big garden.

....

Danny couldn't do it 'cos he didn't want to shut Shoom down, so we got Steve Proctor to play. We run 200 people down. The bloke who owned the place was sitting there at about six in the morning with Boy George, and George was singing 'Karma Chameleon' and this bloke says, 'This is the greatest moment of my life!'

It got to about 8.30 in the morning and everyone was really going for it. There was not one complaint. The police turned up. I've got pictures of this, it's appalling: there's Smiley shorts, bandanas. It's really bad. They said, 'What's happening here then?'

'Oh, we're from London, we're on these coaches here and we're having a party.'

They went, 'Right, there's beer cans in the street, can you pick them up.'

So we walked over there, off our nuts, picked up the beer cans.

They said, 'What time are you finishing?'

We said, 'Er…. 11?'

'Alright then. See you lads!'

A year later they're using truncheons!

Weren't there people walking home and talking to cows?

That was at the East Grinstead party. That was the one party for me where it was like this is it. There'll never ever be anything like this. We were very lucky because we had this great field right on a lake, massive marquee, sold tickets in London, we ran a few coaches and we had about 500 people of the Shoom/Future crowd. Unknown to us there was a huge rave, something like Sunrise, in the next village. The police had spent the whole night trying to shut that down and left us completely alone. We had all the bales of hay and on this lake there were these geese. I can't remember anyone dancing. It was weird, just people sitting there gurning. And these geese came down, a flock of them, through the mist – *schhhhhh* – and all of a sudden all these people started clapping, as if, you know, we'd done this, [laughter] as though they were acid house geese and we'd trained them.

Then there was a big hill and someone said, 'Look at that cow.' There were about four cows on this hill. 'That cow's dancing.' It was about quarter of a mile away. And everyone stopped and were looking. This cow was going [wiggles right leg] and people were going, 'Aw, fucking hell!' The cow was slowly coming down the hill. Suddenly it got really close and you could see it was jacking! And there was people who couldn't look at it, freaked out. Suddenly you could tell it was a pantomine cow. It was Barry Mooncult and someone else. But they hadn't walked into the party and gone 'Weee!' They'd been up on the hill for about half an hour freaking people out.

© DJhistory.com

FAITH 50

JON CUTLER FT. E MAN – It's Yours
JULIAN JABRE – Voodance
JOSH ONE – Contemplation
METRO AREA – 1-4
MONDO GROSSO – Star Suite
DJ GREGORY – Tropical Soundclash
DJ BUCK – Release The Tension
ROBERT OWENS – Tears (Full Intention Remix)
PEACE DIVISION – Black Light Sleaze
ABSTRACT TRUTH – We Had A Thing
KERRI CHANDLER – Atmosphere
CARL CRAIG – Sandstorm
TEN CITY – All Loved Out (Joe Claussell Mix)
THE JACKSONS – We're Almost There
(DJ Spinna Remix)
DUBTRIBE SOUND SYSTEM – Equitoreal
MINIMAL FUNK – My Definition Of House
TEDD PATTERSON – Roots
MONDO GROSSO – Souffles (MAW Mix)
BILLY PAUL – Let 'Em In
QUENTIN HARRIS – My Joy
DJ GREGORY – Elle
BLAZE – My Beat (Derrick Carter Mix)
RPR – Got E's
ABE DUQUE – Disco Lights
FRANKIE KNUCKLES – Only The Strong Survive
AME – Nia
ROBERT OWENS – Walk A Mile In My Shoes
(Henrik Schwarz Mix)
ANE BRUN – Headphone Silence (Dixon Mix)

PHOTEK – Mine To Give (Morales Mix)
DANNY TENAGLIA – Elements
ARGY – Love Dose (Luciano Mix)
TRIANGLE ORCHESTRA – Where's The Tape
GLADYS KINIGHT & THE PIPS – I've Got To
Use My Imagination (Quentin Harris & Timmy
Regisford Mix)
JEROME SYDENHAM & DENNIS FERRER –
Sandcastles
DJ GREGORY – The Joburg Theme
DOUBLE EXPOSURE – Everyman
(Joe Claussell Edit)
DAN ROBBINS – Chanting In The Dark
(Pete Heller Mix)
LINDA CLIFFORD – Changes (Ralphi Rosario Mix)
JEPHTE GUILLAUME – The Prayer
STEVE BUG – Loverboy
DUBTRIBE SOUND SYSTEM – Do It Now
DJ SNEAK – You Can't Hide From Your Bud
GUIDO SCHNEIDER – Transmissions
SHLOMI ABER – Freakside
DONNIE – Cloud 9 (Quentin Harris Mix)
LOS JUGADEROS – What You Doing To This Girl
(Norman Jay Edit)
BOOKA SHADE v. MANDY – Body Language
HERCULES AND LOVE AFFAIR – Blind
(Frankie Knuckles Mix)
BRETT JOHNSON & DJ HEATHER –
Everything's Electric
JILL SCOTT – Scott Free

Compiled by Terry Farley

RECOMMENDED LISTENING

VARIOUS – Faith Vol. 1 (DJ mix)
VARIOUS – Junior Boy's Own: A Boy's Own Odyssey (DJ mix)

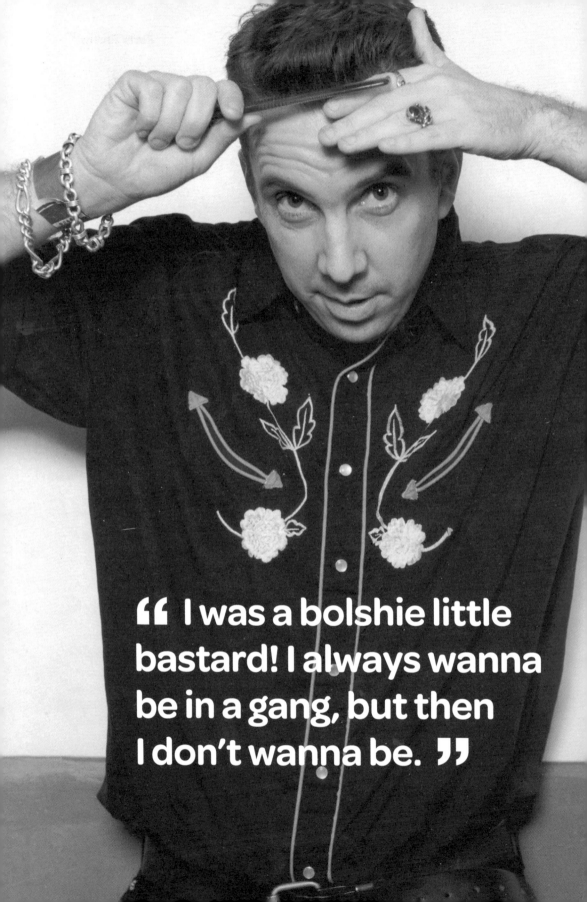

" I was a bolshie little bastard! I always wanna be in a gang, but then I don't wanna be. "

Andrew Weatherall
Electronic punk

Interviewed by Bill in London, May 28, 2009

Inspired as much by '50s rockabilly legend Mac Curtis as the deep house of Mac Thornhill, Andrew Weatherall bequeathed us one of the finest albums of the modern era in *Screamadelica*. In a variety of subsequent guises he went on to produce everything from coruscating techno made for shirts-off German nutters to delicate ambient music perfect for Café Del Mar, and his DJ sets are as notoriously wide and eclectic as his productions.

Weatherall started his DJing career as the bloke with weird records booked to play in second rooms or late on in the proceedings. After regular appearances at early acid club Shoom he found himself suddenly in demand, and at gigs where he was expected to actually make people dance. Working in a Windsor clothes shop by day, by night he'd be either DJing or venting his spleen in the pages of Boy's Own, the fanzine he started with local chums Terry Farley, Cymon Eckel and Steve Mayes.

We meet in the Griffin, a skanky old boozer in Shoreditch owned by Weatherall's *Boy's Own* cohort Eckel, a stone's throw from his studio. Andrew is today sporting a look somewhere between '50s navvy and World War II wing commander.

Tell me something about growing up and your musical interests as a kid.
I was brought up in the suburbs in Windsor and my grandparents lived in Slough. It was suburban but it wasn't too far away, so I could go on raiding parties. I'd jump on a train and in an hour I'd be in London. The great thing about that is you don't take it for granted. You may even have a couple of months to assimilate what you've seen and heard and done. Sometimes when you live in London, you get blasé, it washes over you a little bit. So living in suburbia you had chance to discuss the skirmishes you'd been involved with, which is what I really liked.

So what would a typical trip be then?
I'd save up and then I'd probably go to Kensington Market to a rockabilly shop. I'd go to World's End. I'd do any number of jobs and save up so I could go into town and buy records from the Cage in Beaufort Market in the Kings Road which was the first shop that sold post-punk records, apart from Rough Trade. It was a pop culture thing: clothes, records, haircut, and tattoos!

What did you do for jobs when you left school?
First job I had was a furniture porter for an old school shop called Pyle Brothers. They had no lifts and they had a storeroom on the third floor and they'd buy up bankrupt stock and us four had to unload articulated lorries full of Chesterfields and take them up three flights of stairs. At this time I'd just discovered amphetamine sulphate as well so I was a tad wiry and more than willing to start some sort of fracas on a Friday night. Loads of jobs. My last job was a stagehand building film sets. It was around 1988. I'd work on a film set for a couple of weeks and I was beginning to DJ a bit and there was a bit of dilemma: do I start DJing properly? And I'd been offered a job abroad with this set company and in the end I didn't go because they let me down at the last minute. So if I'd have gone on that trip I probably wouldn't be sitting talking to you now.

Did you see music as an escape from what you'd been doing?
Not really. It was literally, here's a chance to make some money. I like to have money to buy clothes. I thought I'd give the DJing a go. But even when 'Loaded' [by Primal Scream] came out I remember going for a job interview at London Records to be a record plugger or A&R man or something. I still thought it was the latest way to make some money. It felt like another stop-gap. It's the same as the Rolling Stones reflecting on how they started, 'Oh we thought it'd be over in 18 months!' That's how I felt. I'd plough on in my direction and things seem to turn out alright.

When did you first get interested in DJing, what made you want to become one?
It was only quite recently that I considered myself a DJ. I started collecting records when I was 12 or 13 years old and whenever there was a get-together I would be asked, 'Bring your records,' when everyone else was more interested in copping off and drinking party sevens. The next step was, 'Get that bloke with the weird record collection to play some music.' That was a couple of years before Shoom. The same happened at the birth of acid house: 'Call that bloke with the weird records to play at six in the morning.'

I just had that sort of joy I had when I was 11 or 12. I've had the experience of hearing this for the first time and now it's your turn. I was just playing records, I wasn't skilled. I was playing such varied music you couldn't mix it.

But then because my name started to get associated with Shoom, Spectrum and things like that, people would book me without really hearing what I did. They probably booked me so they could put 'Shoom' in brackets. So I was getting booked to play main spots and going down like the proverbial turd in the salad because I'd be playing weird music at six in the morning. So I had to incorporate more and more house and disco tracks and learn how to mix. My first pair of record decks were bought by a record company I did a mix for. I did the sleevenotes for some Italo-disco compilation and my payment was a set of decks. It was about 1990. So it was a gradual progression until about five or six years ago I kind of realised I was a DJ.

❝ The same happened at the birth of acid house: 'Call that bloke with the weird records to play at six in the morning.' ❞

But the thing that probably attracts you is that evangelism of finding interesting stuff and playing it to people.
Yeah... but without straying into righteous zeal territory! You know what I mean? It's almost as good a feeling looking in someone's eyes and seeing their joy of discovery; it's almost like re-living your own joy of discovery. In a way it's a little bit selfish. Although you're sharing stuff, a good part of it is for your own gratification. There's a little bit of selfishness back 'cos you want that feeling back that you'll never get again. It's a bit desperate really! [laughs].

There's also a certain amount of ego involved because it's obviously quite exciting to play records to people. Was that an attractive thing?
Not to start with because a lot of times the DJ was only one step above bottle washer. It was only when people were so desperate for heroes that they thought DJs would be good ones. I'll be honest with you, I did fall for it hook, line and sinker because being such a music fan and buying the *NME* and music magazines, and all of a sudden you find yourself in them, well it can turn a man's head. I did go a bit silly for a number of years. Then you throw the obvious drug into the equation as well, which is super-duper ego-expanding powder and yeah, you do get sucked in. I don't sympathise with people on that star trip but I can empathise with them. You're living in lala-land and people are coming up to you every day and saying how great you are. Hold on a minute, are we so desperate for heroes that we're going to have DJs for heroes? That's not right, it should be something a bit more substantial than that.

....

How did it affect you personally?
Well without going into too much detail, it affected relationships on every level from friends to girlfriend. Just general everyday dealings with human beings. I was a bit arrogant. To be honest, some of that was a defence mechanism. I'd been told I was the best thing since sliced bread and in the back of my mind was this feeling that all these people would find me out. Someone's gonna go, 'Look he's not wearing any clothes!' So partly the arrogance was to put up a wall because of my insecurity. But it's part of getting older, really. The artistic world is full if insecure people and I was just one of them. You get older and become more self-aware. It's nice that people come up and say nice things about what you've done. But you know, sometimes I think I'd rather people think I had a shit back catalogue but thought I was a decent human being.

What were your first musical passions?
Fifties rock and roll and glam rock, without a doubt. It was about the time the film *That'll Be The Day* came out. I would've been 11 or 12. They had these adverts on the cinema and there was 'Poetry in Motion' by Johnny Tillotson, 'Runaway' by Del Shanonn, 'Johnny Remember Me' [by John Leyton], all those kind of things. Look, I'm getting goose bumps talking about it! It sounded like music from another planet. Coupled with a film about blokes on bumper cars with leopard skin drape suits and David Bowie on *Top Of The Pops*.

It's the classic kid in the suburbs. I had a nice upbringing but it was a bit dull. That was like a gateway to a parallel universe. Then a few years later punk came along, then post-punk business, rockabilly revival. Yeah, and I've been on every bandwagon since! [laughs].

How did you meet the *Boy's Own* lot then?
Well I lived in Windsor and they lived in Slough and it was that classic suburban thing of people meeting at the one decent clothes shop. Can't remember what it was called offhand but this guy Johnny Rocca worked there. I met Gary Haisman and Terry Farley there. We used to go to the same sort of discos. Cymon [Eckel] lived there as well. I was really hanging out a lot with Cymon and another guy called Phil Goss, who now lives in Italy. Every Friday, pre-acid house, we used to meet up at 9 o'clock and drop a tab of acid, which is where that post-punk compilation I did for Nuphonic got its name from [*9 O'clock Drop*]. Then we headed into town and went to Le Beat Route or Mud Club or something like that. I gradually got to know Terry over those years going to clubs.

When you started *Boy's Own*, what was it? Was it a club or a magazine or what?
It was a magazine first. Terry was enthralled with *The End*. His words at the time, 'If fuckin' scousers can do it then I'm sure we can!' or some such pep talk. And we did. It was Pritt sticks and cutting things out on my coffee table.

Were you aware of *The End*?
Yeah I'd seen it; I knew exactly what he was talking about. I wasn't into football. [Steve] Mayesy and all that lot, they were into football and they'd get these things from football and I totally got what he was saying. So it was like, let's give it a go.

What stuff were you reading at the time?
Well I can't remember exactly but it would probably involve Camus and Kafka and the usual kind of youthful follies. I was and still am a Joseph Conrad fan. I just saw it as a chance for expression and I'd be able to write about music. It's a fanzine, so it doesn't have to be particularly current, you've got nobody's product to push so you can be quite abstract. I was the Outsider [his pseudonym in *Boy's Own*].

Why did you call your column The Outsider?
Because I was a bolshie little bastard! I always wanna be in a gang but then I don't wanna be. I want the best of both of worlds. So I thought I'd be able to write a sarky piece deconstructing or taking the piss out of everything you're about to read about. I wanted to have my cake and eat it I suppose.

Is that a theme that runs through your whole career?
I'm totally like that. I wanna be accepted but get annoyed when I am. Groucho Marx said, 'I wouldn't want to be a member of any club that accepted me as a member.'

....

How did the ideas come about for *Boy's Own*?
It was literally what anyone had listened to that week or read or what had happened. After acid house kicked in it became the village paper for the acid house scene. There was only two or three clubs! There were pictures of parties where only 2-300 people had been. It was very insular. After a couple of years, John Brown Publishing offered us national distribution and we were like it's pointless, cos people'll just think, 'Silly Cockney cunts.' It would have appeared too cliquey. Obviously people from up north did buy it but they were people that came to the parties. It would have been like making a parochial local newspaper and then selling it throughout the British Isles. It wouldn't work.

How do you feel about it now? It's still revered and a lot of it is still funny.
Yeah, but I don't actually own a copy. There was a certain point – on too many ecstasies – that I gave away most of my possessions, you know what I mean? Most of my test pressings, acetates and everything: 'Yeah, go on, I love you!' [laughs] I've seen bits of it and I think it's alright but there are a bits that I find a bit embarrassing and a bit un self-aware but other people might think were really funny. If you looked back at some of the stuff you wrote 20 years ago you'd probably think the same.

Indeed.
And throw the vernacular of acid house into the equation as well!

And the drugs.
Yeah. It's a good, unpretentious document of those times I think. It would be pretty essential in years to come for people researching the birth of acid house. I'd say it was a jolly good read for historical purposes but for entertainment purposes it would be very dated.

What bound all of you lot together?
A common love of going out and all that that entailed. The music, the clothes, what happened afterwards when you discussed things like books, art, it was the whole social scene that generations before us had had. I just wanted my scene. I was a bit too young for punk. So it was kind of my thing. Again it's that thing I wanted to part of a scene but didn't want nobody to understand! It was that again.

What about places like the Mud Club.
Well it was good, the dressing up was fun but there didn't seem to be any kind of scene although I suppose there was: it was new romantic, what Robert Elms called 'The Scene With No Name'. Actually what it was like is what's it's like round here now [Shoreditch], a weird mish mash of rockabilly and punk. No one's quite sure. You'd go to a gig in the mid '80s and there'd be rockabillies, goths and there's that kind of feel now. While they're looking for something new they're pillaging what's gone on in the past.

Is it less tribal now?
As I see it, I live in London's fashionable Shoreditch so I'd go, 'No, it's like one great big village!' But if I lived on some estate in the north of England where there's a big divide between say, casuals and goths... Some goth kid was killed by kids off an estate recently so it's all very well for me to say it's all fine but you can't get any more tribal than people killing each other.

What effect do you think acid house has had?
It helped push music technology forward. Everyone said it had a great social effect, I don't really think it did. The biggest effect it had was the push and development of music hardware, firstly, and then software. Kids were going out and hearing these records and wanting to make them themselves. I would imagine those that went to those early clubs ended up, a good proportion of them, being involved in music technology. That lit the blue touchpaper for where we are now, where we can sit here and make tracks on our laptops. That's what acid house did. It had a few momentary social consequences, like the poll tax riots and the club laws, but it was only made political by the press.

Do you not think, unconsciously at least, it was political: the idea of reclaiming and remaking communities?

To a certain extent, but a lot of that community was fuelled by ecstasy. It was there and I don't want to downplay it, and I don't want come across as a curmudgeon. It was the same with the '60s; it was a bit of false dawn. It affected people's lives but it didn't usher in a new Age of Aquarius! [laughs]. It really didn't. It depends on whether you want to see breaking into a building and dancing as a political act. It was just another strand, another part of London and Manchester discos.

What effect did punk have on you when it happened? How old were you?
I was 13 in 1976. I remember the day after the Sex Pistols were on *Today* [with Bill Grundy], I had shoulder length hair and I remember sitting in the barbers and pointing to a picture of them in the papers and saying, 'Chop all me hair off!' You can't describe it to younger people. People thought it was the end of civilisation. It was like bomb going off, especially in suburban England. It frightened my parents to death. My dad was a bit of a reprobate himself, he wasn't totally square, but this was just ridiculous. It really put the fear in people. Anything that scares the old folk is good. That's why I'm covered in tattoos. When I was a kid my parents were so against them they thought they were evil, so I gravitated towards them. It's the way youth culture works.

> **❝ There was a certain point – on too many ecstasies – that I gave away most of my possessions. Most of my test pressings, acetates and everything: 'Yeah, go on, I love you!' ❞**

Did you see any parallels between punk and acid house?
Briefly, when it hit the papers, but that was more to do with the fact that it was so drug fuelled. It wasn't the politics or nihilism or against society like punk was. It was the accoutrements that they were against.

For you personally did it have any resonance?
Not really, no. I was always a bit of a confused person. I liked punk but I liked disco music, so the two were always separate. So acid house was the development of my disco side, it wasn't a development of the more political and more abstract musical side. It was a revolution in my disco world rather than my political world.

So did you have compartmentalised little worlds that you dipped in and out of.
Well yeah really! I never got that thing that disco sucked when punk was going on, because I knew all the originals were bored soulboys who used to go to Chaguarama's. That's where you got dressed up. You could go to weekenders dressed like Bryan Ferry or David Bowie and you wouldn't be hassled. It's like that early thing John Lydon said: punk was all about selling trousers! Sorry everybody, it was primarily a London fashion thing. It was bored soulboys and people going to gay discos and wearing mohair jumpers and plastic sandals. Sorry Conflict, GBH and Crass, it was a London trouser thing! [laughs]

Do you think the superstar DJ thing was a betrayal of the whole acid house ethos?
I've looked at certain DJs and thought, 'Fuck, I'm gonna give this up.' I'm not gonna say who but I've been to see some high end DJs and there's times I've come out and I've been embarrassed to say that I'm a DJ. I could've been that person if I'd carried on a certain route. It's probably part of myself I don't like, rather than them. Anything I get angry with in the music industry is often because I don't want to be reminded of the person I was.

Do you think the scene is in a better state now the superstar thing has deflated?
It's still there.

Well it is but it's more fluid than it was.
I think kids have got wise to the fact that you need better heroes than DJs. Even Pete

Doherty's a better hero than Judge Jules, let's be honest, and Pete Doherty's a bit ropey. DJs should be heard and not seen, really. That thing where you're playing [indicates on high] and people are looking at you... it's not what it's about. I like Moodymann and playing behind a screen.

But that actually accentuates everything!
Yeah you're right. You still need that contact, but you don't need to be bathed in light, you don't need to be the centre of attention.

> **❝ I think kids have got wise to the fact that you need better heroes than DJs. Even Pete Doherty's a better hero than Judge Jules, let's be honest, and Pete Doherty's a bit ropey ❞**

How important is mystique in music?
Very important. I was always drawn to the fact I'd never seen a picture of Martin Hannett or Adrian Sherwood. It was years before I saw a picture of either. That added a little bit more substance to things. When I first started I didn't want to use my real first name and I refused to be photographed for years. The first photo shoot I did I wore a medicine hat and a big pair of glasses and a scarf. Anton LeVay was the head of the Church of Satan in San Francisco and he used to play organ in burlesque and strip shows in the 1940s and there'd be a room full of guys watching someone almost naked, but if a woman wearing a pencil skirt walked in every head in the place would turn because they want what's hidden. I'm with Anton on that! [laughs]

What makes a good DJ?
It can be as simple as playing good music. Good music, well programmed. Even if you're playing wildly different music, I try and make some sort of connection or some sort of flow. I don't like to be jarred too much. There has to be a connection, where I can see there's some sort of thought process and not, 'Ooh haven't I got an eclectic record collection?' I want to listen to something in slightly open-mouthed wonder, doesn't matter whether it 's a rockabilly track or techno. Doesn't have to be dazzlingly new. I got hooked on the idea that everything has to be new and original for while. But nothing dates quicker than a new sound. Believe it or not I'm in the Billy Childish camp. Originality is not what is important, it's authenticity.

How did the studio work happen?
Jeff Barrett was managing me and he did Primal Scream's press. He gave me a copy of the album. He said it was getting slated left, right and centre and I came back to him and said I loved it. So he said, 'Why don't you write a review for the *NME*?' He wangled that so I went down to Exeter to see them play and reviewed it – the headline was 'Sex, Lies & Gaffer Tape.' I got on really well with them. Then I'd see them in clubs like the Future. Andrew Innes was in Spectrum one night and he said, 'We've got this track and you can do what ever the fuck you like with it.' That was 'Loaded'. I made one attempt where I reined back a bit because I didn't want to upset them. I played it to them and Innes said, 'No man, fuckin' destroy it!' So I went back into Bart's Studios in Walthamstow with a very talented man called Brian O'Shaughnessy who'd actually produced and engineered the original.

So you never actually worked with the band?
No, and that was pretty much how *Screamadelica* was made as well. I think there was only one time I got it wrong. I did a version of 'Shine Like The Stars' they didn't really like and I went back in and did it again, and I'm really glad I did because it's one of my favourite tracks on there. Obviously they'd have to do overdubs or they'd drop in to see how it was going, but I didn't have the joy of the drummer setting up his kit or the guitarists saying, 'I'm a bit

toppy.' Which is a working method I've applied: have as few musicians in for as little time as possible! Otherwise it gets very tedious.

Were they immediately happy with the results?
Yeah. They might have come in and suggested things. I don't remember really, because it was a very hazy time. It was just people hanging out and making records.

How many things had you done in the studio before?
Not a lot. Happy Mondays, East India Company, maybe St Etienne. Apparently there's a website dedicated to this information.

What was your role?
Well, when I got the demos I knew exactly what Bob [Gillespie] had been listening to to get that song. So I would inject my approximation of that. You know, it's weird but I was listening to 'I'm Coming Down' and I spoke to Bob on the phone and said, 'For some reason I'm getting Pharaoh Sanders, the sax player, don't ask me why.' And he said, 'I've got a Pharaoh Sanders CD in my hand at the moment!'

It was like that. Whether it was a chord progression or a vocal line, I knew exactly what the ingredients were that went into that. So I'd go into the studio and say to the engineers this is why this sounds like it does and play them Big Star or whatever and we'd build it up from that. I was the conductor, basically. 'This is what it should sound like, I'm not sure how to do it, that's why you're here.' I was learning as I was going. I knew what it wanted.

On one track I knew we needed those plastic tubes that kids swing round their heads, it was the only sound I could hear. And we did indeed have five people swinging them round in the studio! But I couldn't have done it without Hugo Nicholson, who would hear my suggestions and say, yes but what about this? So I was open to that. So it was my blueprint even if it did get smudged. Hugo did all my early stuff till about 1994, when Sabres of Paradise started when I worked with Jagz and co.

How did Sabres come about?
Can't remember exactly. I was looking for new people to work with and I got introduced to Jagz and Gary at Full Circle probably. And they knew of a studio in Hounslow West in this really rough council estate. It was like a room inside a room above a newsagent, so you'd never know from the outside it was a studio. There was a pub at the end of the road and the landlord had recently been put away for murdering one of his clientele! It was pretty hardcore. If anyone had known it was a studio it would have been done over in minutes.

Listening back to the music you've done over the years which are the tracks you're most pleased about?
Well there are things that I've done and been a bit embarrassed about over the years, but then you actually hear them still being played. Often the very things that made those records work are the things I don't like: the mistakes and the simplicity and the obviousness of them. I didn't think about them too much when I was making them, but over the years I've thought about structures and so on too much. Brevity? Don't know the meaning of the word, sir! One kitchen sink? Let's have two or three. It's that naivety I like but it's that naivety that makes me go, 'Mmm shouldn't have had that there.' It's like the drum loop on 'Loaded', it's ridiculous. There's a crash on every bar! It's a mistake but it's one of the things that makes it.

One of the things I've learned about the studio is if you think about things too much it's time to stop. I've had some killer tracks that I've noodled out of existence because you always think it's got to have more. Last week I was going through the computer and I found 10 new tracks, basically a whole new album, really good beginnings of songs that we'd got bored with. The stuff I'm doing at the moment has a sound that's almost similar to the early stuff. It's closer to my vision of what I was trying to do 15 years ago. I've got more technical knowledge. So now I've got the best of both worlds, my naive approach but with a bit more technical backup. I've gone backwards in sound a little bit but it's that authenticity over originality! If you do something authentically it somehow ends up sounding more original anyway.

© DJhistory.com

ANDREW WEATHERALL SELECTED DISCOGRAPHY

HAPPY MONDAYS – Hallelujah (remixer)

JAH WOBBLE'S INVADERS OF THE HEART – Bomba (remixer)

THE GRID – Floatation (remixer)

MY BLOODY VALENTINE – Glider (remixer)

PRIMAL SCREAM – Don't Fight It, Feel It (producer)

ST ETIENNE – Only Love Can Break Your Heart (remixer)

BOCCA JUNIORS – Raise (writer/producer)

PERCY X – 3 (remixer)

SABRES OF PARADISE – Smokebelch II (writer/producer)

WOLFGANG PRESS – 11 Years (remixer)

SABRES OF PARADISE – Wilmot (writer/producer)

RED SNAPPER – Hot Flush (remixer)

SABRES OF PARADISE – Tow Truck (writer/producer)

TWO LONE SWORDSMEN – Rico's Helly (writer/producer)

TWO LONE SWORDSMEN – Don't Call It Jerk (writer/producer)

TWO LONE SWORDSMEN – Glide By Shooting (writer/producer)

UZMA – Yab Yum (remixer)

DEATH IN VEGAS – Rekkit (remixer)

ANDREW WEATHERALL – Feathers (writer/producer)

THE DOVES – Compulsion (remixer)

PRIMAL SCREAM – Loaded (producer)

RECOMMENDED LISTENING

PRIMAL SCREAM – Screamadelica

VARIOUS – Andrew Weatherall: Fabric 19

VARIOUS – Andrew Weatherall: Watch The Ride

ANDREW WEATHERALL – A Pox On The Pioneers

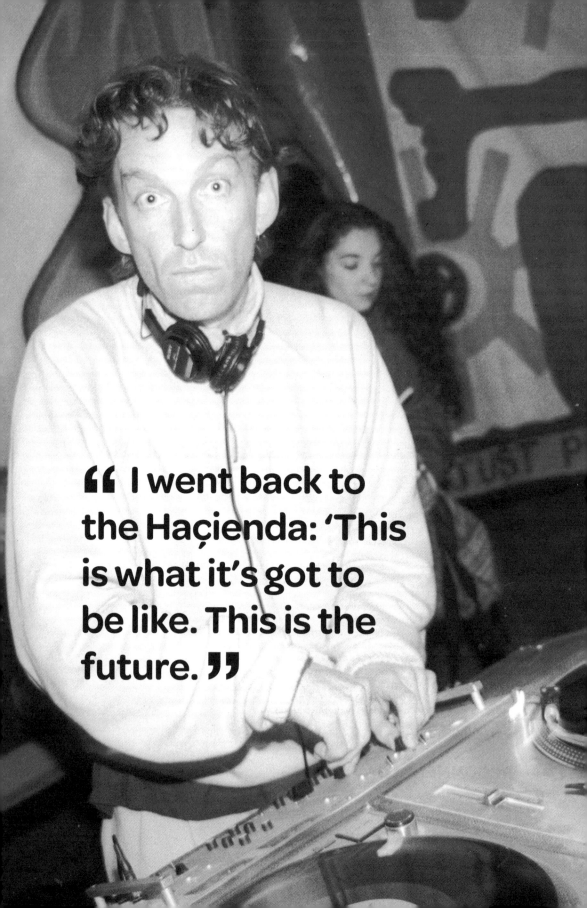

" I went back to the Haçienda: 'This is what it's got to be like. This is the future. "

....

Mike Pickering
Haçienda housemaster

Interviewed by Bill by phone, December 1, 2000

....

For years the Haçienda was a glorious white elephant, opening as a state-of-the-art Manhattan nightclub, with a fancy-pants restaurant, in a town populated by glum students in raincoats. Bands played to a cold, half-empty room and the scallies only came in because there was cheap Stella. But when acid house exploded in 1987, suddenly this immaculately designed glass-roofed shed made complete sense to everyone. While London and the south were still flirting with house, not sure if it would outlast go-go, in Manchester there was no hesitation. Fresh from seeing how things worked in New York, Mike Pickering ripped the microphone out of the DJ booth and set to work.

An ex-punk and ardent football fan from the blue half of the city, Pickering helped build the reputation of the Haçienda well before all this. As part of Quando Quango, his records were championed in venerated clubs like the Music Box in Chicago and the Paradise Garage in New York (where the band also performed). Alongside Jon Da Silva and Graeme Park he led Manchester into a new era. Pickering's post-house band M People enjoyed great success, as well as winning the Mercury Music Prize in 1994.

We talk over the phone a few days after the contents of the Haçienda have been auctioned off in Manchester. Mike is now the proud owner of some wooden dancefloor and two bricks.

How did you come into the orbit of the Factory people?
I met Rob Gretton at 16 years old. We were Manchester City supporters and we got chased by a load of Nottingham Forest supporters in Nottingham. I just jumped in a garden and hid behind a hedge and he did the same thing. That was it then. We were best mates. He managed Joy Division and New Order, though he was a DJ at the time. What really happened with the Haç, I went through the punk times and then I buggered off to Holland and lived in Rotterdam. These people that I met, they squatted this disused water works with a tower. They said that they wanted to do something with this big hall. We cleared it all out and I just started DJing. I was into Chic and Stacey Lattislaw. It was called Rotterdam Must Dance and it became quite a big club night. We put bands on and I put on the second New Order gig after Ian died.

Rob saw it all, and said he was opening this club and he wanted me to help him do it all. I came back six months before it opened but it was just rubble, really. I used to book the DJs, lighting, bands, everything. At that time, I was always going away with New Order and my band Quando Quango and we were often in New York. 'Love Tempo' by Quando Quango was really big in the Paradise Garage. We actually did a PA there, when Larry Levan was DJing. I went to the Loft, and I was gobsmacked by it all, because I was just this little scally. So I went back to the Haçienda and I was, 'This is what it's got to be like. This is the future, you know.' So I pulled out the microphone.

The other thing me and Rob were into was no door policy (apart from keeping the knobheads out), to reverse what was the door policy at the time. I couldn't find a DJ. They all wanted to talk, they were all so programmed. So in the end, I just thought I could do better and started doing the Friday night. It was a real mélange of music at first, everything from salsa, to electro to northern and it really took off.

....

How long did it take from you starting to really getting it going?
It only took about four weeks. I don't know why, but word spread, I suppose this was about 1985.

What about when the first house records started coming over?
That would have been about 1985 or '86. You know, stuff like Wally Jump Jr. and JM Silk. We had a lot of old northern soul boys 'cos it was all 4/4 and quite pacy. I used to do a swap in London at a club called Fever run by Simon Goffe at the Astoria. I got booed off. There were a lot of black guys there, and they were shoving notes into my face saying, 'Stop playing this fucking homo music.' At the Haçienda it was a really black night until ecstasy swept in. I couldn't believe it. About six or seven months later I played for Nicky Holloway at the Trip, which was also at the Astoria, and they were all like bingo-bongo, smiley T-shirts and I was like, 'Wait a minute...?'

> **❝ I was playing everything, a much wider variety of music. As we all got swallowed up – actually that's the wrong phrase isn't it? As we all swallowed it up, it was all house. ❞**

How did the night change from being black to white?
Ecstasy.

Really?
Yeah. Once it exploded, it was weird, you could watch from Friday to Friday and see the crowd change in colour. In those days, most of the black kids would smoke weed, but they weren't into chemicals. But then when ecstasy came in it wiped it all out. It was so quick. It was over in about four or five weeks. It was because it was so packed, and they couldn't do the moves so they retreated to the smaller clubs. It was a shame in one way. In the long run it was a shame.

Did ecstasy change the music you played and the approach you took?
Oh it did.

How?
Before, I was playing everything, a much wider variety of music. As we all got swallowed up – actually that's the wrong phrase isn't it? As we all swallowed it up, it was all house.

I think everyone lost their head because it was so all encompassing.
Yeah, well we used to come out of the Haç, get in the car and put the set on that we'd just done! Nowadays, I think, 'Fucking hell, it must've been really boring.'

When did ecstasy arrive in a big way then?
Early '88, I'd say.

What was the halcyon period for you?
I loved the year or so leading up to the ecstasy explosion. We only had a fire limit of 1,200 but we were getting 1,600, and the thing about it was they were complete music fans. We had some weird records that were big. JM Silk was really big, stuff like 'Jump Back'. Then you'd get things like Whistle's 'Buggin'' and 'Was That All It Was' by Jean Carn, so it was old and new.

Was go-go big?
No. We had Trouble Funk on, but it didn't take off like it did in London. 1988 and '89 were special times, but in different ways. It changed our lives, both personally and professionally. Everyone I know from that period, we all dumped longstanding girlfriends or boyfriends and met the loves of our lives! It was a wonderful wonderful time that period in Manchester.

What do you think of the Haçienda now it's long gone?
I'm glad it's gone and it wasn't taken over by anybody. I think it lived too long anyway. We had a 10 year plan and at the end of that 10 years, it was definitely finished. But it had a great 10 years.

Something puzzled me about that period: why did you never run a sub-label of Factory for all of this stuff coming out of Manchester and the Haç?
A lot of people mentioned it when Factory went into receivership and I was a bit embarrassed about it. I eventually became a junior director of Deconstruction.

Were you taking music to Factory and telling them to sign things?
Well the real truth was Rob Gretton and myself went to Tony Wilson and said – in about 1986 or '87 – and Factory had always had this thing about a lot of us being influenced by funk and electro records. We said, 'Look, we wanna start a subsidiary dance label.' Tony said, 'Dance will never happen.' And of course two years later it did. That was fair enough, though: Tony wanted to stick with what he knew. But I signed Black Box, Felix, Guru Josh – for my sins – and of course M People.

What about 'Voodoo Ray' [by A Guy Named Gerald] and 'Pacific State' [by 808 State]? You must have had early access to them?
Well I put 'Voodoo Ray' on the *North* album that I did on Deconstruction. It was a great souvenir of that time. Tony was really nice about it. He'd come in and congratulate me when another record I'd signed had done well. I was thinking, 'But Tony, you could have had 'em!' It was another quirky Factory thing. There was a lot of wastage of money around that time. But then, in a sense, without that wastage, the Haçienda would never have existed. It was a bit of a folly anyway.

To be fair, it would never have remained open had it had different owners. We didn't have a clue what we were doing. We were open seven nights a week with a haute cuisine

....

restaurant! It was like an alien spaceship had landed in Manchester, and everybody was still in raincoats and listening to the Cure.

Was that one of the incongruous things about it, that it had been opened by Factory, but a lot of what was being played there was black music.
That even extended into 1989 when Madchester came on the scene. I remember sitting in a hotel room with Andy Weatherall one Saturday afternoon. It was like a scene from a film. There was Japanese, Canadian and American film crews all over the street. There must've been about 40 of them on the way from Piccadilly Hotel to Oldham Street. It was fucking hilarious. Then I started doing interviews and this American guy asks me, 'Mike, what puzzles me a little is how you find enough Madchester records with your club open so long?' He thought we only played Stone Roses, Inspiral Carpets and 'baggy' music. So I said, 'Well we play records from Chicago and New York.' He just didn't understand what was happening. I thought, 'Oh God, is this the beginning of the end?' And it was, really.

What's your fondest memory of it now?
1988 and '89. The whole time was just great. Prior to that, on the Friday night, when I had Mantronix playing and then DJing with me, that was quite amazing. Anything during those two years was amazing. I'll tell you another thing, every year for the birthday party, we used to go really over the top: fairgrounds, pontoon bridges, everything.

When did you stop DJing?
Funnily enough at one of the Haçienda birthday parties in 1992. Both myself and David Morales got threatened. I'd said to David beforehand that I'd been thinking of giving up, and people were saying it was because of the success of M People, but it wasn't and I was quite upset by that. People came up saying, 'You're deserting us,' and I had to tell them, 'No, I haven't. It's because I don't want you to all get beaten up and mugged.' I told David this and he said, 'Yeah I knew there was something.' Blow me, at the end of the night, we'd both been threatened: him with a bottle, me with a knife. I thought, 'I'm out of here.' I tried to carry on DJing after that, travelling all over the world, like the modern guys do, but it didn't work for me. I just couldn't do it after that. I'd only ever worked in the same place I always like having my own crowd. I really believe to be a good DJ, you've got to have your own crowd. They come and respect your tastes, and you respect their tastes.

Do you still buy records?
I buy more now. I think you mentioned earlier about not listening to anything but house from 1988 onwards. Before that, I had really wide, eclectic tastes and I found my taste for collecting came back. Now, when I'm not in the studio, I live in second-hand record stores.

When they auctioned off the contents of the Haçienda, did you buy any of it?
I made the highest bloody bid. Even the DJ box went for about a grand. I bought a painting from the Shiva night, which was actually done by my wife, but that actually got up to £3,200. And then I bought a big bit of the dancefloor for £400. What I really wanted was an Anthony Blunt picture, but they'd all gone. I got some bricks. One of the bricks is for Mark Kamins. It's his Christmas present.

HAÇIENDA NUDE NIGHT 20

GINO LATINO – No Sorry
K-OS – Definition of Love
INNER CITY – Do You Love What You Feel (Power 41 In Control Remix)
INNER CITY – Do You Love What You Feel (Power 41 Remix)
ROYAL HOUSE – Get Funky
RAVEN MAIZE – Forever Together
WHITE KNIGHT – Keep It Movin' (Cause The Crowd Says So) (Insane Mix)
SOUND FACTORY – Cuban Gigolo
DIONNE – Come Get My Lovin'
28TH STREET CREW – I Need A Rhythm
ADEVA – Warning
THE BASS BOYZ – Lost In The Bass (Mike 'Hitman' Wilson Mix)
JULIAN 'JUMPIN'' PEREZ & KOOL ROCK STEADY – Ain't We Funky Now
MONIE LOVE – Grandpa's Party (Love II Love Mix)
TONY SCOTT – That's How I'm Living
CHUBB ROCK – Ya Bad Chubbs (Crib Mix)
AKASA – One Night in My Life
KID'N'PLAY – 2 Hype
KENNY 'JAMMIN' JASON & FAST EDDIE – Can U Dance
JUNGLE CREW – Elektric Dance

Compiled by Mike Pickering

RECOMMENDED LISTENING

QUANDO QUANGO – Pigs + Battleships
M PEOPLE – Elegant Slumming

**" When I DJ, I perform
I get into character. "**

Paul Oakenfold
Most successful

Interviewed by Frank in London, Apr 4, 1999

Ambition. Drive. Focus. You can't fault this man's will to succeed. Just like Madonna is a corporation that sings songs, Paul Oakenfold is a businessman who is a DJ. A couple of years ago he put his LA mansion, 'One of the best sited view homes on its own promontory,' on the market for $10 million (having paid a fraction of that). From acid house it's been an inexorable rise: label boss, star remixer, international headliner, superclub resident. Oakey now sells albums in bulk and moves in the world of soundtracks and global brands. And he's still working at mastering the American market, determined to install Perfecto trance in its charts.

A south London chef and ardent soulboy, Oakenfold fell in with soul scene DJ Trevor Fung who remembers a bus ride together to a club in Slough and a lot of questions about how you become a DJ. But a DJ's simple passion for music was never going to be enough; Oakey was always going to need a piece of the action. And as dance music evolved he kept himself at the heart of it. He hustled his way into a transatlantic hip hop job, then with Trevor and his cousin Ian St Paul opened the Project Club in Streatham, using his music biz day-job to fill it with everyone from LL Cool J to Marshall Jefferson. When Trevor and Ian washed up as bar-owners in Ibiza they invited Paul to come over to check out the island's ecstasy-fuelled dancefloors. The trio then imported this Balearic hedonism into rainy Streatham and then the West End. Through all this Oakenfold made sure his was the name that was remembered: DJing up in the club's pulpit-like booth, swathed in smoke, playing with epic self-assurance.

We meet in his offices where he is charming, casual, seemingly off-duty. At the end of the interview a matey handshake and he moves to the next thing in his diary. A check of the time and it's dead on the hour.

You got into the music industry during hip hop. Can you remember the thrill when you first heard it?
Yeah, I can, actually. I was living in New York. That's how I really got into it. I was born and bred in London. I went to New York for a holiday, then two weeks later I actually went back and lived there. Fell in love with the place, the energy, the excitement, just turning on the radio and listening to, like, early Kurtis Blow and Melle Mel and all that. I really got into it. I ended up getting really hooked into hip hop big time. I ended up working for Profile Records in America.

Then when I came back, I was running Profile in Europe. I was head of A&R, so I was looking after Run DMC, all those acts. And I knew Russell Simmons because he managed Run DMC, so then I was also being paid as a consultant to run Def Jam. I'd go into Sony twice a week and say, listen, Beastie Boys, LL Cool J, Jam Master Jay...

And then I was running Champion Records and my first signing was Will Smith – at the time it was Jazzy Jeff and the Fresh Prince – then Salt 'N' Pepa, kind of. When the Beastie Boys, LL came over and toured I was doing all that, and the same with Run DMC, so I really was quite heavily involved even to the point of having a column – I mean, not that that I'm a journalist – but I had a column in *Blues and Soul* called Wotupski.

And that was when you were doing The Project club?
Yeah, I was doing The Project, and it was really funny because we'd have this small club in Streatham and I'd have LL Cool J down, I'd have Run DMC, I'd have all these kind of acts.

And right afterwards house made another huge impact.
Yeah, so then house started coming in. And there was a kind of change in the whole hip hop scene. The violence started to creep in, and lyrically the music was getting really, really heavy, and that didn't appeal to me. And then because I was doing A&R with Champion, I started really getting into house.

What did you think when you first heard it?
I liked the rhythm of it, and the tempo. So I really got into it and then I started signing the records to Champion again, and we did really well on some of the stuff that we put out, and again I just kind of fell into this situation... I've never pretended that I've been an expert on it but because I'd been involved with it at an early stage, London Records hired me as a consultant. So when Farley Jackmaster Funk come over, I ended up running them around all the clubs. I was looking after Steve Hurley who had 'Jack Your Body'. I knew all those Chicago DJs from years ago when I was going to the New Music Seminar.

❝ The DJ is a modern-day entertainer. There's no difference between a band and a DJ. When I perform, they're watching every move. They expect you to deliver. ❞

Why do you think hip hop and then house had such an impact in the UK?
I think because of the rawness, the energy, and because we're always open. British people are always open – more musically open – to change. And we're always striving, musically, for something new. Even now the media are always looking for the Next Big Thing. And even if the Next Big Thing hasn't happened, they'll try and create it.

Ibiza and ecstasy were a huge part of the house explosion, and you were part of bringing that vibe to the UK: the famous Ibiza visit with you, Rampling and Johnny Walker. But what do you think would have happened if that hadn't been added to the mix?
You tell me.

Do you ... well, do you think that music would have been so successful without ecstasy? I mean when house first came out, it was seen as a bit of a fad
Yeah, well, house music was out before... before Ibiza and ecstasy. Ecstasy had been around since '83, '84. I remember, when I was touring America with Mike Pickering, and we went to Dallas, and that's where I first come across Ecstasy. I didn't try it.

Right.
But I met a club owner who'd bought a nightclub from selling ecstasy [laughter]. I remember when I used to go to Paradise Garage, I was, like, 19, and I couldn't understand why everyone could stay up all night [laughter]. They'd serve coffee at like six in the morning, and we'd be in the common room waiting for the coffee. And that was when I first experienced the drugs, but I think that drugs... I think that sometimes you have to look at a bigger picture rather than clubs. Drugs were going on... drugs and music for some reason have been hand in hand from the Beatles to the Rolling Stones...

It's all about losing yourself, isn't it?
I don't want to sit here and praise drugs... but it hasn't been a bad thing. You know, they do open your mind.

Do you think ecstasy was behind the rise of the DJ as a superstar, the kind of DJ worship that goes on?
No.

You don't?
No, not at all.

Where do you think that came from?
It's just... times change. The DJ is a modern-day entertainer. There's no difference between a band and a DJ. When I perform, they dance, but they're watching the DJ, they're watching every move. They expect you to deliver.

DJs are directly in touch, they know what's going on. They're in a club every weekend. More so than a band. DJs make their own music. DJs produce artists. There's a lot of pressure. People pay, good money, and they expect you to deliver. And that's all it is. Times change. It's like supermodels. When we used to go and see fashion shows it was all about the clothes. Now it's about who's walking down the catwalk. It's like... in the last four, five years football's changed so much. Now you've got your Owens and Beckhams that are not just footballers. They're huge stars.

Right.
And it's the same with DJs. For me it's changed in the last two years. Gone are the days of the DJ getting his head down and not taking part with the audience. I truly believe that one of the main reasons for my success is because I work with the crowd. There is that eye contact. I will touch... Because I only do one gig a night, I will take time out to talk to the people. There's direct contact. You know, there's that rapport. You can get close to me. You can get close to footballers. After the game's finished, you know, when they're getting on the team coach, they stand there, they sign photos. Every day people will go down while they're training. You can't get close to pop stars. You can't get close to film stars.

When I DJ, I perform. I get into character. It's not me. They don't want to know if me and you went out last night and got drunk. Tonight I've got to perform. I've got to get into character. I've got to get on stage and I'm a performer, and that's exactly what I do.

What do you mean by get into character?
Well, I get into character. If I've got a hangover, they don't want to know that. They're paying £15 to come and see me; they want the best night of their life. They don't want me just standing there, mixing a few tunes in, and not taking part. That's where DJing's shifted now; that's where it's moved. People want to see a DJ perform. They want that. That's why they all dance towards the DJ, so when you lift your arms up, they will lift their arms up. If you're pointing at them, they feel a part of it. That's what it's all about.

So what do you feel like when you're DJing? Because a lot of DJs say they feel like they're on the dance floor, part of the crowd.
Of course. Of course. That's what we are. The most important thing for me is them. So that's why I have to get into character. You know, I prepare, you know, mentally. I don't want no-one in the booth. I don't want you talking to me while I'm in the middle of DJing. It's like, if you were in a band playing bass, and suddenly someone's come on stage and talking to you while you're playing bass. They want my 100 percent attention, giving my all, to give them the best night of their life. And that means I have to get into character. If I'm down, I have a Red Bull or a shot of vodka, get myself going. You come on, they're all there. They're like, fucking hell, now, this is it!

What about when the adoration gets out of hand? I mean, you must have experienced that.
Well, of course, but you've got to...

How does that feel?
Well, it gets on top. I'm no different to anyone else. I would like to think that I'm a normal, down-to-earth guy and if I'm tired, I'm down, I'm exhausted, but I will... it's part of the job.

Paul Oakenfold

Right.

As a professional DJ, it's part of my job to talk to… and I actually learned this when I was on tour with U2, I learned a lot from watching them and hanging out with their manager. You watch how the band conduct themselves. You see how they take time out to do those things that are important, and you think, 'I can take a little bit of that and put it in my world.' And their world is a surreal world compared to mine. But, you know, you're learning all the time. You'd never meet them, you'd never get close to them, but you would come to a club and I'd see you, and you'd go, 'Alright, Paul?'

What's the biggest number of people you've ever played for?

Well, I did three nights at Wembley, 200,000 a night.

That's the U2 gigs?

That's the U2. And main stage at Glastonbury, when I played between Van Morrison and Peter Gabriel. I don't know how many there was at that. And when I played in Napoli, with U2 again – 120,000. But then they hadn't come to see me. Let's be honest: it was good of U2 to offer me a job to warm up the crowd for them.

How do those huge gigs feel compared with DJing in a club?

It's easier. Because when you've got 100,000 there, you're not expected to make them all dance, so it shifts from making people dance to playing familiar, good tunes. So you come on with Queen, 'Another One Bites The Dust', and you just stand there going like that [waving arms] and then suddenly everyone's singing along, 'cos they all know it. If I'd come on with a trance tune, they'd all be throwing fucking bottles at you. So you adapt.

How does it feel to have control over that many people?

Great! You know. It's a buzz. But you have to be comfortable with it. The hardest thing for anyone is to be comfortable with silence. If you're sitting here with a girl, you've just met her and you're really into her, could you be comfortable with silence?

Awkward silences!

Yeah, so imagine having 1,500 people in front of you and turning off the turntables and just standing there. Sometimes I'll turn off the turntables and I will just stand there, and they're going fucking mad, but you have that control. It's not an ego... it's nothing to do with an ego here... Say you DJ before me, nine times out of 10 a DJ will come on and mix into your last record. I don't.

You turn it down?
I will turn you *off*. So halfway through your record, I'll just turn it so it goes [dying down noise] Suddenly the music goes, so now we go to silence. So everyone's looking and thinks, 'What the fuck's going on? What's going on? What's going on?' I'm now in control because I've got everyone's attention. So now I'm going to take you where I want to take you. And the first record and the last record are hugely important. The first record sets the pace, the rhythm, the direction, and that's your building point. And the last record is the climax, and my style of DJing will leave you really, really on a high climax. I start there and I drop, and then I go up. Other DJs will just play all the hits, all the obvious records. I'm not about that. I'm about education but entertainment.

Right.
You've got to have the education because that's my stimulation from a DJ's point of view. Like going to Cuba [he's just back from playing a secret gig there]. I didn't get paid, we smuggled decks in and we educated them. It's a fine balance really.

Tell me about your remixing. What was the thinking behind your Happy Mondays mixes?
Well, I was doing a club called The Future, and the whole idea was to mix the best of all kinds of music. Now I liked indie dance, rock'n'roll, whatever you want to call it, but the rhythms were always wrong. Because it was live drums, and the B-lines for me were all over the place. The rhythm was wrong for a nightclub. So when we was approached to do mixes, it was all about changing the rhythm. You keep the integrity of the artist, you keep the guitars, but you make it a lot more melodic, so it's a lot more acceptable in nightclubs. That's all it was, really. No secret.

And that's really what you're hired for when you do a remix. They're coming to you as a DJ because you know what makes people dance.
Sure. Exactly! I know how to construct a record to fill a dance floor. I should fucking know it by now! So someone'll play you something, you say, 'That's wrong, that's wrong, that's wrong, take all them out and replace them with this, this, this and this, rearrange it – and it'll work.'

> **❝ The people who came out of that scene are now in a hugely important position, dictating what is going on on a global level. ❞**

What are some of the things you've learned from DJing that you've taken into remixing?
Key sound arrangement. Keys are a very important thing because keys fuck with feelings. Minor keys make you feel down, solemn, sad. If you listen to Sade, how do you feel? You feel emotional. You listen to a major key, a major key makes you feel happy. So you put a really strong top line on a keyboard [sings] and it's in a happy key, you're going to be, like, 'Yeah! I feel happy!' And that's understanding people's feelings. So again, you just adapt that to what you're doing.

Would you say that everything you've learned about music comes from DJing?
Yeah, for sure.

Does it work the other way round, that when you start making records you have a better understanding of playing records?
Yeah.

What kind of things come in there?
My three-hour set is composed and arranged like a record. Intro, your basic body, your break, your drop-down, your build, your climax, your outro. The set is built in a similar style to how I'd make a record. It's a formula that – for me – has worked.

DJs talk about reading a crowd, how do you actually do that?
Watch them.

And what are the signals?
Well, if you're playing a record and they're all starting to lose interest, or you're starting to lose the floor, then it means you're going in the wrong direction, so you need to either play a record that they know to get them back, or you need to move it in another direction.

What did you think of rave culture when it all kicked off?
Great. A culture that brings all kinds of people together – from fucking football hooligans and villains to supermodels and pop stars – all together, under one roof, is great.

The rave movement and – I guess you could call it ecstasy culture – a lot of people used it as a real springboard. Why do you think it was such a motivating force?
Yeah. This huge, huge movement. Those people who came out of that scene are now in a hugely important position, dictating what is going on on a global level. Pete Tong, he's gone from a DJ to running a record company to one of the biggest DJs on Radio 1. Judge Jules, Danny Rampling, myself, I could play to an estimated million people a year. Morales last week won a Grammy. Fucking great, you know. Good luck to 'em. We're in a really, really strong position.

❝ We were onto something new and fresh. You came down and experienced it, you'd go away and tell your mates. It wasn't just a club change. It changed the whole youth culture. ❞

What makes a good DJ?
A good DJ is someone who understands the crowd. Someone who can read a crowd, who can truly understand a lot more how music's made. And having experience and knowledge. There's so many DJs who think it's all about buying the latest records and practising in the room, and just being able to mix. It's so wrong. And especially the new breed of DJs, because I'd say 80 percent of the new kids who are DJs are in it for the money, are in it for the glamour, and just go and buy all the big tunes. That isn't hard to do.

You know, I try so hard to find a good warm-up DJ who's done an apprenticeship and knows how to warm the crowd up, ready for the main DJ, because the most important thing is not an individual, it's the whole night, for me. So if you're on before me and you warm the crowd up right, you've got them to a certain level, I will take them to the next level, then they leave having a great night. It's not about you going in there, playing half the tunes that I'm going to play and you banging it, and then it's like, fucking hell, we've gone there. Now we have to start all over again.

And half the DJs do that. Because a lot of them are fucking egotistic twats, to be honest with you. It's all about them, them, them, and they don't get it. It's not about them, it's about the crowd. And if they truly understand that, and work the crowd and bide their time as a professional, then it will come.

I was DJing years before I ever got a break, before anyone even thought of a DJ, but because I've had that experience and knowledge, I understand it as a trade. They want it now. Everything, you see with society, everyone wants it now. No one thinks about tomorrow. And if you're smart enough to think about tomorrow, you'll be in the business a lot longer.

Definitely.
I got into this for one reason, and one reason only – because I absolutely loved music and I loved playing to people. Whether I earn money out of it or not is irrelevant, because I've never seen myself a 100 percent as a DJ. I was doing other things. DJing was always a love, so I'd be working in an office. I was a chef, so at night I'd come home with a little bit of spare money, I'd buy records, have my deck, I'd be doing it at home. And then I'd be playing at a nightclub. No one gave me a job in a nightclub. I created my own job. I went down to The Project in Streatham and I said, listen, can I have Friday night – because Friday night was dead – I said, can I have Friday night? I'll pay you. So I was paying *them*.

There's one funny thing about DJing: most DJs, however successful they are professionally, they'll all go home and spin records at their own house, just for fun.
I don't do that.

You don't play at home?
No. I don't play at home. I don't listen to dance music apart from preparation
I think 80 percent of DJing is preparation and being aware, but I don't go home and DJ. I will go home and listen to, you know, the new Massive Attack album ...

What do you do to prepare?
I spend a lot of time on arrangement, on putting my records in keys. When I turn up at the club, people think, oh, he's just turned up with boxes, to play his tunes. They don't know what I've done...

All the preparation.
All the preparation. I'm mentally a lot more prepared than a lot of other DJs, I think. And I realise how important they are. I'm no better than anyone else, I'm just more aware of the situation because I study the situation. I try and study how it all comes together and what makes it work. It's just like an actor who does method acting and studies a character... Well, I do that as well. I look at how music's arranged, and what key it's in, and how feelings come from that, and where you can take people, and how you can get that communication and that eye contact. You look at someone in the crowd... it makes their night. If you've got that eye contact and you smile, it's such a simple thing to do but it means the world to them.

In the early days when there were a lot of illegal events and it was all pretty much centred around this new illegal drug – did you ever feel like an outlaw?
Yeah. What I did in Cuba last week I was an outlaw. I could have got banged up, but it's the excitement of it. The downside of that was walking through a fucking field for half a mile with a box of records [laughter]. But no, I mean, when you're standing at four in the morning in the middle of a fucking field with 10,000 people there, and it's going on...

Yeah.
It's a great feeling.

How often did that happen for you?
I used to do them all [the M25 raves].

....

Do any moments stand out in particular?
Yeah. Biology at sunrise, when I played at sunrise, and all of a sudden looked up and I was there, and it was in a valley, and then the sun come up overhead and… It was like eye contact, and it was like… fucking hell! You know, you're just standing there and you think, this is fucking great.

Were there times when you really were an outlaw? Raves you played that got busted? What usually went down?
Well, The police'd turn up and the power supply'd be turned off but luckily enough they never took your records. When I was DJing on Kiss when it was a pirate, every time they raided it, they'd take your records. That was really worrying. And then at raves they started saying, right, we're going to confiscate the DJs' records, and then … you know, that's when it's really worrying because if they do turn up you literally have to run with your records because they're after you. They wanted to try and stop it so they blame the DJ or the promoter. You can't afford to get your records taken away, so you just… I would then stop playing at those places because I didn't want to be put in a situation where I could lose my records …

What was your greatest moment from those years?
Spectrum. My own club that started it really. On one bank holiday Monday we had Heaven, Spectrum had Heaven, which had 1,500 people in. Across the water, *Time Out* voted us the Club of the Year, so we had a marquee with another 1,000 people in, called *Time Out* Spectrum, and then in Manchester we had a Spectrum there. On one night we had three clubs absolutely rammed, and it was just, fucking hell, this has come from nothing. Because I was no-one. I was no-one. We were just doing our own thing.

What was the secret then?
We were onto something new and fresh. You came down and experienced it, you'd go away and tell your mates. It was truly a unique experience. It was completely different from people wearing black, standing there, nicking handbags, listening to hip hop, to all of a sudden wearing baggy trousers, fucking trainers… Anyone could come in as long as they had the right attitude and… just having it. It wasn't just a club change. It was a youth culture change. It changed the whole youth culture.

© DJhistory.com

PAUL OAKENFOLD SELECTED DISCOGRAPHY

HAPPY MONDAYS – Hallelujah (remixer)
CABARET VOLTAIRE – Keep On (remixer)
ELECTRA – Autumn Love (writer/producer)
A SPLIT SECOND – Flesh (remixer)
HAPPY MONDAYS – W.F.L. (remixer)
MOVEMENT 98 – Joy & Heartbreak (writer/producer)
MASSIVE ATTACK – Unfinished Sympathy (remixer)
MOVEMENT 98 – Sunrise (writer/producer)
THE CURE – Close To Me (remixer)
IZIT – Stories (remixer)
U2 – Even Better Than The Real Thing (remixer)
D:REAM – U R The Best Thing (remixer)
ARRESTED DEVELOPMENT – Mr Wendal (remixer)
THE SHAMEN – Move Any Mountain (remixer)
U2 – Lemon (remixer)
NEW ORDER – World (remixer)
GRACE – Not Over Yet (producer/remixer)
OAKENFOLD – Starry Eyed Surprise (writer/producer/mixer)
AFRIKA BAMBAATAA & THE SOUL SONIC FORCE – Planet Rock (remixer)
OAKENFOLD – Zoo York (producer)

RECOMMENDED LISTENING

VARIOUS – Journeys By DJs Marathon (DJ mix)
VARIOUS – Cream Anthems 97 (DJ mix)
VARIOUS – Perfecto Volume 1

" It's the elevation of the DJ from the janitor to the person who pulls the crowds. "

Norman Cook
Pop star

Interviewed by Bill by phone to Brighton, March 3, 1999

Norman Cook brought a slice of rock'n'roll mayhem to '90s dancefloors. Using an array of aliases (of which Fatboy Slim was but one), his uncanny ear for a killer hook, and winning sample, and his unerring understanding of what makes a dancefloor go potty, ensured he spent most of the decade with his arms aloft. His album *You've Come A Long Way, Baby* lodged itself into the upper echelons of worldwide charts (going platinum in the US on the way) and spawned four hit singles and an amazing Spike Jonze video. Along with groups like Prodigy and Chemical Brothers, Cook's high-octane brand of dance music seemed to cross barriers and vastly widened dance music's appeal, taking it into the scrubby hinterland of student dorms and *NME* demographics.

When he started playing, DJs had the same social status as glass collectors. But Mr Cook was lucky. By the time he'd made it big (and Norman made it bigger than most), DJs had reached the exalted status that more usually requires spacesuits and oxygen masks. In this rarified atmosphere the job had more to do with helipads, groupies, souped-up Beemers and Pavlovian DJ trickery than getting on your hands and knees in Crazy Beat looking for rare twelves. At its most bonkers, Norman's Big Beat Boutique on Brighton beach in 2002 drew a reported 250,000 people. Though the mania has subsided somewhat the Fatboy is still a huge festival draw.

Okay. Did you feel aggrieved at the reaction from some quarters when you went from the Housemartins to dance music?
Not at all. I think I proved my mettle by having been a professional DJ playing dance music for three years before the Housemartins. There was a film that the BBC did...

Where you played the Clash breaks?
Yeah, and everyone who was into dance music was like, 'Oh yeah, you're the one in the Housemartins who was doing dance music before the rest of us.' There were only a couple of journalists who didn't realise I'd done dance music before who ever really made much of a deal about it. My conscience is clear. Besides, there wasn't much of a bandwagon to get on when I got on it.

How does being a DJ affect what you do in the studio?
When you're making dance music it helps because when you're DJing you spend untold hours just standing watching people dance. And you begin to realise which bits get 'em going. So when I'm in the studio, I think back to the night before and what kind of things worked with dancers.

What do you learn from DJing?
That goes back to the previous question. You just learn what makes people dance. It doesn't necessarily mean you make great pop music, but if your music's aimed straight at the dancefloor it gives you a head start on everybody else. Also, it gives you a chance to try your tunes out.

What's the secret of your success?
Dogged determination in the face of thinking I was too old for it. Living the life 100 percent. There's tons of people who, when they get older, stop going to clubs. And if you stop going to clubs, you stop making club music really. You can make interesting noodly stuff, but you've got to be out there every weekend to make pure dance music. Putting in those late night hours.

How do you go about making great records?
Again, it's similar to the other one. Just faff about for ages until it sounds good. And remember how you felt when you put a tune on and it rocked the crowd, or a groove that the crowd just totally got into when they've never heard the record before.

Does that translate into the big commercial pop successes you've had?
No, that's kind of a case of just throwing lots of stuff at the ceiling and seeing what sticks. I just do tons of tunes aimed at the dancefloor, and every now and then one of them fits on the radio and the charts. I've tried to make pop records, but they're always appalling. All the Fatboy records are just made for the Big Beat Boutique. It's just lucky that the taste of the crowd there is the same as Radio 1 programmers. That catapults you into a different arena.

❝ Sometimes they just don't advertise me on the flyer because it wouldn't be fair on the people who couldn't get in. ❞

How do you come across the samples for the records. How do you make them fit together so well?
Trial and error. Getting tons of stuff together by going to record fairs, car boot sales, cheap old rubbish. Then getting bits you think might work as a hook. I just have them all on disc and I just try them out until I find ones that work with each other.

What are the things you look for?
Yeah. Hair styles and beards on a band. If they've got long hair and beards, and look like they smoke pot they're likely to make better records.

Like Black Oak Arkansas?
Yeah. Especially those big bands with eight of them in, half white, half black and they look like they all take acid.

Like Tower of Power?
Yeah. Secondly, the more obscure the better, because you have to pay less for the samples [laughs]. The year's quite important too. 1970-1975, those are the best times, because before that the drum sounds weren't very tight. And then after 1977 because disco came in and everything went shit.

What technical aspects do you apply when you make these records? What's the process?
There is no process really, it's just... I dunno, you just sit there for hours making weird noises until you find something that turns you on. I normally start with the rhythm track. Then the hook. Then I see what else is missing.

What differences are there in the business from when you left the Housemartins, to now?
The first thing I noticed was that DJs could play outside of the town they lived in. Because when I started there was no way you'd ever play in another town because the wages you were getting paid wouldn't even cover your train fare. The elevation of the DJ. The DJ is like the new pop star. And pulling people, which meant you got laid more. People at the other end of the country had heard of you. When I started DJing, the DJ was just below glass collector in order of importance in a nightclub. You were just the bloke who stood in the corner and put records on. Over the years the DJ got more and more important.

I dunno, in those days all there was was James Hamilton's column in *Record Mirror* and that was our only network of finding out what anybody else was doing. But no-one was making records and there weren't any stars really, apart from Froggy and Chris Hill. Then when I came back to DJing, it was like, 'God, you can play in London, you can play up North.' *Mixmag* had stopped being a magazine that focussed on wet t-shirt contests sponsored by Malibu UK, so everybody started finding out what other DJs were doing. I suppose it's the elevation of the DJ from being the janitor in the club to being the star and the person who pulled the crowds.

A lot of the stuff you do is hip hop influenced. What impact did that make on you?
That was when I first started going to clubs, when I was 17, and I used to go to a club called Sherry's in Brighton on a Wednesday, which was the big new romantic night. And in amongst the Human League, Blancmange and Depeche Mode, they'd drop like these other weird tracks. And I remember hearing 'Planet Rock' when it first came out. It was like, wow, it's like that and it's funky and whoah! As I started DJing in clubs electro and hip hop were the big forces. My roots in DJing were that music, which is probably why I keep coming back to it.

Is that what made you want to become a DJ?
No I was already a DJ from when I was 15. When I started I was playing punk and new wave and 2-Tone, and then new romantic electronic stuff. But that was when I first getting paid for it. Before that I was just doing weddings, funerals and bar mitzvahs.

When you started making dance records, did you have any idea where it would go as a career?
None. I thought it was a flash in the pan, like skateboarding, and we'd get away with it for a year...

And then you'd be back flipping burgers?
Yeah, right, back to working in the record shop.

What is the buzz personally for you as a DJ?
Making people dance and watching them all having a good time. And you having a good time, too. On a bad night, it's the loneliest thing in the world. You're standing there with a load of people you don't know, sometimes playing records you don't like very much, and all your mates are somewhere else and you're thinking, 'Oh my god, this is horrible.' But on a good night, you're in the middle of a crowd of people, a lot of whom are your mates, and you're having fun. You're the centre of the party. You're making them dance and getting paid to play your favourite records. What a way to make a living, eh? And when you're playing your own records and they're dancing... That's when you start having orgasms.

Do crowds react differently to you because you're a pop star?
I think nowadays they do, yeah.

In what way?
I've kind of avoided being a pop star for ages and I was known on the dance scene, but people wouldn't travel to see me, and when we started the Boutique it was funny... I emerged as the crowd pleaser out of them, but at the same time people started coming down to the club because they've heard of me. But obviously, in the last six months, it's got really silly [sniggers].

How has it got silly?
People going bonkers from the moment I walk on rather than me earning it. You hope you're worthy of it. Nowadays some people not even putting me on the flyer because too many people would turn up. If there's a club that's full already, then I'm on, sometimes they just don't advertise me because it wouldn't be fair on the people who couldn't get in. [Laughs]. I'm serious! I'm like, 'You bastard, why haven't you put me on the flyer?' 'Oh, we couldn't take the roadblock.'

Where has this happened?
A couple of times at the Boutique where everyone knew what the buzz was about the

....

Boutique. We'd been rammed and the queue's famous. And we were like, 'Oh we can't tell them...' I can't tell you where it's happened, because it would give the game away.

Why do you think DJing leads naturally into production?
Well, because most DJs become DJs because they love the music, and if you love the music, you feel you have some of it in you waiting to come out. You're playing tracks that are really simple. You think this is just a couple of samples and a drum machine, I bet I could probably do that. And invariably, you can.

What's the craziest thing that's happened to you, in terms of adulation, sex, drugs, rock'n'roll?
Not much sex. The amount of girls that show you their tits is quite bizarre. People take their clothes off, too. In Japan, in Tokyo once, this bloke climbed on the speaker stack. He looked like Jimi Hendrix. I played 'Crosstown Traffic', and he just took all of his clothes off and danced the whole thing naked, much to the amusement of the other Japanese people.

Did he have an air guitar?
No, but his penis was almost big enough [laughter]. No, I remember, the most ludicrous things have always happened at Manumission. People hanging upside down from the lighting rig with no clothes on. There's a bloke who always carries cardboard cut-out elephants. I remember at one point having a fight with my cardboard cut-out elephant, and he had a cardboard cut-out Darth Vader. And we were having a fight on the dancefloor and this girl, who didn't even know us, came to break it up and she was going, 'Now come on, stop, he's not worth it. And you, Nelly, just go and stand over there and leave it out.'

Do you think you earn your fee?
Er, no. I'm worth some money, and I've put in the years and paid my dues, but sometimes the money I get paid I think, 'Fuck, this is just stupid.' If there's a DJ getting paid £50 and I'm getting paid five grand, I couldn't say I was a hundred times better. I could say I was better than him. I might even say I was twice as good as him, but there's no way that I'm a hundred times better than him.

Sasha once told me he was turning down gigs because he didn't want to do them, but promoters were coming back and offering even more money, despite the fact that the money wasn't an issue.
I'm getting a lot of that at the moment, especially New Year's Eve. I said I didn't wanna do New Year's Eve, because I normally do one on one off. I've just done two on because I got made an offer I couldn't refuse last year, so I said to everyone, 'Look I'm not playing this year.' So they've said, 'OK, we'll double the money.'

'No, I just don't wanna play, I wanna stay at home with my mates.'

And then they double it again, and it just gets to the point where it's like, I've gotta take it. I could take all my mates on holiday for two weeks and pretend it's New Year's Eve. A lot of people think you're just holding out for the right price, when in fact I just want some peace and quiet. It's horrible when they then offer you so much money that you have to do it, because you feel terrible that you're really greedy and that's why you said no, when what you wanted to do was to be left alone and not be offered so much money. But they finally found what your price was. Because everybody does have a price.

Are DJs worthy of superstar status, or is it good marketing?
If they pull the crowds, and the crowds have fun, yeah. If they get away with it, they must be worth it. Promoters aren't stupid. Promoters aren't running an ageing DJ charity. They're paying you that money because they know they'll make more. And they're making it because you're attracting crowds and entertaining them.

How does the punk ethos come into what you do?
The DIY attitude. An irreverence to the rules, like you can make a record that's really repetitive and isn't very musical and was made at home in your bedroom and doesn't have chords, drummers, singers, or anyone who can read a musical note. That, and just enjoying being a little bit naughty, winding people up. 'Oh, you're one of those club people aren't you?'

....

Do you think house has brought the democracy that punk spoke of but didn't deliver?
No, I think it's post-punk. Nothing could out-punk punk. If punk was just 50 people ripping their shirts, then house has failed miserably at being punk. Punk was about freedom. It freed up the thing about eight-minute guitar solos, superstars worshipped by millions. You're right, it is very democratic. But house has carved its own niche. It's got its own language, its own uniform, its own set of parameters. But it's definitely not punk's parameters.

What do you think the difference is?
More based on hedonism and less on rebellion.

Do you think that's its own form of rebellion?
No I just think it comes with the territory. I don't think people are getting off their nuts because they like people thinking they're drug-crazed lunatics, they just like getting off their nuts. And the fact that it winds people up that they do it, and that they're having an exceptionally good time doing it.

> **" In Tokyo once, this bloke climbed on the speaker stack. He just took all of his clothes off and danced the whole thing naked. "**

Do you consider the DJ an artist nowadays?
I think some are [snickers]. Not necessarily though. A lot of my favourite DJs are consummate artists. I think the decks or a sampler give you the same potential as an electric guitar to entertain you, or completely bore you. And in the right hands, a pair of turntables, it's music to my ears. And in the wrong hands, it can be horrible. A lot of DJs put a lot into it, and treat it as an art. And then other ones don't... and are better [more snickers].

Why?
The law of averages. Some people can do a masterpiece after labouring for 20 years on it, and some people, their best work comes off the cuff. Some people do their best DJ set by thinking about it and planning it while other people, the best way they can plan is to get absolutely twatted before they start and be hanging on by a thread. I've seen some great sets by people who couldn't actually stand up, but they could DJ like an angel.

What makes a good DJ or bad DJ?
For me, it's whether they look up or not while they're playing. A good DJ is always looking at the crowd, seeing what they're like, seeing whether it's working, communicating with them, smiling at them. And a bad DJ is always looking down at what they're doing, and just doing their thing that they practised in their bedroom. It's whether they're communicating to the crowd and whether they're receiving the communication back from the crowd.

Do you think there's a correlation between ego and communion in bad DJs?
Yeah, well not even ego because some DJs that are looking up can have much bigger egos and probably deserve to have bigger egos. But it's more about communication than communion.

What have you learnt from DJing?
That I prefer it to playing in a band.

Why?
I feel more comfortable. It's more me. I spent 10 years trying to pretend I was a guitarist or bassist and all the time I was a closet DJ living in denial.

What have you learnt about music from DJing?
Not to take it too seriously and not to ever think that dance music anything more than the soundtrack to people having fun on a Friday and Saturday night. People put it on a pedestal: it's very easy to go up your own arse and think, just because all of these people love what

you're doing, that it's actually some form of art. It isn't. It's just a form of entertainment.

You don't think it's art at all?
I see it as the art of entertainment. But if you ever stop being entertaining, then you quickly realise that there's nothing artful about that. And you normally get a hefty slap on the face from everybody else.

> **"It's easy to think that DJing is actually some form of art. It isn't. It's just entertainment."**

Why do you think dance music has become so international?
Less lyrics. French people can finally make music that English people like because we don't get put off by the fact that it's not in our language. And other countries can listen to English music without being put off by the fact that they've got no idea what we're on about. If there's a hookline, you can just mime along to it, you don't have to know what the story of the song is.

Where do you see dance music going next?
Evolving, just like it's always done. When one field gets a bit boring something else surges a bit. Constantly kind of looking back to the past and recycling.

How do you see yourself in marketing terms as Fatboy Slim. Are majors taking people like you and putting their rock template on it?
It's trying. I have this constant battle and the more popular it becomes, the more ... It's nice that you're promoting me and we're selling albums, but let's not forget that this is what I do. They're always trying to make me put a band together and play as a band. I got offered to do *Letterman* and *Saturday Night Live,* which is a lovely idea, but what would I do? Er, I'm a DJ and it takes two hours to DJ. You can't do it in three minutes. I've had to turn TV shows down because what a DJ does, doesn't work in that environment. I've got to the point now where in America, I'm like, 'Look this is as far as we can take it.' Where it's still dance music. I don't wanna cross over and be a rock act. I don't wanna play in a band. I don't wanna tour.

Do you think they're a little bit blind to the fact that you DJing in a big venue is as good a promotion as Nirvana doing a gig?
No, they know that and it's worked. We're shipping units, as they say. But that's as far as I can take it with the DJing.

Do you think the pressure on them is because they don't understand dance music, so they try and make you adhere to the template they have for selling rock albums?
Mmm. Yeah, probably. But it's the lure of the dollars, because they've finally found a few dance acts that can sell. You know, me and Tom and Ed [The Chemical Bros.], and the Prodigy, where you can sell albums at least and make decent money. They don't know – and we don't know – how far we can take it in the rock field. I've just had a gold album in America and I'm like, 'Fuck, I've never had a gold album in 14 years!' I'm really chuffed. But they're like, 'No, we can make this platinum!'

They want me to play at Woodstock this summer. I said, 'Interesting idea, but it's got to be in a tent.' And they're like, 'No, we can get you on the main stage at Woodstock.' It's just uncharted territory, because dance music's never sold albums before. I think the Prodigy, Underworld and Tom and Ed have opened this new door for dance music and it's great because it's opened the doors for everyone else and it means major labels will plough money into developing dance acts, whereas before they'd be happy licensing the odd 12-inch here and there, but they'd never see them as serious acts and give them serious advances.

Who do you think those people you've mentioned have been selling albums in America?
There's a little element of rock'n'roll in all of us, I think. We're not just studio boffins, we're kind of caning rock'n'roll animals that *Rolling Stone* and *Spin* can write stories about.

We've all had brushes with rock music. There's a couple of guitars in there and that's all the Americans needed to latch on to!

Do you think they need to push it as far away from disco as possible because disco was black and homo and bad?
Yeah, it definitely is. When me and Tom and Ed get on the radio we're always on KROQ, played against Nirvana and REM. But also, there are no stations that cover dance music so...

Do you think that's the right place for you to be on?
No, I think the right place for me to be on would be this dance music station that doesn't exist. It's very strange being taken to interviews in America they always put the station on in the car on the way there saying, 'Yeah, so this is the guy you'll be talking to.' I'm like, 'Hello? I think we're going to the wrong place here! Hootie and the Blowfish? I don't think so!' I don't feel very comfortable in the modern rock arena.

Do you think people like you can help break barriers down in America?
Hopefully, yeah. I don't get called the Band of the '90s quite as much as I did two years ago. When I used to get to a venue, people say, [adopts American accent] 'Hey, are you in Fatboy Slim?' [laughs]

And what's the answer to that?
No. But do you wanna be?

© DJhistory.com

NORMAN COOK SELECTED DISCOGRAPHY

ERIC B & RAKIM – I Know You Got Soul (remixer)
URBAN ALL-STARS – It Began In Africa (mixer)
BEATS INTERNATIONAL – Dub Be Good To Me (writer/producer)
A TRIBE CALLED QUEST – I Left My Wallet In El Segundo (remixer)
CHEEKY BOY – Once In A Plastic Time (producer/editor)
PIZZAMAN – Happiness (writer/producer)
FREAK POWER – Tune In, Turn On, Cop Out (writer/producer)
PIZZAMAN – Trippin' On Sunshine (writer/producer)
FREAK POWER – New Direction (producer)
FATBOY SLIM – Punk To Funk (writer/producer)
THE MIGHTY DUB KATZ – It's Just Another Groove (producer)
JEAN-JACQUES PERREY – E.V.A. (remixer)
THE FEELGOOD FACTOR – The Whole Church Should Get Drunk (writer/producer)
THE MIGHTY DUB KATZ – Magic Carpet Ride (writer/producer)
SON OF A CHEEKY BOY – Comma (producer/editor)
CORNERSHOP – Brimful Of Asha (remixer)
FATBOY SLIM – Praise You (writer/producer)
FATBOY SLIM – Right Here, Right Now (writer/producer)
FATBOY SLIM – Rockefeller Skank (writer/producer)
FATBOY SLIM FT. MACY GRAY – Demons (writer/producer)

RECOMMENDED LISTENING

VARIOUS – On The Floor At The Boutique (DJ mix)
VARIOUS – Big Beach Boutique (DJ mix)
VARIOUS – Fatboy Slim's Greatest Mixes

" The DJ has given the business a massive up-side. "

Pete Tong
Essential selector

Interviewed by Bill and Frank in London, May 13, 1999

Pete Tong is the business – literally. Without him large parts of the industry of dance music would cease to function. Or at the very least need to find themselves another set of wheels. When Britain was dancing itself doolally with pills and thrills, Tong was already stationed in a comfy record company office, closing the deals that fuelled acid house, signing bands and licensing tracks including many of the big tunes of Chicago. He was also instrumental in developing the market for DJ-mixed compilations, one of the few sectors of the music industry that hasn't yet been given up for dead.

Millions know Tongy as the unflappable voice of Radio 1's Essential Selection. Since 1991 he's provided the Friday night pre-club soundtrack as a nation dolls itself up and has a few snifters of vodka. You'll hear him playing future anthems first and giving a giant boost to the fortunes of any single lucky enough to make the playlist.

The interview takes place in his office where he's posted behind a sizeable desk. Dance music has certainly been good to him. Worth a reported £20 million, he picks up about 20 grand a gig, he's married to a Brazilian model and confesses to 'one crippling vice – private jets'. And it's a select group indeed who've become an enduring piece of rhyming slang. It may have occasionally gone a bit Pete for some of us, but certainly not Mr Tong.

When you were broadcasting on pirate radio, did you feel like an outlaw?
Yeah, you did, you were conscious of that. When I started doing pirates it didn't seem to be an illegal thing to do. It was sort of like a hobby and the fact that you were so bothered about doing it and you would bother to go to the great lengths you'd have to go to set it up to do it, it seemed like, 'What do you mean it's illegal?' Obviously it was illegal. I was lucky, I was never there when a raid happened. I was on LWR; I was on Invicta when it was a pirate. LWR was more, sort of, cloak-and-dagger: down back alleyways, knocking on doors and giving passwords sort of thing. When we worked at Invicta, you'd go into a nice little house near Crystal Palace. It was all very luxurious actually! It was like playing records in your bedroom with the sun coming in.

It was almost like a public service rather than a pirate?
Yeah. I think it got a little bit more renegade in the '90s, especially with the inner city stations. Pirates, when I started, it was just, 'There's not enough Robbie Vincent on the radio so let's give them some more.' Whereas pirates these days it's much more, there's not enough drum and bass, there's not enough UK garage; it's much more focused on musical genres.

Is that always going to be their function, filling gaps?
I think so yeah.

Is that because national radio is tightly controlled?
I don't think it's as tightly controlled as it used to be. I don't think running a legal dance station is as easy as people think. I think that's the state of mind in the late '90s: being given a license is one thing, but making a business out of it is another. The principal reason why

....

Kiss has gone all over the place in terms of musical style is because they've got quite a heavy investment and heavy overheads and they've got to deliver a certain amount of listeners to satisfy their advertisers. If they want to play in the Premier League, they've gotta get themselves Premier League capacities. Whereas if they were a niche broadcaster like Choice, they could size down their operation.

The pirate is a romantic ideal, a fascinating thing. But you're catering for a niche. There's no pressure. No-one's getting paid. Everyone's groovy. But as soon as it comes to business and making it work and being legitimate, you've got to make money to pay for it all. It's not quite the Alice In Wonderland-type scenario you think it's gonna be. So I've got a lot of sympathy for Kiss, other than the fact they went off in the wrong direction a little bit at the start. It's no real surprise what's happened to it in the last four or five years. That's what happens to a lot of those American stations: you turn the dial and get every flavour you want, but go back in six months time and they'll all be in a different place.

Is Radio 1 a happy medium in that it doesn't have to deliver in the way a commercial station does?
I think so, yeah. Their mission statement is to champion new music, not to get the biggest audience. Every decision that runs through that building is based around that core set of values and that doesn't involve getting an audience.

How often do you compromise?
I don't ever compromise. I get left alone completely. They expect me to do alright.

Do you get left alone because they haven't got a clue what it is you do, or...
When I first started they were just happy to put me in a room and let me get on with it. It was the Parfitt/Bannister era where they took a lot more interest in what I do. I say I get complete freedom in what I do, the only check they have is that I don't fill up the show with my own records!

Do you think it's a measure of Kiss's success that Radio 1 has absorbed a number of DJs from there, or is it a relative measure of success of dance music?
I think it's a measure of the fact that it became the obvious place to learn your craft.

When did you first come across house?
Someone asked me, 'Was it a holy grail when you discovered it?' And I actually said no, though it was a little bit. The reason I said no was because we didn't go out and discover it. The reality in the late '80s was you were obviously always looking for new music, but your field of vision was totally dictated by what City Sounds or All Ears Records got in. And obviously they imported as much as they could and sold what they did. But that was the reality and those records just started coming in.

Did it take a long time for them to come over?
No not really. It was at the height of the Def Jam mania, stuff like 'My Adidas' by Run DMC, which I signed. If you'd gone to Doo At The Zoo with me and Nicky Holloway playing with Gilles [Peterson] and Bob Masters, you would have heard a mixture of what Gordon Mac calls boogie. Then you'd get 'Rock The Bells' by LL Cool J, Beastie Boys and some Sleeping Bag records. The first house record I got was Sleezy D. But the first one where it was a movement in my head was 'Music Is The Key' by JM Silk. Because soon after there was another JM Silk record and that was an indication of something. Then suddenly we were hungry, give us more, give us more because DJs... you get something like that and it's hard to put something before it and after. So you want more.

It went on from there. It was a change. That's what's kept me going for so long – because you're always looking for the next thing. A fashion junkie in a sense. A music junkie of new trends. So you're playing rap and then six months later everyone is playing rap. Right, what's next? I can't just can't keep doing this when it's in the high street Mecca clubs.

To be fair, and I think it's been quite well documented before, in London we flirted with it a bit. What I was just talking about was 1986 and '87. And at that time I did 'Masterplan' by Diana Brown. We were a bit schizophrenic. And even when there was the infamous Ibiza trip and that threw it a little bit more and we were playing everything from INXS to new beat. Whereas Pickering and Park at the Haçienda were looking down at us, going, 'You fucking southern soul tossers!' To be fair, they were much more on it. The day a house record came in, they chucked all the old ones out.

Was that their taste or the crowd's?
I think that was Mike. You'd have to credit Mike and Graeme. I tell you what it was, I think it was the club. Streamlined, smooth-lines, stark-look. It fitted the club. You hear a rap record in the Haçienda it always seems like it's the wrong room. Whereas house music seemed much more like the right thing to play in it. When you think about T Coy and those early records. A bit of German, a bit of Kraftwerk. They just went with it. They were purist. Even at the Astoria we played some weird records. That wasn't pure house. We were playing new beat.

How long was it before they realised they had a substantial export market?
Straight away. Rocky Jones and Larry Sherman were always over here. Particularly Rocky.

When was the first compilation?
about 1986 or '87.

Wasn't there a tour, too?
The biggest one was when we brought over Jamie Principle. That was '87.

> 66 **Pickering and Park at the Haçienda were going, 'You fucking southern soul tossers!' They were much more on it. The day a house record came in, they chucked all the old ones out.** 99

Did you think when house started coming over that it would be as big as it has been?
I definitely acknowledged it was a seminal moment. I don't think I was the only one. It was dance music's punk rock. It was like Before and After. And the weird thing is I suppose punk had a fundamental influence on rock'n'roll. But it's not as obviously audible in the records today, whereas house music is. House music is everywhere. Still. America's got on it and drifted back off. On a pop level.

Why do you think straight America's never really got into it?
Because it tended not to be artist based. It tended to be producer/writer based.

Do you think that's because they're so old school rock'n'roll that they couldn't get their head around it?
No, I think that's true of here; it's just our market allowed it to happen more quickly. The way you have hits in America is fundamentally different to the way you have hits here. It's just so much bigger. Just look at the English chart: football songs, novelty songs. The disposability of dance music was perfect for it, I suppose. Whereas with America, the notion of singles was practically dead by the '90s. Generally white people in America don't buy singles. Black people do. But they're coming back round to it.

What was the indicator that made you realise that dance music was the new pop?
I suppose when I saw 5,000 people queuing outside the Astoria every Saturday night for three years. And Tribal Gathering. It's just what people wanted. Even Glastonbury years and years ago, walking up what they call the motorway, it was always house and techno there. It's been in the culture so long it just has to be represented in one way or another.

Do you think it's affected the way you market records, singles in particular?
It has done in the past I think. We're probably over the phase now, in the business, where I think in the mid-'90s, every record company went spastic in the same way the American

market went spastic for disco. It doesn't matter who you are, you're going to have a David Morales remix.

There was an awful lot of money thrown at the wall. That's where you got your multiple packs of records. I've moved house a couple of times lately, and the biggest pain in the arse is the record collection legacy. You can thin out. How many of those remixes by artists that are not of the culture do you really need to keep? There's very few. You can literally lose all of them! Never miss them. It's quite sad isn't it, because they all cost a fucking fortune. And how relevant was it? That is when it went mad.

What about compilations. Is that the new way of selling singles?
It's a way of maximising the sales of a record that was probably never destined in its own right to do more than 5-10,000. There's an awful lot of those and when you put those together with 15 other tracks they become a lot more interesting.

> **❝ People bought into trusting the Ministry of Sound logo or trusting Boy George, or trusting me or trusting Sasha. I think that's a massive revolution in the last five years. ❞**

Because there's one thing that the DJ does is filter information. So people buy into the DJ rather than the records now.
People bought into trusting the Ministry of Sound logo or trusting Boy George, or trusting me or trusting Sasha. I think that's a massive revolution in the last five years really.

Are you aware of that in the way you market things?
Very much so. I was asked to do mix albums for Cream and then I was involved with the Ministry for a long time. And I started doing my own ones off the back of the show and it just got to a point where I thought there were too many of them and I can't be on everybody's so I just decided I couldn't really do a DJ compilation for the Ministry and not do it for myself, so that's why there's the *Essential Selection* series. And I'm not on the Ministry any more. But definitely for us, it's big business. There's no question about it. I think they can perform two functions. I still really get off on doing the sort of artistic ones, like David Holmes. The whole cost base is lower and you can do really well selling 30- 40- 50,000. They become catalogue items.

Whereas I'm operating in the other end of the market where you go for hundreds of thousands and the sales are gigantic and happen in a short space of time and I'm not really expecting them to be dug up five years later. I just don't think they will be. Whereas Holmes' album and hopefully Kevorkian's, those sorts of records, they're different. It is a business as much as it is a pleasure, and art, and everything else. Getting back to your original point, packaging up the music, selling it in an attractive fashion. The DJ has given the business a massive up-side, akin to what it's like having an album when you're a 'proper' artist with a hit single.

Is that one of the reasons the DJ has become such a superstar?
Yeah, definitely. It's a really nice, succinct way of charting their ability to entertain, I think. Obviously, it came out of the tape revolution in the early '90s, the bootleg tapes. The hottest thing was a Sasha tape from a club in Coventry, or Renaissance. And that's what people wanted. It still goes on, but nothing like it did. Obviously, you can just walk in a store now. They needed to be legitimised, because it was getting silly, when the DJ wasn't getting paid, the music wasn't getting paid.

It was DMC who did it first wasn't it?
Yeah, and Renaissance, but then they were one of the biggest tapes sources! Do us a tape.

That's what people want. It'll be interesting to see the evolution of online music. That's all very well, and everyone's getting worried about it, but actually what it's gonna do it's gonna splat on the internet; so to suddenly just give Joe Bloggs everything is just so overwhelming. I think what the future will be is they go to Oakey's site or Sasha's site and they'll say select us some music. That's sort of what it's gonna be like in the future: we'll trust those people to give us the tape.

Why hasn't dance music broken in America like it did here?
I think the problem with America is they can't deal with anything that doesn't last that long. The fact that there's no album. I kind of understand why it got in a bit of mess in America. Donna Summer was alright. They got that.

The way the DJ is so exalted now, are they trying to turn the DJ into a rock star?
Yeah, I suppose so yeah. I don't think it's been quite thought through like that. I suppose yeah, that's a fair analogy. I mean, Oakey's over there touring constantly, almost at the expense of what he does here. That's his life. That's something I can't do because I've got a record company. But Carl [Cox] is over there. Sasha and Digweed. Paul's doing it the most.

Yeah, he seems like he's on a mission.
Yeah, it's the same. It's just like taking the thing to the masses. Because there's so much uncharted territory over there. From what he tells me he's being welcomed with open arms everywhere. He's getting to places where no-one's been to. More so than here, that will be the way America markets the mix albums. It'll be like the Grateful Dead. You know, see Oakey and buy the CD on your way out.

What do you think makes a good DJ or a bad one?
I think entertainment is a massive factor. I think now, if you're starting out you're pretty resigned to the fact that you've got to come out with a unique sound. Adam Freeland comes along, makes his mark very quickly and stays very focused. What does Adam Freeland sound like? Breakbeats. Then he's got to take it to the next level, the same way that Sasha can play to 10,000 people at Creamfields last year and rock this place with one record. Adam can't quite do that yet. First its positioning. That's what seems to be the term of reference. When a new DJ comes along, it's, 'What does he sound like? What's he doing that's different?'

I come from a slightly privileged position in that it wasn't like that when I started. It was more about playing music that no-one else played. It was more like a mission. That's what the experience felt like. It wasn't that hard to become a DJ. It wasn't that hard to become well known.

Did it feel more subversive?
Much more in the old days. You don't get that nowadays. In those days it was very much black and white. You were either playing pop music or you were playing jazz-funk. And it was a little bit more covert. You felt like you were in a secret society. *Blues & Soul* was the *Mixmag* of the day and you couldn't buy it anywhere. You had to subscribe to it. Get it in a brown paper bag!

What is the buzz, playing?
It's more that frustrated rock star. That's what it's all about still. People go up to me: is it dying; is it building; is it this; is it that? You just go out to clubs and it's just not really over. Do DJs get paid too much money? Well not really because if they did you wouldn't book them back would you?

Do you think it's still a central part of what you do?
Definitely. I don't know what I'd do on the radio if I didn't play in clubs. I'd feel like a bit of a fraud. I think I've developed a skill to communicate with people and build a radio show, and ebb and flow a radio show. At the same time I don't know why I'd be there if I wasn't out in clubland.

Is it the same feeling of community on the radio show?
I've developed the show to a point where I'm trying to be this umbrella of involvement,

bringing in everybody. I've adopted more of an anchoring role because I think you have to keep inventing yourself. I'm there because I don't feel a fraud, because I'm playing in clubs, but by the same token I'm not suggesting that Bugged Out are doing something good so let's get them on, let's get everybody on and represent. Quite similar to what Westwood does in a way. That's what keeps that show interesting. The show, there's no question, it's the start of the weekend, it's a Friday night thing. That's my GOOD IDEA.

> **❝ One of the problems of being Pete Tong is that you have that huge responsibility to peak the night. I never forgot that. They want to go doolally to their favourite records. ❞**

As music has evolved the DJ has been at the forefront. Why do you think that is?
Because most of us are anoraky, trainspottery vinyl junkies craving for the next thing. I parted company with my ancestors because a lot of them didn't want to change. I came into the Chris Hill thing [the so-called Soul Mafia] as a junior fan and left it because they wouldn't play rap music. It seemed mad to me. They were quite happy to keep regurgitating old soul records. They were a massive influence on me, but... When rap came along, me and Jeff Young we became the embarrassment on the bill at those weekenders. Chris was like, 'Oh fucking hell, here they are with that old racket.' And when house music came along that was the last straw.

House music came along and still to this day hasn't really got a fashion. It's got a state of mind. House music is more a club cultural experience in a different way to hip hop. I know what a DJ looks like because they've usually got a baseball cap on.

So what's next?
I never like to say what's next. I don't think anyone really knows, because we don't decide; that's the fun bit actually. We tend to just be there when it starts to move. I can't put my finger on it, but I know sometimes when I'm coming back from a gig. And this happens every couple of years. There comes a point when you've done your job, people have gone spastic, the club promoter comes up to you at the end of the night and wants you back. You get back in the car and think it didn't rock me, it didn't do me, it didn't get me going. I didn't get an orgasm out of it. And that's because it was too easy. When you do a gig you know what will work, so you always try and go off that a little bit. That sort of feels like the time we're in right now.

One of the problems of being Pete Tong or Judge Jules or whoever is that you have that huge responsibility to peak the night. I never forgot that. You are there to entertain. Education is something we like doing. That's not actually the biggest thing on the night, when people are queuing to get in and paying their money. They want to go doolally to their favourite records.

I've been quite good, throughout my career, at just tripping over that line a little bit. There's a lot of purist house around now that's really good again. Now is that us being boring and suddenly becoming Chris Hills about it and not wanting to change? Maybe a 17 year old might say that. I'm very conscious of that. There's always been something about techno that's never been overground. There's something about what Sasha's doing. And what Carl's doing. And what they like at Bugged Out. What they do at the End. Also what Bangalter does. He plays disco but he plays it like techno.

I almost feel like I've got a puzzle in front of me. Like an algebra thing. There's something in there and I just keep looking at it and keep going back to it, thinking I'll figure it out soon. That's what I wanna do. I go and watch Sasha and there'll be maybe an hour where it's not that good, then suddenly there'll be 10 minutes of brilliance and he's definitely pushing the boat out again.

The goal posts are being moved. What sounded a little odd nine months ago, is the norm now. Norman Cook, funnily enough, he's also broken a whole set of rules. 750,000 albums they've done in America. I've been dealing with this business all my working life and there's a set of rules of what you're meant to do to sell records in America. You're meant to go over and kiss butt, you're meant to go to all the States, you're meant to do this. The guy's been there three times. He's never travelled to more than one state at a time. He's never met anybody apart from the first layer of staff at Astralwerks. He's just broken every rule.

How will the internet change the way we consume music?
There was a massive evolution from vinyl to CD, in a sense that you could buy something more expensive and you got something smaller! People getting used to things is not what life's about. Maybe experiences is what life's about. Less things the better. I've got various sets of friends and you go round to some of them and every single orifice of the house is stuffed with books and records. And you go to other people's houses and there's nothing in them! It's all going to be stuffed on a hard disk somewhere. I suppose what I've got to watch as a business is how people interact with music and what becomes their life.

The internet will be more like cable radio on demand...
Yeah, which gives a great outlet for dance music and DJs, because I do think given infinite choice, you become totally confused. I've interacted recently. My dog-walker wanted a spoken word record by Richard Harris. I just hit the search engine and a place in California had it in. I put my credit card in and it was in Wimbledon in two days. Unbelievable.

© DJhistory.com

PETE TONG'S TOP 10 A&R SIGNINGS

RUN DMC – Walk This Way

JOYCE SIMS – Come Into My Life

FARLEY 'JACKMASTER' FUNK FT. DARRYL PANDY – Love Can't Turn Around

STEVE 'SILK' HURLEY – Jack Your Body

LIL LOUIS – French Kiss

BRAND NEW HEAVIES – Back To Love

ORBITAL – Chime

GOLDIE – Inner City Life

SALT 'N' PEPA – Push It

FRANKIE KNUCKLES – Tears

Compiled by Pete Tong

RECOMMENDED LISTENING

VARIOUS – Essential Selection (Trust The DJ) (DJ-mix)

VARIOUS – Platinum On Black: The Final Chapter (DJ mix)

VARIOUS – FFRR Classics 1988-1998

" I was never comfortable on the cover of magazines. "

Sasha
Son of God?

Interviewed by Bill and Frank in Soho, July 7, 2005

DJing at Fabric before Sasha and you've never seen so many boy's faces. They crowd the booth, then squirm forward as he puts on his first tune. DJs feed off energy and release; it must be strange to be always playing surrounded by scrutiny and obsession. No DJ is as observed, as discussed, as annotated, as Alexander Coe. His sets are picked apart on forums as soon as his decks fall silent; every tune he adds to his box is snapped up by bedroom DJs the world over. His celebrated residency at Shelleys in Stoke on Trent, and later at Mansfield's Renaissance qualified him for the role of DJ messiah, and tapes of his piano-laden house sets spread nationwide. Clubbers adored him, and as clubs became super, *Mixmag* made him their superman. 'SON OF GOD?' was their coverline in 1994 when the magazine elevated him to star status, keen to find DJs who could become celebrities to sell magazines and fill barn-sized dancefloors.

Sasha was the first DJ to have an album of remixes marketed under his own name. The sleevenotes claimed he was blurring the lines between DJ and artist. He was also one of the first global DJs, able to pull a crowd in Sydney or Cape Town as easily as New York or London. He saw out the '90s playing a monthly residency with John Digweed at New York's Twilo.

Despite years of unreal adoration, Sasha remains a pretty level-headed guy. His thoughts on DJing are mostly geared to finding ways to keep himself excited while meeting the expectations heaped on him by his fans. This interview took place when he was first enthralled by Ableton Live, digital DJing software which allows him to side-step the trainspotters a little. The other big news when we spoke was the apparent collapse of the superclub economy.

Is the buzz of DJing still the same for you?
The buzz now, or the buzz when I was 18? The whole scene was different then. Everything was edgier and more underground. It all felt like it could fall apart at any minute. DJing at warehouse parties in Manchester, you never knew what was going to happen. That was a real buzz. I played in Buenos Aires in an outdoor stadium to 23,000 people and they were going fucking mental, it's an amazing buzz. Doing things like my residencies in the States and coming back to play Fabric every now and again. It's still a massive buzz. The fact that I've found something now that's got me interested and excited in the music again is definitely giving me more of a buzz. It's not like in 2003. I wasn't enjoying it, I was just a bit lost I think.

Are you glad to see the superstar craziness crash?
I guess so. I was never comfortable on the cover of magazines. Hated it, hated doing that sort of stuff, but it's part of the game isn't it.

I know you were never comfortable with it, but there was a symbiotic relationship between DJs like you and *Mixmag* and some of the clubs you played at. The three things fed into each other. So obviously it really helped you and your career.
Of course. I'm the first to admit that. As soon as I was on the cover of *Mixmag* I suddenly started getting people from Australia ringing me up to book me. And touring the world.

Without my covers of *Mixmag* I wouldn't have been able to develop my career the way it has. Of course there's that relationship.

Am I glad to see it go? No I'm quite sad about the way it's imploded in Britain. Some of those clubs were great, even though they did get a bit out of control. It was quantity over quality. There were too many big nights going on. And the people who were paying their hard-earned money to go into the clubs weren't getting respected. There were so many mediocre nights on, so much mediocre music being put out. Everybody jumped on this huge bandwagon. It just got big fat and ugly and it needed some air let out of its tyres. It's a shame cos in Britain they've just slashed the tyres completely. The rest of the world is still buzzing.

“ The most outrageous thing was I turned down 50 grand to DJ for two hours. ”

Did you ever feel like you were just a marketing tool?
Not really. But I was definitely shocked at some of the figures flying around, leading up to 2000, in terms of money that was getting offered. It was like what the fuck is going on?

Money offered to you?
To me and to other people, you know these things you hear.

Can you go on record saying what the most outrageous thing was?
The most outrageous thing was I turned down 50 grand to DJ for two hours.

Seriously?
I knew that as soon as I did it I'm going to fucking regret this.

Where was that?
I'm not telling you where it was or who offered me the money but... I was recording my album in Amsterdam. It was the last two weeks that I'd be in the studio and because I hadn't actually DJed for four or five months I knew that in order to get my set together and do it properly I would have had to spend a couple of days sorting things out and I knew that I wouldn't be able to do it properly. What I should have done is just get a load of tunes together, got on a plane and taken the money and run, but I guess I just couldn't in my right mind do that. Daft. Really daft. It was an insane time. Every weekend the amount of competition between clubs in England, it was crazy. And now there are only only five or six gigs in the UK that are worth playing. It's a shame. I used to be able to fill my diary up for three months just touring round the UK.

And it was all those provincial places that were really brilliant, like Mansion in Bournemouth. All these little places out of the way. People used to go potty. That circuit doesn't exist any more. I'm sure people there are going out on Saturday nights, but they're not listening to this sort of music. Or if they are it's a local guy that's playing it and the club owners aren't paying him 10 grand to fill a club.

But the rest of the world's still fucking having it. Especially in the emerging markets like South America and China. It's exciting to go out there now. I'm on my way out to China in November for my second proper tour out there for two or three weeks. It was nuts last time. Beijing and Shanghai.

What size venues do you play?
They've booked me into these ridiculous sized venues. I think they were expecting fireworks to come out of my bum or something. But they booked me into these ridiculous... like the science museum in Shanghai. It was really, I praise the promoters for this tour, the productions were just amazing. Walked in, there's this huge sound system, amazing stages, but completely unfeasible venues. I mean the science museum had never had this sort of music. We didn't start till midnight. The party's supposed to go till four in the morning. Of course by half past midnight the police have turned up and there's guns and riot batons

everywhere. What the fucks going on? So all the parties got shut down apart from the smaller ones. But when I go back we're doing much more realistic venues. I've never ever had to do press conferences like I had to in China. I felt like J-Lo or something. Fifty microphones and cameras everywhere. It's fun though.

Did the superstar thing affect what you were trying to do in the booth?
At certain times it did. When I toured too much. When it was all jammed together. It became this big grinding machine where I was just on tour. And it was never like that when I DJed in Manchester. The furthest I'd go would be Coventry. And I'd have maybe one or two gigs at the weekend and I'd spend all week at home just going through records, and I didn't have a record contract. I didn't have remixes to do. I didn't have an agent, I didn't have all that sort of stuff. My whole week would be built around the next week's set.

Once it became this career that I had, all my free time just got eaten up completely. It became much more of a business, and it was very important that I deliver the goods every Saturday. But I had much less time to prepare that. Which for me is why I embraced the digital side of things. I definitely find a lot of time I'm sat in a car or sat on a train or a plane, all that wasted time I can utilise it now and prepare myself for the next gig. As a travelling working DJ who's constantly touring, I live out of airports, until the digital thing came along there was so much wasted time. But now...

Getting your set together in departure lounges?
Yeah, and doing edits in the departure lounge, making sure each gig has its own special moments. Preparing intros for a certain part of the world, and incorporating some music from that area. Just trying to do something interesting and special for each place. Which I think is important. People get disappointed if they hear a set they've downloaded off the internet, and then three months later you come to play their club and they hear 80 percent of what they've already heard and they've been listening to in their cars for a couple of months.

A hundred years ago a stand up comic could do the same jokes for years because there was no telly. For DJs it's become like everyone's watching you all the time.
Yeah, everyone's watching you. I'm shocked. I'm fucking shocked. Sometimes I'll play on Saturday night and then on Monday morning someone will forward me my tracklisting for the entire night, bar about three fucking tunes. I'm like fucking hell, how do these people know this stuff? Have they got my phone tapped? What's going on? Drives me nuts. Well, it's funny. The good thing about Ableton is you can change things around.

Outwit them.
You can slightly outwit them.

Why do you think you inspire such obsessive adoration?
It's not just me.

It's not just you but it's you in particular.
I definitely get the worst of them. Fucking weirdos.

I DJed with you at Fabric and the build up of 20-year-old boys around the DJ booth...
It's bizarre. If only it was 20-year-old girls. It never is, is it?

Does that disrupt what you do, or are you just used to it?
It is bizarre. When I'm in the club I don't really notice it, unless its one of those booths where they can really get at you, I hate those. I like Fabric especially because I can't see anyone around me and I just get into it on my own. I went through a little phase of looking through the forums but it's bizarre. It's like being sat in a toilet cubicle and you overhear your name and you're not sure if you want to listen in case someone's slagging you off.

Everybody's got a fucking opinion and you can't please these people. It's quite unhealthy. I know a couple of other DJs used to finish their sets and go straight onto the forums and I'm like, what are you doing this for? It's soul-destroying. And they used to get really upset by some of the things that were said. These kids are sat there off their nuts after the club and they've got nothing better to do than just sit there and type crap. I have a look every now and again. It's a good reality check to see where the land lies.

Have any of them stepped over the line and become stalkers?
Yeah. It's happened a couple of times. Its weird because I don't seem to attract stalkers that want to get in touch with me, but they really hassle my managers and my agents and won't stop phoning the office. I've had a couple of people that have invented whole relationships with me, that are just bizarre. They haven't even got my phone number or my email address but they've created this relationship.

What, they pretend they've got some kind of business with you?
Yeah. Its very strange.

You had someone going round Northern Ireland pretending to be you.
That was years ago. He pulled it off, mate. I got to take my hat off to him. I blew the gig out. I don't know if the promoter arranged for this guy to turn up. I'd just shaved my head as well. the only time I've ever done it. Did this complete skinhead, when I was on tour, some kid shaved his head, played the set, apparently walked off with three grand or something. And no-one knew any better until I announced that I wasn't even in the country.

Do you like playing to huge audiences?
I've always struggled playing those big arenas. Apart from the early days when it was just one big acid house family and no-one gave a fuck and you'd play 'Bombscare' next to Denise Lopez, and it was all one sound and it wasn't split up into all the of different genres.

I go to one of those festivals and you see how powerful that trance music thing is. You see 15,000 kids going nutty to one of those classical pieces of music. With a 145 bpm trance beat behind it. It works in that environment, but it's a million miles away from where the scene came from. The only credible music I've ever seen work in that environment is the Chems and Underworld. Underworld especially. They just know how to do it. It's that stadium sound, and they've done it without being cheesy. But they're one of the few that can actually pull it off.

What did it feel like when you first walked into the Haçienda and saw it in action?
I'd been a couple of times before, when it was much more like jacking house music. Before the acid house thing had kicked in and everyone had gone completely bonkers. There was this dance troupe called Foot Patrol and they used to take over the dancefloor. They'd have almost like dance battles in the Haçienda, and it was kind of early Chicago jack house music, and people would get quite dressed up for it.

I didn't go for a couple of months and I went back in and literally acid house had arrived and the whole place was day-glo and smiley faces. And everyone was doing this trance-dancing dance. My chin hit the floor. It was just amazing, the energy in the room. I'd never experienced anything like it. The music sounded like it was from another planet. Yeah, the energy was just shocking. I'd never seen a group of people behave like that before.

How much is what you do based on trying to recapture those moments?
My career has been based on my experiences at the Haç. The way I learnt how to build my DJ sets from people like Graeme Park and Jon DaSilva, and the sound of the Haçienda, especially in those first couple of years, the way they used to mix up all those different styles together, it was just inspiring. I always gravitated towards a more... I liked a lot of the big records they played at the end of the night. I also loved the stuff they played really early on. That idea of playing a long set, I always love doing that. And building that set towards the big records of the night.

My DJ career took off when the Haçienda went off on a certain route. Graeme Park and Mike Pickering veered off to playing a lot of the American records. The Italian stuff was getting all big piano breaks and I loved that, and our sounds really went in different directions. My first year of going to the Haçienda – pretty much religiously on Wednesdays and Fridays – that's what shaped everything really. It was such an influential place: the sound of it, the design of it, the whole way it was done. The advertising they used: Peter

Saville's design for all the posters. It was just everything, it was a blueprint for everything as far as I'm concerned: for the whole scene.

Were you involved in any of those Blackburn raves?
Yeah. I used to go to them and then towards the end I started DJing at them.

Was breaking the law part of the appeal?
Absolutely. We were constantly dodging police. Police and riot vans. It got to the point where the police would be trying to find out where the warehouse was because if the police could get to the warehouse before the ravers they could shut the party down. So they started sending decoy convoys of 200 people, and then the real convoy would head off, get to the warehouse, and then those 200 people would end up getting round there. As long as the party got going it was fine. So it really was dodging the police. Especially at Blackburn. It really did feel like two fingers up at the law. But then they brought in the whole Criminal Justice Bill... There were a lot of reasons why that had to come to a stop. The gangsters moved in up there, it just got really messy, really nasty. Quickly actually.

> **It's happened a couple of times. I've had a couple of people that have invented whole relationships with me, that are just bizarre.**

Did you come down to London at all in that period?
No. I didn't at all. So I missed whatever Shoom was. And I'm sure it was as influential to people down here. I guess if you were in the north it was the Haçienda, down here it was Danny Rampling and Paul Oakenfold.

Do you think with what you and John [Digweed] did in Twilo, you had a taste of that in inspiring America?
Maybe. I think the scene was already really going, developing. I think probably what we did in Orlando a few years before, even though we didn't have a regular club there, but just the fact we were going to Orlando every two or three months and doing these massive parties there. I went out first and then a while later John came out and then the Chemical Brothers. We were some of the first ones to go out there and then it really opened up.

Twilo was more like the jewel in the crown, after eight, nine years of hard work touring the States, to get that gig was wow, to get a residency in New York. At that club as well, which used to be the Sound Factory, it was Junior's club, to get into that place, where Danny [Tenaglia] had been a resident, and Frankie Knuckles, to get that residency and to hold on to it and for it to be so successful. It was really a defining moment.

I guess for people that were just getting into the scene maybe that did shape things. It was such a big huge space, and this low ceiling and this enormous sound system and this really dark room, and those minimal progressive dark records just sounded so brilliant in there.

As soon as the club went that music just seemed to lose its place and it didn't seem to have a home any more. I pretty much stopped playing that sound within six months of that venue stopping. It just didn't fit anywhere any more. The more minimal the records, the darker the records, it just sounded fantastic in there. It really did fit the room. How certain records just work at Fabric and you struggle to make them work anywhere else.

There was also a whole mood change in music around that time as well. Just after 9/11 you started hearing guitars on the dancefloor. It got much more like bootlegs and electroclash came along and the whole sound just became more eclectic.

Is America anywhere nearer to embracing dance music on a mainstream level?
I don't think it ever will. I always said it was never gonna happen, and then a couple of years ago when the trance thing started to get really big, I thought maybe there's a chance that somebody like Tiësto, or somebody of that nature might break through into the top 10, but

then even with his remix of the Sarah McLoughlan thing, the biggest selling trance record ever, it still didn't make an impact. I think a lot of the problem with America is the slow-moving nature of the charts; you have to have such a battle plan in place to get a record up the charts in the States, and you have to sit on it for so long. In its 12th, 13th, 14th, week it'll start to slowly move up the charts, and your record company has to have a whole machine in place to keep going, and then you've got to do the daytime television, you got to do MTV.

Whereas the whole nature of dance music is about hearing stuff you haven't heard before and loving it and slinging it away. When you go to a rock show you want to hear David Bowie do all his old hits. You don't want to hear his new shitty album. But the thing about electronic music is, people want to hear the new stuff. Yeah, they might want a little classic thrown in at the end of the night just for a little smile, but the rest of the night they want to hear shit they haven't heard before.

The idea of an electronic record staying in people's record boxes and on the DJs' playlists for 20, 30, 40 weeks, which is sometimes what it takes for these chart acts to ease their way up the charts, it doesn't work like that. So it's gonna need a Prodigy style act, an Underworld style act, but maybe from America, to really take it home. It's gonna take stars, it's gonna take characters, and that's the one thing dance music's always struggled with: we're all faceless... We all like to sit in the dark. Except for Tiesto, he loves being main stage. It will take somebody like him to break it through, but I don't think he'll be the figurehead of a movement, like it was in the UK.

That's the great thing about the British charts. Everyone's got a shot at it. In the States it's so much more calculated. There's so much more at stake. These big record companies aren't going to allow some shitty little record from a 19-year-old kid in his bedroom to get to number one and knock Beyoncé off who they've invested ten squillion quid in.

> **❝ I was DJing with Josh Wink. He was looping up bits of his set over the top of my bit and sampling bits of mine and we were throwing things backwards and forwards. ❞❞**

What's all the fuss about Ableton? What can you do with it that you can't do with vinyl or CD?
The spontaneous way you can re-edit things is just amazing. I had a problem with it last weekend. I turned up in Greece ready to play and we had no power supply. So I spent about four hours frantically burning CDs, and I went out and DJed on CDs and it was so weird because a lot of the tunes I've been used to playing are only four or five minutes long – I'm grabbing music from lots more diverse sources now – and I don't realise how short they are. In the computer I can loop them up and I'm stretching them out and turning them into eight or nine minutes long. Extending the breakdowns. But when I had to DJ with CDs this weekend and the intro's only eight bars it was really quite all over the place.

And I've only scratched the surface of it. People who use it much more as a live performance thing really start to get into the snippets of sounds and the cut-and-paste element of it. that's when you can come up with some really interesting stuff. You're almost writing and composing little hooks in the club and creating. When I was DJing with Josh Wink, he made me play a lot more cut-and-paste. He was looping up bits of his set over the top of my bit and sampling bits of mine and we were throwing things backwards and forwards and it became this wall of sound, from just snippets. Instead of playing whole tracks. There's so many different ways to approach it,

The problem that it has is the interface is very much a studio interface. It's not very user-friendly. I'm used to it but it took me a good four or five months practising every weekend before it started to feel like DJing. The first few months it didn't feel like I was connected to it. I can understand that might scare people off a bit. I hope Ableton will listen to all the advice on the forums and come up with an interface that's much more DJ-friendly. They're still quite off the mark.

The important thing about technology is when it becomes transparent. Like a CDJ1000 it took about two nights for the thing to become transparent. You don't have to think about it any more. You just reach over and that button does that. With Ableton it took a long time before it became transparent, and you still have to really focus on it. What I've realised in the last month or so is that for a while I was just doing pure Ableton sets and its so draining on your head. Every point in your set you could go a thousand different ways, and its quite daunting.

Isn't that the problem with digital DJing in general – you're paralysed by possibilities?
I had a couple of weekends where I didn't have time to load up my computer so I was going 50/50 between the computer and then playing a couple of CDs and I just found my sets sounded a bit more vibrant that way, and also I enjoyed it more. When you're focusing 100 percent on that computer it can be quite taxing on your brain.

Just navigating all those tunes. With records you've got all those extra cues: the sleeves, the colours, the labels.
Well CD to records is another thing. That's a whole other argument, looking through a record box and you get shapes in your head and colours. And looking through a browser at names of records you really have to stay on top of what things are called. I mean I know what my records are called now. Three or four years ago I never remembered names of tunes at all.

When I've seen you DJ, your box looked like you'd just tipped it in from a dustbin, and then tipped it out again to start, and there's stuff everywhere, stuff not in sleeves... Have you had to alter that?
Yeah, absolutely. It forces you to be a lot more organised. But it means every time I play out it's different. I can play different styles of sets for different clubs and not just go on tour with the same box of records for two months. Now I'm getting a DVD of new music every week. That's 40 or 50 tunes that are going into the pot. It's allowing me to be a lot more on the ball and be playing new music all the time, and also it's really fucking important the position I'm in, 'cos sets get leaked out over the internet and you get slagged so much if you play the same record over and over. There's definitely a pressure to deliver something new and exciting every time you play out.

Because of the way you get so scrutinised?
Right. The fact that I can log into my server anywhere I am in the world and download straight into my laptop and be playing out that night with new music. Before, if I was on tour for a long time I'd have to get sent a box of records from London, I had to make sure I had access to a set of decks. Now stuff goes straight onto my iPod and I'm in a taxi listening to new music and sorting things through. It's definitely allowing me much more freedom to be spontaneous and throw new music in, 'cos I know it, rather than testing stuff out in the club 'cos you don't know it that well.

What do you say to people who say DJs should play vinyl?
I see their argument. My girlfriend really loves vinyl. She's constantly having a go at me and I see the attraction to it. I'm not sitting here saying this is the only way forward. It works for me and I like it. I also really enjoyed playing this weekend off CDs, when I was stuck without the computer. At the end of the day it's DJing.

Someone might have heard me a year ago playing off CDs and then hear a set off Ableton and think Ableton sucks, but maybe they just don't like the music this year. It's just a format of playing records, but it's not the only format. I think Ableton may well be superseded by another technology in the next six months. Maybe Pioneer might come out with something that looks like the CDJ1000 that's got some hard drive in it that loops stuff up automatically. Who knows? As the technology moves forward I'm just embracing it.

To be honest I needed something to help me in my DJing career, 'cos I think I just got to the point where I was a bit, not bored but lethargic. I wasn't feeling too inspired in 2003.

Sasha

I'd just had whole year of 2002 touring my ass off an not really enjoying it. In 2003 I was scratching my head wondering what I was going ton do. And that was when I discovered the Ableton thing. For me it's given me a massive shot in the arm and I'm really enjoying playing out again. I'm excited every weekend to go out and play, 'cos I know I've got a new armoury of tunes, especially when you've got old stuff in there that you haven't played for years, and you can suddenly chop it about and find new records that mix perfectly with it. It's exciting to be able to do that sort of stuff.

Is this a revolution? Is there going to be a real split between people who use things like this – studio techniques live – and people who don't?
I think it's a huge change. Not everyone's going to embrace it. But what it will mean is people are going to start getting used to hearing these kind of sets in clubs, and they're going to start demanding it. So if you turn up with vinyl and start train-wrecking mixes, you're gonna get hammered for it. With DJs like James Zabiela coming through who are really embracing the CDJs and sampling stuff live and really turning a DJ set into something more than just playing two pieces of vinyl, it definitely means the crowd are going to start looking for that sort of stuff.

I'm approaching this from my angle of having DJed for the last 17, 18 years. You give this new technology to an 18-year-old kid who's gonna approach it from a completely new mindset, that's when fireworks will happen. That's when maybe the next sound, the next generation of what a DJ performance is will come through. It probably won't come from me, it'll come from some 18- or 19-year-old kid who's sat in his bedroom right now who's downloaded it from the internet. Who's approaching it from a different musicality sense. A completely different angle.

Ours is probably the last generation that thinks of music as objects. Teenagers now don't have that. So someone with that conception and this equipment is going to be a very different DJ.
Absolutely. They're going to approach it a very different way. Bring it on. It's exciting. but still there are certain DJs who, watching them spin records, is mesmerising. Carl Cox, Jeff Mills. Watching DJ Shadow, I think he's starting to embrace digital as well. Watching the turntablists do their stuff with vinyl. I can't imagine them switching over to a keyboard and a mouse. But I think the technology, the interface of it will catch up.

❝ You give this new technology to an 18-year-old kid who's gonna approach it from a completely new mindset, that's when fireworks will happen. ❞

Someone will come out with an interface where you hardly have to look at the computer. It'll be all in one box and that'll be that. It's definitely the early days for the technology but it is the way for the future. Five years time computers in DJ booths will be completely normal. The idea of having 10,000 records on a hard drive sounds daunting to us now but in five years time that'll be the norm. Everything that's every been made will be catalogued in the DJ booth. So it's gonna be about taste and programming.

And that's really the thing I like. It takes out that whole thing about 'Ooh he can beatmatch, isn't that amazing, he can mix things in key.' Maybe in '94 '95 when we started doing those really long seamless mixes and everyone would be stood around the booth really buzzing on the fact that you're holding mixes together for ages, that doesn't really happen any more. Those kids don't sit there going, 'Oh he's mixing in key.' The only time your mixing is noticed is if you fuck up. Mixing in key is like being able to kick a football if you're a footballer.

This software takes it out of the equation. It takes it back to your ability to programme a night and where to drop a specific record. And also sourcing your music. As I said I've started buying records from all these weird and wonderful record shops. Where I didn't do that before. And it doesn't matter if I've only got a two-minute piece of music. It's going into the computer. I'll just use it and stretch it out and utilise it in my set.

It's blurring the line between production and DJing.

I think at certain points in your set it can get like that. If you're doing a 45-minute live set and you're approaching Ableton like that, as a hybrid of a DJ set and a remix thing, then I think you could do something really exciting. Playing in a DJ Shadow sort of way, grabbing snippets of other peoples records. But you could only keep that up for 45 minutes or an hour maximum, or your head'd be fried. When I play a six-hour set it's only really the last hour or so when I start really getting four or five or six channels going.

Will it help convince people that the DJ is an artist?

I think this goes some way to maybe separate the men from the boys. People who are really into that producing side of things are really going to gravitate towards this. People that aren't interested in it I don't think they'll find it useful. It just blows my head off sometimes when you have these spontaneous ideas and you grab an old record and layer it, and mix in an old classic. I love doing that sort of stuff.

It seems like it's really given you the buzz back.

It has, absolutely. I was definitely in a bad state in 2003. I think I'd achieved in 2002 a lot of goals I'd been heading towards. Touring the states with the Delta Heavy thing, releasing my album, a lot of things happened in 2001, 2002. I got to 2003 and I was, 'Right, what the fuck shall I do now?'

I definitely spent the summer of 2003 treading water I think: musically, and DJing. Not really knowing what to do with myself. And I think in general that year was a big breakpoint for electronic music. We'd been talking about the internet a few years beforehand, but 2003 was the year when the music industry took its first kick in the nuts. And especially for electronic music. Where the fuck is this going? What are we doing now? How's this going to develop? And the software came along and I grabbed hold of it and it definitely showed me a way to move forward and stay interested. It's not like I was bored, 'cos how can you be bored getting flown around the world and playing gigs and stuff, but I was definitely looking for something.

The cultural role of a DJ, you've seen it change from being someone who doesn't get paid very much and does it for a laugh, and then it became this huge thing, and now it's come down to earth...

It's come down to earth in this country. I would understand if you don't travel how it would seem, from this point of view, standing in this country it looks like its all turned to shit, but I travel everywhere and it's fucking vibrant everywhere. It's kicking off everywhere.

You don't get a sense that it's changing? It's still on a high everywhere else?

It is on a high, yeah. It might not be that frenetic madness that was happening around 2000 when there was ridiculous money being offered and everybody was fighting each other for gigs, but its still keeping me really busy.

What's the most preposterous treatment you've ever had as a DJ?

You know... I think just getting flown around in private jets is ridiculous, and it's happened a couple of times. It's nice though, when people roll out the carpet for you.

Didn't you have a police escort somewhere.

Yeah, I've had police escorts in the Philippines. That was brilliant because the traffic was literally not moving for 30 miles, and to get into the town centre it would normally take two or three hours and we got there in 15 minutes. Wish I could request one of those everywhere I went.

What are your ambitions now?

I don't know. I'm scratching my head about that at the moment. I always had plans to move

into production and film scores and that sort of stuff, and I'm not sure now. I spent some time in LA and I don't really see myself living that life. I just don't see it. To become part of that whole film world you have to live there and it changes people in a really weird way.

There are the famous Nick Gordon Brown sleevenotes where he sets you up as an artist. How did you feel when that happened?
I think unless you're making your own records or doing remixes it's very difficult to put your hand up and say that's what you are. But if you're making your own records, producing your own stuff, and also getting into these new technologies where you can be doing your own little re-edits and remixes of songs in the club, it's still a difficult argument to call yourself an artist. But you are putting so much into it. It is a real creative expression. I do think what DJs do is a creative expression. It is art, it is an artform, so I guess we are artists, but I wouldn't really wanna be standing on a soap box shouting about it.

> **❝ I do think what DJs do is a creative expression. It is art, it is an artform, so I guess we are artists, but I wouldn't really wanna be standing on a soap box shouting about it. ❞**

Are there any interesting little scenes that you've come across in your travels? Or are we headed for global homogenisation?
No, if anything, that homogenisation is causing more of these underground pockets to happen. Little fucking after-hours parties in Mexico City that are just amazing. Energy levels through the roof. Dirty and seedy. That's where I have the funnest times. And it's all stuff that's off the beaten track, stuff that isn't written about. And that's where it's at, and that's where it... Those illegal warehouse parties in the beginning, that's where it all came from.

So you're conscious that when you go to these places there's always something very underground and very different.
If I'm doing a big party guarantee there's some dirty little after-hours going on afterwards and its some...

...and the music will be indiginous.
Yeah. Local DJs playing wicked shit I've never heard before. It's healthy, it's thriving, it's out there.

That kind of outlaw attitude, it's embedded in dance culture really.
It's the real shit. Those after-hours parties you hear about that are unannounced or unadvertised. They're the things of dancefloor history and folklore, but they're still going on and they're really important. The commercial end of it will live and die by its sword, and we've been witness to that in the UK. But still that underground thing is going on. You go to the East End of London any Saturday night I guarantee there are loft parties going on, fucked up acid house music playing. Everywhere. Strobe lights, smoke machines. Everywhere.

© DJhistory.com

SASHA SELECTED DISCOGRAPHY

URBAN SOUL – Alright (remixer)

CREATIVE THIEVES – Nasty Rhythm (remixer)

M PEOPLE – How Can I Love You More (remixer)

D:REAM – U R The Best Thing (remixer)

SASHA – Higher Ground (writer/producer/mixer)

HYSTERIX – Must Be The Music (remixer)

BT – Embracing The Sunshine (remixer)

SASHA & MARIA – Be As One (writer)

SASHA – Arkham Asylum (writer/producer)

2 PHAT CUNTS – Ride (writer/producer/mixer)

THE CHEMICAL BROTHERS – Out Of Control (remixer)

MADONNA – Ray Of Light (remixer)

SASHA – Xpander (writer/producer)

JUNKIE XL – Breezer (writer/producer)

GUS GUS – Purple (remixer)

THE CHEMICAL BROTHERS – Out Of Control (remixer)

SASHA/EMERSON – Scorchio (writer/producer)

SASHA – Wavy Gravy (writer/producer)

SASHA – Magnetic North (writer/producer/mixer)

KASABIAN – Underdog (remixer)

RECOMMENDED LISTENING

VARIOUS – Mixmag Live Vol. 3 (DJ mix)

VARIOUS – Sasha, Global Underground 013: Ibiza

SASHA – Airdrawndagger

" We'd get straight-up breaks, speed them up and mix them into the techno. "

Fabio
Hardcore hero

Interviewed by Bill and Frank at Radio 1, February 4, 2005

He's the drum an bass desperado whose demented experiments with breakbeats helped create the first uniquely British dance music genre. Using their club as foundry, Fabio and longtime partner Grooverider planted the roots of hardcore and drum and bass out of a rag-bag assortment of tunes, all glued together by an idiosyncratic DJing style, a ravenous dancefloor and a common denominator: bass. Their seminal residency at Rage, in London's Heaven, began with house and ended with a demonic breakbeat sound that drew from European techno, New York house dubs and reggae-influenced British productions. After its synthesis on the turntables of Fabio and co. it became known as jungle. With a few twists and some journalistic spin it was drum & bass. From his early days as a pirate DJ, Fabio has followed the well-worn path to legality, becoming a Radio 1 jock, firstly at One In The Jungle and now on Fabio & Grooverider. Twenty years later, he's as establishment as an outlaw DJ from Brixton will ever be.

And there are few people who tell stories as well as Fabio. We meet in an anodyne office somewhere in the labyrinth of wonderful Radio 1 where he seems almost part of the furniture. Yet set him a few questions about the old days, the Brixton blues parties, (reggae shebeens named after the old Blue Beat ska label), or Mendoza's after-hours, and we're swiftly transported back with him, so vivid are the tales. As we scamper out into the winter chill, we high five and beam excitedly: a killer interview.

Let's start with where you grew up
I grew up in Brixton, music was always around me. My dad was a record buyer, not a massive collection but a great collection of ska, Motown and stuff like that. Across the board black music. In Brixton growing up it was a massive blues party scene going on. Round the corner from me there was a place called Elland Park. On a Saturday night you could have five, six parties going on, with sound systems. I could hear it from my house. They were in people's houses, or they used to rig up a sound system in old squats. There were a lot of squats in those days. We used to go to a lot of the local blues parties, when I was 13 or 14. I had a whale of a time, man. That got me into going out and being in this place with loud music playing. It was great because the blues scene was the original club scene, on one level: using huge sound systems, having MCs, not mixing, but the whole emphasis on loud sounds.

And this is very much Jamaicans doing over here what they used to do over there?
That's right. We used to go to regular clubs and the sound systems were so crap, and you'd get DJs talking shit all night: 'The next one is, A Ha, "Lean On Me"...' It wasn't like that at all. You'd have the host, the MC, and the guy who used to play music, it was like this *narration*. You weren't that aware of what was going on but it was brilliant.

Growing up in Brixton was great because of the vibe. Brixton's very colourful and you can't really escape the music thing. Music and crime. You had these two areas where you could go if you didn't want to do a nine-to-five. Either be a criminal or be, not necessarily a DJ, but just have something to do with music. The sound systems were great. Weren't no money in it or nothing. Strictly for breaking premises and having a party til 1 o'clock in the afternoon.

....

Did people charge?
They did. They used to charge £2 on the door. The whole thing though was going in and buying drinks. They used to have a little bar set up. It was all very civilised, but it was really dangerous, because we were mixing with hardened Brixton criminals. You stepped on someone's lizard-skin shoes man and it was curtains. For real, serious. It was like *Goodfellas*. You knew: don't fuck with these guys. There was one guy in particular, one dread, he was so smooth and what he used to do was this slow rubbing thing with girls, and he could dance with a girl and skin up a spliff at the same time. We used to watch him, he's the fucking man. It was this whole mad thing. The dangerous thing was a lot of people wanted to be like them. I did as well, but luckily I was more into music than wanting to go out on the rob.

Was it inseparable?
The DJs were the guys who decided we want to set up our sound system here, and play our music. The criminals used to follow them around, 'cos all the girls used to be there. And, of course, wherever there's nice girls there's criminals. It was great, these beautiful women that wouldn't look at you. You never had a chance. We were 14 and they were 21. At around nine in the morning they'd slow it down and you had to ask a girl for a dance. I think I had one dance in the three years I was going to blues parties. I was so nervous I think she walked away half way through it. It was the earliest memory I have of being captured by the whole club thing. Then things kind of moved on, I got into the whole soul scene.

> ❝ **It was great. These beautiful women that wouldn't look at you. And of course, wherever there's nice girls there's criminals.** ❞

Did you think that reggae was your music, cos you grew up here?
I was kind of divided between reggae and soul. In them days, you couldn't really be both. I remember they used to say if you liked soul music you were gay. What happened was a cousin of mine used to go to soul clubs, and she used to sneak me in and I never used to tell anybody. Then at the weekend I used to go to the blues dances. Once a girl said to me: 'I saw you in Crackers on Wardour Street.'
'No you didn't.'
She was like: 'No it was you.'
'It wasn't me.'
'It was you, you were...'
And everybody was like: 'Boy, I hope that weren't you.'
'Nah, a soul club, are you crazy?'
Then I got caught up in it, so when I was 15, 16, I kind of ventured more into going to Crackers and a place called 100 Club, and just getting into the whole soul movement.

Was it the teen disco on a Saturday lunchtime you went to at the 100 Club?
I went to the adults one. I looked 18 when I was about eight. I used to wear a little waistcoat and a shirt. My auntie used to get me in there. This was Friday lunchtime. Telling my mum I'm just popping down the road, I was clubbing, there were girls, everything...

The Friday lunch thing, was it at Crackers?
Yeah. Guy called George Powers and Paul Anderson used to play. Crackers was an amazing club. People used to go there and just dance. Everyone just got on it and there were amazing imports from America. It was fresh and vital at the time.

What was it that attracted you?
I tell you what was so great: it was going into a place and it was mixed. Blues parties were 99 percent black. But this was 50/50. That was the first time I'd ever seen that. It was the first time I saw colour didn't really matter. You could go out with a white girl and it weren't no

big thing. White guy'd go out with a black girl, and you could hang out with white guys. It wasn't an issue. You had white DJs, you had black DJs. It was the first time I'd felt this social thing. You could do what you wanted in Crackers. The DJ never talked and he never mixed, but kind of segued the tracks, so it was this seamless mixture of funk and soul. At the time you didn't know that in 20-odd years you'd still be referring to this place. It was just where you went to on a Saturday afternoon and had a wicked time.

Did you look up to dancers like Peter Francis and Horace?
There was a whole lot of them: Horace and a guy called John O'Reilly who danced for Paul Anderson. So instead of looking up to criminals I was looking up to them. They were getting all the girls. When you're young that's what it's all about. They used to dance and everyone used to crowd round them. They'd walk off with the best looking girl at the end of the night. So it was that same thing: looking up to these guys and thinking I want to be like them. So me and my dancing partner, Colin Dale, we used to go out all over.

If it was such a hot scene, why was there this reggae vs. soul thing?
There were even divides in soul. The jazz dancers used to think we were pussies if you liked funk. There used to be fights with guys coming from rival soul clubs, with jazz boys and soul heads. They'd be like, 'You guys are pussies, all that pussy music you listen to,' and so there used to be regular fights. It was just wanting to belong to a certain clique.

Do you think young black guys got into soul because they were looking for a specific black British identity?
I don't think consciously we were doing that. The blues thing wasn't a movement it was more local. You went to Battersea, Clapham, all over south London there were blues parties. You did used to follow sounds but it wasn't a movement in the way that this [soul clubs] was a movement. This was going out into the West End as well. You've got to remember the West End was the place.

It's neutral. It's not a neighbourhood.
It was a travelling thing. The whole thing getting ready and dressing up as well. We couldn't afford to buy clothes in the West End, so the only way you could go to the West End was to club or buy records. The whole thing of buying imports, of getting things first, that all came from that, more than kind of the reggae scene. They used to play a lot of old stuff, Alton Ellis and stuff like that. It wasn't really a forward moving thing.

It's more about having a dubplate than the latest thing.
Exactly. And it was more localised as well. If you went to a blues dance in Battersea they'd be like, 'You guys aren't from round here.' You could seriously get yourself in trouble. The soul scene was different. You used to meet people from Wembley. We'd be like, 'Wembley, where the fuck's that?' And Ilford. 'Ilford? Never heard of it.' 'We're from Brixton.' 'It's a bit dodgy down there.' Then the whole soul movement, Caister, it took on a whole new lease of life.

Did you get involved in that?
To be fair I didn't. None of use drove, and we used to hear about this Caister thing, but by the time we wanted to get in it was kind of like an exclusive club. It was a very white scene. Caister was 80 percent white. Essex was kind of the bastion of racism. We were like what are these guys doing being into soul music? It was bizarre, it really was.

When did you first start DJing.
I was collecting records, and my buddy Colin Dale was a soul DJ and we'd follow him around. The idea of DJing never really struck my mind. I wanted to be a singer, or be involved in production. I was a real trainspotter. I used to know the serial numbers of certain tracks, and me and my friend, we used to listen to pirate radio from one to five in the morning and try and guess who the producer was: 'Right, who produced this then?' 'Well it sounds like the drums could be Harvey Mason, the bassline could be the Brothers Johnson.'

A lot of the times we were right. DJing never really came into it, until my first gig was at a place called Gossips in the West End, for Tim Westwood who was a soul DJ that we followed. Colin Dale used to do the warm up down there, and Tim phoned me up and was like, 'I really need you to play.' I was like, 'Cool man...'

'Cos he went into the electro thing in a big way.
This was literally months before it happened. When I DJed there it was the most horrific experience. I never thought I'd ever be that scared. I was absolutely bricking it. I didn't enjoy it at all. I walked away thinking, 'Nah I don't want to do this.' Then the early electro scene started and we used to go to Global Village on a Sunday night. But behind this as well was the electronic thing, because we were soul boys, and we were like, 'Man this electronic things taking away the soul of it...' But 'Planet Rock' and all the early Tommy Boy stuff was just irresistible. There was also a guy called Yakamoto...

Riuichi Sakamoto?
Yeah, and he done a tune called 'Riot In Lagos', which was the most incredible tune, even more than 'Planet Rock'. I just caught the bug. Then I was dissed by the soul boys: 'I can't believe you're into this electro shit man.' So I just moved from scene to scene. But the early electro scene I felt honoured to be part of that.

People diss Tim Westwood but that guy was in it from dot, man. He changed the game. He stopped playing the soully kind of things and went full steam into electro. Used to go to Spatz, Saturday afternoon. People would be breaking. We were into the *Wildstyle* thing, all of that shit.

Where was Spatz?
In Oxford St, just opposite 100 Club. Where Plastic People was. Little hovel downstairs. Wicked little space. Great dancefloor and stuff.

How did the house thing come about?
The pivotal point was a pirate station called Faze 1. That was the turning point for everything that's happened to me since. A guy called Mendoza set up a station. This was '84. He said, 'I want all of you local guys to come in and do a show.' It was a Brixton thing, right next to a pub, and he had a shebeen, an after-hours place, downstairs. But this shebeen, no-one ever used to go to. It was our local but he never had any more than six people there on a Saturday night. We used to go there, get pissed, go upstairs and play some music. A great set-up.

I had an afternoon soul show, where I used to play funk and really early house and electro. Then one night he said, 'Listen I got a brother called Chris, man, and he knows some guy called Paul Oakenfold and they've got this mad thing, have you ever heard of Spectrum?'

I said, 'No.'

He said, 'What we're going to try and do, we're gonna do some after-parties.'

So I said, 'Right I'm going to check out Spectrum next week.' The next Monday night we went down there. Me and a couple of lads from Brixton walked in and they were like, 'What the hell is going on here?' We saw everyone with smiley t-shirts, with big eyes, chewing their teeth, and just walking around in another world. My mates fucked off and left me in there. They were like, 'You know what? It's like we've walked into hell. We're going back to Brixton.' I just remember looking up seeing Paul Oakenfold and this smoke, and him being like a fucking god up there. I was like, 'This is absolutely fucking amazing.'

To cut a long story short, they asked me if I would like to play at this after-party. I said, 'What in Mendoza's? You're going to have an after party? No way are they gonna come down there.'

He said, 'The only other guy I know who plays house on the station is Grooverider.'

I said, okay. But I didn't really know Groove that well. Groove was quite arrogant and aggressive and he used to do the night-time shows. Anyway, he said, 'Get down there about 1 o'clock in the morning.' So me and Groove was in there all night, no-one came down; not a dickie bird. Groove had to go work, he was working with computers. He said, 'Listen Mendoza, I'm off.'

So we was loading the records up in the car when we saw these guys walking down the alleyway going [scally northern accent] 'Where's the fookin' party?' He was wearing shorts, in the middle of winter, a union jack tattoo on his back and a skinhead, going, 'I wanna hear some fookin' music, right.' He goes downstairs. We go in, we think we'd better play for this guy or else he's going to kill us or something. He was on his own, just doing this all night [mad dancing moves], putting his head in the speaker, and Mendoza, the club owner, was like, 'It's alright, he's buying drinks, just carry on playing.'

Groove went upstairs, came back and said, 'Oh my god there are hundreds of people down this alleyway.' All of a sudden all these people just rushed in there, everyone was pilled up. It was absolutely rammed. They couldn't fit anyone else in there at all. There was a queue hundreds of people outside. So we decided to make this a regular occurrence, every week! Seriously. We did our own flyers, Groove went out and bought a Ford Cortina for 60 quid and we used to go down to the Trip at the Astoria, and we used to give out flyers there, and the rest is history basically. We had something going on every single week for about two years. That really got us known. Oakey used to come down, Trevor Fung used to come down. We met a lot of the big promoters and we got a lot of work out of it, man. That was really the start of the whole Fabio and Grooverider thing.

🔎 People used to go home and take their kids to school, have a wash and come back at one in the afternoon. It was happy days. 🔎

Did it ever have a name?
No just Mendoza's. It didn't have a name or anything. People didn't give a shit, they knew they could come down there, used to go till four in the afternoon. People used to go home and take their kids to school, have a wash and come back at one in the afternoon. That's what makes me laugh when people say, 'Can you play for two hours?' What!? It was happy days, man. It was great.

What was Spectrum like?
Spectrum was crazy. Spectrum was every single person was out of it, you never seen people out of it before...

How quickly did you catch on to what was going on?
About the third time I went there. It was quite scary, man. It was pretty hellish, and that's why a lot of people turned their back on it because the music was so loud and the lights were so intimidating. The music wasn't soulful. You've got to remember that. The music was this kind of flamenco mixture. And that's why a lot of the urban guys were like, 'Fucking hell!' It was extreme. At the time it was like punk, but 'cos of the background, of listening to electro, we were like this shit, man, is so fucking extreme. And Groove was always extreme. Groove was into Public Image Ltd and stuff like that, so he was, 'THIS IS ME, YEEEAAH!'

How soon did you get him to go down to Spectrum?
Groove is so completely teetotal. So he came down there and was literally in there for half an hour and said, 'I am getting the fuck out of this place. I love the music but this out of the head business is... I'll meet you down at Mendoza's yeah, you stay here.'

I was like, 'OK, yeah cool. Oakey's playing, let me just stare at him, man...'

Anyway, he might have thought I was gay or something... This hero worship, man! I was like, 'No man he's gonna play "Jibaro" in a minute.'

And Groove wasn't so much into Balearic music, Groove was much more into Fast Eddie and the kind of real soulful acid coming out of DJ International and Trax.

So how did Rage start.
Rage was the US thing. Rage used to be on a Thursday and they set up against Spectrum which was a European thing, Rage was a much more...

Weren't Justin Berkmann and people like that involved?
Yeah, Justin Berkmann, Trevor Fung, Colin Faver; and they were much more into the

American thing, the imports, the Trax thing. And they were kind of against the whole Spectrum thing. That was the first divides; very rarely you'd meet people who'd go to Spectrum and Rage.

We knew the barman there, they didn't really have DJs at the Star Bar, they had a guy just playing music, and we met Kevin Millins who ran Rage and he was like, 'Do you guys want to do a little thing down here?' So we started upstairs, but we had such a massive following up there. We used to ram out this place. We'd established ourselves as kind of underground heroes, so we had a following. We didn't know how big because we'd never ventured into the club world. Anyway, Colin Faver and Trevor Fung went to LA and missed their flight back, and Kevin said, 'I'm going to take a chance on you guys tonight downstairs.' We went in there and basically smashed the shit out of the place. The end of the night everyone was going crazy.

> ❝ **We used to get this guy called Danny Jungle lead the dancefloor, going, 'Jungle, Jungle!' and then before we knew it that was the tag.** ❞

But we didn't want to step on Trevor and Colin's toes so we shared the main floor with them. But they were still into the US stuff and we were playing early techno from Belgium and Germany: Frank de Wulf, R&S and stuff like that. We really got into that sound and played it down at Rage, and it wasn't quite going with what Trevor and Colin were doing, but it was getting so popular that we ended up getting the main set there.

We got the Derrick Mays and the Kevin Saundersons and Joey Beltrams giving us dubplates. It turned into the techno place. It wasn't so much hardcore, it was techno. But we'd get these B-side mixes from Masters at Work, and they used to have straight-up breaks on and we used to speed them up and mix them into the techno stuff. We realised anytime we did that we were getting people euphoric, like this is something new.

We used to get this guy called Danny Jungle lead the dancefloor, going, 'Jungle, Jungle!' and then before we knew it that was the tag. Then people started making jungle; Living Dream and Ibiza Records were early labels. We had a set full of this way-out breakbeat stuff. We mixed Prodigy into 'Mentasm' [by Joey Beltram], and things like that. It was just the craziest mixture of extreme madness. Rage turned from being this kind of posey kind of night with loads of girls and loads of well-dressed people, to being ghetto man. We ghettoed out the whole fucking place.

Until it got to the stage where... it kind of got a bit shady. It kind of added to the whole vibe of the night though. You didn't know whether you were gonna get killed down there or not. Great! But then Kevin started to get a bit like, 'Guys, it's getting a bit on top in here, we've really alienated our old crowd.'

Were there any real incidents?
Nothing major, a few rucks, but you used to get a few of the big dealers coming in there. I think the old guard got a bit threatened. Certain DJs, well-known soulful house DJs, actually made formal complaints to him. Unfortunately the night closed because of that. We had a meeting and he said, 'Listen guys you're really going to have to change the music. You're gonna have to go back to playing house because I don't really like the crowd and security are getting a bit...' And he shut the night, man.

When did it close?
I think it closed in '93.

When you were experimenting with the breakbeats were you conscious you were pushing things in a certain direction?
No. We didn't have a fucking clue. It worked, but because we were kind of hated on by the more soulful DJs we thought maybe we are doing the wrong thing. Maybe we have fucked

the night up totally. We were still doing nights where we played more soulful stuff. Rage was a total experiment. We never used to play like that anywhere else. But in that big club where we had carte blanche. It was Fabio and Grooverider's house and we just did what the fuck we wanted.

Looking back on it people aren't that brave any more, and that's probably one of the reasons dance music's got slightly stagnant. No-one would dare do that any more. It really was, at the time, so out there. We really got people's backs up with Rage.

And the press just slagged it...
At the start the press slagged hardcore, 'Charly', things like that. *Mixmag* put it on the cover and basically laughed it off, saying this is a fucking joke. But they loved jungle, cos that cartoonish element wasn't there in jungle. Jungle was very aggressive and quite abrasive. Buju Banton sampled over breakbeats. It was a real ghetto thing. 'Oh it's black music, we love black music, it's the new punk but it's like black punk.' So much bullshit going on.

When did jungle become drum and bass?
That happened in about 1996.

Any explanation?
The whole tag 'jungle' took on a real sinister angle. It just got so smashed in the press. We were like if we're going to carry on we're gonna have to change the name here, 'cos we're getting slaughtered here. The ragga thing kind of went, and it turned into drum and bass. It all fell apart in '98. We were getting totally slagged off for the music, everyone was like drum and bass has died, which was the headline for 18 months. And then garage came along: the death knell for drum and bass. It was the new drum and bass. It was the biggest kick in the teeth for us ever.

And they had all the girls...
Yeah! They had all the girls, it was where all the girls went from the jungle scene. Drum and bass was at its worst. Garage got so big so quickly, and so flavour of the month. Drum and bass was suddenly nothing. We didn't even have a review section in magazines, no drum and bass reviews, never listed any clubs we were doing. It was like we'd died! Come up to modern day now, and drum and bass is as big as its ever been. And I feel this year is a real turning point for the music. It's been around a long time and everyone's got over the fact that we're gonna be here now. We're not going anywhere.

What about the Sunrise parties and outdoor raves you did?
Sunrise was the craziest times, man. I got into it 'cos I knew a few guys that were selling tickets. At my first gig there I did the warm up, the first slot. Colin Faver had the nightmare of nightmares when he was DJing. I don't know what happened but he had a nightmare set. And everyone was throwing things at him. The promoter was like, 'Colin get off. Fabio, have you still got your records?' And I put on 'Strings Of Life', man. I'd never even heard 'Strings Of Life', and I'm not claiming to be the first man to play it but it was the first time it got played at Sunrise. I'll tell you what, everyone stood there, and you couldn't direct this in a film, it was like *Close Encounters* and when it started going [the faster bit], it just went off! I could have played that record all night and everyone would have went home and said, 'I had the best night I ever had in my life.'

What was it like doing business with some of these guys?
These guys would walk away with silly amounts, 700 grand clear profit, without the police

or the tax man knowing anything. You'd have all these people marching into a field and these county police who'd never even seen a black person before, going, 'Oh my goodness, what are these people doing in this field, what shall we do? Shall we call the army?' Then *The Sun* came out with that rave thing and that blew the whole thing apart and they was like, 'Yeah we saw E wrappers, silver wrappers that these druggies take.' It was laughable but it changed everything. It was never quite the same again. After that you got helicopters and police monitoring you, following you around. It was like being subversive. I don't know if it was the time but everyone thought everyone was old bill. It was a really paranoid time.

Did you get a kick out of feeling like an outlaw?
You did. But at the same time towards the end it wasn't fun any more. You were literally being chased through fields with your records, and the feeling that you were gonna get all your records confiscated and it's the end of your career. It wasn't fun any more.

> **We felt glad not to be part of Thatcher's Britain. We don't do nine-to-fives, man. We're outlaws with bandanas on our heads, dancing in the fucking street.**

But the early days...
We used to get a call from headquarters, which was the house round the corner where they sold the tickets, and they wouldn't know where the rave was going to be until nine at night. Convoys 30 or 40 cars, like, 'Where's the party?' Go to the M1, go to Heston services and then you used to get another phone call, it's here, and you'd drive down, and what you'd see was these dark fields and then all of a sudden you'd see one laser. It was like the Batman sign. It's over there! All of a sudden you'd look and there'd be 300 cars behind you.

So you didn't know any more than the punters where it was going to be?
No. And that's why we used to go there. It was so impromptu. You'd see farmers going, 'Fuck off out of my field.' Or in residential areas, in a warehouse, we used to see people sitting with their kids, 'What's going on? This is so scary,' until 11 or 12 in the afternoon.

They were the greatest days man. I'm not going to witness anything like it again. You did feel like a rebel. And you did feel, coming home, 12 o'clock in the afternoon, with a tie-dyed top on, dripping with sweat, walking into a petrol station with bare feet, you did feel like...

You've got to remember this was Thatcher's Britain at the time, and we were like: Fuck Thatcher! Fuck the Tories. So you really did feel like an outsider. We felt glad not to be part of Thatcher's Britain. We're nothing to do with you. We don't do nine-to-fives, man. We're fucking outlaws, we're going around with bandanas on our heads, dancing in the fucking street. You had an allegiance with anyone with a smiley badge. It was like a code. You'd see a smiley badge and you'd be like, 'Yeahh, shhhhh.' It really was like that. It was a secret fucking society man.

© DJhistory.com

RAGE 50

FIERCE RULING DIVA – You Gotta Believe

BLAKE BAXTER – Sexuality

LTJ BUKEM – Music

JOEY BELTRAM – Energy Flash

SMOOTH AND SIMMONDS – The Four Seasons

BLACK DOG – Virtual

RHYTHIM IS RHYTHIM – It Is What It Is

FALLOUT – The Morning After

EGO TRIP - Dreamworld

FLOWMASTERS – Let It Take Control

ARTHUR BAKER FEAT. ROBERT OWENS – Silly Games (Bonesbreak Mix)

LTJ BUKEM – Horizons

CENTERFIELD ASSIGNMENT – Mi Casa

INNERZONE ORCHESTRA – Bug In The Bassbin

LENNIE DE ICE – We Are I.E.

D MOB – That's The Way Of The World (Morales mix)

FINGERS INC – I'm Strong

JOHNNY DANGEROUS - Reasons To Be Dismal

APHRODISIAC – Song Of The Siren

JUNGLE WONZ – The Jungle

DEEP BLUE – The Helicopter Track

BLAKE BAXTER – When We Used To Play

BODYSNATCH – Euphony (Just For U London) (Bodysnatch Remix)

D.A.L. – Strings On A Monster Bass

FABIO AND GROOVERIDER – Rage

ADAMSKI – Killer

FINGERS INC – Distant Planet

GOLDIE – Terminator

BLUE JEAN – Paradise

LEFTFIELD – Not Forgotten

MR FINGERS – What About This Love

TOTAL MADNESS – Petey Wheatstraw

ZERO B – Lock up

RALPHI ROSARIO – You Used To Hold Me

HOUSEMASTER BALDWIN AND PARIS GREY – Don't Lead Me

NEAL HOWARD – To Be Or Not To Be

MARC KINCHEN – MK EP

BOBBY KONDERS – The Poem

LFO - LFO

ZERO B – Rumpelstilstkin

MOBY – Go

VOODOO CHILD – Voodoo Child EP

OB1 – OB1

JIMI POLO – Better Days

RHYTHIM IS RHYTHIM – Strings Of Life

JOEY BELTRAM – Mentasm

TRONIKHOUSE – Hardcore Techno EP

SUEÑO LATINO – Sueño Latino

RON TRENT – Aftermath

STERLING VOID – Runaway Girl

Compiled by Fabio.

"Everyone's looking at each other: 'What the fuck is this?'"

Shut Up And Dance
Into the jungle

Interviewed by Bill and Frank in Hackney, April 27, 2005

British dance music is rarely more than three steps away from a sound system. In Hackney, thunderous cabinets in brick basements are a simple fact of life. And away from the constraints of the more overground nightlife economy, the men who stack up the speakers have a freedom to experiment that regular club DJs can only dream of. It's no surprise then, that sound system culture is the looming force behind many of the UK's dance music innovations.

When hip hop records started arriving on British shores, PJ and Smiley wanted to play them a bit faster than advertised. The tempo suited their crowd and with the duo rapping over the top the speeds slipped gradually up. Even better, this style made for a quick move into production: it's far easier to loop up a breakbeat than to sweat over a drum machine. So, as Shut Up And Dance, PJ and Smiley started making records that matched their parties: speeding breakbeats, daft pop samples, ragga-style MCing.

They still thought of themselves as hip hop kids but in the mad years of acid house they were kidnapped by the rave scene, and their records paved the way for an era of rugged home-grown white labels quake-full of breaks. It's hard to pin an exact starting point on jungle and drum & bass, but without a doubt, Shut Up And Dance were way ahead of the game in sourcing the ingredients.

You guys were doing parties before the whole rave thing happened?
Smiley: Yeah. We started on the sound system thing. Us and [DJ] Hype. Just built a sound. Back then you couldn't just have a record box. You had to have your own sound system if people were going to hear you, take you seriously. The sound started about '82, '83. Then it got more serious about '86, when hip hop blew up.

How long did it take to build?
Smiley: Having a sound system you don't stop. 'Cos things need replacing and adding, maintaining. It's a proper sound system. It's not like where you buy everything.

Soldered with these bare hands! And that was more on the reggae scene?
Smiley: It was everything. I guess you could say we started more as a reggae thing.

Building on traditions that were already here?
Smiley: Yeah, 'cos Hackney, as you know is a big sound system place. For some reason this place just breeds talent in music. All kinds: punk, indie, reggae, rap, whatever it is. Don't know what it is with this area: always has done. From the '60s they say, this area's just been a cauldron of it all.

A lot of blues parties when you were growing up?
Smiley: Yeah, yeah man. I'm sure I was conceived in a blues. It's life really. You just got to live it, the sound thing. We certainly lived it. Earned my stripes and all that.

You had older brothers helping you?
Smiley: Not really. I had an older brother but he wasn't interested in it. It's just something

that's driven me, the love of music. 'Cos you don't earn any money with a sound system, not really.

How did you guys meet?
PJ: We went to school together.

When was your first party with your sound?
Smiley: About 1982.

What was it like?
Smiley: Weird. Good though. We didn't look back 'cos we're still doing it. It was by Lea Bridge roundabout, in a church hall. I found a poster for it. Hype hand drew it. He was nearly in tears when he saw it. Got to frame it.

The name of the sound?
PJ: The sound was called Heatwave.

What kind of stuff were you playing?
Smiley: Mainly reggae and dub I suppose. 'Cos Shaka was very big then. Everybody wanted to be like Shaka. The odd soul thing. The only big hip hop tunes were 'Planet Rock' and 'The Birthday Party', Sugarhill Gang.

SHUT UP AND DANCE RECORDS
53 BELGRADE ROAD
STOKE NEWINGTON
LONDON N16 8DH
SMILEY /PJ

" When we tried to get a deal no-one wanted to know. 'What the fuck is this?' 'Cos it was fast hip hop music, with people rappin. "

Wasn't playing soul a bit controversial on the reggae scene?
Smiley: Not really. A lot of sounds round here played reggae and soul. Obviously some of them put their nose up to it. But we loved it all. So we played it all from the beginning.

You had MCs?
Smiley: Well me and PJ used to MC, and my twin brother as well, but mainly me and PJ. And Hype was the DJ, doing the scratching. We'd select the tunes and he'd put it on.

Was it with two turntables, or an old fashioned sound with one?
Smiley: We started with one, obviously; we didn't get two until '86.

So very much in the tradition of what was going on before?
Smiley: Yeah.

Did people want to hear hip hop? Were there other guys playing it?
Smiley: Not really, because hip hop was so underground back then. People wanted it, but you could only play a few, 'cos a lot of people didn't know what it was. But we definitely dropped hip hop. And we were the first sound to have someone like Hype, cutting up two breaks. And we had a reggae MC, which was my brother, Daddy Earl, and me and PJ rapping. No other sound system had all that. They'd just play records, and maybe do something over the instrumental. We actually did it like a performance, Hype doing his thing on the decks.

So by 1986 you had it developed?
Smiley: We brought the sound all over the country.

Did you have an idea of the way parties worked in New York?
Smiley: We thought we was a hip hop sound system. We obviously wasn't, but we thought we was.

What kind of gigs were you doing?

Smiley: Blues. We had to do our own things. Break into empty houses. My brother was a sparks, so he'd get the lighting going, and Hype would be driving round with whoever, seeing where there's an empty house.

Did people start catching up with your style and doing similar things?
PJ: No-one else even thought about doing the DJing. Well you couldn't do what Hype was doing. He was shit hot. You can't learn that overnight.

When did the tempo start moving up in what you were doing?
Smiley: Good question.
PJ: Great question. I don't know. Obviously from our point of view we always wanted to get people dancing. That's what it was about. A sound system, it's about getting the vibes going, having a good time. So the tempo increased as part of that.
Smiley: It was just before the house explosion. House blew up in about '88 in Hackney – just when the hip hop thing was at its peak. Have you heard of Dungeons up the road? That was the Mecca of where it all started. Easily the biggest rave club in England. On Lea Bridge Road. Fuck the Hacienda, Dungeons was like ten different tunnels, all underground, and each tunnel had a different sound system. All house, acid house, all playing different music. And everyone's obviously off their tits. E's were new. That's where it all really kicked off big time.

Me and PJ, we liked fast hip hop, like what Big Daddy Kane was doing. It wasn't like Beastie Boys hip hop and Run DMC, we liked the breaky stuff, a bit faster. But still we wanted to take it further, because we wanted to be able to dance to it. Not just nod your head. So we made our stuff a lot faster when we started making music properly, about '87.

How fast? I read you'd play Def Jam tunes at about 120, 130 [bpm].
Smiley: Yeah. I'd say about 120, 125, that sort of tempo. That was the sort of rap we made, and it was really alien, unheard of. There weren't even such a thing as hip house back then.

So you were just speeding up records and rapping over the top.
Both: Yeah.

Was this led by you or led by the crowd?
Smiley: Us, definitely.
PJ: Everyone thought we were strange.
Smiley: Even here they thought we were strange. And when we tried to get a deal no-one wanted to know. 'What the fuck is this?' Cos it was fast hip hop music, with people rappin. So when we started making music we thought it had to be like what we liked to do, which was to dance to, not just to spit rhymes or rhyme or write, it had to be a bit more than that. You had to be able to dance to it.

There was this studio had a competition: IMW. Me, him and Hype went to this competition because the winner would get studio time, so we got in the studio, did a demo, and we won a week's studio time to make a record. The record was absolutely shit but we won the studio time anyway.
PJ: It came out on their label. It was one of those government-backed things, like the Prince's Trust but before that.

What was the record like?
[Both laugh]
Smiley: The first one was a double A-side. it was 'My Tennents' and 'Puppet Capers'. That was a pisstake of Run DMC's 'My Adidas'.
Smiley: Yeah. 'Puppet Capers' was more Hype's thing: little snippets of scratches and samples. '...Tennents' was more our side with us rappin'. We made a little video. Which I don't like pulling out, but...
[more laughter]
Smiley: So obviously we wanted to pursue it, get a proper deal, make more demos. No one wanted to know. No major label, no indie, because they were all like, 'This is too fast. This isn't going with the norm.' So we thought fuck you lot we're going to do it all ourselves.

So we did a tune, '5,6,7,8', pressed it up ourselves. Stuck it in the boot of his car, 500 of 'em, went to all the shops up west and round here, to see what they got to say. Within the week, the whole of 'em was sold out. And my younger brother, he was well into house, he was down Dungeons every week and he came home wouldn't stop talking: 'They played your fucking tune, the place was going crazy, you have to come next week.'

Were you going to house clubs at all? Or buying any house records?
Smiley: Oh always did, always bought house records. But we was more going to hip hop things. Everybody who came over from America we'd go and see it, every hip hop jam, that was full of violence, we were always there. We were so deep into hip hop. But I knew about house stuff, knew about Fingers Inc and all these people. We didn't go to no house clubs. But all of a sudden they were playing us. Weird. We found it very strange.

Did that influence the direction you went next?
Smiley: Not really. We just kept doing our thing. This fast hip hop thing – beats sped up, rapping on it. They just wanted more and more of this. We couldn't press enough records. It just went crazy. '£10 To Get In', 'Lamborghini', some of the singles were selling 40- or 50,000. And this was just two guys who wanted a record deal. We had all the big boys coming round, Virgin, Island, coming round with their big cheques. We were like, 'Naw, not big enough.' Who knows what would have happened if we would have signed with them.

When you saw how it was going off, did you become part of the acid house thing?
Smiley: Not really. We was *dragged* into that scene.
PJ: The scene we thought we was in didn't want to know. And this other scene held out its arms to us. We were like, 'But we're this,' and they were like, 'No you're not, you're coming over here mate.' You'd go to a few clubs, check out the vibe. So obviously when you get back to the studio you got more vibes, 'cos you see what they're on about.
Smiley: But we weren't into the four-beat thing, *dumm-dumm-dumm-dumm*. We never did that, always breakbeats.
PJ: Its like when people describe us as rave, we've never made a rave record. The only one is 'Raving I'm Raving.'

Was that an out-and-out pisstake, then?
[laughter]
PJ: It's a classic.
Smiley: 'Cos we never really liked old school ravey hardcore. I never liked that then, I don't like it now. It's weird to be sucked into something. People used to say you're king of raves, king of hardcore. *What?*

The lyrics were fairly ambivalent. They're not exactly celebrating drug culture. It's a satire isn't it?
Smiley: I just thought it was a good idea. Simple and plain. A good idea and it worked.

The story of acid house is usually told in terms of Shoom, Spectrum and the Trip and then the M25 raves, but you're saying there was stuff happening here that was more important.
Smiley: The West End didn't do shit, man. The West End didn't even let black people in their clubs anyway. You can't really talk about the West End in terms of bringing up a music.

But it's where it gets its exposure, so it's what get written about.
Smiley: It's just journalists who don't know fuck all. Trust me, I was there. From the beginning. Hopefully I'm there to the end. Trust me, it's from Hackney. That's where it all started: places like Dungeons, Roller Express, that place in Tottenham... The only thing that really came in the West End was places like the Astoria, but the whole scene had already blown up by then.

Were there a lot of villains about?
Smiley: It all depends on how big the rave was I guess. Obviously it you had a rave and it was a big massive warehouse and it was packed out and you charged a fiver to get in, that means there's money in it. So you gonna get robbed probably. When we had our raves we only charged two quid. That's why we made that song '£10 To Get In', 'cos we thought it

was a bit of an insult to the public. All of a sudden this rave explosion happens and people are charging £10 to get in. And yet people were paying it.

PJ: Willingly. I blame the drugs.

Smiley: Why would you want to pay £10 to get in for four walls and a DJ? It's not some glitzy club, you didn't get a few free drinks at the bar, a buffet at the back. Probably no fucking toilets in there, even. What were you getting for your money? Nothing really. It was a crap sound system, really shit, because the bigger the raves got the worse the sound got.

PJ: That why the remix was '£20...' cos the prices went up.

Did you do any PAs at any of the big raves?

Smiley: Yeeeah. 'Cos the label was so massive then and all the acts were blowing up. People wanted to see us. We only started in late '91, reluctantly, just had to, everyone wanted us to.

" The scene we thought we was in didn't want to know. And this other scene held out its arms to us. 'You're coming over here mate.' "

Tell us about the Ragga Twins and that whole sound.

PJ: That was just more experimentation really. We'd put out three or four singles of our own: '5678', '£10 To Get In', '£20 To Get In'. We thought we can't just carry on releasing our own stuff, we have to sign people up and expand. Try something different. And the Ragga Twins, we knew em from a sound system called Unity. Funnily enough I used to go to school with them as well. Again it's all from the manor.

We had an idea: lets try this reggae thing. We done our hip hop thing, we done our uptempo thing, and we wanted to try the reggae side of it. So we just approached them, had a chat. And they were like, fuck it lets give it a go. We used them on 'Lambourghini'. The intro is from D-man from a sound system tape, and we did 'Spliffhead' and 'Wipe The Needle' with them. Their album was so successful.

Where did the idea come from to combine reggae toasting with techno?

Smiley: When we got the Ragga Twins down I said to 'em, 'What we're going to try and do with you has never been done before.' People might laugh at this. We've always liked you guys as MCs, but what we're trying to do is something different. We wanted to give a reggae injection into it, see if it works. We don't know what they'll think, don't know what's gonna happen. But then, fuckin' hell, they were bigger than us.

Did you have a dancefloor in mind when you were making those records?

Smiley: Exactly what we were doing before, but it had a reggae thing on it.

So it was for your sound, something you could play out at your parties?

PJ: Yeah, we have to like it.

But were you making them for a particular place?

PJ: No it was more, I want to hear a good dance tune, with a reggae vibe on it, that works.

Smiley: Proper reggae vibe as well. It weren't no hold back thing. They were MCing properly on it. It wasn't, 'Oh talk a bit more English.' It was hardcore reggae people full blasting it. And they fucking loved it. They blew up overnight. And that was a rave thing as well.

Smiley: That was in the middle, the core of the rave thing.

Did you start going to those parties then?

Smiley: We had to. To see what the rave people were going to think of this. We thought they might not even like it. But fucking hell, I remember when they played their first tune, 'Hooligan 69', at Dungeons. Everyone's looking at each other: 'What the fuck is this?' With the Prince intro, 'Dearly beloved...' And then the reggae guy jumps in on it and sings... they loved it. Loved it! It just blew up. It was pure experimentation, for me. Pure. Just build and build and build.

....

Looking back it's clear that that was the start of a lot of things. Did you notice people inspired by what you were doing?
Smiley: Yes, yes.
PJ: There were many soundalikes came along. Anything successful people try and jump on and follow it.
Smiley: Fair do's to them,
PJ: It's a compliment really. But obviously it's *diluting* your sound. 'Cos everyone's trying to sound like you. So we had to keep moving the goalposts a bit.

And Hype obviously went on to great success.
Smiley: Hype's like family. When we blew up overnight, he just couldn't believe it. But he was always there in the background. We did loads of John Peel sessions, he was the one on the decks. We always thought: you need to be in the game, you need to work for a record company, couldn't really work for us 'cos we were too tight, too much friends, since five years old. So we got him a job at Kicking Records, and the rest is history.

66 Little Hackney, look what it's produced. I don't know why. Just so much from here. 99

Where would you place what you did in the evolution of what became jungle?
Smiley: Well everyone says that we started it all. I guess you could say that. 'Cos nobody was doing what we were doing. It wasn't a copied thing. It was experimentation all the way.
PJ: From speeding up breaks to putting reggae beats on speeded up breaks.
Smiley: Putting two breaks together. No-one did things like that.
PJ: Putting a beat around the break... It was all new.
Smiley: When it got to about '94, that's when everybody tried to do what the Ragga Twins were doing. This quick jungle with speeded-up breaks and you have to have a reggae sample, or reggae vocal, or reggae bassline. Everything was reggae to a speeded-up break thing. And that went on for a good two years. And that was basically what we'd been doing with the Ragga Twins back in '89, '90.

Who were the people who took it directly from you and took it somewhere else?
Smiley: Good question. Reinforced, they were doing good things. And M-Beat. The only problem with when it all first started there were just so many people doing it, and all they were doing was the same as us but speeding it up. Too fast – noisy, undanceable. Where's the soul in this? It's just noise now.

Were there any particular clubs round here?
Smiley: Yeah. Telepathy at Roller Express championed that sound. Hype was there, Grooverider, Fabio, Brockie, Ron was big then...
PJ: Of all that list, about four of them people are from this area.
Smiley: Jumping Jack Frost, he used to champion that sound as well. There was only a handful, but they were getting all the work. Because it wasn't a DJ world then. Back then everybody wanted to just go out. They didn't want to become a DJ. More people were excited about writing or making the stuff, than playing it. The DJ explosion came after that, like '96, '97. When more people wanted to be DJs.

What do you think makes the UK make music that's so different? I don't think the music you made could have come from anywhere else.
Smiley: I've always said London is the capital of the world for music. I truly believe that. It's not just 'cos I live here. I truly believe that. It's just a place where there's so much talent. Just little Hackney, look what it's produced. I don't know why. Just so much from here.

Do you think it's to do with the sound system tradition? That seems to be the thread that runs through it.

Smiley: From the Jamaicans coming over here, late '50s, early '60s, obviously that plays a part. It must be. It's always had something here. It always will. Don't know why. So many people are on top of their game. And their knowledge of music is good. If you go to America a lot of people don't really know anything. But in London there's so many knowledgeable fanatics here, who just know their shit, whatever kind of music you're talking to them about.

And different kinds of music mix, definitely more than the States.
PJ: You can hear it all here. We've got brilliant radio. In America or most countries you're growing up on chart music, on *Top Of The Pops*. But here, I was brought up as a child on pirate radio. So I got to hear everything underground growing up.

Why did you choose the heavy hitting samples? The trend then was to go for obscure funk records, and you were going for Prince, Suzanne Vega and all that stuff.
Smiley: We've always loved pop stuff. It was what we grew up on. Eurythmics, I saw them at Wembley when I was a kid. I thought Prince was a genius. I've always thought so. Use samples that are good. Just 'cos it's obscure so what? Doesn't mean its good. Use something that's good. Like when was the last time you heard Kate Bush in a sample? Kate Bush is a genius. You should use things like that. I'm a fanatic of music. If it's good I've got it. And I'm gonna use it.

So is there an innate pop sensibility in what you were doing?
Smiley: Not really, because we didn't come with some four-beat thing. If anything we twisted it up. We just brought something different to it.

When drum and bass was a fully formed genre did you think you were still hip hop guys, or did you feel part of the drum and bass scene?
PJ: We still loved our rap, and everything else, but we no longer saw ourself as hip hop, 'cos we knew that's not what it was seen as when we do it. With us, all the music we're into, we just reflect that in *our* music. It don't really get no deeper than that. We just believe what you like you should use. Those ingredients that make the food taste nice: you should put them in the pot, and we do.

© DJhistory.com

SHUT UP AND DANCE SELECTED DISCOGRAPHY

SHUT UP AND DANCE – Lamborghini (Writers/Producers)
SHUT UP AND DANCE - £20 To Get In (Writers/Producers)
SHUT UP AND DANCE – The Green Man (Writers/Producers)
THE RAGGA TWINS – Hooligan 89 (Producers)
SHUT UP AND DANCE – 5, 6, 7, 8 (Writers/Producers)
SHUT UP AND DANCE - Autobiography Of A Crackhead (Writers/Producers)
THE RAGGA TWINS – Spliffhead (Producers)
SHUT UP AND DANCE – Derek Went Mad (Writers/Producers)
RUM & BLACK – Fuck The Legal Stations (Writers/Producers)
SHUT UP AND DANCE FT. PETER BOUNCER – Raving I'm Raving (Writers/Producers)
NICOLETTE – Waking Up (Writers/Producers)
SHUT UP AND DANCE – Save It Till The Morning After (Writers/Producers)
NICOLETTE – Wicked Mathematics (Writers/Producers)
SHUT UP AND DANCE – No Doubt (Writers/Producers)
CEDRIC WINKLEBURGER & THE YELLOW BLUEBERRIES – Take It Easy (Producers)
SHUT UP AND DANCE – Black Men United (Inst.) (Writers/Producers)

RECOMMENDED LISTENING

VARIOUS – Shut Up And Dance

"The tracks got a little funkier, little bit dubbier and the tempo a little faster."

Dreem Teem
Garage mechanics

Interviewed by Bill and Frank at Radio 1, Feb 2, 2005

UK garage is a perfect example of how quickly DJs can breed a new kind of music. From an American style: the 'Jersey sound' of soul and gospel-inspired vocal house (also known as 'US garage' and associated most closely with DJ Tony Humphries), in just a handful of summers, British DJs selectively bred a uniquely British genre. Hot on the heels of drum and bass, from which it took much of its aesthetic and several of its producers, UK garage (or 'speed garage' as it was first called) took this American template, upped the tempo, swapped diva vocals for an MC, and added a taste for billowing sub-bass and super-crisp 'chunky' production.

The Dreem Teem are Timmi Magic, DJ Spoony and Mikee B. All were turned on by acid house, though Mikee has a longer history – he was decksman of hardcore rave stalwarts Top Buzz. The Dreem Teem were part of a wider group of DJs who nurtured UK garage, notably DJ/production duo of Matt 'Jam' Lamont and Karl 'Tuff Enuff' Brown, known together as Tuff Jam. Ending up on Radio 1, however, the Dreem Teem broke garage, originally 'a London thing', far and wide.

Garage had such a momentum that even as it was emerging it was already inspiring further evolutions. Two-step was formed when its four-to-the-floor rhythms were replaced by more funk-derived breakbeats, 'grime' came about when the MCs took centre stage, and when it looked back to the dub reggae and drum and bass of its heritage, dubstep took the floor. There's also 'bassline' a reaction to two-step that took things back to the housier territory of its starting point... as if to emphasise just how fast the sands keep shifting.

Where did you grow up?
Spoony: Born in Hackney, spent most of my formative years in Stoke Newington.
Timmi: Leyton. There was a lot of influences from there at that time. Linden C's from that area, Derek B was from east London, so they were inspirations. There were a lot of clubs playing '80s soul.

Were you old enough to go when Derek B was doing Canning Town.
Timmi: Yeah. Bentleys was the place, Sunday night. It got raided, so yeah, we were old enough at that time.
Mikee: And myself, Mikee B. Bit older. Born in Jamaica, grew up in Hackney, Clapton, Stoke Newington. My music career started when I was at school. Washing cars, getting a bit of money and going to the record shop up the road and standing in the corner, with the big men. I suppose at that time I was about 10.
Timmi: How much were records at that time?
Mikee: I think the records then were... if I said ten shillings...? [laughter].

When were you born then?
Mikee: If I told you... 1957. I'm like 47 now.

And you started on a sound system?

....

Mikee: Yeah... that we threw together. Funky Express. We played over west London with all the big systems, south London.

What kind of music were you playing?
Mikee: Rare groove, soul, lovers rock, Studio One, Treasure Isle, all that kind of music really. Emphasis on the reggae or the soul?
Mikee: More on... soul

And as DJ in Top Buzz you were playing loads of the big raves.
Mikee: '87 to '89, so much happened. Top Buzz, that was me, Jason K and Mad P the MC. We went through that stage of hardcore, and it changed from hardcore into like drum and bass...
Spoony: I remember listening to tapes of Mikee B before I was even old enough to go out. He was an absolute legendary DJ, but he'd just been under the radar. So to hang around Mikee was like being around Tony Humphries, except he was English.

> **❝ I was on pirates from '88, '89. There was not too much presenting, it was all about music; there'd be 10 guys in the studio... ❞**

What were your first experiences of house music?
Timmi: I went to the Trip the first day it opened. Nicky Holloway. I went to the one before that...
Mikee: Shoom.
Timmi: Yeah, Shoom. Little Wednesday night. I went to one Shoom night, then a guy said there's this new night starting up at the Astoria. By then I was already buying a few tunes, and the Trip, the Astoria, it blew me away, the whole attitude to what was going on. It was fire-eaters, jugglers, party animals. Then it was Spectrum on a Monday we used to go to, and Clink Street.

But I think the first time it really got me going on the DJing was going to Camden Palace, seeing the sort of unity between football hooligans, blacks, whites, and everyone raving. That inspired me to say, yeah, this is the sort of thing I could go to. Like Mikee I was into my rare groove, soul and a bit of reggae. And that was what changed me, more of a social thing, more than the music side of it.
Timmi: We used to do Dungeons in Leyton, that was one of the real underground clubs at that time. It really stood out, where it would finish at nine, then it would carry on till mid-day. Mr C used to play there, Rhythm Dr used to play there. Linden C, Rob Acteson, that little crowd.

The DJs that started Feel Real [long-running London house night]?
Timmi: Yeah. I used to play with those guys, Femi B, on the south coast. I should have actually fitted in with that crowd at the time, but I was too busy buzzin' on the south coast.
Spoony: The funny thing was I didn't actually used to go out. When people say the summer of love, I've got all the records from it, but I didn't go to loads and loads of club events. I was totally in it for the music side, not necessarily for the scene and the rave side of it.

Weren't you working at the benefits office in Hackney?
Spoony: I was collecting, buying records at Mr Music in Dalston, from my dear friend Daryl. And it just snowballed from there. But yeah, I was at the Jobcentre for seven years, I had a normal nine-to-five job, I was playing football. I loved my football, I loved my work, and the three had an excellent and perfect synergy for how I wanted to live my life. Had I been going out clubbing at the weekends I wouldn't have played football. I'd have been too hungover to go to work. Work would have been arduous from Monday to Wednesday. As it was it was just perfect.

How did you guys meet?
Timmi: For us guys meeting up, in about '94, '95, we was on a pirate radio, you had Freak FM, and London Underground, which was where we met up. We took our career from there, which was the birth of UK garage.

How did you get involved with the pirates then?
Timmi: It was a natural progression. Coming into London there were so many DJs, the best way to get heard was on a pirate. And it's a community, you'd get on with guys, you'd hear other DJs playing records. I was on pirates from really, really early: '88, '89, so you had all the name DJs who were just coming up: Kenny Ken, DJ Rap, a lot of the drum and bass boys. There was not too much presenting, it was all about music; there'd be 10 guys in the studio...

When were you drawn to the more garagey sound?
Spoony: When I joined I was very much known as the soulful house man on the station. And every now and again I'd sprinkle it with some of the UK stuff. I was definitely known as someone who would play vocals: vocal house and vocal [US] garage. It didn't depend on the tempo, it just had vocals on it. A lot more soulful. And as time went on the tracks got a little bit funkier, little bit dubbier and the tempo a little faster. And the transition was a very smooth one.

Why were you drawn to that kind of sound?
Spoony: Because I guess I was brought up on music and songs and melodies so that's what came naturally to me. The only thing that changed was the tempo. And then if I go all the way back to what my mum listened to: soca music, then she was brought up on uptempo music anyway, so this was just like our uptempo music.

The roots of UK garage are really when house music starts to split into different factions, different scenes.
Mikee: At the big raves you'd get everything: Carly Simon, Phil Collins, anything...
Timmi: Yeah just drop it in the middle of a rave, 'cos everyones buzzin'. But round about that '91 stage you did get a definite definition, where you were either CeCe Peniston, or you were 'Charly' and the Prodigy. People either wanted it hard or they wanted the other thing. And the gulf was too vast. And that's when it started to break away.
Timmi: Beginning of '91 there was a split. Where you either went hardcore, or you went all US-ey. I went on the US path. Sterns [club in Worthing] kind of defined it. If you went to Sterns there were three floors. Top floor you had what now you'd call drum and bass: Dr S Gachet, these sort of people. On the ground floor you'd have Top Buzz, Grooverider, Fabio, Rap, and all the harder DJs. Carl Cox used to do his three decks. That's where he first started to stand out, with his three decks mixing. Carl Cox, got to see him. 'Is it really three decks?' And then the middle floor Mr C, even though he played quite deep, not soulful, but he kept it not as hard. It wasn't banging. And you had people like myself, Frankie 'Shag 'Bones, Femi B, Rhythm Dr, on the middle floor; Harvey from Ministry, Justin Berkmann.

Was there ever a defining moment when you were forced to choose?
Timmi: No. It was nice because people used to move around all the way. People appreciated mixing and they appreciated hearing tunes getting together. Not just what you were playing and who the DJ was, but how they were playing it. Cos no-one had actually become a superstar DJ yet.

So the middle floor had a good following, 'cos it was... more girls, and if you were downstairs you had a bit of Vicks on the back of your neck and weeee you was off. I moved away from that 'cos I liked to have a shirt that didn't sweat so much. You could define the clothing as well. Those who wanted to hang upstairs, with the girls and give it some, and if you wanted to nut off you was downstairs.

But everyone came from the same starting point and stayed in touch with each other.
Spoony: Yeah, and the starting point is house music. And the others are effectively sub-genres. It would have been jungle-house music, it would have been garage-house music, happy hardcore house music, trance-house music. They're all different divisions within

house music. And people just decided they wanted it a little more soulful or a little bit harder, or a little bit more banging, or a little bit more percussive.

In the days of playing in a field, people would come on and play whatever: the big DJ would play the last set and 'Pacific State' by 808 State, and everyone would have their hands in the air. But as you went a few years later, it then started to split down. Happy hardcore had a massive scene, Fabio and Grooverider playin' happy hardcore, but they were some of the biggest DJs around at the time. So everyone still managed to keep their identity, their reputation, but people were being known for playing different brands and strands of house music.

And once you had those splits, all the new bedroom producers started to push things further apart.
Spoony: Yeah, and I noticed it with the garage scene. Once you've got this new music phenomenon, someone sitting in their room says I like that one a little bit more than I like that one. And they're gonna make that kind of record. Then you're gonna have an influx of new producers making that kind of music. And the same goes for every single one of those genres along the line.

Over a matter of six, eight months you're gonna get so many more soulful vocal bumpin' kind of tracks because of the new influx of producers. Before you know it you're playing an hour and a half of a particular type of music. 'Cos the music is now there for you to play.

What do you think the roots of the UK sound were?
Spoony: Funnily, in a paradoxical kind of way, the US. Because you had people like Masters At Work: very sexy percussive with very much a Latin influence. Whereas Smack Productions, Todd Terry or DJ Disciple were making dubbier, clubbier records. And that sound was very much embraced by the UK DJs who thought that the soulful vocal house was a little bit too smooth for 'em.

You'd pick up a Strictly Rhythm record, some people would play side A with a vocal, some people would play the other side with the dub vocal edit, some people would play the straight up dub. So stuff like Barbara Tucker 'Stay Together', four different DJs would play three or four different mixes of the same record.

So there was always a difference between the sound that UK DJs would prefer, compared to someone like Tony Humphries
Spoony: Yeah, because I think the UK clubbers wanted it a little bit more jumpin', a little bit more pumpin' than someone like Tony Humphries. I don't know what it is with us here, maybe the cosmopolitan nature of growing up in London, we can listen to a little bit of Latin, listen to a little bit of something with a tougher edge, little tougher sound in it, because when you walk down the street it could be black, white, Asian, Middle Eastern, and we eat like that as well. We see those programmes on TV, and without realising it means that when you hear bongos or a Spanish guitar it doesn't sound as alien as if we lived in very mini-societies like the States.

Even DJs like Ricky Morrison, who again would play on the same bill, he would still play a little chunkier than Tony Humphries, and then when you had the next wave of UK DJs, like the Dreem Teem and Matt 'Jam' Lamont, they started playing chunkier still. Ricky Morrison might have played half chunky. Dreem Teem or Matt 'Jam' Lamont might have played 75 percent chunky. You'd then get DJs who'd play 100 percent chunky and then DJs who were so chunky you'd have to start calling it something else. It's now morphed into something else.

What would you regard as the first UK garage record?
Spoony: I think rather than try to put my finger on the first I would say the label Nice 'N' Ripe was immediately identified with this new sound. There were other records that were sprinkled about but when you saw a Nice 'N' Ripe record, it was them. It was Grant Nelson, Tony Power, very much responsible for what happened as far as UK garage goes. He was heavily influenced by what was going on Stateside, but as far as bringing the sound here... Whether Christopher Columbus is the greatest discoverer or the greatest pirate depends on which side of the table you're sitting on.

Timmi: One of the first tunes that could define it was a tune on Strictly [Rhythm] called Logic 'Blues For You', and Grant Nelson done a mix, on Nice 'N' Ripe, which was exactly the same tune, just had different sounds, a lot more bright, the British sounds: the sounds that you'd expect in a bit of jungle and drum and bass. Even though it was still housey, it was a lot brighter and a lot heavier on the dancefloor. And that for me is the defining tune. 'Cos there were a lot of DJs that were still trying to make US-sounding tunes, but they were British DJs, and it was like come on, give it a little twist. What we used to do at that time, we defined US against UK, because most of the US DJs would play the vocal mix, but we'd turn it over and play the dub mix and pitch it up.

Who were the Americans at the same sort of time?
Spoony: Terry Hunter, Eddie Perez and Smack Productions, the Mood II Swing boys, Basement Boys. They were all making those records. The bumpier side of vocal house garage.

> 66 **The end of '95 was the defining time for promoters. They said hold on a minute, we've been booking US DJs for thousands, let's try and book these guys instead.** 99

Was there a nightlife split as well?
Well the other thing that defined it: in '93 we couldn't get any work on a Saturday night. Ministry? – oof, out! 'But I got credentials!' 'No!' You'd go to Heaven, Heaven used to have Grooverider and Fabio downstairs... and the garage room? 'No! No!' Feel Real? I knew all the guys, I was like, 'C'mon mate, give us a go.' 'No, no, no!' So our time became Sunday afternoon. Sunday afternoon was a really important time for those who wanted to go out after Ministry, like 9 o'clock, would go to a pub called The Castle, in Elephant and Castle. Or the Frog and Nightgown.
Mikee: I saw Finbarr's missus yesterday as a matter of fact. He used to do the pirate club.
Timmi: The Pirate Club's another one. That's from the early days though. The Frog and Nightgown was probably quite defining. Walked in there one day there was Matt Jam Lamont DJing there, Mickey Sims, DJ Dominic. And their sound was a lot more moodier, a few gangsters, it was an older crowd, loads of birds, a lot of brandy...
Mikee: ...and champagne
Timmi: ...and it was just different. It was a calmer night from a Saturday night.

Had they all been to Ministry?
Timmi: Some had, but some started saying we're not going to Ministry, we're going to start at the Frog and Nightgown. That would go on to around four or five in the afternoon and then people would leave and go to the park in Kennington. I thought, this is me, I'll have some of this. You needed to find a home.

The end of '95 was the defining time for promoters. They said hold on a minute, we've been booking US DJs for thousands, let's try and book these guys instead – who are now getting massive crowds. Mikee's doing a rave called Moschino, at Bagleys, and loads of little things started cropping up, middle of '95. We were still on pirates, we hadn't got together till end of '95, beginning of '96. We got together as the Dreem Teem.

Which pirates?
Timmi: We were on London Underground and Freak FM, but London Underground was the one, 'cos the amount of DJs... most of the main DJs were on it. You had Norris 'da Boss' Windross, you had Dominic, you had Mikee, Spoony and myself, Ramsey and Fen, Jason K, DJ Hermit, a lot of the earlier DJs, the respected DJs in London.

So London Underground was where the sound coalesced on the radio?
Timmi: Yeah. I'd say that was where it really built up on the radio. That just woke up alarm bells

everywhere. The DJs are inspired now, the producers are inspired to make the music. The MJ Coles are now coming in, and that's when you started to get a nice infrastructure of DJs, producers, promoters. Sun City, La Cosa Nostra, The Arches, the Zoo boys started doing some stuff. That's when it started to expand, and a few of us went to Kiss FM. Karl 'Tuff Enuff' Brown, Matt 'Jam' Lamont, brilliant producers at the time. Inspired a lot of the UK garage of the time with their sound.

When Mixmag and DJ first wrote about it they called it 'speed garage'. That wasn't anything that anyone on the scene was using?
Spoony: No.

What did you guys call it?
Spoony: We were just calling it garage or UK garage.

> ## 〞 You were just hit by hundreds of people dancing 500 percent. No-one looking around, they're just in there grooving away. And as a DJ that's all you can ask for. That's everything. 〝

So when did you think here's a completely new style of music?
Spoony: I think before we could say a totally new form of music was not really until the whole MCing thing came onto it. That was when it was rubberstamped that this is now English. This is revolution not evolution.

Where did the whole MC thing come from.
Spoony: You grow up in London you're exposed to lots of musical tastes and cultural tastes. Generally, you grow up as a young black kid, you're gonna hear a lot of reggae, lot of sound systems: people like Saxon, and Unity, or listen to David Rodigan on the radio. Suddenly there's a new kind of music that people want to do their thing on. Kids thought: if Biggie Smalls and Tupac can grab a mic, I'm gonna do it here.

And the cutting and scratching and rewinds. Obviously the music lends itself to those techniques, but were DJs consciously bringing them in?
Spoony: I used to be a hip hop scratch DJ. One day Timmi and Mikee were round the house and I was mixing an acappella and I started scratching it. They were like, 'Can you scratch?' 'It's how I learnt to DJ. I was scratching before I could DJ.' They said, 'We think you should do that in your set. And the rewinds when people really love the record. The rewinds go back to drum and bass, back to dancehall, back to reggae. This is what we were brought up on.

Did you notice a point where there were a lot of disillusioned refugees from the drum and bass scene?
Spoony: Originally MJ Cole was making drum and bass records, but then 'I want there to be music. I want chords and strings and melodies and grooves.' TJ Cases made American R&B music, got disillusioned with that, thought, 'Wow what is this uptempo music with soul, where has this come from?' So all these different people for different reasons, coming from different places, are now jumping into the melting pot.
Timmi: As we got to about '98, '99, you got refugees from everywhere. 'Cos now you had the two-step sound kicking in. 'The Theme' [by DJ Ride] was probably one of the first – breakbeat with a vocal. 'Destiny', by Dem 2. I thought, naw I want to put a ballad, so we did the 'Dreem Teem Theme'. Amira ['My Desire'] was another one that I put a ballad to. That inspired a lot of people, like Artful Dodger. Then Brandy, 'Boys Mind', Architects did a two-step mix and it blew the original out of the water.

Suddenly you had loads of record companies sending R&B mixes. Any tune that was out was getting a two-step remix. So now you go to a club where R&B wasn't massive, never had been, and you'd just see the room two clear out, cos wow, there's energy to this music now. and R&B didn't have the energy that it does now. It was just wine bar music at the time.

What about 'Never Gonna Let You Go'? That was an early one wasn't it?
Timmi: It was but that was an American record, that was an accidental thing. It was two minutes long on the end of Tina Moore's track.

Then everyone started getting real glamorous: the Moschino and the champagne.
Timmi: I never wore that kid of stuff. I just tried to look smart in a shirt...

I remember going to Twice As Nice at the Coliseum and I hadn't seen such flamboyant dressed guys outside of a gay club. Everyone had spent so much time and effort on their clothes.
Spoony: Because you know you're going to get the crème de la crème of women and if you go there looking your part there's a good chance you could be on it. So even if you couldn't be bothered you would be bothered on a Sunday night outside the Coliseum. Sunday night became Saturday night. Sunday night became the night to go out. I'm taking Monday off work, getting the car cleaned on Saturday, I'm getting my hair cut as late as I can on Saturday so it still looks brand new on Sunday, I got a new outfit to wear. Saturday? Not bothered about Saturdays. Sunday night fever.

At the end of the '90s the garage scene had pretty much rounded up every woman in clubland.
Spoony: That's why everyone wanted to come. They didn't necessarily like or understand the music, but Jesus, never seen so many women in one place. And eventually you start liking the records. My brother, he's very much into reggae and dancehall music: 'Nah, I ain't listening to house.'

I said, 'Come down you'll have a good time.'

He came down and all he started talking about was, 'The girls, the girls, the girls, the girls. But what was that record though, the one that sounded alright?' Then he'd ask me about more records, and before you knew it, 'Yeah I need a tape now. 'Cos a girl got into my car and I didn't have none of the music.'

What was the difference in atmosphere compared to early house things you went to?
Spoony: Early house was very much fuelled by drugs. Being someone who doesn't take drugs it was nothing to stand there seeing people poppin' around pills all night. At the Arches, even though people were obviously still taking them, because the music was all melodic it wasn't as if you had to be off your head to enjoy it. You could listen to it on a Wednesday on your way to work, as opposed to something that you just listen to when you're out clubbing.

What was it like playing at the Arches?
Spoony: Electric. Electric. You felt it. You felt the atmosphere, you could touch the atmosphere, you could bottle it. You opened the door, you took a deep breath, and you were just hit by hundreds of people dancing 500 percent. No-one looking around caring who's in there, they're just in there grooving away. And as a DJ that's all you can ask for. That's everything. You felt you were going to play a wicked set because the atmosphere wouldn't let you put a foot wrong.

That was where it really took off then? You couldn't look back.
Tony Humphries came and played at the Arches one week and totally bombed.

....

Wow! Quite a symbolic moment.
Yeah. Maybe the tempo and the energy was too much. He may have been better playing a straight up disco set, as opposed to a mellow soul house set.

But as far as DJ Spoony goes, that was when I started getting a reputation that I was going to come and rock a party. But that was just because the people made me feel that I had to rock the party. I can't fail to.

Were the Tuff Jam guys following a very similar trajectory? Were you aware of them early on?
Spoony: Yeah because they were producing music as Tuff Jam quite early on. These were people that at the time were UK garage's biggest DJs.

They were putting stuff out on Catch quite early.
Yeah. This is even before Catch. I think they had something out on Unda-Vybe, but they were doing their thing before the Dreem Teem were invented.

What's the secret to your success on the radio?
I think we brought another dimension to it. It was no coincidence that we became UK garage's biggest, maybe the three different influences we had. And at the time, when we were on Kiss, we then had a very successful radio show. We were appealing to people who couldn't come to the club and hear us, they could tune in and listen on a Friday night. For that reason we then became UK garage's biggest. All the artists wanted to come on our show, we started getting all the exclusives. It was fun to listen to the show. We weren't attitude kind of people, we'd have a laugh, take the piss out of each other. It sounded like an on-air party.

How did Ayia Napa become the garage party destination?
If you tell people 'no' enough they'll just go off and do their own thing. So Ibiza comes along, we want to go there but you can only listen to harder house music. There's somewhere else where they've got smaller bars – not 5,000 capacity places, they play R&B records, garage, uptempo R&B, the rest is history.

Had it been a popular destination for black London youth from before?
A lot of my footballer friends were going there from years ago but it wasn't a massive destination, just a resort. I had a phone call from Pure Silk 1997, 'Do you want to DJ abroad?' I don't care I'll DJ anywhere. And that was it. the next four years were unbelieveable. You then had a London promoter and they're bringing the feel to the island, as opposed to it being just a local DJ playing in a bar. Just like how Cream or Manumission go to Ibiza, Pure Silk were going to be Ayia Napa's Cream. Then Twice as Nice came, Garage Nation, Garage Heaven... By '99, 2000 it was road-blocked, the planes were packed, the beaches were packed. People booking holidays a year in advance.

© DJhistory.com

TWICE AS NICE 50

GUY SIMONE – You're Mine

AMIRA – My Desire (Dreem Teem Remix)

TJ CASES - Joy

PEACE BY PIECE – Nobody's Business (Dreem Teem Remix)

ROBBIE CRAIG – Lessons In Love

ANTHILL MOB – Plenty More

MOOD II SWING - Closer

TITO PUENTE – Oy Como Va (MAW Mixes)

RIP GROOVE - RIP

SO SOLID CREW – Oh No

MASTER STEPZ – Melody

ARTFUL DODGER FEATURING CRAIG DAVID AND ROBBIE CRAIG – Woman Trouble

WOOKIE – Scrappy

MJ COLE – Crazy Love

K2 FAMILY – Bouncing Flow

NEW HORIZONS – Find The Path EP

TJ CASES – Do It Again

DARYL B – Too Late

GROOVE CHRONICLES - Chronicles Theme

DJ LUCK & MC NEAT – Little Bit Of Luck

SHAWN CHRISTOPHER – Make My Love (Kerri Chandler Mix)

HIGH TIMES – Feel It

M DUBS – Over You

LENNY FONTANA – Spirit Of The Sun (Steve Gurley Remix)

MASTER STEPZ FEATURING RICHIE DAN – R U Ready

BAFFLED – Over U

DEETAH – Relax (Grant Nelson Mix)

KELE LE ROC – My Love (10° Below Mixes)

RIP PRODUCTIONS – Oh Baby

BIZZI – Bizzi's Partee (Booker T Remix)

DREEM TEEM VS. ARTFUL DODGER – It Ain't Enough

M DUBS – Bump 'N' Grind

ROY DAVIS JR. – Gabrielle

MONSTA BOY FEATURING DENZIE - Sorry

RAMSEY & FEN – Love Bug

BRANDY – Angel In Disguise (X Men Remix)

STICKY FEATURING MS DYNAMITE – Boo!

TUFF JAM – History Of House Music

DJ PIED PIPER & THE MASTERS OF CEREMONIES – Do You Really Like It

BRASSTOOTH – Celebrate Life

RESERVOIR DOGS – What To Do About Us

SOUND OF ONE – As I Am (Todd Edwards Dub)

DHL – Favourite Girl

MARISSA – Dedicated To Love

4 DEEP CONNEXTION – Twisted Future

TJR – Just Gets Better

WOOKIE - Battle

DREEM TEEM – Dreem Teem Theme

HARDRIVE – Deep Inside

NORRIS 'DA BOSS' WINDROSS – Funky Groove

Compiled by Spoony

RECOMMENDED LISTENING

VARIOUS – The London Dream Team – In Session (DJ mix)

VARIOUS – Sound Of The Dreem Teem (DJ mix)

❝ It's a huge rush when you're on stage and 10,000 people scream at you. ❞

Tiësto
Stadium superstar

Interviewed by Bill by phone to the Netherlands, Mar 2, 2007

His plan is to take DJing to the next level. And from here, lost in the crowd, it looks like mission accomplished: stadium tours, inroads into the US charts, and the unparalleled spectacle of the 2004 Olympic opening ceremony where he played for a global audience of more than 100 million. There are towns smaller than a Tiësto dancefloor. He is without doubt breathing at a higher altitude than any DJ before him.

But at the risk of sounding like grumpy old rotters, we're not sure that what he does has much in common with the craft's lower levels. He's playing music and people are dancing, but most similarities stop there. DJing is about interacting with a dancefloor full of people, about feeling what they like and coaxing them into something more adventurous, releasing unexpected feelings, or gently teasing out their energy reserves. A large crowd – anything over a few hundred people – is a truly lumbering beast. Playing to 10,000 or more must be roughly akin to trying to pull wheelies in an oil tanker. What keeps a DJ on his toes is the fear of clearing the floor, and that doesn't seem likely here. Stadium superstar he may be – and a thoroughly nice chap – but we reckon Tiësto's already gone comfortably beyond DJing. At the centre of monster events, screaming fans, dazzling lightshows, and a 35-strong tour crew, he puts on records.

Who was your first inspiration as a DJ?
My first inspiration was on a night out in Belgium in 1994, it was a live act and a DJ and the DJ was Sven Väth and the other one was Moby. I decided this was music I really, really like and would like to play.

You must have been listening to dance music before then?
Yes. I was into dance since it started in 1988. I was listening to acid house and all that music.

How did you first come across it, on the radio?
No in a record shop. I was a huge heavy metal fan back in those days [chuckles]. I saw in the shop a sign with 'House Music', so I thought, house music, what is that? I was always curious about new music to listen to and I was like what is this. I discovered *Techno! The New Dance Sound Of Detroit*.

The compilation?
Yeah, and from then on I was sold.

Do you remember guys like Ben Liebrand [Dutch master mixer]?
He was definitely a big influence, because every Friday night he had his own mix show, and every Friday he'd do a really good remix of a current hit. Everybody listened to it. Every Friday night from a 9.15 until 9.30 I think. They were amazing the mixes he did, they were incredible, and I still don't know how he did it. Every week a whole new mix and really good-sounding, too.

....

When was the first time that you played in a club yourself?
The first time was probably in 1989. These were really small, though. The very first time I played was on holiday in a club in Majorca. I brought my records and I was in this bar and I said, hey can I play some records. That was also the first time I heard Lil Louis' 'French Kiss' and I was like, wow this is really special.

What was it about house that appealed to you and converted you from heavy metal?
In the beginning it was the atmosphere. I mean, I went to Club BCM in Majorca and it was just amazing, the atmosphere in there: the dancers, the DJs, it was like nothing you'd heard before, and everything you heard was weird and new. At home I listened to a lot of new beat from Belgium. But what really converted me was that night with Sven Väth, because he played a lot of melodic house music, very trancey, with the symphonies and melancholic sounds which are very close to heavy metal, but more electronic.

Did you have anyone that taught you or mentored you?
Well, the whole DMC period inspired me because on Thursday night in Holland you had a radio show called the Full (??) Show with Terry Marks (sp??) and every week there was a 15-minute mix with a DJ from Holland mixing all the hot records together, a guy called Peter Slaghuis. Those guys were the pioneers, they mixed records for the radio. I learned it myself but I was inspired by what they were doing.

Could you tell what they were doing just by listening?
A little bit. They were more into tape cutting. I wasn't really into that.

The more hip hop style?
Yeah. But the mixing in general inspired me.

> **❝ Slowly I learned more about DJ party organisations. I went on to get more and more famous. ❞**

When was your big break in Holland?
My big break came much later because I started working in a record store selling records to other DJs; it was a store in Rotterdam called Basic Beat. Before that I was in the mixing championship finals. I started mixing there and that went really well and that gave me the inspiration to keep going. Slowly I learned more about DJ party organisations. I went on to get more and more famous.

My big break came in 1998 when I played at a big rave in Holland called Inner City. It was the first big rave that was programmed with normal dance music rather than gabber; stuff like trance, techno and house. It was in Amsterdam in the Rai. I had my big breakthrough. I mixed a compilation for that party which sold about 100,000 copies just in Holland, so people right away knew who I was. Back then there weren't many DJs who did that. Only Global Underground had compilations, but no one from Europe. It helped a lot.

Do you think that the DJ is an artist?
I think the mixing and creation of an atmosphere in a room is definitely art.

What would you say to a rock critic who says you're just playing other people's records?
It's a different kind of art. Of course, you don't always make the music yourself, but you're still making something new out of the records you have. It wouldn't happen if you didn't do it. A really good DJ knows how to time a record and he knows when to play a record. That's a piece of art. Music is all about timing. You can listen to two records when you're in a bad mood and good mood and you will have a different perspective of that record each time. The DJ knows how to make people in a good mood and make them feel euphoric and that's the art of it, and that's very special and not many DJs know how to do that.

Also, nowadays, I make most of the music myself, so there's a big difference to back in the day. The DJ is an artist now. I'm releasing my third album now.

Do you still enjoy playing your own music? I know quite a lot of DJs who have heard their stuff so often in the studio they're bored with it by the time its released.
The response is so intense when I play 'Traffic' or 'Adagio For Strings'. People react so much harder when I play one of my own tracks. It's a big difference and you never get bored of that because you think, 'Yeah, I made that in the studio.' But now people love this track so it's a big compliment.

Of course you don't feel the same way you did the first night you played it, and some nights you fee like – hmmm [unenthusiastic mumbling] but I see myself as a DJ slash crowd pleaser. I play for the people. I'm not an underground DJ like Richie Hawtin who has a totally different kind of art, I think. What Richie does is he creates a painting; okay people, this is my painting whether you like it or not, this is what I do take it or leave it. What I do is start working on the painting then I see what people's opinion is and then I adjust it. That's the big difference between me and other DJs. I want to be interactive with the crowd, and if I feel they want to hear a big tune, I think fuck it; I want everyone to go home with a smile so I give them a big tune…

Why do you think minor keys are so popular in dance music?
It just gives people two kinds of feelings, beautiful, warm and dramatic, and that's what it is. When people are in a good mood you can cry from happiness. When you feel bad about something it helps you to get over stuff. It's just a great feeling to feel that you feel serious but emotional.

So why do you think major keys are used less?
As a producer you really wanna make something that moves people. You want to tickle the brain and the ears and that's much easier with minor keys.

You've obviously achieved a great deal already, so what is the buzz for you now: producing a great song? DJing to a big crowd?
The most exciting thing for me is the total package. Producing the new tracks, and then make an amazing show and blow everybody away. I have a whole new visual show, all directed by me, so I'm definitely involved in that, too. It's an audio-visual package which makes it more exciting for me because back in the day I was just DJing. Now I control the visuals on the screen behind me, the lighting, the special effects. So it's definitely more of a concert than a DJ show.

When I do a DJ show, I turn up in a club, a couple of thousand people, I play my set and that's about it. When I do a concert, everything is directed. I control the music of course. I can mix whatever I want… I travel with a big crew now, three big trucks and a lot of people as well…

How many people are in the crew for a big tour?
Thirty-five people. It's like a big band but only me on stage.

Does that feel bizarre or lonely because you're on your own?
It definitely doesn't feel lonely because I have people around me who help me with everything: the music, the lighting, the sound, and we have a really good crew. I've got eight people around me and they're all really good friends of mine.

Once you start playing though, it's just down to you: you're truly on your own. Do you ever think about it that way?
Not really. It's been growing for years so it went from 100 people to 200 people. It's a huge rush when you're on stage and all those people scream at you, say 10,000 people; it's definitely a feeling…

Better than drugs?
Much better! [laughs]

Do you think the presence of drugs affects the way you DJ?
Well, yeah, it's definitely a different vibe. In the '90s drugs was huge and you heard that

Tiësto

from the crowd, but sometimes people take so many drugs that they didn't get the music any more. I feel nowadays – I don't know how it is in England – but here in Holland, you see the trend to see less people on drugs. It's more accepted as a new musical stream. With other DJs I don't know, but with my show say 70 percent don't take drugs and 30 percent do take drugs. And in '98, '99 it was 80 percent on drugs.

When did you first start playing in the US?
2001. The first real tour was quite amazing because I did the Area 2 tour and I was touring with Moby, David Bowie and Carl Cox. That was my first tour of America. I only met David Bowie for five minutes.

When was the first tour on your own?
I was supposed to do one in September 2001 but I decided September wasn't a good month so let's try October or November, but then the tour came and wasn't so successful because nobody wanted to go out and it was quite dead. Then the year after in 2002 was a big summer tour and then that was my first proper tour that sold out and it went bigger from there.

Didn't you do a huge thing on New Year's Eve in Vegas?
Yes, last year at Orleans Concert Arena. There was 9,000 people, which for Vegas is really big.

Have you had any chart success in the US, because you seemed to have bucked the trend for dance music in America?
Yes I've had success in the *Billboard* charts and my CDs have sold really well from the beginning. The biggest success I had was for 'Delirium Silence', which was also a huge tune in the UK. That was on national radio in the US and the first dance record to be played on national radio in the US. The good thing is, and that's why I'm still growing fast, is because of internet radio. They have dance channels and they are definitely taking over the regular radio stations, so more people have access to dance music now.

Do you feel that DJing leads naturally into producing?
Yeah. I was DJing '95 '96 and I was like, 'Yeah it's great but I really wanna know how to make it.' That's how I started getting into that. I thought, it doesn't sound too hard to make [laughs]. It's just a bass drum and a bassline. So I went to a store bought some stuff and started learning.

How long did it take you?
It took me two years and I got to certain level and could make great demos and they sounded alright, and then I met a guy called Denis and he was much further on than me on the technical side but he didn't have that many ideas on the producing side so we started working together and together we make fireworks. And then we started producing and remixing, and then the 'Silence' track came along and blew up as producers. I've been working with him for seven years now and it's been very good. He's definitely the guy behind Tiësto

The power behind the throne, as we say in England...
Yes, the power behind the throne!

Why do you think that dance music has become such an international force?
I think we are much more ahead in Europe and it's much more accepted by radio and TV. Everybody loves it. If you go to a bar you hear it. It's definitely a different vibe to a rock or hip hop crowd. Everybody wants to be a part of it. I always notice in America when I go to a hip hop club and at the side there'll be a dance room and you notice the difference. Okay so these people are here but they don't really care about the music, and there's no vibe in the room. If you go to the little room where they're playing house music, there's a vibe in there, everybody's singing along much more uplifting.

Do you regard DJing as work or play?
On a bad night when it's really terrible, work, but on a good night, play. Some nights you have where everything goes wrong. I had a night like that in Dubai last week. They oversold the place; there were too many people inside, so they were pushing towards the DJ booth,

so they had 12 security guards around the DJ booth pushing the people away. That, to me, doesn't feel like a party. It felt like I was in a fortress or something. Then you feel like, 'Oh my god I want this night to end so I can forget it.' I would say most of the time it just feels like a party. You meet up in the dressing room with the promoter then go and have a nice dinner and then you go to the party to do what you love. It's amazing that you can get paid for that!

I guess a lot of the people you grew up will be doing ordinary jobs like car mechanic; do you feel blessed in what you're doing?
Blessed. Yes very much. I always feel very lucky. It's amazing you can travel around the world and you meet all these interesting people and you get paid big bucks.

What do you think your greatest achievement is?
It's hard to say at this point. I would say if we were 10 years further on I would like people to say, 'Tiësto, back then, he took the DJ thing to a different level, he broke the boundaries and that's why it is where it is right now.' It's a different place to where the DJ was and I always try and do different things.

How do you think of yourself now, as a DJ, artist, producer?
Definitely still a DJ. I'm still a DJ. But a DJ doesn't cover the whole thing…

But DJing is like the base metal on which everything else is made?
Yeah, that's definitely true. When I'm in the studio I think of how I'm would play the records out. I always think about DJing. I would say a DJ, but there's so much more to it than there used to be, like the visuals, the producing, the remixes, the show element, everything.

" I would like people to say, 'Tiësto, he took the DJ thing to a different level.' "

Tell me about performing at the Olympics in 2004. How did it happen?
It was quite funny. I was playing a gig in Greece in a club in September 2003 and this guy walks up to me and says, 'Hey Tiësto I just heard you play, you're amazing, I want you to play at the opening ceremony of the Olympics.' I looked at him, like, 'Sure pal!' I gave him my management card and told him to get in touch. Back then I was always getting people coming up to me and saying, 'Yeah, I own this big club in London, blah blah.' But then in January he said, 'Okay, we're coming to Amsterdam and we want to meet you and talk about the opening ceremony but you can't tell anyone about it.' They were really interested in 'Adagio for Strings' and all the other classical-influenced stuff and then we talked about the opening concert.

How did it feel when you came to do it, you must have been nervous?
Well yeah. You practise the whole week, so by the time the ceremony comes you're less nervous because you've practised the whole week. But the big opening night with the security and everything, backstage and you see the television and you know the whole world is watching that stadium, like wow, and in 30 minutes I'm going to be in that stadium playing for all the prime ministers of the world and all the people at home watching. It's a crazy feeling.

Do you plan to do club gigs in the future or have you moved away from that?
No what I have now is a perfect combination. We have the big Elements of Life show which we do in 20 or 30 cities. And that's gonna be a full directed show with big hits and big records; a stadium show, an epic show, as far as a DJ could take it, I think. The biggest dance show in the world. But on the side I will play an intimate club gig in the same place, the night before or the night after. And there I play no hits, really deep, experimental stuff, all kinds of other things. Just for myself to do something interesting.

....

When you do the shows what are you actually doing?

Most of the stuff is pre-made. All the records are edited in the studio. The mixes are done. So what I do on stage is basically about the art of mixing so I really mix the record together. That's about it. Everything else is pre-programmed.

What about the visuals, how does that work? Do you have a pre-ordained set to accompany them?

Well yes and no. I want to be spontaneously in control, when to play what. Like I said, the timing of the records is essential. What I do is like five minutes before I will know, so I will coordinate with me guy behind me. I tell him, 'Okay in five minutes I'm going to play "Love Comes Again" and then he says to the visual guy so he gets everything ready and I mix it in and then as the first notes of 'Love Comes Again' coming in – click.

So it's sort of like a mix between club and concert?

Yes.

How has technology affected your performances in the past ten years?

Quite a lot. I said to myself, even in 2001, that vinyl will never die, I was such a vinyl freak. And then the CD came, the legendary Pioneer, and it just changed everything. No more scratched records, no more zooming. It's basically better than vinyl. I always said that only when a CD player can do everything a record player can do will CDs take over. If you see someone playing vinyl now, you just start laughing because you can't imagine playing it any more, at least for the big professional DJs.

66 It's not about a DJ turning up with just his records, but for him to make a whole show. 99

What about digital DJing with programs like Ableton or Serato?

I know how to use Ableton and I've been working with it, but the quality is a little less. I'm definitely gonna use it for when I wanna do a power mix live, like if I wanna mix 15 records in half an hour then I'm gonna use Ableton. But... I do think the art of mixing records is very special and if you don't do that any more as a DJ, it just doesn't feel like you're DJing.

You mentioned the influence of classical music, have you used it much?

I've had my period, but not any more, not at the moment. During 2003 and 2004 that was definitely when I used a lot of classical pieces. That was then but I've moved on to other things. I think the music has moved on too, and things are coming back together again, DJs are not expected to play just house or just trance or whatever, and DJs are mixing it up much more.

How has the internet affected how you work?

In some ways quite a lot, in some ways not at all. As a DJ to buy records it's quite convenient, places like Beatport and for regular albums I got to iTunes. Also back in the day and you played a set in Amsterdam and then the night after in London and then New York, it could be the same set and nobody would know, or care. But now people are like, 'He played the same set as last night!' It makes it more difficult to please people. It's harder to stay fresh, I think, but that's also a good thing too because it's makes you stay sharper.

What was it like being voted the most popular DJ in *DJmag* three years running?

It was great. It was like getting an Oscar. But it doesn't really affect me as a person that much. When I tell my children later I was voted best DJ, but in general it doesn't do anything....

I suppose so, but you said earlier that you liked being a populist DJ and I guess something like this is confirmation of that.

I don't think *DJmag* in general has that much influence, it's more.... It doesn't do much for your career, but it's a very nice compliment. It's a confirmation of where you stand. And the

whole list, it does feel a little strange lately. Fatboy Slim is not even in top 100 and he's sold millions of records. And there are guys in the top 10 and you're like, who is this guy?

Are you allowed to give away any secrets about the live show?
Well, we're thinking about it, and the visuals are definitely going to have a big impact and the lighting show is very special. There's gonna be a lot things that have never been done before on the technical side, it's gonna look amazing. It's going to be something extremely special.

Will you be on your own or will there be other things?
It will be me and other live elements and there will be singers. I hope they can make it! It's going to be the biggest dance show the world has ever seen. That's all I can say about. I don't want to ruin all the surprises.

Earlier on, you said you'd like to be remembered for taking dance music in new directions. Where would you like it to go?
I want DJing and dance music to be just as big as hip hop or rock music is now. It would be nice if dance music blows up in America and I was a part of that.

In a way, America is the last frontier, isn't it?
Yeah, I think it's a winnable battle. To take DJing to another level it's not about a DJ turning up with just his records, but for him to make a whole show. That's my goal.

Where is dance music going?
No idea! All I can say is for myself that it's growing, more people come to my shows, they buy more albums, every year it's been bigger. I hope it never ends. I need new challenges. This year it's the world tour. It lasts a year.

© DJhistory.com

Big thanks to...

Charlie Ahearn, Paul Allen at Anglo Management, Arthur Baker, Daniele Baldelli, Dean Belcher, Enrico Borsetti, Chris Brown, Miguel Bustos, Rudy Cardenas, Phil Cheeseman, Joe Conzo, David Corio, Ian Dewhirst, Jeff Dexter, Chip E, Terry Farley, Marybeth Feeney, Alfredo Fiorito, Camille Fossi, Froggy (RIP), Steve Frost, Pete Haigh, Nicky Holloway, Rick 'The Deck Burglar' Hopkins. François K, Ian Levine, David Lubich, Luis Mario, Trevor Midgely, David Mancuso, Phil Mison, David Morales, Tom Moulton, Clare Munro, Winnie O'Connor, Shane O'Neill, José Padilla, Hector Romero, Charlotte Scott, Nicky Siano, Rosie Stewart, Ian St. Paul, Bruce Tantum, Pete Tong, Yoko Uozumi, Gavin Watson, Clare Woodcock, Carl Woodroffe, Dave Swindells, Ian St. Paul, Jason Bold, Nick Steel, Laura Morris and everyone at Harriman Steel; Andy Singh and Mark McQuillan at Republic of Music; Bill Norris at Central Books, Chris Rees, Jim, Cath, Mel and Peter at Signature Books; Tracy, Fia, Helena and Kevin at C & C Offset, Alban Horrocks at Townsends.

And everyone who helped us put together Last Night A DJ Saved My Life

Special Thanks: Dave Barlow, Ben Ferguson

Without whom etc:
Imogen
Liz

Photo credits

All reasonable efforts have been made to trace and contact copyright holders of the images in this book, but if any have been inadvertently overlooked, we will be pleased to make the necessary acknowledgements at the first opportunity.

6. Frank Broughton
20. Redferns
22. courtesy of Ian Samwell
24. courtesy of Jeff Dexter
38. Getty images
44. Malcolm Robertson
48. courtesy of Terry Noel
51. courtesy of Terry Noel
53. courtesy of Rudy Cardenas
56. Ken Kneitel
59. courtesy of Francis Grasso
63. Frank Broughton
71. courtesy of Francis Grasso
72. courtesy of Carl Woodroffe
80. courtesy of Ian Levine
82. courtesy of Ian Levine
85. courtesy of Ian Levine
86. courtesy of Ian Levine
100. Ian Dewhirst
112. courtesy of David Mancuso
124. Estate of Peter Hujar
134. courtesy of Tom Moulton
144. courtesty Nicky Siano
150. courtesy of Nicky Siano
152. courtesy of Nicky Siano
154. Garth Aikens
164. Joe Conzo
169. Frank Broughton
172. Joe Conzo
176. David Corio
181. Frank Broughton
190. David Corio
202. courtesy of Kool Lady Blue
204. courtesy of Arthur Baker
215. courtesy of Arthur Baker
216. David Corio
224. courtesy DJ Shadow
232. courtesy of Hector Romero
242. courtesy of Chip E

252. photographer unknown
264. Phil Cheeseman
271. photographer unknown
276. courtesy of Hector Romero
286. courtesy of Hector Romero
290. photographer unknown
298. Chris Wahl
306. courtesy of Derrick May
317. courtesy of Derrick May
320. courtesy of Jeff Mills
330. Ian St Paul
334. courtesy of Alfredo
338. courtesy of José Padilla
340. courtesy of José Padilla
344. courtesy of Daniele Baldelli
347. courtesy of Daniele Baldelli
351. courtesy of Daniele Baldelli
352. courtesy of Froggy
358. courtesy of Froggy
361. photographer unknown
362. Dave Swindells
370. courtesy of Terry Farley
384. courtesy of Andrew Weatherall
392. Gavin Watson
394. Kevin Cummins
397. peterjwalsh.com
400. Ian St. Paul
404. Dean Belcher
410. courtesy of Steve Double
418. courtesy of Pete Tong
426. courtesy of Sasha
436. courtesy of Sasha
438. Alexis Maryon
448. photographer unknown
450. courtesy of Dolan Bergin
456. Rankin
466. courtesy of Tiësto
473. courtesy of Tiësto